Communications
in Computer and Information Science 326

Tianyuan Xiao   Lin Zhang   Shiwei Ma (Eds.)

System Simulation and Scientific Computing

International Conference, ICSC 2012
Shanghai, China, October 27-30, 2012
Proceedings, Part I

 Springer

Volume Editors

Tianyuan Xiao
Tsinghua University
Department of Automation
National CIMS Engineering Research Center
Beijing 100084, China
E-mail: xty-dau@tsinghua.edu.cn

Lin Zhang
Beihang University
School of Automation Science and Electrical Engineering
Beijing 100191, China
E-mail: johnlin9999@163.com

Shiwei Ma
Shanghai University
School of Mechatronics Engineering and Automation
Shanghai 200072, China,
E-mail: masw@shu.edu.cn

ISSN 1865-0929   e-ISSN 1865-0937
ISBN 978-3-642-34380-3   e-ISBN 978-3-642-34381-0
DOI 10.1007/978-3-642-34381-0
Springer Heidelberg Dordrecht London New York

Library of Congress Control Number: 2012949601

CR Subject Classification (1998): I.6, I.2, H.4, H.3, C.2, D.2, I.4

Typesetting: Camera-ready by author, data conversion by Scientific Publishing Services, Chennai, India

Printed on acid-free paper

Springer is part of Springer Science+Business Media (www.springer.com)

Preface

The Asia Simulation Conference and the International Conference on System Simulation and Scientific Computing 2012 (AsiaSim & ICSC 2012) was formed to bring together outstanding researchers and practitioners in the field of modeling and simulation and scientific computing areas from all over the world to share their expertise and experience.

AsiaSim & ICSC 2012 was held in Shanghai, China, during October 27–30, 2012. It was constituted by AsiaSim and ICSC. AsiaSim is an annual international conference organized by three Asia Simulation Societies: CASS, JSST, and KSS since 1999. It has now become a conference series of the Federation of Asia Simulation Societies (ASIASIM) that was established in 2011. ICSC is a prolongation of the Beijing International Conference on System Simulation and Scientific Computing (BICSC) sponsored by CASS since 1989. AsiaSim & ICSC 2012 was organized by the Chinese Association for System Simulation (CASS) and Shanghai University. In the AsiaSim & ICSC 2012 conference, technical exchanges between the research community were carried out in the forms of keynote speeches, panel discussions, as well as special sessions. In addition, participants were also treated to a series of social functions, receptions, and networking sessions, which served as a vital channel to establish new connections, foster everlasting friendships, and forge collaborations among fellow researchers.

AsiaSim & ICSC 2012 received 906 paper submissions from eight countries. All papers went through a rigorous peer-review procedure including pre-review and formal review. Based on the review reports, the Program Committee finally selected 298 good-quality papers for presentation at AsiaSim & ICSC 2012, from which 267 high-quality papers were then sub-selected for inclusion in five volumes published in the Springer *Communications in Computer and Information Science* (CCIS) series.

This proceedings volume includes 63 papers covering five relevant topics including modeling theory and technology, M&S technology on synthesized environments and virtual reality environments, pervasive computing and simulation technology, embedded computing and simulation technology, and verification/validation/accreditation technology. All of these offer us plenty of valuable information and would be of great benefit to the technical exchange among scientists and engineers in modeling and simulation fields.

The organizers of AsiaSim & ICSC 2012, including the Chinese Association for System Simulation and Shanghai University, made enormous efforts to ensure the success of AsiaSim & ICSC 2012. We hereby would like to thank all the members of the AsiaSim & ICSC 2012 Advisory Committee for their guidance and advice, the members of the Program Committee and Technical Committee and the referees for their effort in reviewing and soliciting the papers, and the members of the Publication Committee for their significant editorial work. In particular, we would like to thank all the authors for preparing, contributing, and presenting their excellent research works. Without the high-quality submissions and presentations from the authors, the success of the conference would not have been possible.

Finally, we would like to express our gratitude to the National Natural Science Foundation of China, the Japanese Society for Simulation Technology, Korea Society for Simulation, the Society for Modeling and Simulation International, International Association for Mathematics and Computer in Simulation, Federation of European Simulation Societies, Science and Technology on Space System Simulation Laboratory, Beijing Electro-Mechanical Engineering Institute, Shanghai Electro-mechanical Engineering Institute, and Shanghai Dianji University for their support in making this conference a success.

July 2012

Bo Hu Li
Qinping Zhao

AisaSim & ICSC 2012 Organization

Honorary Chairs

Chuanyuan Wen, China   Robert M. Howe, USA   Osamu Ono, Japan
Sung-Joo Park, Korea   Myoung-Hee Kim, Korea   Mahammad Obaidat, USA
Sadao Takaba, Japan   Xingren Wang, China   Zongji Chen, China

General Chairs

Bo Hu Li, China
Qinping Zhao, China

General Co-chairs

Koyamada Koji, Japan   Jonghyun Kim, Korea   Axel Lehmann, Germany
Qidi Wu, China   Song Wu, China   Zicai Wang, China
Xianxiang Huang, China   Khalid Al-Begain, UK

International Program Committee

Chairs

Tianyuan Xiao, China
Lin Zhang, China

Co-chairs

Bernard Zeigler, USA   Tuncer Ören, Canada   Ralph C. Huntsinger, USA

Xiaofeng Hu, China   Fengju Kang, China   Soo-Hyun Park, Korea
Satoshi Tanaka, Japan   Zaozhen Liu, China   H.J. Halin, Switzerland
Xudong Pan, China   Kaj Juslin, Finland   Roy E. Crosbie, USA
Ming Yang, China   Xiaogang Qiu, China   Satoshi Tanaka, Japan
Jin Liu, China   Min Zhao, China   Shiwei Ma, China

Technical Committee

Agostino Bruzzone, Italy   Anxiang Huang, China   Yoonbae Kim, Korea
Yu Yao, China   Fei Xie, USA   Toshiharu Kagawa, Japan

Giuseppe Iazeolla, Italy   Mhamed Itmi, France   Haixiang Lin,
                                                    The Netherlands
Henri Pierreval, France   Hugh HT Liu, Canada   Shengen Zhou, China
Wolfgang Borutzky,   Jong Sik Lee,Korea   Xiaolin Hu, USA
  Germany
Yifa Tang, China   Wenhui Fan, China   Mingduan Tang, China
Long Wang, China   Doo-Kwon Baik, Korea Shinsuke Tamura, Japan
Pierre Borne, France   Ratan Guha, USA   Reinhold Meisinger,
                                                    Germany
Richard Fujimoto, USA   Ge Li, China   Jinhai Sun, China
Xinping Xiong, China   Gary S.H. Tan,   Francesco Longo, Italy
                            Singapore
Hong Zhou, China   Shin'ichi Oishi, Japan Zhenhao Zhou, China
Beike Zhang, China   Alain Cardon, France Xukun Shen, China
Yangsheng Wang, China   Marzuki Khalid,   Sergio Junco, Argentina
                            Malaysia
Tieqiao Wen, China   Xingsheng Gu, China   Zhijian Song, China
Yue Yang, China   Yongsheng Ding, China Huimin Fan, China
Ming Chen, China

Secretaries

Ping Zhang, China
Li Jia, China

Publication Chairs

Huosheng Hu, UK
Fei Tao, China

Special Session Chair

Shiwei Ma, China

Organizing Committee

Chairs

Minrui Fei, China
Yunjie Wu, China

Co-chairs

Ping Zhang, China
Linxuan Zhang, China
Noriyuki Komine, Japan
Kang Sun Lee, Korea

Members

Shixuan Liu, China
Baiwei Guo, China
Yulin Xu, China
Xin Li, China
Qun Niu, China
Shouwei Gao, China

Xiao Song, China
Gang Zhao, China
Tingzhang Liu, China
Li Jia, China
Min Zheng, China

Ni Li, China
Yanxia Gao, China
Shaohua Zhang, China
Xin Sun, China
Ling Wang, China

Awards Committee

Chair

Zongji Chen (China)

Co-chairs

Axel Lehmann (Germany)
Soo-Hyun Park (Korea)
Wakae Kozukue (Japan)

Members

Satoshi Tanaka (Japan)
Sung-Yong Jang (Korea)
Wenhui Fan (China)
Yifa Yang (China)
Xiao Song (China)

Table of Contents – Part I

The First Section: Computing and Simulation Applications in Science and Engineering

The Second Section: Computing and Simulation Applications in Management, Society and Economics

The Third Section: Computing and Simulation Applications in Life and Biomedical Engineering

Table of Contents – Part II

The First Section: Computing and Simulation Applications in Energy and Environment

The Second Section: Computing and Simulation Applications in Education

The Third Section: Computing and Simulation Applications in Military Field

The Fourth Section: Computing and Simulation Applications in Medical Field

Theoretical Study and 3D CFD Simulation of Temperature Distribution through HTST for Orange Juice

Yi Tang, Jing Xie, Jinfeng Wang, Zheng Zhang, and Chaoheng Gu

College of Food Science and Technology,
Shanghai Engineering Research Center of Aquatic-Product Processing & Preservation,
Shanghai Ocean University, Shanghai, 201306, China
kaixinfa@yahoo.cn, jxie@shou.edu.cn, jenniferwjf@126.com

Abstract. Heat sterilization has a long history. However, due to lacking of precise research, the sterilization relies mainly on experience, which leads to uncompleted sterilization or energy wastage. Computational fluid dynamics (CFD) is a tool to study the flow and heat transfer properties of different kinds of fluid. With the development of computer science and the improvement of CFD itself, CFD has been widely used in the industrial engineering. In this work, the CFD is used to study variation of the central temperature of an orange juice model under the HTST sterilization. Compared with the experiment results, the current simulation method is optimized and the error is reduced.

Keywords: orange juice, CFD, numerical simulation, temperature.

1 Introduction

The methods of heat sterilization of juice are divided into pasteurization, high temperature-short time (HTST) sterilization and ultra high temperature (UHT) sterilization. HTST is unlike from others for the sterilization time and temperature is different. The time for HTST is always maintained at several of minutes and at the temperature at 100°C~130°C. Recently, there are many literatures describe the research of HTST in the filed of sterilization for juice and others liquid food [1-3]. However, in the practical production of juice, the sterilization is always uncompleted or overmuch since lacking of research. Therefore, the noxious bacteria always above of standard in quantity or the energy always wasted.

As a tool to study the heat transfer and flow properties of different kinds of fluid, Computational fluid dynamics (CFD) has been widely used in the field of science and technology engineering because of its advantages of changing the simulation condition easily and saving the time and money for experiment. What's more, CFD simulation can predict some factors (e.g. interior velocity, huge pressure, high temperature, etc) which practical experiment probably unable to measure. Now CFD technology has been used in the field of the sterilization of juice. Ghani used CFD and made sure that the area of slowest heating zone (SHZ) in the model [4-6]. Wimalaratne obtained the relation of temperature and pressure in heat sterilization and found that the temperature could reduce when the pressure arrived at 100MPa [7]. Wang used 2D CFD model and

T. Xiao, L. Zhang, and S. Ma (Eds.): ICSC 2012, Part I, CCIS 326, pp. 1–7, 2012.

conducted the simulation to HTST and UHT sterilization and got different consuming times for different heating temperatures of sterilization [8,9]. However, 2D model probably would cause lower accuracy than 3D model, as its disadvantage of analyzing the research plane. Yuan researched the 3D model in heating sterilization for juice, but the experiment for validation lacked [10].

As lacking of simulation methods in the field of sterilization of liquid food, it is necessary to find a optimized method and give reference to further research. This work used CFD and simulated HTST sterilization in a canned model for orange juice by 3D technology mentioned in the previous literature. The central temperature in the model during sterilization was obtained. The computational results were compared with practical experiment and then the simulation method was optimized. After this, the error reduced at last and was within 2%.

2   CFD Simulation Approach

The size of model for HTST sterilization was followed the practical can which was 7.85cm, 2.65cm and 0.15cm for length, radius and thickness of wall, respectively. The physical parameters of juice were given in literature 8, 9, 10, 11 and defined that the density $\rho = 1026 kg / m^3$, the specific heat capacity $C_p = 3880 J /(kg \bullet K)$, the thermal conduction $k = 0.596 W /(m \bullet K)$ and density of heat flow rate $a = 600 W /(m^2 \bullet K)$.

The simulation model was constructed in GAMBIT2.2.30. During the construction process of the model, a cylinder was similar to a can which was built in the software. The boundary of the model can was defined as wall and the fluid in the can was defined as juice. To make the simulation results more close to reality, the wall thickness of real model was measured and set into FLUENT. As the unstructured mesh was more suitable for complicated model than structured model, this article chosed this one to fill the computational can model. Interval size of mesh was set as 0.5 which created 11658 computational cells. The initial temperature was followed as practical condition of 17°C.

Since the temperature in central zone of the can increased slower than other zones, when the central temperature reached the temperature requested, the sterilization was thought to be accomplished. Moreover, the conclusion that temperature of killing deleterious bacterial was not high in pervious research [8,9], and because the low pH could inhibit the growth of bacterial, this work defined that the standard of finishing HTST was when the central temperature arrived at 80°C as mentioned in previous research. Equations which were applied to define simulation condition in this work as table 1 showed [12].

Table 1. The different equations applied in simulation in this study

Different type of equations	Form of expression
Equation of mass conservation	$\dfrac{\partial u}{\partial x} + \dfrac{\partial v}{\partial y} + \dfrac{\partial w}{\partial z} = 0$
Equation of energy conservation	$\dfrac{\partial(\rho T)}{\partial t} + div(\rho u T) = div(\dfrac{k}{c_p} \bullet gradT) + S_T$
Control equation	$\dfrac{\partial(\rho \varphi)}{\partial t} + div(\rho u \varphi) = div(\Gamma \bullet grad\varphi) + S$

In the table 1, where u, v, w was the velocity of flow in X, Y, Z direction during HTST, respectively, and ρ was the pressure in the infinitesimal flow. In table 1, Cp was the specific heat capacity of the juice, k was the heat transfer coefficient and ST was the dissipative term of viscous force to the juice. T, φ and S was the thermodynamic temperature, universal variable, generalized source, respectively.

3   CFD Simulation

After the model was built in GAMBIT, it was inputted into the computational software FLUENT6.2.16. At first, the size of model was adjusted to be agree with the practical model. To get the higher accuracy in the simulation, the solver and the equation (e.g. energy, momentum, residual, etc) were applied 2-order precision. SIMPLE (Semi-Implicit Method for Pressure Linking Equation) algorithm was used to couple the pressure and velocity of the flow and the gravity was activated. In the simulation, properties of fluid were thought to be constant and finite volume method was used for computation. The sterilization temperature in the simulation was 100°C, this showed that wall temperature was set at 100°C.

As there was no flow at the beginning of the heating in the model, the state of fluid was considered laminar flow. The result of simulation at unsteady period was published by TECPLOT 10 and was showed at Fig 1.

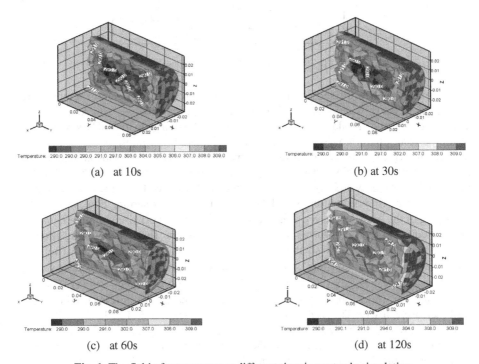

(a)   at 10s   (b) at 30s

(c)   at 60s   (d)   at 120s

Fig. 1. The field of temperature at different time in unsteady simulation

Fig.1 showed the temperature in the central of can was increased slowly in the simulation. When the can was heated after 2min, the temperature in the central of the model was constant.

4   Experiment Verification

To get the realistic variation of central zone, the experiment was taken. The instruments and material used in the experiments were a aluminous can whose size was similar to simulation, multipoint temperature collecting instrument (FLUKE-netDAQ32), thermostatic oil bath (CH1506), computer, thermocouple, iron wire, bracket, rubberized fabric and plastic tube. In the experiment, 4 thermocouples were located around the wall of the model to get the wall temperature at different periods, 1 thermocouple was inserted into the central of tube. When the temperature of oil in the bath was heated to 100°C and became steady, the can was putted into the bath and submersed into the oil. The experiment was repeated for 3 times and the connection of instruments was showed in Fig 2.

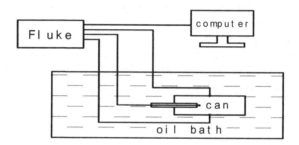

Fig. 2. The connection of instruments

The experiment result showed that it cost 206s to change the central temperature from 17°C to 80°C, which was proved different from the previous simulation result. This is because the simulation was previously used laminar equation. However, there would be some small movements of fluid molecules in the heating progress. Because the dynamic viscosity of the fluid was extremely little and the Reynolds number of the fluid would increase rapidly, the property of flow would probably change from laminar flow to transition flow and finally became turbulent flow even the velocity of fluid was very low. The flow equation would be chosen as k-ε equation, however, at the beginning of the heating, there was no flow in the can, this work used laminar equation as flow equation at first. During the heating process, the fluid need a long time to became the turbulent flow, so the coefficient of C_μ should be modified. The wall temperature of experiment was changed continually, which was different from what expected. This was because the convection strength of oil was much weaker than any other fluid (e.g. water, air, steam, etc), which caused the temperature of fluid near the wall increased slowly. The results of experiment were showed in Fig 3.

Fig 3 showed that the wall temperature changed and was agreed with the formula: $T= 9.4438Ln(t)+34.942$ (where T was the temperature and t was the time). Then the formula was compiled by a UDF program and set into the FLUENT to substitute the constant wall temperature set previously. Fig 3 showed that the central temperature was

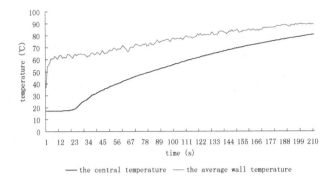

Fig. 3. The temperature variation during the heating process of the experiment

changed at 16s, which proved that the movement in the fluid existed, therefore, the equation of flow should substitute $k\text{-}\varepsilon$ equation for laminar equation and the coefficient of C_μ changed during the heating.

Table 2. The comparison between experiment results and simulation results

time	C_μ	central temperature of experiment (K)	central temperature of simulation (K)	error between simulation and experiment (%)
5th second	liminar	290.05	290	0.02
35th second	10^{-5}	300.44	303.63	1.06
65th second	10^{-5}	315.92	315.78	0.05
105th second	10^{-4}	329.69	329.39	0.09
155th second	10^{-1}	343.32	343.99	0.20
200th second	10^{2}	351.92	350.58	0.38

The simulation result of the optimization computational method was showed at table 2 and reflected the biggest error between the experiment and the optimized simulation was reduced to 1.1%.

The temperature field distribution in model during the different time of heating was showed in Fig 4.

Table 2 and Fig 5 showed that the optimizing simulation results were close to the practical experiment results, which proved that the CFD technology had a high accuracy and was suitable for simulation of HTST by 3D model. Following this method, this work also simulated the heating temperature at 110°C and 120°C, respectively.

The comparison of the central temperature variations between experiment results and simulation results at three different heating temperatures was showed in Fig 5. Both the simulation and experiment results showed that the central temperature of the can rose fast at the beginning of heating and then went up slowly.

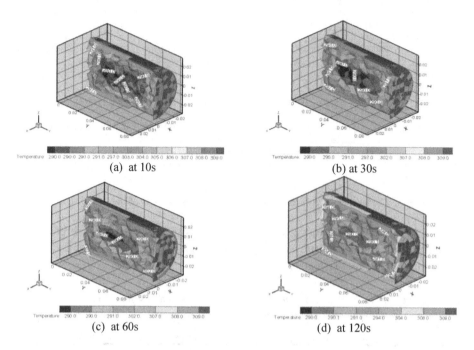

Fig. 4. Temperature field distribution of different period during simulation

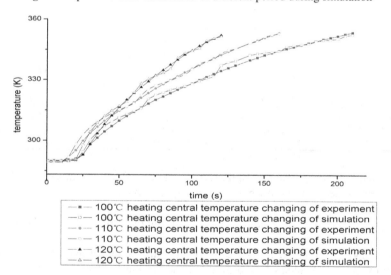

Fig. 5. Central temperature variation of experiment and simulation at different heating temperature

5   Conclusions

This work applied CFD to predict the temperature changing situation of HTST for juice. The simulation results were compared with experiment and conclusions were given as follow:

(1) To explain the property of flow, laminar equation was proved not suitable for this work;
(2) The simulation and experiment results showed the central temperature of the model rose fast at first and then went up slowly.
(3) The error between experiment and simulation in this work was less than 1.1%, which proved that CFD was an useful tool to simulate the HTST and other heating sterilization processes.

Acknowledgements. This research was funded by Luozhaoyao foundation from Shanghai Ocean University, the Scientific Research Foundation for Doctor from Shanghai Ocean University, the Shanghai Committee of Science and Technology Engineering Center Building Project(11DZ2280300) and the Leading Academic Discipline Project of Shanghai Municipal Education Commission (J50704).

References

1. Tomasula, P.M., Kozempel, M.F., Konstance, R.P., et al.: Thermal Inactivation of Foot-and-Mouth Disease Virus in Milk Using High-Temperature, Short-Time Pasteurization. Journal of Dairy Science 90(7), 3202–3211 (2007)
2. Hanson, A.L., Metzger, L.E.: Evaluation of increased vitamin D fortification in high-temperature, short-time–processed 2% milk, UHT-processed 2% fat chocolate milk, and low-fat strawberry yogurt. Journal of Dairy Science 93(2), 801–807 (2010)
3. Huang, J.L., Zhang, M.: Effects of Microwave and HTST Steam Blanching before Drying on Enzymes and Nutrients of Agaricus Bisporus. Drying Technolgy & Equipment 8(4), 150–157 (2010) (in Chinese)
4. Abdul Chani, A.G., Farid, M.M., Chen, X.D.: Theoretical and experimental investigation of Bacillus stearothermophilus in food pouches. Journal of Food Engineering 51(3), 221–228 (2002)
5. Abdul Chani, A.G., Farid, M.M., Chen, X.D., et al.: Thermal sterilization of canned food in a 3-D pouch using computational fluid dynamics. Journal of Food Engineering 48(2), 147–156 (2001)
6. Abdul Chani, A.G., Farid, M.M.: Using the computational fluid dynamics to analyze the thermal sterilization of solid–liquid food mixture in cans. Innovative Food Science & Emerging Technologies 7(1-2), 55–61 (2006)
7. Wimalaratne, S.K., Farid, M.M.: Pressure assisted thermal sterilization. Food and Bioproducts Processing 86(4), 312–316 (2008)
8. Wang, J.F., Tang, Y., Xie, J.: Numerical Simulation of UHT Sterilization on Orange Juice in Can. Journal of Engineering Thermophysics 33(2), 288–290 (2010) (in Chinese)
9. Wang, J.F., Tang, Y., Xie, J.: Optimization of HTST Sterilization Processing for Orange Juice Based on CFD. Food Science 31(22), 115–118 (2010) (in Chinese)
10. Yuan, X.H., Xie, J., Wang, J.F.: Study on high temperature pasteurization and cooling process of orange juice based on CFD technology. Food & Machinery 28(1), 55–58 (2012) (in Chinese)
11. Abdul Chani, A.G., Farid, M.M., Chen, X.D.: A computational and experimental study of heating and cooling cycles during thermal sterilization of liquid foods in pouches using CFD. Journal of Process Mechanical Engineering 217(Part E), 1–9 (2003)
12. Zhang, S.S.: The application of computational fluid dynamic, pp. 6–9. The Huazhong University of Science and Technology (HUST) Press, Wuhan (2011)

Fuzzy Control Strategy for Train Lateral Semi-active Suspension Based on Particle Swarm Optimization

Guangjun Li[1], Weidong Jin[1], and Cunjun Chen[2]

[1] School of Electrical Engineering, Southwest Jiaotong University, Chengdu 610031, China
[2] School of Mechanical Engineering, Southwest Jiaotong University, Chengdu 610031, China

Abstract. Fuzzy control strategy based on PSO was proposed for the complex train lateral suspension model. In this thesis, A17-DOF train lateral semi-active suspension system was modeled by simulink software, and at the same time, fuzzy controller and control rules were designed. Then, the root mean square value (RMS) of train lateral acceleration was used as object function, and membership functions of fuzzy controller's output variable were designed by PSO. The result of the simulation reveals that compared with the traditional fuzzy controller, the values of train lateral acceleration RMS of the front and rear bogies by using the optimized fuzzy controller reduce by 5.05% and 7.75%, respectively. In comparison with the passive suspension, the values reduce by 13.56% and 15.51%, respectively, which is more significant.

Keywords: Train lateral suspension, Fuzzy control, Particle swarm optimization (PSO), Root mean square value (RMS).

1 Introduction

To improve the running stability of high speed trains, it is necessary to reduce the train's lateral vibration. In addition, to minimize the cost and maximize the effect of vibration absorption, semi-active suspension strategy is adopted as an effective way to improve the running stability of train. Therefore, most trains are designed in semi-active suspension structure based on relative algorithms. Often used semi-active suspension control algorithms involve PID, linearization optimization, sky-hook control and robust control. However, influenced by the nonlinear characteristic of train suspension system, these algorithms all has their respective limitations [1].

Fuzzy control is a simple algorithm compared with the above mentioned control methods[2-5]. It bears the characteristic of "artificial intelligence" and does not need an exact mathematic model for the object under control. Therefore, the application of algorithms with arbitrary excitation and complex mathematic models is widely applied and showed great advantage in the design of suspension system. Meanwhile, to improve the effect of fuzzy control, optimized algorithms are often used in the design of fuzzy controller. In literature [6,7], genetic algorithm (GA) and fuzzy control are combined in vehicle suspension control system. The control effect of optimized fuzzy controllers shows an more obvious advantage than that of ordinary fuzzy control. The

T. Xiao, L. Zhang, and S. Ma (Eds.): ICSC 2012, Part I, CCIS 326, pp. 8–16, 2012.

weakness of GA is its complexity. Meanwhile, slow convergence speed is also a factor that influences the optimization effect of fuzzy control. Particle swarm optimization(PSO) is a new algorithm[8]. In comparison with GA, it searches for global optimum solution by following the optimum value that has been searched now and doesn't need the operations of crossover and maturation. In most cases, the application of particle swarm in the optimization can obtain better effect. So, particle swarm is used to optimize fuzzy controllers of train lateral semi-active suspension.

2   Train Lateral Semi-active Suspension Model by Simulink Software

2.1   The Model of Train Lateral Suspension

Lateral vibration of train is caused by the random irregularity of tracks. It is transferred to the car body through the lateral contact between wheels and tracks. In this thesis, a dynamic lateral model of 17 degrees of freedom for a kind of high-speed train is presented as follows[9]:

$$M\ddot{X} + C\dot{X} + KX = G\omega \tag{1}$$

$X = \{ y_{w1}, y_{w2}, y_{w3}, y_{w4}, \psi_{w1}, \psi_{w2}, \psi_{w3}, \psi_{w4}, y_{t1}, y_{t2}, \phi_{t1}, \phi_{t2}, \psi_{t1}, \psi_{t2}, y_c, \phi_c, \psi_c \}$.
The variables of y_{w1}, y_{w2}, y_{w3} and y_{w4} in the above formula are the lateral movement of the 4 wheels respectively; while $\psi_{w1}, \psi_{w2}, \psi_{w3}$ and ψ_{w4} are the yawing movement of 4 wheels respectively. $y_{t1}, y_{t2}, \phi_{t1}, \phi_{t2}$ ψ_{t1} and ψ_{t2} are the lateral, rolling and yawing movements of the two bogies respectively. y_c, ϕ_c, ψ_c are the lateral, rolling and yawing movement of the car body. M、 C and K are the matrixes of quality, damping and stiffness of the whole vehicle, G is the input distribute matrix of tracks and ω is the input of tracks irregularity along and perpendicular to their direction (detailed model and indexes refer to literature[9]). When the value of ω is obviously larger than the gaps between rails and wheels, a lateral movement that may excite the collision between rails and wheels will happen. Meanwhile, the forced wheel vibration of y_{wi} and ψ_{wi} (i =1,2,3,4) produce the vibrations of lateral movement y_{tj}, rolling movement ϕ_{tj} and yawing movement ψ_{tj} (j =1,2) and transfer the vibration to car body and consequently lead to the vibrations of y_c, ϕ_c and ψ_c in car body and bogies. All these three kinds of movements are the major factors that deteriorate the lateral irregularity of speed-raise and high-speed trains. The combination of the three kinds of movement results in the lateral acceleration of a_f and a_r to the front and rear bogies of the car (abbreviated as the front and rear

ends), and is detected by the acceleration sensors installed to front and rear bogies of the car body. The a_f and a_r are expressed as follows:

$$a_f = a_{y_c} - a_{\phi_c} + a_{\psi_c} \tag{2}$$

$$a_r = a_{y_c} - a_{\phi_c} - a_{\psi_c} \tag{3}$$

2.2   Train Lateral Semi-active Suspension Model by Simulink Software

Semi-active suspension is used through the controllers and adjustable dampers in the model. Then, the model is built by simulink software comprising five modules, namely: track irregularity module, car model module, controller module, data input and output module. The relationship of these modules is shown in figure 1.

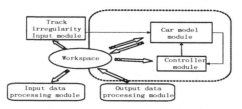

Fig. 1. The relationship of the modules

(1) Track irregularity input module: track irregularity input module involves horizontal irregularity and directional irregularity. According to relative track spectrum formula, the time domain simulation value of track excitation developed from the program in file M is transferred by S function into track irregularity input and added to car models through workspace.

(2) Car model module: Made up by the modules of wheel sets, car body, bogies and combined lateral acceleration, the function of this module is to realize the computation of all differential equations of the 17 freedom degree car model, as well as the calculation of geometric parameters and creeping force, it is a module of intuition. The lateral vibration of train involves lateral vibration, rolling vibration and yawing vibration. The combination of all these three types of vibration will form the lateral acceleration of cars, which is one of the major influences to the lateral stability of a train. Index of car structure is transferred by external M file to this module through workspace.

(3) Controller module: The modules are realized by programming language and S function, this module involves the sections of control algorithm realization and adjustable damper realization by means of semi-active suspension. The function of this module is to realize the computation of controlling algorithm by M file through workspace. When it works, the lateral acceleration of a train is detected by sensors and then sent out as input variables to the controller. The controller adjusts its output variable according to relative algorithms and makes it the input variable of adjustable damper. The damper then output damping to reduce the vibration of train. The adjustable damper is a magnetorheological fluid damper installed between front and

rear bogies and the car body. With coil current as its input variable, the formula between damper coil current I and damper coefficient C [5,9] is as follows:

$$C = 54.3687 * I^3 - 65.2278 * I^2 + 29.9317 * I + 2.4747 \qquad (4)$$

In this formula, $0 \le I \le 1.4$ A.

(4) Input data processing module: The function of this module is to provide all indexes required by the simulation experiment. Indexes to be input include model structure, train speed, track excitation, sampling frequency and simulation time. All these indexes transfer data to track excitation module, control module and car model module through the workspace of Matlab.

(5) Output data processing module: The function of this module is to output the data from the model to the workspace of MATLAB for mapping or statistics computation. Parameters to be output involve the lateral car body acceleration and transverse, rolling and yawing vibrations of car body.

3   Fuzzy Control of Train Lateral Semi-active Suspension

Install same fuzzy controllers to both the front and the rear of the train. Use car body lateral speed v and acceleration a as input to the fuzzy controller, and output i as the input current of adjustable damper. Set a_1 and a_2 as the quantified input variable of the quantified fuzzy controller, and b as its output variable. The universes are $[-1.5, 1.5 \text{ m.s}^{-1}]$、$[-1.5, 1.5 \text{ m.s}^{-2}]$ and $[0, 1.4\text{A}]$ respectively, therefore, the proportional divisors of each variable are: $k_v = a_1 / v = 10$、$k_a = a_2 / a = 2$ and $k_i = b / i = 1$. The fuzzy set of input and output variables involve seven degrees of: negative big (NB), negative intermediate (NM), negative small (NS), zeros (ZO), positive small (PS), positive intermediate (PM) and positive big (PB). The membership function of each fuzzy variables obtained is shown in figure 2 (MF means membership function). According to experience, the 49 control rules can be obtained is shown in table 1.

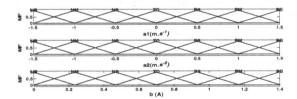

Fig. 2. Membership functions of fuzzy controller

The description of control rule R_j in language variable is [2,3]:

R_j : if a_1 is A_{j1} and a_2 is A_{j2},then b is B_j (j=1,2,...,n)(5) The membership functions of $\mu_{A_{j1}}(a_1)$, $\mu_{A_{j2}}(a_2)$ and $\mu_{B_j}(b)$ are all trigonometric functions. For given a_1^0 and a_2^0, the adaptability is:

$$\tilde{\omega}_j = \mu_{A_{j1}}\left(a_1^0\right) \wedge \mu_{A_{j2}}\left(a_2^0\right) \ (j=1,2,\ldots,n) \tag{6}$$

The output membership function is:

$$\mu_B(b) = \tilde{\omega}_1 \mu_{B1}(b) \vee \tilde{\omega}_1 \mu_{B2}(b) \vee \tilde{\omega}_n \mu_{Bn}(b) \tag{7}$$

Use particle method to de-fuzzy b and then input current I of the damper according to formula (4):

$$b^0 = \int b \mu_B(b)db \ / \int \mu_B(b)db \tag{8}$$

Obviously, n=7 in the paper.

Table 1. Control rules of fuzzy controller

b		a_1						
		NB	NM	NS	ZO	PS	PB	PB
	NB	NB	NB	NB	NM	NM	NS	NS
	NM	NB	NB	NB	NM	NM	NS	NS
	NS	NM	NM	NM	ZO	ZO	PS	PM
a_2	ZO	NM	NM	NS	PS	PS	PM	PM
	PS	NM	NS	ZO	PS	PM	PM	PB
	PM	NS	ZO	PS	PM	PM	PB	PB
	PB	ZO	PS	PM	PM	PB	PB	PB

4   Fuzzy Controller Based on PSO

4.1   Basic Principles of PSO Algorithm

The principle of PSO algorithm is presented as follows: Initialize a group of random particles first (random solutions), and then these particles will search following the optimum particles in the space of solutions to find the optimum solution through iteration. Set the swarm of particles as N, then the position and speed of particle number i in a space of D dimensions is represented as $X^i = (x_{i,1}, x_{i,2}, \cdots, x_{i,D})$ and $V^i = (v_{i,1}, v_{i,2}, \cdots; v_{i,D})$ ($i = 1, 2, \cdots, N$). In iteration, the particle renews itself by following two optimum solutions. The first one is just the optimum solution found by the particle swarm itself (personal best) $P^i = (p_{i,1}, p_{i,2}, \cdots, p_{id})$. The other one is the optimum solution found by the entire swam (global best) marked by P^g. When these two optimum solutions are found, the particle will renew its speed and position by the following formulas:

$$v_{i,j}(t+1) = wv_{i,j}(t) + c_1 r_1[p_{i,j} - x_{i,j}(t)] + c_2 r_2[p_{g,j} - x_{i,j}(t)] \tag{9}$$

$$x_{i,j}(t+1) = x_{i,j}(t) + v_{i,j}(t+1)(j = 1,2,\cdots,D) \tag{10}$$

In the above two formulas, w is inertia factor, c_1 and c_2 are learning factors bigger than 0, r_1 and r_2 are the random number between [0, 1].

4.2 Fuzzy Controller Optimized by Paticle Swarm

Let's divide the fuzzy output variable in figure 2 into 6 areas. As is shown in figure 3, the distances is k_i (i =1, 2, ..., 6) . Using PSO to code k_i will optimize the membership of output variables and then the controller may obtain a better control effect. The sum of $\sum_{i=1}^{6} k_i$ is 1.4 , which can be obtained from Fig. 3;

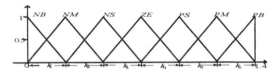

Fig. 3. Coding strategy for membership function

In the design of train lateral semi-active suspension system, it is necessary to consider both front and rear acceleration. Therefore, the sum of mean square root of front and rear acceleration is used as evaluation index[7], and the expression is as follows:

$$J = 0.5 * (\sqrt{\frac{1}{T}\int_0^T a_f^2(t)dt} + \sqrt{\frac{1}{T}\int_0^T a_r^2(t)dt}) \tag{11}$$

The process of PSO is presented as follows:

1) Choose k_i ($0 < k_i < 1.4$) to code and k_i shall satisfy that the sum of $\sum_{i=1}^{6} k_i$ is 1.4.

Set the number of particle swam N =5, number of space dimension D =6. Number of iteration M =10, $c_1 = c_2$ =2, w =0.5 and then initialize the position and speed of particles in the swarm randomly.

2) Encode the fuzzy output variables and sent them to the train lateral suspension model based on simulink. Then use J as objective function to calculate the fitness of each particle, and then store the position and fitness values of each particle into its own pbest. Finally, store the position and fitness values of optimum ones in pbest into gbest.

3) Renew the speed and position of particles according to formula (9) and (10).

4) Compare the fitness values of each particle to the best position that it has experienced, if the result is better, then the best position is identified.

5) Compare all pbest and gbest values and renew pbest;

6) The search will be stopped if all the above stop conditions have been met. The output data is $P^g = [k_i](i = 1,2,\cdots,6)$. If the conditions are not met, the process returns to step 3 and continues to search.

4.3   Optimization Result

With the speed of 270 km/h, the experiment uses American track spectra of class 6 and the duration of simulation is 25 seconds. By optimizing fuzzy controller with particle swarm to iterate for 10 times, the relationship between M (times of iteration) and J (value of objective function) is presented in figure 4. From which we can see that as M increases, value of objective function J reduces from 0.1335 m.s^{-2} of the first iteration to 0.1327m.s^{-2} of the eighth iteration, and finally reaches the global best :[0.77625806261380,0.00660175802301,0.180151753-98366,0.12039046036430 ,0.30999620699222,0.0066-0175802301]. Therefore, k_i (i =1,2,...,6). As a result of the application of floating point numbers the sum of $\sum_{i=1}^{6} k_i$ is approximately 1.4. The fuzzy controller based on PSO is shown in figure 5.

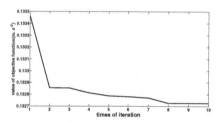

Fig. 4. The objective function optimization

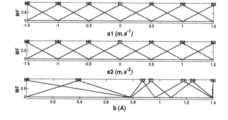

Fig. 5. fuzzy controller based on PSO

5   Simulation Experiment

Under same simulation conditions, a comparison is made between optimized fuzzy control by particle swarm, non-optimized fuzzy control and passive suspension. In this figure, the black solid line stands for optimized fuzzy control; the blue dot line is non-optimized fuzzy control and the green dash dot line is passive suspension. Lateral acceleration of the front and rear bogies is shown in figures 6 and 7 respectively. According to figures 6 and 7, in comparison with non-optimized fuzzy control and passive suspension, fuzzy control based on PSO significantly reduces the peak value of acceleration and the effect of control is better than that of the other two methods.

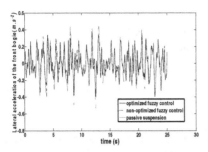
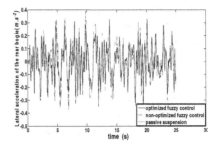

Fig. 6. Lateral acceleration of the front bogie   **Fig. 7.** Lateral acceleration of the rear bogie

The power spectrum density (abbreviated as PSD) is shown in figures 8 and 9 respectively. In these figures, the solid line stands for optimized fuzzy control; the dot line is non-optimized fuzzy control and the dash dot line is passive suspension. From the two figures, we see that the PSD of front and rear lateral acceleration focused on the sensitive section of low frequency. In the low frequency sections below 3 Hz, especially on the two peaks of 0.5493 Hz and 0.7935 Hz, the PSD of optimized fuzzy controller is obviously better than non-optimized fuzzy controller and passive suspension. And the mean square root of acceleration is shown in table 2.

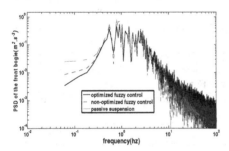
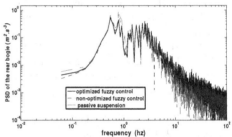

Fig. 8. PSD of the front bogie   **Fig. 9.** PSD of the rear bogie

Table 2. RMS of lateral acceleration

Type of vibration	Optimized control (m/s^{-2})	Non-optimized control (m/s^{-2})	Passive suspension (m/s^{-2})
Front lateral acceleration	0.1428	0.1504	0.1652
Rear lateral acceleration	0.1226	0.1329	0.1451

From which we see that optimized fuzzy control has a better performance. The mean square roots of front and rear lateral acceleration are obviously smaller than that of non-optimized fuzzy control and passive suspension: In comparison with non-optimized fuzzy control, the mean square root of acceleration improves by 5.05% and 7.75% respectively. In comparison with passive suspension, the effect of non-optimized fuzzy control improves by 13.56% and 15.51% respectively. In comparison with passive suspension, the effect of non-optimized fuzzy control is better, and the mean square root of front and rear lateral root improves by 8.96% and 8.41% respectively.

6   Conclusions

In this thesis, a design of train lateral semi-active suspension system with 17 degrees of freedom modeled by simulink software is proposed. Then, a fuzzy controller based on PSO is designed to reduce lateral vibration. The effect of fuzzy controller optimized by particle swarm has improved performance and better exactness. In comparison with non-optimized controllers and passive suspension, both the mean square root of front and rear lateral acceleration and power spectrum density of low frequency section are reduced. The effect of non-optimized fuzzy control is better than that of passive suspension at the same time.

References

1. Li, G.-J., Ding, J.-M., Zhang, C.-F., et al.: Research on fuzzy control method of railway vehicle semi-active suspension system. Modern Manufacturing Engineering (11), 1–4 (2010) (in Chinese)
2. Fan, Z.-P., Yang, J.-W.: Self-Adaptive Fuzzy Control Method for Lateral Vibration of Heavy-Duty Locomotive. China Railway Science 28(3), 68–70 (2007) (in Chinese)
3. Guan, J.-F., Hou, C.-Z., Gu, L., et al.: Adaptive Fuzzy Control for Vechicle Semi-active Suspension Based on Neural-network. Automotive Engineering 25(6), 587–589 (2003) (in Chinese)
4. Cao, T., Li, P., Liu, H.: An Interval Fuzzy Controller for Vehicle Active Suspension Systems. IEEE Transactions on Intelligent Transportation Systems 11(4), 885–895 (2010)
5. Ding, J.-M., Chen, C.-J., Lin, J.-H., et al.: Fuzzy control of lateral semi-active suspension system for high-speed train. Journal of Traffic and Transportation Engineering 9(2), 75–78 (2009) (in Chinese)
6. Guo, J.-H., Li, Y.-D., Li, J.: Design of Fuzzy Logic Controller of Active Suspension Based on Genetic Algorithm. Journal of System Simulation 19(18), 4178–4781 (2007) (in Chinese)
7. Dong, X.-M., Yu, M., Liao, C.-R., et al.: Fuzzy logic control based on hybrid taguchi genetic algorithm for vehicle magneto-rheological suspensions. Journal of Vibration and Shock 29(6), 150–153 (2010)
8. Kennedy, J., Eberhart, R.: Particle swarm optimization. In: Proceedings of IEEE Conference on Neural Networks, pp. 1942–1948. IEEE, Perth (1995)
9. Chen, C.-J., Wang, K.-Y.: Study on modeling of lateral semi-active suspension system of high-speed train. Journal of Vibration and Shock 25(4), 151–153 (2006) (in Chinese)

Design and Implementation
of a Mathematical Simulation Platform

Jianxiang Wang[1], Guanghong Gong[1], Yaofei Ma[1], Haihong Wang[2], and Dezhi Dong[1]

[1] School of Automation Science and Electrical Engineering, Beihang University,
100191 Beijing, China
[2] PLA 91635 Troop,
102249 Beijing, China
wangjx062046@asee.buaa.edu.cn

Abstract. Simulation platform plays an important role in modeling and simulation. Some simulation platforms have already been successfully applied in related fields. In this paper, we propose a structure of a mathematical simulation platform, which is designed for the design and analysis of control systems. Functional modules of the platform, including the design methods and implementation details, are thoroughly illustrated,. This simulation platform has advantages in 1) Simulation resources deployment. 2) Batch simulation with different model parameters. 3) Simulation results post-processing. 4) Simulation model version management. 5) Distributed deployment and nodes monitoring. 6) Generation of report document. Within these functions, the simulation platform may reduce costs and enhance efficiency in developing a simulation application. Finally, an implementation of this structure is provided and an example of an application of this simulation platform is demonstrated as well.

Keywords: Simulation platform, Mathematical simulation, Software structure.

1 Introduction

Simulation technology is used for systems design and analysis in various fields. It is the imitation of a real-world process or system over time[1]. Simulation can be applied to show the eventual real effects of alternative conditions and courses of action. Simulation is also utilized when the real system cannot be engaged, because it may be not accessible, or it may be dangerous or unacceptable, or simply not exist.

Simulation platform which combines the function of modeling and simulation is well used for analysis and verification of real systems. Simulation platform offers the traditional benefits of software construction: Typical simulation platforms share some common points as follow:

- Supporting modeling of target entities or systems.
- Able to configure and generate simulation schemas.
- To run a simulation, set inputs of models as well as get outputs.
- Logging simulation data and displaying result curve synchronously.
- Post-processing or analyzing simulation results.

T. Xiao, L. Zhang, and S. Ma (Eds.): ICSC 2012, Part I, CCIS 326, pp. 17–24, 2012.

The rest of this paper is composed of the following sections. Section 2 illustrates the development history of simulation platform and introduced some typical simulation platforms. Software structure of our simulation platform is thoroughly illustrated in section 3, including key modules design methods and implement technologies. Section 4 shows an implementation of the structure. At last, Section 5 concludes this paper.

2   Related Work

Simulation platform provides a precise environment, access to physically immeasurable variables and rapid redesign and testing[2]. In the past few decades, simulation software absorbed the new method of related disciplines, such as similarity theory, computer networks technology, computer image\graph technology, automatic control, software engineering, system engineering etc. During the infantile period, simulation software was developed for a specified purpose which was not flexible enough to transplant. Later on, with the advancement of computer science, simulation software became versatile that support a category of simulation sharing much common features[3]. Previous work could transplant to a new simulation without paying much effort. Nowadays, simulation becomes a multidisciplinary, intelligent and flexible technology. Even though simulation platform appeared less than two decades, some simulation platform made a great achievement in its field. GAMA[4], a typical agent-based simulation platform applied in geographic information modeling, got great success. Simics[5] is a full system simulation platform which used for hardware and software design. A domestic simulation platform CISE (Components-based Integrated Simulation Environment) is a new generation platform developed by Beijing Simulation Center[6]. CISE is competent of supporting high performance parallel simulation, heterogeneous systems distributed simulation and combat simulation. CISE is composed of graphical modeling module, model components management module, simulation management module, adapter management module and public resources management module. Adapter which maps simulation to specified operating environment is the core to implement integrated modeling. CISE is able to support basic statistical analysis of simulation results either. ModSAF which experts in creating visual effect is a set of simulation software modules and applications that construct Distributed Interactive Simulation (DIS) and Computer Generated Forces (CGF) entities for realistic training, test, and evaluation in the virtual battlefield environment. It contains entities that are sufficiently realistic resulting in the "illusion" that the displayed vehicles are being maneuvered by computers, rather than human crews. ModSAF uses 'selective fidelity' to balance cost, desired performance, and realistic simulation. Therefore, many models include elements of human control that simplify the behavior of the entities[7].

3   Design of a Mathematical Simulation Platform

In order to tackle the deficiencies of previous platforms and facilitate simulation experiments, we design a simulation platform which is competent of running mathematical simulation experiments. This simulation platform is composed of the following modules and tools.

3.1 Model Component Description and Create Tool

Model component description and create tool which could describe the simulation model structures and generate model codes is provided to simplify modeling process. Existed models could be encapsulated by this tool. This tool adopts a unified modeling format which specifies model interface, access method and execute mode. In this way, simulation engine could run the simulation schema without much obstacle. The process of modeling is divided into two parts by this tool:

➢ Model description: model description information is included in a XML format file. Model description follows a rule set called 'model specification' which covers description of input\output data, input\output events and parameter configuration of model.

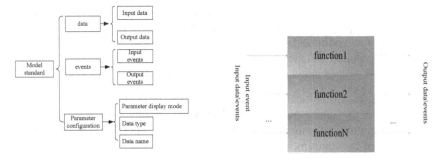

Fig. 1. Model standard of this platform   **Fig. 2.** Model structure of this platform

Inputs and outputs of model are defined by interfaces, while functions of model process the input data (events) and set the output data (events). The model structure that the simulation engine could support is depicted as Fig. 2.

➢ Model codes generation: Model codes generation is an application wizard embedded in Microsoft Visual Studio which could parse the description file and create a VC project framework. The project framework contains interfaces and framework described above. This wizard is coder-oriented that greatly reduce the workload of model developer. The developers are required to complete the function implementation of this model only.

3.2 Simulation Schema Generation and Management Tool

Simulation schema defines the operating mode of experiment, models, parameter configuration of models, interactions and link relationship between models. Simulation schema also includes the deployment information of each model, data record items, simulation time, post-processing configuration etc. This tool is competent of managing existed schema or creating a new one. All available models can be listed in this tool, as well as the available nodes of the local networks and simulation schemas. A selected model is shown in the model linkage area as an instance. The user could link the selected models via an oriented line segment. As for single output model and single input model, the oriented line means directly data exchange, otherwise, data exchange should be configured. The deployment file can be parsed by other components of this platform.

3.3   Deployment and Nodes Monitoring Module

Deployment and nodes monitoring module serves as a network resources administrator of this platform. The functions of this module are listed below:

➢ Detecting available nodes in the workgroup. While a new node joining the workgroup, this node is added to the nodes list and vice versa, and the topological structure of simulation network is changing as well.
➢ Dispatch simulation schema file to selected node. Simulation schema is first generated in central node and the information is contained in the deployment file. After that, deployment file is send to the available node via this module.
➢ Nodes status monitoring. With the technology of socket via UDP, node status is actively reported to the console, including whether the node is running a simulation, existed simulation schemas in the node, etc.

The module is group-multicast structure, the server is binding to the central node (console) while the client placing on other nodes. Each client node periodically broadcasts formatted status message in the local networks via UDP protocol. While the console received the status message, it parses the message and updates nodes list.

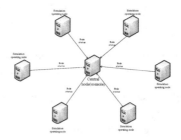

Fig. 3. Nodes monitor topological structure

When launching a simulation, central node dispatches the deployment file to all available nodes. Each node parses the deployment file and executes related tasks. The central node sends out a start command to trigger off simulation.

3.4   Simulation Engine

Simulation engine is able to drive models, distinguish algebraic model[8] from non-algebraic model, determine the solve order, exchange data. As for the distributed environment, communication between simulation nodes, synchronization of actions and time management strategy of simulation advancement are critical factors that affect the efficiency and reliability. Interaction of simulation nodes and time advancement strategy are managed by Run-Time-Infrastructure (RTI). Simulation nodes join the RTI federation as a federate member while running a simulation schema. The simulation nodes subscribe the data and events it needed and publish the data and events it generated. The operating process of simulation engine is depicted in Fig. 4. For centralized environment, data exchange among models is via a shared buffer. Centralized simulation engine is independent of RTI. It appears in the form of a VC project which could debug and test model codes.

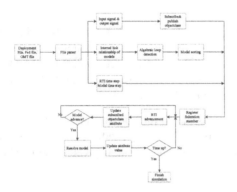

Fig. 4. Operating process of distributed simulation engine

3.5   Simulation Data Log, Display and Simulation Management Tool

Simulation data log and display tool charges of collecting and storing data, drawing results curve synchronously. Besides that, during the whole process of simulation, this tool could manipulate simulation operation. This tool has three functional modules:

➢ Data collecting module. Data collecting module is a RTI based program. This module subscribed all object classes and interaction classes which may appear during the simulation and RTI callback mechanism ensures the synchronization of simulation data. Once the simulation engine updated an attribute value, data collecting module received the value.

➢ Data storage module. Data storage module is an independent thread which could encode the data into a string and put it into files. To guarantee storage efficiency, Berkeley DB is introduced to store and manage data. The access and encode interfaces are encapsulated based on the raw interfaces of Berkeley DB. A decoding interface is provided for simulation results post-processing module.

➢ Data display tool. Data display tool is a C-S structure tool. Data exchange between client and server is developed via a cross-language network service development tool Thrift[9] since curve drawing module is developed with Java while data transporting is a C++ program. By using thrift, the process of socket programming is simplified as a function calling from server to client. An unique index is attached to each model output value for distinguishing data from different models. To enhance transporting rate, a send buffer may contain a bulks of data packages rather than a single one.

3.6   Simulation Results Post-processing and Exception Detection Module

This module is used for analyze simulation data and handle exceptional data. Data analysis part provides various build-in analysis algorithm library and an extension interface of algorithm library. The user could import a new algorithm with extension interface to enrich the post-processing ability. Functions of post-processing part are listed below:

➢   Retrieve simulation data. Before analyze simulation data, this module access simulation data file, acquire specified data from massive simulation data.
➢   Simulation results analysis and post-processing. All available analysis algorithms are to be selected for post-processing result data such as calculating rising time and overshoot of second-order control system.

Exception detection part is used for monitoring exceptional simulation results. Exception handling methods and boundary conditions could be set before simulation. If exceptions were thrown, exception detection may catch and handle it follow the given method.

3.7   Simulation Report Document Generator

While the simulation experiments finished, report generator created a document which includes simulation results and experiment information. Simulation report generator extracts simulation description information from deployment file and then fills the information into a predefined document template. Simulation data and post-processing results are filled into the template as well. Simulation curve, if any, could paste to the template also. While completed, a report document is saved as a WORD file with the extension of .doc.

3.8   Simulation Resources Management Tool

Simulation resources include models, source codes, schema files, configuration files, data files, report documents and other resources related to simulation. Simulation resources management tool has two functional modules:

➢   Simulation model and schema management module. This module manages simulation schema as a logical object to ensure the consistency of simulation schema, model components, model codes, parameter configuration and deployment configuration.
➢   Simulation data management module. After a simulation schema finished, related data files were uploaded to database and mapped to relevant schema.

4   An Implementation of This Platform

We implemented a simulation platform as the structure discussed in Section 3. This platform was first used for control system simulation. Fig. 5 shows the primary UI of the platform. All available simulation schemas, simulation models and nodes are listed in the top left corner of primary UI. Right part of the UI displays the configuration of simulation schema. A typical second-order inverted pendulum control system with 10 groups of parameters is being simulated in this platform. Results curve is being drawing as well. After the simulation, the user could select a post-processing method to analysis the simulation results. Post-processing results and simulation information are filled into a report document template and save as a new word document. Simulation schema files and report documents are stored in resources management data finally.

Fig. 5. Primary interface

5   Conclusions

The simulation platform we developed is applied for system prototype simulation and analysis. This platform may reduce the cost and time of simulation experiment, it may also enhance the efficiency of model development. Simulation resources management provides an effective way to organize resources. Testing results show that this platform excels in batch simulation with variant parameters of simulation model. VC project generator of this platform simplified the model develop and test process. Further developing work will be carried on to extend this platform for the supporting of hardware-in-loop simulation, which requires a mechanism to guarantee synchronization between hardware and software. Besides that, the build-in model library should be enriched with more typical models.

References

1. Banks, J., Carson, J., Nelson, B., Nicol, D.: Discrete-Event System Simulation. Prentice Hall, p. 3 (2001)
2. Gans, N.R., Dixon, W.E., Lind, R.: A hardware in the loop simulation platform for vision-based control of unmanned air vehicles. Mechatronics 19 (2009)

3. Li, B., Chai, X., Zhu, W.: Some Focusing Points In Development of Modern Modeling and Simulation Technology. In: Proceeding of The Symposium on Global Manufacturing & Simulation Technology of the 21st Century (2004)

4. Taillandier, P., Vo, D.-A., Amouroux, E., Drogoul, A.: GAMA: A Simulation Platform That Integrates Geographical Information Data, Agent-Based Modeling and Multi-scale Control. In: Desai, N., Liu, A., Winikoff, M. (eds.) PRIMA 2010. LNCS, vol. 7057, pp. 242–258. Springer, Heidelberg (2012)

5. Magnusson, P.S., Cbristensson, M., Eskilson, J.: Simics: A Full System Simulation Platform. Computer 35(2) (February 2002)

6. Qing, D.-Z., Li, B.-H., Sun, L.: Research of Component-based Integrated Modeling and Simulation Environment. Journal of System Simulation 20(4) (February 2008)

7. ModSAF 5.0 Functional Description Document, ADST-II-CDRL-MODSAF5.0-9800327

8. Geng, H., Yang, G.: Algebraic loop problems in simulation of control systems and the methods to avoid it. Electric Machines and Control 10(6) (November 2006)

9. Thrift official website, http://thrift.apache.org

An Investigation on the Flow Field of a Vortex Cup

Xin Li[1], Shoichiro Iio[2], and Toshiharu Kagawa[1]

[1] Precision and Intelligence Laboratory, Tokyo Institute of Technology, R2-14,
4259 Nagatsuta-chou, Midori-ku, Yokohama, 226-8503, Japan
[2] Dept. of Environmental Science and Technology, Shinshu University, 4-17-1 Wakasato,
Nagano, 380-8553, Japan

Abstract. This work presents a computational fluid dynamics (CFD) calculation to investigate the flow field of a vortex cup. The vortex cup utilizes air swirling flow to achieve handling a work piece without any contact. The numerical calculation was performed using the standard k-ε model and Reynolds stress model (RSM), and the pressure distribution calculated numerically was compared with the experimental results. It is found that RSM can better reproduce the characteristics of experimental results than the standard k-ε model. Based on the calculation results of RSM, the flow field, spatial pressure and velocity distributions inside the vortex cup were clarified. Furthermore, a visualization experiment was conducted by using ink in water with an enlarged cup, in which the flow was observed and confirmed.

Keywords: vortex levitation, vortex cup, non-contact handling, air swirling flow, CFD, RSM.

1   Introduction

When handling and moving work pieces such as semiconductor wafers and glass panels of liquid crystal, pneumatic levitation approaches, which use air flow to apply a lifting force to a work piece, are widely used because air flow is magnetic free, generates little heat, requires no control loop to obtain a stable state and nearly maintenance free for their simple structures [1, 2]. A new pneumatic non-contacting handling approach named vortex levitation has been introduced by the authors [3, 4]. From our previous work it is known that vortex levitation uses a swirling air flow generator called vortex cup to cause negative pressure region to achieve a lifting force, and thereby is able to handle a work piece without any contact and keep a stable levitation under the vortex cup at a certain position that is defined as stable levitation position [3,4]. However, flow phenomena inside the vortex cup are not made clear yet due to the fact that the vortex cup is too small to insert a sensor into it for experiment and measurement. In such a case, the exploitation of computational fluid dynamics (CFD) software for the numerical calculation is an efficient alternative, and may yield better understanding. In this paper, an investigation on the flow field of vortex cup is conducted by using CFD and the numerical result is compared with experiment.

T. Xiao, L. Zhang, and S. Ma (Eds.): ICSC 2012, Part I, CCIS 326, pp. 25–34, 2012.
© Springer-Verlag Berlin Heidelberg 2012

2   Mechanism of Vortex Cup

Similar to cyclones where low pressure is caused by air swirling, vortex cup is able to generate negative pressure by utilising air swirling flow. As can be seen in Fig. 1, the cup is made up of a circular vortex chamber, a tangential nozzle inserted above and an annular flat skirt set on the surrounding. Compressed air is blown through the nozzle into the vortex chamber, and then spins along the circular wall to create a negative pressure in the central area by centrifugal force. Fig.2 shows an experimental result of a typical pressure distribution on the upper surface of a work piece placed under the vortex cup. Here, G is supply mass flow rate and h is the gap thickness between the vortex cup and the work piece. This negative pressure will apply a lifting force denoted by F_l to the work piece so that the work piece can levitate at an equilibrium position where the gravity is balanced by the lifting force. Because air is supplied continuously, the work piece will keep levitating with a very thin gap of hundred micrometers from the vortex cup, through which air can be discharged into the atmosphere. For this reason, the work piece never has any contact with the vortex cup.

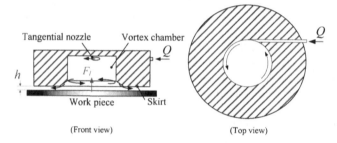

Fig. 1. Sketch of vortex cup

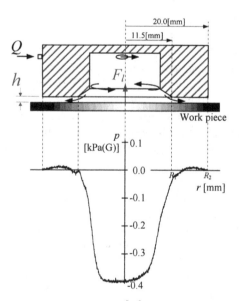

Fig. 2. Pressure distribution (Q=15.7[10^{-5}m^3/s(ANR)], h=0.45 ~ 0.85[mm])

3   Numerical Calculation

The numerical calculation was performed by use of the commercial finite volume flow solver Fluent 6.2. Fig. 3 shows a geometric model for the vortex cup after grid segmentation. A certain amount of air flow is supplied into the vortex chamber via the tangential nozzle and discharged into the atmosphere through the thin gap between the skirt of the vortex cup and the work piece. Therefore, the supply mass flow rate can be specified at the upstream of the tangential nozzle when the inlet boundary condition for calculation is to be defined. However, the outlet boundary condition cannot be set directly at the gap outlet, because the flow status at gap outlet is rather complicated to make it difficult to define the boundary conditions accurately. For this reason, with the sufficiently large space around the vortex cup being considered in calculation, as shown in Fig. 4, the outer surface of this space is defined as pressure outlet boundary with atmospheric pressure. The details of numerical calculation are listed in Table 1.

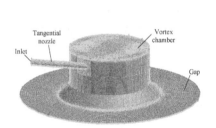

Fig. 3. Geometrical model of vortex cup   **Fig. 4.** Boundary conditions

Table 1. List of calculation conditions

Fluid	Ideal gas
Viscous	Turbulence
Inlet	Mass flow rate (G=18.7[10^{-5}kg/s])
Outlet	Pressure outlet (Atmospheric pressure)
Gap thickness	0.4 [mm]
Wall treatment	Enhance wall treatment
Discretization	Second order upwind
Grid cells	1280000

4   Visualization Experiment

In order to investigate the flow phenomena experimentally, a visualization experiment is conducted. The arrangement of the experimental setup is shown in Fig. 5 [5]. In this experiment, water is used as a working fluid to visualize easily. Water in a head tank with an overflow system goes through the water-supplying pipe, and then is adjusted to appropriate flow rate by hand valves, and enters an enlarged vortex cup placed in a test section from the nozzle. The issued water generates a swirling flow in the cup, and then goes out of the test section through the gap between the cup and the work piece. The overflow system enables stable water supplying. The cup is fixed at the bottom of the test section such that the open-end of the cup is in an upward direction. A plate is placed on the cup as a work piece. As shown in Fig. 6, ink is injected into the water supply pipe connected to the tangential nozzle, such that water flow can be visualized. A sheet light lightens a layer and a camera records the flow.

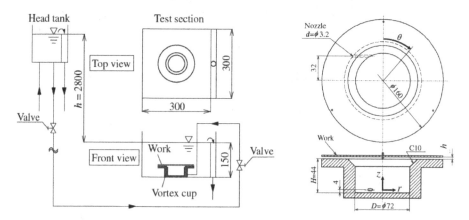

Fig. 5. Apparatus of visualization experiment (left: water circuit; right: enlarged vortex cup)

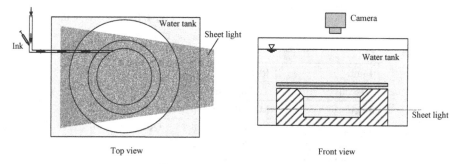

Fig. 6. Apparatus of visualization experiment

5   Results and Discussion

5.1   Turbulence Model

The vortex cup forms a flow field in high-speed swirl in vortex chamber, accompanied with occurrence of turbulence. Turbulence is characterized by the existence of fluctuating velocity fields, which are too computationally expensive to simulate directly in practical engineering calculations since these fluctuations can be of small scale and high frequency. A frequently adopted approach is to describe the flow field by averaging the time of solution velocity, and the fluctuating velocity component is substituted in Navier-Stokes equation as an additional tension term during the process of solution. As for how to treat Reynolds stress, a number of turbulence models have been proposed, but none of which is applicable to all turbulence situations. In this study, two turbulence models are applied respectively to calculate the flow field of the vortex cup, and their results are compared with experimental result. They are the simplest yet the most frequently-used standard k-ε model and the most complicated Reynolds stress model (short for RSM), the main difference of which lies in whether the anisotropy of Reynolds stress is taken into account [6-8].

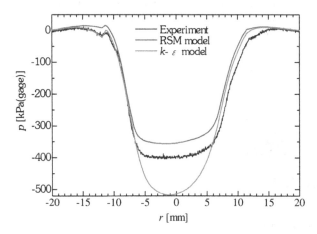

Fig. 7. Pressure distribution (h=0.4[mm], Q=15.7[10^{-5}m^3/s (ANR)])

5.2   Pressure Distribution

In the previous chapter, the pressure distribution on the upper surface of the work piece has been measured through experiment. Next, a comparison between experimental and calculated results is conducted. As shown in Fig. 7, the air spins in vortex chamber and generates centrifugal force, which causes the pressure in the central part to be lower than that in the peripheral region and gives rise to negative pressure. We can see that both of the turbulence models can well reproduce such a phenomenon. From the angle of pressure-distribution shape, however, note that the pressure distribution in the central part appears rather abated, comparing with the intense pressure distribution in the peripheral region. Such a distribution shape failed to be calculated perfectly with standard k-ε model, while the characteristics were well reflected by RSM. Therefore, it is thought that the flow in vortex cup can be better calculated by RSM.

In the meantime, it is noticed that in comparison with experimental results, the calculated results of RSM contained certain error in absolute value of pressure, which was especially prominent around the gap entrance (11.5[mm]<r<15[mm]). This is because of the discontinuous variation in the sectional area of flow passage existed around the gap entrance. Prior research works imply that when the air gets access to a thin gap from relatively capacious space, complicated flow phenomena, such as turbulence of air flow, separation and reattachment, will emerge around the gap entrance [9, 10]. These phenomena are difficult to be reproduced precisely through numerical calculation. However, such an error will not impede the analysis on the main characteristics of the flow field inside the vortex cup.

The following to be discussed is the spatial pressure distribution. Fig. 8 displays the pressure distribution on a vertical cross section, from which it can be seen that there is no significant vertical pressure variation vertically, and the center of pressure distribution deviates from the geometrical central axle. Fig. 9 shows the center of negative pressure. It can be seen that the upper half of the center of negative pressure deviates from the geometrical central axle and is close to nozzle outlet, while the lower half is on the other side of the central axle, which is distant from the tangential nozzle. The reason lies in that the vortex cup has only one tangential nozzle, which renders vortex cup with an asymmetric structure and consequently, induces asymmetric flow field and asymmetric pressure distribution.

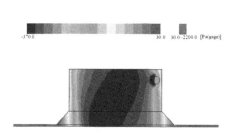
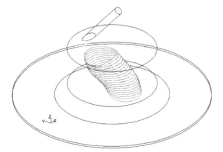

Fig. 8. Vertical pressure distribution   **Fig. 9.** Center of negative pressure

5.3   Velocity Distribution

In this section, the air flow inside the vortex cup is observed based on depicted trajectories through numerical results. If it is presumed that massless particles are invested at nozzle inlet, then the blue lines in Fig. 10 are the flow trajectories of the particles. It can be seen that after air blowing into the vortex chamber via the tangential nozzle, the flow cross section expanded unceasingly while spinning along the circular wall to form swirling flow. Fig. 10 shows that some air get into the gap between work piece and the skirt of the vortex cup after rotating less than one circle in the chamber. Note that the air has a tangential velocity component when entering the gap, but the viscous friction at the narrow gap decreased the tangential velocity component gradually to zero. Therefore, the air flowing through the skirt has bended flow trajectories. It is also noticed that the majority of the trajectories is along the wall due to the existence of centrifugal force, and only a very small part of flow lines might flow towards the central part of the vortex chamber. Fig. 11 displays the spatial position of the center of swirling flow, which exhibits a variation trend nearly identical to that of negative pressure centre shown in Fig. 9. Fig. 12 shows the result of the visualization experiment (top view and front view). After being blown into the cup, the ink flow is similar to the simulation.

In case of swirling flow, it is the tangential flow velocity and its variation and distribution that determine the negative-pressure distribution, lifting force and other properties of the vortex cup. Next, four cross sections were sampled vertically as shown in Fig. 13, and the distributions of tangential velocity component with respect to the geometrical central axle of the vortex cup are sorted and shown in Fig. 14, Firstly, the characteristics of velocity distribution are analyzed based on Fig. 14 (1), from which it can be seen that the air is blown into the chamber with a high speed from the tangential nozzle and forms intensive velocity distribution before the nozzle outlet, while the velocity distribution distant from the tangential nozzle appeared slightly gentler, which results in rather asymmetric distribution at the cross section. As the air swirling downward, Fig. 14(2) and (3) shows that the velocity distribution in all directions became uniform gradually. When air flowing into the gap and advancing radially, as shown in Fig. 14(4), the tangential velocity component of the air decreased gradually to zero under the viscous friction of the thin gap. Also note that all the distributions of four cross sections have a common point, that is, the flow-velocity distribution on the periphery of the vortex chamber is intensive, while that in the central part appears very gentle. This can explain why a rather flat pressure distribution is formed in the central part as described in the previous sections.

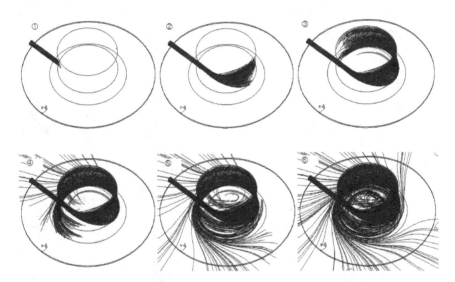

Fig. 10. Swirling flow inside vortex cup

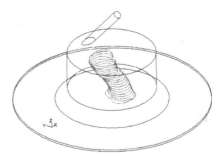

Fig. 11. Center of swirling flow

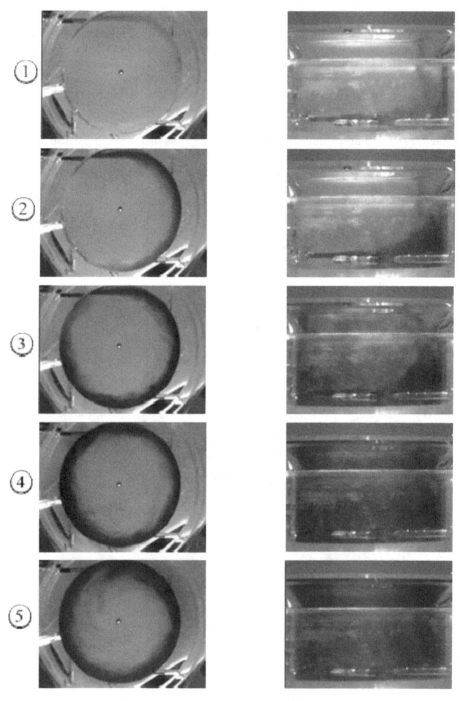

Fig. 12. Visualization result (left: top view, right: front view)

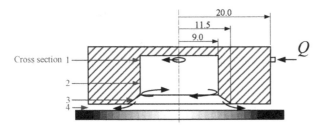

Fig. 13. Position of cross sections

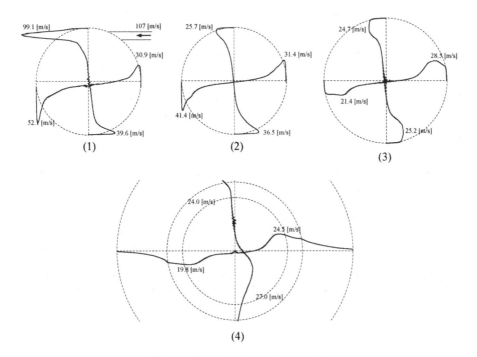

Fig. 14. Tangential velocity distribution

6   Conclusions

In this work, a computational fluid dynamics (CFD) calculation and a visualization experiment were conducted to help us understand the vortex cup and its flow phenomena. Firstly, the numerical calculation was carried out using standard k-ε model and RSM, and the experimental pressure distribution on the upper surface of the work piece is used to verify the numerical results. It is revealed that RSM can reproduce the characteristics of experimental results better than standard k-ε model. Furthermore, we used ink to visualize the flow with an enlarged vortex cup in water. Based on the calculation results of RSM and visualization observation, it is made clear that there is an asymmetric swirling flow field inside the vortex cup, and consequently results in an asymmetric velocity and pressure distribution. In case of swirling flow, the tangential flow velocity and its variation and distribution determine the negative-pressure distribution. In the numerical results, the correspondence of pressure distribution to tangential velocity distribution was confirmed.

References

1. Vandaele, V., Lambert, P., Delchambre, A.: Non-contact handling in microassembly. Precision Engineering 29(4), 491–505 (2005)
2. Brandt, E.H.: Levitation in physics. Science 243(4889), 349–355 (1989)
3. Li, X., Kawashima, K., Kagawa, T.: Analysis of vortex levitation. Experimental Thermal and Fluid Science 32(8), 1448–1454 (2008)
4. Li, X., Tokunaga, H., Cai, M.L., Hunaki, T., Kawashima, K., Kagawa, T.: Research on a non-contact handling system using swirling flow. Japan Fluid Power System 38(1), 1–6 (2007)
5. Iio, S., Umebachi, M., Li, X., Kagawa, T., Ikeda, T.: Performance of a non-contact handling device using swirling flow with various gap height. Journal of Visualization 13(4), 319–326 (2010)
6. Cortes, C., Gil, A.: Modeling the gas and particle flow inside cyclone separators. Progress in Energy and Combustion Science 33, 409–452 (2007)
7. Gupta, A., Kumar, R.: Three-dimensional turbulent swirling flow in a cylinder: Experiments and computations. International Journal of Heat and Fluid Flow 28(2), 249–261 (2006)
8. Fluent Inc.: Fluent manual (2005)
9. Ichikawa, T.: Effect of inlet configuration on annular separation bubble around the inlet corner and viscous radial flow structure between two parallel disks. Daido Institute of Technology 37, 63–75 (2001)
10. Kawaguchi, T.: Entrance loss for turbulent flow without swirl between parallel discs. Trans. of the Japan Society of Mechanical Engineers 36(288), 1341–1348 (1970)

Numerical Simulation and Linear Active Disturbance Rejection Control of Unstable Heat Conduction Systems[*]

Dong Zhao[1], Donghai Li[2,**], Yanzhen Chang[3], and Youqing Wang[1,**]

[1] College of Information Science and Technology, Beijing University of Chemical Technology, Beijing, 100029, China
[2] State Key Lab of Power Systems, Department of Thermal Engineering, Tsinghua University, Beijing, 100084, China
[3] College of science, Beijing University of Chemical Technology, Beijing, 100029, China
lidongh@mail.tsinghua.edu.cn, wang_youqing@mail.buct.edu.cn

Abstract. This paper presents a numerical solution to one-dimensional unstable heat conduction systems with three different boundary conditions, e.g., a thin rod with heat conduction only in the length direction. A finite difference method combined with a physically feasible and high-precision boundary realization approach is employed to calculate the temperature values along the rod under Dirichlet, Neumann, and Robin boundary conditions, respectively. Using the temperature at a desired position, a simple and excellent robustness controller——linear active disturbance rejection control (LADRC) could give an effective actuation on one boundary to get the temperature on the desired position under close-loop control. Finally, the robustness of the proposed controller with respect to external noises and parameter perturbations is also tested.

Keywords: heat conduction systems, distributed parameter systems, finite difference method, boundary control, active disturbance rejection control.

1 Introduction

One-dimensional unstable heat conduction systems modeled by using partial differential equation (PDE) is a typical distributed parameter system (DPS). In fact, many types of diffusion, such as chemical diffusion and electron flow, can be modeled by using similar PDEs. To simulate the one-dimensional unstable heat conduction systems, we should get the solution of PDE. As we all know, in most cases the analytical solution of PDE is difficult and even impossible to obtain. On the other hand, for simulation and control, the numerical solution of PDE is enough; hence we employed a finite difference method to get the numerical solution.

---

[*] This work is supported by the National Natural Science Foundation of China (Grant NO. 51176086, 51076071, and 61074081) and Doctoral Fund of Ministry of Education of China (Grant NO. 20100010120011).

[**] Corresponding author.

T. Xiao, L. Zhang, and S. Ma (Eds.): ICSC 2012, Part I, CCIS 326, pp. 35–46, 2012.

According to Dirichlet, Neumann, and Robin boundary conditions, corresponding integral methods are used to guarantee high precision and physical feasibility.

For controlling and analyzing of DPS, people accustomed to use the transfer function. Using Laplace transform, we can get the transfer function for DPS [1, 2]. However, the transfer function of DPS is usually irrational transfer function, which is infinite-dimensional. Generally it is very hard to realize an infinite-dimensional model and to design a control law directly based on this model. To solve this issue, various model approximation methods were presented [1, 3, 4]. The basic idea of these model approximate methods is the same: using a finite-dimensional model to approximate the infinite-dimensional model. Even though the approximation error could be very small, system's poles and zeros are significantly changed [1]; hence, the performance of the controller based on those approximation models is limited. For a more strict control form, a backstepping method [5] and optimal control [6] were proposed, as these two methods all need accurate mathematical model, for engineering practice, it is very complicated in controller design and the robustness will be quite poor when there exist disturbances. Due to those reasons, the ordinary PDE system should be simulated and model independent control algorithm is a promising way to control this system. Linear active disturbance rejection control (LADRC) is an excellent model independent control algorithm [7, 8]. Through estimating and compensating disturbances automatically, LADRC has great robustness to model-plant mismatch; consequently, it has a significant engineering practical value and can be easily implemented in industrial practice.

In this paper, the following one-dimensional heat conduction system is considered: a thin rod with one endpoint under control and another endpoint having fixed boundary condition. Using the temperature measurements of a given position on the rod, the control signals for the controlled endpoint can be designed according to different boundary conditions and hence the whole temperature profile in the rod could be controlled.

The rest part of this paper is organized as follows. The problem formulation and the numerical solution method are given in section 2. The structure and tuning method of LADRC are introduced in section 3. Some simulation results are presented in section 4. Finally, section 5 offers concluding remarks.

2   Problem Formulation and Numerical Solution

2.1   Problem Description

We consider heat conduction on a thin, homogeneous, and isotropic rod. It is a typical problem of a large class of industrial processes [9, 10]. The length of the thin rod is L and the diameter of the cross section is d. It is just assumed that $L \gg d$, so the temperature at any point of a cross section is the same. The heat conduction is only in the length direction with no heat exchange or heat loss on the cylindrical surface. What is more, the heat source is only in one end and another end is fixed. The constant thermal conductivity is k_0, mass density is ρ and specific heat is c_p. So the temperature $T(x,t)$ at time t and position x from the left hand end [1] is as follow:

$$\frac{\partial T(x,t)}{\partial t} = a\frac{\partial^2 T(x,t)}{\partial x^2}, \quad L > x > 0, \ t > 0,$$

$$T(x,0) = T_0, \ a = \frac{k_0}{c_p \rho}. \tag{1}$$

$T(x,0)$ is the initial temperature, T_0 is normal temperature. In order to simplify the problem, we assume $T_0 = 0$. Different from ordinary differential equation, the solution subjects to initial conditions, PDE needs initial condition and also boundary condition. Now we will introduce the approaches to utilize different types of boundary condition and the numerical calculation method.

2.2   Dirichlet Boundary Condition

Suppose the variable heat source is in the position $x = L$ and we can measure the temperature at the desired position of the rod, the Dirichlet boundary condition becomes

$$T(0,t) = 0, \quad T(L,t) = u(t). \tag{2}$$

First, divide rod in the x direction into N equal parts and the space step is h, define time step as τ, so the heat conduction PDE with initial condition and boundary condition will become

$$\frac{\partial T(nh, j\tau)}{\partial t} = a\frac{\partial^2 T(nh, j\tau)}{\partial x^2},$$

$$T(nh,0) = T_0 = 0,$$

$$T(0, j\tau) = 0, T(Nh, j\tau) = u, \tag{3}$$

$$0 \le n \le N, 0 \le j < m,$$

$$a = \frac{k_0}{c_p \rho}.$$

Use the Crank-Nicholson difference scheme [11] and it is unconditionally stable, as shown in Figure 1. For convenience, T(nh, jτ) in the sequel, so the discrete PDE is as follow:

$$\frac{T(n, j+1) - T(n, j)}{\tau} = \frac{1}{2}a[\frac{T(n+1, j+1) - 2T(n, j+1) + T(n-1, j+1)}{h^2}$$

$$+ \frac{T(n+1, j) - 2T(n, j) + T(n-1, j)}{h^2}],$$

$$n = 1, 2, ..., N-1, \quad j = 0, 1, ..., m-1, \tag{4}$$

$$T(n,0) = 0, \qquad n = 1, 2, ..., N-1,$$

$$T(0, j) = 0, \quad T(N, j) = u(j), \qquad j = 0, 1, ..., m.$$

The truncation error is [11]:

$$R = O(\tau^2) + O(h^2).$$

(5)

If we expand (4) in any two layers along the time direction and rewrite the result into a clear matrix form[11], we will get the final computation formula in (6).

$$AT_{j+1} = BT_j + F, \qquad j = 0, 1, \ldots, m-1,$$

$$T_j = \begin{bmatrix} T(1, j) \\ T(2, j) \\ \vdots \\ T(N-2, j) \\ T(N-1, j) \end{bmatrix}, \ F = \begin{bmatrix} \lambda T(0, j+1) + \lambda T(0, j) \\ 0 \\ \vdots \\ 0 \\ \lambda T(N, j+1) + \lambda T(N, j) \end{bmatrix}$$

$$A = \begin{bmatrix} 2(1+\lambda) & -\lambda & 0 & \cdots & & 0 \\ -\lambda & 2(1+\lambda) & -\lambda & \cdots & & 0 \\ \vdots & \vdots & \vdots & \vdots & & \vdots \\ 0 & \cdots & & -\lambda & 2(1+\lambda) & -\lambda \\ 0 & \cdots & & 0 & -\lambda & 2(1+\lambda) \end{bmatrix},$$

$$B = \begin{bmatrix} 2(1-\lambda) & \lambda & 0 & \cdots & & 0 \\ \lambda & 2(1-\lambda) & \lambda & \cdots & & 0 \\ \vdots & \vdots & \vdots & \vdots & & \vdots \\ 0 & \cdots & & \lambda & 2(1-\lambda) & \lambda \\ 0 & \cdots & & 0 & \lambda & 2(1-\lambda) \end{bmatrix}.$$

(6)

A is one diagonally dominant matrix which ensures the existence of solution to (6). Solving the linear equations about T_{j+1} with initial condition and boundary condition shown in (4), the temperature profile of the rod under Dirichlet boundary condition in any time point will be obtained.

2.3   Neumann Boundary Condition

The Neumann boundary condition is described as below

$$\frac{\partial T(0,t)}{\partial x} = 0, \quad \frac{\partial T(L,t)}{\partial x} = u(t).$$

(7)

The left boundary condition is fixed, $u(t)$ is the time varying right boundary condition. We know that Crank-Nicholson difference scheme is second order accuracy in time and in space direction as shown in (5), for making the accuracy of the boundary numerical solution meets (5), furthermore, guarantees the physically feasible of the solution, an integral method is used[12].

First, we consider the left boundary. Integrating system (1) about x in the left boundary, one gets

$$\int_0^{0.5h} \frac{\partial T(x, j+1)}{\partial t} dx = \int_0^{0.5h} a \frac{\partial^2 T(x, j+1)}{\partial x^2} dx. \tag{8}$$

Where

$$\int_0^{0.5h} \frac{\partial T(x, j+1)}{\partial t} dx = a \frac{\partial T(x, j+1)}{\partial x}\bigg|_{x=0.5h} - a \frac{\partial T(x, j+1)}{\partial x}\bigg|_{x=0}. \tag{9}$$

Refer to (7), (9) becomes

$$\int_0^{0.5h} \frac{\partial T(x, j+1)}{\partial t} dx = a \frac{\partial T(x, j+1)}{\partial x}\bigg|_{x=0.5h} - 0 \approx 0.5h \frac{\partial T(x, j+1)}{\partial t}. \tag{10}$$

Hence, set x=0 for the right hand side of (10), the finite difference form of (10) is obtained

$$T(0, j+1) = \frac{T(0, j) + 2\lambda T(1, j+1)}{1+2\lambda}, \quad \lambda = a \frac{\tau}{h^2}. \tag{11}$$

Now is the right boundary. Integrating system (1) about x in the right boundary, just follow the same procedure from (8) to (10), we will get the numerical solution for the right boundary.

$$T(N, j+1) = \frac{T(N, j) + 2\lambda T(N-1, j+1) + 2\lambda hu(j+1)}{1+2\lambda}, \quad \lambda = a \frac{\tau}{h^2}. \tag{12}$$

Now we can solve the linear matrix equations about T_{j+1} in (6) with boundary conditions shown in (11) and (12) under Neumann boundary condition.

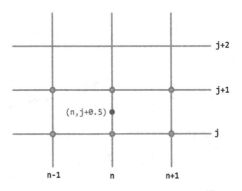

Fig. 1. Illustration of Crank-Nicholson difference scheme. In order to calculate T(n, j+0.5) shown in red 6 points will be involved as shown in green. $1 \le n \le N-1$.

2.4   Robin Boundary Condition

Now we consider a more complex situation.

$$\frac{\partial T(0,t)}{\partial x} - b_1 T(0,t) = 0, \quad \frac{\partial T(L,t)}{\partial x} - b_2 T(L,t) = u(t). \tag{13}$$

Use a same method as in Neumann boundary condition to deal with the left and right boundary conditions[12]. The final calculation expression is shown in (14).

$$T(0, j+1) = \frac{T(0, j) + 2\lambda T(1, j+1)}{1 + 2\lambda + 2\lambda hb_1},$$

$$T(N, j+1) = \frac{T(N, j) + 2\lambda T(N-1, j+1) + 2\lambda hu(j+1)}{1 + 2\lambda - 2\lambda hb_2}. \tag{14}$$

Solving the linear matrix equations about T_{j+1} in (6) with boundary conditions shown in (14), the temperature profile under Robin Boundary condition can be calculated layer by layer.

3   Structure and Tuning Method of ADRC

Active disturbance rejection control (ADRC) was first proposed by Han [7, 13] and are widely used in many fields [14, 15]. In order to simplify the controller structure and reduce controller parameters, based on the concept of bandwidth, Gao used linear gain in place of the nonlinear gain in the control algorithm [8] and which is linear active disturbance rejection control(LADRC). A lot of literature and research work [16, 17] proof that LADRC can also get a excellent performance, what's more, it is easy to use. Inspired by Chen et al. [18] and Chai et al. [19], a second order LADRC can get plants well controlled, as an example, here we just introduce and discuss the second order LADRC.

3.1   The Structure of LADRC

The structure of second order LADRC is illustrated in Figure 2.

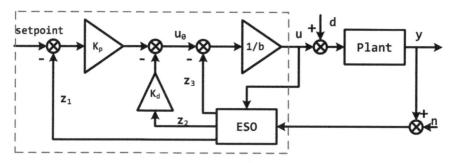

Fig. 2. The structure of second order LADRC

The part in the red dashed line box is the LADRC. Plant is the process to be controlled, d is external disturbance and n is the measurement noise.

LADRC has a key term, extended state observer (ESO). By estimating and compensating the internal (e. g. parameters perturbation or system order changed in plant) and external disturbances (e. g. load fluctuation or noise), the system will be well controlled without accurate mathematical model.

The mathematical expression of second order ESO is shown as follow:

$$\begin{aligned}
e &= y - z_1, \\
\dot{z}_1 &= z_2 + \beta_1 e, \\
\dot{z}_2 &= z_3 + \beta_2 e + bu, \\
\dot{z}_3 &= \beta_3 e.
\end{aligned} \tag{15}$$

Where β_1, β_2 and β_3 are the observer parameters. The control law of LADRC is

$$\begin{aligned}
u_0 &= k_p(r - z_1) - k_d z_2, \\
u &= \frac{u_0 - z_3}{b},
\end{aligned} \tag{16}$$

where r is the setpoint and b is an adjustable parameter. Now we will reveal the secrets of (15) and (16).

First, define the model of the plant as G which can be organized into a simple form

$$\ddot{y} = f + bu. \tag{17}$$

Where y is the process output, u is the process input and f is the whole combined error of G apart from $\ddot{y}$ and bu, no matter the process is linear or nonlinear, low order or high order, time varying or constant, (17) will be established. Then, get the observer represented by (15) well tuned, z_1, z_2, z_3 will track y, $\dot{y}$ and f respectively.

Finally, combined with (15), (17) turns to be

$$\begin{aligned}
z_3 &\approx f, \\
\ddot{y} = f + bu &= f + b\frac{u_0 - z_3}{b} \\
&\approx u_0.
\end{aligned} \tag{18}$$

This is dynamic feedback linearization which makes the control system a simple cascade integral system.

3.2   Tuning Method of LADRC

Based on (16), employ the tuning method in [8, 18]

$$G_c = \frac{\omega_c^2}{(s+\omega_c)^2},$$

$$k_p = \omega_c^2, \quad k_d = 2\omega_c. \tag{19}$$

Where ω_c is defined as control bandwidth [8]. Furthermore, as presented in (20)

$$\frac{z_3}{f} = \frac{\beta_3}{s^3 + \beta_1 s^2 + \beta_2 s + \beta_3},$$

$$\beta_1 = 3\omega_o, \quad \beta_2 = 3\omega_o^2, \quad \beta_3 = 4\beta_2, \tag{20}$$

$$\omega_o = 4\omega_c.$$

Where ω_o is the observer bandwidth [8].

Hence, give an appropriate control bandwidth ω_c, we can get the controller parameters from (19) and observer parameters from (20), finally, monotonously increase b from a small value to a appropriate value which satisfies the dynamic performance.

4   Simulation Result

The numerical solutions and control algorithm are discussed in section 2 and section 3 respectively, now, we will get the one dimensional unstable heat conduction systems controlled with different boundary conditions.

Table 1. Controller parameters of LADRC under Dirichlet(D), Neumann(N) and Robin(R) boundary condition

Parameters	Value(D/N/R)	Parameters	Value(D/N/R)
Setpoint r	1/1/1	β_1	240/168/204
Time step hz	0.01/0.01/0.01	β_2	19200/9408/13872
ω_c	20/14/17	β_3	76800/37632/55488
ω_o	80/56/68	k_p	400/196/289
b	300/21/20	k_d	40/28/34

For simulation study, the length of rod is $L = 2$, desired point $x_d = 1.5$, time step $\tau = 0.01s$, space step $h = 0.05$, time length $t_l = 10s$, $a = 1$. The controller parameters are shown in Table 1.

The simulation results of Dirichlet, Neumann and Robin boundary conditions are shown in Figure 3, Figure 4 and Figure 5 respectively. Subgraph (a), (b), (c) and (d) in figures (Fig 3, Fig 4, Fig 5) illustrate output response to different disturbances. In order to verify robustness of the control algorithm, a $\pm 20\%$ change in parameter a which means thermal diffusivity is added. The results are illustrated in the subgraph (e) and subgraph (f) in the figures (Fig 3, Fig 4, Fig 5). IAE indexes for the conditions in Figure 3, Figure 4 and Figure 5 are in Table 2.

Table 2. IAE index for different conditions under Dirichlet(D), Neumann(N) and Robin(R) boundary condition

Condition	IAE(D/N/R)	Condition	IAE(D/N/R)
Normal	49.33/30.24/20.32	Step and noise	65.51/38.35/27.10
Step disturbance	63.99/32.56/21.77	$a=1.2$	49.03/28.23/18.95
Measured noise	51.36/35.93/26.81	$a=0.8$	50.86/33.28/22.84

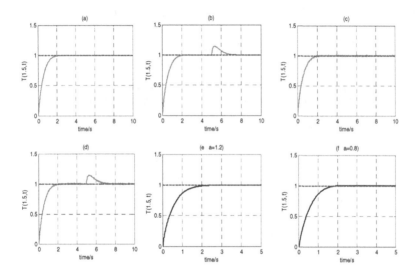

Fig. 3. Output response to different disturbances and robustness testing under Dirichlet boundary condition. The subgraph (a) is a normal condition without any noise or disturbances. A 0.5 step disturbance is added to the control signal u at the time t=5s in subgraph (b). Where in subgraph (c), there exists a measurement noise amplitude [-0.01, 0.01]. The subgraph (d) has all the disturbances existing in subgraph (b) and (c). A +20% change in thermal diffusivity a under Dirichlet boundary condition in (e), where (f) is a -20% situation.

The output response figures (Fig 3, 4, 5) and the corresponding IAE index table (Table 2) all indicate that the controller has excellent disturbance rejection ability and strong robust. Even a 20% change in the key parameter of heat conduction system, the controller still works well. What is more, although the boundary condition is more and more complex, the simulation results show that the performance of the controller is not getting worse and worse but better and better.

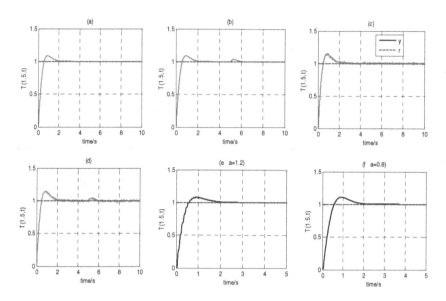

Fig. 4. Output response to different disturbances and robustness testing under Neumann boundary condition. All the testing scenarios are the same with that in Figure 3.

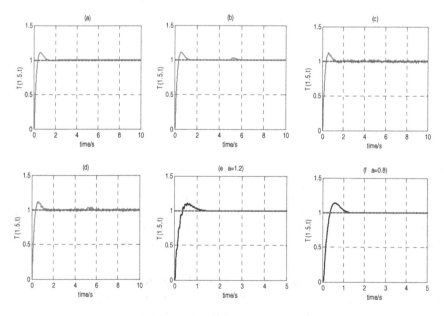

Fig. 5. Output response to different disturbances under Robin boundary condition. All the testing scenarios are the same with that in Figure 3.

5   Conclusions

A finite difference numerical solution with a physically feasible and high precision boundary realization approach is introduced; it is employed to realization the model of one dimensional unstable heat conduction directly without the truncation errors cased by approximation method. What's more, LADRC, a simple, model independent and excellent disturbance rejection ability control algorithm is utilized to control the process of heat conduction. Simulation results indicate that the LADRC has a strong robustness and can produce satisfactory output response under internal and external disturbances. As the model is realized directly, control algorithm is model independent and verified to be strong robustness and excellent disturbance rejection ability, which will easily be implemented from simulation to industrial practice.

References

1. Ruth, C., Kirsten, M.: Transfer Functions of Distributed Parameter Systems: A Tutorial. Automatica 45, 1101–1116 (2009)
2. Zhou, J.P., Lei, Y.J.: Transfer Function Method of Distributed Parameter systems. Science Press, Beijing (2010)
3. Shieh, L.S., Chen, C.F.: Analysis of Irrational Transfer Functions for Distributed Parameter Systems. IEEE Transactions on Aerospace and Electronic Systems 5, 967–973 (1969)
4. Dean, J.S.: Realization of Irrational Transfer Functions. IEEE Transactions on Circuits and Systems—I: Fundamental Theory and Applications 43, 588–591 (1996)
5. Dejan, M.B., Andras, B., Miroslav, K.: Backstepping in Infinite Dimension for a Class of Parabolic Distributed Parameter Systems. Mathematics of Control, Signals, and Systems 16, 44–75 (2003)
6. Ng, J., Dubljevic, S.: Optimal Boundary Control of Parabolic PDE with Time-Varying Spatial Domain. In: Proceedings of the 4th International Symposium on ADCONIP, Hangzhou, China, pp. 216–221 (2011)
7. Han, J.Q.: From PID to Active Disturbance Rejection Control. IEEE Transactions on Industrial Electronics 56, 900–906 (2009)
8. Gao, Z.Q.: Scaling and Bandwidth Parameterization Based Controller Tuning. In: Proceedings of the American Control Conference, pp. 4989–4996. IEEE Press, Denver (2003)
9. Dejan, M.B., Krstic, M., Liu, W.: Boundary Control of an Unstable Heat Equation via Measurement of Domain Averaged Temperature. IEEE Trans. Autom. Control 46, 2022–2028 (2001)
10. Czisik, M.N., Azis, K.: Heat Conduction. Wiley, New York (1993)
11. Gao, Y.C.: Mathematical Physics Equation and Its Numerical Solution. Higher Education Press, Beijing (1983)
12. Li, R.H.: Numerical Solution of Partial differential equation. Higher Education Press, Beijing (2005)
13. Han, J.Q.: Auto-Disturbance Rejection Control and Its applications. Control and Decision 13, 19–23 (1998)
14. Xia, Y.Q., Liu, B.: Active Disturbance Rejection Control for Power Plant with A Single Loop. Asian Journal of Control 14, 239–250 (2012)

15. Xia, Y.Q., Shi, P., Liu, G.P.: Active Disturbance Rejection Control for Uncertain Multivariable Systems with Time-Delay. IET Control Theory Appl. 1, 75–81 (2007)
16. Jeffrey, C., Gao, Z.Q.: Uncertainty Reduction Through Active Disturbance Rejection. In: American Control Conference, Seattle, pp. 3689–3694 (2008)
17. Chen, Z.Z., Zheng, Q., Gao, Z.Q.: Active disturbance Rejection Control of Chemical Processes. In: 16th IEEE International Conference on Control Applications Part of IEEE Multi-Conference on Systems and Control, Singapore, pp. 855–861 (2007)
18. Chen, X., Li, D.H., Gao, Z.Q., Wang, C.F.: Tuning Method for Second-Order Active Disturbance Rejection Control. In: Proceedings of The 30th Chinese Control Conference, Yantai, pp. 6322–6327 (2011)
19. Chai, S.J., Li, D.H., Yao, X.L.: Active Disturbance Rejection Controller for High-Order System. In: Proceedings of The 30th Chinese Control Conference, Yantai, pp. 3798–3802 (2011)
20. Han, J.Q.: Active Disturbance Rejection Control Technique. National Defense Industry Press, Beijing (2008)

Output Power Analysis and Simulations of Resonant Tunneling Diode Based Oscillators

Liquan Wang

Shanghai Institute of Mechanics and Electricity Engineering
412 Guilin Road, Shanghai, China
leo.liqwang@gmail.com

Abstract. Negative differential resistance (NDR) devices such as Esaki tunnel diodes (TD), Gunn diodes and resonant tunneling diodes (RTD) are excellent in the realization of high frequency oscillators. However, for tunnel diodes and RTDs, which have large negative differential conductance, the output power tends to be low due to the DC instability, parasitic oscillations and the small area devices employed. In this paper, the maximum device areas for different NDR oscillator topologies, such as waveguide topology and planar topology, were calculated. The result shows that NDR devices for planar oscillators can be much larger (ranging from 3 to 1600 times) than those could be used in waveguide oscillators. A derivation of the maximum RF output power of a parallel RTD oscillator circuit is given and the simulations show that ~1 mW output power could be achieved at 800 GHz for a single diode oscillator.

Keywords: resonant tunneling diode, planar oscillator, output power analysis.

1 Introduction

Recently, millimetre-wave and submillimetre-wave signal sources are widely required for a variety of applications, such as security and surveillance [1], pollution monitoring and disease detection [2], high-resolution imaging radar [3] and hardware in the loop simulations for army weapon system [4]. Resonant tunneling diode (RTD) is one of electronic devices may be used to build millimetrewave and submillimetre-wave sources. The RTD has been carefully analysed and employed in several high frequency applications. Trigger circuits employing fast switching have been realized up to 110 GHz [5], waveguide oscillators were realised up to 712 GHz [6] and planar oscillators have been reported up to 1 THz [7]. However, the output power levels at high frequency (millimetre-wave) were all low. For example, RF power of -15.5 dBm (28 μW) was measured at 290 GHz [8], and the highest power of -7 dBm (200 μW)at 100 GHz and at 443 GHz, respectively [9], [10]. The reasons for the very low output power of the RTD-based oscillators include small device areas required to suppress low-frequency parasitic bias oscillations [11] and/or the inefficient oscillator circuit topologies employed[12].

RTD oscillators have been implemented in either waveguide technology in planar technology. Reported RTD oscillators implemented in waveguide technology delivered low output power(< -15dBm). This was mainly due the small device areas

T. Xiao, L. Zhang, and S. Ma (Eds.): ICSC 2012, Part I, CCIS 326, pp. 47–55, 2012.

required for suppressing bias oscillations and partly due to impedance mismatch to the load [12].Planar RTD oscillators, on the other hand, eliminate parasitic bias oscillations in an oscillator circuit by employing a shunt resistor to the NDR device [13], [14]. At millimetre-wave and low terahertz frequencies (< 1 THz), planar RTD oscillators have been integrated in slot antennas [14], [15]. The RTD devices are usually integrated at the centre of the slot antenna, a location at which the antenna input impedance is infinity. Therefore the device is mismatched with the antenna load and so the oscillator output power is low. In recognition of this problem, recent work has used devices offset from the slot antenna centre with improved results [10].

In this paper, we calculated the maximum device size for waveguide RTD topology and planar RTD topology, which shows that the planar oscillator topology can employ larger devices compared to those implemented in waveguide topology. Output power analysis based onthe cubic polynomial model [12], [16], [17]for the RTD *I-V* characteristics is carried out. One this basis, predictions on the output power of RTD oscillators in various material designs can be made. It shows that RTDoscillators with single device can delivermillimeterwave and submillimeterwavesources with high output power (~ 1dBm).It is likely to realize RTD based millimeterwavesources with sufficient output power (~ 10 dBm) for applications, such as disease detection and hardware-in-the-loop simulations for millimeterwave radar echo signals, by using power combing topology as illustrated in Ref. [18].

2   Maximum Device Size for Different Oscillator Topology

Fig.1(a) illustrated an equivalent circuit model of an RTD and its typical current-voltage (I-V) characteristicis shown in Fig. 1(b). The equivalent circuitmodel of an RTD includes the parasitic series resistance R_s, series inductanceL_s, voltage-controlled current source $I(V)$ and self-capacitance of the NDR deviceC_n.V_p, V_V,I_P and I_V are the peak voltage, valley voltage, peak current and valley current of the RTD I-V characteristic as shown in Fig. 1(b),respectively. The maximum device area of waveguide RTD oscillator were given by Kidner et al [11], A_{max1}, and Eisele et al [19], A_{max2}, respectively

$$A_{\max 1} = \frac{4C_d}{9L}\left(\frac{\Delta V}{\Delta J}\right)^2 \tag{1}$$

$$A_{\max 2} = \frac{2\rho_s C_d \Delta V}{3L\Delta J} \tag{2}$$

where A_{max1} and A_{max2} are the maximum device areas using different calculating method [11], [19]. $C_d$is the capacitance per unit area of the device,L is the inductance between the bias and device, ΔV is the voltage difference between the peak and valley, ΔJ is the current density difference and ρ_s is the specific contact resistance. The cubic model for the $I-V$ characteristics is used in equation (2) instead of the piecewise linear model used in Ref. [19].

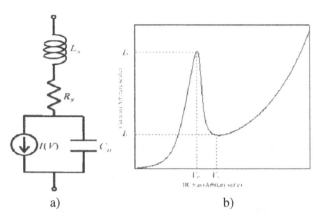

a)   b)

Fig. 1. a) RTD model with series resistance R_s and series inductance L_s. C_n is the device capacitance and $I(V)$ is the voltage controlled current source. b) Typical current-voltage characteristic of a resonant tunneling diode.

Having given the maximum device area of waveguide RTD oscillators, the maximum device area of planar RTD oscillators will also be derived. Fig. 2(a) illustrates ageneric equivalent circuit of planar RTD oscillator topology. R_b and L_b are the bias resistance and inductance, respectively. R_e is the stabilising resistor and C_e is employed as a RF short circuit at the oscillation frequency. L is the inductance used to determine the frequency of oscillation with self-capacitance of the NDR deviceC_n.C_{block} is employed as DC block and R_L is the load.

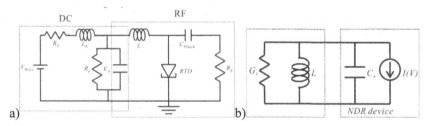

a)   b)

Fig. 2. a) A generic equivalent circuit of planar RTD oscillator topology. b) The simplified RF equivalent circuit of Fig. 2(a).

As illustrated in Fig. 2(a), a stabilising resistor R_e should be used in the planar RTD oscillator design topology in order to suppress the low-frequency bias oscillations [12], [15]and it should satisfy the condition $R_e< 1/G_n$ [15], [20]. For the cubic model for the I-V characteristic of an RTD, $G_n = 3\Delta I/2\Delta V$[17], [20], [21].Therefore, the maximum area of the RTD device used to form an oscillator can be approximated by [12]

$$A_{max 3} = \frac{2\Delta V}{3\Delta J R_e}$$
(3)

The theoretically maximum output power of planar oscillator can be obtained from the NDR device is given in Ref. [12], [21] and it can be written as

$$P_{max} = \frac{3}{16} \Delta I \Delta V = \frac{3}{16} \Delta J A_{max} \Delta V = \frac{\Delta V^2}{8R_e} \qquad (4)$$

For any given material, according to equation (4), since the voltage difference ΔV and current density difference ΔJ are fixed, the maximum RF output power depends on the maximum device area A_{max}. In the calculation of the maximum areas of the NDR devices used in waveguideRTD oscillators (A_{max1} and A_{max2}), a value of inductance L set to 100 pH [12], which is the same value as that wasused to calculate themaximum device areas (A_{max1} and A_{max2}) in Ref. [19]. Forthe calculation of the maximum area of the NDR device used to form a planarRTD oscillator (A_{max3}), a value of resistance R_e is set to 10Ω [12]. Table 1 shows the calculated maximum device areas A_{max1}, A_{max2}, and A_{max3} using equations (1)-(3) respectively for different published InP-based AlAs/InGaAs/AlAs double-barrier quantum-well RTD structures[14], [15], [22].

Table 1. Calculated maximum device areas for some published RTD InP-based RTD structures

Ref.	V_p (V)	V_v (V)	ΔJ (mA/μm^2)	ρ_s ($\Omega \mu m^2$)	C_d (fF/μm^2)	A_{max1} (μm^2)	A_{max2} (μm^2)	A_{max3} (μm^2)
[14]	0.9	1.30	2.75	2.2	3	0.28	0.006	9.7
[15]	1.4	0.9	3	3	5.85	0.72	0.02	11
[22]	0.5	0.75	0.75	48	12.35	6.1	1.32	21.9

From the estimations of maximum device areas for stabilised RTD oscillatorstabulated in Table 1, it is clear that RTD devices for planar RTD oscillators(A_{max3}) can be much larger (ranging from 3 to 1600 times) than those that couldbe used in waveguide RTD oscillators (A_{max1} and A_{max2}). This means the planarRTD oscillators can deliver significantly more power than waveguide RTD oscillators.

3   Output Power Analysis of Planar RTD Oscillators

From the discussion above, it shows that planarRTD oscillators can deliver significantly more power than waveguide RTD oscillators. Therefore, the variationof output power (planar oscillators) with frequency and load conductance will be discussed.

If the series resistor R_s and series inductance L_s are small and can be ignored,the RF equivalent circuit can be drawn as shown in Fig. 2(b) andit canbe described by equation (5) according to Kirchhoff's current law where thecurrent source is represented by a cubic polynomial with a and b both positiveparameters, $a = (3\Delta I)/(2\Delta V)$ andb $= (2\Delta I)/(\Delta V)^3$[16], [21].

$$LC_n \frac{d^2V}{dt^2} + L(G_L - a + 3bV^2)\frac{dV}{dt} + V = 0 \qquad (5)$$

Therefore, the power delivered to equivalent load $G_L(1/R_L)$ as shown in Fig. 2(a)can be given by equation (6) and the maximum   power is given in equation (4) [16], [21].

$$P_L = \frac{2(G_n - G_L)G_L}{3b} \tag{6}$$

However, the R_s and L_s expose a large impact on power delivery when the oscillation frequency of the circuit increases and it will be discussed. The RF equivalent circuit of a planar RTD oscillator (Fig. 2(a))with equivalent load (R'_L) in series with RTD is shown in Fig. 3(a) and Fig. 3(b) illustrates the RF equivalent circuit of a planar RTD oscillator (Fig. 2(a))with equivalent conductance (G'_L) parallel with RTD. The equivalent resistance R'_L and reactance X, and the equivalent conductance G'_L andsusceptance$B$ are described by [12]

$$R'_L = \frac{\omega^2 L^2 G_L}{1 + \omega^2 L^2 G_L{}^2} \tag{7}$$

$$X = \frac{\omega L}{1 + \omega^2 L^2 G_L{}^2} + \omega L_s \tag{8}$$

$$G'_L = \frac{R_s + \dfrac{\omega^2 L^2 G_L}{1 + \omega^2 L^2 G_L{}^2}}{\left(R_s + \dfrac{\omega^2 L^2 G_L}{1 + \omega^2 L^2 G_L{}^2}\right)^2 + \left(\dfrac{\omega L}{1 + \omega^2 L^2 G_L{}^2} + \omega L_s\right)^2} \tag{9}$$

$$B = \frac{\dfrac{\omega L}{1 + \omega^2 L^2 G_L{}^2} + \omega L_s}{\left(R_s + \dfrac{\omega^2 L^2 G_L}{1 + \omega^2 L^2 G_L{}^2}\right)^2 + \left(\dfrac{\omega L}{1 + \omega^2 L^2 G_L{}^2} + \omega L_s\right)^2} \tag{10}$$

where $K = \omega^2 L^2 G_L$ and $\omega = \sqrt{(L - C_n R_s{}^2)C_n} \,/\, [LC_n(1 + R_s G_L)]$.

The circuit of Fig. 3(b) is similar to the circuit of Fig. 2(b) and so the power delivered to equivalent load G'_Las shown in Fig. 3(b) can be given [12], [16], [21]

$$P'_L = \frac{2(G_n - G'_L)G'_L}{3b} \tag{11}$$

Referring to Fig. 3(a), since R'_L is an apparent load resistance due to the external circuit, and R'_L is in series with R_s, the power delivered to the load $R_L$can be expressed by [12]

$$P_L = \frac{2(G_n - G'_L)G'_L}{3b} \frac{R'_L}{R'_L + R_s} \tag{12}$$

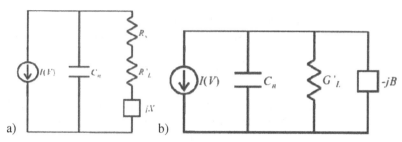

Fig. 3. a) A RF equivalent circuit of Fig. 2(a) with equivalent load (R'_L) in series with the RTD. b) A equivalent circuit of Fig. 2(a) with equivalent conductance (G'_L) parallel with the RTD.

The apparent load G'_L changes with different frequency and so does not presentan ideal load for maximum output power, i.e. output power drops with increasingfrequency. At any given frequency, an optimum value of the oscillator load G_L ofmay be found.

Approximate analysis of output power with frequency of tunnel diode oscillatorswas first provided in Reference [17] in which the equivalent resistance andinductance in equations (7) and (8) were assumed constant in the neighbourhoodof the oscillation frequency. In the analysis presented here, no suchassumptions are made. This analysis, however, does not include the effect ofthe tunnelling and transit times which modify the negative differential conductanceG_n and capacitance C_n of the device with increasing frequency [15]. These are thought to manifest themselves as reactive components in theequivalent circuit, a so-called quantum-well inductance in series with the negativedifferential conductance [22] and additional device capacitance [15]. Therefore theoutput power predicted by equation (12) should be considered as anupper limit on the maximum available output power. This is also because, to date,the intrinsic G_n is only an estimate as it has been impossible to determine it fromthe measured *I-V* curves which are usually distorted by oscillations and this maysoon change with the introduction of the DC and RF characterisation techniquesdescribed in Ref. [23].

4   Simulated Output Power for RTDs

Output power analysis of recently published planar RTD MMIC oscillatorsemploying resistor stabilisation was carried out by using MATLAB. For the oscillators describedin Ref. [15], the layer structure had been grown on a semi-insulating InP substrateand was as follows (from top of the material): n+ -GaInAs (30 nm), n-GaInAs (50 nm), GaInAs (undoped, 5 nm), AlAs, (undoped, 1.5 nm), GaInAs(undoped,4.5 nm), AlAs, (undoped, 1.5 nm), GaInAs (undoped, 5 nm), n-GaInAs(50 nm), n+ -GaInAs (400 nm). The material had a peak current density a $400kA/cm^2$ and a current peak to valley ratio of 3.5~4. The peak-to-valley voltagedifference (estimated from published *I-V* characteristics) was 0.5 V. From theseparameters, the maximum device area was estimated to be 11 μm^2 (using equation(3)) and the device capacitance calculated to be 64.5 fF [12]. R_s was estimated from the specific contact resistance of the Ti/Pd/

Au-Ohmic contacts on n+ InGaAs ($\rho_c = 3 \times 10^{-8}\Omega cm^2$, [12]) and the device area.The simulated output power versus frequency and load conductance is shown in Fig. 4. Here, L rangesfrom 0.4 to 1000 pH and the load conductance G_L ranges from 0.01-0.09 S. The simulation shows that the output power drops with frequency increases and it also varies with the different load conductance.The simulationalso shows that~0 dBm (~1 mW) output power could beachieved at 800 GHz for a single diode oscillator in this material system if the load conductance is set properly.

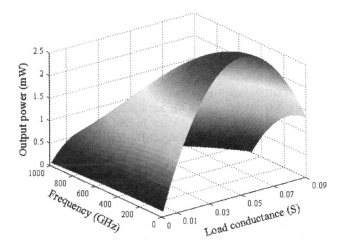

Fig. 4. Simulated output power variation of a planar RTD oscillator with frequency and load conductance by using material in ref. [15]

5   Conclusions

Output power analysis of the parallel RTD oscillator topology has been discussedin this paper. This oscillator topology can be stabilised resistively toeliminate bias oscillations. For a stabilised oscillator at low frequencies, an optimumload can be chosen for maximum output power. At high frequencies, theinfluence of parasitic elements start to dominate the oscillator performance andthe output power reduces (if the low frequency load remains fixed). Analytical expressionsderived for the variation of output power with frequency make it possibleto optimise the oscillator load with increasing frequency, and so maintain a higheroutput power over a larger frequency range. The actual load to the oscillator canbe matched to the optimal load by using impedance matching techniques.

References

1. Appleby, R., Anderton, R.N.: Millimeter-wave and Submillimeter-wave Imaging for Security and Surveillance, Explosives Hidden under Clothing can be Imaged by Submillimeter Waves, but Millimeter Waves are Better Suited for Guiding Helicopter Navigation in Poor Weather. Proceedings of IEEE 95, 1683–1690 (2007)

2. Siegel, P.H.: Terahertz Technology. IEEE Trans. Microw. Theory and Tech. 50, 910–928 (2002)
3. Cooper, K.B., Dengler, R.J., Chattopadhyay, G., Schlecht, E., Gill, J., Skalare, A., Mehdi, I., Siegel, P.H.: A High-Resolution Imaging Radar at 580 GHz. IEEE Microw. and Wireless Components Lett. 18, 64–66 (2008)
4. Kissell, A.H.: An Example of Simulation Use in Army Weapon System Development. In: Simulation Conference Proceedings, Phoenix, pp. 1079–1087 (1999)
5. Ozbay, E., Bloom, D.M.: 110-GHz Monolithic Resonant- tunnelling Diode Trigger Circuit. IEEE Electron Device Lett. 12, 480–482 (1991)
6. Brown, E.R., Soderstrom, J.R., Parker, C.D., Mahoney, L.J., Molvar, K.M., McGill, T.C.: Oscillations up to 712 GHz in InAS/AlSb Resonant Tunneling Diodes. Appl. Phys. Lett. 58, 2291–2293 (1991)
7. Suzuki, S., Asada, M., Teranishi, A., Sugiyama, H., Yokoyama, H.: Fundamental Oscillation of Resonant Tunneling Diodes above 1 THz at Room Temperature. Appl. Phys. Lett. 97, 242102–2421023-3 (2010)
8. Reddy, M., Martin, S.C., Molnar, A.C., Muller, R.E., Smith, R.P., Siegel, P.H., Mondry, M.J., Rodwell, M.J.W., Kroemer, H., Allen Jr., S.J.: Monolithic Schottky-Collector Resonant Tunnel Diode Oscillator Array to650 GHz. IEEE Electron Device Lett. 18, 218–221 (1997)
9. Brown, E.R., Parker, C.D., Calawa, A.R., Manfra, M.J., Molvar, K.M.: A Quasioptical Resonant-tunneling-diode Oscillator Operating above200 GHz. IEEETrans.Microw. Theory Tech. 41, 720–722 (1993)
10. Suzuki, S., Hinata, K., Shiraishi, M., Asada, M., Sugiyama, H., Yokoyama, H.: RTD Oscillators at 430-460 GHz with High Output Power (~200μW) Using Integrated Offset Slot Antennas. In: International Conference on IndiumPhosphide and Related Materials, Kagawa, pp. 1–4 (2010)
11. Kidner, C., Mehdi, I., East, J.R., Haddad, G.I.: Power and Stability Limitations of Resonant Tunnelling Diodes. IEEE Trans. Microw. Theory Tech. 38, 864–872 (1990)
12. Wang, L.: Reliable Design of Tunnel diode and Resonant Tunnelling Diode Based Microwave Sources. PhD Thesis, University of Glasgow (2011)
13. Wallmark, J.T., Dansky, A.H.: Nonlinear Biasing Resistors for Microwave Tunnel-diode Oscillators. IEEE Trans. Microw. Theory Tech. 11, 260–262 (1963)
14. Reddy, M.: Schottky-collector Resonant Tunnel Diodes for Sub-millimeterwave Applications. PhD Thesis, University of California Santa Barbara (1997)
15. Asada, M., Suzuki, S., Kishimoto, N.: Resonant Tunnelling Diodes for Subterahertz and Terahertz Oscillators. Japan. J. Appl. Phys. 47, 4375–4384 (2008)
16. Nahin, P.J.: The Science of Radio: with MATLAB and Electronics Workbench Demonstrations, 2nd edn., pp. 83–94. Springer-Verlag, New York, Inc. (2001)
17. Kim, C.S., Brandli, A.: High Frequency High Power Operation of Tunnel Diodes. IRE Trans. Circuit Theory 8, 416–425 (1961)
18. Wang, L., Wasige, E.: Tunnel diode Microwave Oscillators Employing a Novel Power Combining Circuit Topology. In: 40th European Microwave Conference, EuMA, Paris, pp. 1154–1157 (2010)
19. Eisele, H., Haddad, G.I.: Active Microwave Diodes. In: Sze, S.M. (ed.) Modern Semiconductor Device Physics, ch. 6, pp. 343–407. Wiley, New York (1998)

20. Wang, L., Figueiredo, J.M.L., Ironside, C.N., Wasige, E.: DC Characterisation of Tunnel Diodes Under Stable Non-oscillatory Circuit Conditions. IEEE Trans. Electron Devices 58, 343–347 (2011)
21. Chow, W.F.: Principles of tunnel diode circuits. John Wiley & Sons (1964)
22. Brown, E.R., Parker, C.D., Molvar, K.M., Stephan, K.D.: A Quasioptically Stabilized Resonant Tunnelling Diode Oscillator for the Millimetre and Submillimetre-wave Regions. IEEE Trans. Microw. Theory Tech. 40, 846–850 (1992)
23. Wang, L., Wasige, E.: A design procedure for tunnel diode microwaveoscillators. In: Proc. Int. Conf. Microw. Millim. Technol., Nanjing, vol. 2, pp. 832–834 (2008)

An Approach for Vehicle State Estimation Using Extended Kalman Filter

Liang Tong

Mechanical and Electrical Engineering School,
Beijing Information Science and Technology University, Beijing, China
Tongliang@tsinghua.org.cn

Abstract. In order to meet the high cost requirement of some vehicle states measured directly in vehicle active safety control system, an approach using the Extended Kalman Filter to estimate lateral and longitudinal velocity is proposed. Firstly, a vehicle dynamic model with 3 DOF, including longitudinal, lateral and yaw motions is built with MATLAB/SIMULINK. Secondly, the vehicle state estimation algorithm by the extended Kalman state observer based on the nonlinear vehicle model is achieved and the states of longitudinal, lateral acceleration and yaw rate for the vehicle are estimated online. Finally, the estimated results are compared with the results obtained from CarSim using the same parameter to verify the practicality of the proposed method.

Keywords: vehicle, extended kalman filter, state estimation.

1 Introduction

In recent years, people are paying more and more attention to the safety performance gradually with the increasing vehicle quantity and the increasing traffic accident number when they plan to buy a car.

Based on the Anti-lock Braking System (ABS) and Acceleration Slip Regulation, the development of a new type of vehicle active safety control system called the Vehicle Stability Control system (VSC) that is the field of automotive active safety research focus has been applied on many foreign sedan [1-2].It not only integrates all the features of ABS and ASR, but also maintains vehicle stability in the extreme conditions. According to the characteristics and control system, the world's manufacturers put forward different names in the research and development of the vehicle stability control, such as Electronic Stability Program (ESP), Dynamic Stability Control (DSC),vehicle stability control (VSC),etc., but its composition and functions is about the same.

Vehicle stability control is mainly based on the various parameters (e.g. lateral acceleration, yaw rate) of the motion to determine the appropriate control strategy and achieve the safety of vehicles traveling on the active control. Usually, the car state of motion can be measured through a variety of vehicle sensors. Constrained by the current technical level, some important variables need to use much more expensive equipment to measure (such as speed, yaw rate),or could not take direct measurements (such as the side slip angle), parameter estimation problem is the best solution to meeting a vehicle stability control system requirement.

T. Xiao, L. Zhang, and S. Ma (Eds.): ICSC 2012, Part I, CCIS 326, pp. 56–63, 2012.

The classical Kalman filtering technique (KF) which is an online vehicle state estimation can solve this problem and   has been widespread used in many fields. The Kalman filter dynamics results from the consecutive cycles of prediction and filtering. The dynamics of these cycles is derived and interpreted in the framework of Gaussian probability density functions. However, the Kalman Filter is only used to the estimate the signal of the linear systems because of the basis on a linear stochastic differential equation. In fact, the speed of the vehicle has significantly impact on the movement characteristics, so often needs the nonlinear models in order to more accurately describe the movement of vehicles. A non optimal approach to solve the problem, in the frame of linear filters, is the Extended Kalman filter (EKF) [3].The EKF implements a Kalman filter for a system dynamics that results from the linearization of the original non-linear filter dynamics around the previous state estimates. In this research field,Wenzel et al. investigated the application of the DEKF (Dual Extended Kalman Filter) for estimating state and parameters of the vehicle, while Best proposed a method for joint state-and-parameter estimation in parameter estimation [4].

Since the tire model of dynamic is complicated, making the EKF algorithm for solving process becomes very complicated, and thus has an impact on the real time state estimation. Therefore, based on the vehicle dynamic model with 3 DOF, the extended Kalman state observer has been designed through estimation algorithm of vehicles yaw rate, vertical speed and sideslip angle. The results show that the algorithm is better real-time computing, and the estimated effect is better.

2   Non-linear Three-Freedom Vehicle Model

The purpose of this paper is to develop an estimation method for the vehicle driving state based on a three degree-of-freedom vehicle. However, before trying to do the implementation of the estimation by using the extended Kalman filter to estimate lateral and longitudinal velocities, pitch, it is critical to specify the model that can be used for the simulation of the vehicle. Such model will be derived in this paper.

2.1   Three Degrees of Freedom Vehicle Model

This paper proposed a 3 DOF vehicle model based on the vehicle 2 DOF model by increasing a longitudinal motion which contains not only the longitudinal speed, but also the lateral speed and yaw rate. The structure of the vehicle model is shown in Fig.1[5-8].

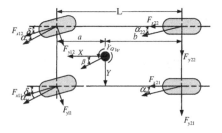

Fig. 1. The structure of the vehicle model

The state equations of the vehicle are as follows:

$$\begin{cases} \dot{Yaw} = \dfrac{a^2k_1+b^2k_2}{I_xu}Yaw+\dfrac{ak_1-bk_2}{I_z}\beta-\dfrac{ak_1}{I_z}\delta \\[2mm] \dot{\beta} = (\dfrac{ak_1-bk_2}{mu^2}-1)Yaw+\dfrac{k_1+k_2}{mu}\beta-\dfrac{k_1}{mu}\delta \\[2mm] \dot{u} = Yaw*\beta*u+a_x \end{cases} \qquad (1)$$

Where m represents the total mass of the vehicle(kg),Yaw is the yaw rate (rad/s),u is the longitudinal velocity respectively (m/s),I_z is the moment of inertia of the vehicle about its yaw axis $kg*m^2$,a is the distance from the center of gravity to the front axle(m),b is the distance from the center of gravity to the rear axle(m), δ is the front steer angle(rad),k_1 and k_2 are lateral stiffness of the front and rear wheel(N/rad), β is the side slip angle, a_x is the lateral acceleration (m/s^2).

2.2   Tire Model

Tire model is the important sub-model of the whole vehicle because the major force and torque to the vehicle is come from the tire, such as longitudinal braking force and driving force, side force and cornering force, aligning torque and invert torque, etc.Tire model is to describe a function between these forces, torques, slip rate, slip angle, roll angle, vertical load, road friction coefficient and vehicle speed. Pacejka Magic Formula model and Dugoff tire model are good models to use [9-10].For Dugoff tire model of a single wheel, it is essential to know the friction coefficient to have a tire model.

The side leaning angles of the every wheel are as follows:

$$\alpha_{fi} = \delta - \tan^{-1}\left[\frac{V_y+a*\dot{Yaw}}{V_x \mp 0.5*B_1*\dot{Yaw}}\right],(i=left,right) \qquad (2)$$

$$\alpha_{fi} = \delta - \tan^{-1}\left[\frac{V_y+a*\dot{Yaw}}{V_x \mp 0.5*B_1*\dot{Yaw}}\right],(i=left,right) \qquad (3)$$

The magnitudes of the front and rear axle velocities are as follows:

$$V_{fi} = \sqrt{(V_y+0.5*a*\dot{Yaw})^2+(V_x \mp 0.5*B_1*\dot{Yaw})^2},(i=left,right) \qquad (4)$$

$$V_{ri} = \sqrt{(V_y-0.5*b*\dot{Yaw})^2+(V_x \mp 0.5*B_2*\dot{Yaw})^2},(i=left,right) \qquad (5)$$

Therefore, the resultant front and rear friction coefficients are as follows:

$$\mu_{resi} = [C_1(1-e^{-C_2 S_{resi}}) - C_3 S_{resi})\tilde{\lambda} \tag{6}$$

Where C_1, C_2 and C_3 are the Burckhardt coefficients. In the case of the known characteristics of the road, road friction coefficient is only dependent on the lateral and vertical slip rate. For the system studied in this paper, tire longitudinal force and lateral force are decided by the following equations:

(1)The front and rear longitudinal and lateral wheel slips are as follows:

$$\begin{bmatrix} S_{xij} \\ S_{yij} \end{bmatrix} = \frac{1}{V_{fl}} \begin{bmatrix} \omega_{ij} * R_w * \cos\alpha_{ij} - V_{ij} \\ \omega_{ij} * R_w * \cos\alpha_{ij} \end{bmatrix}, (i = left, j = right) \tag{7}$$

(2) The resultant front and rear wheel slips are as follows:

$$S_{resi} = \sqrt{S_{xi}^2 + S_{yi}^2}, (i = 1, 2, 3, 4) \tag{8}$$

(3) Now, the front and rear longitudinal and lateral tire forces can be known accurately. The tire-force equations are as follows:

$$\begin{bmatrix} F_{xi} \\ F_{yi} \end{bmatrix} = \frac{\mu_{resi}}{S_{resi}} F_{zi} \begin{bmatrix} S_{xi} \\ S_{yi} \end{bmatrix}, (i = 1, 2, 3, 4) \tag{9}$$

3   Vehicle States Estimation

Usually the car state of motion can be measured through a variety of vehicle sensors to take. Due to constrained by the current technical level, some important variables need to use more expensive equipment to measure (such as speed, yaw rate), or could not take direct measurements (such as the side slip angle), parameter estimation problem is to be solved on a vehicle stability control system design. An extended Kalman filter (EKF) [11] is used to estimate the vehicle state.

The EKF process is represented by a nonlinear state space description incorporating state and measurement difference equations as follows:

In (10) and (11) the nonlinear function f relates the state vector $x(t)$ and the input vector $u(t)$. The measurement vector h relates the state to the measurements. Vectors $w(t)$ and $v(t)$ denote the superimposed process and measurement noise, respectively. The variance of $w(t)$ and $v(t)$ are Q and R, respectively. For the system model, EKF process as [12]:

$$\dot{x}(t) = f(x(t), u(t), w(t)) \tag{10}$$

$$y(t) = h(x(t), v(t)) \tag{11}$$

Step 1: The state equation and measurement equation of the vehicle
The state equation of the vehicle is (1), and the measurement equation is as follows:

$$y(t) = h(x(t), v(t)) = a_y = \frac{ak_1 - bk_2}{mu} Yaw + \frac{k_1 + k_2}{m} \beta - \frac{k_1}{m} \delta \tag{12}$$

Step 2: The linearization of the model

$F(t)$ and $H(t)$ are the Jacobian matrix which are derivative of nonlinear function $f(x(t), u(t), w(t))$ and $h(x(t), v(t))$, $\triangle t$ is the sampling time.

$$F(t) = \begin{bmatrix} \frac{\partial f_1}{\partial x_1} \cdots \cdots \frac{\partial f_1}{\partial x_m} \cdot \\ \cdots \cdots \cdots \cdots \\ \frac{\partial f_m}{\partial x_1} \cdots \cdots \frac{\partial f_m}{\partial x_m} \end{bmatrix} \quad H(t) = \begin{bmatrix} \frac{\partial h_1}{\partial x_1} \cdots \cdots \frac{\partial h_1}{\partial x_m} \\ \cdots \cdots \cdots \cdots \\ \frac{\partial h_m}{\partial x_1} \cdots \cdots \frac{\partial h_m}{\partial x_m} \end{bmatrix} \tag{13}$$

$$\Phi(t) = e^{F(t)*\Delta t} \approx I + F(t)*\Delta t \tag{14}$$

The state equation of the vehicle substitutes into the (13),and you can get the state matrix and the measurement matrix as follows:

$$F(t) = \begin{bmatrix} \frac{a^2 Yaw + b^2 \beta}{I_s u} & \frac{ak_1 - bk_2}{I_s} & -\frac{Yaw(a^2 k_1 + b^2 k_2)}{I_s u^2} \\ \frac{ak_1 - bk_2 - mu^2}{mu^2} & \frac{k_1 + k_2}{mu}_x & \frac{2(ak_1 - bk_2)Yaw}{mu^3} - \frac{\beta(k_1 + k_2)}{mu^2} + \frac{k_1 \delta}{mu^2} \\ \beta u & Yaw*u & Yaw*\beta \end{bmatrix} \tag{15}$$

$$H(t) = \begin{bmatrix} (ak_1 - bk_2)/(mu) \\ (k_1 + k_2)/m \\ -(ak_1 - bk_2)/(mu^2) \end{bmatrix} \tag{16}$$

Step 3:Choosing an initial value for $x(t_0)$ and $p(t_0)$ and take the process shown as Fig.2 to achieve EKF filter recursive algorithm.

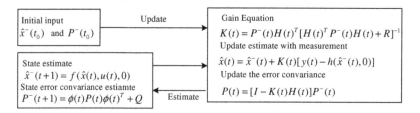

Fig. 2. Working process of EKF

Based on the above equation of state vehicle model and measurement equation,we can design the extended Kalman filtering.We defined the state vector as $x=[Yaw, \beta, u]$,the measurement vector as $y=[a_y]$ that incorporates all the measurement values,the input vector as $u=[\delta, a_x]^T$,the process noise covariance $Q=I_3$,the measurement noise covariance as $R=[10000]$,the initial value for error covariance as

$p^-(t_0)=I_{3x3}$ and the initial value for $x^-(t_0)=[0,0,26.4]$ through the two-lane condition [13-14].

On the Matlab/Simulink platform,the model is achieved and the estimation algorithm is shown in Fig.3.The estimated results are compared with the actual vehicle parameters obtained by MSCCarsim software.

The special vehicle dynamics simulation software named MSCCarsim,which is developed through numerous research experiments with higher accuracy,is used to overcome the difficulty and costly expense for achievement of the vehicle experiment data.The software combines traditional and modern multi-body vehicle dynamics modeling methods towards characteristic of parametric modeling for vehicle dynamics simulation software,including three-part graphic database of full- vehicle model, the direction and speed control and the external conditions (including the road information,drag,etc.)[15].With the simple and easy to understand user interface in Carsim,users can view full-vehicle model,simulation and results,so can use the simulation software quickly and accurately to provide a reference for engineering design.

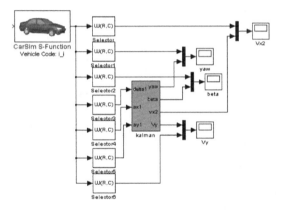

Fig. 3. Vehicle state estimation on the simulink platflorm

4   Simulink Results

The tire forces, the vehicle state histories, and the friction coefficient of the road govern all aspects of the vehicle motions and are important for vehicle simulation, handling evaluation, control system design, and safety measures. In this paper, the simulation model is a three degree-of-freedom of a full-vehicle model [16]. The estimated results are compared with the actual vehicle parameters obtained by MSCCarsim software.

In this paper, the initial speed is 25Km/s, road friction coefficient is 0.3, the sampling time is 0.001s. The steering angle and longitudinal acceleration as input variables, and lateral acceleration as a measurement output are fed into EKF observer in Fig. 4.

Actual vehicle parameters are obtained by MSCCarsim software and the estimated results of the longitudinal and lateral velocities compared with the actual values are shown in Fig. 5 and Fig. 6. It can be seen from the results that the estimated value has a good match with the actual yaw rate, sideslip angle and the speed as the steering angle and longitudinal acceleration of the changes. Therefore, the estimates states of EKF follow the actual states properly, even in the face of cornering conditions.

The estimated results of the yaw speed and the side slip angle compared with the actual values are shown in Fig. 7 and Fig. 8, respectively. Through those responses, it can be seen that the derived model could represent the vehicle dynamics well. The differences of these values can be accepted based on some assumption when the dynamic vehicle models were derived and the estimation processed were involved by some noises.

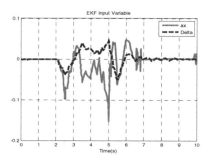

Fig. 4. The input variables into EKF

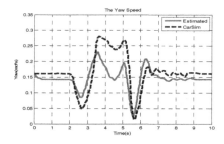

Fig. 5. The yaw rate

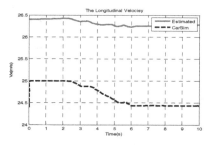

Fig. 6. The longitudinal velocity

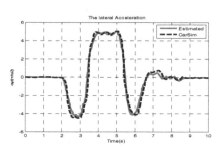

Fig. 7. The lateral acceleration

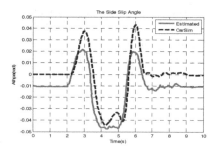

Fig. 8. The side slip angle

5   Conclusion

In this paper, a three degrees-of-freedom nonlinear vehicle model was developed. In the absence of commercially available transducers to measure some state variables, this paper proposes the estimation method for vehicle state histories and yaw rate using EKF. The obtained state estimate values can be used for advanced feedback control to make intelligent driving decisions. The comparison between the estimated results and the simulated Carsim model confirms the validity of the model, in which all the state variables follow the Carsim response well. Therefore, we can estimate more state variables to provide more comprehensive, accurate state parameters for the research and development of automotive control systems.

References

1. Onoa, E., Asanoa, K., Sugaia, M., Itob, S., Yamamotob, M., Sawadac, M., Yasui, Y.: Estimation of Automotive Tire Force Characteristics Using Wheel Velocity. Control Engineering Practice 11, 1361–1370 (2003)
2. Rajamani, R.: Vehicle Dynamics and Control. Springer, New York (2006)
3. Liu, C.-S., Peng, H.: Road Friction Coefficient Estimation for Vehicle Path Prediction. Vehicle System Dynamics 25, 413–425 (1996)
4. Pohl, R.S., Reindl, L.: The Intelligent Tire Utilizing Passive SAW Sensors Measurement of Tire Friction. IEEE Transactions on Instrumentation and Measurement 48(6), 1041–1046 (1999)
5. Wilkin, M.A., Manning, W.J., Crolla, D.A.: Estimation of non-linear friction force between tyre and roadapplied to a performance vehicle. In: AVEC 2004, pp. 387–392 (2004)
6. Christopher, R., Carlson, J., Gerdes, C.: Nonlinear Estimation of Longitudinal Tire Slip Under Several Driving Conditions. In: Proceedings of AVEC 2002, Hiroshima, JP (September 2002)
7. Abe, M., Kano, Y.: Side-slip control to stabilize vehicle lateral motion by direct yaw
8. Ray, L.R.: Nonlinear State and Tire Force Estimation fro Advanced Vehicle Control. IEEE Transaction on Control System Technology 3(1), 117–124 (1995)
9. Hiraoka, T., Kumamoto, H., Nishihara, O.: Sideslio Angle Estimation and Active Front Steering System Based on Lateral Acceleration Data at Centers of Percussion with Respect to Front/Rear Wheels. JSAE Review 25, 37–42 (2004)
10. Dugoff, H., Fancher, P.S., Segal, L.: Tyre performance characteristics affecting vehicle response to steering and braking control inputs. Final Report, contract CST-460, Office of Vehicle System Research, US National Bureau of Standards (1969)
11. Shi, K.L.: Speed estimation of an induction motor drive using an optimized extended Kalman filter. IEEE (2000)
12. Kalman, R.E.: A new approach to linear filtering and prediction problems. Transaction of the ASME-Journal of Basic Engineering, 35–45 (1960)
13. Cherouat, H., Diop, S.: Vehicle velocity estimation and vehicle body side slip angle and yaw rate observer. In: Proc. IEEE Internat. Symposium Industrial Electronics, ISIE 2005, Mini Track on Automotive (2005)
14. Simon, D.: Kalman filter with state equality constraints. IEEE (2002)
15. Jazar, R.N.: Vehicle Dynamis:Theory and Application. Springer, New York (2008)
16. Grewal, M.S., Andrews, A.P.: Kalman Filtering: Theory and Practice Using Matlab, 2nd edn. John Wiley and Sons, Inc. (2001)

Equilibrium Simulation of Power Market with Wind Power Based on CVaR Approach

Jing Li, Xian Wang, and Shaohua Zhang

Key Laboratory of Power Station Automation Technology, Department of Automation,
Shanghai University, Shanghai 200072, China
zhongguosidafaming@163.com

Abstract. High wind power penetration in power systems will significantly increase risks faced by the conventional generators in the deregulated electricity markets. This will further affect these generators' risk preferences and strategic behaviors. Based on conditional value at risk (CVaR), an equilibrium model of electricity market with wind power is developed taking into account the conventional generators' risk preferences. The model is performed by Monte Carlo simulation and nonlinear complementary method. The impacts of wind power volatility and generators' risk preferences on generators' strategy behaviors and equilibrium results are analyzed and the efficient frontier of generators' expected profit – CVaR is provided. The simulation results show that, the equilibrium market price will increase with the increase of wind power uncertainty; the increase of conventional generators' risk aversion will also lead to an increase in the expected market price; if generators collude with others, they will be more conservative.

Keywords: electricity market, wind power, risk preference, CVaR.

1 Introduction

With the dramatic increase in demand for green and renewable power resources, wind power has been widely used around the world in recent years[1]. However,.[1]large-scale wind power penetration in power systems will inevitably increase risks faced by conventional generators due to wind power's features of strong randomness, volatility and intermittence [2]. Moreover, it will affect these generators' risk preferences and strategic behaviors. In recent few decades, many new methods for risk measuring have been put forward in financial field, such as value at risk (VaR) and CVaR which have been applied successfully in predicting and controlling the risk of financial market [3]. Equilibrium models using game-theoretic behavioral assumptions are broadly employed to research on strategic behaviors and market power analysis of oligopolistic electricity markets[4]The Cournot model[5] and the linear supply function equilibrium (LSFE) model [6] are used most extensively at present. In a word, it has great theoretical and practical significance to research on an equilibrium

[1] This project is supported by National Natural Science Foundation of China (No.70871074).

T. Xiao, L. Zhang, and S. Ma (Eds.): ICSC 2012, Part I, CCIS 326, pp. 64–73, 2012.

model of electricity markets with wind power taking into account the conventional strategic generators' risk preferences based on CVaR.

Amounts of researches have been conducted on risk modeling in single generator's or purchaser's optimization problem in the power market. The mean-variance utility theory is used in order to model the generator's or purchaser's risk preference[7], while the CVaR theory is employed to analyzed the risk decision-making problems of the generator or purchaser[8]-[9]. Reference [10] provides the efficient frontier curve of the expected profit and standard deviation through solving the Mean-CVaR approach to solve the medium-term decision-making problem faced by a power retailer[11].

Amounts of researches have been conducted on risk modeling in single generator's or purchaser's optimization problem in the power market. The mean-variance utility theory is used in order to model the generator's or purchaser's risk preference[7], while the CVaR theory is employed to analyzed the risk decision-making problems of the generator or purchaser[8]-[9]. Reference [10] provides the efficient frontier curve of the optimization model of generator's bidding combination. M. Carrion proposed a bi-level programming approach to solve the medium-term decision-making problem faced by a power retailer[11].

The research on risk decision-making equilibrium problem of multiple generators has been conducted rarely. Taking into account the conventional strategic generators' risk preferences, an equilibrium model of electricity markets with wind power is developed. The CVaR theory is employed to model the conventional generators' risk preferences. The impacts of generators' risk preferences and wind power fluctuation on the output, expected profit, CVaR and the market price of conventional generators are researched in details. Numerical examples are presented to verify and analysis the validity of the model.

2   The CVaR of the Profit

VaR and CVaR are widely used for risk assessment in financial engineering and risk management areas in recent years. $\pi(x, y)$ represents profit function, where the decision vectors $x \in X \in R_n$ and $y \in R_m$ are random vectors. $q(y)$ represents the probability density of y. The probability of the profit being lower or equal to a given value of ζ is:

$$\Psi(x, \zeta) = \int_{\pi(x,y)\leq\zeta} q(y)dy \tag{1}$$

$\Psi(x, \zeta)$ is a function which is non-decreasing and continuous on the right. For a given confidence level of α, which is between 0 and 1, $\zeta_\alpha(x)$ represents the VaR of the revenue function $\pi(x, y)$ when decision is x. $\zeta_\alpha(x)$ is defined as:

$$\zeta_\alpha(x) = \max\{\zeta \in R \mid \Psi(x, \zeta) \leq 1 - \alpha\} \tag{2}$$

It represents the smallest possible profit which is generated by decision x under the confidence level of α. For stochastic problems, VaR has the additional difficulty of requiring the use of binary variables for modeling. CVaR is proposed by Rockafellar and Uryasev[12], which can be modeled by the simple use of linear constraints. CVaR is the expected profit not exceeding the measure $\zeta_\alpha(x)$ which is called Value-at-risk (VaR). In fact, this is what the investors care most, so CVaR can be defined as:

$$\phi_\alpha(x) = E\{\pi(x, y) \mid \pi(x, y) \le \zeta_\alpha(x)\}$$

$$= \frac{1}{1-\alpha} \int_{\pi(x,y) \le \zeta_\alpha(x)} \pi(x, y) q(y) dy \tag{3}$$

A relatively simple function [12] is introduced because the expression of $\zeta_\alpha(x)$ which is included in formula (3) is difficulty to calculate:

$$F_\alpha(x, \zeta) = \max\{\zeta - \frac{1}{1-\alpha} \int_{y \in R^m} [\zeta - \pi(x, y)]^+ q(y) dy\} \tag{4}$$

The integration of formula (4) is calculated by using Monte Carlo simulation to produce a set of sample data. $y_1, y_2, \ldots, y_s$ are assumed to be sample data of y. ρ_s is the probability of every sample. So the estimated value of function $F_\alpha(x, \zeta)$ is:

$$\tilde{F}_\alpha(x, \zeta) = \max\{\zeta - \frac{1}{1-\alpha} \sum_{s=1}^{K} \rho_s [\zeta - \pi(x, y^s)]^+\} \tag{5}$$

Therefore CVaR can be obtained by solving the following optimization problem[18] using the auxiliary variable η_s :

$$CVaR(x, \zeta) = \max_{x, \zeta}\{\zeta - \frac{1}{1-\alpha} \sum_{s=1}^{K} \rho_s \eta_s\} \tag{6}$$

s.t. $-\pi(x, y^s) + \zeta - \eta_s \le 0 \quad s = 1, \cdots, K$

$\eta_s \ge 0, \quad s = 1, \cdots, K$

The optimized ζ is the VaR. The meaning of VaR and CVaR obtained from formula (6) is opposite to the loss function. So the larger VaR and CVaR are, the smaller the risk is.

Fig.1 illustrates the concept of CVaR. The value of α is commonly set between 0.90 and 0.99. α is set to be 0.95 in this paper.

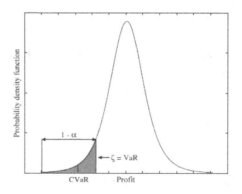

Fig. 1. VaR and CVaR illustration

3   Equilibrium Model of Spot Market with Wind Power Based on CVaR Approach

3.1   Model Assumptions

Suppose that there are n strategic conventional generators and a certain number of wind power units in a power market, the market demand at time period t is expressed by the following linear inverse demand function:

$$p = a - bD \tag{7}$$

where, p is the market price at time t; a and b are constant coefficients taking values greater than 0; D is the market demand at time t.

The conventional generators have the following quadratic cost functions:

$$C_i(Q_i) = \alpha_i Q_i + 0.5 \beta_i Q_i^2 \tag{8}$$

where, Q_i is generator i's output; α_i and β_i are cost parameters taking values greater than 0.

The wind power generators are assumed to be price-takers and the output of wind power units in time t, Q_ω is a random variable. Wind speed v is assumed to follow Weibull distribution:

$$f(x; \lambda, k) = \begin{cases} \dfrac{k}{\lambda}(\dfrac{x}{\lambda})^{k-1} e^{-(x/\lambda)^k} & x \geq 0 \\ 0 & x < 0 \end{cases} \tag{9}$$

Where, x is a random variable, $\lambda > 0$ is the scale parameter, $k > 0$ is the shape parameter. The output of wind power can be calculated by $Q_\omega = 0.5\rho A v^3 C_p$, so the output of wind power is proportional to air density ρ, wind area A, wind energy utilization coefficient C_p of wind turbine and three times of wind speed v. Setting a group of λ and k, and using Monte Carlo method to generate 500 speed data, a group of wind power can be obtained by $Q_\omega = 0.7646 v^3$ [13]. The total demand of electric power market is equal to the output of the conventional generators and wind power units. So the market demand D satisfies:

$$D = \sum_{i=1}^{n} Q_i + Q_\omega \tag{10}$$

the inverse demand function in (7) can be reformulated as follows:

$$p = a - b(\sum_{i=1}^{n} Q_i + Q_\omega) \tag{11}$$

n strategic conventional generators who have risk preferences are supposed to participate in market competition with Cournot mode. Each power generator needs to make a compromise between profit and risk in the hope of gaining maximum profit while making the risk they face as small as possible. The output restriction of generators and the capacity restriction of transmission network are not considerated in this paper.

3.2   Equilibrium Model of Spot Market and Its Solution

The profit of generator i is equal to the payment for its production quantities at the market prices, minus its generation costs, that is:

$$\pi_i(Q_i, Q_\omega) = pQ_i - \alpha_i Q_i - 0.5\beta_i Q_i^2 \tag{12}$$

Substituting (11) into (12), the expected profit of generator i can be calculated as follows:

$$E[\pi_i(Q_i, Q_\omega)] = \sum_{s=1}^{K} \rho_s[a - b(\sum_{i=1}^{n} Q_i + Q_{\omega,s})]Q_i - \alpha_i Q_i - 0.5\beta_i Q_i^2 \tag{13}$$

Generator i's decision problem can be formulated as the following utility-maximization problem by considering the risk preference of generation $i(i=1,..,n)$ and using formula (6) and (13):

$$\begin{aligned}
Max_{Q_i} J_i &= E[\pi_i(Q_i, Q_\omega)] + \delta_i \cdot CVaR_i(Q_i, \zeta_i) \\
&= \sum_{s=1}^{K} \rho_s[a - b(\sum_{i=1}^{n} Q_i + Q_{\omega,s})]Q_i - \alpha_i Q_i - 0.5\beta_i Q_i^2 + \delta_i[\zeta_i - \frac{1}{1-\alpha}\sum_{s=1}^{K} \rho_s \eta_{is}]]
\end{aligned} \tag{14}$$

subject to:

$$-\{[a - b(\sum_{i=1}^{n} Q_i + Q_{\omega,s})]Q_i - \alpha_i Q_i - 0.5\beta_i Q_i^2\} + \zeta_i - \eta_{is} \leq 0 \qquad s=1,2,\cdots,K \tag{15}$$

$$\eta_{is} \geq 0 \qquad s = 1,2,...,K \tag{16}$$

$$Q_i \geq 0 \tag{17}$$

where, J_i is generator i's utility function; δ_i is generator i's risk preference factor. $\delta_i = 0$ means that generator i is risk neutral, $0 < \delta_i < 1$ indicates that generator i is risk averse and the degree of generator i's risk aversion will increase with increasing δ_i.

The Cournot equilibrium model taking into account the conventional strategic generators' risk preferences is composed of n decision problems like (14)-(17).

Obtaining the first order partial derivative of each generator's decision-making model and using NCP-function $\varphi(a,b) := a + b - \sqrt{a^2 + b^2}$, the KKT conditions of generator i's decision problem can be derived as follows:

$$(Q_i) \quad : \quad \begin{aligned} &\not{Q}_i - \{\sum_{s=1}^{K} \rho_s[a - b(\sum_{i=1}^{n} Q_i + Q_{\omega,s})] + \sum_{s=1}^{K}(-\rho_s b Q_i) - \alpha_i - \beta_i Q_i + \\ &\sum_{s=1}^{K} \gamma_{is}[a - b(\sum_{i=1}^{n} Q_i + Q_{\omega,s}) - b Q_i - \alpha_i - \beta_i Q_i]\} = 0 \end{aligned} \tag{18}$$

$$(\zeta_i) \quad : \quad \delta_i - \sum_{s=1}^{K} \gamma_{is} = 0 \tag{19}$$

$$(\eta_{is}, \forall s) : \quad \varphi(\eta_{is}, \frac{\delta_i \rho_s}{1-\alpha} - \gamma_{is}) = 0 \tag{20}$$

$$(\gamma_{is}, \forall s) : \quad \varphi([a - b(\sum_{i=1}^{n} Q_i + Q_{\omega,s})]Q_i - \alpha_i Q_i - 0.5\beta_i Q_i^2 - \zeta_i + \eta_{is}, \gamma_{is}) = 0 \tag{21}$$

The equilibrium solution of the model can be obtained by considering first order optimal condition (KKT) of all conventional generators' decision-making problems.

4   Numerical Examples

Consider a power market, the coefficients in the market demand function in a certain time period (1h) are assumed to be: a=$80/MWh , b=1.0$/MW^{2}h. The KKT conditions of generator i's decision problem is solved by MATLAB programming.

4.1   The Equilibrium Results of Two Symmetric Conventional Generators

4.1.1   Impacts of the Standard Deviation of Wind Speed on Equilibrium Results
Suppose that there are two symmetric conventional generators in the power market. The cost parameters of generator $i(i=1,2)$ are: α_i =10.0$/MWh, β_i =1.0$/MW^{2}h. The maximum output of wind power is assumed to be 30MW. The standard deviation of wind speed is 1,2,3,3.5,4,4.5,5 when λ and k are set to be (10.43,12.0), (10.80,5.8),(11.08,3.7),(11.17,3.13), (11.24,2.7), (11.28,2.36), (11.29,2.1),respectively.
   The impacts of wind speed fluctuation on equilibrium results when the generators' risk preferences are different are given in Table 1. From Table 1, it can be found that: firstly, VaR and CVaR will decrease with increasing the standard deviation of wind speed, indicating an increase in the risk faced by generators. Secondly, to avoid risk, the generator will decrease its output by strategic bidding, leading to an increase in the expected market price. Thirdly, the more risk aversion generator will decrease its output quickly, causing a decrease in its expected profit, while the output of the less risk aversion generator is reduced relatively little, its expected profit will increase benefit of the higher energy price. Finally, when the wind power fluctuation is larger (σ_ω > 3.5 in this case), CVaR of generator 2 is larger than generator 1, indicating that the effect of sacrificing profits to reduce risk of the more risk aversion generator is more obvious.

Table 1. Impacts of the standard deviation of wind speed on equilibrium results

| σ_ω (m.s^{-1}) | Generator 1 $\delta_1 = 0.05$, | | | | Generator 2 $\delta_2 = 0.8$ | | | | |
	output (MW)	expected profit ($/h)	VaR ($/h)	CVaR ($/h)	output (MW)	expected profit ($/h)	VaR ($/h)	CVaR ($/h)	expected market price ($/MW·h)
1	15.58	371.33	325.28	307.90	14.86	358.27	314.56	298.09	41.53
2	15.57	374.54	244.83	210.88	13.66	346.58	226.06	196.78	41.79
3	15.56	379.94	143.17	125.02	12.40	325.12	133.65	119.23	42.00
3.5	15.55	381.39	136.89	85.65	12.15	323.22	127.35	88.58	42.07
4	15.43	382.54	80.48	75.44	11.63	317.07	82.77	78.97	42.18
4.5	15.37	383.86	77.51	58.21	11.34	312.67	80.92	66.70	42.33
5	15.35	385.27	53.46	51.21	11.13	308.84	62.60	60.98	42.95

4.1.2   Expected Profit-CVaR Efficient Frontier of Generator

When the degree of generator 1's risk preference δ_1 is set to be 0.01, the expected profit and CVaR of generator 2 is calculated with the degree of generator 2's risk preference δ_2 changes from 0 to 1, at the confidence level of 0.95, the efficient frontier of generator's expected profit and CVaR is given in Fig. 2 (λ and k is set to be 11.29 and 2.1 in this case).

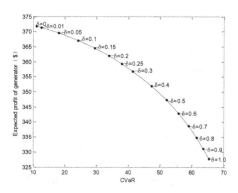

Fig. 2. Efficient frontier of Expected profit-CVaR

Dots in figure 2 represent generator 2's expected profit and CVaR at different risk preference. From Fig. 2, it can be seen that the CVaR of generator will increase with increasing the degree of generator's risk aversion. This means that increasing generator's risk aversion can effectively reduce its profit risk. However, the expected profit of generator will decrease with increasing the degree of generator's risk aversion. The effect of sacrificing part of profit to avoid risk is more obvious when the degree of generator's risk aversion is smaller.

4.2 The Equilibrium Results of Three Asymmetric Conventional Generators

Suppose that there are three asymmetric conventional generators in the power market in order to verify the model further. Two parameters of Weibull distribution is set to be $\lambda=11.08$, $k=3.7$. The cost parameters of generator i ($i=1, 2, 3$) are shown in Table 2.

Table 2. Cost parameters of generators

generator	α_i($/MWh)	β_i($/MW^{2}h)
G1	12.0	1.0
G2	10.0	1.5
G3	8.0	2.0

4.2.1 Impacts of Generator 3's Risk Preference on Equilibrium Results

When the degrees of generator 1's and 2's risk aversion $\delta_1=\delta_2=0$, the changes of each generator's expected profit and CVaR with the degree of generator 3's risk aversion δ_3 changes from 0 to 1 are given in Fig. 3 and Fig. 4, respectively.

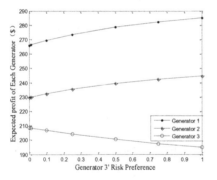
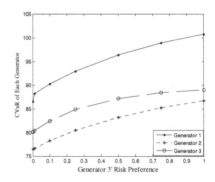

Fig. 3. Impact of generator 3's risk preference on expected profit of each generator

Fig. 4. Impact of generator 3's risk peference on CVaR of each gnerator

From Fig. 3 and Fig. 4, it can be found that generator 3's expected profit will decrease but its CVaR will increase with increasing generator 3's risk aversion, however, its rivals' expected profit and CVaR will increase, it means that the risk faced by each generator is reduced. Generator 3 reduces risk at the cost of sacrificing its own profit, but the effect on its rivals is that increasing its rivals' profit and reducing its rivals' risk. If the three asymmetric generators don't collude with others and the generators would change their risk preferences, the less conservative a generator is, the more profit it can get.

4.2.2   Impacts of Generators' Risk Preferences on Equilibrium Results

The changes of each generator's expected profit and CVaR with the degrees of the three generators' risk aversion δ_i ($i = 1, 2, 3$) change from 0 to 1 at the same time are given in Fig. 5 and Fig. 6, respectively.

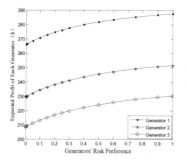
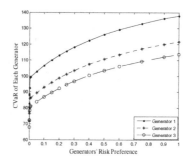

Fig. 5. Impacts of generators' risk preferenceon expected profit of each generator

Fig. 6. Impacts of generator' risk preferenceon CVaR of each generator

From Fig. 5 and Fig. 6, it can be seen that the expected profit and CVaR of each generator will increase with increasing the degrees of the three generators' risk aversion, indicating that their profits will grow larger and risk will be smaller. It means that if the generators would change their risk preferences and collude with others, they all choose to be more conservative.

5   Conclusions

High wind power penetration in power systems will significantly increase risks faced by the conventional generators in the deregulated electricity markets. This will further affect these generators' risk preferences and strategic behaviors. Taking into account the conventional strategic generators' risk preferences, a Cournot equilibrium model of electricity markets with wind power based on CVaR is developed in this paper. The impacts of generator's risk preference and wind power fluctuation on equilibrium results are analyzed by numerical simulation. The conclusions are as follows:

Firstly, the risk faced by generator will increase with increasing the wind speed fluctuation. To avoid risk, the generator will decrease its output by strategic bidding, leading to an increase in the expected market price. Secondly, the expected profit of the larger risk aversion generator will decrease with increasing the wind speed fluctuation, while the expected profit of the smaller risk aversion generator will increase. Thirdly, when wind power is a certain value, as the degree of a generator's risk aversion goes up, the generator will sacrifice part of its expected profit to reduce its profit risk. The smaller the generator's risk aversion is, the bigger risk the generator can reduce by sacrificing part of profit. Finally, if the generators would change their risk preferences, they will be less conservative as they don't collude with others, and will be more conservative as they collude with others.

References

1. Smith, J.: Wind power: present realities and future possibilities. Proc. IEEE 97, 195–197 (2009)
2. Botterud, A., Wang, J., Miranda, V., Bessa, R.J.: Wind power forecasting in U.S. electricity markets 23, 71–82 (2010)
3. Zhang, Q., Wang, X.: Hedge Contract Characterization and Risk-Constrained Electricity Procurement. IEEE Trans. on Power System 24, 1547–1558 (2009)
4. Helman, U.: Market power monitoring and mitigation in the US wholesale power markets. Energy 31, 877–904 (2006)
5. Chen, H., Wong, K., Nguyen, H., Chung, C.Y.: Analyzing oligopolistic electricity market using coevolutionary computation. IEEE Trans. on Power System 21, 143–152 (2006)
6. Wang, X., Li, Y., Zhang, S.: Oligopolistic equilibrium analysis for electricity markets: a nonlinear complementarity approach. IEEE Trans. on Power System 19, 1348–1355 (2004)
7. Liu, M., Wu, F.F.: Managing price risk in a multimarket environment. IEEE Trans. on Power System 21, 1512–1519 (2006)
8. Conejo, A., Raquel, G., Carrion, M.: Optimal involvement in futures markets of a power producer. IEEE Trans. on Power Syst. 23, 703–711 (2008)
9. Dahlgren, R., Liu, C., Lawarrée, L.: Risk assessment in energy trading. IEEE Trans. on Power Syst. 18, 503–511 (2003)
10. Conejo, A.J., Garcıa-Bertrand, R.: Forward Trading for an Electricity Producer. IEEE 4, 89–93 (2008)
11. Carrion, M., Arroyo, J.M., Conejo, A.J.: A Bilevel Stochastic Programming Approach for Retailer Futures Market Trading 24, 1446–1456 (2009)
12. Rockafellar, R., Uryasev, T.: Optimization of Conditional Value-at-Risk. Journal of Risk 2, 21–42 (2000)
13. Wang, S., Xu, Q.: Modeling of Wind Speed Uncertainty and Interval Power Flow Analysis for Wind Farms. Automation of Electric Power Systems 33, 82–86 (2009)

High-Accuracy Magnetic Rotary Encoder

Shuang Wang[1], Jie Jin[1], Tiecai Li[2], and Guoying Liu[3]

[1] School of Mechatronic Engineering and Automation, Shanghai University,
Shanghai, 200072, China
wang-shuang@shu.edu.cn
[2] School of Electrical Engineering and Automation, Harbin Institute of Technology,
Harbin, 150001, China
[3] Shanghai RENLE Science & Technology Co., Ltd, Shanghai, 200072, China

Abstract. A high accuracy magnetic rotary encoder for the speed sampling is designed, including both the hardware structure and the magnetic field analysis. For improving the magnetic field distribution of a magnetic encoder and lower the harmonic of output signals, the hardware structure with the magnetic collector is proposed. Aiming at decreasing the output deviation of the magnetic encoder, the signal correction algorithm based on the least squares estimation is put forward. In order to achieve an accurate measurement of a rotor velocity and a position, the signal decoding algorithm based on the closed-loop position tracking system is designed. The simulation and experiment results are provided to demonstrate the effectiveness and practicability of the proposed method.

Keywords: magnetic rotary encoder, least squares estimation, signal correction.

1   Introduction

Position sensor is a key part of the servo control system. The commonly used sensors are including hall sensors, photoelectric encoder, rotating transformer and inductive synchronizer, etc. Hall sensors are widely used in the square wave brushless dc motor commutation control and low accuracy of speed control. Rotating transformer[1] and inductive synchronizer have a large size. Photoelectric encoder[2] with a mature technology has a poor seismic performance, and an easy aging. Its structure and principle limits the application in bad working conditions with water, dust, etc. Magnetic encoder based on the magnetoresistance and photoelectric encoder have the following advantages: no contact position detection structure makes it can be reliable work in oil, dust, temperature transform strong, as well as in the bad conditions; Not using light-emitting diodes makes it has long service life, less consumption, simple structure, better impact resistance, high reliability; Based on the control algorithm, magnetic encoder can get a high resolution, so in recent years, the encoder research field is getting widely attention[3-8]. Magnetic encoder has two kinds of structure: a single pole type and a multi pole type. Multi pole type magnetic encoder has a relatively complicated manufacturing process. Improved of its resolution is realized by increasing the pole pairs. But the factors of the manufacturing process, product

T. Xiao, L. Zhang, and S. Ma (Eds.): ICSC 2012, Part I, CCIS 326, pp. 74–82, 2012.

volume, leakage magnetic field distribution and so on, which are limited the improvement of the resolution.

This paper proposes a new magnetic encoder design scheme based on the hardware structure included the rotating magnetic poles and additional set of magnetic collector, pair of orthogonal voltage signals with low harmonic components can be obtained. The voltage signals are carried up the rotor position information. The signal correction algorithm based on the least squares estimation and the signal decoding algorithm based on the closed-loop position tracking system is designed. By which, the deviation between the hall sensor output signal and the ideal signal has been corrected and position angle has the precise tracking measurement.

2 Magnetic Field Design

In the ideal case, an isotropic ring magnet which relatively magnetic conductance equal to 1 has been parallel magnetization in a constant magnetic field, and makes the centerline of the magnet ring in the quadrature to the direction of the magnetic field, so the magnet ring has a two-pole magnetic field. The magnetic flux density is $\vec{B}$, Fig. 1 shows the magnetic field distribution of the magnet ring. Hall A and B are two linear hall-effect sensors orthogonal that placed on the space. The installation direction is vertical with the magnets surface. Therefore only the radial component of the magnetic field is induced in the hall sensors and the voltage is in the output. The direction of a positive horizontal axis is assumed to be the rotor zero position. The rotor rotates counter-clockwise. θ is the rotor current position.

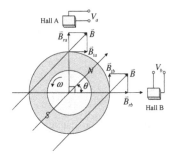

Fig. 1. Magnetic Field Distribution of the Magnet Ring

So the output voltage of hall A and B are given respectively:

$$\begin{cases} V_a = R_H \dfrac{I\left|\vec{B}\right|\sin\theta}{\delta_H} \times 10^{-8} = V\sin\theta \\[4mm] V_b = R_H \dfrac{I\left|\vec{B}\right|\cos\theta}{\delta_H} \times 10^{-8} = V\cos\theta \end{cases} \tag{1}$$

In the formula, V is the constant of the sensor. R_H is the hall materials coefficient; I is the exciting current; δ_H is the thickness of the hall element; B is the magnetic flux density.

In an ideal condition, the hall element is placed in the tangential direction of the stator surface. If the stator and the rotor with the magnets are coaxial mounting, then only the radial magnetic field produced by magnets is induced by the hall sensor. When there is the system deviation produced by the installation, the output of the hall sensor will be affected by the tangential component of the magnetic field. Thus harmonic signals are produced. In order to suppress harmonic signals, and to improve the installation precision, a novel method is adopted in this paper. The magnetic collector is installed in the sensor hardware as an additional set. By which, the weight of the radial magnetic field component is improved and the tangential one is reduced.

The ring magnet, which the outer diameter is 7.5mm, the inner diameter is 4mm and the height is 3mm, has been magnetized along the tangential direction. The space distribution of the air-gap magnetic field is shown below in Fig.2(a). As shown in Fig.3(a), the position which radius is 13.5mm in the air gap, the radial magnetic field component and the tangential magnetic field component are the orthogonal sine curves with the same amplitude of 0.045T. In this paper, an iron ring, which the outer diameter is 16.5mm, the thickness is 1.5mm, the height is 3mm, is concentric placed outside the magnet. The hall element is placed inside the iron ring. The air-gap magnetic field distribution between the hall element and the ring is shown below in Fig.2(b). Due to the constraint of the magnetic field effect by setting the iron ring, the magnetic field distribution is compared with that of no iron ring structure. The radial component and the tangential component are the orthogonal, but no longer the amplitude equal. As shown in Fig.3(b), the radial component amplitude of the air-gap magnetic field is close to 0.092T where radius is 13.5mm, the amplitude of tangential component is 0.01T.

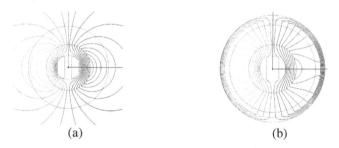

(a)   (b)

Fig. 2. Distribution of air-gap magnetic field

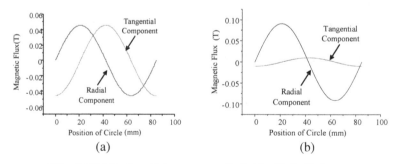

(a)   (b)

Fig. 3. Distribution of air-gap magnetic field with R=13.5mm

The amplitude of the air gap radial magnetic flux density is increased after joined an iron ring, thus it reduced the hall element sensitive error with respect to magnetic field tangential component.

The above analysis is focus on the field distribution that influenced by the iron ring under an ideal assembly condition. The harmonic caused by the magnet eccentricity will be discussed. Fig. 4 shows the magnetic field distribution with 0.1mm eccentricity which is between the center of magnet and stator axis, the bias of the flux density amplitude is close to 1%. The second harmonic amplitude of radial magnetic field component is 0.0013T, about 1.4% of the fundamental harmonic amplitude. When the magnet eccentricity is 0.2 mm, as shown in Fig. 5, the bias of the flux density amplitude is 2.4%. The second harmonic amplitude of radial magnetic field component is 0.0025T, about 2.7% of the fundamental harmonic amplitude.

From the above analysis, we can conclude that the air gap magnetic field has been optimized by joined the magnet collector, the magnet eccentricity can be limited within 0.1mm by the mechanical processing precision, the weight of the harmonic composition in the radial magnetic field component proportion is very small. So the bias of the amplitude, the phase, and the dc offset between the hall sensor output signal and the ideal orthogonal signal, which produced by the error of hall assembly location and the inconsistent characteristics of the hall device, will be the major factor of signal error.

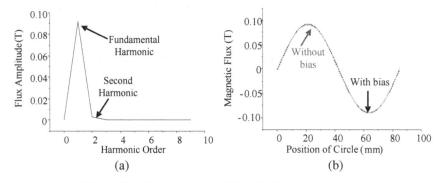

Fig. 4. The air-gap magnetic field with 0.1mm eccentricity

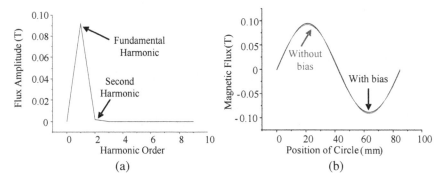

Fig. 5. The air-gap magnetic field with 0.2mm eccentricity

3   Signal Correction Algorithm

Considering the bias, output signal of hall sensor that can be expressed as follows:

$$\begin{cases} u_{sin} = k_a \sin\theta + u_a \\ u_{cos} = k_b \cos(\theta + \varphi) + u_b \end{cases} \tag{2}$$

In the formula, u_{sin}, u_{cos} is the hall sensor output voltage signals respectively; k_a, k_b is sine and cosine signal gain respectively; u_a, u_b is the offset of output voltage signals respectively.

For the deviation of the input signal, the rotor current position cannot be accurately tracked. Because the discrepancies are caused by the mechanical assembly and the hall device individual characteristics, these discrepancies are approximately constant and do not change with time. Therefore, the hall sensor output signals will be given pretreatment as the system is powered on to define the deviation parameters. Then the input signal will be compensated using the deviation parameters when the system is in the operation. So the system no longer needs the deviation parameters to update online, thus the calculation will be greatly reduced.

The specific algorithm described as follows. For $\sin^2\theta + \cos^2\theta = 1$, so:

$$\begin{aligned} Y = 1 &= \frac{1}{k_b^2 \cos^2\varphi}(u_{cos} - u_b)^2 + \frac{1}{k_a^2 \cos^2\varphi}(u_{sin} - u_a)^2 + \frac{2\sin\varphi}{k_a k_b \cos^2\varphi}(u_{cos} - u_b)(u_{sin} - u_a) \\ &= a_1 u_{sin}^2 + a_2 u_{cos}^2 + a_3 u_{sin} u_{cos} + a_4 u_{sin} + a_5 u_{cos} = U \times A^T \end{aligned} \tag{3}$$

In the formula, Y is [n×1] matrix which values both are equal to one, U is [n×5] measured values array, $u(i)$ is the i- times the measured value.

$$U = \begin{bmatrix} u_{sin}^2(1) & u_{cos}^2(1) & u_{sin}u_{cos}(1) & u_{sin}(1) & u_{cos}(1) \\ \cdots & \cdots & \cdots & \cdots & \cdots \\ u_{sin}^2(n) & u_{cos}^2(n) & u_{sin}u_{cos}(n) & u_{sin}(n) & u_{cos}(n) \end{bmatrix} \tag{4}$$

$A = [a_1, a_2, a_3, a_4, a_5]$ is coefficient array, corresponding elements are:

$$\begin{cases} a_1 = \dfrac{k_b^2}{k_a^2 k_b^2 \cos^2\varphi - k_a^2 u_b^2 - k_b^2 u_a^2 - 2k_a k_b u_a u_b \sin\varphi} \\[2mm] a_2 = \dfrac{k_a^2}{k_a^2 k_b^2 \cos^2\varphi - k_a^2 u_b^2 - k_b^2 u_a^2 - 2k_a k_b u_a u_b \sin\varphi} \\[2mm] a_3 = \dfrac{2k_a k_b \sin\varphi}{k_a^2 k_b^2 \cos^2\varphi - k_a^2 u_b^2 - k_b^2 u_a^2 - 2k_a k_b u_a u_b \sin\varphi} \\[2mm] a_4 = \dfrac{-2k_b^2 u_a - 2k_a k_b u_b \sin\varphi}{k_a^2 k_b^2 \cos^2\varphi - k_a^2 u_b^2 - k_b^2 u_a^2 - 2k_a k_b u_a u_b \sin\varphi} \\[2mm] a_5 = \dfrac{-2k_a^2 u_b - 2k_a k_b u_a \sin\varphi}{k_a^2 k_b^2 \cos^2\varphi - k_a^2 u_b^2 - k_b^2 u_a^2 - 2k_a k_b u_a u_b \sin\varphi} \end{cases} \tag{5}$$

By the least square estimation:

$$\min[S(\hat{a}_{1,2\ldots 5})] = \min[\sum_{i=1}^{n}(y_i - \sum_{j=1}^{5} u_{ij}\hat{a}_j)^2] \tag{6}$$

$$\sum_{i=1}^{n} u_{ij} y_i = \sum_{i=1}^{n} u_{ij} \sum_{k=1}^{5} u_{ik} \hat{a}_k = \sum_{i=1}^{n} \sum_{k=1}^{5} u_{ij} u_{ik} \hat{a}_k \tag{7}$$

Namely:

$$U^T \times Y = (U^T \times U) \times \hat{A}^T \tag{8}$$

Thus the estimate of the deviation can be expressed as:

$$\begin{cases} \hat{\varphi} & = arc\sin(\dfrac{\hat{a}_3}{2\sqrt{\hat{a}_1 \hat{a}_2}}) \\[2mm] \hat{u}_a & = \dfrac{\hat{a}_3 \hat{a}_5 - 2\hat{a}_2 \hat{a}_4}{4\hat{a}_1 \hat{a}_2 - \hat{a}_3^2} \\[2mm] \hat{u}_b & = \dfrac{\hat{a}_3 \hat{a}_4 - 2\hat{a}_1 \hat{a}_5}{4\hat{a}_1 \hat{a}_2 - \hat{a}_3^2} \\[2mm] \hat{k}_a & = \dfrac{2\sqrt{\hat{a}_2 (4\hat{a}_1 \hat{a}_2 - \hat{a}_3^2 - \hat{a}_3 \hat{a}_4 \hat{a}_5 + \hat{a}_2 \hat{a}_4^2 + \hat{a}_1 \hat{a}_5^2)}}{4\hat{a}_1 \hat{a}_2 - \hat{a}_3^2} \\[2mm] \hat{k}_b & = \dfrac{2\sqrt{\hat{a}_1 (4\hat{a}_1 \hat{a}_2 - \hat{a}_3^2 - \hat{a}_3 \hat{a}_4 \hat{a}_5 + \hat{a}_2 \hat{a}_4^2 + \hat{a}_1 \hat{a}_5^2)}}{4\hat{a}_1 \hat{a}_2 - \hat{a}_3^2} \end{cases} \tag{9}$$

Then according to the following correction algorithm, the estimates of the orthogonal signals can be expressed as:

$$\begin{bmatrix} \sin\hat{\theta} \\ \cos\hat{\theta} \end{bmatrix} = \begin{bmatrix} \dfrac{1}{\hat{k}_a} & 0 \\[2mm] \dfrac{\sin\hat{\varphi}}{\hat{k}_a \cos\hat{\varphi}} & \dfrac{1}{\hat{k}_b \cos\hat{\varphi}} \end{bmatrix} \begin{bmatrix} u_{\sin} - \hat{u}_a \\ u_{\cos} - \hat{u}_b \end{bmatrix} \tag{10}$$

4   Decoding Algorithm

In order to decode the position information, the algorithm of solving arctangent function can be used. This method is simple, but the position is obtained by the open loop control mode. The precision is low and the resistance to noise interference ability is poor as well. At the position where the angle θ is between 90° and 270°, cosθ is near to zero. The angle θ can hardly be estimate. In this paper, the closed-loop position tracking algorithm is used for the real-time speed extraction. Control system diagram is shown in figure 6.

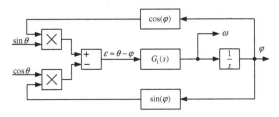

Fig. 6. Block Diagram of The Position Closed-loop Interpolator

In Fig.6, $G(s)$ is the prior transfer function of the position tracking controller; θ is the current position, the position information contained in the orthogonal signals; φ is the tracking position signal; ε is the error signal; ω is the estimation of speed signal.

T is the sampling time. Though the equation of algorithm can be expressed as follows:

$$\varepsilon = \sin\theta\cos\varphi - \cos\theta\sin\varphi = \sin(\theta - \varphi) \tag{11}$$

While $\theta - \varphi \to 0$,

$$\varepsilon = \sin(\theta - \varphi) \approx \theta - \varphi \tag{12}$$

In the figure, $G_1(s) = (2\xi\omega_n s + \omega_n^2)/s$, the transfer functions can be expressed as:

$$\begin{cases} G_\theta(s) = \dfrac{\varphi(s)}{\theta(s)} = \dfrac{2\xi\omega_n s + \omega_n^2}{s^2 + 2\xi\omega_n s + \omega_n^2} \\[2ex] G_\omega(s) = \dfrac{\omega(s)}{\theta(s)} = \dfrac{s(2\xi\omega_n s + \omega_n^2)}{s^2 + 2\xi\omega_n s + \omega_n^2} \end{cases} \tag{13}$$

5   Experimental Results

Fig.7(a) shows the original output signal of the encoder without signals correction, the curve CH1 is the cosine signal, the curve CH2 is the sine signal. Fig.8 shows the harmonic distribution with the Fast Fourier Transform (FFT). The fundamental frequency is 17Hz and the fundamental harmonic amplitude is 65dB. The harmonic components of two signals are similar, the second harmonic and the third harmonic are the main harmonic composition. Fig. 8(a) shows the harmonic distribution of the cosine signal, the content of the second harmonic is 0.18% of the fundamental harmonic, the third harmonic content is 0.21% of the fundamental harmonic; Fig. 8(b) shows the harmonic distribution of the sine signal, the content of the second harmonic is 0.22% of the fundamental harmonic, the third harmonic content is 0.25% of the fundamental harmonic. Fig.7(b) shows the sampling sine and cosine signals by using a 12 bits A/D converter. The wave CH1 and CH2 is the sine and cosine signal of the sensor output without correction, respectively, the wave CH3

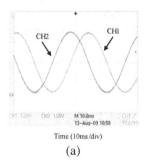

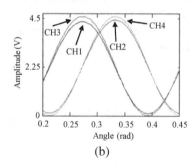

Time (10ms/div)

(a)

(b)

Fig. 7. Sine and Cosine Signals

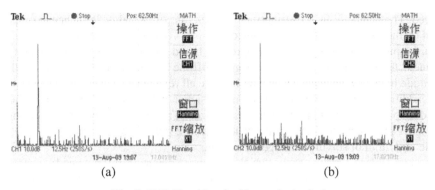

Fig. 8. FFT Algorithm for Harmonic Analysis

and CH4 is the sine and cosine signal with correction, respectively. It can be observed that the original ones without correction have a large amplitude bias and dc offset. With the proposed correction algorithm, the sinusoidal distortion of the signals is lowered and the orthogonality is improved.

In the experiment, the magnetic encoder is coaxially connected with a 5000 lines photoelectric encoder and a motor rotor shaft. The motor rotation speed is 100rpm. Fig.9(a) shows the output angles of the magnetic encoder and the photoelectric encoder. The CH1 shows the output position angle of the magnetic encoder, and the CH2 shows the photoelectric encoder output angle. Fig.9(b) shows the angle difference between the output of the magnetic encoder and the photoelectric one. The maximal relative error is closed to 0.09rad. Fig.9(c) shows the speed output signals of the magnetic encoder and the photoelectric encoder at 100rpm. The CH1 shows the speed output of the magnetic encoder, the CH2 shows the speed signal with the photoelectric encoder. The speed fluctuation range at the test condition is within 1.5% of the reference speed.

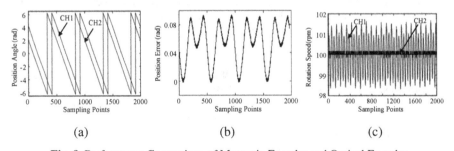

Fig. 9. Performance Comparison of Magnetic Encoder and Optical Encoder

6   Conclusion

This paper proposed a novel design scheme of magnetic rotary encoder. By the design of the additional iron ring outside the magnet, the radial magnetic field intensity has been enhanced in the air gap and the tangential magnetic field intensity has been reduced. The magnetic field distribution has been improved and its influence to output signal by the harmonic has been restrained.

Furthermore, the signal correction algorithm based on the least square estimation is designed, the output sine and cosine signals offline correction to the dc offset, the amplitude bias, and the phase angle gain bias are all realized.

In addition, the magnetic encoder output signal decoding by using a designed closed loop position tracking algorithm is realized. The proposed decoding algorithm has higher precision and has better anti-interference performance compared with the simple algorithm of solving arctangent function.

The experimental results show that the proposed magnetic rotary encoder scheme has higher precision, and can replace some kinds of optical encoder and potentiometer in position detection equipment field.

Acknowledgments. This work is financially supported by the National High-tech R&D Program of China (863 Program) #2011AA04A105 and the University Young Teachers Program of Shanghai respectively.

References

1. Bergas-Jané, J., Ferrater-Simón, C., Gross, G., Ramírez-Pisco, R., Galceran-Arellano, S., Rull-Duran, J.: High-Accuracy All-Digital Resolver-to-Digital Conversion. IEEE Transactions on Industrial Electronics 59(1), 326–333 (2012)
2. Boggarpu, N.K., Kavanagh, R.C.: New Learning Algorithm for High-Quality Velocity Measurement and Control When Using Low-Cost Optical Encoders. IEEE Transactions on Instrumentation and Measurement 59(3), 565–574 (2010)
3. Van Hoang, H., Jeon, J.W.: An Efficient Approach to Correct the Signals and Generate High-Resolution Quadrature Pulses for Magnetic Encoders. IEEE Transactions on Industrial Electronics 58(8), 3634–3646 (2011)
4. Van Hoang, H., Le, H.T., Jeon, J.W.: A new approach based-on advanced adaptive digital PLL for improving the resolution and accuracy of magnetic encoders. In: IEEE/RSJ International Conference on Intelligent Robots and Systems, IROS 2008, pp. 3318–3323 (2008)
5. Le, H.T., Van Hoang, H., Jeon, J.W.: Efficient method for correction and interpolation signal of magnetic encoders. In: 6th IEEE International Conference on Industrial Informatics, INDIN 2008, pp. 1383–1388 (2008)
6. Lin, Q., Li, T., Zhou, Z., Wang, S., Guo, H.: Application of the Magnetic Encoder in Actuator Servo System. In: International Conference on Mechatronics and Automation, ICMA 2007, pp. 3031–3035 (2007)
7. Hwang, S.H., Lee, J.H., Kim, J.M., Choi, C.: Compensation of analog rotor position errors due to nonideal sinusoidal encoder output signals. In: 2010 IEEE Energy Conversion Congress and Exposition (ECCE), pp. 4469–4473 (2010)
8. Shen, L.: DSP-Solution for High-Resolution Position with Sin/Cos-Encoders. In: 2010 International Conference on System Science, Engineering Design and Manufacturing Informatization (ICSEM), vol. 2, pp. 285–288 (2010)

An Adaptive Slope Compensation Circuit
and Its Application

Chen Guanghua, Wang Fengjiao,Wu Changqian, Qin Long,
Ma Shiwei, and Zeng Weimin

School of Mechatronics Engineering and Automation,
Shanghai University, Shanghai 200072, China
chghua@shu.edu.cn

Abstract. To solve the over-compensation problem in the current mode PWM switch power, a new adaptive slope compensation circuit is proposed in this paper. In the circuit, the difference between the output and input voltage is positively correlated with the duty cycle of switch signal, which is used to generate the control signal varying with the duty ratio. The control signal is used to control the gate voltage of MOS operating in linear region, which changes the linear drain-source resistance. With clamping circuit, a proportional ramp voltage with controllable slope is produced and amplified for compensation system by two stage amplifier. This compensation voltage is almost ideal, which can reduce the negative effect of over-compensation farthest. This circuit is applied to an LED driver IC and simulated in Cadence with CSMC 0.5um BiCMOS library. The results show that the boost driver circuit using adaptive compensation has about 28% dynamic response time reducing compared with the settled slope compensation. Therefore, the proposed compensation circuit can improve system's dynamic responsibility effectively.

Keywords: switch power, adaptive slope compensation, current mode PWM, LED driver.

1   Introduction

Switch power IC is quickly developing for its high conversion efficiency and wide application. The voltage control mode and the current control mode are two main control modes in switch power. Because of faster dynamic response, easier compensation structure and wider gain bandwidth, the current control mode is used more than the other. The current control mode is a double closed loop system. The control voltage of the outside loop is compared with the voltage signal obtained from inside loop every cycle. When duty cycle of switch signal is over 50%, a second harmonic generation generates in the current feedback, which may make whole system uncontrolled.

To resolve the second harmonic generation problem, slope compensation is usually used in the circuit. If compensation is too weak to make the system stable, control

T. Xiao, L. Zhang, and S. Ma (Eds.): ICSC 2012, Part I, CCIS 326, pp. 83–93, 2012.

loop still has no function. Therefore, the slope compensation in formerly design is always in safe range. However, this safe range is too conservative generally and can result in over-compensation. Over-compensation will increase the restraint of switch current, which reduces the drive ability of system. Over-compensation also will affect the dynamic response of system. Considering these, several slope compensation circuits are designed to change the level of compensation according to system's status [1-9]. The sectional slope compensation proposed by Chaodong Ling [3] is one of the changeable slope compensation. Because the limit of section's amount, the problem of over-compensation is only resolved partly. The compensation circuit proposed by Lu Jiaying[4] is a dynamic compensation structure which strengthen the stability and the responsibility of system, but it is not a real adaptive slope output, and it also causes a loss in the power.

An adaptive slope compensation circuit is proposed in this paper. In the circuit, a control signal varying with output voltage is produced according to the positive correlation between duty ratio and output voltage. The signal is used to control the gate voltage of MOS, which changes the linear resistance from source to drain. With clamping circuit, a proportional ramp voltage is produced and varying with the resistance of MOSFET. Finally, the ramp voltage is amplified by two stage amplifier, and outputted for compensation system. The signal is almost ideal and can reduce the negative effect of over-compensation farthest.

2   Second Harmonic Generation and Its Compensation

In the current mode PWM boost structure, as Fig.1 shows, a switch signal is generated from comparator to control system's work status. A disturbance Δi_0 is produced on the inductance's current and becomes Δi_1 after one switch cycle. The new disturbance Δi_1 is expressed as

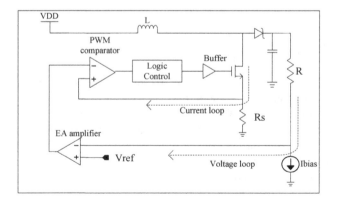

Fig. 1. Schematic diagram of current mode PWM boost structure

$$\Delta i_1 = \Delta i_0 \left(\frac{m_2}{m_1} \right)^1 \tag{1}$$

where m_1 is the slope of inductance current's rise side, and m_2 is the slope of inductance current's drop side, which is showed in Fig.2. After N cycles, the disturbance is given in the following form

$$\Delta i_N = \Delta i_0 \left(\frac{m_2}{m_1} \right)^N \tag{2}$$

When duty cycle D is less than 50%, namely $m_2 < m_1$, then $(m_2 / m_1) < 1$, which means Δi_N is convergent. When duty cycle is over 50%, as shows Fig.3, $(m_2 / m_1) > 1$, which means Δi_N is divergent.

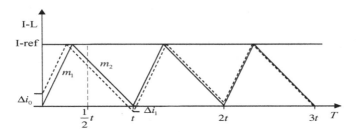

Fig. 2. Current loop oscillation for duty cycle less than 50%

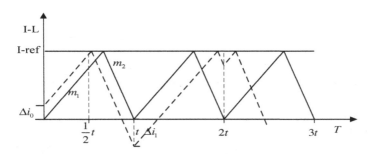

Fig. 3. Current loop oscillation for duty cycle greater than 50%

If Δi_N is divergent, the inductance current must be distorted, which makes the system lose its function. To resolve this problem, a slope signal with same cycle of switch signal is usually added to the input of comparator to compensation the disturbance, as shown in Fig.4. Thus, after one cycle, the disturbance Δi_1 is given by

$$\Delta i_1 = \Delta i_0 \left(\frac{m_2 - m_c}{m_1 + m_c} \right)^1 \tag{3}$$

In equation (3), m_c is the slope of compensation signal. So Δi_N can be expressed as follows

$$\Delta i_N = \Delta i_0 \left(\frac{m_2 - m_c}{m_1 + m_c} \right)^N \tag{4}$$

From the above expression, one can see that the condition of the stability of the converter is given by

$$\left(\frac{m_2 - m_c}{m_1 - m_c} \right) < 1 \tag{5}$$

Using the equation $D \cdot m_1 = (1 - D) m_2$, Equation (5) is expressed explicitly as

$$\frac{m_c}{m_2} > \frac{2D-1}{2D}, \qquad \left(\frac{1}{2} < D < 1 \right) \tag{6}$$

Equation (6) is the final qualification that the slope signal must meet to compensate.

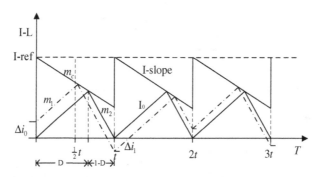

Fig. 4. Current disturbance's variation with slope compensation

For the facility in circuit design, traditional slope compensation circuit usually has a compensation signal with slope $m_c = 75\% m_2$, which can make sure of the current signal being convergence after few cycles. However, $75\% m_2$ is just an empirical value. The real value needed for system can be gained from the deduction below.

According to the definition of inductance current, the slope of the current variation can be expressed as

$$m_2 = \frac{Vout - Vin}{L} \tag{7}$$

In Fig.1, because the current of inductance cannot change instantly, the equation is expressible as follows

$$\left[Vin - (V_{RS} + V_S) \right] \cdot D = (Vout - Vin) \cdot (1 - D) \tag{8}$$

In equation (8), V_{RS} is the voltage of feedback resistance, and V_S is the voltage between source and drain of switch MOSFET. Substituting equation (7), (8) into equation (6) gives

$$m_C > \frac{V_{RS} + V_S - Vin}{L} \cdot \left[1 + \frac{1}{2(D-1)}\right] \tag{9}$$

To assure the system stability, supposing that maximum duty cycle of switch is 80%, equation (9) is the condition compensation slope m_c should meet.

From the above, the value of compensation signal's slope which ensures the system's stability must be in the shadow area in Fig.5, which can be summarized as follows

$$m_C \begin{cases} \geq 0 & 0 < D < 50\% \\ > \dfrac{V_{RS} + V_S - Vin}{L} \cdot \left[1 + \dfrac{1}{2(D-1)}\right] & 50\% < D < 80\% \end{cases} \tag{10}$$

It is obvious that the slope compensation with $75\% m_2$ ramp (as curve B shows) is excessive to the minimum value of compensation slope when duty cycle is less than 80%, especially less than 50%. It will make the average current of inductance be decreased, and the efficiency of switch power be reduced too. As a result, the dynamic response time of the system is increased, which is absolutely unexpected for the designer of the power.

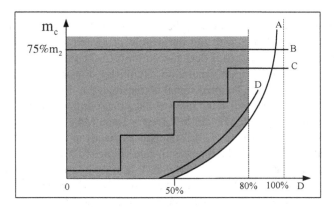

Fig. 5. Slope curve of various compensation methods

To decrease the disadvantage influence of over-compensation, a sectional compensation circuit is proposed by Lu Jiaying[4], whose slope of compensation signal is described by curve C in Fig.5. Compared with settled compensation, sectional compensation reduces the level of over-compensation, but it also can be improved considerably. Such as curve D shown in Fig.5, the slope of compensation signal is zero when duty cycle is less than 50%, and is along with curve A when duty cycle is more than 50%. Obviously the curve D is the optimal compensation slope value.

3   Adaptive Slope Compensation Circuit

A new slope compensation circuit is proposed in this part to get optimal compensation. As the structure shown in the Fig.6, the circuit is composed with three parts. Firstly, the circuit generates a control voltage V-CON which is changed with the difference between the output and input voltage. Secondly, V-CON is used to control the slope of compensation signal. Thirdly, the circuit takes advantage of two stages amplifier to adjust output range and driver ability.

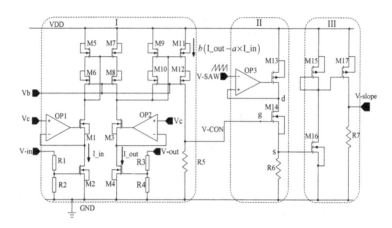

Fig. 6. Diagram of adaptive slope compensation circuit

In the control mode of switch power, the difference between the output and input voltage is positive correlative with the duty cycle of switch signal. The difference detected by the circuit is used to reflect the duty cycle. The circuit in the left dash frame in Fig.6 is a control signal generation circuit. R1~R4 are used to sample the input and output voltage. The sampled signal is transmitted to M2 and M4's gate. M2 and M4 work as OTA to transform the input voltage into current signal. The amplifier OP1 and OP2 composing with M1 and M3 keep M2 and M4's drain voltage up with OP1 and OP2's input V_C, where V_C is supplied by bandgap circuit. These circuits make the current of M1 and M3 be linear with gate voltage of M2 and M4[6]. Thus, it is also be linear with V-in and V-out. MOSFET M5-M12 form two groups current mirror circuit. First group mirror makes the current of M9 reflect the difference between I_out and I_in (which just is the current of M1 and M3). The second group current mirror loads the difference on R5. From Fig.6, one can see that the current of R5 is expressed as

$$I_{R5} = b(I\_out - a \times I\_in)$$ (11)

In equation (11), a is the proportion value between M7's and M5's width and b is the proportion value between M11's and M9's width. I_in and I_out stand for the current of M2 and M4, and can be expressed as

$$I\_out = \beta_4\left(\frac{R4}{R3+R4}\times V\_out - V_T - \frac{V_C}{2}\right)V_C \tag{12}$$

$$I\_in = \beta_2\left(\frac{R2}{R1+R2}\times V\_in - V_T - \frac{V_C}{2}\right)V_C \tag{13}$$

In equation (12) and (13), β is input MOSFET's transconductance parameter, and V_T is the threshold voltage. Substituting equation (12), (13) into equation (11), R5's current is given by

$$I_{R5} = b\left[\beta_4\left(\frac{R4}{R3+R4}\times V\_out\right) - a\times\beta_2\left(\frac{R2}{R1+R2}\times V\_in\right)\right]V_C - b(\beta_4 - a\beta_2)\left(V_T + \frac{V_C}{2}\right)V_C \tag{14}$$

Assuming that $\beta_4 = a\times\beta_2$, and $\dfrac{R4}{R3+R4} = \dfrac{R2}{R1+R2} = k$, equation (11) can be simplified as

$$I_{R5} = b\beta_4 k(V\_out - V\_in)V_C \tag{15}$$

Multiplying I_{R5} to R5, V-CON is found to be

$$V - CON = V_{R5} = R_5\times b\beta_4 k(V\_out - V\_in)V_C \tag{16}$$

Obviously, V-CON is linear with the difference between input and output voltage. In equation (16), proportion coefficient k is used to limit the input voltage's range. This means only when D is more than 50%, M2 and M4 start to work, otherwise, V-CON is zero.

The middle part's circuit of Fig.6 is a proportion circuit. It use V-CON to control the resistant of MOSFET which operating in linear region. The amplifier OP3 and M13 compose a clamping circuit to keep V_D consistent with the negative input of OP3. According the input-output curve of a MOSFET shown in Fig.7, the curve's slope is almost invariable when V_{DS} is less than V_{GS}-V_{th}, and the curve's slope is in inverse proportion to V_{GS}. Because the slope of input/output curve indicates the resistant of device, one can regard the MOSFET as a linear resistor. Furthermore, the resistance of the resistor is also in inverse proportion to V_{GS}.

When V_D is less than V_{GS}-V_{th}, using Rm14 to replace the resistance of MOS, the source voltage of M14 V_S can be expressed as

$$V_S = \frac{R_6}{R_6 + R_{m14}}\times V_D \tag{17}$$

In equation (17), assuming that $\dfrac{R_6}{R_6 + R_{m14}} = n$. Because V_D is the same as V-SAW, when V-SAW is supplied with a sawtooth wave, and whose maximum is less than V_{GS}-V_{th}, V_S must be a proportional part of V-SAW. The proportion parameter n is in proportion to V-CON.

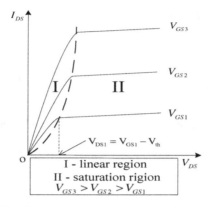

Fig. 7. I-V characteristic curve of MOSFET

Finally, the voltage of V_S is amplified by a two stage amplifier. The compensation slope signal V-slope is the output on R7. M16 and M17 are two common source amplifiers which increase the driver ability, and adjust the output voltage into a suitable range. M15 is acted as the first stage's load with diode structure. In the end, the output voltage V-slope is the compensation signal, whose slope is controlled by the difference between the output and input voltage.

4   Simulation and System Verification

In order to test the validity of the theoretical evaluation, simulations are used to test the performances of the circuit above in Cadence Spectra. By means of setting R1-R4, proportion parameters k and n, the input/output results of the compensation block are shown in Fig.8. At the start, signal V-slope is 0. After V-out reached 6.774V, the compensation circuit begins to output a sawtooth wave, and its amplitude increases with V-out almostly in linear relationship. So V-out can be expressed as

$$Vout = a \cdot m_c + b \tag{18}$$

where m_c is each sawtooth wave's slope, a and b are constants. The input and output voltage of the DC-DC boost converter can be expressed explicitly as following

$$Vin = (1 - D)Vout \tag{19}$$

Substituting equation (19) into equation (18) gives

$$m_c = \frac{Vin}{a(1-D)} - \frac{b}{a} \tag{20}$$

In equation (9), ignoring V_{RS} and V_S, equation (9) is found to be

$$m_c > \frac{V\_in}{2L(1-D)} - \frac{V\_in}{L} \tag{21}$$

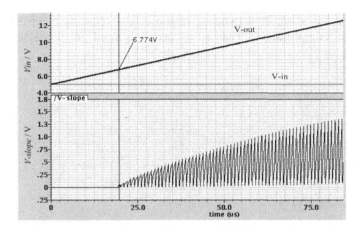

Fig. 8. Output diagram of slope compensation

Setting the resistance to meet the conditions, namely $a = 2L$, and $b / a < Vin / L$, equation (20) is similar with equation (21), and whose curve is the closest to curve A than any other curves in Fig.5. So the compensation structure proposed in this paper is the most optimal than not only the 75% m_2 slope compensation, but also Lu Jiaying's sectional compensation in decreasing the over-compensation.

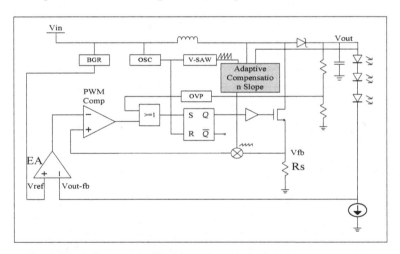

Fig. 9. Block diagram of LED driver IC with adaptive slope compensation

This adaptive compensation circuit is applied in an LED driver IC to test its performance. The chip's structure diagram with PWM current control mode is shown in Fig.9 [10]. The chip is simulated in CSMC 0.5um CMOS model. Fig.10 shows the output voltage curve of the chip. The time used to stabilize the output voltage is 2.456ms. When the adaptive compensation block is replaced by a traditional compensation circuit with 75% m_2 slope, the dynamic response time is increased to 3.418ms, as Fig.11 shows. Obviously, the boost driver circuit using adaptive compensation has about 28% dynamic response time reducing compared with the settled slope compensation. That is a great advanced in improving system's performance.

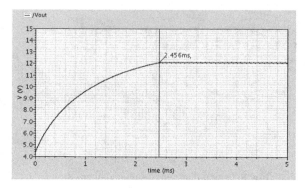

Fig. 10. System's dynamic response with adaptive slope compensation

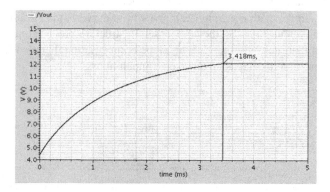

Fig. 11. System's dynamic response with fixed slope compensation

5   Conclusions

An adaptive slope compensation circuit is proposed to resolve the second harmonic generation problem in this paper. Transconductance amplifiers are used to get control voltage which changed with the difference between the input and output voltage in the circuit. The control voltage is used to control the gate voltage of MOS operating in linear region, which changes the linear drain-source resistance. With clamping circuit, a proportional ramp voltage with controllable slope is produced, and amplified by two stage amplifier. Compared with traditional compensation circuit with settled slope compensation, even the section compensation circuit, the compensation voltage of the proposed design is almost ideal, which can reduce the negative effect of over-compensation farthest. This circuit is applied to the LED driver IC and simulated in Cadence with CSMC 0.5um BiCMOS library. The results show that the boost driver circuit using adaptive compensation has about 28% dynamic response time reducing compared with the settled slope compensation. Therefore the proposed compensation circuit can improve system's dynamic responsibility effectively.

Acknowledgments. The research is supported by the Development Special Fund of Shanghai Software & Integrated Circuit Industry, Innovation Program of Shanghai Municipal Education Commission (12ZZ083) and Postgraduate Innovation Fund of Shanghai University.

References

1. Lai, W.J., Chen, C.L., et al.: High-Efficiency Slope Compensator (HSC) with Input-Independent Load Condition Identification in Current Mode DC/DC Buck Converters. In: Energy Conversion Congress and Exposition, pp. 2897–2900 (2009)
2. Li, Y.M., Lai, X.Q., et al.: An adaptive slope compensation circuit for buck DC-DC converter. In: 7th International Conference on Digital Object Identifier (ASICON 2007), pp. 608–611 (2007)
3. Ling, C.D., Wen, C.Q., et al.: Design of a Novel Nonlinear Slope Compensation Circuit for Peak Current-mode Boost DC-DC Converter. In: International Conference on Anti-Counterfeiting Security and Identification in Communication (ASID), pp. 63–66 (2010)
4. Lu, J.Y., Wu, X.B.: A Novel Piecewise Linear Slope Compensation Circuit in Peak Current Mode Control. In: IEEE Conference on Electron Devices and Solid-State Circuits(EDSSC), pp. 929–932 (2007)
5. Yang, Y.Z., Xie, G.J.: Research and design of a self-adaptable slope compensation circuit with simple structure. In: IEEE International Conference on Intelligent Computing and Intelligent Systems (ICIS), pp. 333–335 (2010)
6. Jeong, W.J., Park, J., et al.: LED Driver IC with an Adaptive Slope Compensation Technique. In: International Conference on Green Circuits and Systems (ICGCS), pp. 709–712 (2010)
7. Shibata, K., Pham, C.K.: A Compact Adaptive Slope Compensation Circuit for Current-Mode DC-DC Converter. In: Proceedings of 2010 IEEE International Symposium on Circuits and Systems (ISCAS), pp. 1651–1654 (2010)
8. Zhong, J.M., Liu, S.L.: Design of Slope Compensation Circuit in Peak-current Controlled Mode Converters. In: 2011 International Conference on Electric Information and Control Engineering (ICEICE), pp. 1310–1313 (2011)
9. Yang, Y.Z., Xie, G.J., et al.: Research and Design of a white LED driver chip applied in backlight. In: 2010 10th IEEE International Conference on Solid-State and Integrated Circuit Technology (ICSICT), pp. 506–508 (2010)
10. Lu, J.Y., Wu, X.B.: A PWM Controller IC for LED Driver Used to Multiple DC-DC Topologies. In: Asia-Pacific Power and Energy Engineering Conference, pp. 1–4 (2009)

The Structure Optimization of Spherical Plain Bearings Based on Taguchi Method

Xuejin Shen, Yunfei Liu, Yufeng Huang, and Deguo Li

Department of Mechanical Automation Engineering,
Shanghai University, Shanghai 200072, China
shenxj@shu.edu.cn

Abstract. The self-lubricating spherical plain bearings is one type of sliding bearings, and it is widely used in the modern industry area. The structural optimization and design about it is complicated. The taguchi method based on orthogonal experiment is a steady design method in engineering, and it is used for structural size determination of self-lubricating spherical plain bearings in selected range for parameters matching. Many optimum proposals are formed, and the optimization goals are the maximum value of contact pressure and the maximum Mises stress difference value of the inner ring and the outer ring. Then, the error component is used to simulate the fluctuation of optimization goals. Two sets of signal-to-noise values are worked out. The final prioritization scheme is determined by computing the multiple SN values, and a new idea is provided to solve the similar problems.

Keywords: Structural optimization, Taguchi method, Spherical plain bearings, Finite element analysis.

1   Introduction

Taguchi method was created by Genichi Taguchi who was a famous Japanese quality engineer in 1970s[1,2]. It is based on orthogonal experiment, and it is a steady design method of the engineering. New products and new process which are developed using this technology will be more stable and reliable, and have a strong anti-interference ability. It makes individual performance characteristics to reach the set minimum requirements, and gets the optimal multi-performance characteristics at the same time.

Spherical plain bearings are plain bearings, mainly composed of an inner ring with the outer sphere surface and an outer ring with the inner sphere surface. Generally they are used for slower swing movement, tilt movement and rotation. As a general-purpose machine parts, spherical plain bearings with self-lubricating fabric liner, which are simply named as self-lubricating bearings as follows, have good thermal stability, high carrying capacity, long life, flexible rotation, maintenance-free (solid lubrication), and other characteristics. Now they are widely used in aviation, aerospace, electric power, transportation, biomedical engineering, etc, especially in requirements of heavy load and swing movement[3~6].

T. Xiao, L. Zhang, and S. Ma (Eds.): ICSC 2012, Part I, CCIS 326, pp. 94–102, 2012.

Fig. 1 is a self-lubricating bearings chart. dk is spherical diameter, B is the width of inner ring, and C is the width of outer ring. This paper is to optimize the design for the size of the self-lubricating bearings, which are spherical diameter, the width of inner ring, and the width of outer ring, while the other secondary factors can be determined in accordance with experience.

Under the same assembly size and working conditions, which are the load of 158kN, the oscillating frequency of 12 times / min, the swing angle of +25° ~ -25°, and ambient temperature of 25°C, the paper attempts to do an initial discussion about optimization design of self-lubricating spherical plain bearings.

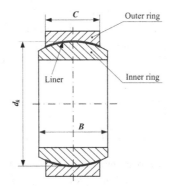

Fig. 1. Schematic diagram of self-lubricating spherical plain bearing

2   Principles and Procedures of Structural Optimization

In this paper, the design for the structure optimization of self-lubricating bearings is steady design, the optimization goals are contact pressure and Mises stress difference value (Mises stress D-value for short) between outer ring and inner ring. The structure optimization is based on the pursuit of the best performance of bearings, and its basic principles are as follows:

(1) The signal-to-noise (SN) ratio (SNR for short) is used as the robustness index, the best optimization program is found by calculating the SNR, and the largest SNR is the best design.
(2) Error component is used to simulate the fluctuation, and error analysis is done for every structure optimum proposal, so as to achieve the goal of robust design.
(3) Orthogonal table is used as a tool to do the internal design and external design, in order to significantly reduce the program number.
(4) According to the degree of the importance of various performance goals, the different weight distribution coefficients are determined, then the integrated SNR is calculated, and the program which has the largest integrated SNR is the optimal solution what we want.

The basic procedures of the structural optimization design, which is based on the Taguchi method, are system design, parameter design and tolerance design[7]. In the process of steady design, system design is the basement, and parameter design is the core.

3   Structural Optimization Method and Procedures

3.1   System Design

Self-lubricating bearings are widely used in many automation equipment and construction machinery. Its main failure modes are wear failure and contact fatigue failure. We believe that the contact pressure value and the D-value of Mises stress are the key indicators of bearings wear and contact fatigue. The goals of structural optimization are the contact pressure value and the D-value of Mises stresses. Their functions are as shown in Eq. (1) and Eq. (2):

$$D_1 = f_1(d_k, B, C) \quad .$$ (1)

$$D_2 = f_2(d_k, B, C) \quad .$$ (2)

Where D_1 is the contact pressure between inner ring and outer ring, D_2 is the D-value of Mises stress, d_k is the spherical diameter size of bearings, B is the width of inner ring, and C is the width of outer ring.

Structure parameters of self-lubricating bearings contain lots of aspects, the consideration here is the spherical diameter, and width dimensions of the inner and outer ring. Analysis of a large number of calculations shows the following relationship between the structure dimensions (factors) and the optimization target (output characteristics).

(1) The contact pressure and D-value of Mises stress will both increase while the size of the diameter is too large or too small, and there is an intermediate value which makes the contact pressure to minimize, and also there is an intermediate value which makes the D-value of Mises stress to minimize.
(2) While the width size of outer ring increases, the contact pressure gradually decreases and gradually tends to a set value, and the difference of maximum Mises stresses of the inner and outer rings will also increase.
(3) While the width dimensions of inner ring change within a certain range, the maximum contact pressure will change at a certain range, but the contact pressure range is very small. While the inner ring width size increases, the difference of maximum Mises stress of the inner and outer rings will increase.

Discussions above are only the impacts of single structural parameters on self-lubricating bearings performances. During integrated optimization design, the structural parameters and their combinations can be done to reduce the contact pressure and D-value of Mises stress of inner ring and outer ring.

3.2   Parameter Design

Based on the design variables and objective functions, the corresponding orthogonal tables as the inner table and the outer table are selected, and the controllable and error factor level tables are determined in accordance with the bearing structure size and the error range of possible changes. Then we could get the objective function values of the outer table. Still further, the SNR of the maximum contact pressure and D-value of maximum Mises stress could be found, and the maximum value is selected as the preferred program through the comparition of SNR in the inner table.

(a) Develop the factor level table
We selected structural parameters of the spherical diameter d_k, inner ring width B and outer ring width C as the design variables. According to the design requirements and bearing structure, we determine the centers of each factor level values, they are $A_0=126$ mm, $B_0=36$ mm, and $C_0=30$ mm. The interval of the various factors between the two levels are taken respectively as 1 mm, 2 mm and 2 mm, which constitutes three levels. The controllable factors in the level of the table are as shown in Table 1.

Table 1. Controllable factor level table

Variable factors / Serial number	Inner diameter of outer ring d_k (mm)	Width of inner ring B (mm)	Width of outer ring C (mm)
1	A_0-1	B_0-2	C_0-2
2	A_0	B_0	C_0
3	A_0+1	B_0+2	C_0+2

(b) SNR calculation
The SNR η is used to evaluate the advantages and disadvantages of assessment indicators (objective function or multi objective evaluation function). According to target characteristics of the design (contact pressure and D-value of the Mises stress are as small as possible), the SNR formula of look small features is adopted as follows[8]:

$$\eta = -10\log\frac{1}{n}\sum_{i=1}^{n}\left(\frac{D_i}{100}\right)^2 \tag{3}$$

Where D_i is the evaluation function (objective function), the number of samples $i = 1, 2, ..., n$. Max (η) corresponds to the minimum value of the objective function, min (D).

(c) Inner design
Table 1 is for the experimental program without considering the interaction of three factors and three levels. By designing the inner table as the orthogonal table, rearranging the factors level menu order, and seating by number, you can have nine different mixes of programs, such as shown in Table 2.

Table 2. Program design table

Program number j	Inner diameter of outer ring d_k	Width of inner ring B	Width of outer ring C
1	A_0-1	B_0-2	C_0-2
2	A_0-1	B_0	C_0
3	A_0-1	B_0+2	C_0+2
4	A_0	B_0-2	C_0
5	A_0	B_0	C_0+2
6	A_0	B_0+2	C_0-2
7	A_0+1	B_0-2	C_0+2
8	A_0+1	B_0	C_0-2
9	A_0+1	B_0+2	C_0

(d) Error factor level table

Table 3. Error factor level table

level \ factors	Inner diameter of outer ring d_k (mm)	Width of inner ring B (mm)	Width of outer ring C (mm)
1	$X_0-0.2$	$Y_0-0.5$	$Z_0-0.5$
2	X_0	Y_0	Z_0
3	$X_0+0.2$	$Y_0+0.5$	$Z_0+0.5$

In order to achieve the purpose of robust design, the corresponding error factors can make it easy to calculate the SNR under the conditions of various programs. Considering the corresponding error factors, which come from three structural parameters fluctuate, we could simulate the fluctuation of different programs through importing the error factors. The appropriate error value is taken based on the fluctuation of d_k, B and C. And the three factors and three levels of error table are worked out by imitating table 1(program 1 of table 2 is as an example, and the other programs are no longer listed). In order to facilitate the formulation, take $X_0=A_0-1$, $Y_0=B_0-2$, $Z_0=C_0-2$, shown in Table 3.

(e) Outer design

Still using the orthogonal table to do the external design of outer table, nine groups of values are adopted as the centers, which are arranged in the orthogonal table. Nine orthogonal tables can be shaped in the same way as table 2.

Only one outside design table is listed (shown in Table 4, it is outside design table of program 1), the other eight forms are similar. The objective function value (D_{1i}, D_{2i}) and the SNR η_{11}, η_{21} are got for program 1, as shown in Table 4. Similarly, SNR of other programs can be calculated based on various programs of external design tables.

Table 4. The objective function computation of program 1

Test number i	Inner diameter of outer ring d_k	Width of inner ring B	Width of outer ring C	The maximum value of contact pressure D_{1i} (10^7pa)	D-value of maximum Mises stress D_{2i} (10^7pa)
1	X_0-0.2	Y_0-0.5	Z_0-0.5	7.029	1.682
2	X_0-0.2	Y_0	Z_0	6.928	1.729
3	X_0-0.2	Y_0+0.5	Z_0+0.5	6.873	1.657
4	X_0	Y_0-0.5	Z_0	6.959	1.724
5	X_0	Y_0	Z_0+0.5	6.905	1.630
6	X_0	Y_0+0.5	Z_0-0.5	6.936	1.623
7	X_0+0.2	Y_0-0.5	Z_0+0.5	6.910	1.680
8	X_0+0.2	Y_0	Z_0-0.5	6.898	1.606
9	X_0+0.2	Y_0+0.5	Z_0	6.901	1.629
$\eta_{11} = -10\log\dfrac{1}{9}\sum\limits_{i=1}^{9}(\dfrac{D_{1i}}{100})^2$				23.19	/
$\eta_{21} = -10\log\dfrac{1}{9}\sum\limits_{i=1}^{9}(\dfrac{D_{2i}}{100})^2$				/	35.58

4   The Results and Discussion of Optimization

According to the SNR formula of look small features, nine sets of SNR under the condition of the internal table can be calculated by calculating the objective function value of each external table. The targets are the maximum contact pressure and

Table 5. SNR calculation results

Program number j	Inner diameter of outer ring d_k	Width of inner ring B	Width of outer ring C	SNR of contact pressure η_{1j}	SNR of mises stress η_{2j}
1	A_0-1	B_0-2	C_0-2	23.19	35.58
2	A_0-1	B_0	C_0	23.65	36.13
3	A_0-1	B_0+2	C_0+2	23.98	36.47
4	A_0	B_0-2	C_0	23.76	36.44
5	A_0	B_0	C_0+2	24.16	37.12
6	A_0	B_0+2	C_0-2	23.33	35.97
7	A_0+1	B_0-2	C_0+2	24.28	36.05
8	A_0+1	B_0	C_0-2	23.44	35.55
9	A_0+1	B_0+2	C_0	23.90	36.29
$Max(\eta_{1j})$				24.28	/
$Min(\eta_{1j})$				23.19	/
$Max(\eta_{2j})$				/	37.12
$Min(\eta_{2j})$				/	35.55

D-value of the maximum Mises stress, and their corresponding SNR calculation results are shown in Table 5.

In the limited range of parameters, by multi-parameter matching, we can form multiple options, as shown in Table 5. In order to get a group of determined structure size optimal value of self-lubricating bearings, normalized theory is adopted to do the calculation. Using formula (4) and formula (5), SNR of contact pressure and D-value of Mises stress were converted into dimensionless form. Normalized SNR calculation results are shown in Table 6.

$$\varepsilon_{1j} = \frac{\eta_{1j} - Min(\eta_{1j})}{Max(\eta_{1j}) - Min(\eta_{1j})} \tag{4}$$

$$\varepsilon_{2j} = \frac{\eta_{2j} - Min(\eta_{2j})}{Max(\eta_{2j}) - Min(\eta_{2j})} \tag{5}$$

where ε_{1j} and ε_{2j} are normalized SNR calculation results, $Max(\eta_{1j})$ is the maximum SNR of contact pressure, $Min(\eta_{1j})$ is the minimum SNR of contact pressure, $Max(\eta_{2j})$ is the maximum SNR of D-value of Mises stress, and $Min(\eta_{2j})$ is the minimum SNR of D-value of Mises stress. Normalized SNR calculation results are shown in Table 6, program number j=1, 2, 3......, 9.

Table 6. Dimensionless numerical calculation results table

Program number j	SNR of maximum contact pressure	Normalized SNR ε_{1j}	SNR of maximum Mises stress	Normalized SNR ε_{2j}
1	23.19	0	35.58	0.019
2	23.65	0.422	36.13	0.369
3	23.98	0.725	36.47	0.586
4	23.76	0.523	36.44	0.567
5	24.16	0.890	37.12	1
6	23.33	0.128	35.97	0.268
7	24.28	1	36.05	0.318
8	23.44	0.229	35.55	0
9	23.90	0.651	36.29	0.471

The weight coefficients of the maximum contact pressure and D-value of maximum Mises stresses are considered. And combined with normalized SNR in table 6, looking for the optimization program when the integrated SNR is maximum. The main failure mode of self-lubricating bearings is wear and tear, and lots of experimental studies have shown that the contact pressure can indirectly reflect the wear amount of self-lubricating bearings. Therefore, it is set that the proportion of contact pressure is bigger for the optimization here. The relationship between integrated SNR ε_{1j} and ε_{1j} is as follows:

$$\varepsilon_j = 0.6\varepsilon_{1j} + 0.4\varepsilon_{2j} \tag{6}$$

Integrated SNR ε_j is shown in table 7 in accordance with formula (6).

Table 7. Table of integrated SNR

Program number j	Inner diameter of outer ring d_k	Width of inner ring B	Width of outer ring C	Integrated SNR ε_j
1	A_0-1	B_0-2	C_0-2	0.001
2	A_0-1	B_0	C_0	0.4
3	A_0-1	B_0+2	C_0+2	0.670
4	A_0	B_0-2	C_0	0.541
5	A_0	B_0	C_0+2	0.934
6	A_0	B_0+2	C_0-2	0.184
7	A_0+1	B_0-2	C_0+2	0.727
8	A_0+1	B_0	C_0-2	0.137
9	A_0+1	B_0+2	C_0	0.579

Considering the calculation results in Table 7, maximum integrated SNR ε_j is selected, and the program which can meet the condition is program 5. At this point, the contact pressure and D-value of Mises stress of self-lubricating bearings are optimal overall. According to the results, the best program for optimizing the structure of self-lubricating bearings is: d_k=126mm, B=36mm, C=32mm.

When doing the statistical analysis of internal table, two methods are common, one is range analysis, and another is the analysis of variance. Range analysis is easy to use and the calculation amount is relatively small. Besides, it is more widely applied in practice. The following range analysis method is for analyzing the SNR, as shown in Table 8. Where, T1, T2 and T3 are respectively the sum of SNR for each column in Table 1. Range analysis results in Table 8 could show that the impacts of outer ring width and bearing diameter are bigger than the inner ring width.

Table 8. Range analysis sheet of SNR

Variable \ Item	Spherical diameter d_k	Width of inner ring B	Width of outer ring C
T1	1.071	1.269	0.322
T2	1.659	1.471	1.520
T3	1.443	1.433	2.331
Mean of T1	0.357	0.423	0.107
Mean of T2	0.553	0.49	0.507
Mean of T3	0.481	0.478	0.777
Range R	0.196	0.067	0.670

5   Conclusions

Based on the basic idea of the Taguchi method, combined with finite element analysis of self-lubricating bearings, the experimental programs of the three factors and three levels are designed, and the system design and parameter design are done. By calculating the SNR of every program of internal table, two performance goals, which are maximum contact pressure and D-value of maximum Mises stress, attain optimal overall when d_k=126mm, B=36mm, C=32mm. And it is gotten that the impacts of outer ring width and bearing spherical diameter on optimal goals are bigger than one of the inner ring width through range analysis.

Acknowledgements. This work was financially supported by the COSTIND of China (JPPT-115-3-1338), Innovative Team Program of Universities in Shanghai (B.48-0109-09-002) and High and New Engineering Program of Shanghai (D.51-0109-09-001).

References

1. Taguchi: Introduction of Quality Engineering. Translation and Publishing Corporation in China, Beijing (1985)
2. Taguchi: Painting of Experimental Design. Nine Good, Ltd., Tokyo (1977)
3. Sautter, S., Haden, H.R., Kottwitz, B.: Spherical Plain Bearings for on and off Road Vehicles. Bearing Technology: Analysis, Development, and Testing. Society of Automotive Engineers, 11–26 (1985)
4. Qu, Q.W., Liu, Y.Y., Zhong, Z.Y., Guo, X.P.: Design Characteristic and Analysis for the Spherical Plain Bearing. Lubrication Engineering 04, 102–105 (2004) (in Chinese)
5. Germaneau, A., Peyruseigt, F., Mistou, S., Doumalin, P., Dupre, J.C.: 3D Mechanical Analysis of Aeronautical Plain Bearings: Validation of a Finite Element Model from Measurement of Displacement Fields by Digital Volume Correlation and Optical Scanning Tomography. Optics and Lasers in Engineering 48(06), 676–683 (2010)
6. Germaneau, A., Peyruseigt, F., Mistou, S., Dalverny, O., Doumalin, P., Dupre, J.C.: Verification of a Spherical Plain Bearing Finite-element Model Using Scattered Light Photoelasticity Tests. Journal of Engineering Tribology 222(05), 647–656 (2008)
7. He, M.H.: Taguchi Method in the Monocrystalline Silicon Solar Cell Production Process Optimization. Nanjing University of Technology and Engineering, Nanjing (2009) (in Chinese)
8. Ge, J.Q., Jia, T.B., Zhao, Z.M., Yang, T.: On Parameters Optimization of Trajectory Correction Submunition Using Taguchi Method. Journal of Projectiles, Rockets, Missiles and Guidance 28(06), 211–214 (2008) (in Chinese)

Research on Weight Functions of Electromagnetic Flowmeter in Open Channels

Shiyi Yin and Bin Li

School of Mechatronics Engineering and Automation,
Shanghai University, Shanghai 200072, China

Abstract. Starting with the basic principles of the weight function related with the electromagnetic flowmeter(EMF), the modeling and the theoretical analysis of the weight function in open channels are proposed, and three main respects which affect the weight function of the EMF in open channels, including the model of the electrodes, the flow liquid level and the shapes of cross sections, are emphasized employing the finite element simulation technology. The distribution characteristics and the statistical properties of the weight function are studied and the conclusions are given, which fill the blanks in the field of the basic research on the weight function in open channels.

Keywords: Weight function, Electromagnetic flowmeter, Open channel, Finite element simulation.

1   Introduction

With the increasing attention to the water resource, the measurement for the discharge in open channels is required in the field of the water conservancy and pollution treatment. The instrument technology of the EMF in open channels, regarded as the technology of the multi-parameter flow measurement, is always the research topic of great challenge in the field of the discharge measurement where the fluid has the conductivity and contains the floating debris. The flow instrument based on the principle of the electromagnetic induction becomes one of the reasonable solutions for the measurement in open channels because of its high precision and stability.

In the 1980s, the instrument technologies for the flow measurement in open channels were widely studied in the developed countries, and the technical reports[1][2] on the methodologies of the flow measurement were drafted by ISO in 1990. The researches on the flow instrument technologies based on the principle of the EMF were further made in the last decade. For instance, the technology of the EMF in partially filled pipes has been investigated for ten years in Germany[3]. Besides, many well-known companies, such as ABB[4], Krohne[5], Yokogawa, etc, promoted the performance of the EMF. However, the basic researches on the dry calibration for the EMF in open channels were less mentioned, and one of the major problems is the determination of the weight function.

T. Xiao, L. Zhang, and S. Ma (Eds.): ICSC 2012, Part I, CCIS 326, pp. 103–111, 2012.
© Springer-Verlag Berlin Heidelberg 2012

The flow in open channels, which is different from the common pipe flow, has various wetted cross sections in shape, and the liquid level is changeable according to the actual working condition. Thus, the distribution of the weight function is not deterministic, with the nonlinear characteristics of the induced voltage on the electrodes presented which directly affect the measurement accuracy of the discharge in open channels. In addition, the determination of the weight function strictly depends on the applied electrode models of the EMF in open channels which mainly include the parallel point-electrode and the long electrode. It follows that the effect of the shape and the position for the standard electrode is also an essential point in the basic research on the EMF in open channels. Based on the statements above, starting with the theory of the weight function for the EMF in open channels, three important factors, including the electrode model, the liquid level and the wetted cross section, are involved, and the relevant conclusions of the weight function for the EMF in open channels are obtained with the finite element numerical simulation employed.

2   Weight Function of EMF in Open Channels

2.1   Theoretical Background of the Weight Function

The basic measurement principle of the EMF is the Faraday's law of electromagnetic induction. In 1954, the first analytical study for the EMF was performed by Shercliff[6] based on the two-dimensional rectilinear flow and the uniformly distributed magnetic field. The microscopic characteristics of the induction electromotive force were demonstrated with the weight function method he proposed which is now widely used in analyzing the EMF. In 1970, Bevir[7] made further progress on the weight function theory with the virtual current introduced, which can be regarded as the extension of the weight function.

Precisely, the flow measurement of the EMF fulfills the integral expression as follows,

$$U_{AB} = U_A - U_B = \int_{\tau} \overrightarrow{W} \cdot \overrightarrow{v} d\tau . \tag{1}$$

where U_{AB} is the potential difference between two electrodes, τ is the space volume of the flowing fluid, $\overrightarrow{W}$ is the weight vector, $\overrightarrow{v}$ is the velocity vector of the fluid. According to Eq(1), it demonstrates that the weight function not only reflects the degree of the contribution of the flow signal generated from the motion of the flow through the magnetic field, but also describes the attenuation coefficient of the induced voltage caused by the geometric position and shape of the electrode in the effective domain.

In Bevir's theory, the weight vector in Eq(1) can also be expressed as

$$\overrightarrow{W} = \overrightarrow{B} \times \overrightarrow{j} . \tag{2}$$

where $\vec{B}$ is the magnetic flux vector, and $\vec{j}$ is the current vector, which characterizes the current density on condition that the unit current passes from the positive electrode to the negative electrode. However, the current does not exist in the flow channel with the practical application of the EMF, and thus the current is called "virtual current".

Generally, there are no electric power and magnetic source inside the sensor, and the electrical potential φ and magnetic potential F within the flow area satisfies the Laplace's equations,

$$\begin{cases} \nabla^2\varphi = 0 \\ \nabla^2 F = 0 \end{cases} \tag{3}$$

and the virtual current density $\vec{j}$ and magnetic flux vector $\vec{B}$ can be further denoted by

$$\begin{cases} \vec{j} = -\nabla\varphi \\ \vec{B} = -\nabla F \end{cases} \tag{4}$$

According to (2)(4), the weight function is obtained by the following equation,

$$\vec{W} = \nabla F \times \nabla \varphi = \begin{vmatrix} \dfrac{\partial F}{\partial y} & \dfrac{\partial F}{\partial z} \\ \dfrac{\partial \varphi}{\partial y} & \dfrac{\partial \varphi}{\partial z} \end{vmatrix} \vec{X_e} + \begin{vmatrix} \dfrac{\partial F}{\partial z} & \dfrac{\partial F}{\partial x} \\ \dfrac{\partial \varphi}{\partial z} & \dfrac{\partial \varphi}{\partial x} \end{vmatrix} \vec{Y_e} + \begin{vmatrix} \dfrac{\partial F}{\partial x} & \dfrac{\partial F}{\partial y} \\ \dfrac{\partial \varphi}{\partial x} & \dfrac{\partial \varphi}{\partial y} \end{vmatrix} \vec{Z_e}. \tag{5}$$

where $\vec{X_e}, \vec{Y_e}, \vec{Z_e}$ are the unit vectors respectively in Cartesian coordinate system.

From Eq(5), the solution of the weight function is mainly determined by the distribution of the electric potential φ and the magnetic potential F, which directly depend on the boundary condition of the electromagnetic sensor.

2.2   Theoretical Analysis of the Weight Function for EMF in Open Channels

In the situation of the open channel, the Cartesian coordinate system is established as Fig 1.

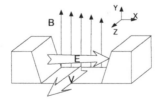

Fig. 1. The Cartesian coordinate system established for the EMF in open channels

The three-dimensional EMF can be simplified to the two-dimensional case under the tolerant error condition, and the weight function can be easily analyzed and calculated. The ideal cylinder model is assumed in this paper, with the cross section of the electrodes selected as the principal plane. The magnetic field is concerned uniform, and the type of the fluid is the axial rectilinear flow. On the basis of the coordinate system established and the assumption above, the mathematical expressions are presented as

$$B_X = B_Z = 0 \quad B_Y = B . \tag{6}$$

$$V_X = V_Y = 0 \quad V_z = V(x, y) . \tag{7}$$

With the effect of the axial direction neglected, the weight vector is degenerated as $W(x,y)$, which can be obtained from Eq(5)(6).

$$W(x, y) = \frac{\partial \varphi}{\partial y} B_X - \frac{\partial \varphi}{\partial x} B_Y = -\frac{\partial \varphi}{\partial x} B . \tag{8}$$

The boundary condition of the EMF in open channels is considered to be further analyzed in order to get the potential function φ, which mainly consists of three aspects below,

(1) There is no normal current on the boundary because of the insulated condition of the wall, which means the component of the potential function along the insulated wall is zero.
(2) The boundary conditions on the electrodes are treated as the values of the potential function which demonstrate the positive and negative voltages.
(3) The boundary condition on the gas-liquid surface fulfills the constraint that the normal current does not exist on the free surface and the normal component of the potential function is zero.

According to the description of the statement (1)(2)(3), based on the Cartesian coordinate system established, the mathematical physics equation of the potential function on the cross section of the electrodes is obtained,

$$\nabla^2 \varphi = 0 \quad \text{in } \Omega$$

$$\varphi = \begin{cases} + U \\ - U \end{cases} \quad \text{on } \Gamma_1 \tag{9}$$

$$\frac{\partial \varphi}{\partial y}\bigg|_{y=H} = 0 \quad \text{on } \Gamma_2$$

$$\frac{\partial \varphi}{\partial n} = 0 \quad \text{on } \Gamma_3 .$$

where Ω is the flow domain, Γ_1 is the boundary of the electrodes, Γ_2 is the boundary of the free surface, Γ_3 is the boundary of the insulated wall, U is the voltage amplitude on the electrodes, and H denotes the liquid level of the fluid.

In view of Eq(9), the distribution of the flow in open channels is asymmetrical which leads to the relevance between the distribution of the weight function and the liquid level, and the boundary condition is directly affected by the shape of the wetted cross section in open channels. Besides, the distribution of the potential function is determined by the shape and the position of the electrodes, which causes the nonlinear characteristics of the weight function, and the relation between the induced voltage on the electrodes and the flow velocity is also nonlinear.

3   Numerical Simulation of the Weight Function

The solution of the weight function for the EMF in open channels depends on the acquisition of the potential function. From Eq(9), the boundary condition of the potential function is the mixed boundary, including the Dirichlet boundary and the Neumann boundary. It is hard to obtain the analytical solution of the Laplace's equation with the mixed boundary by means of the mathematical methodologies. However, with the development of the computer technology, the numerical simulation is introduced in many science fields, and the finite element methodology, regarded as a common numerical analysis tool, is widely used in the solution of various partial differential equations which involve most situations of the physical field. Thus, the weight function of the EMF in open channels is studied in this paper with the finite element numerical simulation employed and Matlab R2010 is chosen as the simulation platform.

3.1   Effects of the Electrode Shape and Position on the Weight Function

In the case of the measurement for the EMF in open channels, two kinds of the electrodes are mainly used, which consist of the parallel point electrode and the long electrode. For convenience to compare, the weight function in the partially filled pipes is selected as the research object, and two typical kinds of the electrode models mentioned above are simulated respectively. In the practical application, the electrodes should be submerged to obtain the induced signal, however the electrodes should not be placed close to the bottom of the pipe for better sensitivity when the liquid level is high. Thus, the electrode position of the senor is generally set at 10% of the pipe diameter. In addition, at least three pairs of the point electrodes are chosen to guarantee the measurement accuracy. Based on the analysis above, the distributions of the senor electrodes are arranged as Table 1, and the mappings of the weight function in the flow domain are obtained with the numerical simulation employed in Fig 2.

Table 1. The senor model based on the distribution of the electrodes

Sensor type	Pairs of the electrodes	Normalized height of the point electrodes				
		1	3	5	7	9
Long electrode	1					
Parallel point electrode I	5	√	√	√	√	√
Parallel point electrode II	4	√	√	√	√	
Parallel point electrode III	3	√	√	√		

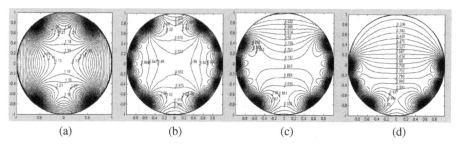

(a)   (b)   (c)   (d)

Fig. 2. The mappings of the weight function (a) long electrode (b) parallel point electrode I (c) parallel point electrode II (d) parallel point electrode III

According to the grid number and the numerical solution of the weight function, the average weight function is defined as

$$\overline{W} = \frac{1}{N}\sum_{i=1}^{N} W_i . \qquad (10)$$

where N is the grid number. In view of Eq(10), the average weight functions of the different sensors are respectively calculated in Table 2.

Table 2. Average weight functions of different sensor models

Sensor type	Long electrode	Parallel point electrode I	Parallel point electrode II	Parallel point electrode III
Average weight function	1.1393	1.4064	1.4776	1.4883

3.2   Effects of the Liquid Level on the Weight Function

The liquid level of the fluid is generally changeable in open channels with the practical working condition, which affects the gas-liquid boundary condition of the

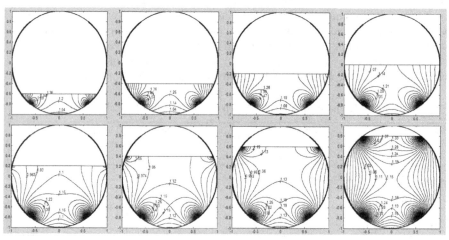

Fig. 3. Mappings of the weight function for long electrode model(liquid level from 20% to 90%)

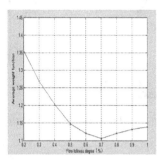

Fig. 4. The average weight functions for long electrode model(liquid level from 20% to 100%)

weight function. For the further research on the effect of the liquid level, the numerical simulations are made with the electrode position selected, from 10% to 90%. Considering the 10% of the diameter is the limit position of the long electrodes, the solutions of the weight function from 20% to 100% are chosen as the samples for analysis, and the average weight functions are also calculated.

3.3   Effects of the Wetted Cross Section on the Weight Function

There are many types of the cross sections for open channels. For the convenience of the construction and the management, the shape of the cross section is generally regular, such as the rectangle, the trapezium, U type, etc. The specific form of the cross section is determined by the local terrain and the material of the open channel, which makes the difference of the solution domain for the weight function. In the paper, three common cross sections are involved, with the long electrode model employed, in which the electrodes are placed from 10% to 90% of the pipe diameter, and the numerical simulations are made to obtain the mapping of the weight function as well as the average weight function. The cross sections selected have the same size in height and width as that of the partially filled pipe in Fig 5, where B=H=D, D is the diameter of the pipe in open channels.

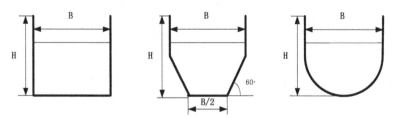

Fig. 5. The cross sections of the open channels involved

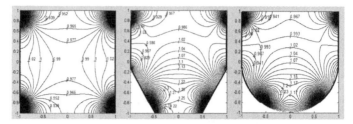

Fig. 6. The mappings of the weight function in different open channels

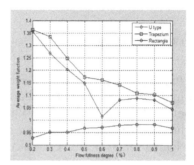

Fig. 7. The average weight functions of different cross sections

4   Conclusions

The finite element numerical simulations demonstrate that the shape and position of the electrodes, the liquid level and the shape of the wetted cross section have great effect on the weight function of the EMF in open channels. The analysis of the numerical simulation results are made based on the standard that the unit average weight function has no error, and the conclusions are obtained below.

(1)   From the perspective of the electrode shape and the electrode position, the performance of the long electrode is better than that of the parallel point electrode. Besides, the average weight function decreases with the increased pairs of the electrodes in the application of the parallel point electrode. To some extent, the long electrode is the derivative of the parallel point electrode, which can be regarded as the electrode with the infinite pairs.

(2)   The nonlinear characteristics of the weight function in open channels are presented with the changeable liquid level. In view of Fig 4, the average weight function accordingly decreases with the increasing fluid fullness degree which leads to the wider coverage of the electrodes. When the fluid is in high fullness degree, the effect of the electrode coverage is reduced, and the width of the gas-liquid surface determined by the liquid level becomes the main factor which affects the weight function. Thus, the constraint of the gas-liquid boundary condition is weakened with the decreasing surface width, and the average weight function is accordingly increased.

(3)   The shape of the wetted cross section also affects the distribution of the weight function. In all the common regular cross sections, the average weight function of the round pipe is the largest compared with the others, for its geometric speciality that the pipe has the sealing property and more constraints of the boundary condition are bought out.

The effects of various factors on the weight function in open channels are proposed in this paper, and the conclusions obtained by the finite element numerical simulations are of the universality. However, the problem that the optimal selection of the electrode shape and position still remains to be studied in further researches.

References

1. ISO/TR 9824-1: Measurement of liquid flow in open channels. Part 11:Free surface flow in closed conduits. Part11A: Methods of measurement. ISO (1990)
2. ISO/TR 9824-1: Measurement of liquid flow in open channels. Part 11:Free surface flow in closed conduits. Part11B: Specification for performance and installation of equipment for measurement of free surface flow in closed conduits. ISO (1990)
3. Godley, A.: Flow measurement in partially closed conduits, Flow Measurement and Instrumentation 13(5-6), 197–201 (2002)
4. ABB Inc: Electromagnetic Flowmeter for Full Pipe and Partially Full Pipelines (2001)
5. Krohne Inc.: Electromagnetic flowmeter in partially filled pipes for water and waste water (2002)
6. Shercliff, J.A.: The theory of electromagnetic flow-measurement. Cambridge university press, London and New York (1962)
7. Bevir, M.K.: The theory of electromagnetic flowmeter. J. Fluid Mech. (43) (1970)
8. Zhang, X.Z.: The virtual current of an electromagnetic flowmeter with partially filled fluid. Measurement Science and Technology 9, 1852–1855 (1998)
9. Zhang, X.Z.: A method for solving Laplace's equation with mixed boundary condition in electromagnetic flow meters. J. Phys. D: Appl. Phys. 20, 573–576 (1989)
10. Hu, L., Zou, J.: Divisionally analytical solutions of Laplace's equations for dry calibration of electromagnetic velocity probes. Applied Mathematical Modeling 33, 3130–3150 (2009)

Engineering Modeling and Simulation for New Estimation of Aircraft's Dynamic Angles

Zhao Wu and Lixin Wang

School of Aeronautic Science and Engineering,
Beijing University of Aeronautics and Astronautics, Beijing 100191, China

Abstract. The measurement of aircraft's dynamic angles is difficult and inaccurate due to the precarious flight environment. This paper brings forward and amends a new estimation of aircraft's angle of attack and sideslip angle based on the basic of INS/GPS data. Through engineering modeling of closed-loop flight simulation framework and estimation method, the result shows obvious rationality and veracity.

Keywords: Modeling, Pilot model, INS/GPS, Angle of Attack, Sideslip Angle.

1 Introduction

Aircraft's angle of attack and sideslip angle are two important condition parameters to the flight control and navigation, which affect the flight safety and campaign ability. However, because of bird strike, hailstone and some other disturbances, the conventional measuration of these two angles is not working well.

In recent years, many researches have been made on measuration of these two angles. NASA Langley Research Center empoldered and tested Flush Air Data System[1], which needs some high precision hardware yet.

This paper aims to bring forward and amend a new estimation of aircraft's angle of attack and sideslip angle on the basic of INS/GPS data, which can be easily obtained. Moreover, in order to validate this method, modeling of aircraft and angle estimation has been done.

2 Modeling of Flight Simulation

In order to get the INS/GPS data, aircraft simulation framework has been modeling, primarily including pilot model and aircraft's kinetic equations.

2.1 Pilot Modeling

Pilot model is one part of the flight simulation framework, which can correctly operate the aircraft's control stick and accelerator pedal to accomplish the flight task. Longitudinal pitch is a familiar flight motion with the obvious variety of angle of attack. In this motion, pilot model control the pitch angle accurately via operating elevator and eliminate the sideslip via operating aileron. Figure 1 shows the structure of pilot model for longitudinal pitch(see the dashed part in figure 1).

T. Xiao, L. Zhang, and S. Ma (Eds.): ICSC 2012, Part I, CCIS 326, pp. 112–117, 2012.

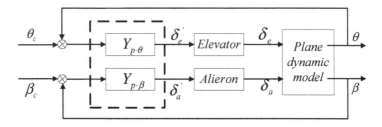

Fig. 1. Pilot model for longitudinal pitch

In the above figure, the pilot control expression and can be described by McRuer's linear model[2]. The value of parameters in the models can be gotten via debugging.

$$Y_{p \cdot \theta}(s) = \frac{-1.5e^{-0.1s}(0.4s+1)}{(0.1s+1)}, \qquad Y_{p \cdot \beta}(s) = \frac{-0.9e^{-0.1s}(0.5s+1)}{(0.1s+1)} \qquad (1)$$

In the longitudinal pitch motion, the flight control goal and can be set as figure 2.

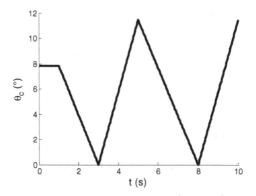

Fig. 2. Pilot control signal θ_c of longitudinal pitch

2.2   Plane Kinetic Equation

In order to avoid bizarre in the process of simulation when the pitch angle θ close to 90°, quaternion is introduced to plane rotational kinetic equations[3]. In these equations, the attitude angles (θ, ϕ and) used to denote the flight stance of aircraft were replaced by quaternion(e_1, e_2, e_3 and e_4).

$$e_1 = \cos\frac{\psi}{2}\cos\frac{\theta}{2}\cos\frac{\phi}{2} + \sin\frac{\psi}{2}\sin\frac{\theta}{2}\sin\frac{\phi}{2} \qquad (2)$$

$$e_2 = \cos\frac{\psi}{2}\cos\frac{\theta}{2}\sin\frac{\phi}{2} - \sin\frac{\psi}{2}\sin\frac{\theta}{2}\cos\frac{\phi}{2} \qquad (3)$$

$$e_3 = \cos\frac{\psi}{2}\sin\frac{\theta}{2}\cos\frac{\phi}{2} + \sin\frac{\psi}{2}\cos\frac{\theta}{2}\sin\frac{\phi}{2} \qquad (4)$$

$$e_4 = -\cos\frac{\psi}{2}\sin\frac{\theta}{2}\sin\frac{\phi}{2} + \sin\frac{\psi}{2}\cos\frac{\theta}{2}\cos\frac{\phi}{2} \qquad (5)$$

3   Modeling of Angle Estimation

The principal idea of the estimation for these two angles is calculating the velocity of wind v_w and the velocity of aircraft v_g, and then getting the angle of attack and sideslip angle by following expressions[4]:

$$\alpha = arctan\left(V_{axb}/V_{axb}\right), \quad \beta = arcsin\left(V_{ayb}/V_a\right), \quad V_a^2 = V_{axb}^2 + V_{ayb}^2 + V_{azb}^2 \qquad (6)$$

Where the velocity of airspeed v_a can be gotten by

$$V_{axb} = V_{gxb} - V_{wxb} \quad V_{ayb} = V_{gyb} - V_{wyb} \quad V_{azb} = V_{gzb} - V_{wzb} \qquad (7)$$

Therefore, the most important part of the angle estimation model is calculating the velocity of wind, primarily including following sub-models (Figure 3).

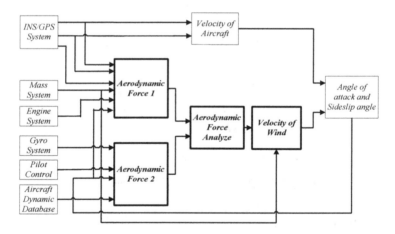

Fig. 3. The framework of angle estimation

3.1   Computation of Aerodynamic Force 1

Aerodynamic force 1 $[D_1, C_1, L_1]'$ is the sum of the wind force and operation force controlled by pilot. Some article[5] pointed out, the total force that aircraft suffered, calculating from the airplane's acceleration doesn't contain its gravity. However, acceleration is the representation of the total force that some object suffered. Thus, The aerodynamic force 1 can be gained from the total force that aircraft suffered $\overrightarrow{F_{tot}}$, engine thrust $\vec{T}$ and aircraft's gravity $\vec{G}$. The detailed expressions as follows:

$$\overrightarrow{F_{tot}} = m\overrightarrow{a_b} = \begin{bmatrix} T_{xb} \\ T_{yb} \\ T_{zb} \end{bmatrix} + \begin{bmatrix} G_{xb} \\ G_{yb} \\ G_{zb} \end{bmatrix} + L_{ba} \begin{bmatrix} D_l \\ C_l \\ L_l \end{bmatrix} \qquad (8)$$

where, L_{ba} is the transform from wind reference frame to body reference frame:

$$L_{ba} = \begin{bmatrix} \cos\alpha \cdot \cos\beta & -\cos\alpha \cdot \sin\beta & -\sin\alpha \\ \sin\beta & \cos\beta & 0 \\ \sin\alpha \cdot \cos\beta & -\sin\alpha \cdot \cos\beta & \cos\alpha \end{bmatrix} \qquad (9)$$

3.2   Computation of Aerodynamic Force 2

Aerodynamic force 2 $[D_2, C_2, L_2]$ is the operation force controlled by pilot, which can be gotten by aircraft's nonlinear aerodynamic database as follows:

$$C_X = C_X(\alpha,\ \beta,\ \delta_e) + \Delta C_{Xlef}(\alpha,\ \beta) \cdot (1 - \frac{\delta_{lef}}{25}) \\ + \frac{c_{ref}q}{2V_a} \left[C_{Xq}(\alpha) + \Delta C_{Xqlef}(\alpha) \cdot (1 - \frac{\delta_{lef}}{25}) \right] \qquad (10)$$

$$C_Y = C_Y(\alpha,\ \beta) + \Delta C_{Y \cdot lef}(\alpha,\ \beta) \cdot (1 - \frac{\delta_{lef}}{25}) + \Delta C_{Y\delta,\,30}(\alpha,\ \beta) \frac{\delta_r}{30} \\ + \frac{b_{ref}p}{2V_a} \left[C_{Yp}(\alpha) + C_{Y \cdot lef}(\alpha) \cdot (1 - \frac{\delta_{lef}}{25}) \right] \\ + \left[\Delta C_{Y\delta_a 20}(\alpha,\ \beta) + \Delta C_{Y\delta_a 20lef}(\alpha,\ \beta) \cdot (1 - \frac{\delta_{lef}}{25}) \right] \frac{\delta_a}{20} \\ + \frac{b_{ref}r}{2V_a} \left[C_{Yr}(\alpha) + \Delta C_{Yrlef}(\alpha) \cdot (1 - \frac{\delta_{lef}}{25}) \right] \qquad (11)$$

$$C_Z = C_Z(\alpha,\ \beta,\ \delta_e) + \Delta C_{Zlef}(\alpha,\ \beta) \cdot (1 - \frac{\delta_{lef}}{25}) \\ + \frac{c_{ref}q}{2V_a} \left[C_{Zq}(\alpha) + \Delta C_{Zqlef}(\alpha) \cdot (1 - \frac{\delta_{lef}}{25}) \right] \qquad (12)$$

$$\begin{bmatrix} -D_2 \\ C_2 \\ -L_2 \end{bmatrix} = L_{ab} \begin{bmatrix} q_{bar}SC_X \\ q_{bar}SC_Y \\ q_{bar}SC_Z \end{bmatrix} \qquad (13)$$

where, L_{ab} is the transform from body reference frame to wind reference frame:

$$L_{ab} = L_{ba}^{T} \qquad (14)$$

3.3   Aerodynamic Force Analyze

The aerodynamic force 1 and 2 is analyzed and that the force caused by wind can be obtained in this part as following expressions:

$$\begin{bmatrix} F_{w \cdot xb} \\ F_{w \cdot yb} \\ F_{w \cdot zb} \end{bmatrix} = L_{ba} \cdot \begin{bmatrix} -(D_1 - D_2) \\ C_1 - C_2 \\ -(L_1 - L_2) \end{bmatrix} \tag{15}$$

3.4   Computation of Wind Velocity

The velocity of wind can be obtained from the force caused by wind, which is calculated in the part of aerodynamic force analyze:

$$\begin{bmatrix} V_{w \cdot xb} \\ V_{w \cdot yb} \\ V_{w \cdot zb} \end{bmatrix} = \begin{bmatrix} \int \frac{F_{w \cdot xb}}{m} \cdot dt \\ \int \frac{F_{w \cdot yb}}{m} \cdot dt \\ \int \frac{F_{w \cdot zb}}{m} \cdot dt \end{bmatrix} + \begin{bmatrix} C_1 \\ C_2 \\ C_3 \end{bmatrix} \tag{16}$$

4   Result and Conclusion

On the foundation of above discuss, the aircraft simulation framework and the estimation model of angle of attack and sideslip angle have been established. Figure 4 and 5 show the result of simulation (stationary wind in the simulation) and estimation of those two angles.

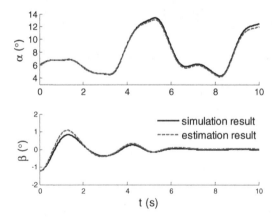

Fig. 4. The results of simulation and estimation of dynamic angles

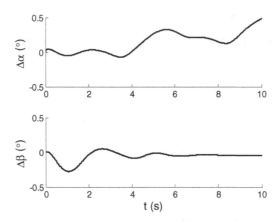

Fig. 5. The error between simulation result and estimation result

The result of simulation and estimation in figure 4 and 5 show the rationality of this aircraft simulation framework and the veracity of estimation method of angle of attack and sideslip angle with INS/GPS data. Moreover, more comprehensive checkout to this estimation method is necessary.

References

1. Sephen, A.W., Roy, J.D., John, M.F.: In-flight demonstration of a real time flush airdate sensing (RT-FADS) system. NASA/TM-104314-1995
2. Wu, Z.: The estimation of aerodynamic angle on the basic of INS/GPS data. Beijing University of Aeronautics and Astronautics, Beijing (2010)
3. Zhang, L.: The research on evaluating stall flying qualities. Beijing university of aeronautics and astronautics, Beijing (2007)
4. Fang, Z., Chen, W., Zhang, S.: Aircraft flying dynamics. Beijing University of Aeronautics and Astronautics press, Beijing (2005)
5. Song, S., Deng, J.: Estimation of angle of attack and sideslip angle on the basic of INS/GPS data, vol. 23(2). Northwest industry university transaction, Xi'an (2005)

Trajectory Tracking Controller of Small-Scale Helicopter Based on Backstepping

Shuai Tang, ZhiQiang Zheng, JianBin Ye, and Qi Wang

College of Mechatronics and Automation,
NationalUniversity of Defense Technology, Changsha, 410073, China
tangshuai@nudt.edu.cn

Abstract. This paper presents a backstepping control design procedure for a small-scale helicopter. The objective is to control the small-scale helicopter to realize the autonomous tracking of the predefined trajectory which consists of the position and the yaw angle. The controller is derived based on Lyapunov stability theory. An approximate helicopter model is adopted and the flapping dynamic of the main rotor is considered. The main idea is to decouple the translational dynamics and the rotational dynamics through solving an equation when the desired yaw angle is predefined. Simulation results show that the performance of the proposed controller is acceptable.

Keywords: unmanned helicopter, backstepping, trajectory tracking.

1 Introduction

Helicopter can take off and land vertically, and can perform flight ranging from hovering to airplane-like cruising with agility and maneuverability. These qualities have made them indispensable vehicles for a variety of applications, such as border patrol, intelligent traffic monitoring, rescue services, 3D mapping, power line inspection, fire front monitoring, and so on[1]. Today, many research communities havepaid their attention on small-scale helicopter. As a small, dynamically fast and unstable system, a small-scale helicopter makes an excellent test bed for nonlinear control experiments. Meanwhile, as a highly maneuverable machine, it also is an excellent test bed for path planning algorithms for autonomous robots[2]. Compare with the full-scale helicopter, small-scale helicopter is much more affordable and easier conduct research.

The controller design and implementation for autonomous helicopter has become one of the most interesting and challenging problems in control society. The main difficultyis the highly nonlinearity between the main rotor and the fuselage. In order to improve the control performance, researchers have proposed many different appro-aches, such as PID[3], LQR[4], and $H\infty$robust control[5]. However, the linear approaches are valid in the neighborhood of the trim point. On the other hand, the nonlinear con-trol can coverwider range of flight envelopes; meanwhile, it requires more accurate knowledge of the plant. In recent years, many papers deal with the

T. Xiao, L. Zhang, and S. Ma (Eds.): ICSC 2012, Part I, CCIS 326, pp. 118–127, 2012.

helicopter fight control based on nonlinear approaches. In [6], the analysis shows that exact feedback linearization of the system dynamic suffer from unstable zero dynamics. In that paper, an approximate feedback linearization is adopted based on approximate dynamic model. In [7], dynamic inversion combined with neural networks was used to complete the helicopter flight control design. Based on dynamic inversion, an approximate linear model was obtained and the controller can be designed by linear control theory. The neural networks was used to compensate the inverse model error.

In most designs, it is common practice to neglect the effect of the parasitic forces associated with the torques production. After this simplification, the model becomes a cascade feedback form and it's convenient to conduct backstepping design. In [8], the authors develop velocity and position tracking algorithm based on a similar backstepping control for a general rigid body. In [9],backstepping controller is completed using dynamic extension,which treats the thrust of the main rotor and its first derivative as the state variables of the system, and the forces and moments are treated as system inputs. Reference [10] proposes a new idea, controlling the magnitude and the direction of the main rotor thrust to stabilize the position dynamic, and eventually design a backstepping controller.

This paper presents a different nonlinear backstepping controller designed for small-scale helicopter. The main objective is to control the helicopter to track a predefined trajectory which consist of position and yaw angle. Considering the flapping dynamic is very important in small-scale helicopter dynamics, it is considered and the control inputs, the longitudinal cyclic pitch and the lateral cyclic pitch is derived through Lyapunov method directly. The main idea is decouple the translational dynamics and the rotational dynamics through solving an equation when the desired yaw angle is predefined. Then, after the desired force presented in the inertial frame is determined, the desired Euler angle and main rotor thrust can be determined directly. The same as other references, an approximate mathematic model is adopted.

The paper is organized as follows. In Section 2, the mathematic model of small-scale helicopter is introduced. The backstepping-based flight control of a small-scale helicopter is discussed in Section 3. The simulation results are given in Section 4, and Section 5 presents the conclusion of this paper.

2   Small-Scale Helicopter Model

The small-scale helicopter can be described by a hybrid model which contains the nonlinear rigid body dynamics and the dynamics of the rotor. The position of the gravity center of the helicopter, in the inertial frame, is notated by $\mathbf{P}=[x,y,z]T$; the linear velocity of the gravity center in the inertial frame is given by$\mathbf{v}=[vx,vy,vz]T$; the angular velocity of the helicopter represented in the body frame is $\omega=[p,q,r]T$; the attitude is denoted by Euler angles $\eta=[\varphi,\theta,\psi]T$. The body frame and inertial frame are shown in Fig.1. Actually, using the Euler angles represent the attitude kinematics, there are singularities when the pitch angle equal to$\pm90°$. Here, it is assumed that the flight condition will never reach the singularity.

2.1   Rigid Body Dynamics

The nonlinear rigid body dynamics in terms of the translational and rotational dynamics are given by:

$$\begin{cases} \dot{\mathbf{P}} = \mathbf{v} \\ m\dot{\mathbf{v}} = \mathbf{R}(\mathbf{\eta})\mathbf{f_b} + mg\mathbf{e}_3 \\ \dot{\mathbf{\eta}} = \pi\omega \\ I\dot{\omega} = -\omega \times I\omega + \mathbf{M} \end{cases} \tag{1}$$

Where the m is the mass of the body and I is the inertia matrix. $\mathbf{e}_3$ is a unit vector along the z axis of the inertia frame. $\mathbf{R}(\mathbf{\eta})$ is the rotation matrix from the body frame to the inertia frame. It is parameterized with respect to the three Euler angle roll(φ), pitch(θ), yaw(ψ). And the third equation of (1) is the attitude kinematics, where π is a 3×3 matrix also with respect to the Euler angle and it can be written as:

$$\mathbf{R}(\mathbf{\eta}) = \begin{bmatrix} c\theta c\psi & s\varphi s\theta c\psi - c\varphi s\psi & c\varphi s\theta c\psi + s\varphi s\psi \\ c\theta s\psi & s\varphi s\theta s\psi + c\varphi c\psi & c\varphi s\theta s\psi - s\varphi c\psi \\ -s\theta & s\varphi c\theta & c\varphi c\theta \end{bmatrix}, \pi = \begin{bmatrix} 1 & s\varphi t\theta & c\varphi t\theta \\ 0 & c\varphi & -s\varphi \\ 0 & s\varphi/c\theta & c\varphi/c\theta \end{bmatrix} \tag{2}$$

the notation $\mathbf{f_b} = [F_X, F_Y, F_Z]^T$ means all the external forces without the gravity and $\mathbf{M} = [M_X, M_Y, M_Z]^T$ means the moments acting on the center of mass of the body due to the rotor, the fuselage and empennage.

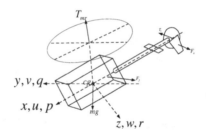

Fig. 1. Body frame and inertial frame

2.2   Forces and Moments

For helicopter, the dominant forces and moments for control come from the main and tail rotor. The forces in the body frame and the moments due to the rotor are given in [1] as follow under the assumption of small flapping angles:

$$\begin{bmatrix} F_x \\ F_y \\ F_z \end{bmatrix} = \begin{bmatrix} -T_{mr}a \\ T_{mr}b + T_t \\ -T_{mr} \end{bmatrix}, \begin{bmatrix} M_x \\ M_y \\ M_z \end{bmatrix} = \begin{bmatrix} (K_\beta + T_{mr}H_{mr})b - T_tH_t \\ (K_\beta + T_{mr}H_{mr})a \\ M_Q + T_{mr}bD_{mr} + T_tD_t \end{bmatrix} \tag{3}$$

Where T_{mr} and T_t are the thrusts of the main rotor and the tail rotor respectively, K_β is the constant of rolling and pitching moment hub stiffness. The notation H_{mr}, H_t, D_{mr}, D_t are the arms of the main rotor and tail rotor thrust with respect to z axis and x axis. M_Q

is the main rotor anti-torque and it can be approximately computed using the follow equation in [11].

$$\begin{cases} C_Q = C_T(\lambda_i - \dfrac{w}{\Omega R}) + \dfrac{C_{D0}\sigma}{8}(1 + \dfrac{7}{3}\dfrac{u^2 + v^2}{(\Omega R)^2}) \\ M_Q = C_Q \rho (\Omega R)^2 \pi R^3 \end{cases} \tag{4}$$

Where C_T is the thrust coefficient, C_Q is the anti-torque coefficient, σ is the solidity and C_{D0} is the profile drag coefficient of the main rotor.

If it is assumed that the dynamics of inflow can be neglected, actually many researchers treat it like this. Under this assumption, there exists an algebraic relationship between the main rotor, tail rotor thrusts and the collective inputs. For the main rotor, the thrust T_{mr} can be written as:

$$\begin{cases} T_{mr} = (w_{blade} - v_i) \dfrac{\rho \Omega R^2 C_{la}^{mr} b_{mr} c_{mr}}{4} \\ v_i^2 = \sqrt{(\dfrac{\hat{v}^2}{2})^2 + (\dfrac{T_{mr}}{2\rho\pi R^2})^2} - \dfrac{\hat{v}^2}{2} \end{cases} ,\text{where} \begin{cases} \hat{v}^2 = u^2 + v^2 + w_r(w_r - 2v_i) \\ w_{blade} = w_r + \dfrac{2}{3}\Omega R \delta_{col} \\ w_r = w + ua - vb \end{cases} \tag{5}$$

The readers can get more information from [12] and the tail rotor has a similar result. If the thrust is known, the collective input corresponding can be computed from the above equation.

In addition, the force and moment result from the fuselage and empennage are too small and are neglected to simplify the model.

2.3   Flapping Dynamics

In helicopter society, the main rotor dynamics can be modeled by two coupled first-order differential equations when the high-order terms are neglected, which represent the longitudinal and lateral flapping motions of the tip-path-plane. For the small-scale helicopter, the main difference is that the main rotor is augmented by a stabilizer bar, which acts as a secondary rotor with much smaller aerodynamic surface and larger time constant. It is installed 90-degree lagged and used to dampen the flapping motion. To simplify the model, the stabilizer bar dynamics can be lumped into the main rotor dynamics[13]. In this paper, the flapping dynamics is represented by:

$$\begin{cases} \dot{a} = -q - a/\tau + A_{\delta lon}/\tau \delta_{lon} \\ \dot{b} = -p - b/\tau + B_{\delta lat}/\tau \delta_{lat} \end{cases} \tag{6}$$

In the above equations, τ is the lumped time constant, $A_{\delta lon}, B_{\delta lat}$ are the control gains. Here the inputs $\delta_{lon}, \delta_{lat}$ are the pitch angles of the swash plate and the dynamics of the servo is not considered.

3   Trajectory Tracking Controller Design

The design goal is to find a feedback control laws for $\delta_{col}, \delta_{lon}, \delta_{lat}, \delta_{ped}$ to track the predefined trajectory. The desired trajectory is represented by desired position $\mathbf{P}^d$ and desired yaw angle ψ^d. It is reasonable under the assumption that the flapping angles a, b and T_t/T_{mr} is small, the forces and moments related are not considered. In this paper, the controller is design using backstepping technique and the whole design process is presented as follow:

As the first step in backstepping, the position error was selected as the first error item δ_1.

$$\delta_1 = \mathbf{P} - \mathbf{P}^d \tag{7}$$

Where $\mathbf{P}^d$ is the desired position. Let the starting Lyapunov Function be

$$V_1 = \delta_1^T \delta_1 / 2 + k_I \left[\int_0^t \delta_1 d\tau \right]^T \left[\int_0^t \delta_1 d\tau \right] / 2 \tag{8}$$

Taking the time derivative of V_1, then,

$$\dot{V}_1 = \delta_1^T (\mathbf{v} - \dot{\mathbf{P}}^d) + k_I \left[\int_0^t \delta_1 d\tau \right]^T \delta_1 \tag{9}$$

Let $\mathbf{v}$ be the visual control and define $\mathbf{v}^d$ as the desired velocity of the helicopter. If $\mathbf{v}^d$ is chosen as

$$\mathbf{v}^d = \dot{\mathbf{P}}^d - k_p \delta_1 - k_I \left[\int_0^t \delta_1 d\tau \right]^T \tag{10}$$

Where k_P and k_I are the positive control gains. If $\mathbf{v} = \mathbf{v}^d$, Then,

$$\dot{V}_1 = \delta_1^T (-k_p \delta_1 - k_I \left[\int_0^t \delta_1 d\tau \right]^T) + k_I \left[\int_0^t \delta_1 d\tau \right]^T \delta_1 = -k_p \delta_1^T \delta_1 \leq 0 \tag{11}$$

The integration term is used to guarantee the convergence of the tracking error[16]. Let $\delta_2 = \mathbf{v} - \mathbf{v}^d$ be the error between the actual and the desired value of velocity. The process of the backstepping continues by expanding the Lyapunov Function as:

$$V_2 = V_1 + \delta_2^T \delta_2 / 2 \tag{12}$$

Similarly, the time derivative of (14) is

$$\begin{aligned}
\dot{V}_2 &= \delta_1^T (\mathbf{v} - \dot{\mathbf{P}}^d) + k_I \left[\int_0^t \delta_1 d\tau \right]^T \delta_1 + \delta_2^T \dot{\delta}_2 \\
&= -k_p \delta_1^T \delta_1 + \delta_2^T [\mathbf{R}(\eta)\mathbf{f_b} / m + g\mathbf{e}_3 - \ddot{\mathbf{P}}^d - k_p (v - \dot{\mathbf{P}}^d) - k_I \delta_1] + \delta_1^T \delta_2
\end{aligned} \tag{13}$$

For the control of air vehicle, if the translational and rotational dynamics are treated separately, the Euler angles can be treated as the control input of the translational dynamics together with the external forces. From this point view, define the expanded input

$$\mathbf{u}_o = \mathbf{R}(\eta)\mathbf{f_b} / m \tag{14}$$

Also, let $\mathbf{u}_{od}$ be the desired value of $\mathbf{u}_o$ and is determined by desired Euler angle η^d and thrust $\mathbf{f}_{bd}$. Select

$$\mathbf{u}_{od} = -g\mathbf{e}_3 + \ddot{\mathbf{P}}^d + k_p (v - \dot{\mathbf{P}}^d) + (k_I - 1)\delta_1 - k_2 \delta_2 \tag{15}$$

Where k_2 is a positive feedback gain. Then,

$$\dot{V}_2 = -k_p \delta_1{}^T \delta_1 - k_2 \delta_2{}^T \delta_2 \leq 0 \tag{16}$$

The desired input of the trajectory controller is the desired position $\mathbf{P}^d$ and yaw angle ψ^d, so we can solve the desired roll angle φ^d, pitch angle θ^d, and thrust f_{bd} from equation (16). Under the assumption above mentioned, $\mathbf{f}_b = [0,0,f_b]^T$ and $\mathbf{u}_o = \mathbf{R}_3(\eta) f_b / m$, $\mathbf{R}_3(\eta)$ is the third column of $\mathbf{R}(\eta)$.

The δ_{col} can be calculated from equation (5) using the state variables. In order to derive the control law for the rotational dynamics, the third error item is defined as

$$\delta_3 = \eta - \eta^d \tag{17}$$

And the new Lyapunov Function is selected as

$$V_3 = V_2 + \delta_3{}^T \delta_3 / 2 \tag{18}$$

Define $F_o = g\mathbf{e}_3 - \ddot{\mathbf{P}}^d - k_p (v - \dot{\mathbf{P}}^d) - k_t \delta_1$, the time derivative of (18) is

$$\dot{V}_3 = \dot{V}_2 + \delta_3{}^T \dot{\delta}_3 = -k_p \delta_1{}^T \delta_1 - k_2 \delta_2{}^T \delta_2 + \delta_2{}^T (\mathbf{u}_o - \mathbf{u}_o^d) + \delta_3{}^T (\pi\omega - \dot{\eta}^d) \tag{19}$$

Here, we have the following relation about $\mathbf{R}_3(\eta)$.

$$\mathbf{R}_3(\eta) = \begin{bmatrix} \cos\varphi\sin\theta\cos\psi + \sin\varphi\sin\psi \\ \cos\varphi\sin\theta\sin\psi - \sin\varphi\cos\psi \\ \cos\varphi\cos\theta \end{bmatrix} \tag{20}$$

It is easy to examine that $\mathbf{R}_3(\eta)$ is a differential continuous function of η. And the norm of the partial derivative of $\mathbf{R}_3(\eta)$ satisfy

$$\left\| \frac{\partial \mathbf{R}_3}{\partial \eta} \right\|_F = \sqrt{2 + c^2 \varphi s^2 \theta} \leq \sqrt{3} \tag{21}$$

Thus $\mathbf{R}_3(\eta)$ satisfy the Lipschitz condition on the argument with respect to η. Then

$$\left\| \mathbf{R}_3(\eta) - \mathbf{R}_3(\eta^d) \right\| \leq L \left\| \eta - \eta^d \right\| \tag{22}$$

Where L is the Lipschitz constant. Using this characteristic of $\mathbf{R}_3(\eta)$, we can get the following relationship

$$\left\| \mathbf{u}_o - \mathbf{u}_{od} \right\| = \left\| \mathbf{R}_3(\eta) - \mathbf{R}_3(\eta^d) \right\| \left\| f_b \right\| / m \leq \left\| f_{max} \right\| L \left\| \eta - \eta^d \right\| / m \tag{23}$$

$\| f_{max} \|$ is the maximum of the thrust due to the main rotor, which is determined by the power of engine. Define $k_u = \| f_{max} \| L / m$, select ω as the visual control input, and define the desired angular rate ω^d:

$$\omega^d = \pi^{-1}(\dot{\eta}^d - k_3 \delta_3) \tag{24}$$

Here k_3 is a positive control gain. Then , if $\omega = \omega^d$, submitting (23) into (19), we get

$$\begin{aligned} \dot{V}_3 &= -k_p \delta_1{}^T \delta_1 - k_2 \delta_2{}^T \delta_2 - k_3 \delta_3{}^T \delta_3 + \delta_2{}^T (\mathbf{u}_o - \mathbf{u}_o^d) \leq -k_p \|\delta_1\|^2 - k_2 \|\delta_2\|^2 - k_3 \|\delta_3\|^2 + k_u \|\delta_2\|\|\delta_3\| \\ &= -k_p \|\delta_1\|^2 - (\sqrt{k_2} \|\delta_2\| - \sqrt{k_3} \|\delta_3\|)^2 - (2\sqrt{k_2 k_3} - k_u) \|\delta_2\|\|\delta_3\| \end{aligned} \tag{25}$$

It is clear that as long as $2\sqrt{k_2 k_3} - k_u \geq 0$, the time derivative of V_3 satisfy $\dot{V}_3 \leq 0$.

Select the fourth error item as

$$\delta_4 = \omega - \omega^d \tag{26}$$

And the Lyapunov Function is

$$V_4 = V_3 + \delta_4^T \delta_4 / 2 \tag{27}$$

Differentiate equation (27), then

$$\dot{V}_4 = \dot{V}_3 + \delta_4^T \dot{\delta}_4 = -k_1 \delta_1^T \delta_1 - k_2 \delta_2^T \delta_2 + \delta_2^T (u_o - u_o^d) + \delta_3^T (\pi \omega^d - \dot{\eta}^d) + \delta_4^T (\dot{\omega} - \dot{\omega}^d) + \delta_3^T (\pi \delta_4) \tag{28}$$

Select $\dot{\omega}$ as the visual control input, and define the desired value of $\dot{\omega}$ named

$$\dot{\omega}^c = \dot{\omega}^d - k_4 \delta_4 - \pi^T \delta_3 \tag{29}$$

Here k_4 is a positive control gain. Similarly, the derivative of V_4 is semi-negative definite. Actually, submitting (29) into the fourth equation of (1), we can calculate the desired moment

$$M^d = I\dot{\omega}^c + \omega \times I\omega \tag{30}$$

And the desired thrust of tail rotor T_{td}, flapping angles a^d, b^d also can be determined. Then, the input of tail rotor δ_{ped} is known. In this paper, we want to consider the flapping dynamics of the main rotor, the process of backstepping is not over, and the fifth error item is selected

$$\delta_5 = \dot{\omega}_{xy} - \dot{\omega}_{xy}^c \tag{31}$$

The operator $(\bullet)_{xy}$ means that the third item of $(\bullet)$ is set to be zero. The Lyapunov Function is

$$V_5 = V_4 + \delta_5^T \delta_5 / 2 \tag{32}$$

The time derivative of (32) is

$$\dot{V}_5 = -k_P \delta_1^T \delta_1 - k_2 \delta_2^T \delta_2 + \delta_2^T (u_o - u_o^d) + \delta_3^T (\pi \omega^d - \dot{\eta}^d)$$
$$+ \delta_4^T (\dot{\omega}^c - \dot{\omega}^d) + \delta_3^T (\pi \delta_4) + \delta_4^T \delta_5 + \delta_5^T (\dot{\omega}_{xy} - \dot{\omega}_{xy}^c) \tag{33}$$

Considering (28), it is true that the first 6 items of (33) is below zero. The focus is to check the last two items. Then

$$\dot{V}_5 \leq \delta_4^T \delta_5 + \delta_5^T (\dot{\omega}_{xy} - \dot{\omega}_{xy}^c) = \delta_4^T \delta_5 + \delta_5^T ([-(I^{-1}(\dot{\omega} \times I\omega))_{xy} - (I^{-1}(\omega \times I\dot{\omega}))_{xy} + (I^{-1}\dot{M})_{xy}] - \dot{\omega}_{xy}^c) \tag{34}$$

If $(I^{-1}\dot{M})_{xy}$ satisfies

$$(I^{-1}\dot{M})_{xy} = (I^{-1}(\dot{\omega} \times I\omega))_{xy} + (I^{-1}(\omega \times I\dot{\omega}))_{xy} + \dot{\omega}_{xy}^c - (\delta_4)_{xy} - k_5 \delta_5 \tag{35}$$

Then the condition of stability is satisfied. Differentiating the following equations

$$\begin{cases} M_x = K_\beta b \\ M_y = K_\beta a \end{cases} \tag{36}$$

And together with (35), $\delta_{lon}, \delta_{lat}$ can be calculated. By this time, all of the control inputs are determined. The process of backstepping is completed.

Table 1 The parameters of helicopter[12]

Parameter	Description	Parameter	Description
$m=9.5kg$	helicopter mass	$\tau_s=0.2236s$	time constant
$I_{xx}=0.305kg.\ m^2$	rolling moment of inertia	$K_\beta=138$	main rotor stiffness
$I_{yy}=0.684kg.\ m^2$	pitching moment of inertia	$\Omega=193rad/s$	main rotor speed
$I_{zz}=0.787kg.\ m^2$	yawing moment of inertia	$\Omega_{tr}=922rad/s$	tail rotor speed
$A_{\delta lon}=0.593$	Gain from δ_{lon} to a	$B_{\delta lat}=0.593$	Gain from δ_{lat} to b

4   Simulation

Several computer simulations are presented in this section to check the performance of the proposed controller.The parameters of the small-scale helicopter are given in Tab 1.In all simulations, we select a helix trajectory ascending in the z axis. The velocity of the desired trajectory is

$$\dot{\mathbf{P}}^d = v\begin{bmatrix} \cos\psi^d & \sin\psi^d & -0.3 \end{bmatrix}^T, \dot{\psi}^d = \omega_o \qquad (37)$$

In the first simulation, we check the tracking performance when the trajectory move slowly, $v=2m/s$ and $\omega_0=20deg/s$. The initial position errors are given by $\delta_1=[2,2,0]^T$ and the yaw angle error 30 deg. The simulation results are shown in Fig. 2. From the results, we can conclude that in this condition, the backstepping controller performed very well, there are short settle time and small overshoot.

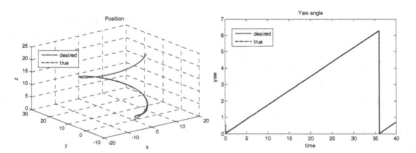

Fig. 2. Simulation results of slow trajectory

In the second simulation, we want to investigate the performance of the controller when the desired yawing rate and the line velocity is large. In this case, $v=6m/s$ and$\omega_0=40deg/s$. The initial position errors are also given by$\delta_1=[2,2,0]^T$ and the yaw angle error 30 deg.The simulation results show in Fig. 3 indicate that the controller can tracking the predefined trajectory fast and accurately.

The third simulation is designed to check the performance when there is a large initial error. In this case, $v=6m/s$and$\omega_0=40deg/s$. The initial position errors are also given by$\delta_1=[10,0,0]^T$and the yaw angle error 30 deg. The results are presented in Fig. 4. It shows that in this case the controller also can drive the helicopter to track the fast trajectory. Therefore, we can conclude that the performance of the backstepping controller is well.

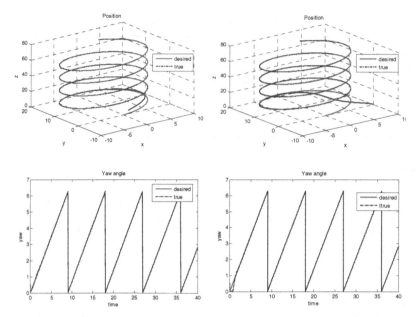

Fig. 3. Results of fast trajectory   **Fig. 4.** Results of large initial error

5   Conclusions

In this paper, a different backstepping trajectory tracking controller is designed. Because the relationship between the thrust and the collective input is an algebraic relationship, it's easy to determine the collective input.We decouple the translational dynamics and the rotational dynamics through solving an equation when the desired yaw angle is predefined. The simulation results show that the proposed controller has very well performance. On the other hand, the mathematic model we adopted is a approximate model, there are some differences between the true helicopter. How to design an adaptive control to eliminate the effect of the differences is the focus of the future works.

References

1. Mettler, B.: Modeling small-scale unmanned rotorcraft for advanced flight control design in Department of Mechanical Engineering. Carnegie Mellon University (2001)
2. Kim, S.K., Tilbury, D.M.: Mathematical modeling and experimental identification of a model helicopter (1998)
3. Mettler, B., Kanade, T., Tischler, M.B., Messner, W.: attitude control optimization for a small-scale unmanned helicopter. In: AIAA Guidance, Navigation, and Control Conference and Exhibit. Denver, CO (2000)
4. Gavrilets, V.: Autonomous Aerobatic Maneuvering of Miniature Helicopters. MIT (2003)

5. Civita, M.L.: Integrated Modeling and Robust Control for Full-Envelope Flight of Robotic Helicopters in Department of Mechanical Engineering, Carnegie Mellon University, Pittsburgh (2002)
6. Sastry, T.J.K.A.S.: Output Tracking Control Design of a Helicopter Model Based on Approximate Linearization. In: Proceedings of the 37th IEEE Conference on Decision & Control, Tampa, Florida, USA (1998)
7. Johnson, E.N., Kannan, S.K.: Adaptive Flight Control for an Autonomous Unmanned Helicopter. In: AIAA Guidance, Navigation, and Control Conference and Exhibit, Monterey (2002)
8. Ahmed, B., Pota, H.R., Garratt, M., Wing, R.: UAV Position Control using Backstepping. In: Proceedings of the 46th IEEE Conference on Decision and Control, New Orleans, LA, USA (2007)
9. Lee, C.-T., Tsai, C.-C.: Improvement in Trajectory Tracking Control of a Small Scale Helicopter via Backstepping. In: Proceedings of International Conference on Mechatronics, Kumamoto, Japan (2007)
10. Raptis, I.A., Valavanis, K.P., Moreno, W.A.: Nonlinear Backstepping Control Design for Miniature Helicopters Using the Rotation Matrix. In: 17th Mediterranean Conference on Control & Automation, MakedoniaPalace, Thessaloniki, Greece (2009)
11. Gavrilets, V., Mettler, B., Feron, E.: Nonlinear Model for a Small-Size Acrobatic Helicopter. In: AIAA Guidance Navigation,and Control Conference and Exhibit, Montreal, Canada (2001)
12. Cai, G., Chen, B.M., Dong, X., Lee, T.H.: Design and implementation of a robust and nonlinear flight control system for an unmanned helicopter. Mechatronics (2011)
13. Cai, G., Chen, B.M., Lee, T.H.: Comprehensive Nonlinear Modeling of an Unmanned-Aerial-Vehicle Helicopter. In: AIAA Guidance, Navigation and Control Conference and Exhibit. AIAA, Honolulu (2008)

Study on General Effectiveness Evaluation Platform for Combat Aircraft

Chao Wang[1], Ni Li[2], Haipeng Kong[2], and Huifeng Li[1]

[1] School of Astronautics
Beijing University of Aeronautics and Astronautics
Beijing, China
[2] School of Automation Science and Electrical Engineering
Beijing University of Aeronautics and Astronautics
Beijing, China
wangchao@sa.buaa.edu.cn

Abstract. The analysis of combat simulation system effectiveness is achieved by synthesizing reasonable indicators that based on demands of evaluation. To meet increasing requirements for evaluation, this paper designs and develops an Effectiveness Evaluation Platform for Combat Simulation System (EEPCSS), which can serve different combat simulations. EEPCSS obtains its generality by many methods, such as constructing the specification of evaluation models, providing typical evaluation models with universal interfaces for various combat simulation systems, building the index systems automatically, analyzing of test data, recording and replaying of evaluation process, synthesizing of indexes, and generation of evaluation results. As an application instance, EEPCSS is conducted to evaluate the performance of aircrafts in combat simulation. The evaluation result proves that EEPCSS can work effectively in solving practical problems.

Keywords: effectiveness, evaluation,simulation, platform, aircraft.

1 Introduction

The effectiveness evaluation of combat simulation is playing a key role in the study of weapon equipment system. The US and the Former Soviet Union have set up research institutes on cannons and fighter planes since 1960s. China also has done a deep research on assessments of airborne weapons and combat aircrafts in air warfare [1]. Nowadays, effectiveness evaluation is no longer a pure military issue, but one involving economy, finance, science, technology and other fields. However, the present evaluation systems are more designed to serve one specific combat simulation system and constrained to some combat conditions. For example, the evaluation for command and control integrated system in missile defense process cannot assess the damage ability of missiles; the assessment for aircrafts is not suitable for anti-ship missiles. There are various evaluation models for different combat simulation systems with multiple weapon platforms and all these test data that evaluation models need come from separate simulation systems. There has grown up an urgent need for a general platform, which can automatically call evaluation models through analyzing

T. Xiao, L. Zhang, and S. Ma (Eds.): ICSC 2012, Part I, CCIS 326, pp. 128–136, 2012.

test data generated by various simulation systems. This paper, in collaboration with some applied theory and technologies of current effectiveness evaluation systems, builds a general effectiveness evaluation platform which can solve a variety of multiple combat simulation evaluation problems using EEPCSS. This platform can free evaluators from messy work in assessing the combat simulation systems from scratch, accelerate the process of evaluation and improve the reuse of evaluation models, index systems, test data, evaluation configurations, and so forth.

The remainder of this paper is organized as follows. Section 2 gives an overview of EEPCSS. Section 3 to Section 5 describe the related key technologies of EEPCSS in detail. Section 6 discusses the typical index system of combat aircrafts. Finally, Section 7 implements an application instance for damage ability evaluation of combat aircrafts, which verifies the reasonableness and flexibility of EEPCSS.

2   The Overall Structure of EEPCSS

The overall structure of EEPCSS consists of three main layers illustrated in Fig.1. The bottom one is the background service layer which provides schedulable storage and algorithm resources for the application of EEPCSS.

The middle one is evaluation logical layer including the synthesis of index systems as well as the managements of evaluation models, index systems, test data, evaluation configuration and evaluation results. The management of evaluation models is composed of its specification, invoking and analysis, and abundant evaluation models provided by EEPCSS. The management of index systems realizes the automatically loading and hierarchically building of index system trees. Management test data analyzes and loads data stored when simulations of different weapon systems are proceeding. These test data are eventually converted into input information for evaluation models separately. Evaluators are allowed to quickly perform the evaluation by just updating changed items since configurations management not only records all the configurations and data generated in evaluation process but also replays the process through analyzing the configured files. The relative weights of evaluation indexes are attained in the comprehensive assessment module with the participation of experts, whose opinions have a vital influence on calculated values of evaluation and capability matrixes. When the evaluation processes are finished, outcomes of evaluation models are synthesized with relative weights into final results which are gathered together to the management of evaluation results.

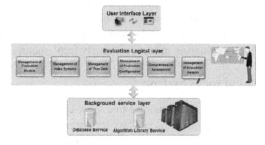

Fig. 1. The overall structure of EEPCSS

The components in logical layer are interdependent and cooperative with each other. Besides, all these components are closely linked to background service layer.

The top one is the user interface layer which is oriented to practical assessment requirements. EEPCSS can accomplish the evaluation task for different evaluation models which come from various simulation systems using these three layers.

The top one is the user interface layer which is oriented to practical assessment requirements. EEPCSS can accomplish the evaluation task for different evaluation models which come from various simulation systems using these three layers.

3   Design of Background Service Layer

The background service layer includes database service and algorithm library service providing the substantial and necessary supports for EEPCSS. The database library stores evaluation models, index systems, test data, configuration files and evaluation results. In the meantime, the algorithm library service covers different evaluation integration models such as WSEIAC model, power series model and Analytic Hierarchy Process (AHP) model. All the evaluation models are encapsulated in DLLs (Dynamic Link Library) regarding the specification of model interfaces, which can be flexibly invoked. EEPCSS manages these models using a relational database, which also stores auxiliary information in addition to model files. The auxiliary information covers external messages which allow evaluators to extend or specify, and internal messages queried by calling model query interface.

4   Design of Evaluation Logical Layer

The evaluation logical layer is a connecting link between the background service layer and the user interface layer, which is responsible for logical task in EEPCSS. It includes managements of evaluation models, index systems, test data, evaluation configuration and evaluation results as well as the comprehensive assessment. The rest of this section will describe each part in detail.

4.1   Management of Evaluation Models

The management of evaluation models specifies the evaluation model interfaces, through which EEPCSS could inherit and invoke the evaluation models conveniently. The specification of evaluation models enables the evaluators to enrich the model library, through which evaluation models are easily implemented their interfaces.

4.2   Management of Index Systems

Index systems are displayed in forms of a tree view control, among which every node contains its attribute information, as well as its parent's. According to index system information, indexes are classified into separated tree views and they achieve their hierarchical relations from their parents' attributions.

4.3   Management of Test Data

EEPCSS builds a XML file to record test data when simulation systems were running, which stores the evaluation model instances' object class attributes and interaction parameters of current combat simulation system. These test data are recognized by these instances and simulation steps. EEPCSS provides evaluators with a vivid chart, which displays the variation tendency of some attribute or parameter when some simulation was proceeding. The chart will wait for evaluations to input simulation steps or its interval for current evaluation model, after that an input file for current evaluation model is generated by screening of chosen test data files according to selected steps. This input file has filtered information that is not concerned in this evaluation, so it is a brief version of all selected test data files, which is customized for the evaluation model more than a rearrangement of the instance's data sets and simulation steps.

4.4   Management of Evaluation Configuration

The management of configuration includes recording segment and replay segment. EEPCSS also uses a XML file to record configuration details of evaluation process, such as the mapping of evaluation models, test data, parameters and simulation steps in addition to the information of simulation project and index system. The mapping relation is implemented by organizing a series of configured indexes, each of which on one hand, marks the test data files, current evaluation model and parameter messages it needs, on the other hand, also stores the detail data sets in the same structure as the input files discussed before.

In the meantime, EEPCSS supplies an assist tool for new evaluation processes, which reuses previous typical cases for similar systems. For such circumstances, evaluators just need to update the changed configuration and data sets to accomplish a new evaluation rapidly.

4.5   Comprehensive Assessment

EEPCSS first decompose the effectiveness problem into a hierarchy of more easily comprehended and calculated sub-indexes, each of which can be analyzed independently. Once the hierarchy is built, experts systematically evaluate its various indexes by comparing them to one another two at a time, with respect to their impact on an index above them in the hierarchy. In making the comparisons, experts use their judgments about the indexes' relative meaning and importance. It is the essence of the AHP that expert judgments, and not just the underlying information, can be used in performing the evaluations.

After this process experts' judgment matrixes are converted to relative weights. While the power series model synthesizes the index system to obtain final outcomes and capability matrixes combined with the relative weights.

4.6   Management of Evaluation Results

The result of assessment is a series of sets coming from evaluation processes. All these sets are aggregated in a result file, which contains the information about the simulation project and the configuration as well as the entire index system with calculated values and capability matrixes solved through comprehensive assessment. Database in background service layer is in charge of storing and managing these files, which provide references and comparisons for later evaluations.

4.7   The Overall Work Flow

These various files managed by evaluation logical layer are indispensable to a simulation project, which is complex set to describe the whole simulation system. Besides those files just mentioned, a simulation project also includes scenario files, weapon models, Federation Executive Data (FED) files etc.

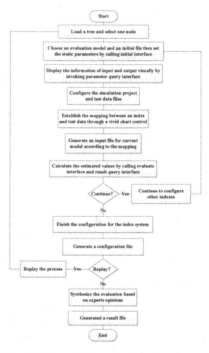

Fig. 2. The work flow of evaluation process

At the end of this section, this paper presents the work flow of evaluation process as shown in Fig2 and discusses the interactions of each section. When an evaluation process starts, EEPCSS loads an index system tree automatically, then waits for evaluators to select one index to assess, who also can change the tree or build a new one from scratch. EEPCSS would list the existing evaluation models which are allowed to expend as well in reference to model interfaces. Then, static parameters of current evaluation model are set by calling an initial file and this model's initial interface. After that, parameter query interface is called to analyze the model's input and output information, which is visually exhibited in user interface layer. Evaluators are needed to configure test data files at this moment, which are classified by simulation projects. A chart is design to assist the mapping between index and test data vividly, after which EEPCSS generates an input file for the evaluate interface. Finally, the evaluate interface and the result query interface are invoked to accomplish the evaluation process for this index. Evaluators just need to repeat these procedures until the entail tree's evaluation is completed. A configuration file is used to record and replay all these procedures while this evaluation process is proceeding. Experts' views are acted on index system tree, by means of which an evaluation result file is organized with both the calculated values of evaluation indexes and the consideration of synthesis of relative weights.

EEPCSS provides a user-friendly interface geared to practical evaluation applications comprising the management of evaluation models, a variety of files, experts' opinions and enriched tools.

5   Typical Effectiveness Evaluation for Combat Aircrafts

Weapon System Effectiveness Industry Advisory Committee (WSEIAC) model is adopted to establish the index system of combat aircrafts. This paper takes a deep research on the capability of aircraft for the reason that availability and dependability in WSEIAC merely concern combat simulation system itself. EEPCSS divides this problem into five factors consisting of survivability, supportability, command ability, breakthrough ability and damage ability [2] [3] as shown in Fig3. It just lists main indexes and many sub models have been left out, which is not concerned in this paper but can be attained from other published papers.

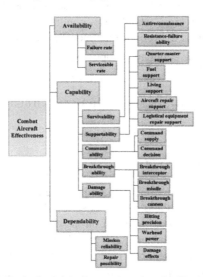

Fig. 3. Typical models for combat aircraft effectiveness

The paper only introduces a possible solution and typical evaluation models for the assessment of combat aircraft. EEPCSS is an open system, whose index systems and evaluation models are easily extended. It is just a general platform but with which evaluators are ability to freely construct evaluation systems for any demands.

5.1   Survivability Mode

The survivability model of aircrafts is to describe the minimum level to maintain its' inherit combat capability under the condition of some specific devastating attack. This model is shown as (1) on the assumption that an aircraft of one side is parking at a launching pad, then an hostile plane throws an aerial bomb to the aircraft [4] [5].

$$P_{sur}=P_{rt}+(1-P_{rt})\times P_{rd} \tag{1}$$

Where P_{sur}, P_{rt}, and P_{rd} are respectively the survivability, anti-reconnaissance and resistance-failureability.

5.2   Supportability Model

On evaluating survivability model of combat aircrafts, five sub-capabilities are taken into account, which are quarter-mastersupport, fuelsupport, livingsupport, aircraft-repairsupport, and logistical-equipment support [6]. All these sub-capabilities are independent to each other and consequently the weights sum is adopted into this model as follows [7]:

$$C_{sup} = \sum_{i=1}^{n} w_i C_{supi} \tag{2}$$

Where w_i is the weight of sub-capability and C_{supi} is the capability index.

5.3   Command Ability Model

Command ability model is consists of command decision and command supply as is illustrated in (3), Where C_{com1} stands for command decision, C_{com2} stands for command supply, and β is the proportional coefficient of importance ratio between the command design and the command supply [8].

$$C_{com} = \begin{cases} 0,0 \le C_{com1} <0.3 \cup 0 \le C_{com2} <0.3 \\ C_{com1}[1+\dfrac{0.698}{\beta-0.698}(0.698)-e^{C_{com2}}],0.3 \le C_{com1} <0.6 \cup 0.3 \le C_{com2} <0.6, \\ C_{com1},C_{com1} \ge 0.6 \cup C_{com2} \ge 0.6 \end{cases} \tag{3}$$

5.4   Breakthrough Ability Model

Interceptors, missiles and cannons are common interceptions of combat aircrafts. This model supposes that all these three means exist simultaneously. The model assumes that one side's fighters are swooping down on his opponent, whose radar detects the fighters. If interceptors that opponent send failed the mission, missiles and cannons will be dispatched to stop the fighters. This leads to the formula [9] [10]:

$$P_{break}=(1-P_d)+P_d\times P_{breakplane}\times P_{breakmissile}\times P_{breajcannon} \tag{4}$$

Where P_{break} stands for the calculated value of this model, P_d stands for detection ability of opponent's radar, $P_{breakplane}$, $P_{breakmissile}$ and $P_{breakcannon}$ respectively mean the breakthrough capabilities to interceptors, missiles and cannons.

5.5   Damage Ability Model

The damage ability plays a key role in effectiveness evaluation, which is visual reflection of battle field. This evaluation model is based on the assumption that one side's planes are attacking a target of hostility's. These planes launch missiles, when targets expose.

6   Application Instance

An example of evaluation for warhead power is given to testify the capacity of EEPCSS in terms of its reasonableness and flexibility. This example assumes that a combat aircraft of one side intends to attack a control tower of its opponent, whose length is 12m, width is 9m and armor thickness is 0.1m. The aircraft sends two air-to-surface missiles of some type (AGM-130) named "AGM-130A" and "AGM-130B". Missiles of this type are 0.4572m in diameter, 0.21m in warhead charge radius, 90kg in warhead charge weight and 3.6g/cm^3 in charge density. These static parameters are set by invoking evaluation models' initial interface, while other simulation data needed for evaluation are achieved by analyzing test data files, according to evaluator's selection for simulation steps, through a vivid chart. The index system tree builds automatically after the evaluator selecting the index system. Evaluation models' input and output information is gained by calling its parameter query interface and then display in the user interface layer.

A FED (Federation Executive Data) file is used to provide object and interaction classes as well as their attributes and parameters.Fig4illustrates the entail process that an evaluator is configuring the simulation steps for "Warhead Deflection in X Axis", which is the Object attribute of "AGM-130A". A graphical chart is used to show the variation tendency of this attribute when some simulation was proceeding. The final step's data which is 16th in the chart is selected as input data to fit the definition of warhead power.

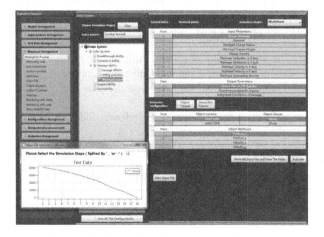

Fig. 4. Configuration of evaluation process

According to the input file, EEPCSS evaluates that armor-piercing probability is 1.00, overpressure/specific impulse probability is 0.826 and damage probability of integrated condition is also 0.826. Repeat these procedures to complete the evaluation of the whole index system tree and then complete the comprehensive assessment.

7   Conclusion

This paper develops an EEPCSS which provides a bunch of evaluation tools. Then the paper describes its structure in detail. Managements of evaluation models, index systems, test data, configuration and evaluation results as well as comprehensive assessment are applied in EEPCSS. To verify the performance of EEPCSS, a practical evaluation process of warhead power is carried out in the platform, which proves that EEPCSS can work effectively in solving practical problems. Further work will be concentrated on enriching evaluation model library and practical functions, improving its intelligence, as well as expanding the range of applications, so as to provide more supports for multiple combat simulation system effectiveness evaluations.

Acknowledgement. The work is supported by both the Graduate Student Innovation Practice Foundation of BeiHang University in China and National Nature Science Foundation of China-"Study on parallel intelligent optimization simulation with combination of qualitative and quantitative method" (61004089).

References

1. Hu, X., Lan, G., Shen, Z., Zhao, W.: The Analysis Methodology of Weapon Equipment Effectiveness. Northwestern Polytechnical University Press, Xi'an (2001) (in Chinese)
2. Feng, Y., Yang, X., Wang, W.: Architecture of combat missiles simulation evaluation system. Journal of National University of Defence Technology 21(1A), 17–20 (1999) (in Chinese)
3. Malaek, S.M., Sajjadi Kia, S.: Effectiveness of Human Pilot Energy Expenditure on PilotEvaluation of Handling Qualities. In: AIAA, pp. 2004–5363 (2004)
4. Ball, R.E.: The Fundamentals of Aircraft Survivability Analysis and Design. AIAA Education Series, New York (1985)
5. Woodford, S.: The Minimization of Combat Aircraft Life Cycle Cost through Concepture Design Optimization. PhD thesis, Cranfield University, College of Aeronatics (1999)
6. Hong, Z.: New Technology for Military Aviation and New Technical Equipment. Aviation Industry Press, Beijing (1997) (in Chinese)
7. Ma, S.: Comprehensive Support Project. Defence Industrial Press, Beijing (1995) (in Chinese)
8. Wu, Z.: Outline of Command and Control Systems. National University of Defence Technology Press, Changsha (1992) (in Chinese)
9. Gu, B.: Invisible Effectiveness of Penetration Fighters 27(5A), 127–135 (2005) (in Chinese)
10. Ray Persing, T., Dube, T., Jeff Slutz, G.: Impact of Aircraft Flight Dynamics Modeling Technique on Weapon System Beyond-Visual-Range Combat Effectiveness. In: AIAA, pp. 2003–5689 (2003)

Fuzzy Sliding Mode Variable Structure Controller for Hypersonic Cruise Vehicle

Chengbin Lian, Liubao Shi, Zhang Ren, and Xingyue Shao

Science and Technology on Aircraft Control Laboratory,
Beihang University
Beijing, P.R. China, 100191
WilliamChengbin@gmail.com

Abstract. For airbreathing hypersonic vehicle, the hypersonic cruise conditions with strong nonlinearity, parameter uncertainties, the higher requirement of control accuracy characteristics, to establish a control oriented model, and by using Lyapunov method were designed with different time scale of double loop control system. In order to solve the chattering problem of sliding mode control, this paper integrates fuzzy control with the idea of sliding mode variable structure control, and had researched the fuzzy sliding mode variable structure controller design method. This method can not only guarantee the system stability, but also restrain chattering. In the MATLAB for the control system of simulation test, the feasibility of the method is demonstrated.

Keywords: Hypersonic cruise vehicle, Fuzzy variable structure control, Fuzzy logic.

1 Introduction

In the United States X-43A validation machine as the typical representative of a waverider for configuration, scramjet powered hypersonic cruise vehicle (HCV) successful test flight represents the hypersonic technology development to a new stage. With HCV rapid response capacity and by virtue of its high speed, to perform rapid, long-range precision strike missions, which improve weapon attack suddenly and effective. Its powerful strategic deterrent to become a research focus of many countries[1]. Its typical aerodynamic shape as shown in figure 1:

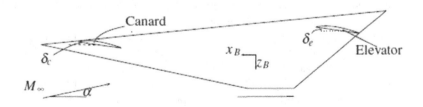

Fig. 1. .The typical HCV aerodynamic shape

T. Xiao, L. Zhang, and S. Ma (Eds.): ICSC 2012, Part I, CCIS 326, pp. 137–146, 2012.

HCV stability in flight and the precise attack depends on the guidance and control system, The guidance and control system is the aircraft's central, which is the aircraft flight safety and complete the mission of basic guarantee. Control of such aircraft to the following features and difficulties: the complexity of the flight environment, the span of the flight envelope, the dynamic characteristics of variable, strict control and other new features. From the control theory point of view, as a control object HCV aircraft model is nonlinear, multivariable, instability, non-minimum phase, the significant characteristics of input and output cross-coupling and model uncertainty. For this class of nonlinear, strong coupling, time-varying object control, using the small disturbance theory to obtain feature points on the linear time invariant model, and for each feature point on the linear model using mature dominant control theory to design a linear controller, then interpolated and scheduled the linear controller, finally we got the full envelope control law. The United States of America hypersonic flight test machine X-33, X-43A used is the gain scheduling for the classical PID control[2,3]. The robustness, poor self-adaptive, and multi-mission of the classical control methods, which is difficult to adapt the HCV complex flight environment. Nonlinear control methods can provide better solutions, such as feedback linearization, sliding mode control, backstepping nonlinear suboptimal control method, based on state Riccati equation method, and intelligent control, etc.

Variable structure control to solve the robustness of HCV aircraft control system provides an effective method[4,5]. The sliding mode variable structure system is invariant, that is, it has nothing to do with the system perturbations and external disturbances[6]. But its drawback is to produce high frequency chattering, this buffeting may activated for unmodeling high-frequency component of the system and even cause system instability. For this disadvantage, a more simple approach is the saturation function method, namely in the area of origin of the discontinuous sign function using continuous function alternative. In order to further improve the control performance, many scholars combinded fuzzy control (a suitable nonlinear control of uncertain systems) and sliding mode variable structure control to overcome the disadvantages of buffeting, which to form a more practical method of fuzzy variable structure control[7-9]. Fuzzy control is an intelligent control method which based on the fuzzy set theory, fuzzy linguistic variables and logical reasoning as a tool, which can use human experience and knowledge, to intuitive reasoning into the decision-making. It does not require the object of which mathematical models ,which take full advantage of the knowledge and experience of control experts, it also has a certain robustness.

There are mainly two ways of the combination of fuzzy control and variable structure control: mixed mode and integration mode. Mixed mode refers to the fuzzy variable structure control, which used variable structure controller, and fuzzy controller for the auxiliary parameters or uncertainty compensation. Model of integration refers to the variable structure fuzzy control, which used the structure of the fuzzy controller, and sliding mode variable and its derivative information as input of the fuzzy system. Fuzzy inference directly input the amount of control which can guarantee the sliding mode reaching condition[10].

In this paper, fuzzy control uesed to adjust the variable structure control law, which we could got design method of fuzzy sliding mode control[8]. In this paper, we fusioned the idea of fuzzy control and sliding mode variable structure control, and based on system status relative position of the sliding surface to design fuzzy controller. The fuzzy sliding mode variable structure control method is applied to design the HCV attitude control law for aircraft hypersonic cruise stage. Finally, the simulation can demonstrate feasible of HCV cruise fuzzy variable structure attitude controller.

2   Control Oriented Modeling of HCV

In the HCV cruise phase, HCV aircraft center of mass motion is achieved through a change in attitude. The guidance system was calculated to achieve flight trajectory tracking of 3 flow angle (angle of attack and sideslip angle, and the bank of angle) attitude instruction, flight control system design task is to realize the guidance angle instruction attitude tracking. Therefore the design of control systems need to established a model dynamics equation in the flow angle.

For control system design, we usually simplify the vehicle dynamics of the six degrees of freedom, deleted some unimportant iterms, so the controller design is to simplify. Under the influence of severe aerodynamic heating in hypersonic flight, the traditional angle of attack measuring device can not be used. It is difficult to accurately measure the actual wind speed, angle of attack and sideslip angle in practical engineering are usually based on the flight velocity estimation, which was considered is the angle between the body coordinate system and the velocity coordinate system. The kinetic equation for the flow angle[11]:

$$\dot{\phi} = \omega_x \cos\alpha \sec\beta + \omega_z \sin\alpha \sec\beta \tag{1}$$

$$\dot{\beta} = \omega_x \sin\alpha - \omega_z \cos\alpha \tag{2}$$

$$\dot{\alpha} = -\omega_x \cos\alpha \tan\beta + \omega_z \sin\alpha \tan\beta + \omega_y \tag{3}$$

In the HCV aircraft cruise phase of flight, sideslip angle is zero, then the type (1)~(3) is:

$$\begin{bmatrix} \dot{\phi} \\ \dot{\beta} \\ \dot{\alpha} \end{bmatrix} = \begin{bmatrix} \cos\alpha & 0 & \sin\alpha \\ \sin\alpha & 0 & -\cos\alpha \\ 0 & 1 & 0 \end{bmatrix} \times \begin{bmatrix} \omega_x \\ \omega_y \\ \omega_z \end{bmatrix} \tag{4}$$

Because HCV is the Symmetry surface vehicle, then $J_{xy}, J_{yz}, J_{xz} = 0$, $J = diag\{J_{x1}, J_{y1}, J_{z1}\}$, we can get rotation of the attitude dynamics equation:

$$\begin{bmatrix} \dot{\omega}_{x1} \\ \dot{\omega}_{y1} \\ \dot{\omega}_{z1} \end{bmatrix} = \begin{bmatrix} 1/J_{x1} & 0 & 0 \\ 0 & 1/J_{y1} & 0 \\ 0 & 0 & 1/J_{z1} \end{bmatrix} \begin{bmatrix} M_{x1} \\ M_{y1} \\ M_{z1} \end{bmatrix} + \begin{bmatrix} c_2 \omega_{y1} \omega_{z1} \\ c_4 \omega_{x1} \omega_{z1} \\ c_5 \omega_{x1} \omega_{y1} \end{bmatrix} \tag{5}$$

Where: $c_2 = (J_{y1} - J_{z1})/J_{x1}$, $c_4 = (J_{z1} - J_{x1})/J_{y1}$, $c_5 = (J_{x1} - J_{y1})/J_{z1}$, $\omega_{x1}, \omega_{y1}, \omega_{z1}$ is absolute angular velocity in the body coordinate system component. J_x, J_y, J_z, J_{xy} is the moment of inertia. M_{x1}, M_{y1}, M_{z1} is the moment components acting on the aircraft body frame, α is angle of attack, β is Sideslip angle, ϕ is bank of angle, $\omega_x, \omega_y, \omega_z$ is absolute angular velocity in the body coordinate system of components, which can be measured by the gyroscope.

3   Fuzzy Sliding Mode Variable Structure Control Method

The sliding mode variable structure control is that when the system state through the different areas of the state space, the structure of the feedback controller in accordance with certain rules changes, which making the control system has a certain degree of adaptation to intrinsic parameter variations and external environment of the controlled object such as disturbancecapacity to ensure system performance indicators to achieve the desired requirements. The control system is robust to the uncertainties that exist in the system, In fact the variable structure controller is actually a nonlinear controller.

The sliding mode variable structure controller design is usually in two steps: the design of sliding surface and design of variable structure control law. For the tracking control problem, the control goal is makes the tracking errors converge 0. Combining the fuzzy control and traditional sliding mode control combination constitutes the fuzzy variable structure control. Fuzzy variable structure control can not rely on the system model, which could maintaining the advantages of a conventional fuzzy controller, at the same time fuzzy variable structure control can also weaken the chattering which cautched by simple sliding mode control system. Therefore, fuzzy variable structure is a kind of intelligent controller which could control the difficulty of modeling of complex objects effectively in the uncertain environment.

The fuzzy controller structure is a multi-input single-output fuzzy system.which designed with two inputs, one output multi-input single-output fuzzy system. Constructed a stability of linear sliding surface in the error phase plane two, four quadrants:

$$s = \dot{e} + ce = 0 \tag{6}$$

Where: tracking error $e = O_d - O$ is the difference between reference output and the actual output, $c > 0$ is the design parameters of the sliding surface, which made the tracking error of the sliding surface is asymptotically stable.

In phase plane will transformat coordinate axis, see Figure1. Sliding surface $s = 0$ as the vertical axis, the vertical line of the sliding surface. $s_\perp$ as the horizontal axis For a moment the state point T, $d_1 > 0$ as the distance from system trajectory to the sliding mode surface, and $d_2 > 0$ as the distance from for T in the sliding mode plane projection to the origin of the distance. Using the derivative of the error and error with the traditional fuzzy controller as an input variable, fuzzy variable structure controller to select the d_1 and d_2 as input variables:

$$d_1 = \frac{|ce + \dot{e}|}{\sqrt{1 + c^2}}, d_2 = \frac{|c\dot{e} - e|}{\sqrt{1 + c^2}} \tag{7}$$

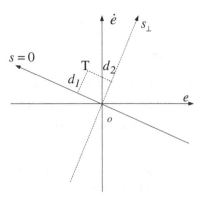

Fig. 2. Fuzzy input variable

The output variable is defined as the maximum available to control the ratio of $0 \leq k \leq 1$, therefore, fuzzy system input and output is greater than 0, greatly reduces the number of rules. Input normalization ratio factor $1/d_{1,\max}, 1/d_{2,\max}$ as design parameters, so that the input, output space are located in [0,1], which could be according to the practical system regulation. Deal input, output space with the same uniform fuzzy segmentation, and divided them into7 fuzzy sets N, P1, P2, P3, P4, P5, P6.We chose simple, practical triangular and trapezoidal membership function, as shown in figure 3:

The core of fuzzy control is the establishment of the fuzzy rule table. For two inputs, there are seven fuzzy sets respectively, so that there are total of 49 rules. The design of fuzzy control rules as shown in Table 1:

Table 1. Fuzzy control ruler

$\dfrac{d_1}{d_{1,\max}}$							
$\dfrac{d_2}{d_{2,\max}}$	N	P1	P2	P3	P4	P5	P6
N	N	P1	P2	P3	P4	P5	P6
P1	N	P1	P2	P3	P4	P5	P6
P2	N	P1	P2	P3	P4	P5	P6
P3	P1	P1	P2	P3	P4	P5	P6
P4	P1	P1	P2	P3	P4	P5	P6
P5	P1	P2	P2	P3	P4	P5	P6
P6	P2	P2	P3	P4	P4	P5	P6

When the system trajectory from the sliding surface is far, the output of the controller is mainly composed of d_1 to decide, namely the state from the sliding surface is far, require a larger control system trajectory to pull the sliding surface. When the system trajectory towards the sliding surface approaches the process, the needed control is reduced. When the system trajectory from the sliding surface is very close, the output of the controller is mainly composed of d_2 to decide, namely the state at a distance from the origin, which need a slightly greater control acceleration error convergence process, so as to the origin of the approach, control should be reduced.

Fuzzy reasoning using Mamdani max-min rule, and the defuzzification calculation for output by using gravity method. Finally, the obtained fuzzy sliding mode variable structure controller control surfaces such as shown in Figure 4 below:

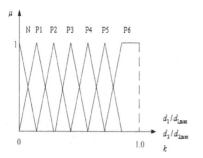

Fig. 3. Membership function   **Fig. 4.** Fuzzy control surface

The fuzzy controller output is the maximum available control scaling factor, therefore the actual control signal size need to multiply the maximum available volume control to meet the physical limitations of the actuator. While the direction of the exerted control depends on the sliding mode variable s symbol, which makes the applied control can make the error state to the sliding mode plane approach.

4   Cruise Phase Attitude Controller Design

HCV fuzzy sliding mode control block diagram shown below:

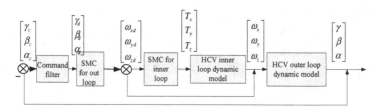

Fig. 5. Cruise phase attitude control system structure

Guidance system gives the three flow angle guidance command to meet the scramjet's normal working conditions during the HCV aircraft cruise phase. In order to avoid reference instruction mutations, and to solve the contradiction between the tracking overshoot and fast, a very effective method is to design command filter. command filter is a pre-filter for smooth command , which could make the tracking error in the controllable range of the object. Guidance command after it will get the attitude command which HCV flight control system is required to track. Fuzzy sliding mode variable structure controller according to the deviation between the practical attitude and the command attitude to generated control moment, to track the guidance command.

Because the command may be mutated, if tracked on the guidance command directly, there may cause HCV aircraft scramjet engine flameout because of large transient error, therefore command filtering is very important. According to the scramjet work characteristics, this paper set the sideslip angle equal to zero, and designed attack of angle command filter and bank of angle command filter are both 2-order linear system with velocity and position limitation.

$$\ddot{X}_d = 2\varsigma\omega_n[S_R(\frac{\omega_n^2}{2\varsigma\omega_n}[S_M(X_c) - X_d]) - \dot{X}_d] \tag{8}$$

Where: S_M is the position saturation function, S_R is the velocity saturation function, X_c is the required posture command which is given for the guidance system, X_d is the filtered reference instruction, and ς, ω_n, respectively, for the damping ratio and natural frequency.

4.1   The Outer Loop Sliding Mode Controller Design

HCV outer loop kinematic equations as formula (1)-(3), angular rate vector ω generated by the inner dynamics model of HCV as a virtual angular rate command ω_c as input, and use the output of the HCV outer loop kinematics equation as tracking the movement direction angle feedback. According to the necessary bandwidth, the compensated outer loop movement tracking error is limited to (via a suitable control) a sliding surface of the form:

$$\sigma = \gamma_e + K_1 \int_0^t \gamma_e d_\tau = 0, \sigma \in R^3 \tag{9}$$

Where, $\gamma_e = \gamma_c - \gamma$, $\gamma = [\alpha \quad \beta \quad \phi]^T$, $\omega = [\omega_x \quad \omega_y \quad \omega_z]^T$, $K_1 = diag\{k_{1i}\}$, $K_1 \in R^{3\times3}$。

The outer ring sliding mode controller generates angular rate command ω_c, make the system along the $\dot{\gamma} = R(\gamma)\omega$ trajectories converge, and reach the sliding surface in finite time $\sigma = 0$.

The dynamic sliding mode $\dot{\sigma}$ in type (8) is described as:

$$\dot{\sigma} = \dot{\gamma}_c - R(\gamma)\omega_c + K_1\gamma_e \tag{10}$$

Using the Lyapunov direct method to design the outer loop sliding mode controller, select the Lyapunov functionis $V = 0.5\sigma^T\sigma$ and its derivative is:

$$\dot{V} = \sigma^T\dot{\sigma} = \sigma^T[\dot{\gamma}_c - R(\gamma)\omega_c + K_1\gamma_e] \tag{11}$$

In order to ensure the asymptotic stability of the system, the following Lyapunov differential inequality is limited to:

$$\dot{V} \le -\rho\sigma^T SIGN(\sigma) = -\rho\sum_{i=1}^{3}|\sigma_i| \,,\, \rho > 0 \tag{12}$$

According to the last type, the required angular rate command ω_c which is used to ensure the asymptotic stability is defined as follows:

$$\omega_c = \mathbf{R}^{-1}(\gamma)[\dot{\gamma}_c + \mathbf{K}_1\gamma_e] + \mathbf{R}^{-1}(\gamma)\rho SIGN(\sigma) \tag{13}$$

Where:

$$SIGN(\sigma) = [sign(\sigma_1), sign(\sigma_2), sign(\sigma_3)]^T \tag{14}$$

The time spand on reach the sliding surface which shown on tape (8) f as follows:

$$t_r = \max_{i\in[1,3]} \frac{|\sigma_i(0)|}{\rho} \tag{15}$$

Among them, the $\rho > 0$ and t_r, is the arrival time of the design parameters to describe the sliding surface.

4.2   Inner Sliding Mode Controller Design

HCV inner mathematical model such as equation(5), the purpose of the design of the inner sliding mode is in order to produce the desired torque command T. controller to track a given angular rate commands ω_d. In addition to addressing the tracking problem of the inner loop is defined as follows:

$$\lim_{t\to\infty}\|\omega_{id}(t) - \omega_i(t)\| = 0 \,,\quad i\in \overline{1,3} \tag{16}$$

Sliding mode controller also makes the system showing the linear   decoupling motion on the sliding surface.

Inner HCV equation of motion as follows:

$$\mathbf{J}_0\dot{\omega} = -\Omega\mathbf{J}_0\omega + T \tag{17}$$

Where T is the control moment generated by the inner controller.

The goal is to design a controller T to make the sliding surface stability to zero.

$$\sigma = \omega_e + \mathbf{K}_2\int_0^t \omega_e d_\tau \,,\quad s\in \mathbf{R}^3 \tag{18}$$

Where, $\omega_e = \omega_c - \omega$, $\mathbf{K}_2 = diag\{k_2\}$, $\mathbf{K}_2 \in \mathbf{R}^{3\times3}$.

For the two ring with a sufficient amount of time, by setting different value $\mathbf{K}$, the inner loop sliding mode motion shown in the type (16) was designed faster than the outer ring.

Sliding mode surface type (18) dynamic equation is defined as follows:

$$\dot{\sigma} = \dot{\omega}_e + \mathbf{K}_2\omega_e = \dot{\omega}_c - \dot{\omega} + \mathbf{K}_2\omega_e$$
$$= \dot{\omega}_c + \mathbf{J}_0^{-1}\mathbf{\Omega}\mathbf{J}_0\omega - \mathbf{J}_0^{-1}T + \mathbf{K}_2\omega_e \tag{19}$$

Using Lyapunov direct method in the design of sliding mode controller, we chose Lyapunov equation is:
$V = 0.5s^T J_0 s$, its derivative is:

$$\dot{V} = s^T J_0 \dot{s}$$
$$= s^T J_0 (\dot{\omega}_c + \mathbf{J}_0^{-1}\mathbf{\Omega}\mathbf{J}_0\omega - \mathbf{J}_0^{-1}T + \mathbf{K}_2\omega_e) \tag{20}$$

The following Lyapunov differential equation must meet in order to ensure the asymptotic stability of the system equations:

$$\dot{V} \le -\eta s^T SIGN(s) = -\eta \sum_{i=1}^{3}|s_i|, \quad \eta > 0 \tag{21}$$

The sliding surface (19) to reach a zero set-up time is defined by the following formula:

$$\tau_r \le \max_{i \in [1,3]} \frac{|s_i(0)|}{\eta} \tag{22}$$

Where $\eta > 0$ and τ_r is the design parameters which describe the arrival time.

Consider the last inequality, the required moment command which to ensure the asymptotic stability is described as follows:

$$T = \mathbf{\Omega}\mathbf{J}_0\omega + \mathbf{J}_0\dot{\omega}_c + \mathbf{J}_0\mathbf{K}_2\omega_e + \tilde{\rho}SIGN(s) \tag{23}$$

The T substitution (20) type, we got:

$$\dot{V} = -\tilde{\rho}s^T SIGN(s) \le -\eta \sum_{i=1}^{3}|s_i| \tag{24}$$

Where $\tilde{\rho} \ge \eta$.

5   Control System Simulationsing

In order to verify the cruise phase attitude controller design, according to the HCV cruise phase of guidance angle α_c , and γ_c tracking in SIMULINK simulation. Angle of attack command filter $\varsigma_\alpha = 1, \omega_{n\alpha} = 10$, bank of angle command filter $\varsigma_{\gamma_v} = 0.7, \omega_{n\gamma_v} = 10$, speed limit is $\pm 5°/s$, input normalized scale factor is $1/d_{1,max} = 10, 1/d_{2,max} = 20$. Simulation of the initial conditions: in 25km altitude, speed of 6 Ma, initial angle of attack for $3°$.

Figure 6 demonstrate, using fuzzy sliding mode variable structure controller can make the attitude tracking error of less than 0.02rad, the controller has robustness and can tolerate parameter error and interference. The control of rudder deflection are also in its physical limit, no saturation phenomenon, but the actuator rate must be fast enough, the simulation of the speed limit is set $100°/s$.

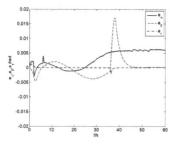

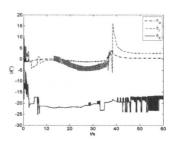

Fig. 6. Attitude tracking error   **Fig. 7.** Rudder command

The simulation also found that the fuzzy controller input and output membership function had large influence on the control performance of the system. Therefore, we can optimize the membership functions using genetic algorithms to further improve the control performance and robustness of fuzzy variable structure controller.

Acknowledgments. This study has been supported by the Science and Technology on Aircraft Control Laboratory at the Beihang University, and based upon work supported under the National Natural Science Foundation of China (90916003,91116002) and 111 project(B07009).

References

1. Yang, Y., Li, S., Yang, J.: A Brief Discussion of hypersonic vehicle and its key technologies. Advances in Mechanics 37(4), 537–550 (2007)
2. Davidson, J., Lallman, F., Mcminn, J.D., et al.: Flight Control Laws for NASA's Hyper-X Research Vehicle. In: AIAA Guidance, Navigation, and Contronol Conference and Exhibit. (1999)
3. Fidan, B., Mirmirani, M., Ioannou, P.A.: Flight dynamics and control of air-breathing hypersonic vehicles: review and new directions. In: International Space Planes and Hypersonic Systems and Technologies, Norfolk, VA (2003)
4. Shtessel, Y.B., McDuffie, Y.J., Jackson, J.: Sliding mode control of the X-33 vehicle in launch and re-entry modes. In: AIAA Guidance Navigation and Control Conference and Exhibit., pp. 1352–1362. AIAA, Reston (1998)
5. Hall, C.E., Shtessel, Y.B.: RLV sliding mode control system using sliding mode observers and gain adaptation. In: AIAA Guidance, Navigation and Control Conference and Exhibit., pp. 5437–5451. AIAA, Austin (2003)
6. Sheng-Yuan, M.G., Huo, W.: Design method of adaptive fuzzy sliding-mode controllers for a class of uncertain multi-input nonlinear systems. Control and Decision 16(5), 535–539 (2001)
7. Wu, S.F., Engelen, C.J.H., Mulder, J.A.: Fuzzy logic based full-envelope autonomous flight control for an atmospheric re-entry spacecraft. Control Engineering Practice (11), 11–25 (2003)
8. Ha, Q.P., Nguyen, H., Rye, D.C., et al.: Fuzzy sliding mode controllers with applications. IEEE Transactions on Industrial Electronics 48(1), 38–46 (2001)
9. Utkin, V.I.: Sliding Mode Control Design Principles and Applications to Electric Drives. IEEE Transactions on Industrial Electronics 40(1), 10–22 (1993)
10. Zhao, H.: Reentry dynamics and guidance, pp. 84–86. National University of Defense Technology Press, Changf Sha (1991)

Grid Current Control Strategy Based on Internal Model Control and Repetitive Control

Jianming Huang, Li Fu, Fuqiang Xu, and Chunhua Wu

Shanghai Key Laboratory of Power Station Automation Technology,
Department of Automation, Shanghai University, Shanghai 200072, China

Abstract. In this paper, a new grid current control strategy based on internal model control and repetitive control is designed. The performance characteristic and operation principle are analyzed   according to the basic principle of internal model control and the dynamic mathematical model of three-phase photovoltaic grid-connected inverters. Because the harmonic current caused by the dead-time effect and the periodic disturbance of the grid can not be eliminated by internal model control, a composite control strategy with internal model control and repetitive control is proposed in the paper. Internal model control can simplify the controller's parameters and ensure the dynamic quality of the system. Repetitive control is able to restrain the dead-time effect and the periodic disturbance of the grid. It can also reduce the total harmonic distortion of the grid-connected current. The simulation results show that the proposed control strategy has good dynamic and steady-state performance and can restrain the periodic disturbance as well.

Keywords: Three-phase grid-connected inverters, Internal model control, Repetitive control, Dead-time effect.

1   Introduction

With the increasing serious energy and environmental problems, distributed grid generation technology is drawing more and more attention. The technology has become an important part of the energy strategy of sustainable development [1-5]. As the interface connecting renewable power generation systems and power network, the control performance of grid inverter can affect the grid power quality directly [6-8]. Therefore, the research of high performance grid inverter control strategy has the important practical significance.

Internal model [9-11] control can be widely used in electric drive system with a lot of advantages, such as lower model accuracy requirement, better system tracking regulation performance and strong robustness, etc. However, the traditional internal model method can not solve the problems of grid current harmonic caused by power devices dead zone effect or grid voltage distortion. Base on internal model control and repetitive control, this paper put forward a composite grid current control strategy. The internal model control that put in inner controller can simplify the design of controller parameter, enhance the system robustness and improve the controlled object frequency characteristics. The repeated control[12-14] can improve system steady state performance, eliminate the influence of periodic disturbances by dead zone effect or

T. Xiao, L. Zhang, and S. Ma (Eds.): ICSC 2012, Part I, CCIS 326, pp. 147–156, 2012.
© Springer-Verlag Berlin Heidelberg 2012

grid voltage distortion, improve the grid power quality. This strategy makes the system with good dynamic and static performance to meet photovoltaic grid control performance requirements.

2   The Principle of Internal Model Control

The equivalent internal model control feedback structure is described in Fig.1, which consists of the controlled object model $G(s)$, the controlled object internal model $\hat{G}(s)$, internal model controller $C_{IMC}(s)$, interference item $D(s)$, the equivalent feedback controller of internal model controller $F(s)$.

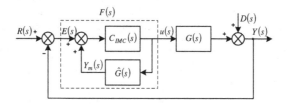

Fig. 1. Structure of internal model control and equivalent feedback control

It is known that the internal model control has the following characteristics.

I   Adjustment output deviation caused by disturbance $D(s)$.

II   Adjustment output deviation caused by mismatch of model and control object ($\hat{G}(s) \neq G(s)$).

III   When the model and control object matches ($\hat{G}(s) = G(s)$), and $C_{IMC}(s)=G^{-1}(s)$, the system can suppress any interference ($D(s)$) and can track without deviation for any input $R(s)$.

The output $Y(s)$ is represented by:

$$Y(s) = \frac{C_{IMC}(s)G(s)}{1 + C_{IMC}(s)[G(s) - \hat{G}(s)]} R(s) + \frac{1 - C_{IMC}(s)\hat{G}(s)}{1 + C_{IMC}(s)[G(s) - \hat{G}(s)]} D(s) \tag{1}$$

If the model is accurate ($\hat{G}(s) = G(s)$), and $C_{IMC}(s)= G^{-1}(s)$, $Y(s)= R(s)$ can be available, the output of the system always equal input, free from any interference.

When the prediction model of control object is known, the internal model controller is given in equation (2).

$$C_{IMC}(s) = \hat{G}^{-1}(s)L(s) \tag{2}$$

Where $L(s)$ is calculated by:

$$L(s) = diag[\frac{\lambda_1^n}{(s + \lambda_1)^n}, \frac{\lambda_2^n}{(s + \lambda_2)^n}, \cdots, \frac{\lambda_k^n}{(s + \lambda_k)^n}] \tag{3}$$

The positive integer n should be adopted large enough to make $L(s)$ positive. When the forecasting model $\hat{G}(s)$ and the actual object are consistent, the closed-loop bandwidth only relies on the parameter λ_i. Therefore, the system can be stable by adjusting the parameters of $L(s)$, and it can obtain the desired dynamic quality and robustness.

3   Internal Model Control of Grid Current

3.1   Design of Internal Model Controller for Grid-Connected Current

The transfer function of the output voltages and the grid-connected currents is given as following, without considering the effect of the power grid.

$$\begin{bmatrix} i_d(s) \\ i_q(s) \end{bmatrix} = \begin{bmatrix} R+Ls & -\omega L \\ \omega L & R+Ls \end{bmatrix}^{-1} \begin{bmatrix} u_d(s) \\ u_q(s) \end{bmatrix} \tag{4}$$

In equation (4), the transfer function of the three-phase grid-connected inverter does not exist zero on right half plane, it can be approximated as a first order system at high frequency. Therefore, the current internal controller ($C_{IMC}(s)$) of three-phase grid-connected inverter can be gotten.

$$C_{IMC} = \hat{G}^{-1}(s)L(s) = \begin{bmatrix} \hat{R}+\hat{L}s & -\omega\hat{L} \\ \omega\hat{L} & \hat{R}+\hat{L}s \end{bmatrix} \frac{\lambda}{s+\lambda} I \tag{5}$$

Where the estimated value of the filter L is $\hat{L}$, the estimated value of the equivalent resistance is $\hat{R}$.

The feedback controller is obtained from equation (5), which is shown in equation (6).

$$F(s) = [1 - \frac{\lambda}{s+\lambda}]^{-1}\hat{G}^{-1}(s)\frac{\lambda}{s+\lambda} = \frac{\lambda}{s}\begin{bmatrix} \hat{R}+\hat{L}s & -\omega\hat{L} \\ \omega\hat{L} & \hat{R}+\hat{L}s \end{bmatrix} \tag{6}$$

The internal model block diagram of grid-connected inverter can be obtained as Fig.2.

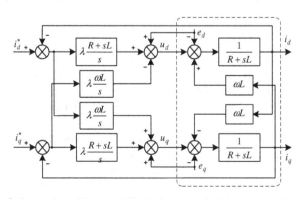

Fig. 2. Internal model control block diagram of grid-connected inverter

It can be derived from Fig.2:

$$P'(s) = \frac{Y(s)}{R(s)} = \frac{C_{IMC}(s)G(s)}{1 + C_{IMC}(s)[G(s) - \hat{G}(s)]} \tag{7}$$

Where $C_{IMC}(s) = \hat{G}^{-1}(s)L(s)$, $L(s) = \frac{\lambda}{s + \lambda}I$, $Y(s) = \begin{bmatrix} i_d \\ i_q \end{bmatrix}$, $R(s) = \begin{bmatrix} i_d^* \\ i_q^* \end{bmatrix}$.

3.2　　Steady-State Analysis of Current Internal Model Control

According to the theorem of steady-state final value, considering step input, step disturbance and the reference model mismatches with the actual object, the steady-state error of internal model control is given in equation (8).

$$E(s) = R(s) - Y(s) = \frac{1 - C_{IMC}(s)\hat{G}(s)}{1 + C_{IMC}(s)[G(s) - \hat{G}(s)]}[R(s) - D(s)] \tag{8}$$

It can be obtained from steady-state final value theorem that the steady-state without deviation can be also achieved by the internal model control under the slope reference input and slope disturbance interference, if the controller $C_{IMC}(s)$ meets the demand

$C_{IMC}(0) = \hat{C}^{-1}(0)$ and $\dfrac{d}{ds}\left[C_{IMC}(s)\hat{G}(s)\right]\Big|_{s=0} = 0$.

$$\frac{d}{ds}[C_{IMC}(s)\hat{G}(s)]|_{s=0} = \frac{d}{ds}[\hat{G}^{-1}(s)L(s)\hat{G}(s)]|_{s=0} = \frac{d}{ds}[\frac{\lambda}{s+\lambda}]|_{s=0} \neq 0 \tag{9}$$

However, it can be known from equation (9) that the partial derivative of the product of current internal model controller $C_{IMC}(s)$ and internal model $\hat{G}(s)$ can not meet above conditions. Thus, when the model parameter mismatches, current internal model control can not eliminate the affection of dead-time effect [15], [16] and the periodic disturbance of the grid.

4　　Composite Control Strategy and Controller Parameter Design

4.1　　Composite Control System

The dead zone effects and the network voltage distortion occur with industrial frequency cycle repeatedly. Repetitive control is one wave control technology based on internal model principle, which can eliminate wave tracking error caused by periodic disturbance effectively and has been used widely in inverter power supply and active power filter field.

　　Fig.(3) is the current-loop control diagram of internal model with plug-in repetitive controller for three-phase grid-connected inverter.

　　In Fig.3, $G_r(z)$ is the discrete transfer function of the repetitive controller. $\Delta i(z)$ is the input current error signal of the repetitive controller. $\Delta i_o(z)$ is the output signal.

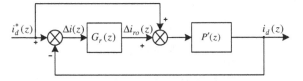

Fig. 3. Current-loop control diagram with plug-in repetitive controller

$P'(z)$ is the discrete transfer function of the closed-loop current based on internal model controller, which is given in equation (10).

$$P'(z) = z|P'(s)| = z\left|\frac{C_{IMC}(s)G(s)}{1 + C_{IMC}(s)[G(s) - \hat{G}(s)]}\right| \quad (10)$$

Fig.4 is the block diagram of repetitive controller with a discrete transfer function as following.

$$G_r(z) = \frac{C(z)z^{-N}}{1 - Q(z)z^{-N}} \quad (11)$$

where $N=f_s/f$, f_s is the sampling frequency of grid-connected inverter, f is the base wave frequency of network voltage, $Q(z)$ is a stability improving link which can be a low-pass filter, also can be a constant a little less than 1(usually takes 0.95). $C(z)$ is a filter to compensate the frequency characteristics of the controlled object, which has a decisive impact on the performance of repetitive control system.

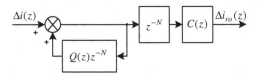

Fig. 4. Block diagram of repeat control

According to the frequency characteristics of the controlled object, compensator $C(z)$ can be made of one or more links of repetitive control gain K_r, advanced process z^k and the filter $S(z)$, which is given in equation (12).

$$C(z) = K_r z^k S(z) \quad (12)$$

4.2   Parameter Design of Internal Model Control

When the model mismatch ($\hat{G}(s) \neq G(s)$), the system (the generalized controlled object $P'(s)$) approximates as a closed-loop one-order system with a bandwidth of λ without considering the effect of the power grid, which is given as following.

$$P'(s) \approx \frac{\lambda}{s + \lambda} \quad (13)$$

For a one-order system, the relationship between the rising time of step response t_γ and the coefficient λ is given:

$$t_\gamma = \ln(9/\lambda) \approx 2.2/\lambda \tag{14}$$

The sampling frequency of the system is $6400 \times 2\pi$ rad/s , selected λ is 4000 rad/s . The transfer function of current loop $P'(z)$ corrected by internal model controller can be obtained in z domain, as following in equation (15).

$$P'(z) \approx \frac{0.4647}{z - 0.5353} \tag{15}$$

It can be known from the frequency characteristics of current loop, the system has good amplitude-frequency characteristics after correction by internal model controller. However, when the gain value is 0 in mid-low frequency, there are phase distortion. The amplitude-frequency gain reduction is slow in high frequency range and the high harmonic suppression is not effective.

4.3   Parameter Design of Repetitive Controller

It needs to design a compensator $C(z)$ to compensate the phase in mid-low frequency and enhance the amplitude-frequency gain attenuation in high frequency, as well as to improve the stability and anti-high-frequency interference of the system.

The parameters of repetitive controller are given: $Q(z)$ is 0.95, the cut off frequency w_n of filter $S(z)$ is 5000 rad/s (a little more than the cut off frequency 4000 rad/s of inner-loop current), the damping ratio ξ of filter $S(z)$ is 0.5. The transfer function of the second-order filter $S(s)$ in s domain is given as following.

$$S(s) = \frac{\omega_n^2}{s^2 + 2\xi\omega_n s + \omega_n^2} = \frac{2.5 \times 10^7}{s^2 + 5000s + 2.5 \times 10^7} \tag{16}$$

The transfer function of the discrete second-order filter in z domain is:

$$S(s) = \frac{0.2278z + 0.1749}{z^2 - 1.055z + 0.4578} \tag{17}$$

Take the order of z^k $k = 3$, the effect of phase compensation at mid-low frequency is very effective. It can be found that the phase lag at mid-low frequency can be compensated well and the system will not be affected by the phase advance of high frequency noise because the high frequency noise has been attenuated effectively.

5   Simulation Results

A simulation experiment has been designed in Matlab/Simulink to verify the correction of the proposed control scheme. The simulation parameters have been given: the line voltage of three-phase power supply is 380 V/50 Hz, DC bus voltage is 600 V, switching frequency of the system is 6.4 kHz, filter inductor is 10 mH, equivalent resistance is 1 Ω, the simulation model is shown in Fig.5.

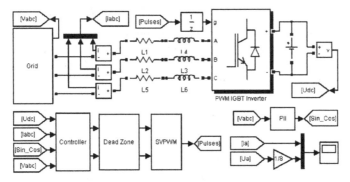

Fig. 5. Simulation Model

5.1   Simulation Performance of Single Internal Model Control

Assume that there is not distortion in grid voltage and the PWM dead-time is not considered, the simulation experiments are studied for mutations of current instruction, amplitude change of grid voltage, and parameter change of filter inductor, the simulation results is shown in Fig.6~7.

Fig.6 is the simulation result of d axis current at given mutation from 5A to 10A at 0.1s and returning to 5A at 0.2s, it can be found that the change of given current is tracked quickly by internal model control. Fig.6(b) is d-q axis current with an ideal decoupling effect.

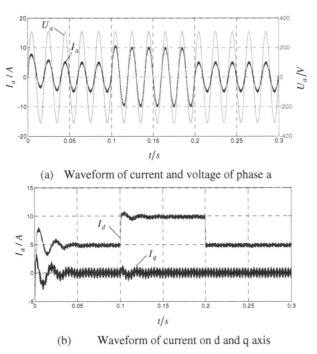

(a)   Waveform of current and voltage of phase a

(b)   Waveform of current on d and q axis

Fig. 6. Simulation results of the reference current change from 5A to 10A, from 10A to 5A

Fig.7 is the simulation results of grid voltage dropping 20% at 0.15s and returning to normal at 0.25s. It can be found that the current increases instantaneously and returns to normal during a grid cycle when grid drops, and the current decreases instantaneously and also returns to normal during a grid cycle. It verifies that internal model control has a good performance with anti-grid disturbance.

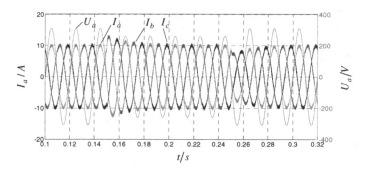

Fig. 7. Simulation results of grid voltage change from 100% to 80%, from 80% to 100%

5.2   Simulation Performance of Repetitive Control

Fig.8(a) and Fig.8(b) are the simulation results considering PWM dead-time and grid voltage distortion by internal model control and repetitive control, where internal model control is adopted before 0.1s and the repetitive control and internal model

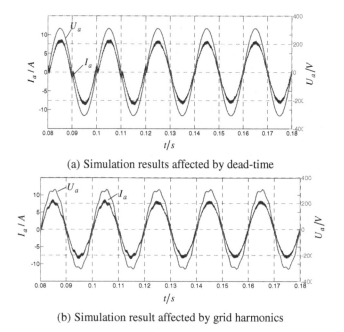

(a) Simulation results affected by dead-time

(b) Simulation result affected by grid harmonics

Fig. 8. Simulation results of current-loop control with nonlinear perturbation

control operate together after 0.1s. It can be found that the problems of dead-time effect and grid-connected current harmonic caused by grid voltage distortion can not be solved by single internal model control. When repetitive control is added at 0.1s, the influence of dead-time effect and grid-connected current harmonic caused by grid voltage distortion are eliminated after a grid cycle delay, and the quality of grid current is ensured.

6   Conclusion

In this paper, according to the basic principle of internal model control and three-phase photovoltaic grid-connected inverter's mathematical model, a grid-connected current control strategy based on internal model control has been designed. In the strategy of current control based on combined internal model and repetitive control, the internal model control has advantage to design the anti-disturbance and enhance the robustness of the system; the repetitive control can improve the steady performance of the internal model control, enhance the quality of grid-connected current, and obtain good dynamic and static performance of the system. Finally, the simulation results showed that the proposed control strategy has good dynamic and steady-state performance and can restrain the periodic disturbance.

Acknowledgments. This research is supported by the National Natural Science Foundation of China (Grant No.51107079) and Shanghai Key Laboratory of Power Station Automation Technology, "11th Five-Year Plan" 211 Construction Project .

References

1. Blaabjerg, F., Teodorescu, R., Liserre, M., et al.: Overview of Control and Grid Synchronization for Distributed Power Generation Systems. IEEE Transactions on Industrial Electronics 53(5), 1398–1409 (2006)
2. Nigim, K.A., Zobaa, A.F.: Development and opportunities of distributed generation fuelled by renewable energy sources. International Journal of Global Energy Issues 26(3), 215–231 (2006)
3. Nissen, M.B.: High performance development as distributed generation. IEEE Potentials 28(6), 25–31 (2009)
4. Li, D.H., Wang, H.X., Zhu, X.D., et al.: Research on several critical problems of photovoltaic grid-connected generation system. Power System Protection and Control 38(21), 208–214 (2010)
5. Hou, S.Y., Song, X., Sun, T., et al.: A novel topology of fault-tolerant three-phase four-switch grid-connected inverter based on space vector hysteresis control. Power System Protection and Control 39(21), 138–144 (2011)
6. Huang, J.J., Zhang, H., Zhang, A.M., et al.: Research on the new current control strategy based on the grid-connected inverter. Power System Protection and Control 39(20), 137–140 (2011)

7. Guo, X.Q., Wu, W.Y., Zhao, Q.L., et al.: Current Regulation for Three-phase Grid-connected Inverters Based on Proportional Complex Integral Control. Proceedings of the CSEE 29(15), 8–14 (2009)
8. Shang, L., Dan, S., Hu, J.B., et al.: Predictive Direct Power Control of Three-Phase Grid-Connected Voltage-Sourced Inverters. Transactions of China Electrotechnical Society 26(7), 216–222 (2011)
9. Zhuang, Y.X., Chen, S.X.: Current Regulation or Vector-Controlled Induction Motors Based on Adaptive Internal Model Control. Transactions of China Electrotechnical Society 15(2), 61–65 (2000)
10. Song, C.H., Hu, D., Ke, J.: Application of internal model control to current regulator. Electric Power Automation Equipment 28(4), 15–18 (2008)
11. Deng, F.J., Cai, X.: Double Closed-loop PWM Rectifier based on Internal Model Control. Power Electronics 42(6), 60–62 (2008)
12. Li, L.B., Zhao, Z.G., Zhao, Z., et al.: Study on three-phase photovoltaic grid-connected inverter system based on compositive control. Power System Protection and Control 38(21), 44–47 (2010)
13. Su, M., Wang, H., Sun, Y., et al.: Design of Three-phase Four-leg Inverter Based on Modified Repetitive Controller. Proceedings of the CSEE 30(24), 29–35 (2010)
14. Wang, S.R., Lü, Z.Y.: Research on Repetitive Control Method Applied to Grid-connected Inverter With LCL Filter. Proceedings of the CSEE 30(27), 69–75 (2010)
15. Lai, Y., Shu, F.: Optimal common-mode voltage reduction PWM technique for inverter control with consideration of the dead-time effect-part: basic development. IEEE Trans. on Industry Application 40(6), 1605–1612 (2004)
16. Chen, L.H., Peng, F.Z.: Dead-Time elimination for voltage source inverters. IEEE Transactions on Power Electronics 23(2), 574–580 (2008)

An Analytical Design Method for the Missile Two-Loop Acceleration Autopilot

Hui Wang[1,2], De-fu Lin[2], Jia-xin Wang[2], and Tao Song[2]

[1] School of Aeronautic Science and Engineering,
Beijing University of Aeronautics & Astronautics, 100191 Beijing, China
[2] School of Aerospace Engineering,
Beijing Institute of Technology, 100081 Beijing, China
wh20031131@126.com

Abstract. According to the missile longitudinal dynamics expressed as the state space matrix form and the defined dynamics coefficient notations, the missile body transfer functions are deduced in detail. Using the thought of pole allocation, a detailed analytical methodology for designing the two-loop acceleration autopilot has been proposed. To get the exact gain crossover frequency of the autopilot, an unconstraint optimization problem is outlined. The design and simulation results show that the two-loop acceleration autopilot can stabilize the missiles with different static margins very well.

Keywords: missile, two-loop autopilot, analytical methodology, static margin.

1   Introduction

The missile lateral autopilots have been introduced in tactical missiles over the past several decades [1-2]. The lateral autopilots control the missile body by elevator and rudder to generate the required acceleration according to the guidance demand which is following some guidance laws, such as proportional navigation, augmented proportional navigation, trajectory shaping, etc.. In some Russia missile design, one accelerometer and one angular acceleration gyro are used and the accelerometer has to be positioned in the rear section of the missile for structural reason. Nevertheless, the lateral autopilots with one accelerometer and one angular rate gyro are always more common in homing guidance missiles [3-4].

The design goal of the missile autopilots is to use the sensed quantities to produce a stable fast response which robustly follows the guidance command signals over a wide range of flight profiles at large bound altitude [5]. Many design methods for the missile autopilots have been studied deeply, for example, pole-place, linear quadratic regulator (LQR), H-infinity, etc.[6-10]. In this paper, an analytical design process for the two-loop acceleration autopilot has been proposed and a design example is given for the missiles with three different static margins.

2   Missile Dynamics

A missile's longitudinal dynamics can be described using the short period approximation of the longitudinal equations of motion. Written in differential equation notation, the basic missile longitudinal plant is [3].

T. Xiao, L. Zhang, and S. Ma (Eds.): ICSC 2012, Part I, CCIS 326, pp. 157–165, 2012.

$$\dot{\alpha} = \dot{\vartheta} - b_\alpha \alpha - b_\delta \delta_e$$
$$\ddot{\vartheta} = -a_\omega \dot{\vartheta} - a_\alpha \alpha - a_\delta \delta_e$$
$$\alpha = \vartheta - \theta \qquad\qquad (1)$$
$$a_y = V\dot{\theta}$$
$$a_{ym} = a_y + c\ddot{\vartheta} = Vb_\alpha \alpha + Vb_\delta \delta_e + c\ddot{\vartheta}$$

where, c is the distance from the accelerometer position to the airframe center of gravity (CG) and a positive c means that the accelerometer is located ahead of CG.

Three possibilities of a_α are:

(1) $a_\alpha > 0$, the airframe is static stable;
(2) $a_\alpha = 0$, the airframe is critical static stable;
(3) $a_\alpha < 0$, the airframe is static unstable.

For a_δ, there also exist two possibilities. When a_δ is over zero, it means that the missile is rear controlled; when a_δ is less than zero, it means that the missile is canard controlled.

The variables and notations are defined in Table 1.

Table 1. Variables and notations

a_α (s^{-2})	a_δ (s^{-2})	a_ω (s^{-1})	b_α (s^{-1})	b_δ (s^{-1})
$\dfrac{-m_z^\alpha qSL}{J_z}$	$\dfrac{-m_z^{\delta_e} qSL}{J_z}$	$\dfrac{-m_z^{\bar{\omega}_z} qSL}{J_z}$	$\dfrac{c_y^\alpha qS}{mV}$	$\dfrac{c_y^\delta qS}{mV}$
$q(pa)$	$S(m^2)$	$L(m)$	$J_z(kgm^2)$	$m_z^\alpha, m_z^{\delta_e}, m_z^{\bar{\omega}_z}, c_y^\alpha, c_y^{\delta_e}$
Dynamic pressure	Referenc e area	Referenc e length	Moment of inertia	Normal moment and force coefficient
ϑ (rad)	$\dot{\vartheta}$ (rad/s)	$\ddot{\vartheta}$ (rad/s^2)	α (rad)	θ (rad)
Body pitch angle	Body pitch angular rate	Body pitch angular acceleration	Angle of attack	Trajectory angle
$\dot{\theta}$ (rad/s)	$\delta_e(rad)$	$V(m/s)$	a_y (m/s^2)	$m(kg)$
Trajectory angle rate	Elevator	Velocity	Acceleration	Mass of the missile

Written in state space matrix form, the basic missile plant is

$$\dot{x} = Ax + Bu , \; y = Cx + Du \qquad\qquad (2)$$

where, $x = \begin{bmatrix} \alpha & \dot{\vartheta} \end{bmatrix}^T$, $y = \begin{bmatrix} a_{ym} & \dot{\vartheta} \end{bmatrix}^T$,

$$A = \begin{bmatrix} -b_\alpha & 1 \\ -a_\alpha & -a_\omega \end{bmatrix}, \; B = \begin{bmatrix} -b_\delta \\ -a_\delta \end{bmatrix}, \; C = \begin{bmatrix} Vb_\alpha - ca_\alpha & -ca_\omega \\ 0 & 1 \end{bmatrix}, \; D = \begin{bmatrix} Vb_\delta - ca_\delta \\ 0 \end{bmatrix}.$$

According to the Laplace transformation, the state Eq. (2) may be written as

$$sx(s) - x(0) = Ax(s) + Bu(s)$$
$$y(s) = Cx(s) + Du(s)$$
(3)

That is

$$y(s) = C(sI - A)^{-1}[Bu(s) + x(0)] + Du(s)$$
(4)

For a 2×2 matrix Q, the inverse of Q may be obtained by using

$$Q = \begin{bmatrix} a & b \\ c & d \end{bmatrix}, Q^{-1} = \frac{1}{ad - bc}\begin{bmatrix} d & -b \\ -c & a \end{bmatrix}$$
(5)

Solving for $(sI\text{-}A)^{-1}$ gives

$$(sI - A)^{-1} = \frac{1}{(s + b_\alpha)(s + a_\omega) + a_\alpha}\begin{bmatrix} s + a_\omega & 1 \\ -a_\alpha & s + b_\alpha \end{bmatrix}$$
(6)

and substituting Eq. (6) into (4) yields

$$y(s) = G\delta_e(s) + G_0 x(0)$$
(7)

$$G = C(sI - A)^{-1}B + D = \begin{bmatrix} G_{ym}(s) \\ G_{\dot\vartheta}(s) \end{bmatrix}$$
(8)

$$G_0 = C(sI - A)^{-1} = \begin{bmatrix} C_{011}(s) & C_{012}(s) \\ C_{021}(s) & C_{022}(s) \end{bmatrix}$$
(9)

where,

$$G_{ym}(s) = \frac{A_2' s^2 + A_1' s + A_0'}{s^2 + (b_\alpha + a_\omega)s + (a_\alpha + a_\omega b_\alpha)}, \quad G_{\dot\vartheta}(s) = \frac{-a_\delta s - (a_\delta b_\alpha - a_\alpha b_\delta)}{s^2 + (b_\alpha + a_\omega)s + (a_\alpha + a_\omega b_\alpha)},$$

$$G_{011}(s) = \frac{(Vb_\alpha - ca_\alpha)(s + a_\omega) + ca_\alpha a_\omega}{s^2 + (b_\alpha + a_\omega)s + (a_\alpha + a_\omega b_\alpha)}, \quad G_{012}(s) = \frac{(Vb_\alpha - ca_\alpha) - ca_\omega(s + b_\alpha)}{s^2 + (b_\alpha + a_\omega)s + (a_\alpha + a_\omega b_\alpha)},$$

$$G_{021}(s) = \frac{-a_\alpha}{s^2 + (b_\alpha + a_\omega)s + (a_\alpha + a_\omega b_\alpha)}, \quad G_{022}(s) = \frac{s + b_\alpha}{s^2 + (b_\alpha + a_\omega)s + (a_\alpha + a_\omega b_\alpha)},$$

$$A_2' = (Vb_\delta - ca_\delta), \quad A_1' = Va_\omega b_\delta - c(a_\delta b_\alpha - a_\alpha b_\delta), \quad A_0' = -V(a_\delta b_\alpha - a_\alpha b_\delta).$$

When the accelerometer is positioned to the airframe CG, the value of c is zero and $G_{ym}(s), G_{011}(s), G_{012}(s)$ can be simplified as

$$G_y(s) = \frac{V[b_\delta s^2 + a_\omega b_\delta s - (a_\delta b_\alpha - a_\alpha b_\delta)]}{s^2 + (b_\alpha + a_\omega)s + (a_\alpha + a_\omega b_\alpha)}, \quad G_{011}(s) = \frac{Vb_\alpha(s + a_\omega)}{s^2 + (b_\alpha + a_\omega)s + (a_\alpha + a_\omega b_\alpha)},$$

$$G_{012}(s) = \frac{Vb_\alpha}{s^2 + (b_\alpha + a_\omega)s + (a_\alpha + a_\omega b_\alpha)}.$$

Thus

$$\frac{a_{ym}(s)}{\delta_e(s)} = G_{ym}(s), G_y(s) = G_{ym}(s)\big|_{c=0}, \frac{\dot{\vartheta}(s)}{\delta_e(s)} = G_{\dot{\vartheta}}(s) \qquad (10)$$

$$a_{ym}(s)\big|_{\alpha(0),\dot{\vartheta}(0)} = G_{011}(s)\alpha(0) + G_{012}(s)\dot{\vartheta}(0) \qquad (11)$$

$$\dot{\vartheta}(s)\big|_{\alpha(0),\dot{\vartheta}(0)} = G_{021}(s)\alpha(0) + G_{022}(s)\dot{\vartheta}(0) \qquad (12)$$

Define the new notations:

$$A_2 = \frac{-b_\delta}{a_\delta b_\alpha - a_\alpha b_\delta} \quad , \quad A_1 = \frac{-a_\omega b_\delta}{a_\delta b_\alpha - a_\alpha b_\delta} \quad , \quad \omega_m = \sqrt{a_\alpha + a_\omega b_\alpha} \quad , \quad \zeta_m = \frac{a_\omega + b_\alpha}{2\sqrt{a_\alpha + a_\omega b_\alpha}} \quad ,$$

$$k_{\dot{\vartheta}} = -\frac{a_\delta b_\alpha - a_\alpha b_\delta}{a_\alpha + a_\omega b_\alpha}, \quad T_\alpha = \frac{a_\delta}{a_\delta b_\alpha - a_\alpha b_\delta} \quad .$$

Neglect the accelerometer position c, Eq.(10) may be expressed as

$$\frac{a_y(s)}{\delta_e(s)} = Vk_{\dot{\vartheta}}\frac{A_2 s^2 + A_1 s + 1}{s^2/\omega_m^2 + 2\zeta_m s/\omega_m + 1} \quad , \quad \frac{\dot{\vartheta}(s)}{\delta_e(s)} = \frac{k_{\dot{\vartheta}}(T_\alpha s + 1)}{s^2/\omega_m^2 + 2\zeta_m s/\omega_m + 1} \qquad (13)$$

The missile dynamic coefficients are shown in Table 2[3].

Table 2. Missile dynamic coefficients

$V(ms^{-1})$	$a_\alpha(s^{-2})$	$a_\delta(s^{-2})$	$a_\omega(s^{-1})$	$b_\alpha(s^{-1})$	$b_\delta(s^{-1})$	$c(m)$
500	500	500	3.0	3.0	0.36	0.5

Fig.1 gives the response of α, $\dot{\vartheta}$ and a_y when an initial value of $\alpha(0)=3°$ and $\dot{\vartheta}(0)=5°/s$ exists respectively.

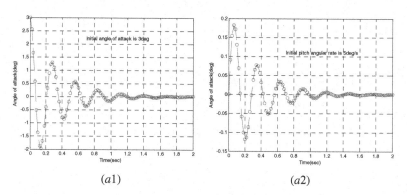

(a1)   (a2)

Fig. 1. Response of α, $\dot{\vartheta}$ and a_{ym} for initial value of $\alpha(0)$ and $\dot{\vartheta}(0)$

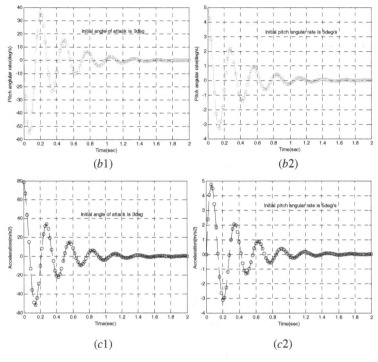

(b1)   (b2)

(c1)   (c2)

Fig. 1. (*Continued.*)

3   Design of the Two-Loop Acceleration Autopilot

The two-loop acceleration autopilot in which the accelerometer provides the achieved acceleration information and the rate gyro is used to act as a damper, known as the classical two-loop autopilot, is shown in Fig.2.

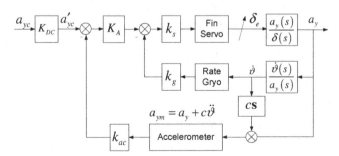

Fig. 2. The two-loop acceleration autopilot

In Fig.2, k_s is the gain of the fin servo while k_g and k_{ac} are the gain of the rate gyro and accelerometer respectively. K_{DC}, K_A, k_g are the autopilot parameters which need to be designed.

Due to the fair separation that exists between the missile body frequency and the frequency of the hardware (such as actuator, rate gyro and accelerometer), there only a small influence on the phase in the low frequency region. Therefore, the dynamics of the actuator, rate gyro and accelerometer are ignored here [8].

When neglect the dynamics of the fin servo, rate gyro and the accelerometer, the closed-loop transfer function of the two-loop autopilot can be written as

$$\frac{a_y(s)}{a_{yc}(s)} = K_{DC} \frac{a_y(s)}{a'_{yc}(s)} = K_{DC} \frac{K(A_2 s^2 + A_1 s + 1)}{s^2 / \omega^2 + 2\zeta s / \omega + 1} \tag{14}$$

According to Fig.2, the open-loop and closed-loop transfer functions can be expressed as following

$$G_{op.}(s) = \frac{M'_2 s^2 + M'_1 s + M'_0}{s^2 / \omega_m^2 + 2\zeta_m s / \omega_m + 1} \tag{15}$$

where

$$\begin{cases} M'_2 = k_s k_{ac} k_{\dot\vartheta} K_A (VA_2 + cT_\alpha) \\ M'_1 = k_s k_{\dot\vartheta} (k_{ac} K_A VA_1 + ck_{ac} K_A + k_g T_\alpha) \\ M'_0 = k_s k_{\dot\vartheta} (k_g + k_{ac} K_A V) \end{cases} \tag{16}$$

$$G_{cl.}(s) = \frac{K_{DC} k_s K_A V k_{\dot\vartheta} (A_2 s^2 + A_1 s + 1)}{(s^2 / \omega_m^2 + 2\zeta_m s / \omega_m + 1) + (M'_2 s^2 + M'_1 s + M'_0)} \tag{17}$$

Let the denominator of Eq. (15) and (17) be equivalent, one obtains

$$\left(\frac{s^2}{\omega^2} + \frac{2\zeta}{\omega} s + 1\right) = \left[\frac{1}{\omega_m^2(1+M'_0)} + \frac{M'_2}{1+M'_0}\right] s^2 + \left[\frac{2\zeta_m}{\omega_m(1+M'_0)} + \frac{M'_1}{1+M'_0}\right] s + 1$$

Then

$$\begin{aligned} \frac{1}{\omega^2} &= \frac{1}{\omega_m^2(1+M'_0)} + \frac{M'_2}{1+M'_0} \\ \frac{2\zeta}{\omega} &= \frac{2\zeta_m}{\omega_m(1+M'_0)} + \frac{M'_1}{1+M'_0} \end{aligned} \tag{18}$$

Define the new gains

$$\begin{cases} K'_{\vartheta A} = k_s k_{\dot\vartheta} K_A \\ K'_{\vartheta G} = k_s k_{\dot\vartheta} k_g \end{cases} \tag{19}$$

Combining Eqs. (16), (18) and (19) gives

$$\begin{aligned} \omega^2 / \omega_m^2 - 1 &= K'_{\vartheta A} k_{ac} (V - VA_2 \omega^2 - cT_\alpha \omega^2) + K'_{\vartheta G} \\ 2\omega\zeta_m / \omega_m - 2\zeta &= K'_{\vartheta A} k_{ac} (2\zeta V - VA_1 \omega - c\omega) + K'_{\vartheta G}(2\zeta - T_\alpha \omega) \end{aligned} \tag{20}$$

Eq. (20) can be further expressed as

$$P = MK'$$ (21)

where

$$P = \begin{bmatrix} \omega^2 / \omega_m^2 - 1 \\ 2\omega\zeta_m / \omega_m - 2\zeta \end{bmatrix}, \quad K' = \begin{bmatrix} K'_{\vartheta A} \\ K'_{\vartheta G} \end{bmatrix}, \quad M = \begin{bmatrix} k_{ac}(V - VA_2\omega^2 - cT_\alpha\omega^2) & 1 \\ k_{ac}(2\zeta V - VA_1\omega - c\omega) & 2\zeta - T_\alpha\omega \end{bmatrix}.$$

Combining Eq. (19) and (20) yields

$$K' = M^{-1}P$$ (22)

or

$$\begin{bmatrix} K_A & k_g \end{bmatrix}^T = M^{-1}P / k_s k_{\vartheta}$$ (23)

where

$$M^{-1} = \begin{bmatrix} (2\zeta - T_\alpha\omega)/\Delta & -1/\Delta \\ -k_{ac}(2\zeta V - VA_1\omega - c\omega)/\Delta & k_{ac}(V - VA_2\omega^2 - cT_\alpha\omega^2)/\Delta \end{bmatrix}, \quad \Delta = \Delta_1 + \Delta_2,$$

$$\Delta_1 = k_{ac}V\omega(-T_\alpha - 2\zeta\omega A_2 + T_\alpha\omega^2 A_2 + A_1), \quad \Delta_2 = ck_{ac}\omega(T_\alpha^2\omega^2 - 2\zeta\omega T_\alpha + 1).$$

One of the main purposes of the missile control system is to track the normal acceleration command. In order to insure the zero steady state error, using the terminal value theorem gives

$$\lim_{s \to 0}\left(a_y / a_{yc}\right) = 1$$ (24)

Then, we get

$$K_{DC} = 1/\left(k_s K_A Vk_{\vartheta}\right)$$ (25)

However, in the past, the gain crossover frequency ω_{cr} of the open-loop system would be put forward as the design parameter but not ω. Actually, there exist a bijection between ω and ω_{cr}

$$\omega_{cr} \doteq f(\omega)$$ (26)

In the design, we can define the objective function with the desired ω_{cr} and calculate the actual ω'_{cr} every time, that is

$$\min\left|\omega_{cr} - \omega'_{cr}\right|$$ (27)

Then an unconstraint optimization problem can be outlined to obtain the exact ω_{cr} value [11].

4   Simulation Analysis

As restricting terms of the autopilot performance, the parameters of the actuator, rate gyro and accelerometer are list in Table 3 [12].

Table 3. Parameters of the actuator, rate gyro and accelerometer

	Damp (ζ)	Frequency (*rad/s*)	Phase lag (*deg*)		
			40(*rad/s*)	45(*rad/s*)	50(*rad/s*)
Actuator	0.65	220	13.7	15.5	17.3
Rate gyro	0.65	300	10.0	11.3	12.6
Accelerometer	0.65	300	10.0	11.3	12.6
Total phase lag			23.7	26.8	29.6

According to the design method in part III, the desired gain crossover frequency and damp of the autopilot are set as ω_{cr}=45.0 (*rad/s*), ζ=0.75. The design results are shown in Table 4.

Table 4. The design results

a_α	K_{DC}	K_A	k_g	Gm(dB)	Pm(deg)	ω_{cr}(rad/s)
500	8.02	0.00013	0.067	12.3	67.6	45.0
0	1.17	0.0011	0.082	11.3	48.3	45.0
-500	0.67	0.0013	0.072	10.4	36.5	45.0

Note that, a_α=500,0 and -500 means that the missile is static stable, critical static stable and static unstable respectively.

Fig.3-Fig.5 gives the simulation results for different static margin missile and the outputs are acceleration, angle of attack and elevator angle respectively. It is shown that the two-loop acceleration autopilot can stabilize a static stable, critical static stable or static unstable missile very well and achieve to the desired performance.

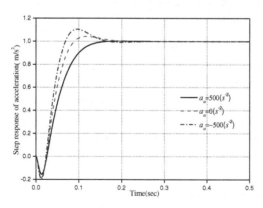

Fig. 3. Unit step response of the accelerometer for different a_α

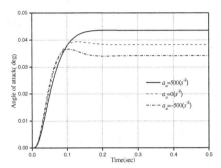 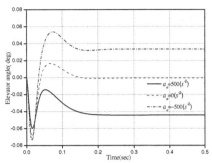

Fig. 4. Response of angle of attack   **Fig. 5.** Response of elevator angle

5   Conclusion

It has defined the missile longitudinal dynamics coefficient notations and deduced the missile body transfer functions according to the state space matrix equations and Laplace transformation. A detailed analytical design process for the two-loop acceleration autopilot has been developed which is some what like the thought of pole-place. The analysis results show that the autopilot can control missiles with different static margins very well.

References

1. Zarchan, P.: Tactical and Strategic Missile Guidance, 5th edn., pp. 483–539. AIAA Inc., Lexington (2007)
2. Devaud, E., Siguerdidjane, H., Font, S.: Some control strategies for a high-angle-of-attack missile autopilot. Control Engineering Practice 8, 885–892 (2000)
3. Garnell, P.: Guided weapon control systems, pp. 95–113. Beijing institute of technology, Beijing (2003)
4. Ghosh, S., Datta, K.K., Goswami, S.K., et al.: A parameter plane design methodology for three loop missile autopilot. Journal of The Institution of Engineers (India) 86, 213–219 (2006)
5. Buschek, H.: Design and flight test for a robust autopilot for the IRIS-T air-to-air missile. Control Engineering Practice 11(1), 551–558 (2003)
6. Wang, H., Lin, D.F., Qi, Z.K.: Design and analysis of missile three-loop autopilot with pseudo-angle of attack feedback. Systems Engineering and Electronics 34(1), 92–98 (2012)
7. Lin, D.F., Fan, J.F., Qi, Z.K., et al.: Analysis and improvement of missile three-loop autopilots. Journal of Systems Engineering and Electronics 20(4), 844–851 (2009)
8. Fan, J.F., Lin, D.F., Zh, S., et al.: Control of static unstable airframes. Journal of Systems Engineering and Electronics 21(6), 1063–1071 (2010)
9. Mracek, C.P., Ridgely, D.B.: Missile longitudinal autopilots: comparison of multiple three loop topologies. In: AIAA Guidance, Navigation, and Control Conference and Exhibit, San Francisco, pp. 917–928 (2005)
10. Mracek, C.P., Ridgely, D.B.: Missile longitudinal autopilots: connections between optimal control and classical topologies. In: AIAA Guidance, Navigation, and Control Conference and Exhibit, San Francisco, pp. 698–727 (2005)
11. Fan, J.F., Xia, Q.L., Qi, Z.K.: Design and Comparison of Classical Topologies for Static Unstable Missile Autopilots. In: 2008 Chinese Control and Decision Conference, pp. 3659–3664 (2008)
12. Nesline, F.W., Nesline, M.L.: How autopilot requirements constrain the aerodynamic design of homing missiles. In: American Control Conference, San Diego, pp. 716–730 (1984)

Study on Holon Environment Model in Battle Deduction Simulation System

Hong Han[1,2*], Fengju Kang[1,2], Huizhen Yang[1,2], and Shengjie Wang[1,2]

[1] Marine College of Northwestern Polytechnical University, Xi'an, China
[2] National Key Laboratory of Underwater Information Process and Control, Xi'an, China
hanhong_1984@163.com

Abstract. The battle deduction simulation system is usually designed as MAS (Multi-Agent System). Environment modeling is considered as the most important process in constructing a MAS. The MRM (Multi-Resolution Modeling) technique is used to build the simulation entity models. In order to construct environment model with multi-resolution in the battle deduction simulation system, a classification of battlefield environment is proposed and a battlefield environment modeling method based on the concept of Holon is put forward. This method uses the cooperation of Holon to make environment model form a dynamic hierarchical structure, which has the characteristics of multi-resolution. This environment model is able to offer environmental information with corresponding resolution for the multi-resolution entity model in the battle deduction simulation system.

Keywords: Holon, battlefield environment, battle deduction, simulation, multi-resolution.

1 Introduction

The battle deduction simulation is a battle hierarchy of the war simulation. It's a typical complex system with large numbers of intelligent entities. These entities form a complex hierarchy by the countermeasure and cooperation among them or by the external command. And these entities advance the simulation system by the interaction among them [1]. According to the characteristic of the battle deduction simulation system, the system is designed as MAS (Multi-Agent System). It's favorable for the study of the characteristics of the complex system, such as intelligence, nonlinear and emergence. When constructing MAS, the environment, as a independent factor, has the function of providing the space for Agents, communicating with Agents and offer reference for the behavior of Agents. Thus the environment becomes a first-order abstraction in MAS [2]. At present, most research considered environment as a holistic structure. And this point of view restricted the interaction efficiency between Agent and environment. Sebastian Rodriguez considered the environment as a entity with network structure, posed a topology-based Holon environment model to solve the problem of

---

* Hong Han (1984-), male, doctoral graduate student, research in system simulation.

T. Xiao, L. Zhang, and S. Ma (Eds.): ICSC 2012, Part I, CCIS 326, pp. 166–171, 2012.

constructing a large scale environment model [3]. This model is suitable for the environment that has network topology, such as roads and traffic, whereas most environments in battle deduction haven't the network characteristic. And for there are lots of entities executing and interacting during the deduction, the MRM (Multi-Resolution Modeling) technique is used to ensure that entities distributed in different hierarchy could execute efficiently and interact correctly. By using MRM technique, the interactions between entities and environment may change alone with different resolution. To provide the proper environment information and interact with entities, the environment model must be flexible. To build the large scale and multi-layer environment model in the battle deduction simulation system, consequently posed a Holon-based dynamic hierarchical environment modeling technique.

2   Holon

What is Holon? The word was coined by Arthur Koestler in his book *The Ghost in the Machine*. It means *whole-part* literally. Holon describes a phenomenon that an independent entity, which contains several parts, is a part of another entity. *Whole* means an entity is independent and has certain functions. It can cooperate with other *wholes*. *Part* means an entity is part of a *whole*. *Part* is controlled by *whole*. Each *part* has certain functions, and the cooperation of *parts* form the function of *whole*. According to all the above, Holon is a recursive concept. One Holon contains several Holons, meanwhile, this Holon is a part of some other Holon.

In the familiar biology, a organism is formed by some entities with certain functions and objectives. For instance, cell always acts according to its own rules. Many independent cells form an organ which acts according to its own rules, and different organs form an organism finally. See from this example, cells and organs both have autonomy and cooperatives. They belong to the different hierarchies of a organism. Organ is a cellulous whole, meanwhile, is a part of an organism. This entity in hierarchy, which has the concept of whole and part synchronously, is a typical Holon.

From analysis above, the two basic characteristics of Holon are autonomy and cooperative. One Holon tends to be a part of another Holon while it keeps its own independent characteristics. This tendency masks a holarchy with specific object have a dynamic hierarchy. The layer of this hierarchy is changed by observer's viewpoint. The layer of a Holon will keep changing between whole and part till the observer's viewpoint doesn't change anymore. By this dynamic hierarchy, holarchy shows a relative independence on different granularity levels. But see from the whole viewpoint, the characteristics of one granularity provide service for the higher level.

3   Holonic Environment Model in Battle Deduction Simulation System

The analysis of the modeling object is required before building the Holon environment model of the battle deduction simulation system. In the battle deduction simulation system, the environment where entities execute can be divided into five types: terrestrial environment, marine environment, atmospheric environment, electromagnetic environment and space environment [4]. The terrestrial environment includes position, elevation, surface friction coefficient, surface temperature, humidity and the surface material, and other important parameters; The marine environment includes position, depth, water temperature, salinity, sea water visibility, sea surface wind speed, waves, noise, topography, and other important parameters; The atmospheric environment includes position, elevation, climate, visibility, and other important parameters; The electromagnetic environment includes position, elevation and electromagnetic field, and other important parameters; The space environment includes position, elevation, space object, high-energy particles, the sun's activity and electromagnetic activity, and other important parameters.

In order to interact with Agent entities in simulation environment, consider environment model as an active entity. Every environment model contains certain areas of the battlefield environment data, and also can interact with Agent entities. The environment model can receive the effect from Agent entities, feed back the physical effectiveness to Agent entities, and update their own internal state based on a true environment evolution rules constantly. The environment model needs to cooperate with other ones to create new functions and characteristics. According to above analysis, set up five different environment Holons as shown in figure 1. As can be seen from the graph, these five environment Holons are similar in function. All of them have function of receiving interaction, feedback and evolution, but internal parameters and methods are different. So in order to ensure the flexibility of model design, proposed a basic environmental model. The five environment Holons are expanded from the basic environmental model, each environment Holon can be designed respectively according to the characteristics of oneself.

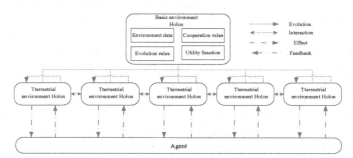

Fig. 1. Environment Holons in the battle deduction simulation system

After the establishment of single Holon environment model, now consider how to use the Holon characteristics to provide a dynamic hierarchical environment model for multi-resolution entities in the battle deduction simulation system. The so-called multi-resolution modeling technology refers to creating models with different precision for the same object, and ensures that the models with different resolution of the object could keep the consistency of the features in time and space during the process of operation. In the battle deduction simulation system, the resolution of the simulation object model from high to low respectively is: equipment level, platform level and formation level. According to different resolution of the entity, the environment model must also provide Holon with corresponding resolution. In the simulation operation, the entity of equipment level such as missile, etc, the position change of the entity is fast, and entity such as sensor, requires environment data of high accuracy. But their function range of the environment generally is small, so the environment Holon should have data of high precision and data exchange capacity of high speed, and it contains environment of small range. The entity of platform level such as ship, plane, involves environment with larger scale, but the environment data accuracy is reduced and the position change of entity is slower, so the environment Holon should have data of general accuracy and data exchange ability of general speed. The entity of formation level involves the environment with the largest scale, environment data accuracy is further reduced, therefore the environment Holon has a minimum data precision and data exchange ability, but the maximum range. After modeling the environment Holon with different accuracy, formed a hierarchy as shown in figure 2. During the system execution, entities with different resolution could request data and interact with environment Holon of corresponding levels.

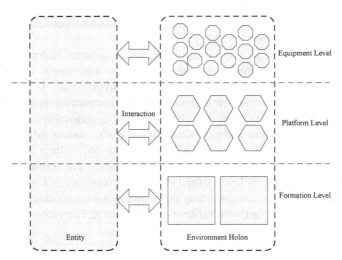

Fig. 2. Multi-resolution hierarchy of environment Holon

In the process of simulation, how does the environment Holon provide models of different resolution? Actually we just need to establish environment Holon with the highest resolution, which is of the equipment level. When the entity of the platform level needs to interact with environment Holon, using the collaborative properties of Holon, a platform level environment Holon is formed by the cooperation of the lower level Holon. The new environment Holon model aggregates the high resolution model, reduces the accuracy of data and enlarges the environment scale. Thus, this new environment Holon is suitable for the platform level. By the same token, when the entity of the formation level needs to interact with environment Holon, an environment Holon with larger scale will be formed by the cooperation of Holon formed by the platform level Holon. This cooperation between environment Holons should be transparent to simulation entities.

In the point of view of entities, no matter what environment Holon level they need, the environment model can accurately provide the environment Holon meets their requirements of the resolution. So, the aggregation method, which forms higher level environment Holon by the cooperation of lower level Holon, makes the environment model have a dynamic hierarchy. And this method provides a multi-resolution environment model for the battle deduction simulation system.

Meanwhile, the environment Holon of the highest level is essentially the one of bottom level. It just shows the features of a high-level Holon through the cooperation of low level Holon. The high level entities don't need to know the detail of the low level operation, because they just need to interact with the environment Holon of corresponding level. But in the bottom level, models are always running, because it needs the cooperation of multiple Holon of bottom level to guarantee the validity of high level Holon model. This hierarchy is very similar to the relationship between cells and organs of an organism. When we need to study the function of an organ, we don't care about how the cells within this organ work. But just because of those cells work properly, they make this organ has its own function. Therefore, Holonic environment model primely solve the consistency problem between environment models of different resolution.

And one more thing to be noticed, the cooperation between Holon environments not only provides an environment model that has dynamic levels, but also is the foundation for the correct operating of the battlefield environment. As mentioned, the Holon models of the battlefield environment are built according to five types, and these Holon models also interact with each other. Such as atmospheric change affects some parameters of the land and sea. Cooperation exists among different types of Holon environments, and this cooperation is same as the cooperation of single Holon environment, it only exists in the same level Holon. The correctness of the cooperation between different levels of the Holon environment can not be guaranteed because of the difference of its containing range and performance characteristics, and this kind of cooperation is not reasonable and unnecessary. Therefore, the interaction between the different level Holon environments is banned.

4   Conclusion

This paper put forward a battlefield environment modeling method based on the concept of Holon. This method uses the cooperation of Holon to make environment model form a dynamic hierarchical structure, which has the characteristics of multi-resolution. This environment model is able to offer environmental information of corresponding resolution for the multi-resolution entity model in the battle deduction simulation system. This method provides a new modeling method for the development of the environment model in the battle deduction simulation system. And this paper is only a summary of this method, the specific technical details will be introduced in a future paper.

Acknowledgments. This paper is supported by the foundation of "National key laboratory of underwater information process and control Foundation (9140c2305041001)", "Foundational Research of Northwestern Polytechnical University (NWPU2011JC0242)", and "Supporting Technology of Shipping Pre-research (11J4.1.1)".

References

1. Han, H., Kang, F., Yao, L.: The Framework Design of Weapon Effectiveness Evaluation Simulation System for Navy. Fire Control and Command Control 12, 195–197 (2011)
2. Weyns, D., Schumacher, M., Ricci, A., Viroli, M., Holvoet, T.: Environments in multiagent systems. The Knowledge Engineering Review 20(2), 127–141 (2005)
3. Rodriguez, S., Hilaire, V., Koukam, A.: Holonic Modelling of Environments for Situated Multi-Agent Systems. In: The Second International Workshop on Environments for Multiagent Systems, Utrecht, Netherlands (2005)
4. Ye, C.: Research on Key Techniques of Multi-agent Platform for Distributed Simulation of Complex System. National University of Defense Technology, Changsha, Hunan, P.R.China (2006)
5. Koestler, A.: The Ghost in the Machine. M. Hutchinson (1967)
6. Rodriguez, S., Hilaire, V., Koukam, A.: Towards a methodological framework for holonic multi-agent systems. In: Fourth International Workshop of Engineering Societies in the Agents World, Imperial College London, UK (EU), pp. 29–31 (Octubre 2003)

Improved Virtual Leader Based Formation Control for Nonholonomic Multi-UUV

Lili Hao[1, 2], Hao Gu[1], Fengju Kang [1, 2], Huizhen Yang[1, 2], and Xiaolong Yang [1, 2]

[1] School of Marine, Northwestern Polytechnical University, Xi'an 710072, China
[2] National Key Laboratory of Underwater Information Process and Control,
Xi'an 710072, China
onceinthemoon@163.com

Abstract. In older to solve the potential singularity problem brought from the polar coordinate representation, and eliminate the offset caused by off-axis point in the feedback linearization formation control approach, a novel improved virtual leader based formation control for nonholonomic multi-UUV is proposed, the kinematics model of which is established using Cartesian coordinates. Then, the global-level formation control is transformed into the problem that the followers track their virtual leader. Next, a globally dynamic feedback tracking controller is designed based on the direct Lyapunov method. Finally, simulation results are given to demonstrate that the proposed model and controller are feasible.

Keywords: nonholonomic multi-UUV, improved virtual leader method, formation control, direct Lyapunov method.

1   Introduction

Each UUV in the multi-UUV system is an independent agent, how to coordinate and control them is the key to improve the overall performance of the system. Recently, there has been much research activity focusing on coordinated control of multiple autonomous vehicles. As one of the research topics, the formation control is studied extensively with the applications in mobile robots [1], unmanned aerial vehicles (UAVs) [2, 3], and autonomous underwater vehicles (AUVs) [4]. A variety of strategies and approaches have been proposed for formation control in the literature. They can be roughly categorized as behavior based [5], leader-following [6, 7], and virtual structure [8], reinforcement learning [9], to name a few.

The behavior based approach is to assign the behavior which is derived by weighting relative importance of each behavior (e.g. obstacle and collision avoidance, target attraction). This strategy is simple but difficult to analyze its behavioral performance mathematically and guarantee precise. The leader-following method only needs to specify the leader's trajectory and the desired relative positions and orientations between leaders and followers. Thus, there is no obvious feedback. The virtual structure approach can evolve as a rigid body in a given direction with some given orientation and maintain a rigid geometric relationship among multiple UUVs,

T. Xiao, L. Zhang, and S. Ma (Eds.): ICSC 2012, Part I, CCIS 326, pp. 172–180, 2012.

however, requiring the formation to act as a virtual structure limits the potential applications. Reinforcement learning method has a higher intelligence and adaptive capacity, but it is slow to learn. In this paper, a method combining the virtual structure and leader-follower formation control for multi-UUV system is proposed, namely virtual leader control method. It is not only simple to implement, but also making the formation control problem as an extension trajectory tracking problem, and introducing feedback to ensure the stability.

The main challenge of the virtual leader method comes from the selecting of representation of the kinematics model and the formation control method. A few models have been presented in the literature [10, 11], which primarily use a polar coordinate based representation. However, the polar coordinate representation has a potential singularity problem, i.e., the denominator of the derived controller may be zero at sometime instant. But, Cartesian coordinate representation is found that it can avoid the possible singular points of polar coordinate representation [12].A controller by input-output linearization is presented in [13], but it need to select an off-axis point in the forward direction of UUV, whereas the off-axis leads to offset, and this method is only stable locally. A globally stable but complicated sliding mode or backstepping based controller is presented in [14, 15]. In this paper we exploit Cartesian coordinate presentation and derive a new kinematics model for the virtual leader configuration of nonholonomic multi-UUV system. Based on this new model, we use the direct Lyapunov method to derive a globally, not just locally, stable controller for the whole system.

This paper is organized as follows. In Section 2, we derive a new kinematics model using Cartesian coordinates for the virtual leader configuration of nonholonomic multi-UUV system. In Section 3, a globally stable controller is designed using the direct Lyapunov method. The stability of the whole system is analyzed as well. The simulation results are included in the section 4 to analyze the proposed formation control algorithms. Finally, this paper ends with conclusions and future work in Section 5.

2 Modeling for the Virtual Leader Configuration of Nonholonomic Multi-UUV System

2.1 Formation Shape Description

In the multi-UUV formation system, each UUV not only is independent, but also should know whom it should follow, and its position in the specified formation, therefore we defined the formation parameter matrix H as follows:

$$H = \left[H_{s1} \, H_{s2}...H_{sn} \right]_{3 \times n}, s = 1,2,3$$
$$H_{sj} = \left[i \quad l_{ijd} \quad \psi_{ijd} \right]^T, j = 1,2,...,n \tag{1}$$

Where, H_{sj} is described as the formation information of UUV R_j, which consists of three parts: i is the number of leading UUV, l_{ijd} and ψ_{ijd} are the desired relative distance and angle between the leader and follower, respectively.

There can be only one leader, who is responsible for navigating motion for other UUVs in the system. It also can be composed of two or more leaders, that is, there can be some local leader- follower relationships. But we must notice that one follower at least should be corresponding to a leader. The designed formation shape description has two advantages: one is that it can achieve the topology construction, and increase the flexibility for changing formation shape; the other is that this method designs priority for each UUV, to an extent. It does not affect the overall formation effect when one UUV fails, then the fault tolerance of the system is improved.

2.2   System Modeling Using Cartesian Coordinates

In this paper, we just consider the planar motion of UUV. The basic kinematics model of UUV can be written as

$$\dot{P} = \begin{bmatrix} \dot{X} & \dot{Y} & \dot{\psi} \end{bmatrix}^{T} = \begin{bmatrix} \cos\psi & 0 \\ \sin\psi & 0 \\ 0 & 1 \end{bmatrix} \begin{bmatrix} v & w \end{bmatrix}^{T} . \qquad (2)$$

Where, P is the matrix which includes the position and yaw angle in the inertial coordinates(X-Y), the linear velocity and angular velocity is denoted by $q = \begin{bmatrix} v & w \end{bmatrix}^{T}$.

UUV here has the nonholonomic constraint and satisfies the pure rolling without sliding movement, namely

$$\begin{cases} \dot{X}\sin\psi - \dot{Y}\cos\psi = 0 \\ \dot{X}\cos\psi + \dot{Y}\sin\psi = v \end{cases} . \qquad (3)$$

Usually, when the multi-UUV executes tasks, the commander system will preplan the path for the main UUV according to the task demand and environment information. Then the leader UUV navigates on a desired waypoint, its corresponding followers should form the desired relative distance and angles with the leader finally. Therefore, we use the virtual leader to represent the desired point of the follower in the formation. The virtual leader configuration of two UUVs is shown as Fig.1.

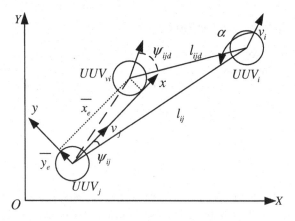

Fig. 1. Virtual leader configuration of two UUVs

From Fig.1, we can get the position and yaw angle of virtual leader by formula (4)

$$P_{vi} = \begin{bmatrix} X_{vi} \\ Y_{vi} \\ \psi_{vi} \end{bmatrix} = \begin{bmatrix} X_i - l_{ijd}\cos(\psi_i - \psi_{ijd}) \\ Y_i - l_{ijd}\sin(\psi_i - \psi_{ijd}) \\ \psi_i \end{bmatrix} . \quad (4)$$

Where (X_i, Y_i), ψ_i are the position and yaw angle of leader, respectively. (X_{vi}, Y_{vi}), ψ_{vi} are the position and yaw angle of virtual leader, respectively. l_{ijd} and ψ_{ijd} are the desired relative distance and angles with the leader.

It can be seen from Fig.1, if we wish the following UUV_j keep the desired relative distance l_{ijd} and angle ψ_{ijd} with the leader, we can design to control the UUV_j tracking the virtual leader UUV_{vi} instead.

Define three error states as

$$P_e = \begin{bmatrix} X_e \\ Y_e \\ \psi_e \end{bmatrix} = \begin{bmatrix} X_{vi} - X_j \\ Y_{vi} - Y_j \\ \psi_{vi} - \psi_j \end{bmatrix} = \begin{bmatrix} X_i - l_{ijd}\cos(\psi_i - \psi_{ijd}) - X_j \\ Y_i - l_{ijd}\sin(\psi_i - \psi_{ijd}) - Y_j \\ \psi_{vi} - \psi_j \end{bmatrix} . \quad (5)$$

To eliminate such singular points caused by the polar coordinates (v_i, α), we next assign a Cartesian coordinate system (x-y) fixed on the follower body UUV_j, as shown in Fig.1. When the follower rotates, we have a rotation of the x-y axes. Then, we can obtain the transform matrix T as follows:

$$T = \begin{bmatrix} \cos\psi_j & \sin\psi_j & 0 \\ -\sin\psi_j & \cos\psi_j & 0 \\ 0 & 0 & 1 \end{bmatrix} . \quad (6)$$

In order to describe the relative position between the virtual leader and follower in Cartesian coordinates, we need to project the relative distance of the follower from the virtual leader along the x and y directions. Thus, we denote the position and attitude error in the Cartesian coordinates $\overline{P}_e = \begin{bmatrix} \overline{x}_e & \overline{y}_e & \overline{\psi}_e \end{bmatrix}^T = TP_e$. Then the error dynamics can be written as

$$\dot{\overline{P}}_e = \begin{bmatrix} \dot{\overline{x}}_e \\ \dot{\overline{y}}_e \\ \dot{\overline{\psi}}_e \end{bmatrix} = \begin{bmatrix} \omega_j \overline{y}_e + v_i \cos\overline{\psi}_e - v_j + l_{ijd}\omega_i \sin(\overline{\psi}_e - \psi_{ijd}) \\ -\omega_j \overline{x}_e + v_i \sin\overline{\psi}_e - l_{ijd}\omega_i \cos(\overline{\psi}_e - \psi_{ijd}) \\ \omega_i - \omega_j \end{bmatrix} . \quad (7)$$

The global trajectory tracking for multi-UUV can be considered that designing the control laws for $q_j = \begin{bmatrix} v_j & w_j \end{bmatrix}^T$ to make $\lim_{t \to 0} \begin{bmatrix} \overline{x_e} & \overline{y_e} & \overline{\psi_e} \end{bmatrix}^T = 0$. The frame of tracking control system is shown as Fig.2.

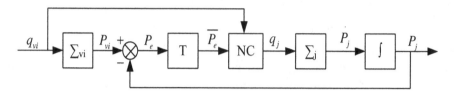

Fig. 2. Frame of tracking control system

In Fig.2, the NC module is nonlinear controller, namely the designing controller in the next section. Σ_j is the controlled UUV_j system, as formula (2). Σ_{vi} represents the kinematics model of virtual leader.

3   Controller Design by Direct Lyapunov

In section 2, we proposed a virtual leader based formation control method. The kinematics model is established in Cartesian coordinate system. This method contributes directly to transform the formation control problem into the tracking problem. So in this section, we focus on designing the tracking control law.

To use the direct Lyapunov method, we select a candidate Lyapunov function as follows:

$$V(\overline{x}_e, \overline{y}_e, \overline{\psi}_e) = \frac{1}{2}\overline{x}_e^2 + \frac{1}{2}\overline{y}_e^2 + \frac{1}{2}\overline{\psi}_e^2 \quad . \tag{8}$$

$$
\begin{aligned}
\dot{V}(\overline{x}_e, \overline{y}_e, \overline{\psi}_e) &= \overline{x}_e \dot{\overline{x}}_e + \overline{y}_e \dot{\overline{y}}_e + \overline{\psi}_e \dot{\overline{\psi}}_e \\
&= \overline{x}_e \left(v_i \cos\overline{\psi}_e - v_j + l_{ijd}\omega_i \sin(\overline{\psi}_e - \psi_{ijd}) \right) + \overline{\psi}_e \left(\omega_i - \omega_j + \overline{y}_e v_i \int_0^1 \cos(s\overline{\psi}_e)ds \right. \\
&\quad \left. + \overline{y}_e l_{ijd}\omega_i \int_0^1 \sin(s\overline{\psi}_e - \psi_{ijd})ds - \overline{y}_e l_{ijd}\omega_i \cos\psi_{ijd} \right)
\end{aligned} \tag{9}
$$

Clearly $V \geq 0$, and only when $\begin{bmatrix} \overline{x}_e & \overline{y}_e & \overline{\psi}_e \end{bmatrix}^T = \begin{bmatrix} 0 & 0 & 0 \end{bmatrix}^T$, $V = 0$. Select $q_j = \begin{bmatrix} v_j & w_j \end{bmatrix}^T$, where

$$v_j = v_i \cos\overline{\psi}_e + l_{ijd}\omega_i \sin(\overline{\psi}_e - \psi_{ijd}) + k_1 \overline{x}_e \quad . \tag{10}$$

$$\omega_j = \omega_i + \overline{y}_e v_i \int_0^1 \cos(s\overline{\psi}_e)ds + \overline{y}_e l_{ijd}\omega_i \int_0^1 \sin(s\overline{\psi}_e - \psi_{ijd})ds - \overline{y}_e l_{ijd}\omega_i \cos\psi_{ijd} + k_2\overline{\psi}_e \tag{11}$$

In which, $k_1, k_2 > 0$.

Proposition: for any continuous and bounded linear velocity v_i and angular velocity ω_i of leader, the proposed control laws in (10) and (11) can make the system (7) stable, namely, as $t \to \infty$, $\begin{bmatrix} \overline{x}_e & \overline{y}_e & \overline{\psi}_e \end{bmatrix}^T = \begin{bmatrix} 0 & 0 & 0 \end{bmatrix}^T$ is globally asymptotically stable equilibrium point.

Substituting (10) and (11) into (9), we have $V(\overline{x}_e, \overline{y}_e, \overline{\psi}_e) = -k_1 \overline{x}_e^2 - k_2 \overline{\psi}_e^2 \leq 0$.

Therefore, according to the Lyapunov stability theorem of autonomous systems, we find that the proposed control laws in (10) and (11) can make the followers approach their virtual leader, achieve and maintain the relative distance and angle between the leader and followers as desired as well. In other words, the whole system is stable.

Due to lack of global information, the position error $\begin{pmatrix} \overline{x}_e & \overline{y}_e \end{pmatrix}$ is not easily measured or obtained directly. Then, we can educe $\begin{pmatrix} \overline{x}_e & \overline{y}_e \end{pmatrix}$ by the relative distance l_{ij} and angle ψ_{ij} between the follower and leader, then, in actual condition, we can use formula (12) to instead.

$$\begin{cases} \overline{x}_e = -l_{ijd} \cos(\psi_e - \psi_{ijd}) + l_{ij} \cos \psi_{ij} \\ \overline{y}_e = -l_{ijd} \sin(\psi_e - \psi_{ijd}) - l_{ij} \sin \psi_{ij} \end{cases}. \tag{12}$$

4   Simulation

To verify the present new model and controller, we simulate the motion of five UUVs as shown in Fig.3. The main parameters which include formation matrix H, initial positions $\begin{bmatrix} X_0 & Y_0 \end{bmatrix}^T$ of the five UUVs, and control law parameters k_1, k_2 are set as follows:

$$H = \begin{bmatrix} 0 & 1 & 1 & 1 & 1 \\ 0 & 200 & 200 & 400 & 400 \\ 0 & -\dfrac{\pi}{6} & \dfrac{\pi}{6} & -\dfrac{\pi}{6} & \dfrac{\pi}{6} \end{bmatrix}, \begin{bmatrix} X_0 \\ Y_0 \end{bmatrix} = \begin{bmatrix} 2500 & 2800 & 2400 & 2500 & 2000 \\ 2500 & 2400 & 2200 & 2300 & 2500 \end{bmatrix}, k_1 = 0.5, k_2 = 0.001$$

The initial scenario is set as following: at first, UUV1 receives the command from the higher level and becomes a leader going along a straight line with slope $K = 1$ and at a constant linear speed $v_i = 30m/s$, angular velocity $\omega_i = 0$ rad/s. When $X_1 = 3500m$, the angular velocity will be changed to $\omega_i = -2\pi/1000$ rad/s, and the followers form and keep a constant relative angle and distance with respect to the leader UUV1.

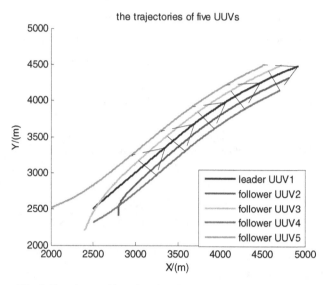

Fig. 3. Forming and keeping the chevron shape for the five UUVs

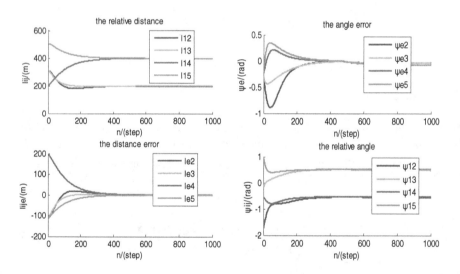

Fig. 4. The relative distance and error   **Fig. 5.** The angle error and relative angle

From Fig3, we can find that the UUV1 could sail according to the initial scenario, and the other UUVs formed and kept the chevron shape with the UUV1 successfully. In order to analyze the following precision, the curves of relative distance l_{ij} , relative angle ψ_{ij} and error matrix P_e is shown in Fig4 and Fig5. It can be seen that the other UUVs can follow the leader and keep the desired the relative angle and distance accurately, and the designed model and controller are demonstrated correct.

5   Conclusion

In this paper, we present an improved virtual leader based formation control for nonholonomic multi-UUV. The contributions of this method are that a new kinematics model is established by using Cartesian coordinates, and a globally stable controller is derived using the Lyapunov direct method. The benefits of our proposal lie in eliminating the potential singularity brought from polar coordinate representation and offset caused by off-axis point in the common feedback linearization formation control approach. The effectiveness of proposed method and controller is verified by simulation results finally. This research will provide technical support for developing the multi-UUV combat simulation system. The future research work will focus on taking into consideration of the dynamic model of UUV, and communication delay.

Acknowledgments. This work is supported by the National Key Laboratory fund of Underwater Information Process and Control, China (9140C2305041001) and the ship pre-research support technology foundation, China (11J4.1.1).

References

1. Cao, K.-C.: Formation Control of Multiple Nonholonomic Mobile Robots Based on Cascade Design. In: 48th IEEE Conference on Decision and Control and 28th Chinese Control Conference, Shanghai, pp. 8340–8344 (2009)
2. Karimoddini, A., Lin, H., Chen, B.M., Lee, T.H.: Hybrid formation control of the Unmanned Aerial Vehicles. Mechatronics 21, 886–898 (2011)
3. Hu, Z.-W., Liang, J.-H., Chen, L., Wu, B.: A Hierarchical Architecture for Formation Control of Multi-UAV. Procedia Engineering 29, 3846–3851 (2012)
4. Xiang, X., Liu, C., Lapierre, L., Jouvencel, B.: Synchronized Path Following Control of Multiple Homogenous Underactuated AUVs. J. Syst. Sci. Complex. 25, 71–89 (2012)
5. Antonelli, G., Arrichiello, F., Chiaverini, S.: The NSB control: a behavior-based approach for multi-robot systems. PALADYN Journal of Behavioral Robotics 1, 48–56 (2010)
6. Morbidi, F., Consolini, L., Prattichizzo, D., Tosques, M.: Leader-Follower Formation Control as a Disturbance Decoupling Problem. In: Proceedings of the European Control Conference, Kos, Greece, pp. 1492–1497 (2007)
7. Li, X., Xiao, J.: Robot Formation Control in Leader-Follower Motion Using Direct Lyapunov Method. International Journal of intelligent Control Systems 10, 244–250 (2005)
8. van den Broek, T.H.A., van de Wouw, N., Nijmeijer, H.: Formation Control of Unicycle Mobile Robots: a Virtual Structure Approach. In: 48th IEEE Conference on Decision and Control and 28th Chinese Control Conference, Shanghai, pp. 8328–8333 (2009)
9. Akramizadeh, A., Menhaj, A., Menhaj, M.-B.: Multi-agent Reinforcement Learning in Extensive Form Games with Complete Information. In: 2009 IEEE Symposium on Adaptive Dynamic Programming and Reinforcement Learning, pp. 205–211 (2009)
10. Cui, R., Ge, S.S., How, B.V.E., Choo, Y.S.: Leader-Follower Formation Control of Underactuated AUVs with Leader Position Measurement. In: 2009 IEEE International Conference on Robotics and Automation, Kobe, Japan, pp. 979–984 (2009)

11. Guo, J., Lin, Z.: Adaptive Leader-Follower Formation Control for Autonomous Mobile Robots. In: Marriott Waterfront, Baltimore, MD, USA, pp. 6822–6827 (2010)
12. Raghuwaiya, K.S., Singh, S.: Formation Control of Mobile Robots. World Academy of Science, Engineering and Technology 60, 762–767 (2011)
13. Dai, Y., Tran, V.-H., Xu, Z., Lee, S.-G.: Leader-follower formation control of multi-robots by using a stable tracking control method. In: First International Conference of Advances in Swarm Intelligence, pp. 291–298 (2010)
14. Defoort, M., Floquet, T., Kökösy, A., Perruquetti, W.: Sliding-Mode Formation Control for Cooperative Autonomous Mobile Robots. IEEE Transactions on Industrial Electronics 55, 3944–3953 (2008)
15. Chen, Y.-Y., Tian, Y.-P.: A backstepping design for directed formation control of three-coleader agents in the plane. International Journal of Robust and Nonlinear Control 19, 729–745 (2009)

An Image Processing Method for Grains Counting

Wencheng Wang[1,2,*] and L. Wang[2]

[1] College of Information and Control Engineering, Weifang University, Weifang China
[2] School of Control Science and Engineering, Shandong University, Jinan, China
wwcwfu@126.com

Abstract. In the process of quality analysis of grains, number counting is one of the key steps for agricultural production. After the introduction of the traditional counting methods, an approach based on computer version and image processing technique is proposed in this paper. The overall structure including hardware and software of system is introduced firstly. Then, the image processing methods are described in details, which are mainly composed of gray transformation, denoising, binary conversion, mathematical morphology analysis, et al.. Finally, an experiment is conducted to test the validity of the algorithm, and the result shows that this method is effective and can realize the automatic grain counting.

Keywords: image processing, grain counting, computer version, morphology.

1   Introduction

Grain seeds selecting plays an important role in agricultural production, it is one of the main methods to increase grain yield and quality [1-2]. So, how to count the number of grains quickly and analyze the grains quality exactly has been paid more and more attention in recent years. In general, the grain counting step is accomplished by manual, although it can ensure accuracy to some extent, it is slowly and consumes a lot of manpower resources. If the eyes work for a long time, that will cause fatigue and then result in large counting errors. Although semi-automatic photoelectric counter appeared in subsequence, it is still easy to aging hardware and has poor accuracy, which will bring about great uncertainty to the quality estimation of grains [3]. With the rapid development of information technology, computer vision detecting technology has been used in the quality detecting of some particles by scholars. Inspired by this, this paper presents an automatic grain counting method based on computer version and image processing technology. It can not only solve the difficulties of the traditional manual counting, but also improve the working efficiency, which is significant for improve the quality of agricultural products[4].

The rest of this paper is organized as follows. Section 2 introduces the framework of hardware and principle of system. The next section describes the

---

* Corresponding author.

T. Xiao, L. Zhang, and S. Ma (Eds.): ICSC 2012, Part I, CCIS 326, pp. 181–185, 2012.

key steps of image processing methods, which can realize the grain counting through a series of operations. In section 4, some experimental results are analyzed with some real examples. Finally, the last section gives some concluding remarks.

2   Hardware of System

As shown in Fig.1, The physical hardware of system is mainly composed of image acquisition unit, image analysis unit, and auxiliary unit. Image acquisition unit includes light source, camera and image acquisition card, it can get the digital image for processing. Image analysis unit mainly composed of computer and application software, it is the core of grain counting system. Auxiliary unit includes vibrating mechanism and control system, it can make the grains distribute evenly.

The working process of system is as follows. Firstly the grains are put into the container, then the vibrating mechanism works to make the grain spreading out uniformly; After that, the digital camera acquires grain information; Image acquisition card is installed in the computer's motherboard expansion slot, it translates the signals to digital information and sends them to computer; Because of the uncertainty and differences of illumination in cross-section of each particle, so the light source is often used for obtain the better performance[5-7]. In addition to this, the printer is sometime used as the output device.

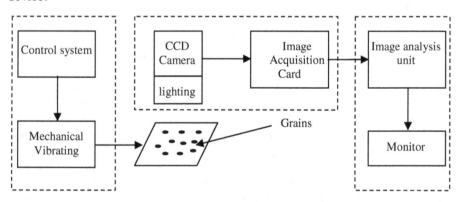

Fig. 1. The whole structure of system

3   Software Design

In this system, the software design is very important. It is mainly composed of image gray transformation, denoising, binarization, labeling processing, et al.. They are described in the following section in detail.

3.1   Gray Transformation

Because the acquired image by digital camera is a color image, namely RGB(Red, Green and Blue) image with color and brightness information, it is relatively a time consuming task. So it needs changing to gray image. The essence of transforming RGB image to gray image is to calculate gray pixel value I of gray image by 3 components R, G and B of a pixel[8-10]. The computation formula is as follows.

$$I = \omega_R \times R + \omega_G \times G + \omega_B \times B \qquad (1)$$

Where $\omega_R = 0.30$, $\omega_G = 0.59$ and $\omega_B = 0.11$ are the weight values of components R, G and B, respectively. Since the human eyes are the most sensitive to green and the minimum sensitive to blue, so when $\omega_G > \omega_R > \omega_B$, it will obtain a reasonable gray image. Fig. 3 shows the original image and the gray image after gray transform.

3.2   Image Denoising and Enhancement

During the course of obtaining images, due to various factors, the resulting image will always infected with some noise information more or less, which will deteriorate the image quality of the information. So, it needs denoising. In this work, median filtering is adopt for reducing the noise. That is, using the window with odd points, the value of center point is instead with the median in this window.

The formula is as follows.

$$g(x, y) = median\{ f(i - k, j - l), (k, l) \in W\} \qquad (2)$$

Where W is the window selected, which is with the size of 3×3, 5×5 or 7×7, et al.. This method can restrain disturbing pulses and point like noise and keep image edge better.

3.3   Image Binarization

Binarization processing is used for distinguishing the background and objectives clearly. It exist many methods, such as bimodal method, iterative method, OTSU method, gray stretch method et al.. Because the processed image histogram has two peaks obviously, the foreground and background gray scale are also similar to normal, so we select the histogram method to obtain the threshold. The common methods are bimodal method and iterative method. Iterative method's operation is stable, but with large operations; bimodal method is simple and easy to implement and suitable for online real-time image processing system.

Suppose original image is $f(x, y)$, Binary image is $g(x, y)$,threshold is T ,then:

$$g(x, y) = \begin{cases} 1 & f(x, y) \geq T \\ 0 & f(x, y) < T \end{cases} \tag{3}$$

3.4   Connected Components Labeling

In order to compute the number of grains, the binary image needs to do label processing. Label processing is giving the same label to the regions in which the pixels connected to each other. While the connectivity in different areas of the pixel given different labels. Therefore, the number of connected areas in an image will obtained through computing the number of labels in different areas.

4   Experiment

In order to test the validity of proposed method, we realized the algorithm with Matlab, and experiments are conducted according to this principle. The experiment result is shown in figure 2. Where Fig.2(a) is the source image, Fig.2(b) is the binary image, Fig.2(c) is the counting result of grains, and it is labeling with '+' . The counting number is 84, and it is agree with the actual number.

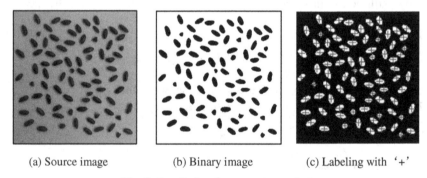

(a) Source image   (b) Binary image   (c) Labeling with '+'

Fig. 2. Result of grain parameter analysis

In the fact, there may be little counting error between computer and manual. The main reason is the overlapping among the grains. It needs better vibrating mechanism and segmentation method to overcome this problem.

5   Conclusions

In this paper, an approach based on computer version and image processing technique is proposed for grains counting. The overall structure system is introduced firstly. Then, the image processing methods are described in details, which are mainly composed of gray transformation, denoising, binary conversion, mathematical morphology analysis, et al.. Finally, the experiment is conducted to test the validity of the algorithm, and the result showed that this method is effective and can realize the automatic grain counting. This can not only reduce the work intensity of people, but increased the efficiency greatly. This method also can be applied to other fields and provide a reference for the other studies.

Acknowledgements. This work has been supported by Doctoral Scientific Research Foundation of Weifang University (2012BS26) and Technology Development Plan of Weifang City (2011119).

References

1. Wu, Y., Pan, Y.: Cereal grain size measurement based on image processing technology. In: 2010 International Conference on Intelligent Control and Information Processing, pp. 209–212 (2010)
2. Liu, T., Liu, G., Liu, T.: Ontology-based Grain Emergency System. Advances in Information Sciences and Service Sciences 3(5), 27–35 (2011)
3. Wang, W.C., Cui, X.J.: Study on Correction Method for Uneven Illumination Particle Image. Journal of Weifang University 11(6), 131–135 (2011)
4. Zhao, P., Li, Y.: Grain Counting Method Based On Image Processing. In: International Conference on Information Engineering and Computer Science (ICIECS), pp. 1–3 (2009)
5. Lu, Y.: Study for Automatic Grain Insect Counting System Based on Image Processing. Microcomputer Information 23(24), 311–312 (2008)
6. Song, Q., Xu, K., Xu, J.: Automatic counting technique for steel bars based on image processing. Iron and Steel 39(5), 34–37 (2004)
7. Huang, H., Hsiao, C.: Image Inpainting based on Illumination Variation and Structure Consistency. International Journal of Advancements in Computing Technology 3(6), 1–9 (2011)
8. Islam, M.J., Jonathan Wu, Q.M., Ahmadi, M., et al.: Investigating the Performance of Naive- Bayes Classifiers and K- Nearest Neighbor Classifiers. Journal of Convergence Information Technology 5(2), 13–37 (2010)
9. Weicker, J.: Efficient image segmentation using partial differential equations and morphology. Pattern Recognition 34(9), 1813–1824 (2001)
10. Zhou, Y., Zeng, L., Liu, J.: A method for automatic colony counting based on image processing and its realization. Journal of Data Acquisition & Processing 18(4), 460–464 (2003)

Design and Realization of Vision-Based Landing Simulation Verification System for UH Based on Vega Prime / MFC

Zhijia Sui[1,2], Yongmei Cheng[1], Tao Wang[2], Ruonan Kong[1,2], and Yazhou Yue[2]

[1] School of Automation, Northwestern Polytechnical University, Xi'an Shaanxi, 710072, China
[2] Science and Technology on Aircraft Control Laboratory,
Flight Automatic Control Research Institute, Xi'an Shaanxi, 710065, China
suizhijia@sina.com

Abstract. In order to reduce the number of flight test of the visual landing navigation verification system, reduce the cost of research and shorten the development cycle, the visualization simulation system based on virtual reality technology is demanded. An vision-based landing simulation verification system for UH based on Vega Prime / MFC was put forward. Firstly, the overall framework of the system was designed and the interaction among modules was introduced. Then a detailed description of each module function was given, and explanation of the cooperation target detection and UH position and orientation parameters were further carried out. Finally, a MFC-based Vega Prime view of the driver to achieve visualization of vision-based landing simulation verification system was developed. The simulation results show that the system can effectively unfold the cooperation target detection and UH position and orientation solving process in an intuitive, continuous and real-time pattern, and realize the simulation-testing function. It provides a good simulation platform for practical engineering applications.

Keywords: Vega Prime, MFC, Unmanned Helicopter, Vision-based Landing.

1 Introduction[1]

With the development of our aviation industry, UH (Unmanned Helicopter) with the characteristics of vertical takeoff and landing, hovering, low-altitude and low-speed flight is being applied in more and more areas. In the whole process of the UH flight navigation, safe landing is a very important stage [1]. Many conventional landing patterns, such as satellite navigation and guidance, ground control to guide, are susceptible to interference such as human factors and electronic countermeasures, which lead to navigation failure. Research of the safe autonomous landing navigation has become an urgent to settle key technology of the field of UAV [2].

[1] Foundation item: National Natural Science Foundation of China (61135001); Aeronautical Science Foundation of China(20100853010).

During the landing process of manned helicopter, the pilot can rely on the information provided by the eye to determine the position and orientation relationship between helicopter and landing platform. Using computer vision technology to simulate the pilot's vision and the vision algorithms on airborne camera to obtain the environmental scene image to process and analyze, we can estimate the relative position and attitude of the UH landing point, thus guide the UH to accomplish autonomous landing. Compared with other methods, vision-based landing navigation has many strong advantages, for example, high precision, low cost, flexibility and anti-electromagnetic interference [3].

Considering visual landing navigation technology is not yet mature, it needs to build its verification system. To reduce development costs, the number of flight tests and shorten the development cycle, a visualization simulation system based on advanced simulation technology and virtual reality is demanded [4].

The landing process of UH can be divided into several phases. This article assumes that the UH relies on GPS or other navigation device to be guided to the landing vicinity of the target, and ground target is always in the camera imaging plane. On this basis, taking use of the Vega Prime and MFC technology, we design and implement a vision-based landing simulation verification system for UH. The system shows the whole process of UH landing, and the vision-based landing simulation data are presented to the research and development personnel intuitively, which help them to verify the design of vision-based landing navigation.

2   System Framework Design

Vision-based landing simulation verification system for UH based on Vega Prime / MFC consists of four parts: Vega Prime module, MFC interface display module, cooperation target detection module, and UH pose decoding module. In the Vega Prime modules, we design a flight path of the helicopter approach and landing, use Creator modeling tools to establish an H-type cooperation target model and embed the camera model in aircraft model, and realize functions of shooting of camera and photos derived. In cooperation target detection module, we use the Harris corner detection algorithm, and realize corner extraction and sorting of the H-type cooperation target, and pass the detection results to the UH pose decoding module. In UH pose decoding module, we first use linear algorithm for solving the pose parameters. Then use the results of the linear solver as the initial value of the nonlinear algorithm for iterative optimization. Finally, the optimized results will be the six pose parameters of UH. MFC interface display module includes a system initialization interface and information display, which can realize very good human-machine interaction function and simulation results can be displayed in two, three-dimensional in a dynamic way. Figure 1 shows the structure chart of vision-based landing simulation verification system for UH based on Vega Prime / MFC.

Complex data exchange relationship is existed between each module of vision-based landing simulation verification system for UH. MFC interface displays module provides initialization settings for Vega Prime modules. Camera model of Vega Prime modules sends images to the cooperation target detection module, and split-screen displays the scene on the screen. Cooperation target detection module extracts and sorts of the corner for real-time image and the corner pixel information will be sent to the helicopter position and posture solver module. It uses camera model parameters and corner pixel information camera model parameters and corner pixel information to calculate the position and posture of the helicopter, and send the result to the MFC interface display module to be display. The relationship between the modules of data exchange is shown in Figure 2.

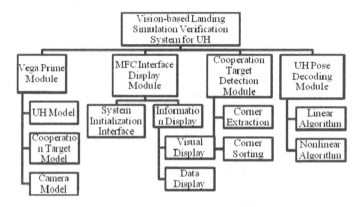

Fig. 1. Structure Chart of the System

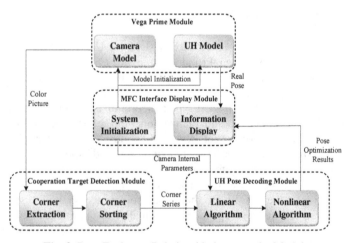

Fig. 2. Data Exchange Relationship between the Modules

3   Design of Modules

3.1   Vega Prime Module

Vega Prime (referred to as VP) and Creator is a perfect combination for visual simulation development launched by MultiGen-Paradigm [5]. VP can be used to render the battlefield simulation, entertainment simulation, urban simulation, training simulators and computing visualization and other areas of visual simulation, and then realize the join of environmental effect and the control of interactive. Creator is a real-time 3D modeling tools, which can build a rich three-dimensional visual model library [6].

The main function of VP module is to render the scene of the UH landing, including the sky, wind driving, cloud floating, airport topography, camera, cooperation target, UH trails and other special effects. VP module development process can be divided into three parts: building visual simulation model library, designing LynX Prime graphical interface and visual simulation application development. The design framework of VP module is shown in Figure 3.

Cooperation target model is produced by Creator, and then imports the .fit format into the VP module. At the same time, the camera model is embedded in the aircraft model. When it is far from cooperation target, camera works in anterior visual shooting mode, when near, the mode of the camera switches to look-down mode to shoot cooperation target. At the same time, we design and develop a UH landing trajectory of VC++, from the non-stop into hovering to close the goal of cooperation, and finally vertically landing, which truly performing the landing process of UH, providing the user a multi-screen multi-angle observation, so that observers are like roaming in the scene.

3.2   MFC Interface Display Module

The MFC interface display module shows the final result of the simulation verification of vision-based landing system. Thus, it's necessary to design the interface depending on the purpose of the simulation. The MFC interface display module of this system can initialize entities like camera and UH, and display three-dimension scene for the UH landing, environment, special effect, simulation result, etc. The concrete functions are as follows:

(1) Display the vision-based landing process of UH real-timely;
(2) Display images taken by the camera continuously in multi-screen;
(3) User can set parameters, change viewpoint and perspective dynamically with the system interactively through external equipment such as menu, keyboard and mouse;
(4) Display true pose of UH and their estimated value in the form of lists;

The design of system interface is based on single document frame of MFC, roughly divided into two parts: display area and control area. As shown in Figure 4.

The main display area of the interface is view window which is responsible for 3D scene display. The bottom left corner of the interface is the display area of UH pose, which shows the comparison result of true the value and the estimated value. So the simulation and verification function has been reached.

In the control area, the display part can control the beginning, suspension and exit of the simulation, observe switching of object and scene, choose viewpoint and perspective, show the size of windows. The main function of parameter initialization in the menu is to set the initial positions of UH, focal length of cameras, etc. As shown in Figure 5.

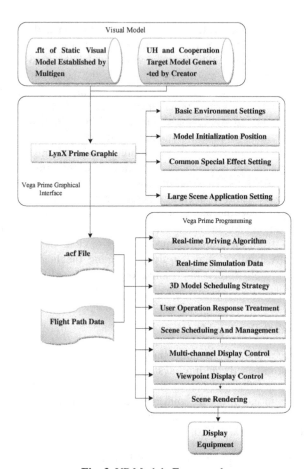

Fig. 3. VP Module Framework

Fig. 4. MFC Display

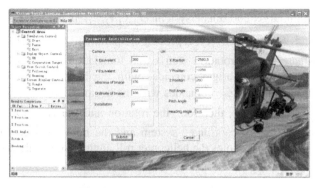

Fig. 5. Parameter Initialization

3.3   Cooperation Target Detection Module

The goal of cooperation target detection module is extracting image points which are feature corners from images correctly, rearranging the image points according to the actual order in cooperation target, getting feature corners coordinates in landing coordinate and image coordinate and their corresponding relations.

Firstly, scanning the given region progressively, separating red region of cooperation target from other regions by using threshold, generating grayscale images which have the same value with images red color. After that, executing Harris corner detection and ordering the corners, signing those corners which have maximum distance with triangle of cooperation target on H-type as 1. Then, scanning the columns and signing other corners. Finally, export pixel values of the corners according to priority. Figure 6 shows the results of corner detection and ordering.

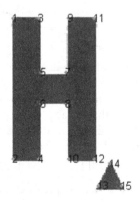

Fig. 6. Results of corner detection and ordering

3.4   UH Pose Decoding Module

The coordinate system of UH landing is shown in Figure 7. $O_B X_B Y_B Z_B$ is the body axes coordinate system; $O_C X_C Y_C Z_C$ is the camera coordinate system; $O_W X_W Y_W Z_W$

is the cooperation target coordinate system, $O_D X_D Y_D Z_D$ is the local plane coordinate of VP. R_W^C and T_W^C, respectively, represent cooperation target coordinate system to camera coordinate system rotation matrix and translation vector. At any time, the camera coordinate system origin coincides with the body axes coordinate system origin and the optical axis Z_C coincides with the negative direction of the body axis Z_B (pointing to the ground), therefore, the rotation and translation transform do not exist between the camera coordinate system and the body axes coordinate system. α, β, γ, respectively, denotes the helicopter roll angle, pitch angle and yaw angle.

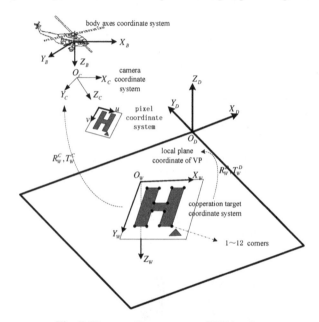

Fig. 7. The coordinate system of UH landing

This article uses 12 corners information of H-type to solve the position and attitude of UH. The landing icon is flat, in theory, as long as four points in general position (any three points are not collinear), there are non-zero solutions, the selection of 12 points is aim to smooth noise by the least square method.

Firstly, we utilize Courtney's method [7] to solve the helicopter rotation matrix R_W^C and translation vector T_W^C relative to the cooperation target coordinate system. Then we use R_W^C to solve the Euler angle, thus get the position and attitude parameters of camera relative to the landing platform. However, only six independent parameters are achievable, the linear solution process is severely affected by noise. In order to search for more accurate solution, a nonlinear method is utilized to optimize the results of the linear algorithm. This method has the advantage of simple projection relation, good robustness at the expense of several singular value decomposition and more computational burden.

Then convert the position and attitude parameters which relative to cooperation target coordinate system to the position and attitude parameters which relative to VP local coordinate system for the purpose of result comparison. According to the solution of rotation matrix $R_W^C = [r_{ij}]_{3\times3}$ and translation vector T_W^C by the method of linear algorithm, the UH position and attitude angle relative to cooperation target coordinate system are as follows:

$$[x_w \quad y_w \quad z_w]^T = -(R_W^C)^{-1}T_W^C \ . \tag{1}$$

$$\begin{cases} \alpha = -\arcsin r_{31} \\ \beta = \arctan(r_{32}/r_{33}) \\ \gamma = \arctan(r_{21}/r_{11}) \end{cases} . \tag{2}$$

As known, the plane of cooperation target coordinate system $O_W X_W Y_W$ is parallel to the plane of VP local coordinate system $O_D X_D Y_D$, included angle as θ, cooperation target coordinate origin in VP local coordinate system as $(t_{wx}^d, t_{wy}^d, t_{wz}^d)$. Thus the UH position under the VP local coordinate system is as follows:

$$\begin{bmatrix} x_d \\ y_d \\ z_d \end{bmatrix} = R_W^D(x_w, y_w, z_w) + T_W^D$$

$$= \begin{bmatrix} \sqrt{x_w^2 + y_w^2}\cos(\theta - \arcsin(x_w/y_w)) \\ \sqrt{x_w^2 + y_w^2}\sin(\theta - \arcsin(x_w/y_w)) \\ -z_w \end{bmatrix} + \begin{bmatrix} t_{wx}^d \\ t_{wy}^d \\ t_{wz}^d \end{bmatrix} . \tag{3}$$

Finally, comparing the position and attitude dates of UH in VP local coordinate system which achieved from helicopter position and attitude solver module with real dates, with the results of visual feedback to the user, will achieves the simulation function.

4   Vega Prime Program Design Based on the Framework of MFC

MFC is the encapsulation of the Window API, which can greatly simplify development work. It is application framework based on the document/view structure, and it has become the mainstream framework of the Windows application development. The constructed visual simulation test system in this paper is using MFC framework for Vega Prime application development.

A basic Vega Prime application work process includes five steps: initialization, definition, construction, frame cycle and quit. Therefore, there are two problems in MFC with Vega Prime program need to be solved: the scene will be rendered to MFC view window; find out the position of completing system frame cycle.

In MFC, there are two ways to realize the VP frame cycle [8]. One is to use the timer, the other is to open up new work thread. The former method is simple, but during operation in the window of VP, sometimes it can't response and normal refresh the 3d scene, which affects the real-time simulation. So we take the latter method to realize VP frame cycle. As MFC and VP are both running with news cycle mechanism, So Vega Prime program based on MFC must solve the problem of communication between them. The best way to solve the problem is to use multithreading technology. MFC thread has two kinds: the User Interface thread and Worker Thread. The user interface thread is used for processing news response, realizing news cycle in the thread; worker thread has nothing to do with the user interface, which is used for big quantity of calculation.

VP needs real-time rendering cycle and time-consuming calculation process. Therefore, we create working thread for VP, and put the five stages of basic work process in the thread.

In the end of the application, make sure to turn off the Vega Prime worker thread first. Because Vega Prime worker thread will create other threads for the turn of the picture and object model rendering. So directly exiting main thread will cause abnormal.

5   Simulation Results and Analysis

We make the visual landing navigation simulation towards UH vertical drop stage on the "Vision-based Landing Simulation Verification System for UH based on Vega Prime / MFC". The simulation results are shown in Figure 8. This simulation system can display shooting images of airborne camera in real-time, and the real pose of UH and estimated pose of the vision-based landing navigation system on the interface, so that developers can test and analyze the visual landing navigation algorithms.

Figure 9 and figure 10 are the simulation results of position and rotation estimate of UH in the vertical drop stage. Comparing the estimate of visual landing navigation system with true value of the motion estimate of a given track, the pose error decreases with the decrease of the decline in height. In the final 5m to the cooperation goal in relative height, the position error can be controlled in 10cm, posture error can be controlled in 2 degrees. So, the estimate posture and position of UH are consistent with the theoretical value well. The simulation results prove the effectiveness and correctness of the system.

Fig. 8. Visual simulation results

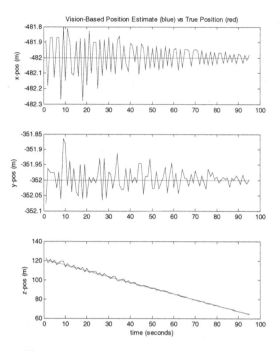

Fig. 9. Position estimates of vision-based landing

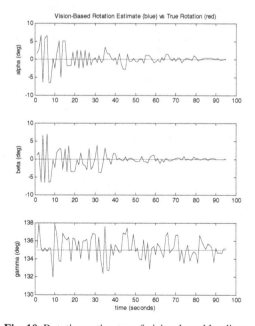

Fig. 10. Rotation estimates of vision-based landing

6   Conclusions

Based on the advanced simulation technology and virtual reality technology, the main framework of Vision-based Landing Simulation Verification System for UH based on Vega Prime / MFC is given in this paper. The Vega Prime module, MFC interface display module, cooperation target detection module and helicopter pose decoding module consist of the simulation system, with clear structure, the function modular, easy to expand, easy to be realized, etc. The system implement the visualization simulation environment with virtual reality tool software Creator, Vega Prime and VC++, can be used to verify the visual landing navigation correctness. The system changes the digital information into intuitive, graphical image form and simulation process changing along with the time and spatial change, which helps developers to better analysis the relationship among the landed platform, the plane and the camera, to improve the design of visual landing system, to reduce development cost, flight testing time, test cost and to shorten the development cycle.

References

1. Chen, L., Chen, Z.J.: Study on Simulation System for Vision-based Autonomous Landing of Unmanned Combat Aerial Vehicles. Journal of System Simulation 18, 1815–1819 (2006)
2. Dong, C.Y., Wang, J., Wang, Q.: Design and Development of Carrier Aircraft Landing Visualization Simulation System. Journal of System Simulation 20, 4626–4629 (2008)
3. Li, Z.H., Wang, W., Cui, J.G.: Study on Visual Simulation of Aircraft Horizontal Tail based on Creator and Vega. In: 2011 International Conference on Electrical and Control Engineering, Yichang, pp. 3678–3682 (2011)
4. Li, Z.H., Zhang, S.J., Cui, J.G., et al.: Visual Simulation of Flight Attitude Based on MFC and Vega. In: 2010 International Forum on Information Technology and Applications, Kunming, vol. 2, pp. 130–133 (2010)
5. Multigen-Paradigm, Inc.: Vega Prime desktop Tutor, USA, pp. 10–82 (2009)
6. Multigen-Paradigm, Inc.: Multigen Creator Desktop Tutor, USA, pp. 10–82 (2009)
7. Wang, Z.Y.: The Design of Scene Simulation System based on MFC Programming Framework. In: 2nd IEEE International Conference on Advanced Computer Control, Shenyang, vol. 3, pp. 302–305 (2010)
8. Courtney, S., Orriid, S., Sastry, S.S.: A Vision System for Landing an Unmanned Aerial Vehicle. In: Proceedings of the 2001 IEEE International Conference on Robotics & Automation, Seoul, pp. 1720–1727 (2001)

Design and Experiment of Adaptive Active Vibration Control System for Aircraft Framework

Wei Sun, Zhiyuan Gao, Di Tang, and Xiaojin Zhu[*,**]

School of Mechatronics Engineering and Automation, Shanghai University,
Shanghai, 200072, P. R. China
mgzhuxj@shu.edu.cn

Abstract. Hypersonic aircraft with a high velocity and super maneuverability has become a hot spot in current research of near space aircraft. To suppress the aircraft's vibration during its running process, an active vibration control system for aircraft framework is designed in this paper based on the adaptive filtering algorithm. To start with, an adaptive filtering algorithm – filter-x least mean square (FXLMS) algorithm is presented. Then the hardware configuration and software development are introduced in detail. Meanwhile, the piezoelectric smart structure is used for detecting and driving. The measurement and control system designed in this experiment has 8 input channels and 8 output channels which are able to process off-line identification, on-line identification and real-time control. By choosing reasonable parameters and distributing channels logically, an adaptive active vibration control is imposed. Finally, the experimental performance verifies the feasibility of FXLMS algorithm and the validity of the designed control system.

Keywords: adaptive control, active vibration control, near space aircraft.

1   Introduction

In recent years, with the rapid development of material technology, control technology and propulsion technology, the application and development of near space aircraft for civilian uses and military uses are gradually taken into consideration[1, 2]. Due to the defects of strong flexibility and low damping, if there is no control of vibration, the entire system's processing will suffer from disastrous consequences[3].

Once a conventional structure is manufactured, it will be affected passively by the environment, rather than dynamically monitoring the aircraft's performance or responding to the change of surroundings[4]. Contemporarily in the smart structure field, the appearance of the piezoelectric intelligent material breaks a brand new path for active vibration control. The material has advantages such as being light in weight, low power dissipation, high response speed and easy to arrange execute components, which has promising prospects in application[5].

---

[*] Corresponding author.
[**] This research is supported by program of National Nature Science Foundation of China (90716027; 51175319), and Shanghai Talent Development Fund (No.2009020).

This paper designs an experimental platform of simulative near space aircraft system. Active vibration control based on adaptive filter feed-forward algorithm-FXLMS is researched by distributing logical signal paths. And the experiment results demonstrate that the adaptive active vibration control system can effectively suppress external disturbance during its operating process.

2   Adaptive Vibration Control

An active vibration control system usually has measuring uncertainties due to its construction. Thus, an adaptive control method needs to be implemented in the control system. The cores of the adaptive vibration control system are the adaptive filter and the adaptive filtering algorithm. At present, the FXLMS algorithm with Multiple Input and Multiple Output (MIMO) is widely used (Fig.1 shows the structure) [6].

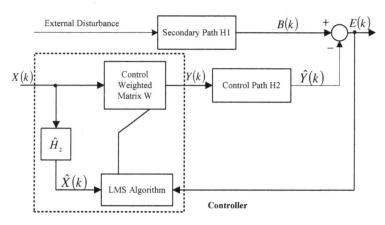

Fig. 1. The structure of FXLMS algorithm with MIMO

In Fig.1, $X(k)$ is reference signal, $Y(k)$ is input signal, $\hat{Y}(k)$ is External disturbance response vector, $E(k)$ is residuals offset vector, $X(k)$ is the filter signal of $X(k)$ to $\hat{H}_2$, and $\hat{H}_2$ is the structural model of the control path H2.

MIMO control method is an adaptive procession which is in searching for the optimal weight matrix W. There are M controllers outputting control signals onto the M actuators, and finally making the mean sum square of the Error response signal in the L monitoring points reach the minimum values.

According to the relationships between every part of the structure in Fig.1, the operation process of FXLMS algorithm is as follows (1)-(3).

$$Y(k)=W(k)X(k) \tag{1}$$

$$E(k)=B(k)+\hat{X}(k)W(k) \tag{2}$$

$$W(k+1)=W(k)-\mu\hat{X}{}^{\mathrm{T}}(k)E(k) \tag{3}$$

3   Model and Structure of the Experimental Platform

3.1   Hardware Configuration

The experimental aircraft model includes an aluminum alloy frame and an aircraft model framework structure. It has a sensor network with groups of piezoelectric sensors and an actuator network with groups of piezoelectric actuators. The frame which can be installed or lifted vibration exciters is qualified with high stability and sturdiness. The piezoelectric sensors and the piezoelectric actuators are separately pasted to avoid interference of the control voltage during MIMO process.

The hardware configuration of the experimental measurement and control system platform includes a vibration exciter, several piezoelectric-driven power amplifiers, several charge amplifiers, a digital oscilloscope, an A/D acquisition card, a D/A output card, a high performance computer, a arbitrary function signal generator and a signal power amplifier. The hardware and the structure diagram of the system are shown in Fig.2 and Fig.3.

Fig. 2. Active vibration control platform

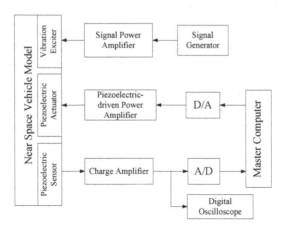

Fig. 3. The structure diagram of the active vibration control platform

(1) Charge Amplifier

Compared with the voltage amplifier, the charge amplifier has higher sensitivity, signal-to-noise ratio and more working reliability. In this control system, a YE5852A low noise charge amplifier is applied. The maximum output charge quantity of this amplifier is 106pC, and the noise voltage is lower or equal to 5μV.

(2) Digital Oscilloscope

A GDS-840C digital oscilloscope is used in this system. The digital oscilloscope is connected to the charge amplifier to acquire the structural vibration response signals, so as to measure or revise data.

(3) Data Acquisition Card A/D

In this experiment, a 12-bit PCI-1712A/D convertor is used. It has 16 digital output channels and 1MHz sampling rate. The acquisition card is connected to the computer via PCI bus, which can meet the demand of MIMO and real-time identification.

(4) High-performance Computer

The main control computer is in charge of extracting and analyzing the vibration signals from A/D. After processing the signals with FXLMS algorithm, the computer output the control signals through D/A convertor. In this paper, a Founder I500-7255 computer is used. It is convenient to be operated with all kinds of programming language, such as graphical MATLAB Simulink and LabVIEW.

(5) Analog Output Card D/A

A 14-bit PCI-1724U D/A convertor is applied in the experiment. It has 32-bit isolated analog output channels. Similar to the A/D card, the analog output card is connected to the main control computer.

(6) Piezoelectric-driven Power Amplifier

Piezoelectric-driven power amplifier is used to amplify the multiple signals from the D/A card, and output them to every group of piezoelectric actuator to produce controlling force to the aircraft model. The vibration system is in need of a particular power amplifier, which is compositive and miniaturized, to supply with energy to the piezoelectric actuators. Fortunately, a brand new high-voltage power amplifier is developed independently. The power amplifier is based on APEX-PA95 amplifier chip with 35/70 times magnification and 0~5 KHz response frequency. It is extremely suitable for aero-space structure monitoring and controlling [7].

(7) Vibration Exciter

A vibration exciter is used to vibrate the aircraft. It is connected to the aircraft model with joint levers. Multiple vibration exciters can also be used to produce vibrational excitation to the framework at the same time. In this experiment a JZK-10 modal vibration exciter is applied due to its small volume, light weight, wide frequency coverage and high reliability.

(8) Signal Generator and Signal Power Amplifier

The system uses Angilent-33220A function signal generator to produce signals, and applies the function signals to the vibration exciter via YE5872 signal power amplifier in order to simulate all kinds of vibrating conditions. The function signal generator applied in this experiment is able to produce all kinds of signals such as 20MHz sine wave, square wave as well as 64K-point wave.

3.2   Development of the Computer Software

The software of measurement and control system in this experiment is developed in Microsoft Visual C++ 6.0. It is mainly used to realize the functions such as signal collecting and processing, control algorithm and output the results to D/A. In addition, the software is convenient in data saving and operating. The flow chart of the software is shown as follows.

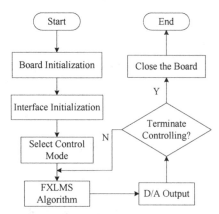

Fig. 4. The flow chart of the upper computer software

4   Result Analyzing and Verification

4.1   Parameter Selecting and Channel Distributing

In this research, an 8-input and 8-output adaptive multiple-channel filtering experiment is used in the structural active vibration control. Among the channels, the 3rd path and the 4th path are used for measuring and controlling the two wings of the near space aircraft model respectively, while the other six channels are used for measuring and controlling the body framework. In the experiment, some practical control operations are implemented in testing the first four orders of bending vibration modes. After being controlled, the response of one order is gradually suppressed. When the vibrating frequency suddenly changes and produces another order mode, the algorithm is able to suppress new structural response rapidly after readjusting the weights. Thus it proves that this control method not only has high correcting rate, but is perfectly adaptive to the exterior changes as well.

4.2   Verification of FXLMS Algorithm

In the verifying process, a random frequency is chosen among the first four order modes as vibrating frequency. The frequency is 20.70Hz. The reference signal is the vibration signal and the off-line identification results are used as parameters of controlling channels. The length of the filter is 24 and the convergence step size μ is 0.0002. Confined to the length of the thesis, the paper focuses on the vibration control of four channels. The four channels are 1st channel, two channels on the both wings (3rd channel and 4th channel) and 6th channel. The effects of vibration control are shown as follows (Fig.5 ~ Fig.7).

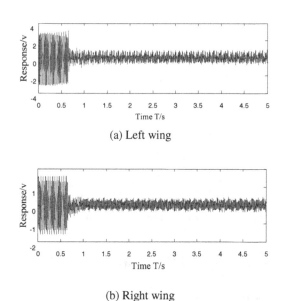

(a) Left wing

(b) Right wing

Fig. 5. Time history of the left and right wings vibration response

Fig.5 and Fig.6 show the response time history of the left and the right wings, the channel 1 and channel 6. The vibration can be suppressed in about 0.7 seconds; Fig.7 shows the square root of all the least mean-square errors' sum in the 8 channels. According to Fig.5~ Fig.7, the entire system's response obviously declines, which means the vibration response of the structure is effectively suppressed.

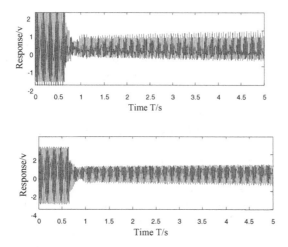

Fig. 6. Time history of the channel 1 and channel 6 vibration response

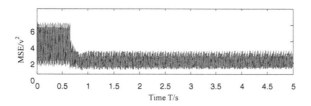

Fig. 7. Vibration suppression performance

5   Conclusions

Active adaptive vibration control system for aircraft framework is designed in this paper. By analyzing the FXLMS algorithm, an 8-input and 8-output adaptive control system is designed, and the hardware configuration as well as software development is presented. Then the designed control system is applied to the active vibration control experiment with simulative near space aircraft. As the experimental result demonstrates, the designed measurement and control system is able to meet the requirements of adaptive vibration control in multiple channels and has remarkable suppressing performance.

Acknowledgments. This paper is sponsored by program of National Nature Science Foundation of China (90716027; 51175319), Shanghai Talent Development Fund (No.2009020), Mechatronics Engineering Innovation Group project from Shanghai Education Commission, Shanghai University "11th Five-Year Plan" 211 Construction Project and Shanghai Key Laboratory of Power Station Automation Technology.

References

1. Yang, F.-D., Yang, W.-D.: Analysis and Study on Effectiveness of Near Space System. Journal of the Academy of Equipment Command & Technology 19, 63–67 (2008)
2. Xue, Y.-J., Li, T.-F.: Development of Near Space Aircraft and Analysis of the Key Technology. Winged Missiles Journal 02, 32–36 (2011)
3. Quan, W.-Z., Fang, M.-X.: Flutter Study of Wing-Fuselage Combination of Supersonic Aircrafts. Noise and Vibration Control 06 (2010)
4. Liu, T.-X.: Smart Structure and Its Use in Space Aircrafts. Spacecraft Engineering 13, 27–31 (2004)
5. Xing, F., Zhang, R.-H.: Research and Prospect of Vibration Control Technology of Smart Structure. Mechanical Management and Development 03, 41–42 (2011)
6. Wang, C.-Y., Wu, Y.-F., Yang, H.: Design and Experiment of Multi-Channel Adaptive Active Noise Control System. Measurement & Control Technology 30, 57–63 (2011)
7. Zhu, X.-J., Cao, H., Lu, M.-Y., Shao, Y.: Development of Piezoelectric Power Amplifier Based on PA95 Chip. Piezoelectrics & Acoustooptics 30, 561–563 (2008)

Model Reconstruction Using B-Spline Surfaces

Wei Li[1], Zhuoqi Wu[2], Shinoda Junichi[3], and Ichiro Hagiwara[4]

[1] College of Mathematics and Statistics,
Nanjing University of Information Science & Technology, Nanjing 210044, China
[2] School of Mechanical Engineering, Shanghai Jiao Tong University,
Shanghai 200240, China
[3] Interlocus,Inc. Kanagawa, Japan
[4] Department of Mechanical Sciences and Engineering,
Graduate School of Science and Engineering, Tokyo,
Institute of Technology Tokyo, Japan
liwei2009@hotmail.com

Abstract. Recently, some results of the G^1 continuity conditions for B-splines surfaces have been presented. These G^1 conditions can be used in the reconstruction of bicubic and biquintic smooth B-splines surfaces with a single interior knots. However, the C^1 continuity conditions of B-spline surfaces with arbitrary degrees have not been solved. In this paper, we obtain the C^1 continuity conditions between two adjacent B-spline surfaces with arbitrary degrees. We also present a practical scheme of reconstructing model using the C^1 continuity conditions in reverse engineering.

Keywords: Modeling reconstruction, B-spline surface, C^1 continuity condition.

1   Introduction

In the field of computer-aided design (CAD), computer graphics, geometric modeling, and reverse engineering, the reconstruction of model with smooth parametric curves and surfaces from a set of scanned 3D data is an important problem. As we know, the B-splines and the non-uniform rational B-splines (NURBS) have become a standard for the representation of free-form parametric curves and surface. In recent years, the study of the geometric continuity conditions of B-spline and NURBS surface have been received improvements [1-5]. Shi et al. [1-2] gave the G^1 continuity conditions of adjacent bicubic B-spline surfaces and convergent G^1 continuity conditions of adjacent biquintic B-spline surfaces with single interior knots, and also described a scheme how to reconstruct bicubic and biquintic smooth B-splines surfaces with G^1 continuity over arbitrary topology. We pay an interest on the C^1 continuity conditions that join B-spline patches in an easy and effective way.

The paper is consisted of as follows. Section 2, we present the C^1 continuity conditions between two adjacent B-spline patches. Section 3 develops a practical scheme of reconstructing model with smooth B-spline surface. In section 4, some examples are given to show the results of implementing the scheme, then give conclusions and future work.

T. Xiao, L. Zhang, and S. Ma (Eds.): ICSC 2012, Part I, CCIS 326, pp. 205–210, 2012.

2 C^1 Continuity Conditions of B-spline Surfaces

Suppose two B-spline surface patches (see [6]) be defined by

$$S_1(u,v) = \sum_{i=0}^{n}\sum_{j=0}^{m} N_{i,p}(u)N_{j,q}(v)\mathbf{P}_{i,j},$$

$$S_2(u,v) = \sum_{i=0}^{n}\sum_{j=0}^{m} N_{i,p}(u)N_{j,q}(v)\mathbf{Q}_{i,j}.$$

(2.1)

The p×q are the degrees of the B-spline surfaces, the { $\mathbf{P}_{i,j}$ } and { $\mathbf{Q}_{i,j}$ } are the control points, and the { $N_{i,p}(u)$ } and { $N_{j,q}(v)$ } are the B-spline basis functions.

Suppose $S_1(u,v)$ and $S_2(u,v)$ have common boundary curve (see Fig.1)

$$\Gamma(v) = S_1(0,v) = S_2(0,v)$$

This is called the two B-spline surfaces patches are C^0 continuity on their common boundary curve.

Since

$$S_1(0,v) = \sum_{j=0}^{m} N_{j,q}(v)\mathbf{P}_{0,j},$$

$$S_2(0,v) = \sum_{j=0}^{m} N_{j,q}(v)\mathbf{Q}_{0,j},$$

we obtain

$$\mathbf{P}_{0,j} = \mathbf{Q}_{0,j} \quad j = 0, \ldots, m.$$

(2.2)

In order to get the C^1 continuity condition between $S_1(u,v)$ and $S_2(u,v)$, their cross boundary tangent vectors $C_1(v)$ and $C_2(v)$ in direction u along the common boundary curve $\Gamma(v)$ can be calculated as follows

$$C_1(v) = \left.\frac{\partial S_1(u,v)}{\partial u}\right|_{u=0} = p\sum_{j=0}^{m}\frac{\mathbf{P}_{1,j}-\mathbf{P}_{0,j}}{u_{p+1}-u_1}N_{j,q}(v),$$

$$C_2(v) = \left.\frac{\partial S_2(u,v)}{\partial u}\right|_{u=0} = p\sum_{j=0}^{m}\frac{\mathbf{Q}_{1,j}-\mathbf{Q}_{0,j}}{u_{p+1}-u_1}N_{j,q}(v).$$

(2.3)

If two surfaces are C^1 continuous on their common boundary curve, their cross boundary tangent vectors $C_1(v)$ and $C_2(v)$ should be equivalent for any v, that is

$$\left.\frac{\partial S_1(u,v)}{\partial u}\right|_{u=0} = \left.\frac{\partial S_2(u,v)}{\partial u}\right|_{u=0} \tag{2.4}$$

We can get

$$\mathbf{P}_{1,j} - \mathbf{P}_{0,j} = \mathbf{Q}_{1,j} - \mathbf{Q}_{0,j} \qquad j = 0, \ldots, m. \tag{2.5}$$

So, equations (2.5) are the C^1 continuity conditions for two surfaces their common boundary .

The C^1 continuity conditions of two adjacent B-spline surface patches are directly represented by the relevant three columns control points near and on the common boundary (see Fig. 1).

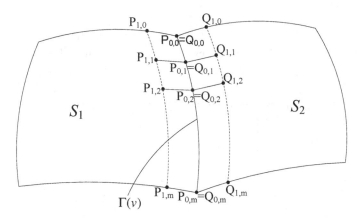

Fig. 1. Two B-spline surface patches with common boundary curve $\Gamma(v)$

3   Model Reconstruction Using B-Spline Surface

In this section, we describe a scheme of model reconstructing according to the C^1 continuity conditions above.

3.1   Joining Patches Smoothly at Common Corner

Suppose a set of B-spline surface patches $\{S_i\}$ ($i = 0, \ldots, r$) have common corner point $\mathbf{P}$ as shown in Fig. 2.

Let $\mathbf{A}_i$ ($i = 0, \ldots, r$) be the closest control point to $\mathbf{P}$ of common boundary, $\mathbf{B}_i$ ($i = 0, \ldots, r$) be the closest control points to $\mathbf{P}$ next to the common boundary curve.

Fig.2 shows that patches S_r and S_0 share a common boundary, and we will discuss how to join these patches at the common corner point $\mathbf{P}$ smoothly in three steps as follow.

1. Determine the normal vector of the tangent plane at the common corner point **P**.

Let $\mathbf{n}_i(\mathbf{P})$ $(i = 0, \ldots, r)$ be the normal vector of S_i at **P**, the common normal vector at **P** can be decided as

$$n(P) = \sum_{i=0}^{r} n_i(P) \Big/ r \qquad (3.1)$$

2. Determine the tangent points $\mathbf{A}_i$ $(i = 0, \ldots, r)$.

All control points $\mathbf{A}_i$ are projected onto the common tangent plane, and they are still represented as $\mathbf{A}_i$.

3. Determine the control points $\mathbf{B}_i$ $(i = 0, \ldots, r)$.

On tangent plane, make lines pass through point $\mathbf{A}_i$ and let the line be perpendicular to the line $\overline{\mathbf{A}_i\mathbf{P}}$. Then calculate the intersecting points of two lines. Let these intersecting points be the control points next to the common boundaries as shown in Fig. 2.

Since all control points $\mathbf{A}_i$ and $\mathbf{B}_i$ are decided on the tangent plane, the surface patches $\{Si\}$ $(i = 0, \ldots, r)$ are joined in C^1 continuity.

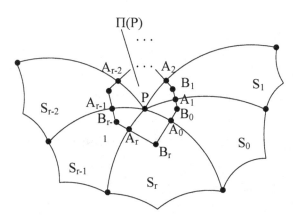

Fig. 2. The patches meet at a common corner **P**

3.2   Joining Patches Smoothly along Common Boundary

The remained control points of common boundary will be determined by C^1 conditions (2.5) as follow. That is how to determine the new control points $\mathbf{P}_{1,j}$ and $\mathbf{Q}_{1,j}$ $(j = 1, \ldots, m\text{-}1)$:

On tangent plane of $P_{0,j}$, makes a line $L(P_{0j})$ passing through point $P_{0,j}$ and let $L(P_{0j})$ be perpendicular to the line $\overline{P_{0,j-1}P_{0,j+1}}$. Let new $P_{1,j}$ and $Q_{1,j}$ (j = 1, ..., m-1) satisfy the C^1 continuity conditions:

$$P_{1,j} - P_{0,j} = Q_{1,j} - Q_{0,j} \qquad j = 1, ..., m-1.$$

4   Implementing Results and Conclusions

The scheme presented in section 3 has been successfully implemented in a number of examples over an arbitrary topological type of geometric model.

Here, we give the results of a model of mobile in Fig.3-4.

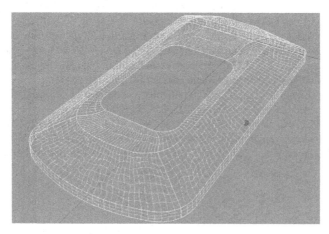

Fig. 3. A mobile model scanned data

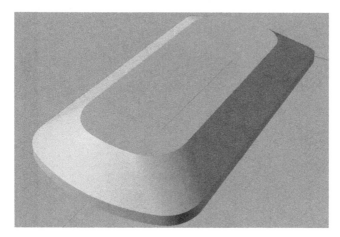

Fig. 4. The reconstructed mobile model consists of eight of B-spline patches joining with C^0 and C^1 continuity

As conclusions, in this paper, we have obtained the C^1 continuity conditions between two adjacent B-spline surface patches. By the C^1 continuity conditions, we have developed a scheme for reconstructing a smooth tensor product B-spline surface of a geometric model. The scheme has been implemented successfully and effectively.

Acknowledgement. Several parts of the research work were carried out by the support of Grants-in-Aid for scientific research(category C) under Grant No. 22560135.We acknowledge its aid dearly.

References

1. Shi, X., Wang, T., Yu, P.: Reconstruction of convergent G^1 smooth B-spline surfaces. Computer Aided Geometric Design 21, 893–913 (2004)
2. Shi, X., Wang, T., Yu, P.: A practical construction of G^1 smooth biquintic B-spline surfaces over arbitrary topology. Computer-Aided Design 36, 413–424 (2004)
3. Shi, X., Yu, P., Wang, T.: G^1 continuous conditions of biquartic B-spline surfaces. Journal of Computational and Applied Mathematics 144, 251–262 (2002)
4. Che, X., Liang, X., Li, Q.: G^1 continuity conditions of adjacent NURBS surfaces. Computer Aided Geometric Design 22, 285–298 (2005)
5. Milroy, M.J., Bradley, C., Vickers, G.W., Weir, D.J.: G^1 continuity of B-spline surface patches in reverse engineering. Computer-Aided Design 27(6), 471–478 (1995)
6. Piegl, L., Tiller, W.C.: The NURBS Book, 2nd edn. Springer, Berlin (1997)

Consideration of Origami Design Clothing

Eri Nakayama, Sachiko Ishida, Liao Yujing, and Ichiro Hagiwara

Organization for the Strategic Coordination of Research and Intellectual Property,
Meiji University, 1-1-1, Higashi-Mita, Tama-ku, Kawasaki City, 214-8571
tz12007@meji.ac.jp

Abstract. Several Applications of Origami have been tested in industrial areas, however, in design area, Origami design is found only in lamp shade and wrapping. In clothing Origami design hasn't been practically applied before. In this paper, a conical Truss model is introduced as an application of skirt designs, and the simulation software from 2D to 3D is considered. Later the measurement of brain wave is conducted for observers who see the simulation screen, and by examining the correlation between each feature of clothing and brain wave α, we can detect the most healing design for clothing.

Keywords: Origami, conical truss model, healing, brain wave α.

1   Introduction

In the area of Origami Engineering conical truss core panel has been applied to solar panel and the strengthened floor panel for automobile. In this paper, conical truss model is applied to clothing design which add the value of clothing novelty. Traditional way of folding is only used for collar, trouser cuff, and skirt tuck as function, while as design there exists only pleats skirt. Pleats skirt is popular in girls school uniform which give people the impression that they are conservative and formal. While in this paper, we aim that more movable design which could heal them.

2   Conical Truss Model

2.1   Drawing Way of Conical Truss Model

It has been already proved by Dr.Nojima that the pattern where reverse spiral structured conical is folded flat by making a complete rotation in 360 degrees could be drawn as Fig.1(a). Conical typed reverse spiral structure is drawn in several patterns according to degrees α, β, γ Fig.1(b) and the parallelogram form. However, the developable and foldable pattern which can be put into practical use is only model(a). Therefore in this paper, we consider only the pattern(a). Firstly the condition that the elements which constitute the pattern(a) is represented as formula (1). N is the number of triangle which stand in the circle and an angle of Φ degrees is the center angle of pattern. An angle of β degrees can be arbitrary degree but to be

---

T. Xiao, L. Zhang, and S. Ma (Eds.): ICSC 2012, Part I, CCIS 326, pp. 211–215, 2012.

folded flat it has the restriction related with an angle of α degrees. The fun shaped pattern is found to be drawn in curving lines, however in Fig.1(b) all lines which constitute each triangle are straight. Therefore, the way of drawing whole of the pattern is firstly drawing both the diagonal lines which divide equally the arch of fun shaped pattern and parallel lines with arch ones. Secondly, all adjacent points are connected with straight lines. In this way the pattern(c) is completed by drawing step by step which is composed of triangles which have the same rate of agreement in the direction of center orderly. In this paper the development of automatic drawing pattern software is proposed restricted to this kind of pattern, and based on the measurement results whether the observer feels healing or not the design which could give healing with observer is proposed. We focus on clothing design especially skirt because it is designed more simply.

$$\alpha = \left(2\pi - \Theta\right)/2N \tag{1}$$

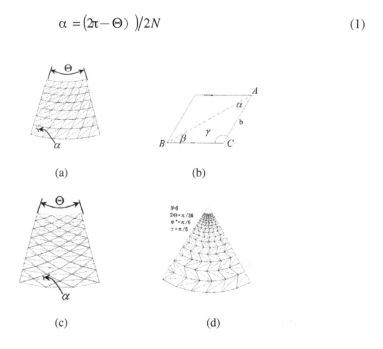

Fig. 1. (a),(b),(c) Development of foldable conical shell, (b) one element

2.2   Algorithm Used for Origami Software

The software for creating pattern has already been developed by Mitani. He publish in his website the editor for flat Origami(ORIPA, 2009) for free. However, the function of this editor is drawing folding lines on ORIPA referring to the marked lines on paper after developed and displaying the estimated completion on ORIPA by which the correctness of folding lines drawn on ORIPA is confirmed. It means that ORIPA is not the software which can realize the estimation based on only pattern. While there is another software; Freeform Origami(Tachi,2010) which can deal with only rigid Origami. By using Freeform Origami, the simulation from 2D to 3D of conical truss model is tried to be failed. This failure seems to result from in folding procedure the side is bent. Therefore we try to develop both editor and simulation software and proceed to apply them to conical truss model.

2.3   Automatic Transformation of Cylindrical Truss Model

The pattern of conical truss model is obtained by transforming cylindrical truss model by defining vertical angle as an angle of ϕ degrees. The way of transformations are shown in Fig.2.

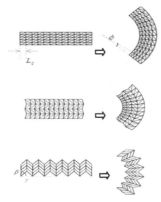

Fig. 2. The transformation from cylindrical to conical   truss   model development

3   Development of 2D to 3D Simulation Software

The final aim is the development of 2D to 3D simulation software. It has been tried by many researchers, but it has never been realized because of complex properties of Origami. In this paper, we fold conical truss model by paper and find the gradual moving. The appearance is shown in Fig.3.

Fig. 3. The real moving of conical truss from 2D to 3D

3.1　Application to Clothing Design

Considering the contents mentioned above we have to imagine the possibility of the real clothing created on the basis of simulation. The serious problem is that how to keep vertical pleats which is affected easily with gravity. For this problem we will approach from 2 viewpoints as material and processing. From material viewpoint, polyester is appropriate because it has the property of high thermo-plasticity. As a result, it become possible to make shape of clothing keeping in the state of wearing. From processing viewpoint, it is necessary to compensate pattern according to curving lines of human body, for example, women body style has curving around waist and hip, so the pattern is to be modified as clothing fits to body.

3.2　Design Providing Observers with Healing

For estimating the psychological effect clothing give to observers, we use the measurement for brain wave. Mind Set (developed by Neuro Sky) can measure how much each frequency is occurring each interval. We focus on wave α (8-13Hz)which indicated how much a subject feels relaxed. On the other hand we pick up the features which constitute of skirt; shape, texture, color, the number of steps, and curving degree. After that we convert into numerals those features for computing. And, we investigate the relative relationship between each feature and the feeling of subject.

3.3　Measurement of Brain Wave

We obtained data of brain wave by using Neuro Sky. Fig.4 is drawn based on the date which is measured each 0.5 second for each frequency(interval 1.0). Fig.5 is drawn by using the algorithm included in this software which has close result on the basis of brain wave α. We will watch the meditation level while observers see clothing.

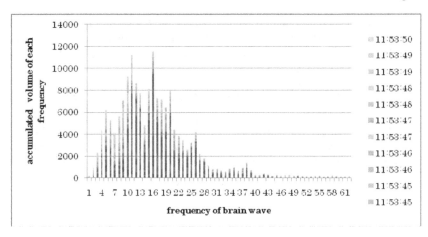

Fig. 4. Accumulated frequency of brain wave for certain period

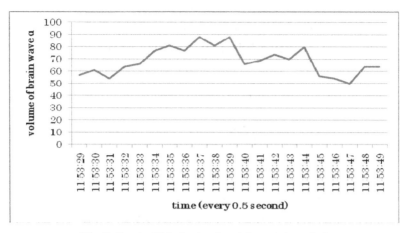

Fig. 5. Graph of Meditation Level for certain period

4   Conclusions

After experiment of mentioned in 2.3 section, the features which are related more with healing feeling are detected. And, by arranging the features for the design to provide observers with healing more we can determine the most healing design of Origami design skirt. When we propose people the skirt design, we are going to hear their impression, and confirm the design actually is best design for healing. Here we only consider the straight folding lines, however when we pursue healing design the curving design should be more suitable. So, in next paper we are to adapt both straight and curving folding lines for clothing design.

Acknowledgement. Several parts of the research work were carried out by the support of Grants-in-Aid for scientific research(category S) under Grant No.20226006.We acknowledge its aid dearly.

References

1. Kamata, Y., Ito, K., Kawamura, T., Honda, T., Matsuki, Y., Ishimura, T.: The development of foldable PET bottle. JSME Dynamics and Design Conference, CD-ROM, September 5-9, Koumi City (2011)
2. Nojima, T.: The creation of foldable conical shell. JSME (editing C) 66(647), 349–355 (2000)

Comprehensive Optimization for Raised Floor Structure Using Origami Engineering

Yang Yang[1] , Zhizhen Xia[2], Xilu Zhao[3], Sunao Tokura[4], and Ichirou Hagiwara[1]

[1] Institute for Advanced Study of Mathematical Science, Meiji University, Kanagawa, Japan
{tz12014, ihagi }@meiji.ac.jp
[2] Tokyo Institute of Technology, Tokyo, Japan
xiazzpal@hotmail.com
[3] Saitama Institute of Technology, Saitama, Japan
tyoukiroku@gmail.com
[4] Tokura Simulation Research Corporation
tokura@kk.iij4u.or.jp

Abstract. Multi-core panel is widely used in raised floor structure. However, it has the disadvantage of heavy weight. In this paper, the authors try to reduce the weight of the raised floor structure by replacing multi-core panel with truss core panel, which is a well-known lightweight structure using origami engineering. The intension and stiffness of truss core panel for raised floor model are investigated. The multi-core panel and the truss core panel are compared by running impact test and load test. Response Surface Method (RSM) is used to optimize the shape of truss core panel. The explicit FEM software LS-DYNA is used to solve impact-load analysis. The results show that 23.69% weight reduction is achieved for exiting multi-core panel of raised floor by using truss core panel.

Keywords: Origami Engineering, Raised Floor, Comprehensive Optimization, Impact, Load, Truss Core Panel, Multi-Core Panel.

1 Introduction

Raised floor has been widely used as an elevated floor above a solid substrate to store wiring freely, an essential part of the infrastructure of today's information economy[1]. The weight reduction of raised floor is preferred, in order to reduce the manufacturing cost of mass production and to alleviate the burdens of buildings[2].

At present, the raised floor actually used is glued to a surface plate with a plate on which multi-cores are arranged. The multi-core is formed like a hemispheric convex. However, the weight of the existing multi-core type raised floor structure needs to be reduced for economic reasons. Therefore, it is necessary to understand the mechanical characteristic of raised floor under different conditions of usage, and to optimize the raised floor structure based on the industry testing standards of JAFA(Japan Access Floor Association) [3].On the other hand, origami engineering is the scientific study of the techniques of origami, a traditional Japanese craft, and the attempt to apply the

T. Xiao, L. Zhang, and S. Ma (Eds.): ICSC 2012, Part I, CCIS 326, pp. 216–227, 2012.

craft to engineering problems. It was proposed by Taketoshi Nojima of Kyoto University and advanced by Professor Ichiro Hagiwara of the Tokyo Institute of Technology, who launched a research group on origami engineering in the Japan Society for Industrial and Applied Mathematics. Origami engineering is leading to the development of strong yet lightweight structure[4]. From the prospect of application to origami-engineering, we direct our attention to truss core panels as less weighty structure. They have better aspects in bending stiffness and in shear strength[5]~[7]. Saito investigated the relation between the geometrical pattern and mechanical characteristic of truss core panel and found that geometrical parameters have obvious effect on the bending stiffness and on the in-plane shear strength[8]. Togura confirmed the formability of truss core panel employing a simple press method of nonlinear analytical simulation and using multi-purpose dynamic analysis software LS-DYNA[9]. Togura announced the results of doing shape optimization to improve impact energy absorption ability of the truss core panel by using LS-DYNA[10]. However, so far there are no studies of truss core panel that apply the technology to the development of raised floor structure.

In this paper, based on the JAFA testing standards, considering static load and impact at the same time, we replace multi-core panel with truss core panel and utilize multi-purpose dynamic analysis software LS-DYNA under condition that the performances of the residual deformation when elastic deformation recovered completely after the impact and the maximum deformation of the static load are not worse than the exiting multi-core panel structure. We also optimize design of the new truss core panel type raised floor structure to seek the lightest floor structure by using the optimization method of Response Surface Methodology.

2   Raised Floor Structure and Analysis Model's Settings

Fig. 1 shows the exiting multi-core type raised floor structure, which consists of two parts. The surface of raised floor is a plat with edge length 500mm (below, this plat is called top plate), and the back of raised floor is the multi-core type panel with edge length 500mm (below, this panel is called bottom plate). The top plate and the top of cores in the bottom plate of raised floor are connected by spot welding. The material used is the steel plate SPCE, and we use the specific values shown in Table 1 for structure analysis.

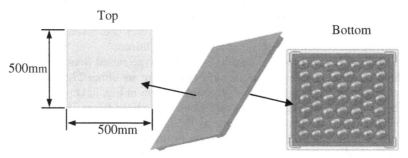

Fig. 1. Multi-core Type Raised Floor Panel Structure

In this study, the geometric dimensions such as width, height and so on are not changed, and the face plate is the same. Replacing multi-core type bottom plate influenced greatly by bending stiffness with truss core panel type, not only considering conditions of static load and impact based on the JAFA testing standards but also maintaining the performance of the exiting raised floor structure or equivalent, we will discuss the lightest raised floor structure in detail by adjusting the geometrical shape or thickness of truss core type floor.

Table 1. Material Properties of Raised Floor Panel Structure.

Young's modulus	205.66 GPa
Poisson's ratio	0.33
Density	7.84×10^{-6} kg/mm^3
Yield stress	270 MPa

3   Proposition for Truss Core Panel Type Raised Floor Structure

The truss core panel is a structural material invented based on the research work of space filling feature for regular tetrahedrons or regular octahedrons[5]~[7].The truss core panel applied in this study, is a combination of a flat plate and a triangular pyramid panel in which triangular pyramids are arranged in the form of staggered pattern. The feature of the basic structure of truss core panel is shown in Fig. 2.

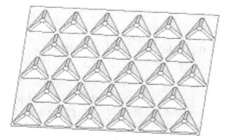 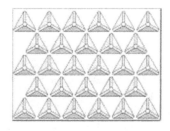

Fig. 2. Truss Core Panel Structure

The shape and dimension of the existing multi-core type raised floor, and that of the truss core panel type raised floor proposed in this paper, are shown in Fig. 3 and Fig. 4 respectively. The dimension of both whole structures is of a similar square with edge length 500mm×500mm corresponding to use conditions.

Fig. 3 shows the structure of the multi-core panel type raised floor. The height of hemisphere type core is 22mm, and the radii of the core are either 27.5mm or 30mm, and they are properly arranged as those positions shown in Fig. 3. On the other hand, Fig. 4 shows the structure of the truss core panel type raised floor. The height of the truss core in the bottom plate is the same as the height (22mm) of hemisphere type core in the multi-core panel. The edge length on the top of core is r and the edge length on the bottom of core is R. The chamfer length is a. The cores are arranged in the form of staggered patter in the whole truss core panel.

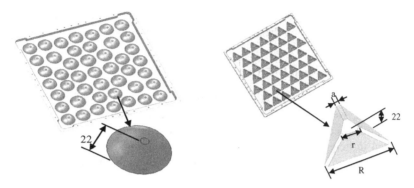

Fig. 3. Current Multi Core Panel Type   **Fig. 4.** Proposed Truss Core Panel Type

For the actual floor structure, the top plate is linked to the vertices of cores in the bottom plate by spot welding method. In the analysis model of this paper, we set the spot welding modeling using beam element and make it possible that the nodes (the spot welding points) of both ends of beam elements can be put on the arbitrary positions of the shell element sides as shown in Fig. 5.

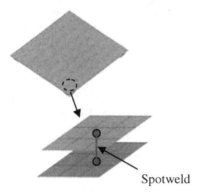

Spotweld

Fig. 5. Definition of Spot Weld using Beam Element

For the existing raised floor structure, the thickness of top plate is 1.4mm and the thickness of bottom plate is 1.0mm. In this research, the flexural rigidity, impact characteristic of the structure and etc. is improved by applying the truss core pane as an alternative to the multi-core panel; and the main purpose is to reduce the thickness of the core as much as possible to realize lightweight of the whole structure.

4   Analysis Method of Impact and Static Load

In order to synthetically optimize the raised floor structure considering the residual deformation of the impact and the maximum deformation of the static load concurrently, it is necessary to calculate the residual deformation of the impact and the maximum deformation of the static load, and to do optimization analysis of the floor structure shape based on the both analysis results of impact and static load.

4.1   Analysis of Residual Deformation by Impact

Complying with the testing standards of "Performance Assessment of the Free Access Floor" of JAFA, we build the impact analysis model as shown in Fig. 6, where the four corners of raised floor structure are fully fixed. The sandbag of 30kg freely falls from 250mm in height in a vertical direction and then impacts the raised floor. The contact area between the sandbag and the panel is a 220mm diameter circular form.

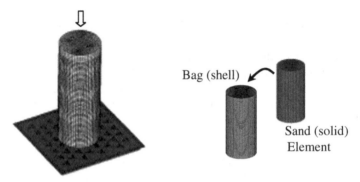

Fig. 6. Impact analysis model   **Fig. 7.** Sand bag analysis model

Here, the sand is modeled by three-dimensional solid element, and its material characteristics is defined by "*MAT_NULL command" in LS-DYNA. The value of material characteristics is shown as follows:

Mass density $1.7 \times 10^{-6} kg/mm^3$
Pressure cutoff $-100N$
Young's modulus $2.1 \times 10^5 N/mm^2$
Poisson's ratio 0.3

Here, because the Young's modulus and the Poisson's ratio are used when calculating the touch force between the sand and the floor, their values are assigned as above when considering the material characteristics of floor.

On the other hand, in order to consider the pressure effect of the sand, the equation of Bulk Modulus of Elasticity (K) is given as follows:

$$K = \frac{E}{3(1-2\mu)} . \qquad (1)$$

where the Young's modulus (E) of sand is $7000N/mm^2$, and the Poisson's ratio (μ) is 0. Therefore, the Bulk Modulus of Elasticity (K) of sand is $23333.33N/mm^2$.

If only a mass of sand dropped, it will splatter over the surface of the floor. Therefore, in order to simulate the impact experiments as faithfully as possible, as shown in Fig. 7, making model for the bag which wrapped the mass of sand wrap from outside by using thin shell element, and assuming that the material characteristics value of the bag as isotropic elastic medium the values are given as follows:

Mass density $1.0 \times 10^{-6} kg / mm^3$

Young's modulus $5.0 \times 10^3 N / mm^2$

Poisson's ratio   0.3

In addition, we set the contact condition between the sand and the bag as the follows rules: The sand does not leak from the bag; the sandbag does not pass through the floor when the sandbag is dropping; and it is possible to transmit the load simultaneously through the contact conditions.

It takes a considerable amount of time to compute impact analysis of sandbag' dropping by repetitive calculation in chronological order. In order to save the analysis time, we compute the speed when the sandbag reaches the floor from height $h = 250mm$ with the following equation:

$$v = \sqrt{2gh} .$$ (2)

And the acceleration of gravity is $g = 9800mm / s^2$.

The impact analysis starts with the state that the sandbag is in touch with the floor and the initial speed of the sandbag is calculated using equation (2). The impact position is the central part of the top veneer, that is, the weakness rigidity part of floor. When the analysis ends, the area of impact is the center part of top plate for the weakness stiffness part of floor. So we evaluate the residual deformation using the central point of circular impact area as the evaluation point. In the actual impact analysis, we analyze repetitively from the moment of the impact starting to 40msec in chronological order, and then take the sandbag away. After the floor recovers from elastic deformation completely, we evaluate the residual deformation.

4.2   Analysis of Maximum Deformation by Static Load

Fig. 8 shows the model of static load analysis which is the same as impact analysis model made according to the testing standards of "Performance Assessment of the Free Access Floor" of JAFA. The four corners of raised floor structure are fully fixed. In the actual static load experiment, a 50mm diameter cylinder with 3000N load is put on the center area of top veneer of floor.

As shown in Fig. 8, the contact state between the pressurizer and the surface of floor is complex. In order to analyze the distribution of contact force accurately, it is necessary to set nonlinear contact condition between the pressurizer and the surface of floor and analyze it in detail. However, from the standpoint of optimal design and for the reason that obtaining more accurate displacement value would cost more analysis time, it is important to grasp variation trend of the displacement as soon as possible.

Here, checking the specific dimension, we notice that, the edge length of floor is 500mm, which is 10 times of the diameter of pressurizer (50mm). According to Saint Venant's principle, it is thought that the load diameter has great effect on the maximum deflection of mechanical characteristic of the whole structure, and the load distribution depending on contact state has little effect on it.

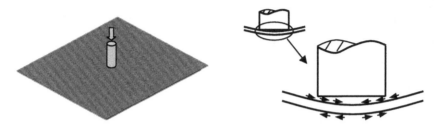

Fig. 8. Static analysis model

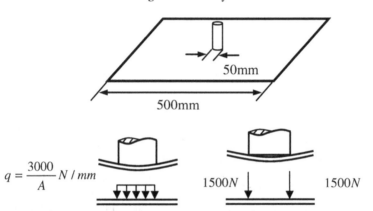

Fig. 9. Uniform load and 2 points concentrated load

Table 2. Comparison of Displacement with Difference Load Conditions

	Centre-point deflection	Deflection difference
Uniform load	7774414063/EI	
2 points concentrated load	7699218750/EI	−0.967%

Here, in order to verify the correct load setting quantitatively, about the contact state of pressurizer and the surface of floor, when the deflection of central point on the raised floor reached the maximum or minimum values that as shown in Fig. 9, the uniformly-distributed load and the two-point concentrated load are used as the load distribution respectively. We use the actual floor dimension and deflection equation of material mechanics to estimate the deflection of these two extreme load cases. As shown in Table 2, the results suggest that the effect of the deflection on the central point of floor by different load distributions is within 0.967%.

Therefore, the static analysis problem of this research, that can apply distribution of load which corresponding to the largest deflection, as putting 3000N uniform load on the 50mm diameter circular area at the center of the floor surface. Thus it can be evaluating of output as the maximum deformation of deflection of the central point on the floor surface.

5   Light-Weight Design by Comprehensive Optimization

5.1   Model's Settings of Comprehensive Optimization

The optimization question considering concurrently with the residual deformation of impact and the maximum deformation of static load is expressed as follows:

$$\text{Find} \quad x = [t_1, t_2, r, R, a/r]^T$$

$$\text{Min.} \quad W = f(x)$$

$$\text{S.T.} \quad 0.7mm \leq t_1 \leq 1.4mm$$

$$0.6mm \leq t_2 \leq 1.0mm$$

$$15mm \leq r \leq 30mm \tag{3}$$

$$50mm \leq R \leq 58mm$$

$$0.1 \leq a/r \leq 0.5$$

$$D_I \leq [D_I]$$

$$D_S \leq [D_S]$$

In this expression, there are five design variables $x = [t_1, t_2, r, R, a/r]^T$, t_1 is the thickness of top plate, t_2 is the thickness of bottom plate, and as shown in Fig. 4, r is the edge length on the top of core, R is the edge length on the bottom of core, a/r is the ratio of the chamfer length a and the top edge length r. The variation range of each design variable is shown in expression (3). The target function $W = f(x)$ is to find the minimum weight of the raised floor structure. D_I is the residual deformation of impact. $[D_I]$ is the acceptable value for the residual deformation of impact. According to the principle that the performance of new floor structure is not worse than that of the existing raised floor, $[D_I]$ is set at the value 4.27mm which is the residual deformation of the existing multi-core type raised floor by impact. D_S is the maximum deformation of the static load. $[D_S]$ is the acceptable value for the maximum deformation of the static load, and it is set at the value 3.22mm which is the maximum deformation of the existing multi-core type raised floor by static load.

We can find the lightest truss core type raised floor through solving the optimization expression(3) within the variation range of design variable, under the premise that the residual deformation of impact and the maximum deformation of the static load for the new floor structure are better than the existing multi-core type raised floor.

5.2   Optimization Method of Response Surface

To analyze the response (residual deformation, maximum deformation, etc.) of design variable change is essentially to solve a nonlinear problem in the expression (3). And the analysis time is considerably long.   Since the design space is complex, we decide to use Response Surface method[11] as the optimization technique.

When the Response Surface method is used to solve the optimization expression (3), it is done based on the following calculation procedures. Firstly, it is necessary to choose an appropriate orthogonal table following the design parameter and variation range. Here we use the L27 orthogonal table to generate sample data to make the response surface for optimization. Secondly, we use these sample data to change the structure models respectively, and then do the analysis of the impact and the static load analysis respectively with these structure models. From the analysis results, we obtain the residual deformation, the maximum deformation and the weight of structures which are necessary for the optimization calculation. Finally, we organize the one-to-one relationship between sample data and characteristic value, and create the interpolation approximate formula called Response surface. Lastly, the optimized solution is obtained by doing the optimization calculation using the approximate formula.

This optimized solution is obtained by using the interpolation approximate formula. Now we have to build the truss core panel type raised floor structure with the optimized design variable and then to confirm the accuracy of the optimized calculation through doing the impact analysis and the static load analysis by using LS-DYNA.

5.3   Optimized Result

We get the optimized result by using Response Surface method to analyze the optimization expression (3). We build the truss core type raised floor structure with this optimized result, and then do confirmation analysis using LS-DYNA. Table 3 shows the results of the confirmation analysis. The optimized truss core type raised floor structure is shown in Fig. 10. As shown in Fig. 10, with the chamfer becoming rather larger, the hexagon top surface of primary truss core becomes closer to triangular shape.

Comparing the optimization result in Table 3 with the optimization expression (3), the design variables and the constraint condition are all within the acceptable range. In addition, the weight of raised floor has been reduced by 23.69% by changing the raised floor structure from multi-core type to truss core type and adjusting parameters to appropriate shapes. Additionally, the residual deformation of impact and maximum deformation of the static load have been improved by 3.98% and 3.42% respectively.

Table 3. Comparison of Initial Multi Core Type and Optimal Truss Core Type of Raised Floor Structures

	Multi core type	Truss core type	Change (%)
Thickness of Face plate (t_1)	1.4mm	1.0mm	
Thickness of Back plate (t_2)	1.0mm	0.9mm	
Length of upper edge of core (r)		18mm	
Length of lower edge of core (R)		58mm	
Wide of cut corner (a)		8.59mm	
Wight of raised floor (W)	5.53kg	4.22kg	-23.69%
Residual displacement of impact load (D_I)	4.27mm	4.10mm	-3.98%
Displacement of static load (D_S)	3.22mm	3.11mm	-3.42%

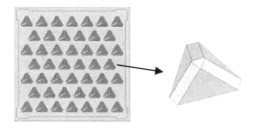

Fig. 10. Optimized Truss Core Type Raised Floor Structure

6   Consideration for Optimization Result

The validity of the optimization result, as well as the mechanical characteristic and the effect of the raised floor changing from multi-core type to truss core type, will be discussed as follows.

Firstly, the effect of the change for the load contact area of core that as shown in Fig. 11, when the load (impact load or static load) travels along the top plate to the core parts, for the truss core type, the top surface is a flat triangular shape close to hexagonal shape and the contact area becomes much larger. But for the multi-core type, the contact shape is close to point contact. Therefore, compared to the multi-core type, the local deformation of the truss core type is comparatively difficult to generate, and such structure is also useful for reducing the weight of the structure.

(a) Before optimization (b) After optimization   (a) Before optimization (b) After optimization

Fig. 11. Comparison of Multi Core and Truss core under Press Load

Fig. 12. Comparison of Multi Core and Truss core

Secondly, the effect of the change for the wall geometry of core that as shown in Fig. 11, analyzing the wall geometry from the geometric configuration of three-dimensional conformation, the wall cross-section of multi-core type core is arc-shape and it is a comparatively weak constitution of resistance-reaction force for deflection. On the other hand, for the truss core type core, the wall cross-sections are structured of rectangle or trapezium supporting each other mutually in an oblique direction like three-dimensional truss structure, and such structure is thought that it reinforce resistance-reaction force for deflection greatly. This becomes one of the reasons why the structure lightening can be achieved.

Furthermore, it is about the appropriate three-dimensional conformation of core and the form change of truss core type core before and after the optimization that is shown in Fig. 12: before optimization, the top surface and the bottom surface are similar parallel hexagonal shape, the wall surfaces are rectangle or trapezium. In contrast, after optimization, the top surface is close to triangle, the bottom surface is hexagon, the wall surfaces are intersected with rectangle or triangle. It is considered that the most effect on resistance-reaction force for deflection on the wall surface is the arrangement of broken curve. It is considered that comparing with the core form before optimization, the core form after optimization has relatively better stability because the top surface and the wall surface after optimization are formed of stable triangle.

7   Conclusions

Considering the residual deformation of impact and the maximum deformation of the static load based on the JAFA testing standards, we utilized the truss core panel of typical structural material invented from origami-engineering to replace the existing multi-core type raised floor. And we designed lightweight structure of truss core panel type raised floor structure.

(1) According to the optimization result, it is feasible to build raised floor using truss core panel instead of multi-core type panel. Under the premise that the characteristics of impact and static load for the truss core type structure are better than the existing multi-core type raised floor, we achieved 23.69% weight reduction than the existing multi-core type raised floor. Additionally, the residual deformation of

impact and maximum deformation of the static load have been improved by 3.98% and 3.42% respectively.

(2) It is made clear that, utilizing the truss core panel type instead of the exiting multi-core type, the load contact area of top surface on the core became larger; the local deformation rigidity became relatively stronger. Additionally, the shape of the wall surface is not of arc, but close to the three-dimensional truss structure supporting each other in an oblique direction. Therefore, the resistance-reaction force for deflection of the raised floor is considerably reinforced.

(3) From the optimization result of truss core type raised floor, we could predict that, comparing with the exiting truss core panel, the optimized raised floor has the most stability as the top surface of triangle, the bottom surface of hexagonal, and the wall surface of rectangle or triangle mutually support one another.

In future study, we will discuss the new raised floor of truss core type which is confirmed performance in this study around the forming process.

Acknowledgments. Several parts of the research work were carried out by the support of Grants-in-Aid for scientific research(category S) under Grant No.20226006.We acknowledge its aid dearly.

References

1. Nakamura, M., Hashimoto, Y., Kanoh, S.: A Survey on Raised Access Floor with Fixed Height. Architectural Institute of Japan, 693–694 (2003)
2. Nishimura, H.: Lightening technology in the object-making. Form Tech Rev., 19–24 (2008)
3. Performance assessment of free access floor based on test method of free access floor (JIS A 1450:2009) Japan Access Floor Association, pp. 6–11 (2009)
4. http://sciencelinks.jp/content/view/656/260/
5. Nojima, T.: Panel and Its Manufacturing Method. Japanese Patent (2005)
6. Nojima, T., Saito, K.: Plate and Piece of Plate. Japanese Patent (2005)
7. Hagiwara, I.: From Origami to "Origamics". The Japan Journal 5(3), 22–25 (2008)
8. Saito, K., Nojima, T., Hagiwara, I.: Relation between Geometrical Patterns and Mechanical Properties in Newly Developed Light-Weight Core Panels. Transactions of the Japan Society of Mechanical Engineers A 74(748), 1580–1586 (2008)
9. Tokura, S., Hagiwara, I.: Forming Process Simulation of Truss Core Panel. Transactions of the Japan Society of Mechanical Engineers A 74(746), 81–87 (2008)
10. Tokura, S., Hagiwara, I.: Shape Optimization to Improve Impact Energy Absorption Ability of Truss Core Panel. Transactions of the Japan Society of Mechanical Engineers A 76(765), 24–31 (2010)
11. Zhao, X.: New Aspects for Development of Optimization System from The Point of Design Site. In: Proceedings of the Conference on Computational Engineering and Science, vol. 12, pp. 129–132 (2007)

3D Origami Structure Design and Simulation by Parametric Origami Module

Yujing Liao[1], Xilu Zhao[2], Sachiko Ishida[1], and Ichiro Hagiwara[1]

[1] Institute for Advanced Study of Mathematical Science, Meiji University, Kanagawa, Japan
{tz12009,tz12013,ihagi}@meiji.ac.jp
[2] Saitama Institute of Technology, Saitama, Japan
tyoukiroku@gmail.com

Abstract. The purpose of this paper is to propose a Parametric Origami Module and relevant methods, which are able to expand the complex three-dimensional origami structure into a plane only by the topological relation matrix TP and node position coordinate matrix GP. Furthermore, an extended data structure for POM is proposed as well. In this study, we are not limited to the particular conditions for design origami structure such as Ori-tatami folding and axial symmetry. Plenty of three-dimensional origami structures are analyzed from the geometrical perspective and the common features among them are extracted. In the end, we compare the proposed method with others in further discussion and confirm its effectiveness.

Keywords: 3D Origami Structure, Parametric Origami Module, Origami Engineering.

1 Introduction

In recent years, in order to be able to make the metal plate simply by pressing process, utilizing excellent performance of bending stiffness and in shear strength, origami structure as new lightweight structure have been developed, and which have more application s and samples in engineering. Many researchers have been researching on origami structure from different point of view as well[1],[2].

Nojima published related results from discussions of Plane Filling Form, Space Filing Form, Ori-tatami , Spiral rotation facet structure[3]-[5] and etc. From practical point of view, Robot J. Lang developed a simulation system [6] under geometric restrictions by using computer technology, and Miyazaki developed origami simulation system which was able to fold virtual paper in three-dimensional space [7]. It is necessary to consider shape form and folding lines configuration of origami structure for such customized simulation software system. The development of these results related research has been carried on [8],[9] whereas they were specialized to be held under the Ori-tatami conditions that can be flat foldable.

On the other hand, Mitani was not limited to conditions of folding, took the axial symmetry three-dimensional origami structure as study object, proposed a three-dimensional origami design method for axial symmetric shape [10],[11]. By

T. Xiao, L. Zhang, and S. Ma (Eds.): ICSC 2012, Part I, CCIS 326, pp. 228–240, 2012.

imputing fold line on the two-dimensional plane, the software is able to generate crease pattern in plane and 3D data of axial symmetric three-dimensional origami automatically was developed.

In the following discussion, if it as a technique for designing origami structure is not practical. Since the geometrical composition of the general 3D origami structure is very complicated, that establishing design method of the general practical 3D origami structure and developing new origami structure have becoming important issue.

In this study, we are not limit to specific conditions, such axial symmetry and Ori-tatami; Plenty more 3D origami structure are analyzed from a geometric point of view, the common feature is extracted out and parametric origami module with extended data structure is proposed.

2   Parametric Origami Module proposal

As shown in Fig. 1, there is an 3D origami structure design example of snake like shape. The 3D origami structure and the corresponding crease pattern in plane is shown in Fig. 1 (a) and (b), respectively. In the same figure, solid line represents mountain line whereas dot line represents valley line of origami. Moreover, pay attention to the node exists in the plane which is shown by the white circle dot, it is easy to confirm that fundamental structure composed of three mountain lines and one valley line is existing , which is regarded as common geometric feature as shown in Fig. 1(c).

Here, the fundamental structure in Fig. 1(c) is shown connecting relationship between node and the others. Thus by giving coordinate value to each node, it is possible to express portion of the origami structure freely.

In this study, the fundamental structure which is shown in Fig. 1(c) is called Parametric Origami Module (hereafter is shorted as POM). Ordinarily, such POM alike features are able to be extracted as many different types for complex 3D origami structure. POM with the fewest node number which is suitable for 3D origami structure use has been investigated. First of all, in the case of one mountain line and one valley line, or two mountain lines and one valley line, there will an unstable curved surface and them are not able to be applied as POM for 3D origami structure. However, in the case of three mountain lines and one valley line which is shown in Fig. 1(c), straight lines are between nodes and make each facet as stable plane.

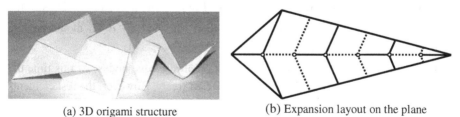

(a) 3D origami structure   (b) Expansion layout on the plane

Fig. 1. Snake type 3D origami structure and parametric origami module

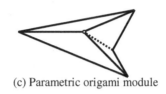

(c) Parametric origami module

Fig. 1. (*Continued*)

Certainly the other type POM should be considered, whereas in this study, the minimum nodes POM of which three mountain lines and one valley line has been focused on; and the expanded POM has been considered as well.

2.1   Composition of POM

TP and GP are defined as follows for general 3D origami structure. TP is the abbreviation for topologic parameter and GP is the abbreviation for Geometric Parameter as well.

$$TP = \begin{Bmatrix} 1 & P_1^{(1)} & P_2^{(1)} & P_3^{(1)} & P_4^{(1)} \\ 2 & P_1^{(2)} & P_2^{(2)} & P_3^{(2)} & P_4^{(2)} \\ \cdots & \cdots & \cdots & \cdots & \cdots \\ i & P_1^{(i)} & P_2^{(i)} & P_3^{(i)} & P_4^{(i)} \\ \cdots & \cdots & \cdots & \cdots & \cdots \\ n & P_1^{(n)} & P_2^{(n)} & P_3^{(n)} & P_4^{(n)} \end{Bmatrix} \quad GP = \begin{bmatrix} 1 & x_1 & y_1 & z_1 \\ 2 & x_2 & y_2 & z_2 \\ \cdots & \cdots & \cdots & \cdots \\ i & x_i & y_i & z_i \\ \cdots & \cdots & \cdots & \cdots \\ n & x_n & y_n & z_n \end{bmatrix} \quad (1)$$

In this equation, n is node sequence number of 3D origami structure; $P_1^{(i)}, P_2^{(i)}, P_3^{(i)}, P_4^{(i)}$ are number of node which node i connect with, and node i is regarded as center node of element i. x_i, y_i, z_i ($i = 1,2,......,n$) is node coordinate. The composition of TP matrix of Eq.(1) is explained as follows.

(1) The node number of node i connected with is four or three ; when it equals three, the fourth element $P_4^{(i)}$ is set 0.

(2) Connection relationship of nodes is contained in element of i row. The end of valley line is regards as the first element $P_1^{(i)}$ as usual, and set up elements $P_2^{(i)}, P_3^{(i)}, P_4^{(i)}$ by mountain line end in anti-clockwise order. Thus in the way as: valley line end $i - P_1^{(i)}$, mountain line end $i - P_2^{(i)}$, mountain line end $i - P_3^{(i)}$, mountain line end $i - P_4^{(i)}$.

(3) There is the case of valley end is not exist on all the edge nodes. At this time the node of first element $P_1^{(i)}$ is able to be selected freely. However, the rest elements should follow anti-clockwise order.

Here, for simplicity, detail of POM is utilizing the 3D origami model shown in Fig. 2. The coordinate of eight nodes in the same figure are becoming as the following:

$$GP = \begin{bmatrix} 1 & 0 & 0 & 0 \\ 2 & -55.54 & 0 & -81.95 \\ 3 & -99.00 & -90.93 & -52.5 \\ 4 & 99.00 & 0 & 0 \\ 5 & -99.00 & 90.93 & -52.50 \\ 6 & 154.54 & 0 & -81.95 \\ 7 & 198.00 & 90.93 & -52.50 \\ 8 & 198.00 & -90.93 & -52.50 \end{bmatrix} \qquad (2)$$

While the structure shape changing TP matrix remains as it was, only GP matrix changed and new shape is obtained.

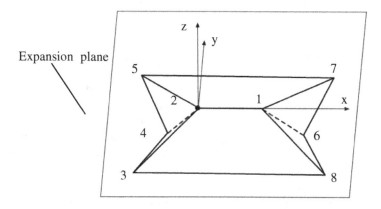

Fig. 2. A 3D origami model with expansion plane

After that, it is that extract adjacent nodes to make TP matrix for each node. About the node located on the edge, if number of them is not enough fill element of 0. For the sample of 3D origami structure in Fig. 3, the node sequences are obtained as follows:

$$\{1,2,3,4,5\}\ \{2,1,5,3,0\}\ \{3,1,2,8,0\}\ \{4,6,7,1,8\}$$
$$\{5,1,7,2,0\}\ \{6,4,8,7,0\}\ \{7,4,6,5,0\}\ \{8,4,3,6,0\} \qquad (3)$$

Here, wrote Eq.(3) by the order of center node number of each POM, the node connecting relationship matrix is obtained as follow:

$$TP = \begin{bmatrix} 1 & 2 & 3 & 4 & 5 \\ 2 & 1 & 5 & 3 & 0 \\ 3 & 1 & 2 & 8 & 0 \\ 4 & 6 & 7 & 1 & 8 \\ 5 & 1 & 7 & 2 & 0 \\ 6 & 4 & 8 & 7 & 0 \\ 7 & 4 & 6 & 5 & 0 \\ 8 & 4 & 3 & 6 & 0 \end{bmatrix} \qquad (4)$$

It is possible that represent 3D origami structure that shown in Fig. 3 by using TP matrix in Eq.(4) and GP relationship in Eq.(3).

2.2   Extension of POM

Furthermore, if a POM is not typical construction of 'Three mountain lines and One valley line' , the TP matrix and GP matrix are defined as follows:

$$
TP = \begin{Bmatrix}
1 & P_1^{(1)} & \cdots & P_J^{(1)} & P_T & P_{J+1}^{(1)} & \cdots & P_K^{(1)} \\
2 & P_1^{(2)} & \cdots & P_J^{(2)} & P_T & P_{J+1}^{(2)} & \cdots & P_K^{(2)} \\
\cdots & \cdots & \cdots & \cdots & & \cdots & & \cdots \\
i & P_1^{(i)} & \cdots & P_J^{(i)} & P_T & P_{J+1}^{(i)} & \cdots & P_K^{(i)} \\
\cdots & \cdots & \cdots & \cdots & \cdots & \cdots & \cdots & \cdots \\
n & P_1^{(n)} & \cdots & P_J^{(n)} & P_T & P_{J+1}^{(n)} & \cdots & P_K^{(n)}
\end{Bmatrix}
\qquad
GP = \begin{Bmatrix}
1 & x_1 & y_1 & z_1 \\
2 & x_2 & y_2 & z_2 \\
\cdots & \cdots & \cdots & \cdots \\
i & x_i & y_i & z_i \\
\cdots & \cdots & \cdots & \cdots \\
n & x_n & y_n & z_n
\end{Bmatrix}
\tag{5}
$$

Although the GP matrix kept the same construction as mentioned above, the TP matrix became a little bit complicated. Here, P_t represents a flag bit which is able to be distinguished from node number, thus it is capable to make a distinction between mountain line nodes and valley line nodes; For the reason that node number is larger than one, the value of it uses -1 in usual.J and K in the equation represents sequence number for different node. Before the tag bit are valley line nodes whereas after are mountain line nodes. However, we assume that the structure consists of the same type POM so the mix type POM is not considered. As a result , the application range of POM is extend and a sample of it is given in the later chapter.

Moreover, for the reason that the node connecting relationship between structure and crease pattern have not change, both of TP matrix are the same.

In this study, the combination of TP matrix and GP matrix is defined as POM of 3D origami structure. In other words, because the one-to-one relationship existed between POM and 3D origami structure, the complex structure is able to be handled in the mathematic form of simple matrix.

3   Unfolding Algorithm of 3D Origami Structure by POM

When unfolding a 3D origami structure into a plane, since the connecting relationship between nodes is unchanged, using a same matrix TP, in order to match coordinate of each node after unfolding, it is require that update GP matrix.

Here, technique of generating crease pattern is shown. Before unfolding POM origami structure is shown in Fig. 3 (a), unfolding crease pattern by POM is shown in Fig. 3 (b). Before and after, the equivalence relationship between angle formed by two sides of POM for 3D structure and crease pattern is existed:

$$
\theta_i = \theta_i' \quad (i = 1,2,3,4) \tag{6}
$$

In addition, in order to unfold the structure into a flat plane, it is necessary to meet condition as follow:

$$\theta_1 + \theta_2 + \theta_3 + \theta_4 = 360° \tag{7}$$

Based on Eq.(7), the previous section unfold the structure to the plane following as below. Here, for simplicity as the previous section, explain unfold algorithm by using the 3D origami model shown in Fig. 2.

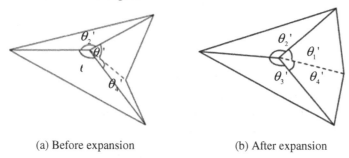

(a) Before expansion   (b) After expansion

Fig. 3. Angles between edges in the POM

(1) Select a arbitrary edge of the 3D origami structure as beginning of expansion. Determine a plane for expanding which is including the selected edge. For the sample in Fig. 2, internal edge1-4 is regarded as beginning edge of expansion, and xy-plane is regarded as expansion plane. The structure before expanding and expansion plane are shown in this figure. At this time, connection relationship is kept the same as Eq. (2).

(2) Confirm that the structure is able to be expanded or not. The POM upon node 1 is able to be expanded when all the angles around node 1 $\theta_{415} + \theta_{512} + \theta_{213} + \theta_{314} = 360°$ satisfied Eq. (6). In the same way, the POM upon 4 is able to be expanded.

(3) In a row there are four nodes elements in TP matrix, thus there are two POM existing. A node which connecting with four nodes is called internal node, whereas a node connecting with three nodes is called boundary node. Then carry on the expansion calculation for the POM upon node 1. First of all, for the reason that the node 4 is already located on the expanding plane, edge 1-4 is taken as base one for expanding connected node 5 in counter clockwise direction. The included angle θ_{415} formed by edge1-4 and edge1-5 of the structure is calculated as follow:

$$\theta_{415} = \arccos \frac{\overrightarrow{14} \cdot \overrightarrow{15}}{\left|\overrightarrow{14}\right|\left|\overrightarrow{15}\right|} \tag{8}$$

In this equation, $\overrightarrow{14} = \left[v_{x14}, v_{y14}, v_{z14}\right]^T$ is the vector from center node1 to node4, $\overrightarrow{15} = \left[v_{x15}, v_{y15}, v_{z15}\right]^T$ is the vector from center node1 to node5.

Secondly, in the expanding plane, along the direction starting from node 1 and the same as vector $\overrightarrow{14}$, identical length as $\left|\overrightarrow{15}\right|$ vector $\overrightarrow{15'} = \left[v_{x15'}, v_{y15'}, v_{z15'}\right]^T$ is made as the follow equation:

$$\vec{15'} = \left|\vec{15}\right| \frac{\vec{14}}{\left|\vec{14}\right|} \tag{9}$$

In addition, rotate vector $\vec{15'}$ of angle θ_{415} in the expanding plane, the expanding edge 1^*-5^* is obtained.

$$\vec{1^*5^*} = \begin{bmatrix} \cos\theta_{415} & \sin\theta_{415} & 0 \\ -\sin\theta_{415} & \cos\theta_{415} & 0 \\ 0 & 0 & 1 \end{bmatrix} \vec{15'} \tag{10}$$

Here, superscript* means expanded in the plane. Regarding expanded edge 1^*-5^* as base edge, by similar process, connected node 2 is able to be expanded in counter clockwise direction. And then is based on edge 1^*-2^* and expand node 3 by similar process. As result, all nodes of the POM upon node 1 as center are expanded on plane entirely.

The GP matrix and the structure in this step is shown in Eq.(11) and Fig. 4, respectively.

$$GP = \begin{bmatrix} 1 & 0 & 0 & 0 \\ 2 & v_{x12'}\cos\theta_{512} + v_{y12'}\sin\theta_{512} & -v_{x12'}\sin\theta_{512} + v_{y12'}\cos\theta_{512} & z_{12'} \\ 3 & v_{x13'}\cos\theta_{213} + v_{y13'}\sin\theta_{213} & -v_{x13'}\sin\theta_{213} + v_{y13'}\cos\theta_{213} & z_{13'} \\ 4 & 99.00 & 0 & 0 \\ 5 & v_{x15'}\cos\theta_{415} + v_{y15'}\sin\theta_{415} & -v_{x15'}\sin\theta_{415} + v_{y15'}\cos\theta_{415} & z_{15'} \\ 6 & 154.54 & 0 & -81.95 \\ 7 & 198.00 & 90.93 & -52.50 \\ 8 & 198.00 & -90.93 & -52.50 \end{bmatrix} \tag{11}$$

Here, in order to check whether the expansion to plan is done or not, angle $\theta_{415}^*, \theta_{512}^*, \theta_{213}^*, \theta_{314}^*$ was calculated and this result satisfied the Eq. (5), which is shown that node 1 regarded as center node POM was able to expand into the plane.

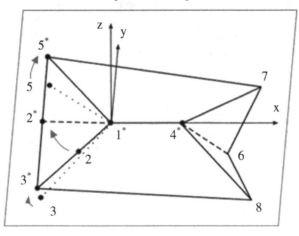

Fig. 4. Expanded point 5, 2 and point 3

(4) After expanding one POM, it is the expansion for adjacent POM. At this time, it is starting from the edge which connecting with center node of each POM. In this example, edge4-1 is regarded as base one, and expanding connected node 8 in counter clockwise direction. And then based expanded edge 4^*-8^* and expanding node 6 into the plane; Based expanded edge 4^*-6^* and expanding node 7 into the plane. Till now all nodes of the POM upon node 4 as the center are expanded into the plane. Here, confirm expansion condition (6) for current POM, satisfied and finished expansion.

The GP matrix and the structure of which POM upon node 4 as the center is expanded into the plan is shown in Eq.(12) and Fig. 5, respectively. Obviously, the z coordinates in the 3rd column of the matrix have became 0.

In addition, there are only 2 POMs of the structure that shown in Fig. 2. At this point, the three-dimensional origami structure is expanded into the plane entirely. Moreover, the expansion algorithm is able to be used for the extended POM data structure as well. In this way, by changing value of the node which is regarded as a parameter, it is able to generate 3D origami structure series of different shapes.

$$
GP = \begin{bmatrix}
1 & 0 & 0 & 0 \\
2 & -99.00 & 0 & 0 \\
3 & -99.00 & -105.00 & 0 \\
4 & 99.00 & 0 & 0 \\
5 & -99.00 & 105.00 & 0 \\
6 & 198.00 & 0 & 0 \\
7 & 198.00 & 105.00 & 0 \\
8 & 198.00 & -105.00 & 0
\end{bmatrix}
\tag{12}
$$

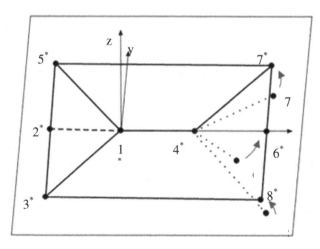

Fig. 5. Expanded Points 8,6 and 7

4   The Design Procedure of Design 3D Origami Structure by POM

The design procedure is divided into three parts as the following.

(1) Make 3D shape or make origami structure based on POM from point cloud. This part is design of 3D origami structure and decides basic composition as shape of it.
(2) Make POM information from given shape. More specifically, repeating for each node, TP matrix elements and GP matrix elements are generated automatically by the system. Also, checking expansion condition for each POM in GP matrix and modification are carried on.
(3) Add or remove POM if it is necessary. In this step it is adjusting for fishing design of the 3D origami structure obtained in step (2).

5   Verification of the Proposed Method by Samples

We have developed a system that able to design and generating three-dimensional origami structure by using proposal of POM. The interface of the system is shown in Fig. 6(a).

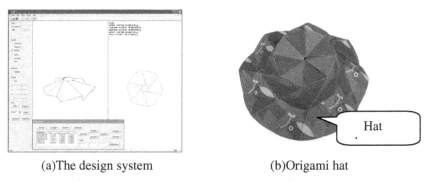

(a)The design system   (b)Origami hat

Fig. 6. The system inter face and origami hat sample

A sample of origami hat along is shown in Fig. 6(b), and the procedure is:

(1) Made one POM which is shown in Fig. 7 (a). The node of the POM is V0, V1, V2, V3 and V4. Here, the length d of the N- regular polygon(In this case n=8.) which is interior part of the hat along is utilized. The coordinates of node V3, V0, V4 were obtained. According to interior angle θ of the N-regular polygon and angle condition in Eq.(7), the coordinates of node V1, V2 were obtained.
(2) Use the edit function of the system, make POM rotate angle θ around the circumferential direction and duplicate new POM of seven times. (Fig. 7 (b))
(3) Close the outer periphery of the hat along. (Fig. 7(c))
(4) Delete repeating vertexes and edges, In addition adjust node number, the hat along finished.

The obtained TP matrix and GP matrix of which corresponding structure of the hat along are shown in Fig. 7(c), Eq. (12), respectively.

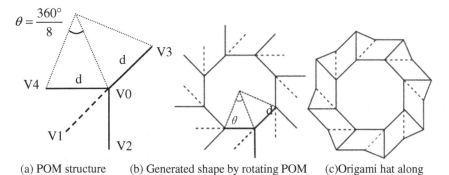

(a) POM structure   (b) Generated shape by rotating POM   (c)Origami hat along

Fig. 7. POM and hat along of origami structure

$$
TP = \begin{bmatrix}
1 & 2 & 3 & 4 & 22 \\
2 & 24 & 3 & 1 & 0 \\
3 & 2 & 5 & 1 & 0 \\
4 & 5 & 6 & 7 & 1 \\
5 & 3 & 6 & 4 & 0 \\
\cdots & \cdots & \cdots & \cdots & \cdots \\
22 & 23 & 24 & 1 & 19 \\
23 & 21 & 24 & 22 & 0 \\
24 & 23 & 2 & 22 & 0
\end{bmatrix}
\quad
GP = \begin{bmatrix}
1 & 8.40 & 0.00 & 0.00 \\
2 & 10.86 & -5.94 & 0.00 \\
3 & 14.34 & -2.46 & 0.00 \\
4 & 5.94 & 5.94 & 0.00 \\
5 & 11.88 & 3.48 & 0.00 \\
\cdots & \cdots & \cdots & \cdots \\
22 & 5.94 & -5.94 & 0.00 \\
23 & 3.48 & -11.88 & 0.00 \\
24 & 8.40 & -11.88 & 0.00
\end{bmatrix}
\tag{13}
$$

Here, by using the functionality of the design system, while changing the angle as shown in Fig. 8, it is able to generate the folding process of the hat along portion. The GP matrix in Eq.(12) stored changing coordinate of each node whereas the TP matrix in Eq.(12) is kept the same values during folding process.

Fig. 8. Origami hat along structure shape and GP matrix in the process of folding back

For the top of the origami hat, the typical POM definition is not enough to represent the 3D structure although its portion is in one type similar composition. However, the extension of POM is able to be appropriate for this problem. By the rotation of one extended POM, the 3D structure is represented as shown in the left of Fig. 9, which is satisfied the expansion condition of Eq. (7).

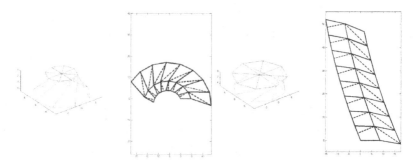

Fig. 9. 3D structures and crease patterns by extension of POM

And then, by the expansion algorithm the crease pattern of it is obtained   near the 3D structure in the left of Fig. 9. Moreover, by adjusting parameters of POM, it is easy to obtain structure serials whereas TP matrix kept the same. For example, a new 3D structure of top hat and its corresponding crease pattern are shown in the right of Fig. 9 only by changing parameters. The advantage of POM is obvious.

6   Comparison with Conventional Design Methods

Here, in order to verify the effectiveness and advantage of the proposed method, the comparison from different point of view has been doing as follows.

(1) With respect to design method, the origami design proposal by Robot J.Lang from reference 8 to be discussed. The design method of it, which is not able to applied for the origami pattern as shown in Fig. 9. That is, the origami structure is necessary to perpendicular to the base plane and composing Ori-tatami two facets have to be symmetric as well. Thus the applied range of the proposal has been greatly restricted. In addition when carries on design, user has to image the structure in 3D space and create projection of it in a base plane. Thus it is difficult to image the final shape of the structure at the beginning, user should be experiential and design process is time-consuming.

On the other hand, applied the proposal of this study, based on local POM generated from internal nodes in the system, TP and GP matrix are added or modified whereas the 3D origami structure is corresponding to them of one-to-one relationship.

The proposed method is not only deal with intermediate between 3D origami structure and crease patter, but also able to verify expanding condition and generate 3D origami structure directly.

(2) With respect to data structure, for storing hat sample along in Fig. 7 by the proposed 3D origami design method in reference 7, data information of three layers are necessary: Fi represents facet information, Ei represents edge information, and Vi represents vertex information.

By using the proposed method in this study, as data structure, GP and TP obtained as follows: When using the proposed method of this study to represent 3D origami structure, only by TP matrix and GP matrix are enough and data structure became simpler. Speed for searching necessary node for processing is able to be faster, and algorithm complexity became simpler. Moreover, facet information is included in GP and TP matrix without data information lost.

(3) With respect to applying range, a design system has been developed which is regarded axial symmetry origami structure as research object in reference 10. However, the input point array must be on the same plane of it. The sample in Fig. 8 is not satisfy this condition, so that it is not able to be generated by this method. On the other hand, by applied the proposed method of this study, there is not limitation by geometric condition, such as axial symmetry, and it is able to represent complex 3D origami structure by GP and TP matrix of POM.

7 Conclusions

In this study, design general 3D origami structure is regarded as research object, design method based on parametric origami model is proposed and the system for verify it has been developed. In addition, about the proposed design method specific discussions from instances are listed as follows:

(1) POM composed of geometric parametric GP and topologic parametric TP matrix for design 3D origami structure has been proposed.Moreover, extension of POM of data structure is complemented and enlarge the apply range for POM. Complex structure is able to be applied by it through parameters.
(2) The algorithm for design 3D origami structure and generate crease pattern based on POM was proposed, the expansion condition is able to be checked on the interface of the developed system and the effectiveness of the proposal was verified.
(3) From the actual design results of rotating and cylindrical 3D origami structure, the appropriateness of the POM based 3D origami structure design proposal is confirmed.

That Development and discussion on generating appropriate complex structure by utilizing POM will be the next issue.

Acknowledgments. Several parts of the research work were carried out by the support of Grants-in-Aid for scientific research(category S) under Grant No.20226006.We acknowledge its aid dearly.

References

1. Nojima, T.: Analytical Modeling of Origami and Its Applications: Mainly for Engineering Applications. The Japan Society for Industrial and Applied Mathematics 18(4), 271–284 (2008)

2. Hagiwara, I.: State-of-the-Art of Origami Engineering. Journal of the Japan Society for Simulation Technology 29(3), 80–81 (2010)

3. Saito, K., Nojima, T.: Modeling of New Light-Weight, Rigid Core Panels Based on Geometric Plane Tilings and Space Filling. Transactions of the Japan Society of Mechanical Engineers A 73(735), 1302–1308 (2007)

4. Nojima, T.: Foldable Tubes and Conical Shells Consisting of Differently Shaped Elements: Origami-Modelling of Non-Circular Tubes and Conical Shells. Transactions of the Japan Society of Mechanical Engineers C 68(667), 1015–1020 (2002)

5. Nojima, T., Kamei, T.: Origami-Modellings of Foldable Conical Shells Consisting of Spiral Fold Lines. Transactions of the Japan Society of Mechanical Engineers C 68(667), 1009–1014 (2002)

6. http://www.langorigami.com/science/computational/treemaker/treemaker.php

7. Miyazaki, S.: An ORIGAMI Playing Simulator in the Virtual Space. Journal of Visualization and Computer Animation 7(1), 25–42 (1996)

8. Lang, R.J.: A Computational Algorithm for Origami Design. In: SCG 1996 Proceedings of the Twelfth Annual Symposium on Computational Geometry, USA (1996)

9. Tachi, T.: Geometric Considerations for the Design of Rigid Origami Structures. In: Proceedings of the International Association for Shell and Spatial Structures (IASS) Symposium 2010, China (2010)

10. Mitani, J.: A Method for Designing 3D Origami Which Envelop an Axisymmetric Shape. Journal of the Japan Society for Simulation Technology 29(3), 114–120 (2010)

11. Mitani, J.: Geometric Modeling With Developable Surfaces and Designing of Origami. Journal of the Japan Society for Computational Engineering and Science 16(2), 2541–2544 (2011)

A Number of Key Technologies
in Ocean Wave Modeling and Simulation

Jianhua Xu[1,2], Hao Gu[1], Dinghua Wang [1,2], Fengju Kang[1,2], and Huizhen Yang[1,2]

[1] Marine College of Northwestern Polytechnical University, Xi'an 710072, China
[2] National Key Laboratory of Underwater Information Process and Control, Xi'an
`flyingcondor@163.com`

Abstract. Given the requirements for ocean wave three-dimensional visual simulation, and in combination with theory and engineering it expatiates, visualization key technologies such as ocean wave numerical simulation based on the modified linear dual superposition method, vertex array-based wave surface rendering method and light effect simulation into the details, and using DirectSound technology it achieves a sound simulation of the different sea conditions. The simulation results show that the ocean wave three-dimensional display is of high fidelity, good real-time and abundance sound, and thus is of great significance in ocean development and combat simulation.

Keywords: ocean wave, modeling, simulation, visualization, sound.

1   Introduction

Ocean wave is a very complex natural phenomenon, in terms of time and space, which has irregular and non-repeatability. The different causes led to all kinds of ocean wave, ocean wave caused by wind occur most frequently, it's the greatest impact on ocean phenomena. Ocean wave three-dimensional visual simulation technology make ocean wave mathematical simulation digital information become intuitive and the form of graphic images, change over time and space and interact with drilling platforms, ships and other artificial systems, enable researchers to grasp the overall evolution of the process and found its internal rules, thus it enrich the marine scientific research. How to make fidelity and real-time two key indicators can simultaneously meet the demand, which has been exploring target[1-6].

With rapid development of computer technology, in this paper, combining theory with engineering, it explicate numerical simulation technology, real-time rendering technology, light effect simulation technology and associated sound technology into the details.

2   Modeling Theory Method of Random Ocean Wave

Different forms of ocean wave modeling method is usually different, the paper discuss ocean wave model away from the coast, such ocean wave depends on the wind as the

T. Xiao, L. Zhang, and S. Ma (Eds.): ICSC 2012, Part I, CCIS 326, pp. 241–249, 2012.
© Springer-Verlag Berlin Heidelberg 2012

driving force, gravity as a restoring force, and does not consider the influence of seabed topography and the coastline. For this ocean wave research is generally from two areas, one on the fluctuations of ocean wave from a fluid mechanics point of view to discuss the state of ocean wave within the particle motion, the linear wave theory is also known as small-amplitude wave theory. Another is that the randomness of the wave action of the theory of random ocean wave, characterized by wave action as a random process (function), the use of stochastic process theory to analyze the statistical characteristics of the wave action in all cases. Obviously, the latter approach will be conducive to rapid visualization of simulation. Because of the general wave environment simulation must be introduction of a variety of three-dimensional model. The artificial system entities separate ocean wave image refresh rate to 50/s is required to ensure that the frame rate of the entire visual system is greater than 24/sec, which cause wave model selection problem.

2.1   Spectral Method Based on Linear Stochastic Theory

The theory of random ocean wave is divided into linear and nonlinear. Among them, the linear random wave theory is widely used in the simulation of the marine environment. Ocean wave phenomenon as a random process and the statistical characteristics of its characteristic is the primary means of random ocean wave. The first-order distribution of the random process (or first-order joint distribution) function to describe the first-order statistics (or the concept of joint statistics) the nature, Pierson, the first use Rice on the theory of radio noise in wave research, and introduce the power spectrum into random ocean wave research, so far, this method has developed into one of the main spectral method. To date, researchers have proposed various wave model based on this method, these models of wave-plane displacement assume that a random amplitude and phase of a number of mutually independent linear small amplitude wave superposition, whose result is ergodic stable normal random process. This procedure describes ocean wave, which constitute the linear (normal) random ocean wave theory. From the actual observation, the full growth of deep-water storms usually becomes linear or weakly nonlinear, wave surface displacement distribution is also approximate to a normal distribution, linear random wave model can be exported to the statistical distribution of a series of wave elements, ocean wave spectrum is an important statistical properties of random ocean wave, which contain not only the rich second order ocean wave information, but also directly give ocean wave energy distribution relative to frequency and direction, ocean wave spectrum for ocean wave forecasting, ocean and Marine engineering, ship design and so on has important practical significance. Therefore, the spectral method is a powerful tool to study ocean wave and its related issues.

The present study in-depth is ocean wave frequency spectrum and directional spectrum. Ocean wave spectrum $S(\omega)$ defined as the Fourier transform of the fixed-point of a smooth process wave surface displacement covariance function. Linear random ocean wave surface displacement of the mean is generally taken to be 0, so the Fourier transform of the correlation function $R(\tau)$ the covariance function is taken as

$$S(\omega) = \mathrm{Re}\,\frac{1}{2\pi}\int_{-\infty}^{\infty} R(\tau)\exp(-i\omega\tau)d\tau = \frac{1}{\pi}\int_{0}^{\infty} R(\tau)\cos\omega\tau d\tau \qquad (1)$$

Its inverse transform is

$$R(\tau) = \mathrm{Re}\,\int_{-\infty}^{\infty} S(\omega)\exp(i\omega\tau)d\tau = 2\int_{0}^{\infty} S(\omega)\cos\omega\tau d\omega \qquad (2)$$

$S(\omega)$ is a even function which the one side ($\omega \geq 0$) is enough to represent the entire function, so the unilateral spectrum can be defined in the wave, which use double side of the spectrum value to represent the symmetrical distribution $\omega = 0$ bilateral spectrum. The purpose of doubling is to make unilateral spectra and bilateral spectra have the same wave surface displacement variance, which show the unilateral spectral and bilateral spectrum gives the same energy. It is difficult to derive theoretically the ocean wave spectrum, existing ocean wave spectral models are empirical or semi-empirical semi-theoretical.

2.2   Amendments to the Linear Superposition Model

Ocean wave mathematical models created according to the above theory, get optimization and correction using the commonly linear dual superposition model based on the direction spectral inversion method of the linear stochastic theory, by the method, visual ocean wave is closer to the true ocean waveform.

Under stable sea conditions ocean wave is considered ergodic random process, and its fluctuation can be seen as a simple cosine wave superposition by ranging from unlimited multiple amplitude, frequency and initial phase. The common mathematical model Longuet-Higgins, and double superposition model. Longuet-Higgins, only to simulate ocean wave of the main wind direction, dual superposition model based on Longuet-Higgins model consider the actual ocean wave as wave mixing from different directions. he following formula:

$$\zeta(x, y, t) = \sum_{m=1}^{M}\sum_{n=1}^{N} a_{mn}\cos[k_{mn}(x\cos\theta_{mn} + y\sin\theta_{mn}) - \omega_{mn}t + \varepsilon_{mn}] \qquad (3)$$

Among, ζ is wave height, a_{mn} is composition wave amplitude, is the number of composition wave, θ_{mn} is composition wave direction angle, ω_{mn} is composition wave frequency, ε_{mn} is early phase of the composition wave, the wave parameters of the various components can be selected wave spectrum.

Wave spectrum on behalf of the wave energy relative to the composition of the distribution of the wave frequency is relatively easy by observing the JONSWAP spectrum formula proposed by Germany, Britain and other countries are as follows:

$$S(\omega) = \alpha \frac{g^2}{\omega^5} \exp[-1.25(\frac{\omega_0}{\omega})^4] \gamma^{\exp[-\frac{(\omega-\omega_0)^2}{2\sigma^2\omega_0^2}]} \tag{4}$$

Due to the small amplitude linear wave superposition, the crest of ocean wave generated is smooth, while real ocean wave even under calm ocean condition has more pointed crests and relatively flat troughs, let alone when a storm come, crests become more sharp , curled or broken. Therefore, the simulation waveforms should be amendatory:

1) The horizontal position of the grid points should be Changed and the same height of ocean wave should be maintained, in particular, when ocean wave in the trough, the horizontal direction should be stretched, at the peak the horizontal direction should be contracted.
2) According to the wind speed set in the model, sea surface mesh vertices interval between sampling points should be dynamically changed, when wind speed is smaller, the sampling point interval should be appropriately amplified, when the wind speed increases, the sampling point interval is appropriately reduced.

3   Wave Surface Rendering Method Based on the Vertex Array

Figure 1, to complete the three-dimensional shape of ocean wave, using the triangle mesh, all objects in OpenGL are described as an ordered collection of vertices, rendering primitives, you need to call the OpenGL function if you select 32400 points to draw 180 degree wave surface grid, at least need to call 32402 function, you first call glBegin() function, and then successive draw each vertex, the last call to glEnd() function. In addition, the additional information (polygon boundary line flag, texture mapping and surface normal, etc.) makes an increase of some function such as glTexcoord2f(), glNormal3f() acts call for each vertex, which makes a function call more than 3 times , increase in system overhead, and slow down the graphics rendering speed. The rendering process includes an array of activation, the array specified data and rendering.

4   Expedite the Processing of Multi-GPU-Based Parallel

Real-time has improved; we should seek a variety of soft and hardware acceleration from a technical methodology to achieve the acceleration of calculation and drawing. The software architecture or code optimization can accelerate software, reducing the computation improve rendering speed; hardware acceleration starts from improving the computing performance and processing mode for fast calculation and drawing.

With the development of high-speed computing power of the GPU (graphics processor), parallel computing, and pixel processing power, programmable graphics hardware acceleration technology become a mainstream direction to improve the visual simulation speed. GPU delivers the geometry processing and rendering, which can greatly improve the speed of graphics rendering, but the architecture of the GPU is a highly parallel single instruction multiple data instruction execution system, GPU is different from CPU, and their respective instructions are also different, the code can not be directly transplantation. According to the displayed object, using GPU acceleration, we should come up with GPU-based algorithms and data processing to achieve hardware-based rendering and accelerate the drawing.

5   Simulation of Sea Surface Lighting Effects

The pros and cons of the lighting effects or the lighting effects, will directly affect the fidelity of sea scenes. At present, the simulation of the sea surface light has three ways, from simple to complex: light map, using the OpenGL lighting model and using realistic graphics complete light on the different lighting effects.

As people are very familiar with the specula highlights on the real object, which provides a very important visual cues about surface curvature. Cube maps provide an intuitive way to render stable specula highlights. More specula highlights can be encoded into a cube map texture, they can get through the surface of the reflection vector. Without calculating the color of each vertex and interpolating on the surface, the hardware only calculate the reflection vector (much faster than computing the actual specula reflection contribution) to get the texture coordinates. Figure 1: Lighting effects.

Fig. 1. Lighting effects

6   Ocean Wave Sound Simulation Based on DirectSound

Realistic spatial sound synthesis in the auditory channel can not only greatly enhance the immersion effect in the environment, but also enhance visual effects and rendering.

6.1   Classify of Ocean Wave Sound

There are variety of natural ocean wave sound, according to the characteristics of ocean wave, the sound of ocean wave classify into intermittent sound and continuous sound. Continuous sound has the sound of ocean wave fluctuations and the sound made by the ship sailing in ocean wave etc.; intermittent sound has the sound of ocean wave breaking and the sound of ocean wave hitting the reef.

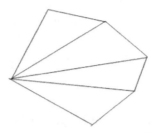

Fig. 2. Triangle mesh rendering

6.2   Components of DirectSound

Microsoft DirectX is a series of low-level programming interface for high-quality multimedia applications, DirectSound is an important component, as it can quickly play a sound, manipulate all of the hardware resources at a higher level, and in the absence of any supporting truly reproduce the sound effect[7]. The DirectSound usually apply Visual C++, Delphi, the Visual Basic and other development tools for the platform.

A sound buffer object is on behalf of a sound source, which can be either static sound buffer object or dynamic. Once starting we need to build the sound buffer object, whose number is the same as the playing sound at the same time. When the sound buffer object played, DirectSound get data from each buffer, and then mix in the "main buffer". When mixing, it will perform all the necessary format conversion. At the same time, it will deal with all the special effects. After mixing in the "main buffer", the sound is sent to the output device[8]. When the hardware buffer and hardware mixing equipment is idle, DirectSound automatically give sound object away in the hardware memory as much as possible. Sound objects stayed in the host system memory mix together by DirectSound and are set into a hardware mixer in the way of the sound stream and sound object in the hardware buffer.

6.3   Ocean Wave Sound Simulation Achievement

According to the characteristics of ocean wave sound, we select the appropriate DirectSound class to achieve the simulation of the different ocean wave sound.

1) Continuous wave sound simulation

Continuous ocean wave sound is related to the speed of sea breeze class or ships, using the DirectSound component real-time synthesis sound can be generated natural and smoother sound with better interactivity. CSinGenerator and CEngineVoiceSim, these two classes can achieve dynamic sound data generation and playback, and continuous ocean wave sound simulation, the process is shown in Figure 3.

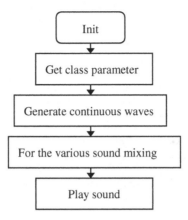

Fig. 3. Flow of continuous sound simulation

2) Intermittent ocean wave sound simulation

Intermittent ocean wave sound such as ocean wave cracked sound has a short duration, often repeat and is irrelevant or less with the sea breeze grades and ship speed, therefore it is not necessary to calculate, we only need to record the sound directly into a sound file saved to sound files library, bring up the appropriate file when needed and play the sound through DirectSound components. This approach not only made the sound natural and realistic, and also reduce amount of calculation and enhance real-time.

CDSBuffer object used to read ocean wave sound data files and package the playback control interface. When ocean wave sound need to playback, we call PlaySound (DWORD the dwFlags). When the sound disappears, we call StopSound() to stop playing. ControlRightAndLeftVolume (BOOL val) is set to play left and right channels. Concrete realization of the process is shown in Figure 4.

6.4   Sound and Visualization Synchronization

In multimedia simulation, video graphics and audio sound synchronization match is very important. When ocean wave sound and ocean wave view generate on the same platform, the system configuration need sufficient data processing capability and easier synchronization, as in each frame, the images and sounds data can be real-time changed and generated, and ocean wave sound data and ocean wave view data is stored. When the three-dimensional ocean wave sound and ocean wave view generated on a separate platform, both through real-time synchronization mechanism.

We can achieve the fusion of sound and image synchronization.

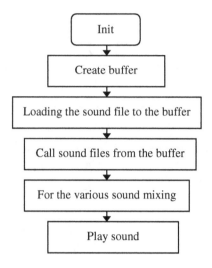

Fig. 3. Flow of intermittent sound simulation

6.5   Experimental Results

Typical ocean wave three-dimensional visual simulation screen show in Figure 5, with common accelerated graphics the PC frame rates is greater than 60/s, which meet the realistic and real-time requirements.

Fig. 4. Simulation of ocean wave

7   Conclusions

Ocean wave modeling, simulation, visualization and sound simulation technology research, along with the improvement of computer performance, so that ocean wave three-dimensional visualization develops to a new level. The next research goal of the field is how to solve the realistic modeling of the interaction between ocean waves of ups and downs with the ship sailing.

Acknowledgements. This work supported by the ship pre-research support technology foundation, China (11J4.1.1) and the basic research foundation of Northwestern Polytechnical University, China (NWPU2011JC0242).

References

1. Gamito, M., Kenton Musgrave, F.: An Accurate Model of Wave Refraction over Shallow Water. Computers & Graphics 26, 291–307 (2002)
2. Lanza, S.: Animation and Display of Water in ShaderX^3: Advanced Rendering with DirectX and OpenGL, Engel, W. (ed.) Charles River Media (2004)
3. Yuan, J., Jia, J., Meng, C.: Dynamic Vision Emulation of Ocean Wave. Advances in Marine Science 23, 498–503 (2005)
4. Ren, H., Yin, Y., Jin, Y.: Realistic Rendering of Large-Scale Ocean Wave Scene. Journal of Computer-Aided Design & Computer Graphics 20, 1617–1622 (2008)
5. Xu, D., Zou, Y., Xiong, Z., et al.: Research on the Visual the Simulation the System of Martial Marine Environment. Computer Simulation 23, 171–175 (2006)
6. Wen, Z., Liu, Z., Liang, W.: Real-time Rendering of Ocean Special Effects Based on GPU. Computer Engineering and Design 31, 4426–4429 (2010)
7. Microsoft Inc.: DirectSound Programming Guide Version 8.0. USA: Microsoft Inc. (2001)
8. Yueqi, Guila, C., et al.: Study on Real-time Audio the Simulation the Using of DirectSound. Computer Simulation 18, 47–50 (2001)

Simulation of Skip-Glide Trajectory
for Hypersonic Vehicle in Near Space

Zhifu Shi[1], Daizhong Zhou[2], Shunhong Wang[1], and Lefei Pan[1]

[1] Xi'an Research Institute of Hi-Tech Hongqing Town, Xian, 710025, China
[2] Aircraft Design Institute GAIG, AnShun, 561000, China
npuhawk@163.com

Abstract. The periodic skip-glide trajectory models for hypersonic vehicle in near space were brought out and simulated in this paper. Firstly, the basic concepts of hypersonic vehicle and different trajectory modes were introduced in detail. Then, the three degrees of freedom model of hypersonic vehicle was given. Lastly, the model was simulated and analyzed using MATLAB. The difference changing trend of periodic trajectory, velocity, effective range, trajectory obliquity and dynamic pressure are given. How the main factors such as trajectory obliquity, launch orientation affect the periodicity was also studied. The primary simulations show that the periodic trajectory of hypersonic vehicle helpful in studying new space vehicle.

Keywords: Hypersonic vehicle, Near space, Trajectory simulation, Periodic Skip-glide.

1 Introduction

Near space generally refers to the altitudes range between 20 and 100 km, which is the region between the maximum flight altitude for aircraft and the minimum flight altitude for space orbiter vehicles [1]. The region includes the stratosphere region, the middle atmosphere region and part of the ionosphere region form bottom to top. With the development of science and technology , the demand of future information war and the improvement of the "four-dimensional" missile defense system of land, sea, air and space, the traditional ballistic missiles flight mode of high-speed and high-altitude, and cruise missiles flight modes of low-speed and low-altitude face with severe challenges for missile survival and penetration. In the past four decades there has been a considerable amount of interest in developing hypersonic vehicles of near space for a host of applications. U.S.Department of defense not only includes the near space vehicle (NSV) in the unmanned aircraft system for the first time in "Unmanned Aircraft systems Roadmap 2005-2030" [2], but also include the NSV in the space simulation for the first time in Schriever-III space war game in 2005. The typical NSVs of U.S include X-43, common aerial vehicle, etc [3]. For near space hypersonic vehicle, the hypersonic vehicle with boost -glide trajectory has been widely concerned, such as the common aerial vehicle (CAV) and X-series vehicles of U.S. And the Russia is developed and successfully tested a new type of nuclear missile system which, it not only can fly like a

T. Xiao, L. Zhang, and S. Ma (Eds.): ICSC 2012, Part I, CCIS 326, pp. 250–258, 2012.

cruise missile, but also can fly like ICBMs [4]. For boost-glide trajectory, Yong mi-en and others of National University of Defense Technology have conducted a preliminary analysis, and provided out the middle motion equation of the boost - gliding missile [5]. Gu Liang-xian et al of Northwestern Polytechnical University have researched and analysis the skip-gliding trajectory using lifting body shape for conventional missiles and several times ignition technology of the final stage engine in [6]. Li Yu and others of Harbin Institute of Technology have study the whole trajectory optimization problem for boost-glide missile using piecewise optimization method in [7]. The key technologies covered by the boost-glide trajectory have been summarized in [8]. This article focuses on analysis the trajectory characteristics of no-power skip-glide vehicles in near space. The emphasis is built and analysis the periodicity skip-glide trajectory mathematical model based on the analysis of boost-skip-glide trajectory in detail. The study has showed that the boost-skip-glide trajectory of near space high dynamic vehicle in this paper combinative the advantages of ballistic missile and cruise missile. It can use the defects of the existing missile defense system effectively and can meet the strategic thinking of global quickly reach, efficient penetration and precision attack. If the existing intercontinental ballistic missile adopts the boost-skip-glide trajectory, it will be a new missile which has advantages on range and survival over compared with conventional ballistic missile and cruise missile.

2   Basic Concepts and Modes of Boost-Glide Trajectory

Boost-glide trajectory is a vehicle which can be sent to predetermined height and has a small inclination of the trajectory by the booster rocket, then the warhead enter into the atmosphere along the elliptical trajectory by the free flight section. It can realize the long-range periodic skip-glide to increase range and improve the penetration performance rely on aero dynamic control at reentry stage through designing the aerodynamic shape of warhead reasonably. The fly process can be broadly divided into boost phase, periodic skip phase and gliding phase. The boost phase refers to the vehicle can be sent to predetermined height at specified speed by boost rocket. The periodic skip phase refers to the vehicle can conduct periodic skip many times in near space range rely on aerodynamic control, which is the main phases and is the most significant phase different from ballistic missiles and cruise missiles. The gliding phase refers to the vehicle can reduce the speed dip angle after the vehicle reaches the predetermined position, and then attack the target quickly. The concept of boost-glide was first proposed by Eugene Sanger who is come from German. Sanger designed the "Silbervogel" hypersonic concept vehicle in 1993[9], which can be sent to the near-Earth orbit altitude from the ground by liquid rocket engine, then the vehicle glide back to the surface by a series of damped oscillation curves skip and gliding mode. Xuesheng Qian has designed a hypersonic rocket aircraft which speed can reach to 12Ma at California Institute of Technology Jet Propulsion Laboratory in 1949, which is actually a glide intercontinental transport system by rocket propelled and reentry. The two modes are showed in Figure 1. Eggers has also studied the performance of the various kinds of skip-glide trajectory of long-distance hypersonic vehicle and got a series of results and distance estimation method of skip-glide trajectory [10].

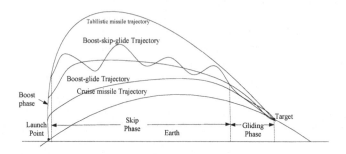

Fig. 1. Trajectory figure of boost-skip-glide ballistic

3   Mathematician Model of High Dynamic Boost-Glide Vehicle

3.1   Atmosphere Model

Near space containing the stratosphere, the atmospheric middle-tier and low thermal areas, it is the most dramatic changes in the atmosphere of the region. When the vehicle flying in the near space, it will be affected by aerodynamic and aerodynamic moment, so the atmosphere parameters can affect the flight performance seriously. Here we take the aerodynamic data of CAV-H as an example. The atmospheric density, sound velocity and other atmospheric data model of aerodynamic calculation using the 1976 U.S. standard atmospheric model. Taking into account the gravitational field changes with altitude, so we can using gravity potential height H takes the place of the geometric height h, the definition of potential height as follows:

$$H = \frac{1}{g_0} \int_0^h g_0 (\frac{R_0}{R_0 + h})^2 dh \tag{1}$$

he relationship between potential height and geometric height as follows:

$$H = \frac{h}{1 + h / R_0} \tag{2}$$

Here $R_0 = 6371.000 km$ is the average radius of the Earth.

3.2   Thrust Model

The vehicle rely mainly on rocket propelled engine to provide the thrust at boost phase, the rocket propelled engine can eliminate the influence of atmospheric drag through fuel consumption, so the system is a variable mass system. Here the boost engine can adopt the three rocket propelled model. Suppose the thrust and propellant second's consumption is taken as constant. The thrust model as follows:

$$P = \dot{m}u_e + S_e(p_e - p_H) \tag{3}$$

Here $\dot{m}$ denotes the propellant mass seconds consumption, u_e denotes the gas exhaust velocity at nozzle cross, p_e denotes the gas static pressure, p_H denotes the atmosphere static pressure which change with height, S_e denotes the cross area of engine nozzle.

The vehicle has not thrust at glide phase. The aerodynamic shape of the vehicle suppose to be lift body and the data can reference CAV-H.

3.3   Kinematics Model

Consider the effects of Earth's rotation and flat rate, based on "instantaneous equilibrium" hypothesis, ignoring attached to Chicago's power and control force, we can build the three degrees of mass point moment particle equations based on the launch coordinate system as follows[11]:

$$\begin{bmatrix} \dot{V}_x \\ \dot{V}_y \\ \dot{V}_z \end{bmatrix} = \frac{G_B}{m} \begin{bmatrix} P \\ 0 \\ 0 \end{bmatrix} + \frac{G_V}{m} \begin{bmatrix} -X \\ Y \\ -Z \end{bmatrix} + \frac{g_r}{r} \begin{bmatrix} x + R_{ox} \\ y + R_{oy} \\ z + R_{oz} \end{bmatrix} + \frac{g_{w_e}}{w_e} \begin{bmatrix} w_{ex} \\ w_{ey} \\ w_{ez} \end{bmatrix} - A_m \begin{bmatrix} x + R_{ox} \\ y + R_{oy} \\ z + R_{oz} \end{bmatrix} - B_m \begin{bmatrix} V_x \\ V_y \\ V_z \end{bmatrix} \tag{4}$$

$$\begin{bmatrix} \dot{x} \\ \dot{y} \\ \dot{z} \end{bmatrix} = \begin{bmatrix} V_x \\ V_y \\ V_z \end{bmatrix} \tag{5}$$

Here x, y, z denote the positional component respectively, V_x, V_y, V_z denote the velocity component respectively, G_B, G_V are denote the transformation matrix between body coordinate system, velocity coordinate system and launch coordinate system respectively, m denotes the mass of the vehicle, P denotes the thrust, r denotes the geocentric radius, g_r denotes the projection of the gravitational acceleration on the geocentric radius, R_{ox}, R_{oy}, R_{oz} denote the components of the launch position geocentric radius in launch coordinate system, w_e denotes the speed of the Earth's rotation, and g_{w_e} denotes the projection of gravitational acceleration on the direction of rotation of the earth.

X,Y,Z are aerodynamic drag, aerodynamic lift and lateral force of the vehicle respectively, and the expression are showed as follows:

$$\begin{cases} X = C_X(\dfrac{1}{2}\rho V^2)s \\ Y = C_Y(\dfrac{1}{2}\rho V^2)s \\ Z = C_Z(\dfrac{1}{2}\rho V^2)s \end{cases} \tag{6}$$

$$V = \sqrt{V_x^2 + V_y^2 + V_z^2} \tag{7}$$

Here s denotes the reference area of the vehicle, ρ denotes the atmosphere density which is related with vehicle height, C_X, C_Y, C_Z denote the aerodynamic drag coefficient, the aerodynamic lift coefficient and the lateral force coefficient respectively. If we ignore the impact of the Reynolds number, then the coefficients value are related with angle of attack and Mach number of the vehicle which can be determined by the method of interpolation or fitting of the aerodynamic data.

$$\begin{cases} C_X = f_X(\alpha, Ma) \\ C_Y = f_Y(\alpha, Ma) \\ C_Z = f_Z(\alpha, Ma) \end{cases} \tag{8}$$

Mach number of the vehicle is the ratio between the speed of the vehicle and the sound speed at different height in near space:

$$M = \frac{V}{a} = \frac{V}{20.0468\sqrt{T}} \tag{9}$$

Here T is the temperature in the near space at different height.

A_m and B_m are matrix of centrifugal force and Coriolis inertia force matrix respectively, the expression as follows:

$$A_m = \begin{bmatrix} -(w_{ey}^2 + w_{ez}^2) & w_{ex}w_{ey} & w_{ex}w_{ez} \\ w_{ex}w_{ey} & -(w_{ex}^2 + w_{ez}^2) & w_{ey}w_{ez} \\ w_{ex}w_{ez} & w_{ey}w_{ez} & -(w_{ex}^2 + w_{ey}^2) \end{bmatrix} \tag{10}$$

$$B_m = \begin{bmatrix} 0 & -2w_{ez} & 2w_{ey} \\ 2w_{ez} & 0 & -2w_{ex} \\ -2w_{ey} & w_{ex} & 0 \end{bmatrix} \quad (11)$$

Here w_{ex}, w_{ey}, w_{ez} are the components of Earth's rotation speed in the launch coordinate system.

3.4   Control Model

The active phase of boost-skip-glide trajectory can adopt program ballistic and can be controlled by flight path angle. The periodicity skip phase and gliding phase using no-power, so it can adjust the flight attitude rely on the aero-surfaces and made a certain angle of attack, thus control the flight trajectory.

4   Simulations and Analysis

4.1   Simulation of Trajectory

For the mathematician model of high dynamic boost-glide vehicle, we can make simulation under a set of initial parameter. Suppose the longitude and latitude of the launch point is (750, 250), launch azimuth is 450, initial obliquity of trajectory is 600, the simulation step is 1sec. We can get the curves of space three-dimensional trajectory, height curve change with time, range curve with time, speed curve change with time, obliquity angle curves change with time and dynamic pressure. All curves are showed in Figure 2-8 respectively.

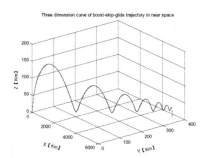

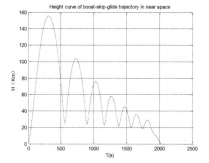

Fig. 2. Space three-dimensional trajectory curve

Fig. 3. Flight height curve with time

Figure 2 and figure 3 show that the vehicle can realize periodicity skip with reduction and shock mode. The periodicity skips range approximately 4650.1km, which is 78.1% of the total range. The vehicle enter into gliding phase after reentry into atmosphere, the gliding range is 357km, which is about 6% of the total range. Figure 4 and Figure 5 show that the vehicle has flight 5954km in 33.7 minute, the average speed

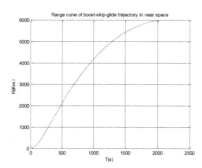

Fig. 4. Range curve with time

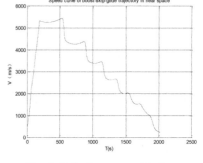

Fig. 5. Velocity curve with time

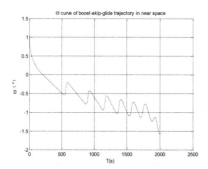

Fig. 6. obliquity angle curve with time

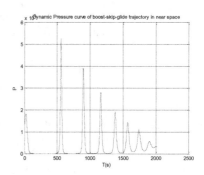

Fig. 7. Dynamic pressure curve with time

attach to 8.68Ma, the maximum speed is 5394.1m/s, approximately 15.9Ma after boost phase. Figure 6 shows that the obliquity angle is periodicity change in the near space, and it turn into small quickly after enter into gliding phase, so it can attack target rapidly. Figure 7 shows that the dynamic pressure is also periodicity change, which also explains that the periodicity skip trajectory of the vehicle is controlled by aerodynamic in near space.

4.2   Parameter Sensitivity Analysis

In order to analysis the affection of initial parameter on boost-glide trajectory, we can make sensitivity analysis on initial parameters. If we keep the other parameter unchanged, only change initial launch azimuth or initial obliquity angle of vehicle respectively. The analysis results are showed as Figure 8-9 respectively.

Figure 8 shows that the affection of launch azimuth on trajectory is very significant. The smaller the launch azimuth, the maximum flight height and bounce amplitude is significantly increased, but the times of bounces less. With the launch azimuth angle increases, the trajectory is smooth, and increases the number of bounces. The free phase range and total range have obvious difference with different launch azimuth, but the total range is not monotonic change with the launch position. So we should find the best launch azimuth.

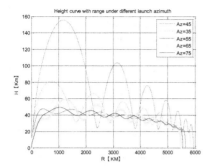

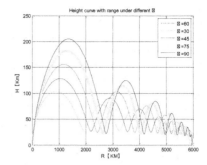

Fig. 8. Height curve with range (different launch azimuth)

Fig. 9. Height curvel with range (different obliquity angle)

Figure 9 shows that the affection of obliquity angle is not significant. Although when the initial obliquity angle is bigger, the free flight range increases and reentry phase range reduces, the maximum flight height and bounce amplitude is also increased, but the entire trajectory is similar. And the total range various is not obvious, or monotonic change with obliquity angle.

5   Conclusions

The models of the periodicity skip trajectory are studied in this paper and the preliminary simulations are made. We have mainly analysis the change condition of flight height, speed, obliquity angle, range and dynamic pressure. We also make quantitative analysis and comparison of initial parameter which is how to effect on the trajectory. The simulation results show that the periodicity skip trajectory can increase the range, increase mobility and thereby increasing the probability of penetration. But the initial parameter choose can effect the trajectory significantly. So we will optimization the trajectory under the constraints of overload, attack speed at terminal, thermal and so on in the future.

References

1. Knoedler, A.J.: Lowering the High Ground: Using Near-space Vehicles for Persistent ISR (2005)
2. Unmanned Aircraft systems Roadmap 2005-2030, Office of the Secretary of Defense (2005)
3. Corporation T.P. A Common Aero Vehicle Model, Description, and Employment Guide (EB/OL) (2003), http://www.dtic.mil/matris/sbir/sbir041/srch/af031a.doc
4. Preston, C.H., Pines, D.J., Eggers, R.L.: Approximate Performance of Periodic Hypersonic Cruise Trajectories for Global Reach. Journal of Spacecraft 35(6) (1998)
5. Yong, E.-M., Tang, G.-J., Chen, L.: Schematic study of mid-course trajectories for the boost-glide missiles. Journal of National University of Deffense Technology 28(6), 6–10 (2006)

6. Zhao, J.-S., Gu, L.-X., Gong, C.-L.: Design and optimization of hypersonic skip-glide trajectory. Journal of Solid Rocket Technology 32(2), 123–126 (2009)

7. Li, Y., Yang, Z.-H., Cui, N.-G.: A study of optimal Trajectory for Boost-glide Missile. Journal of Astronautics 29(1), 66–71 (2008)

8. Ma, Y., He, L.-S.: Study on Key Problems of Realizing Hypersonic Skip Trajectory. Journal of Ballistics 21(1), 35–38 (2009)

9. Saenger Bomber (2005), http://www.astronautix.com/lvs/saenger.htm

10. Eggers, A.J., Allen, J.H., Neice, S.E.: A Comparative Analysis of the Performance of Long-Range Hypervelocity Vehicles. NACA Technical Report 1382, Ames Aeronautical Laboratory (1958)

11. Zhang, Y., Xiao, L.-X., Wang, S.-H.: Trajectory of ballistic missile. National University of Defense Technology Publish (1999)

Current Trends and Issues of Origami Engineering

Ichiro Hagiwara

Organization for the Strategic Coordination of Research and Intellectual Property,
Meiji University, 1-1-1, Higashi-Mita, Tama-ku, Kawasaki, 214-8571, Japan
ihagi@meiji.ac.jp

Abstract. Japanese Origami craft is very beautiful, and the term "Origami" is translated into Origami in English. There have been many Origami creators appearing from Japan, however their craft work is not created on the basis of geometry but born from imagination they possess. As a result, only honeycomb is developed by British referring to star festival decoration of Japan. This situation is shameful for Japanese engineers. In this paper, many Origami crafts based on geometry are introduced. Taking these crafts into consideration, two facts are to be verified. One is that dire-core based on space filling geometry surpasses in some features than honeycomb, and the other is that judging from the fact plants grow up spirally, reverse spiral structure which has the same structure as them is superior as energy absorption member.

Keywords: truss core, reverse spiral cylindrical structure.

1   Introduction

It is necessary to create new Origami and examine CAD, computational mechanics comprehensively for applying various materials such as paper and metal to real Origami goods. Concretely shown as in the below figure there are phases about details to be examined; ① Origami creation on the basis of biotechnology, ② the technique which can exalt sensitivity, ③ computational mechanics, ④ manufacturing etc. Namely the steps is firstly creating various shapes in phase①, and next creating CAD model from the shape obtained in phase ①, finally correcting the shape or sometimes feeding back to phase ① in aesthetic viewpoint. IT technologies of Origami is to promote the imagination of phase ① furthermore. The shape obtained in this way is appropriated functionally in phase ③ (computational mechanics).Here, it will become necessary to collaborate closely with not only phase ② however also phase ④ (manufacturing processing). It is because the function and manufacturing processing can't easily consistent each other. And also, close discussion with industrial world is essential to promote Origami engineering.Fig.2 displays the Origami created on the basis of plants. Here, two examples about truss core structure and reverse spiral cylindrical Origami structure are explained which are obtained by unifying four technologies mentioned above.

T. Xiao, L. Zhang, and S. Ma (Eds.): ICSC 2012, Part I, CCIS 326, pp. 259–268, 2012.
© Springer-Verlag Berlin Heidelberg 2012

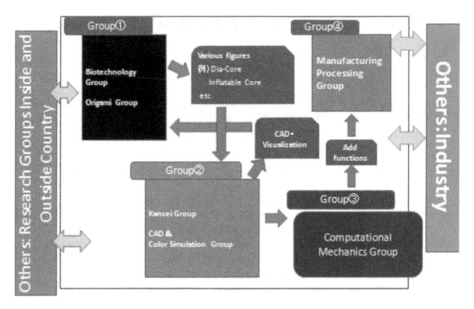

Fig. 1. Flow of Research and Development

2   Truss Core

Fig.3 shows various types are obtained by operating dire-core base, corner cut, andmenri which are created based on space filling theory displayed in Fig.3 and Fig.4 .In this case CAD supporting is effective.

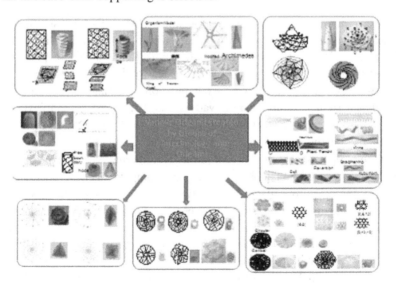

Fig. 2. Origami based on plants

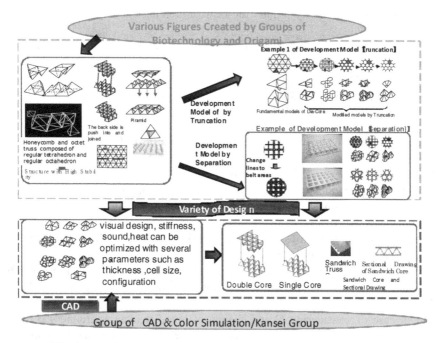

Fig. 3. Dire-Core Base and Various types obtained by Origami Operation

(a) tile pattern observed in building   (b) 11 kinds of uniform tessellation composed of regular polygon

Fig. 4. Plane filling shape

2.1   Phase of Creation/ CAD/ Computational Mechanics

Fig.6 shows the situation where core rigidity, vibration, impact, and bending compression property are optimized which are obtained by space filling of tetrahedron and octahedron specially named as truss core.Fig.7 shows the analytical procedure of bending compression property. Firstly the flow of creating bending analytical model is written as below.

Trimming the press-forming completion and then mapping onto mesh for bending analysis

Copying panel and reverse upside down one sheet

Jointing two pieces of truss core panels

Defining the spot welding in the apex of triangle pyramid

Creating 3 points bending model

Trimming written in above ① is constituted of two tasks as below.

Defining trim line

Dividing and Re-meshing shell elements on trim line

And, the mapping means stress, deformation, and mapping of board thickness distrihoweverion from mesh for press forming(detailed mesh) analysis to noisy mesh for bending analysis,

Concerning the definition of spot welding mentioned above ④,the apex of triangle pyramid is welded in case of real panel.

In simulation, the modeling method of spot welding (free node spot welding)which

combines beam elements and the restrict condition of freedom degree of nodes is applied.

Here in case of considering C and change of board thickness, around 1.6 times strength has been shown, however the effect of work hardening is more significant than the one of board thickness change.

In reduction integral calculus element (BT element) , even if considering work hardening, only 80 percentage of strength of complete integral element (BD element) can be achieved. It is because in BT element warpage is not reflected on element rigidity.

As mentioned above, advanced computational mechanics is essential.

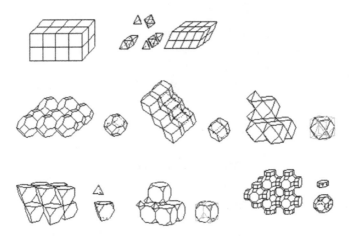

Fig. 5. Space filling shape

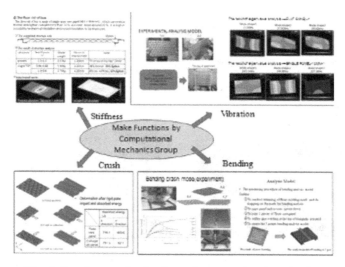

Fig. 6. Function creation in phase of computational mechanics

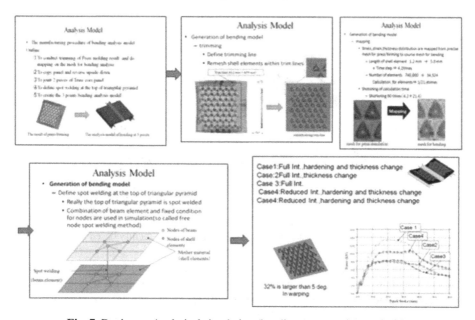

Fig. 7. Device on Analytical simulation (bending compression analysis)

2.2 Forming Phase of Truss Core Structure

As far mass production has been conducted only in the corrugate method and Wiring method of honeycomb shown in Fig.8, while in this paper mass production as in Fig.9 is achieved for truss core. This product was developed by Shiroyama Industry Co., Ltd. on the basis of the world's first multistep forming.

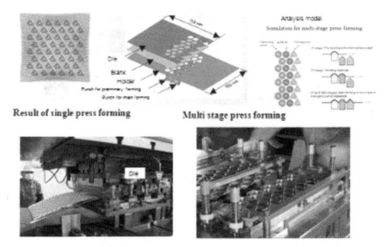

Result of single press forming   Multi stage press forming

floor structure by the analysis model of multi stage forming

Fig. 8. Two manufacturing methods for star festival decoration and honeycomb

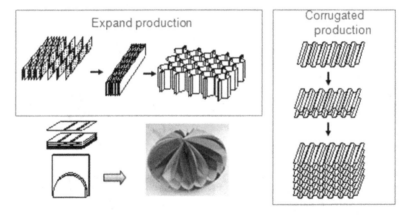

Fig. 9. Multistep forming simulation and Mass production facility based on that

Concerning the panel made from resin with high formability, shape is selected freely by vacuum forming, while concerning panel made of metal it is difficult to form deep crevice part, and so it is necessary to apply special forming such as traditional superplastic forming and facing hydro-forming. Manufacturing cost of these forming are highand for trying to diffusion to broad area as new light weight means, we had aimed new forming technique at a lower price, as a result we've just succeeded in developing multistep press forming which can make it possible to create at a lower price by support of computational mechanics. (1)~(5).

Firstly the solar cell panel composed of single truss core developed by this facility is adopted in Town Hall Sagamihara city(6), and continuously there has been one plan of mass adoption from United States big enterprise. Concerning heliostat for solar heat generation, current frame made of glass and steel is abolished and the structure using truss core plans to be adopted in Mitsubishi Heavy Industries Co., Ltd as Japanese original. In the near future, OA floor composed of truss core is to be sold.

3   In Case of Reverse Spiral Cylindrical Origami Structure

3.1   Forming Phase of Truss Core structure

Fig.10 shows foldable and deployable reverse spiral cylindrical model. In this figure, α represents the number of polygon sides and β shrinks at very low load when it meets formula (1) in this figure and β shrinks by generating much reaction force while turning around, when it doesn't meet that. We investigated whether the former can be applied to beer can and pet bottle and the latter can be used for automobile energy absorption. In automobile collision, the hollow Half cut typed member which does sport welding between hat typed panel and flat panel is lifeline, however even if the member break ideally, its own space become bulky, so it crush as long as only 70 percentage of its own length. In crash zone it is desirable for member to crush as long as it can. Therefore the use of this RSC has been proposed. In test model created on the basis of CAD data generate tearing at the edge part as shown in Fig.11.Therefore,by applying subdivision the improvement of forming proper has been obtained as well as aesthetic effect.

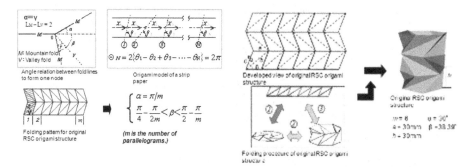

Fig. 10. RSC development and Origami theory

Fig. 11. RSC Origami structure

While in specification of Fig.12, the amount of load is generated less than expected. Then, the process where from cylinder type RSC is expressed automatically was contrived which had made optimal analysis with many parameters possible with RSC changing successively in the course of optimization. As a result, the design specification with 1.8 times more energy absorption than traditional structure on the condition of the same weight has been found. This feature can be advantage in effective for crew injury index for longer crush period, because reaction power can be controlled by oblique folding lines and crush with rotating proved as in Fig.14 The term "without bead" in this figure means that s feature is essential for the current half cut type member to generate satisfactory crush mode(6),(7).

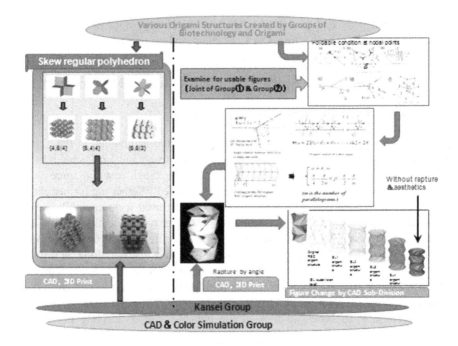

Fig. 12. Forming improvement and Aesthetic effect by Subdivision

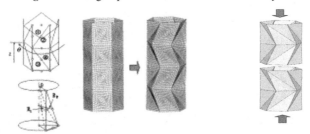

Fig. 13. Realization RSC from Cylinder   **Fig. 14.** Strong points of RSC

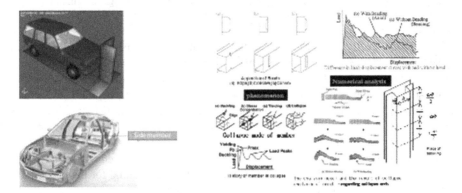

Fig. 15. The Condition of crash control by adopting side member and beat

3.2   Forming Phase

RSC can be created by hydro-forming as proved in Fig.16(8),so house makers are interested in RSC. While in automobile companies which are strict with budged control,RSC is still under consideration about adoption and it hasn't been accepted immediately. Therefore as shown in Fig.17, if the traditional half cut type side structure obtains the same property as RSC, it is estimated that more excellent property at lower cost will be achieved.

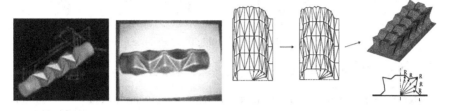

Fig. 16. Test RSC   **Fig. 17.** Half cut typed structure from RSC

Half cut type member can't rotate as RSC does, because it's structure is joint by spot welding between one sheet of foldable panel and one sheet of flat panel. Then, as shown in Fig.17 by making multistep at the direction of axis and creasing along inclined direction, it has been found that transformation tendency same as RSC is generated inside internal each step and between each step. In short terms, same as RSC, crush deformation mode and reaction force can be controlled freely with end and oblique folding lines, and by appropriate design specification collision energy absorption property has been improved and the result has been also yielded that member is resistant to oblique directional load(9).

Automobile companies are concerned extremely with this member. It has demonstrated the significance that traditional structure should also be reconsidered from the viewpoint of Origami one. Furthermore, this new half cut type member provides very effective crush mode shown as in Fig.18 not only in the traditional case of installing under floor and but also inserting member between truss core in electric automobile.

It is occasionally difficult for Origami form to be processed at low price. If so, it is the important aspect of Origami Engineering that the structure processed at low price is transformed into Origami form and as a result higher performance can be obtained. This example is displayed as in Fig.18(b).

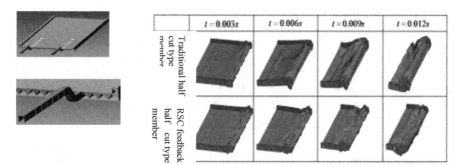

(a)Concept of truss core electric automobile   (b)high performance of half cut type RSC

Fig. 18. Undertaking of Space utility by applying truss core into electric automobile

Acknowledgement. Several parts of the research work werecarried out by the support of Grants-in-Aid for scientific research(category S) under Grant No.20226006.We acknowledge its aid dearly.

References

1. Tokura, S., Hagiwara, I.: Manufacturing Simulation of Truss Core Panel. Transactions of the Japan Society of Mechanical Engineers (Edit A) 74(746), 1379–1385 (2008)
2. Tokura, S., Hagiwara, I.: A Study for Bending Stiffness of Truss Core Panel with Work Hardening Effect Derived from Forming Simulation. Transactions of the Japan Society of Mechanical Engineers (Edit A) 75(753), 588–594 (2009)
3. Saito, K., Takeda, K., Tokura, S., Hagiwara, I.: Relation between Geometrical Patterns and Press Formabilities in Newly Developed Light-Weight Core Panels. Transactions of the Japan Society of Mechanical Engineers (Edit A) 75(751), 111–117 (2009)
4. Tokura, S., Hagiwara, I.: Forming Process Simulation of Truss Core Panel. Journal of Computational Science and Technology 4(1), 25–35 (2010) (Release Date: March 30, 2010)
5. Tokura, S., Hagiwara, I.: A Study for the Influence of Work Hardening on Bending Stiffness of Truss Core Panel. J. Appl. Mech. 77, 031010-1–031010-6 (2010)
6. Hagiwara, I., Tsuda, M., Kitagawa, Y., Futamata, T.: Method of Determining Positions of Beads, United States Patent, Patent Number 5048345

Design and Simulation for the Single Leg of the Six Degrees of Freedom Vibration Isolator

Yongliang Zhang, Baiwei Guo[*], and Xiuyun Meng

Key Laboratory of Dynamics and Control of Flight Vehicle, Ministry of Education,
Beijing Institute of Technology, Beijing 100081, China
gbw@bit.edu.cn

Abstract. With the development of space technologies, the optical payload requirement on the pointing accuracy becomes higher and higher. The active vibration isolation is an effective way to improve the pointing accuracy of the optical load, and the six freedoms Stewart Platform is widely adopted in the active vibration isolation for spacecrafts. The double-layer structure is adopted for the single leg of the Stewart Platform and the parameters of the passive part are optimized by the GA algorithm. For the active part, the L1 method is used for solving the problems in the vibration isolator because of the impact load. The simulation results indicate the effectiveness of the L1 method for solving the problem.

Keywords: GA algorithm, parameters optimization, L1 method, double-layer structure, active vibration isolation.

1 Introduction

The satellite platforms being used as the carriers of the payloads suffer complex disturbance from the space dynamic environment. On one hand, the disturbances from the space environment may disturb the attitude motion of the payload; on the other hand, the active part of the satellite platform may produce disturbances on the stability of the LOS. The performance of the payload may degenerate because of the factors above. Then adding the coupler between the satellite platform and the payload is an effective way for solving the problem. Many researchers pay their attentions to the configuration and control strategy of the coupler and get fruitful research results, such as reference [6], [7], [8], [9], etc. Among the results, the orthogonal Stewart configuration and the decentralized control strategy is commonly used. On the basis of the research results, attentions are paid to designing the configuration and the controller of the single leg in the Stewart platform. The double-layer structure is adopted as the configuration of the single leg and the GA algorithm is used to optimize the parameters.

---

[*] Corresponding author.

T. Xiao, L. Zhang, and S. Ma (Eds.): ICSC 2012, Part I, CCIS 326, pp. 269–276, 2012.

In order to control the shock load which the coupler may suffer, the L1 optimal method is used to design the controller. At last, the related simulations are done for verification.

2   Optimization of the Parameters

There are a lot of research results about the design of the controller for the vibration isolator, but few papers focus on the optimizing the parameters of the passive part. As we know, optimizing the parameters of the passive part is important to improve the overall performance of vibration isolation. As for the optimization of the double-layer structure, the linear optimization algorithm is invalid because there are lots of parameters to be optimized and nonlinear relation among the parameters. In the paper, the GA algorithm is selected to deal with the problem because of its stable convergence in global optimization. The value ranges of the parameters are chosen considering the weight limit and the realizable characteristic of the parameters.

The following factors are taken into consideration to determine the objective function :(1) the frequency range (2) the vibration spectrum of the satellite. So the objective function to be optimized is formula (1.1)

$$\int_0^{w_0} \|T(jw)\| \|G(jw)\| dw .$$ (1.1)

where $T(jw)$ is the transfer function of the single leg and $G(jw)$ is the weighted function which is defined as the vibration frequency spectrum of the satellite in the paper, namely,

$$G(s) = \frac{160}{0.002337s^3 + 0.05282s^2 + 0.3981s + 1}$$ (1.2)

The figure 1 is the structure chart of the passive part of the double-layer vibration isolator:

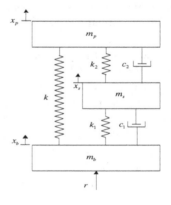

Fig. 1. The structure chart of the passive part

So the transfer function of the passive part can be got by the vibration equation, namely formula (1.3), and the output equation, namely formula (1.4)

$$M\ddot{x} + C\dot{x} + Kx = Wr \tag{1.3}$$

$$y = C_q x + C_v \dot{x} \tag{1.4}$$

Where

$$M = diag(m_b, m_s, m_p) \qquad W = \begin{bmatrix} 1 & 0 & 0 \end{bmatrix}^T$$

$$C = \begin{bmatrix} c_1 & -c_1 & 0 \\ -c_1 & c_1+c_2 & -c_2 \\ 0 & -c_2 & c_2 \end{bmatrix} \qquad K = \begin{bmatrix} k+k_1 & -k_1 & -k \\ -k_1 & k_1+k_2 & -k_2 \\ -k & -k_2 & k_2+k \end{bmatrix}$$

$$C_q = \begin{bmatrix} k & k_2 & -k-k_2 \end{bmatrix} \qquad C_v = \begin{bmatrix} 0 & c_2 & -c_2 \end{bmatrix}$$

The value ranges of the parameters are defined as follows:

$m_s \in \begin{bmatrix} 0 & 1 \end{bmatrix}$, $k_1 \in \begin{bmatrix} 0 & 1000000000 \end{bmatrix}$, $k_2 \in \begin{bmatrix} 0 & 1000000000 \end{bmatrix}$, $c_1 \in \begin{bmatrix} 0 & 1000 \end{bmatrix}$, $c_2 \in \begin{bmatrix} 0 & 1000 \end{bmatrix}$, $k \in \begin{bmatrix} 0 & 10000 \end{bmatrix}$

Considering the characteristics of the GA algorithm, the logic diagram of optimization is built as follows:

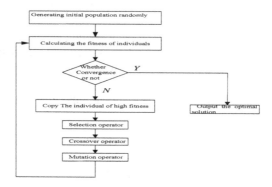

Fig. 2. The flow chart of the GA algorithm

Then ,the optimization result is got,   namely

$$m_s = 0.267, \ k_1 = 8.7 \times 10^8 \ k_2 = 7.0 \times 10^5, \ c_1 = 120, \ c_2 = 350, \ k = 800$$

Introducing the parameters above into formula (1.3) and formula (1.4), the transfer function of the passive part can be gotten.

Then choosing the disturbance signal built according to the vibration frequency spectrum of the satellite, so the time process of the output can be plotted, such as figure 3.

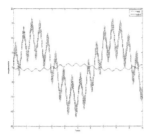
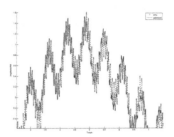

Fig. 3. The contrast of the output and the   **Fig. 4.** The contrast between the two systems
input

From the figure 3, the output signal is smaller 20dB than the disturbance signal. In order to explain the optimized result, the optimized system is compared with the system in the literature [4]. After the comparison in figure 4, the conclusion can be drawn: the performance of the optimized system in vibration isolating is better than the system's in the literature [4].

3   Design of Controller

The payloads are often subjected to the shock load when the spacecrafts are flying in the orbit, such as liquid sloshing, the large angle maneuvers of the spacecraft and the movement of the solar panels, etc. The problems should be taken into consideration in the design of the controller for the vibration isolator. The L1optimal algorithm is adopted to design the controller in order to deal with the problems effectively.

Theoretical basis:

The design of the l1 optimal controller for the vibration isolation system can be expressed as follows:

$$\min_{K\ stable} \left\| \begin{matrix} S(s) \\ T(s) \end{matrix} \right\|_A \qquad \begin{aligned} s.t \quad & \dot{x} = Ax + Bu + Dw \\ & y = Cx \\ & w(t) \in \Delta \end{aligned} \qquad (2.1)$$

Where $S(s) = P_w(I + P_uK)^{-1}$ is the transfer function from shock disturbance to the output of the system and $T(s) = P_wK(I + P_uK)^{-1}$ is the transfer function from shock disturbance to the input of the system's controller. The figure 5 is the block diagram of the system.

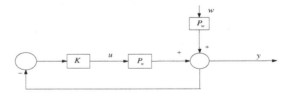

Fig. 5. The block diagram of the system

According the theory of l1optimal algorithm, the solution of the l1optimal problem is non-rational. The implementation and application of the controller are difficult and if one solves the l1 optimal problem directly. So the solution of the L1 optimal problem can be got indirectly by making the system discrete so as to get the continuous controller which can be implemented easily. Then, the l1 optimal problem can be obtained which is equivalent to the original problem.

$$\min_{Kstable} \left\| \Phi(z) \right\|_{A_d} = \min_{Kstable} \left\| \begin{matrix} S(z) \\ T(z) \end{matrix} \right\|_{A_d} \tag{2.2}$$

The discrete controller $K(z)$ can be acquired by solving the formula (2.2) and then the continuous controller can be acquired by making the discrete controller $K(z)$ continuous.

The figure 6 is the schematic of the double-layer vibration isolation system.

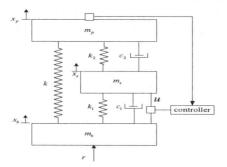

Fig. 6. Schematic of the system

Its vibration equation and output equation are as follows:

$$M\ddot{x} + C\dot{x} + Kx = Eu + Wr \tag{2.3}$$

$$y = C_q x + C_v \dot{x} \tag{2.4}$$

where, the definitions of M、C、K、W、C_q、C_v are same with the above and $E = \begin{bmatrix} 1 & -1 & 0 \end{bmatrix}^T$.

Introducing the parameters into the vibration equation and output equation, the natural frequencies and the transformation matrix can be got as follows:

$$\omega = \begin{bmatrix} 0 & 62 & 57123 \end{bmatrix}$$

$$\Phi = \begin{bmatrix} 1.00 & 1.00 & 1.00 \\ 1.00 & 0.99 & -749.12 \\ 1.00 & -10.01 & 0.0008 \end{bmatrix}$$

There will be elastic modes and rigid modes in the systems if their constraints are incomplete. As for the double-layer vibration isolation system, there is only one rigid mode .The positive definite subsystem should be extracted from the positive semi-definite system in order to control the system effectively. In the paper, the model reduction method is adopted.

Taking x_i as the principal modes of the system, so any non-zero vibration modes can be expressed as follows:

$$Y = \sum_{i=1}^{n} \alpha_i X_i \tag{2.5}$$

Then introducing the transformation

$$D = I - \sum_{j=1}^{r} X_j X_j^T M \tag{2.6}$$

where r is the number of the rigid mode and I is a unit matrix, and transforming Y to X by the matrix D, where X is the elastic mode. As for the matrix D, there are $n - r$ columns which are linearly independent. The matrix P can be built by selecting any $n - r$ columns which are independent from the matrix D. Introducing the equation $X = PZ$ into the vibration equation and the output equation, the new system can be got as follows:

$$M_0 \ddot{z} + C_0 \dot{z} + K_0 z = E_0 u + W_0 r \tag{2.7}$$

$$y = C_{q0} z + C_{v0} \dot{z} \tag{2.8}$$

Where $M_0 = P^T M P$ $K_0 = P^T K P$ $C_0 = P^T C P$ $E_0 = P^T E$ $C_{q_0} = C_q P$ $C_{q_0} = C_q P$

The Eigen values and eigenvectors (λ_i, X_i) of the initial systems can be got by the transformation $X_i = PZ_i$, $i = r+1, \cdots, n$ after getting the Eigen values and eigenvectors of the new systems.

So the 11 optimal problem of the double-layer vibration isolation system can be expressed as follows:

$$\min_{K\text{稳定}} \left\| \begin{array}{c} P_w (1 + P_u K)^{-1} \\ P_w K (1 + P_u K)^{-1} \end{array} \right\|_{A_d} \tag{2.9}$$

Where P_w is the transfer function from the disturbance to the output and P_u is the transfer function from the actuator to the output and K is the controller.

The problem can be expressed in the following way by the *Youla* method.

$$\Phi = \begin{bmatrix} P_w \\ 0 \end{bmatrix} - \begin{bmatrix} P_u \\ 1 \end{bmatrix} Q P_w \tag{2.10}$$

So the problem can be solved by the method in the reference [3] and the discrete controller can be got.

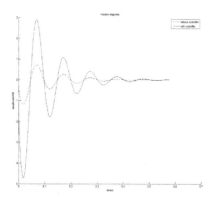

Fig. 7. Effect of the control

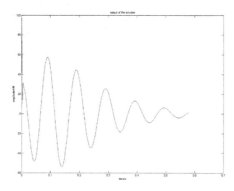

Fig. 8. Actuating force

4   Conclusion

Some simulation is done in order to verify the validity of the l1 optimal method. Taking the unit impulse as the input of the system and the force acting on the payload as the output of the system, the curve of the output and the curve of the force which is exerted by the actuator can be got.

The performance of the passive part in vibration isolating increases 10% by optimizing the parameters of the passive part comparing with others. From the simulation result, one can draw a conclusion that the controller which is designed by the L1 optimal method can make the system effective when it suffers the shock load and the peak of the response becomes smaller four times than original. But even now, there are shortages in the design of the controller, such as lacking of the characteristic of the actuator and the sensors. In the further research, lots of attentions should be paid to the problems.

References

1. Zhang, J., Li, N., et al.: Integration vibration control. Science press, Beijing (2005)
2. Li, H.: Vibration theory and engineering application. Beijing institute of technology press, Beijing (2006)
3. Diaz-Boblillo, I.J., Dahleh, M.A.: Minimization of the Maximum Peak-to-Peak Gain: the General Multiblock Problem. IEEE Trans. Auto. Contr. 38(10), 1459–1482 (1993)
4. Liu, L., Wang, B.: Multi Objective Robust Active Vibration Control for Flexure Jointed Struts of Stewart Platforms via H∞ and μ Synthesis. Chinese Journal of Aeronautics 21, 125–133 (2008)
5. Zhou, D., Wu, P.: Intelligent Control. Chongqing university press, Chongqing
6. Jafari, F., McInroy, J.E.: Orthogonal Gough-Stewart Platforms for Micromanipulation. IEEE Transactions Robotics and Automation 19(4), 595–603 (2003)
7. Li, W., Huang, H.: Space-based Precision Tracking and Pointing Stewart Platform with Key Technologies. Aerospace Control 28(4), 92–96 (2010)
8. Cobb, R.G., Sullivan, J.M., Das, A.: Vibration isolation and suppression system for precision payloads in space. Smart Mater. Struct. 8, 798–812 (1999)
9. Yang, C., Huang, Q., Han, J.: Decoupling control for spatial six-degree-of-freedom electro-hydraulic parallel robot. Robotics and Computer-Integrated Manufacturing 28, 14–23 (2012)

Analysis and Implementation for the Algorithm Based on Combinatorial Relaxation for Computing the Structure Index of DAE

Yan Zeng[1,2], Xuesong Wu[1], and Jianwen Cao[1]

[1]Laboratory of Parallel Software and Computational Science of Software,
Institute of Software Chinese Academy of Sciences, Beijing, 100190, China
[2] Graduate University of Chinese Academy of Sciences, Beijing, 100049, China
zengyan_616@yahoo.cn, xuesongwu@msn.cn,
caojianwen@gmail.com

Abstract. As the society industrialized, mathematical modeling and simulation become increasingly important in the product design. At present, the multi-domain unified modeling with Modelica is a mainstream technology in the field of complex systems. Modeling of complex physical systems with Modelica often produces a high-index differential algebraic equation (DAE) system. It needs to be transformed to low-index DAE before solving it. The structure index reduction algorithm is one of the popular index reduction methods. But in some special circumstances, its solution may be incorrect. At present, combinatorial relaxation algorithm is a widely used method for solving the problem. Solving maximum weighted matching is one of important problems of the combinatorial relaxation algorithm. This paper describes the combinatorial relaxation algorithm and proposes three different implementations of Hungarian algorithm for the maximum weighted matching problem. The theory results are consistent with the experiment results,

Keywords: Modelica, DAE, Combinatorial Relaxation, Hungarian algorithm.

1 Introduction

With the society industrialized, the modeling and simulation technology plays an important role in the product design. It is an important technology for testing and analyzing the technical performance of products. But as the functions and components of products become complex and relate to multi-domain, it is more and more difficult to design products. The traditional single-domain simulation technology cannot meet the requirements of designing complex products. At present, the multi-domain unified modeling is a main-stream technology for researching the complex system. Modelica[1,2] is a multi-domain and equation-based unified modeling language. It constructs a mathematical model by describing component rules, simulating component behaviors and using the intuitive structure of physical system. It is convenient for engineers designing and developing products. But, it puts up a

T. Xiao, L. Zhang, and S. Ma (Eds.): ICSC 2012, Part I, CCIS 326, pp. 277–286, 2012.
© Springer-Verlag Berlin Heidelberg 2012

difficult problem to the solvers, as it produces a high-index Differential Algebraic Equation (DAE) system. It couples Ordinary Differential Equation, Differential Equation, State Equation, Parametric Equation, Conditional Transfer Equations and Stochastic Process, so the high-index DAE system always includes hundreds or tens of thousands of algebraic equations.

It is difficult to solve such large-scale and high-index DAE system directly. At present, there are four low-index DAE systems which can be solved directly. Index reduction method is always used to reduce a high-index DAE to a low-index DAE. Index reduction algorithm based on structure index[3] is a kind of mainstream method to reduce such DAE system, i.e. Pentelides algorithm[4]. In some special cases, this algorithm will result an incorrect solution. In order to overcome the drawback, Kazuo Murota has proposed a combinatorial relaxation algorithm based on matrix, matroid and combinatorial optimization theory. This algorithm includes three phases: compute the structure index by solving the maximum weighted matching of the bipartite graph, test the equations of the structure index and the differential index and correct the incorrect. As the high index DAE produced by Modelica modeling and simulation is always large scale, computing the structure index is an important partition of the combinatorial relaxation algorithm. This paper presents combinatorial relaxation algorithm, and for the large-dense bipartite graph, it analyzes the key algorithm for solving the maximum weighted matching based on theory and experiment. It proposes three different implementations of the Hungarian algorithm. Compared with the theory analysis, the experiment results conform to them. From the experiment, it can take advantage of different implementations for different DAE systems to complement the structure index reduction of the high-index DAE.

This paper is organized as follows. Section 2 describes the structure index reduction algorithm and its drawback. It consists of the existed index reduction algorithms based on structure index, the case of incorrect solution and its reason. The section 3 provides the combinatorial relaxation algorithm and its key technology. It also presents and compares three different implementations of the Hungarian algorithm. The section 4 compares and analyzes three implementations by experiment results. The importance of the structure index reduction algorithm based on combinatorial relaxation algorithm and the research direction in the future are presented in section 5.

2   Index Reduction Based on Structure Index

According to indices, there are two categories of DAE: high-index DAE and low-index DAE. The index of high-index DAE is larger than one, and the one of low-index DAE is less than or equal to one. At present, only ODE or some special high-index DAE can be solved directly. Index reduction is a process of transforming the high-index DAE into equivalence low-index DAE or ODE which can be solved directly. Based on Modelica modeling, it always produces a high-index DAE system. As it is difficult to be solved directly, the index reduction algorithm plays an important role in the modeling and simulation platform based on Modelica. This section presents the classical structure index reduction algorithm and its drawback.

2.1   Index Reduction Algorithm

The structure index reduction algorithm is on basis of matriod and graph[5]. It analyzes the structure index of DAE, tests a matrix subset of the DAE repeatedly, and then computes the differential for the equation subset and modifies the bipartite graph of the DAE. At last, it produces a low-index DAE system. The algorithm is on basis of graph theory and symbol processing of correlation matrix. Compared with the traditional numerical method, it has less symbol processing and lower computational complexity. So it is widely applied to industry, such as OpenModelica. There are many implementations of structure index reduction algorithm, such as Pantelides, Dummy Derivatives and so on.

2.2   Drawback

It is valuable for using the structure index reduction algorithm to solve the high-index DAE in practice, but it has a drawback. As it just considers the structure of equations, it produces uncompleted reduction or excessive reduction, when the differential index does not consist with the structure index. So it has an incorrect solution at last. The drawback of the method in some special case is presented in [6]. Next, we analyze the drawback of the structure index reduction algorithm through a simple example, the definitions of differential index and structure index refer to [3].

Given a circuit model (Figure 1.), it consists of an AC power, two ohmic resistances (the value of resistances are R_1 and R_2), one capacitor C, one inductor L. The state vector of the circuit model can be described as $\mathbf{x} = (i_1, i_2, i_3, i_4, i_5, u_1, u_2, u_3, u_4, u_5)^T$. In which, $i_1....i_5$ stand for electric current and $u_1....u_5$ stand for potential drop.

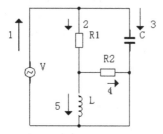

Fig. 1. Circuit Model

Based on Modelica modeling and simulation, the equation system of the circuit model is $A\mathbf{x} = \mathbf{b}$, see as Formula (1). In which, $\mathbf{x} = (i_1, i_2, i_3, i_4, i_5, u_1, u_2, u_3, u_4, u_5)^T$, $\mathbf{b} = (0,0,0,0,0,V,0,0,0,0)^T$. It gains a new coefficient matrix A by doing Laplace transformation for the coefficient matrix A and transforming the differential variables to algebraic variable.

$$\begin{cases} i_1 - i_2 + i_5 = 0 \\ -i_1 + i_3 + i_4 + i_5 = 0 \\ -u_1 - u_2 - u_4 = 0 \\ u_2 + u_3 - u_5 = 0 \\ -u_3 + u_4 = 0 \\ -u_1 = V \\ R_1 i_2 - u_2 = 0 \\ R_2 i_3 - u_3 = 0 \\ L(di_4 / dt) - u_4 = 0 \\ C(du_4 / dt) - i_5 = 0 \end{cases} \tag{1}$$

After calculating indices of the DAE, the structure index is 1 and the differential index is 2. The structure index and differential index are different. At this time, if we use structure index reduction algorithm to reduce index, the result may be incorrect.

The drawback of this index reduction algorithm limits applications of this algorithm on the software based on Modelica. During the modeling process, if the drawback is ignored, it may result an incorrect DAE, and the solution of the DAE may be wrong at last. In order to improve the applicability and accuracy of this algorithm, it is very important and valuable to check and correct the incorrect.

3   Algorithm

At present, checking and correcting the incorrect produced by structure index reduction algorithm is a research hotspot. At home and abroad, many researchers have made deep researches. Based on matrix, matroid and combinatorial optimization theory, Kazuo Murota, Satoru Iwata and Izumi Sakuta have devised combinatorial relaxation algorithm. This algorithm uses mathematical method, i.e. polynomial matrix, standard matrix and so on, to check and correct the incorrect. So the high-index DAE can be stably transformed to low-index DAE. Next, we will describe the combinatorial relaxation algorithm, key algorithms and their implantations.

3.1   Combinatorial Relaxation Algorithm

Given a bipartite graph $G(A)$ of the DAE, the algorithm includes three phases.

Phase 1: Compute $\hat{\delta}_k(A)$ by solving the weighted-matching problem in $G(A)$ using an efficient combinatorial algorithm, such as Hungarian method (see [7] [8]).

Phase 2: Test whether $\delta_k(A) = \hat{\delta}_k(A)$ or not by checking four matrix rank constraint conditions (see as $(r_1) \sim (r_4)$).

(r_1) rank $A^*[R,C] \geq k$

(r_2) rank $A^*[I^*,C] = |I^*|$

(r_3) rank $A^*[R,J^*] = |J^*|$

(r_4) rank $A^*[I^*,J^*] \geq |I^*| + |J^*| - k$

The highest degree δ_k, tightness coefficient matrix A^*, rank(A), I^*, J^* are defined in [9]. If $\delta_k(A) = \hat{\delta}_k(A)$, the structure index equals to the differential index, stop. Otherwise, the structure index and the differential index are different, go to Phase 3.

Phase 3: According to the formula $A'(x) = U(x)A(x)V(x)$, modify matrix A to A' such that $\delta_k(A') = \delta_k(A)$ and $\hat{\delta}_k(A') \leq \hat{\delta}_k(A) - 1$. Put $A := A'$ and go to Phase 1.

For combinatorial relaxation algorithm to check and correct the incorrect produced by the structure index reduction algorithm, converting DAE system to the frequency domain via the Laplace transformation gives rise to matrix pencils $A(s)$ [10] in s. The structure indices of the matrix pencil provide useful information for the initial value problem on the DAE system, and they are determined by the maximum degree of minors. For the structure index reduction algorithm and combinatorial relaxation algorithm, they construct a bipartite graph corresponding to matrix A, and then compute an upper bound $\delta_k(A)$ on the maximum degree of minors by solving the maximum weighted matching. $\delta_k(A) = \max\{\deg \det A[I,J] \mid |I| = |J| = k\}$, $A[I,J]$ is the sub-matrix of $A(s)$ with the row set I and column set J. Through testing the tightness of the upper bound, the combinatorial relaxation algorithm can check the incorrect produced by the structure index reduction algorithm.

From above description, we can see that solving the weighted-matching problem of bipartite graph is a key point of the combinatorial relaxation algorithm. Hungarian algorithm is a classical algorithm for it and KM is an improved algorithm based on Hungarian algorithm. Next, we will introduce and compare three different implementations of Hungarian algorithm in details.

3.2   BFS Single-Augmented

The idea of BFS (Bread-first search) is: given a graph G and origin vertex s, search all edges in G to find all vertices u being arrived from s, and compute the distances between s and u. That is, it finds the vertices with distance k starting from s firstly, and then finds the vertices with distance $k+1$ starting from s. BFS always extends the border between discovered and undiscovered vertices along the span direction.

The process of searching single augmenting path by BFS shows in Algorithm 1:

Algorithm 1. BFS single-augmented Method

Input: bipartite graph $G = (X, Y, E)$

Output: the maximum matching M

Step 1: Initialize.

Step 2: Select an unmatched vertex x from X, and search all un-matched vertices $y(y \in Y)$ arrived from vertex x with distance $k, k+1, k+2, k+3\ldots$. If there is a find out a shortest augmenting path and modify the match M. Repeat this step until there is no vertex y satisfying the conditions.

Step 4: If there is no augmenting path in G, stop, and output the maximum matching M. Otherwise go to Step 2.

The Hungarian algorithm is a polynomial time algorithm. It updates the matching when it finds an augmenting path, and the edges of matching M is increased by one, so there is at most n times for searching augmenting path. For the adjacent matrix, the time complexity of searching for one augmenting path by BFS is [11]. So that, the time complexity of the Hungarian algorithm, searching for single augmenting path by BFS, is.

3.3   DFS Single-Augmented

Depth-first search is another common graph algorithm, and it obeys the search strategy searching a graph deeply as possible. During the search process of DFS, for the current vertex u, if there is an un-searched edge with the starting point u, continue searching along this edge until all edges with the starting point u are searched. Back to the parent vertex of u, and continue to search all other edges until all vertices being arrived from origin vertex are found. If there are un-found vertices, select one as an origin vertex, and repeat above steps until all vertices are found.

The process of searching single augmenting path by DFS shows in Algorithm 2:

Algorithm 2. DFS singled-augmented Method

Input: bipartite graph $G = (X, Y, E)$

Output: the maximum matching M

Step 1: Initialize.

Step 2: Select an un-matched vertex x from X, and search for all vertices y $(y \in Y)$, which are abject to x and not matched by x. If it finds such a vertex y_i, it finds an augmenting path. Then mark the vertex y_i being matched and modify the matching M, stop the recursion.

Step 3: If there is no augmenting path in graph G, stop and output the maximum matching M. Otherwise go to Step 2.

This method needs to search augmenting path for n times, and the time complexity of searching for an augmenting path by DFS is. So the time complexity of the Hungarian algorithm, searching for single augmenting path by DFS, is Multi-augmented Hopcroft and Karp put up an idea of finding multi-augmented path in 1972. That is, at the step of searching for augmenting path, it searches for more than one shortest augmenting path concurrently, rather than one shortest augmenting path. All the shortest augmenting paths form into a maximal augmenting path set S, and then augment these paths in S concurrently.

The process of searching for multi-augmented path shows in Algorithm 3:

Algorithm 3. Multi-augmented Method

Input: bipartite graph $G = (X, Y, E)$ Output: the maximum matching M Step 1: Initialize Step 2: Select all un-matched vertices from X and form into a set S. Then for the vertex x_i in S, search un-matched and different vertex y_j ($y_j \in Y$) arrived from vertex x_i with distance k, respectively. Add y_j into the maximum augmenting path set P. Step 3: Along with all augmenting paths p ($p \in P$), augment them by DFS. For every path, if there is an un-matched vertex y_k ($y_k \in Y$) arrived from x_i and on the augmenting path p_i finds out an augmenting pat. Step 4: If there is no augmenting path in graph G, stop and output the maximum matching M. Otherwise go to Step 2.

All the shortest augmenting paths searched by the BFS in every time have same length. With the executing of the algorithm, the length of the shortest augmenting paths increases gradually. At last, it needs times to gain the maximum matching [12]. For augmenting the path in set P by DFS, its time complexity is. Therefore, the time complexity of the Hungarian algorithm, searching for multi-augmented paths, is.

3.4   Comparison

The bread-first search technology has no backtracking operation, but the depth-first search technology has, so for the Hungarian algorithm, BFS single-augmented method is faster than DFS single-augmented method. As it needs to storage all vertices produced during the bread-first search, but the depth-first search does not, the memory needed by BFS single-augmented method is more than DFS single-augmented method. Multi-augmented method combines DFS technology and BFS technology, so it is faster than DFS single-augmented method, but slower than BFS single-augmented method. The memory needed by multi-augmented method is more than DFS single-augmented method, but less than BFS single-augmented method.

4   Experiment

Modeling of complex physical systems with Modelica usually produces a high-index DAE system. Before using the combinatorial relaxation algorithm, construct a bipartite graph $G = (X, Y, E)$ for the DAE system. The vertex x_i in the set X stands for the i-th equation, and the vertex y_j in the set Y stands for the j-th variable. In these examples, we use adjacent matrix $G[n][n]$ to storage the relationship between differential algebraic equations and variables. The rows stand for the differential algebraic equations X, and the columns stand for variables. Set $|X| = |Y| = n$, $|E| = m$ the edge stands for the relationship between the i-th differential algebraic equation and the j-th variable.

In the three examples, the data scales respectively are: (1) $n = 600$, $m = 600 * 600$; (2) $n = 6000$, $m = 6000 * 6000$; (3) $n = 10000$, $m = 10000 * 10000$. Experiment environment is: Linux platform(Debian 4.4.5-8), Intel(R) Xeon(R) CPU X5472 @3.00GHz, Memory 16 GB, Compiler gcc version 4.4.5. The experiment results show in "Table 1".

Table 1. The experiment results of three implementations

Examples Run time(s)	Case 1 $n = 600$ $m = 600 * 600$	Case 2 $n = 6000$ $m = 6000 * 6000$	Case 3 $n = 10000$ $m = 10000 * 10000$
DFS single-augmented method	0.11s	72.12s	549.87s
BFS single-augmented method	0.04s	6.9s	28.32s
Multi-augmented method	0.05s	7.96s	34.61s

The "Table 1" shows, for the dense bipartite graph, BFS single-augmented method is the fastest, multi-augmented method is later, and DFS single-augmented method is the slowest. In the examples, the runtime ratio of BFS single-augmented method and multi-augmented method is stable, and it keeps up about 83%. The runtime ratio of BFS single-augmented method and DFS single-augmented method is about 35%-5%. The runtime ratio of multi-augmented method and DFS single-augmented method is about 50%-6%. With the scale increasing, the difference of runtime between BFS single-augmented method, multi-augmented method and DFS single-augmented method are more and more large respectively. The experiment results conform to the theory analysis. According to the experiment results, for the large-scale bipartite graph, BFS single-augmented method and multi-augmented method are better than DFS single-augmented method.

5   Conclusion

Modeling of complex physical systems with Modelica usually produces a high-index DAE system. In order to solve it directly, it needs to transform high-index DAE to low-index DAE. Structure index reduction algorithm is a mainstream algorithm for reducing index. But it has a drawback: the low-index DAE may be an incorrect, when there is a difference between structure index and differential index. Combinatorial relaxation algorithm can detect and correct the incorrect, so it makes up the drawback. Combinatorial relaxation algorithm is help for improving the adaptability and robustness of the structure index reduction algorithm. This paper presents the combinatorial relaxation algorithm and analyzes one key problem of the algorithm: solving maximum weighted matching of bipartite graph. For the large-scale bipartite graph, three different implementations of Hungarian algorithm are proposed. The experiment results conform to the theory analysis: BFS single-augmented method is the fastest, multi-augmented method is later, and DFS single-augmented method is the slowest. With the scale increases, the runtime of the three methods are very long. In the future, we will consider parallelizing the three different implementations and implementing the combinatorial algorithm efficiently. At last, the high-index DAE can be solved correctly and efficiently.

Acknowlegements. This research has been supported by National Natural Science Foundation (61170325).

References

1. Akesson, J., Arzen, K.-E., Gafvert, M.: Modeling and optimization with Optimica and JModelica.org-Languages and tools for solving large-scale dynamic optimization problems. Computers & Chemical Engineering 34(11), 1737–1749 (2010)
2. Li, P., Li, Y., Seem, J.E.: Modelica-Based Dynamic Modeling of a Chilled-Water Cooling Coil, HVAC & R Research (2010)
3. Yang, H.: Index Reduction Algorithm Studies for High Index Differential Algebraic Equation Produced from Modelica Modeling Software, Beijing. ISCAS (2009)
4. Pantelides, C.C.: The Consistent Initialization of Differential-Algebraic Systems. SIAM Journal on Scientific and Statistical Computing 9(2), 213–231 (1988)
5. Murota, K.: Matrices and Matroids for Systems Analysis. Springer, New York (2000)
6. Ungar, J., Kröner, A., Marquardt, W.: Structural analysis of differential-algebraic equation systems — Theory and application. Computers & Chemical Engineering 19, 867–882 (1995)
7. Lawyer, E.L.: Combinatorial Optimization: Networks and Matroids. Holt, Rinehart and Winston (1976)
8. Tarjan, R.E.: Data Structures and Network Algorithms. In: SIAM Regional Conference Series in Applied Mathematics, vol. 44 (1983)
9. Zhang, W.: The Research and Analysis of Structural Index Reduction Algorithm via Combinatorial Relaxation, Beijing. ISCAS (2009)

10. Iwata, S.: Computing the Maximum Degree of Minors in Matrix Pencils via Combinatorial Relaxation, pp. 476–483. ACM (1999)
11. Cormen, T.H., Leiserson, C.E., Rivest, R.L., Stein, C.: Introduction to Algorithms, 2nd edn. China Machine Press (2007)
12. Hopcroft-Karp algorithm,
    http://en.wikipedia.org/wiki/Hopcroft%E2%80%93Karp_algorithm

Design and Analysis of Missile Two-Loop Autopilot with Angle of Attack Feedback

Jiang Wang, Zhe Yang, and De-fu Lin

School of Aerospace Engineering, Beijing Institute of Technology,
Beijing 100081, China
wjbest2003@163.com

Abstract. In order to eliminate the static error of the classic two loop autopilot, the PI compensator is introduced into the control system. To enhance the robustness of two loop autopilot with PI compensator, an angle of attack feedback is introduced into the system. Using the method of pole-place, the controller parameters of different two loop autopilot topologies are deduced. The analytical results show that a well designed two-loop autopilot with PI compensator can introduce a zero in numerator which counteracts the first-order inertial loop in denominator. However, the two-loop autopilot with PI compensator and angle of attack feedback introduces the phase-lead compensation in the feedback-loop. The zero cannot cancel the first-order inertial loop in denominator, and it is dominated by the first-order inertial loop. This kind of autopilot topology has better robustness than others.

Keywords: two loop autopilot, PI compensator, angle of attack feedback, missile.

1 Introduction

Classical control techniques have dominated missile autopilot design over the past several decades. Most guided missile systems employ acceleration and rate feedback together with proportional and integral control to stabilize the missile and to track the guidance command signals [1]. That is to say, the design goal of these autopilots is to use sensed quantities to produce a stable fast response which robustly follows the input command. The gains of these autopilots are obtained at a variety of linearized flight conditions and have to be scheduled by appropriate algorithms to account for the changing environment [2].

As a representative example, the classic two loop lateral autopilot topology has been studied for many years in tactical missile design. The lateral autopilot is helpful to maintain the near-constant steady state aerodynamic gain, increase the weathercock frequency and damping, reduce cross-coupling between pitch and yaw motion, etc [3].

In this paper, the controller parameters of different two loop autopilot topologies are deduced using the method of pole-place. In order to eliminate the static error of classic two loop autopilot, the PI compensator is introduced into the control system. To enhance the robustness, angle of attack feedback is also introduced and the contribution

T. Xiao, L. Zhang, and S. Ma (Eds.): ICSC 2012, Part I, CCIS 326, pp. 287–296, 2012.

of PI compensator and angle of attack feedback is discussed. Finally, the essence of two loop autopilot with PI compensator and with angle of attack feedback is revealed.

2   Missile Dynamics

A missile's longitudinal dynamics form a SIMO (single-input multi-output) design model. It can be described as short period equations of motion. Written in differential equation notation the basic missile plant is

$$
\begin{cases}
\ddot{\vartheta} = -a_\omega \cdot \dot{\vartheta} - a_\alpha \cdot \alpha - a_\delta \cdot \delta \\
\dot{\theta} = b_\alpha \cdot \alpha + b_\delta \cdot \delta \\
\dot{\alpha} = \dot{\vartheta} - \dot{\theta} \\
a_y = V \dot{\theta}
\end{cases}
\tag{1}
$$

Table1. shows the defined variables and notations.

Table 1. Variables and notations

V	a_y	a_α	a_δ	a_ω	b_α	b_δ
Velocity (m/s)	Acceleration (m/s^2)	s^{-2}	s^{-2}	s^{-1}	s^{-1}	s^{-1}

ϑ	$\dot{\vartheta}$	$\ddot{\vartheta}$	$\dot{\theta}$	α
Body pitch Angle (rad)	Body pitch angular rate (rad/s)	Body pitch angular acceleration (rad/s^2)	Rate of trajectory angle (rad/s)	Angle of attack (rad)

Written in three-dimensional state space, the basic missile plant is

$$
\begin{aligned}
\dot{x} &= Ax + Bu \\
y &= Cx + Du
\end{aligned}
\tag{2}
$$

where

$$
x = \begin{bmatrix} \alpha \\ \vartheta \\ \dot{\vartheta} \end{bmatrix}, \; y = \begin{bmatrix} a_y \\ \vartheta \\ \dot{\vartheta} \end{bmatrix}, \; A = \begin{bmatrix} -b_\alpha & 0 & 1 \\ 0 & 0 & 1 \\ -a_\alpha & 0 & -a_\omega \end{bmatrix}, \; B = \begin{bmatrix} -b_\delta \\ 0 \\ -a_\delta \end{bmatrix}
$$

$$
C = \begin{bmatrix} Vb_\alpha - ca_\alpha & 0 & -ca_\omega \\ 0 & 1 & 0 \\ 0 & 0 & 1 \end{bmatrix}, \; D = \begin{bmatrix} Vb_\delta - ca_\delta \\ 0 \\ 0 \end{bmatrix}, \; u = [-\delta]
$$

where c is the distance form the accelerometer position to the airframe center of gravity (CG) and a positive c means the accelerometer is located ahead of CG.

The controllability matrix is given by

$$Q_c = \begin{bmatrix} B \\ AB \\ A^2B \end{bmatrix}^T = \begin{bmatrix} -b_\delta & b_a b_\delta - a_\delta & -b_a^2 b_\delta + a_a b_\delta + a_\delta b_a + a_\omega a_\delta \\ 0 & -a_\delta & a_a b_\delta + a_\omega a_\delta \\ -a_\delta & a_a b_\delta + a_\omega a_\delta & -a_a b_a b_\delta - a_a a_\omega b_\delta + a_a a_\delta - a_\omega^2 a_\delta \end{bmatrix} \tag{3}$$

Reference [4][5] has proved that $rank(Q_c) = 3$, that is to say, the missile plant is completely controllable.

The output acceleration is

$$a_y = (Vb_\alpha - ca_\alpha)\alpha - ca_\omega \dot{\vartheta} + (Vb_\delta - ca_\delta)\delta \ (m \cdot s^{-2}) \tag{4}$$

3 Pole-Place for Different Topologies Two-Loop Autopilots

3.1 Classil Two-Loop Autopilot

In reference [3], the classic two loop autopilot has no PI compensator. Using pole-place and state feedback technology, we get

$$K = \begin{bmatrix} k_1 \\ k_2 \end{bmatrix}^T = \begin{bmatrix} \dfrac{k_{ac} k_s (Vb_\alpha - ca_\alpha)}{[1 + k_{ac} k_s (Vb_\delta - ca_\delta)]} \\ \dfrac{k_s (k_g - ck_{ac} a_\omega)}{[1 + k_{ac} k_s (Vb_\delta - ca_\delta)]} \end{bmatrix}^T \tag{5}$$

$$\begin{cases} k_{ac} = k_1 / k_s [(Vb_\alpha - ca_\alpha) - k_1 (Vb_\delta - ca_\delta)] \\ k_g = k_2 / k_s + k_{ac} (k_2 (Vb_\delta - ca_\delta) + ca_\omega) \end{cases} \tag{6}$$

where K is the state feedback matrix, k_{ac} is the forward loop gain, k_g is the inner damping-loop feedback gain and k_s is the gain of fin dynamics.

The closed-loop gain is

$$K_G = \frac{k_{ac} V (a_\delta b_\alpha - a_\alpha b_\delta)}{(k_g + k_{ac} V)(a_\delta b_\alpha - a_\alpha b_\delta) - (a_\alpha + a_\omega b_\alpha) / k_s} \tag{7}$$

Generally speaking, in the design, k_s is set to -1. For tail control and static stable missiles, $a_\omega > 0$, $b_\alpha \gg b_\delta > 0$, $a_\alpha > 0, a_\delta > 0$ and a_α, a_δ is approximately at the same quantitativeness, we get $K_G < 1$ and there exists static error in the classic two-loop autopilot.

In classic two-loop autopilot, the output acceleration can not match the command acceleration and the variety of missile aerodynamics has great effect on the closed-loop gain. It is one of the main disadvantages of the traditional two-loop autopilot.

3.2   Classic Two-Loop Autopilot with PI Compensator

In engineering, in order to eliminate the static error, the PI compensator was often introduced into the control system. As the conventional way, a two-loop lateral autopilot with PI compensator using an accelerometer and rate gyro is shown in Figure.1. Given the state feedback matrix as $K = \begin{bmatrix} k_1 & k_2 & k_3 \end{bmatrix}$, we get $y = (C - DK)x$.

Here the control input can be written as

$$
\delta = \begin{bmatrix} \left[k_{ac} K_P (Vb_\alpha - ca_\alpha) - k_{ac}V(K_P/T_i) \right] / \left[1 - k_{ac}K_P (Vb_\delta - ca_\delta) \right] \\ k_{ac}(K_P/T_i)V / \left[1 - k_{ac}K_P (Vb_\delta - ca_\delta) \right] \\ \left(ck_{ac}(K_P/T_i) - ck_{ac}a_\omega K_P + k_g \right) / \left[1 - k_{ac}K_P (Vb_\delta - ca_\delta) \right] \end{bmatrix}^T \begin{bmatrix} \alpha \\ \vartheta \\ \dot{\vartheta} \end{bmatrix}
\tag{8}
$$

We obtain

$$
\begin{bmatrix} k_1 \\ k_2 \\ k_3 \end{bmatrix}^T = \begin{bmatrix} \left[k_{ac} K_P (Vb_\alpha - ca_\alpha) - k_{ac}V(K_P/T_i) \right] / \left[1 - k_{ac}K_P (Vb_\delta - ca_\delta) \right] \\ k_{ac}(K_P/T_i)V / \left[1 - k_{ac}K_P (Vb_\delta - ca_\delta) \right] \\ \left(ck_{ac}(K_P/T_i) - ck_{ac}a_\omega K_P + k_g \right) / \left[1 - k_{ac}K_P (Vb_\delta - ca_\delta) \right] \end{bmatrix}^T
\tag{9}
$$

$$
\begin{cases}
K_P = \dfrac{-(k_1 + k_2)}{k_{ac}(Vb_\alpha - ca_\alpha) - k_{ac}(k_1 + k_2)(Vb_\delta - ca_\delta)} \\[2mm]
T_i = \dfrac{k_{ac}VK_P}{-k_2 + k_{ac}k_2(Vb_\delta - ca_\delta)K_P} \\[2mm]
k_g = -k_3 + k_{ac}k_3(Vb_\delta - ca_\delta)K_P + ca_\omega k_{ac}K_P - ck_{ac}(K_P/T_i)
\end{cases}
\tag{10}
$$

Because of the introduced of PI compensator, the closed-loop gain is 1 and the variety of missile aerodynamics has no effect on the steady state gain.

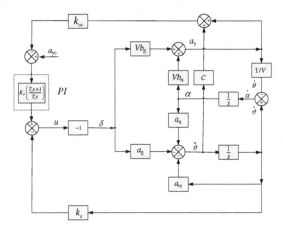

Fig. 1. Two-loop lateral autopilot with PI compensator

3.3   Two-Loop Autopilot with Angle of Attack Feedback

In section 3.2 we have know that PI compensator has eliminated the static error and the variety of missile aerodynamics has no effect on the closed-loop gain. In practice, the angle of attack may be over the maximum limit especially for air-to-air missiles and the robustness of this kind of autopilot topology is not very strong [3]. So, we will improve the autopilot topology and introduce a feedback loop in the classic two-loop autopilot with PI compensator as shown in Figure2.

The transfer function from $\dot{\vartheta}$ to α is

$$G_{\dot{\vartheta}}^{\alpha}(s) = \frac{k_{\alpha}(B_1 s + 1)}{k_{\dot{\vartheta}}(T_{\alpha}s + 1)} \qquad (11)$$

where, $\dfrac{k_{\alpha}}{k_{\dot{\vartheta}}} = \dfrac{a_{\omega}b_{\delta} + a_{\delta}}{a_{\delta}b_{\alpha} - a_{\alpha}b_{\delta}}, T_{\alpha} = \dfrac{a_{\delta}}{a_{\delta}b_{\alpha} - a_{\alpha}b_{\delta}}, B_1 = \dfrac{b_{\delta}}{a_{\omega}b_{\delta} + a_{\delta}}$

We have know that a_{α} and a_{δ} are large value, a_{ω}, b_{α}, b_{δ} are small value and $b_{\alpha} \gg b_{\delta} > 0$.

For simplify, $\dfrac{k_{\alpha}}{k_{\dot{\vartheta}}} \approx \dfrac{a_{\delta}}{a_{\delta}b_{\alpha}} = \dfrac{1}{b_{\alpha}}, T_{\alpha} \approx \dfrac{a_{\delta}}{a_{\delta}b_{\alpha}} = \dfrac{1}{b_{\alpha}}, B_1 \approx 0$,

then we get

$$G_{\dot{\vartheta}}^{\alpha}(s) \approx \frac{1}{s + b_{\alpha}} \qquad (12)$$

The PI compensator controller parameters is the same as in section 3.2, except K_P.

$$K_P = \frac{-(k_1 + k_2) - 1}{k_{ac}(Vb_{\alpha} - ca_{\alpha}) - k_{ac}(k_1 + k_2)(Vb_{\delta} - ca_{\delta})} \qquad (13)$$

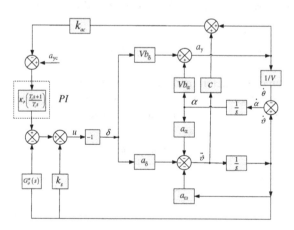

Fig. 2. Two-loopl lateral autopilot with PI compensator and angle of attack feedback

4   Autopilot Analysis and Comparison

4.1   Two-Loop Autopilot Design

In the flight control system, the accelerometer feeds back achieved acceleration information into the autopilot while the rate gyro feeds back airframe body rate information. The autopilot gains, $\begin{bmatrix} K_P & T_i & k_g \end{bmatrix}$, must be chosen to satisfy some designer-chosen criteria.

Missile design engineers would like to let the denominator closed-loop transfer function of third-order autopilot have the form

$$p(s) = (\tau s + 1)\left(\frac{s^2}{\omega^2} + \frac{2\mu}{\omega}s + 1\right) \tag{14}$$

which has made the polynomial a real pole ($-1/\tau$) times a quadratic.

Missile engineers would like to put forward the time and frequency-domain mixed performance index in terms of τ, μ and ω.

In engineering, the crossover frequency of open-loop system ω_{CR} would be put forward as the design parameter [6][7]. Actually, there exists a bijection between ω and ω_{CR}

$$\omega_{CR} \doteq f(\omega) \tag{15}$$

We redefine the objective function with the required ω_{CR} and calculate the actual ω'_{CR} every time.

$$\min|\omega_{CR} - \omega'_{CR}| \tag{16}$$

From the point of view of pole assignment, the desired closed-loop system poles can be determined as follows

$$P = \left[-1/\tau \quad -\mu\omega + j\omega\sqrt{1-\mu^2} \quad -\mu\omega - j\omega\sqrt{1-\mu^2}\right] \tag{17}$$

For given airframe parameters and performance index, it can decide the desired poles and the autopilot gains. The corresponding control parameters are defined in Table 2. Where, ω_s and μ_s are fin dynamics parameters.

Table 2. Control parameters

V	a_α	a_δ	a_ω	b_α	b_δ	c	ω_s	μ_s
1140	72.4	471	1.5	1.27	0.477	0.66	150	0.7

Set $\tau = 0.3s$, $\mu = 0.7$, $\omega_{CR} = 40rad/s$ and the input is unit g step. The design results are shown in Table 3. and Figure3.

Table 3. Design results for FOUR two-loop autopilot topologies

	Two-loop Autopilot Topologies	GM (dB)	PM (deg)	ω_{CR} (rad/s)
1	Classic two-loop	7.38	33.9	39.9
2	Two-loop with PI compensator	7.35	33.4	39.4
3	Two-loop with PI compensator & angle of attack feedback	12.1	44.0	39.5
4	Two-loop with PI compensator & simplified angle of attack feedback	11.1	41.4	40.2

To holding ω_{CR} as 40rad/s, classic two-loop and two-loop with PI compensator autopilots have smaller GM and PM than two-loop autopilots with PI compensator and (simplified) angle of attack feedback. That is to say the later two topologies autopilots have higher robust. The cost is that two-loop autopilots with PI compensator and (simplified) angle of attack feedback respond slower than the former two topologies autopilots.

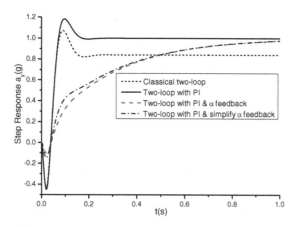

Fig. 3. Step response of different two-loop topologies

4.2   Angle of Attack and Actuator Analysis

During transient process, the need of angle of attack and fin resource for classic two-loop autopilot and two-loop autopilot with PI compensator is larger than two-loop autopilot with PI compensator and angle feedback, The simulation results shown in Figure4. and Figure5. validate the analysis.

The later topology autopilot is benefit to let the plant to use less angle of attack and fin deflection to achieve larger acceleration and make the missiles get better maneuverability. It is especially important for advanced air-to-air missiles which have specially demand for large angle of attack and also strict limit of angle of attack.

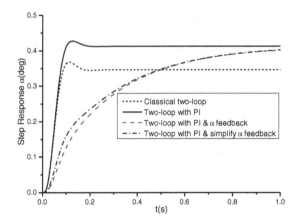

Fig. 4. Step response of α for different two-loop topologies

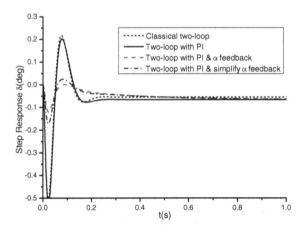

Fig. 5. Fin deflection of different two-loop topologies

4.3   PI Compensator Analysis

According to the analysis method in reference [4], the equivalent "airframe" of pure airframe adding with well-designed damping can be expressed as $G(s)$ and neglect

c, shown in Figure6(a)~(b). Where, $\quad T = T_i\left(1 + \dfrac{1}{K_P V b_\alpha}\right) > T_i$.

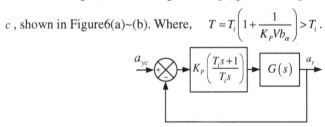

Fig. 6(a). A equivalent two-loop topology with PI compensator

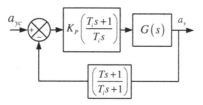

Fig. 6(b). A equivalent two-loop topology with PI compensatorand angle of attack feedback

The closed-loop transfer functions of two topologies are similar, shown as follows.

Two-loop with PI: $\dfrac{K_P(T_i s+1)G(s)}{K_P(T_i s+1)G(s)+T_i s}$

Two-loop with PI and α feedback: $\dfrac{K_P(Ts+1)G(s)}{K_P(Ts+1)G(s)+T_i s}$

Therefore, though there is a slow pole in the closed-loop system, a well designed two-loop autopilot with PI compensator introduces a zero in numerator to try to counteract the first-order inertial loop in denominator. But for two-loop autopilot with PI compensator and angle of attack feedback, it introduces phase-lead compensation in the feedback-loop and the zero can not cancel the first-order inertial loop in denominator and it approaches a first-order inertial loop.

4.4   Robustness Analysis

Reference[3] has pointed out that the robustness of two-loop with PI compensator is not very strong especially at high frequency. When angle of attack feedback is introduced, the system is dominated by the first-order inertial loop which is determined by PI compensator and the variety of aerodynamic parameters has little effect on the control system, so two-loop topology with PI compensator and angle of attack feedback has strong robustness.

Table 4. lists the four closed-loop transfer functions. Wherein, the fin dynamics was set as -1 to inspect the results more clearly. Two-loop autopilot with PI compensator introduces an approximate-canceling zero-pole pair, $(s+3.6)$ and $(s+3.5)$, while the zero and pole of the later autopilot topology is $(s+16.5)$ and $(s+3.6)$ or $(s+11.3)$ and $(s+3.2)$ which is not an canceling zero-pole pair.

Table 4. Closed-loop transfer function

	Two Loop Autopilot Topologies	Closed-loop transfer function
1	Classic two-loop	$\dfrac{-0.62\,(s+35.1)\,(s-33.6)}{(s^2+41.3s+870.3)}$
2	Two-loop with PI	$\dfrac{-0.62\,(s-33.6)\,(s+35.1)\,(s+3.6)}{(s+3.5)\,(s^2+38.5s+735.5)}$
3	Two-loop with PI & angle of attack feedback	$\dfrac{-0.11\,(s-33.6)\,(s+35.1)\,(s+16.5)}{(s+3.6)\,(s^2+35.5s+622.8)}$
4	Two-loop with PI & simplified angle of attack feedback	$\dfrac{-0.18\,(s-33.6)\,(s+35.1)\,(s+11.3)}{(s+3.2)\,(s^2+36.8s+719.2)}$

Use the residue-analyze technology, Figure7. shows the results more directly.

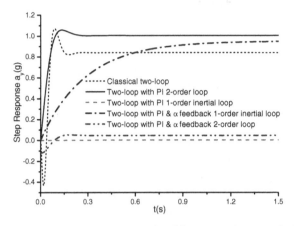

Fig. 7. Response of separate loops for different two-loop topologies

5   Conclusion

The introduced of angle of attack feedback for two-loop autopilot with PI compensator let the missile to use less angle of attack and fin deflection to achieve larger acceleration and better maneuverability during transient process. The PI compensator eliminates the system static error and makes a two-loop autopilot with PI compensator approaches a classic two-loop autopilot with an approximate-canceling zero-pole pair. The two-loop topology with PI compensator and angle of attack feedback is dominated by the first-order inertial loop, thereby it responds slower than the two-loop topology with PI compensator.

References

1. William Nesline, F., Zarchan, P.: Robust Instrumentation Configurations for Homing Missile Flight Control. AIAA, 209–219 (1980)
2. Buschek, H.: Design and flight test of a robust autopilot for the IRST-T air-to-air missile. Control Engineering Practice 11, 551–558 (2003)
3. Garnell, P.: Guided weapon cont rol systems. Revised by Qi Zaikang, Xia Qunli. Beijing institute of technology, Beijing (2003)
4. Defu, L.: Analysis and improvement of missile three-loop autopilots. Journal of Systems Engineering and Electronics 20(4), 844–851 (2009)
5. Fan, J.-F.: Design and Comparison of Classical Topologies for Static Unstable Missile Autopilots. In: 2008 Chinese Control and Decision Conference, pp. 3659–3664 (2008)
6. Fan, J.-F.: On Control for Static Unstable Missiles. In: Proceedings of the 26th Chinese Control Conference, pp. 464–468 (2007)
7. Zarchan, P.: Tactical and Strategic Missile Guidance, 4th edn., pp. 70–73. AIAA Inc., Virginia (2002)

Iterative Learning Control of Batch Processes Using Adaptive Differential Evolution Algorithm

Guohua Zhang, Kai Yuan, and Li Jia*

Shanghai Key Laboratory of Power Station Automation Technology,
Department of Automation, College of Mechatronics Engineering and Automation,
Shanghai University, Shanghai 200072, China
jiali@staff.shu.edu.cn

Abstract. Considering the potentials of iterative learning control as framework for industrial batch process control and optimization, an iterative learning control based on adaptive differential evolution algorithm is proposed in this paper. At first, quadratic criterion-iterative learning control with adaptive differential evolution algorithm is used to improve the performance of iterative learning control. In addition, the strategy of eliminating error using iterative algorithm is employed to drive the solution to the optimal point. As a result, the proposed method can avoid the problem of falling into local extreme points when solving the objective function with multiple local extreme points, which usually exists in traditional gradient-based iterative learning control. Lastly, example is used to illustrate the performance and applicability of the proposed method.

Keywords: batch process, adaptive differential evolution algorithm, iterating learning control.

1 Introduction

Recently, batch processes have been used increasingly in the production of low volume and high value added products, such as special polymers, special chemicals, pharmaceuticals, and heat treatment processes for metallic or ceramic products [1-3]. For the purpose of deriving the maximum benefit from batch process, it is important to optimize the operation policy of batch processes. Therefore, optimal control of batch processes is very significant. However, optimal control is often suboptimal acquiring from off-line process model when applied into the real process because of the mismatching.

To overcome the aforementioned problem in optimal control, Iterative learning control (ILC) has been used in the batch-to-batch control. In the past decade, the development of iterative learning control is rapidly promoted. There are some research results in this field. Jia and Shi proposed a novel neuro-fuzzy model-based iterative learning control methodology for batch processes with uncertainties, and proved its global convergence based on the Lyapunov approach [4]. Zhou and Wang

---

* Corresponding author.

T. Xiao, L. Zhang, and S. Ma (Eds.): ICSC 2012, Part I, CCIS 326, pp. 297–303, 2012.
© Springer-Verlag Berlin Heidelberg 2012

presented an iterative learning model predictive control algorithm for a class of continuous or batch processes with periodic strong disturbances [5]. Zhang and Xiong came up with an iterative learning control method using batch wise updated linearised models aiming to adapt the model to process variations and the current operating condition [6]. In general, the solution to the optimization problem in iterative learning control can be easily solved using classical mathematic method. But the optimization control technology based on traditional gradient algorithm may fall into the local extreme point and can't solve the problem efficiently when dealing with multiple objective functions.

With the development of artificial intelligence technology, the differential evolution algorithm has good advantage of rapid convergence and stability [7, 8], and shows a huge potential for the dynamic optimization of batch process. Thus, an iterative learning control based on adaptive differential evolution algorithm is proposed in this paper. Quadratic criterion-iterative learning control with adaptive differential evolution algorithm is used to improve the performance of iterative learning control. In addition, the strategy of eliminating error using iterative algorithm is employed to drive the solution to the optimal point. Furthermore the proposed method can avoid the problem of falling into local extreme points when solving the objective function with multiple local extreme points.

The rest of this paper is organized as follows. In Section 2, the iterative learning control of batch process using adaptive differential evolution algorithm is presented. Section 3 introduces the proposed adaptive differential evolution algorithm for batch process. Simulation example is given in Section 4, followed by the conclusion given in Section 5.

2   Iterative Learning Control of Batch Process Using Adaptive Differential Evolution Algorithm

Differential Evolution Algorithm (DE) was proposed by Storn and Price in 1995 [9, 10]. Like Genetic Algorithm (GA), the population of DE consists of N members searching in D-dimensional space. The population is defined as $X = \{X_i \mid i = 1, 2, ..., N\}$ and the ith member is represented as $X_i = [X_{i,1}, X_{i,2}, ... X_{i,D}]$. The basic operators of DE contain mutation, crossover and selection.

The mutation operation is

$$V_i = X_{r_1} + F(X_{r_2} - X_{r_3}) ,$$ (1)

where $V_i = [V_{i,1}, V_{i,2}, ... V_{i,D}]$ is mutation vector, $r_1 \neq r_2 \neq r_3 \neq i$, $F \in [-2 \ \ 2]$ is shrinkage factor.

The crossover operation is implemented to enhance the population's diversity by

$$Z_{i,j} = \begin{cases} V_{i,j}, & p_t \leq CR \\ X_{i,j}, & p_t > CR \end{cases} ,$$ (2)

where $Z_i = [Z_{i,1}, Z_{i,2}, ... Z_{i,D}]$ is crossover vector $p_t \in [0\ 1]$ and $CR \in [0\ 1]$ is cross-over probability factor.

The selection is employed to generate a new population by

$$X'_i = \begin{cases} Z_i\ , & f(Z_i) < f(X_i) \\ X_i\ , & others \end{cases}, \tag{3}$$

where X'_i is the ith new population individual, $f(\cdot)$ is the objective function used to compute the fitness values.

In this paper, DE is employed into the iterative learning control for batch process. The proposed method makes use of the characteristic of repetition as shown in Fig.1.

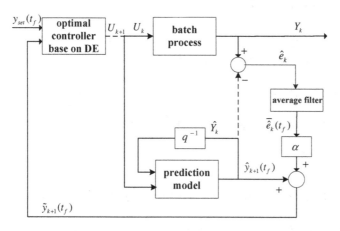

Fig. 1. Iterative learning control for product quality base on DE

where k is batch index, t is the batch discrete-time and t_f denotes a period of one batch. $y_{set}(t_f)$ is the desired value, U_k is input sequence and $\mathbf{Y}_k$ is corresponding output sequence.

The model prediction error is

$$\hat{e}_k(t_f) = y_k(t_f) - \hat{y}_k(t_f)\ , \tag{4}$$

where $y_k(t_f)$ is the product quality measured at the end of the kth batch, and $\hat{y}_k(t_f)$ denotes the model prediction of the kth batch.

On the basis of iterative control principle, the model prediction error of all historical batches can be employed to revise model prediction by

$$\tilde{y}_{k+1}(t_f) = \hat{y}_{k+1}(t_f) + \alpha \cdot \overline{\hat{e}}_k(t_f)\ , \tag{5}$$

where $\alpha(0 < \alpha < 1)$ is iterative correction factor, $\overline{\hat{e}}_k(t_f)$ is generated by the average filter, and $\overline{\hat{e}}_k(t_f)$ is formulated by

$$\bar{\hat{e}}_k(t_f) = \frac{1}{k}\sum_{m=1}^{k}\hat{e}_m(t_f) = \frac{1}{k}\sum_{m=1}^{k}(y_m(t_f) - \hat{y}_m(t_f)) \ , \tag{6}$$

In order to maximize the product quality at the end of each batch, a quadratic objective function is defined as:

$$\min_{U_{k+1}} J(U_{k+1}, k+1) = \| y_{set}(t_f) - \tilde{y}_{k+1}(t_f) \|_Q^2 + \| U_{k+1} - U_k \|_R^2 \ , \tag{7}$$

where $Q = \lambda_q \cdot I_n$ and $R = \lambda_r \cdot I_n$ are positive weighted matrixes.

The steps of the optimal controller based on DE algorithm are as follows:

Step 1: Set $k = 1$ and initialize $U_1, \hat{e}_1, Q, R$ and α.

Step 2: Input U_k into the batch process and measure the product quality $y_k(t_f)$, then calculate the model prediction $\hat{y}_k(t_f)$ of U_k.

Step 3: Compute $\hat{e}_k(t_f)$ and $\bar{\hat{e}}_k(t_f)$ according to eq.(4) and eq.(6).

Step 4: Use DE to obtain the optimal input sequence U_{k+1} in eq.(7).

Step 5: Return to Step 2 until the terminate condition is satisfied.

3   Adaptive Differential Evolution Algorithm for Batch Process

t_f is devided into T intervals, and the input and output sequences are respectively formulated as $U_k = [U_{k,1}, U_{k,2}, ..., U_{k,T}]$ and $Y_k = [Y_{k,1}, Y_{k,2} \cdots Y_{k,T}]$, where k denotes the batch index, $Y_k \in R^T, U_k \in R^T$ and $y_k(t_f) = Y_{k,T}$.

In this paper, the ADE's population is defined as $UK = [UK_1, UK_2, ..., UK_N]$, $UK_i = [UK_{i,1}, UK_{i,2}, ..., UK_{i,T}]$, and $UK_{i,j} \in [u_{min} \ u_{max}]$, where u_{min} and u_{max} denote the lower bound and the upper bound of the input variable respectively.

During the gth evolution iteration in the kth batch, the ith population individual is computed according to the control parameter $\{F_{i,g}, CR_{i,g}\}$ and objective function eq.(7). The procedures are as follows:

Mutation operation:

$$V_i = UK_{r_1} + F_{i,g}(UK_{r_2} - UK_{r_3}) \ , \tag{8}$$

Crossover operation :

$$Z_{i,j} = \begin{cases} V_{i,j}, & p_t \le CR_{i,g} \\ UK_{i,j}, & p_t > CR_{i,g} \end{cases} \ , \tag{9}$$

Validation for search scope :

$$Z_{i,j} = \begin{cases} Z_{i,j}, & u_{\min} \leq Z_{i,j} \leq u_{\max} \\ u_{\min}, & Z_{i,j} < u_{\min} \\ u_{\max}, & Z_{i,j} > u_{\max} \end{cases} \quad , \tag{10}$$

Selection operation :

$$UK_i' = \begin{cases} Z_i, & J(Z_i, k+1) < J(UK_i, k+1) \\ UK_i, & others \end{cases} \quad , \tag{11}$$

Compute the adjustable parameters for the $(g+1)$th iteration by eq.(12) and eq.(13):

$$F_{i,g+1} = F_{\min} + \beta \left(\frac{J(UK_i', k+1) - \min_{q=1}^{N}[J(UK_q', k+1)]}{\max_{q=1}^{N}[J(UK_q', k+1)] - \min_{q=1}^{N}[J(UK_q', k+1)] + \delta} \right)^{\theta} \quad , \tag{12}$$

$$CR_{i,g+1} = \frac{CR_{\max}}{\chi + \gamma \left(\frac{J(UK_i', k+1) - \min_{q=1}^{N}[J(UK_q', k+1)]}{\max_{q=1}^{N}[J(UK_q', k+1)] - \min_{q=1}^{N}[J(UK_q', k+1)] + \delta} \right)^{\theta}} \quad , \tag{13}$$

where $F_{\min}$ and $CR_{\max}$ are respectively the minimum shrinkage factor and the maximum crossover probability factor ; δ is a arbitrarily small positive real; the parameters of θ, β, χ and γ are adaptive factors of ADE, $\theta \in [0\ 1]$, β, χ and γ are positive integers.

4   Illustrative Example

The proposed algorithm is applied to a typical batch reactor A $\xrightarrow{k_1}$ B $\xrightarrow{k_2}$ C [11, 12]:

$$\begin{cases} \dot{w}_1 = -4000 \exp\left(\frac{-2500}{T_p}\right) \cdot w_1^2 \\ \dot{w}_2 = 4000 \exp\left(\frac{-2500}{T_p}\right) \cdot w_1^2 - 6.2 \times 10^5 \exp\left(\frac{-5000}{T_p}\right) \cdot w_2 \end{cases} \quad , \tag{14}$$

where w_1, w_2 denote respectively dimensionless concentration for product A and product B; $T_p \in [298\,K\ 398\,K]$ is the reactor temperature. The initial reaction condition is: $w_1(0) = 1, w_2(0) = 0$. The control objective is to manipulate the reactor temperature T_p to control the concentration of B at the end of each batch.

To verify the effectiveness of the proposed algorithm, three experiments are implemented and the parameters are shown in Table 1 and Table 2.

The simulation results are given in Table 3 and Fig. 2, and showed that the proposed method is better than other two methods.

Table 1. The parameters of three experiments(Exp. 1: optimize product quality using DE; Exp. 2: optimize product quality using DE based iterative learning control; Exp. 3: optimize product quality using the proposed method)

	N	D	G_{max}	F	CR
Exp.1	30	10	80 iterations	0.6	0.5
Exp.2	30	10	8 iterations/batch	0.6	0.5
Exp.3	30	10	8 iterations/batch	adaptive	adaptive

Table 2. The parameters of Exp.3

F_{min}	R_{max}	β	χ	γ	θ	δ
0.5	0.5	0.1	1	2	0.25	1×10^{-10}

Table 3. The Simulation Results of Three Experiments

	Maximum	Minimum	Average Error
Exp. 1	0.6072	0.6034	0.00428
Exp. 2	0.6091	0.6085	0.00115
Exp. 3	0.6094	0.6091	0.00064

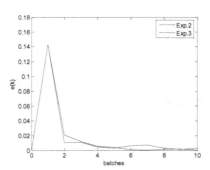

Fig. 2. e(k)-batches curves

5   Conclusions

An iterative learning control based on adaptive differential evolution algorithm was proposed in this paper. Quadratic criterion-iterative learning control with adaptive differential evolution algorithm was used to improve the performance of iterative learning control. In addition, the strategy of eliminating error using iterative algorithm was employed to drive the solution to the optimal point. Moreover, the proposed method can avoid the problem of falling into local extreme points when solving the objective function with multiple local extreme points. The results showed the proposed method has better performance.

Acknowledgments. This work is supported by National Natural Science Foundation of China (No.61004019) and Doctoral Program of Higher Education of China (20093108120013).

References

1. Lu, N., Wang, F., Gao, F., Wang, S.: Statistical Modeling and Online Mo-nitoring for batch processes. Acta Automatica Sinica 32(3), 400–410 (2006)
2. Liu, H., Jia, L., Liu, Q., et al.: Batch-to-batch Control of Batch Processes Based on Multilayer Recurrent Fuzzy Neural Network. In: Proceedings of the International Conference on Intelligent Systems and Knowledge Engineering, p. 1369. Atlantis Press, Paris (2007)
3. Zhang, J.: Batch-to-batch Optimal Control of a Batch Polymerisation Process Based on Sta-cked Neural Network Models. Chemical Engineering Science. 63(5), 1273–1281 (2008)
4. Jia, L., Shi, J., Song, Y., Chiu, M.: A Novel Neuro-Fuzzy Model-Based Run-to-run Control for Batch Processes with Uncertainties. In: 2009 Chinese Control and Decision Conference (CCDC 2009), pp. 5813–5818 (2009)
5. Zhou, M., Wang, S., Jin, X., Zhang, Q.: Iterative Learning Mo-del Predictive Control for a Class of Continuous/Batch Processes. Chinese Journal of Chemical Engineering 17(6), 976–982 (2009)
6. Zhang, J., Xiong, Z.: Delautre Guillaume and Alexandre Lamande.: Batch to Batch Iterative Learning Control of a Fed-Batch Fermentation Process. Advances in Intelligent and Soft Computing 125, 253–260 (2012)
7. Storn, R., Price, K.: Differential Evolution: a Simple and Efficient Adaptive Scheme for Global Optimization over Continuous Spaces (EB/OL) (October 25, 2010), http://www.icsiberkeley.edu/~storn/TR-95-012.pdf
8. Yüzgeç, U.: Performance Comparison of Differential Evolution Techniques on Optimization of Feeding Profile for an Industrial Scale Baker's Yeast Fermentation Process. ISA Transactions 49(1), 167–176 (2010)
9. Storn, R., Price, K.: Differential Evolution–a Simple and Efficient Adaptive Scheme for Global Optimization over Continuous Spaces. International Computer Science Institute, Berkley (1995)
10. Goudos, S.K., Baltzis, K.B., Antoniadis, K., Zaharis, Z.D., Hilas, C.S.: A Comparative Study of Common and Self-adaptive Differential Evolution Strategies on Numerical Benchmark Problems. Procedure Computer Science 3, 83–88 (2011)
11. Ray, W.H.: Advanced Process Control. McGraw-Hill, M. New York 1 (1981)
12. Jia, L., Cheng, D., Shi, J., Chiu, M.: Particle Swarm Optimization Algorithm Based Iterative Learning Algorithm for Batch Process. Control Engineering of China 18(3), 341–344 (2011)

Modeling and Simulation on Information Spreading Based on Networks of Mobile phone

Fang Zhang[1,2], Guangya Si[1], and Pi Luo[1]

[1] National Defense University, No.3(A), Hongshankou, Haidian District, Beijing, China
[2] Sergeant School of the Second Artillery Engineering University, No.12,
Fangongting South Street, Qingzhou China
sunny7201@163.com

Abstract. It is an advancing subject to research information communication by modeling and simulation and then to research the correlation of information propagation oriented at war gaming such as public opinion and rumor etc, which possesses important theoretical and practical values. The paper summarizes the current research and appliction state of modeling and simulation in the field of information spreading, points out the existing difficult problems in our study, and introduces the methods and key technology of modeling and simulation.

Keywords: Networks, Mobile Phone, Information Spreading, Modeling and Simulation.

1   Introduction

With the prominently increasing position and role of the information dissemination by the mobile phone as a means of information dissemination affects the international society in political, economic, military, technological and cultural fields, which requires full use of the information conditions in social studies including all possible visualized, and quantitative qualitative experimental means.

2   Method

The information spreading system based on the mobile phone is a complex aggregates with a variety of systematical elements behaviors, processes and their interaction and integration. In view of the highly integrated characteristics of complexity of the information communication based on networks of handsets, as the system structure of the nonlinear and the information dissemination process dynamic variety of the mobile phone information transmission at the macro level , and the individual attributes of heterogeneity and behavioral uncertainty at the microscopic level, we use integrated modeling simulation method based on complexity theory to research mobile phone network information dissemination problem. The logical structure is shown in Fig. 1, which includes three logical levels. The Agents layer is a

T. Xiao, L. Zhang, and S. Ma (Eds.): ICSC 2012, Part I, CCIS 326, pp. 304–312, 2012.

heterogeneous Agents model, including mobile phone users, communication base station, media and control Agents. The relationship layer is the abstract description for the complexity factors of the structure of the system, which can be described by Internet. Thus, this network is the important channel of "information flow". The information flow layer bears the communication behaviors which are powers that supports the evolution of the whole system and can be described the psychological and communication behaviors of the Agents to describe the intelligent and adaptive of various types of Agents.

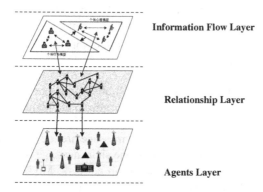

Information Flow Layer

Relationship Layer

Agents Layer

Fig. 1. Conceptual model based on networks of handsets

3   Models

A prototype system of information spreading includes three keys: mobile phone network model based on the interpersonal relationship, individual mental model based on attitude and individual behavior model based on the mobile phone network.

3.1   The Network of the Mobile Phone

We make a mobile phone network based on the interpersonal relationship and theory of complex network to reflect these complex and dynamic kind of social relationships.

Relationships Among Persons. The relationships of mobile phone user are abstracted into three categories: natural relations, namely family and kinship relationship; communication relationship, a relationship among Agents with similar cognitive level, value concept, political inclination, such as classmates, colleagues and so on; stochastic relation, a temporary relationship which could build exchange relationship.

Interpersonal Relationship Network of Persons. We use different algorithms to generate natural, exchange and random networks. The natural relation network is a fully coupled network model based on the family relationship.

The communication network depends on two custom parameters, one is similarity factor s_{ab}, and the other is uncertainty factor ε. If W^τ is the definition of weight vector of individual attributes, M is the same or similar numbers of individual attributes, and the individual and the similarity between a and b can be expressed as $s_{ab} = \Sigma M / W^T$. The uncertainty factor ε tells us that two individuals with similar or same attributes are not necessarily to establish communication relationship. Letting $\varepsilon \in [0,1]$ and giving threshold T ($T = 0.618$), if $s_{ab} > \varepsilon \times T$, and if there is no communication connecting edge between a and b , communication edges is established between a and b , and the communication network is established. Repeating the above steps among the Agents to establish.

The temporary relationship networks is established by the near distance principle and expressed by individual distance between two Agents, giving a threshold η, if the individual distance between two Agents is less than threshold η, the two individuals establish a stochastic relation.

The Network Model of Mobile Phone. The mobile phone network model includes two parts: one is the network of mobile phone and mobile phone short message; the other is the network of mobile phone blog.

The mobile phone and mobile phone short message are the basic and main modes. The network of mobile phone and mobile phone short message is a weighted network based on the generated interpersonal relationship network. Model generation process is as follows : Using the only serial number as the Agent's mobile phone number, other connected Agents' mobile phone numbers as the Agent's the mail list, the weighted transmission network is established according to the mail list; weight of natural relation edges is 1, weight of communication relation edges is the clustering coefficient of entry points; the evolution of the network comes from the increasing of the mobile phone users and the new communication relationship from stochastic relationship. The network model is static in the form, but is also dynamic during the information dissemination process. Mobile phone blog is the short message communication between the mobile phone and corresponding micro-blog network, and this communication is not necessarily based on the existing interpersonal relationship. Therefore, the micro-blog network model, based on BA model algorithm, uses the micro-blog users as points, the paid attention as edges to form a scale-free network.

3.2   The Individual Mental Model Based on Attitude

From results of the dissemination, one of the ultimate effects of communication is to change audience's attitude which is a psychological process. Therefore, we establish psychological model in which the attitude is the core and the psychological change is described as cognitive, emotional, behavioral tendency of three psychological processes.

Basic Parameters. The key parameters of the model are defined as follows:

Attitude: $x \in [x_1, x_2]$, $x_1 \in [0, +1]$, $x_2 \in [0, +1]$, the two dimensions are direction and direction strength;

Cognitive: $r \in [r_1, r_2]$, $r_1 \in [0,+1]$, $r_2 \in [0,+1]$, the two dimensions are attention and comprehension;

Emotion: $y \in [y_1, y_2]$, $y_1 \in [0,+1]$, $y_2 \in [0,+1]$, the two dimensions are valence and arousal;

Behavioral Intention: $h \in [h_1, h_2]$, $h_1 \in [0,+1]$, $h_2 \in [0,+1]$, the two dimensions are extraversion (outward - inward) and stability;

Information: $i = [i_1, i_2, i_3]$, $i_1, i_2 \in [0,+1]$, $i_3 = [1,+10]$, three dimensions are importance and uncertainty, and crisis degree.

According to voice information and text information, we establish two psychological models responding to the different psychology effect coming from different mobile phone information.

Psychology Model Based on Straightforward Dialog. If the cognitive elicited by outside information is defined as input of the system, behavioral intention, change of attitude as parameter of the system, the every time attitude state as states of the system, new emotion as output of the system for, the nonlinear model can be established:

$$\begin{cases} X(x_1', x_2') = \varphi(X(x_1, x_2), H(z_1, z_2), Y(y_1, y_2)) + \phi(d, H(z_1, z_2), Y(y_1, y_2)) \\ Y(y_1', y_2') = f(\beta, Y(y_1, y_2), X(x_1, x_2)) \end{cases}$$

Among them, $X(x_1, x_2)$ is the individual initial attitude status, d is the reaction from outside information, $Y(y_1, y_2)$ is the individual's initial emotion, φ is the changed component of attitude from attitude by itself, ϕ is the changed component of attitude from external stimulation, $H(z_1, z_2)$ is the behavior tendency, and β is the emotion attenuation factor, which β is larger value, generally take 0.1 because of the more obvious emotional changes.

Let $d = (min(r_1 + r_2, i_1 + i_2) - max(r_1 - r_2, i_1 - i_2)) \times (1 + lg\, i_3 / 10)$

The model only considers the influence of attitudes from emotion and personality, not considering changes caused by the properties of attitude, so φ can be described as $\varphi = \alpha \times X(x_1, x_2) \times Trust_{ab}$

Among above, $\alpha = e^{-(YS_y^r + HS_h^r)}$, S_y、S_h express respectively the influence matrix of attitudes from emotion and behavioral tendency, and $S_y = [S_{y11}, S_{y12}]$, $S_{y11}, S_{y12} \in [-1,+1]$;

$S_h = [S_{h11}, S_{h12}]$, $S_{h11}, S_{h12} \in [-1,+1]$。

$Trust_{ab}$ is the trust factor of recipient to sender, which can be defined as $Trust_{ab} = i_1 \times i_2 \times w_{ab}^2$, and w_{ab} is the weight of the interpersonal relationship between the recipient and the sender.

Let

$$\phi = \begin{cases} \exp^{YS_{yh} + HS_{hi}} & d & d > 0 \\ \exp^{-(YS_{yh} + HS_{hi})} & d & d < 0 \end{cases}$$

Among above, S_{yi}、S_{hi} respectively, express impact factors of emotion, behavior tendency from external stimuli, and

$$S_{yi} = [S_{yi11}, S_{yi12}], \quad S_{yi11}, S_{yi12} \in [-1,+1] \quad ; \quad S_{hi} = [S_{hi11}, S_{hi12}], \quad S_{hi11}, S_{hi12} \in [-1,+1]$$

The output of new feeling is $f = (1-\beta)y(y_1, y_2) + X(x_1, x_2)D \times e^{hi}$

Among above, D is the mapping matrix of the attitude and emotion, and $D = S_y^T$.

Model experimental results show that psychological model based on text information considering various influence factors of the individual psychology under the text information can comprehensively simulate human's psychological changes, and the psychological changes the model simulated are consistent with human psychological variation. Therefore, the algorithm of psychological model based on text information is credible and can be used to make corresponding Agent psychology in communication to study on modeling and simulation of mobile phone information propagation.

Psychology Model Based on Indirect Exchanging. Dissemination of voice information is directly and more bidirectional, timely and interactive. When communicating, both Agents can constantly amend and change opinions according to each other's response. Many factors such as cognitive, emotional, different original attitudes determine that mutual influence between Agents is asymmetric; moreover, emotions of both Agents are more easily influenced based on voice information.

According to related psychological parameters of Agent m and Agent n, let asymmetric impact factor

$$d_{mn} = min(y_{m1} + y_{m2}, y_{n1} + y_{n2}) - max(y_{m1} - y_{m2}, y_{n1} - y_{n2})$$

Let effect function m to n be $f(m,n)$ and effect function n to m is $f(n,m)$

If $d_{mn} > y_{n2}$, then $f(m,n) = Trust_{nm} \times (d_{mn}/y_{m2} - 1)$, Otherwise $f(m,n) = 0$;

If $d_{mn} > y_{m2}$, then $f(n,m) = Trust_{mnm} \times (d_{mn}/y_{n2} - 1)$, Otherwise $f(n,m) = 0$;

$Trust_{nm}$ and $Trust_{mn}$ is respectively trust degree that n to m and m to n, and

$Trust_{nm} = r_{n1} \times r_{m2} \times i_3 \quad Trust_{mn} = r_{m1} \times r_{n2} \times i_3$

Namely, the individuals know the less information about the event, the more unstable emotions and attitudes will be, the more influenced the individuals will be. So, the change of mood of m and n is

$$y'_m = y_m + f(n,m) \times (y_n - y_m) \quad y'_n = y_m + f(m,n) \times (y_m - y_n)$$

If $y'_m > 0.5$, $x_m = x_m + y'_m \times h_{m1} \times h_{m2}$, Otherwise $x_m = x_m - y'_m \times h_{m1} \times h_{m2}$

If $y'_n > 0.5$, $x_n = x_n + y'_n \times h_{n1} \times h_{n2}$, Otherwise $x_n = x_n - y'_n \times h_{n1} \times h_{n2}$

Psychological models based on the voice information mainly focus on individual psychological changes when individuals directly interact in certain cognitive and behavioral tendency and the asymmetry action of the emotional factors. Model results show that the individual psychological changes conform to psychological research findings, consistent with reality intuitively, have certain credibility and can be used in the related fields of study.

3.3 Individual Behavior Model

The intelligence and adaptive of all Agents is reflected in behavior of Agents. In the information communication research, we must describe behaviors of all kinds of Agents, such as the acceptance of information. The essence of the behaviors effects on states of Agents which is a process that makes Agents interaction into behaviors.

Propagation Model of Mobile Phone Users Agents. The behavior property of mobile phone users Agents refers mainly to information dissemination pathways, such as phone calls, short messages and micro-blogs. Phone calls and short messages are required functions, and micro-blogs are optional. Another property is preference or characteristics when Agents use mobile phone (such as using little of mobile phone but using less phone calls but more short messages), and the preference of micro-blog users is more obvious.

Mobile phone communication model is described as follows: A selects B according to the connection weights to make a telephone calling to B, then B accepts the calling with the probability p_{JAB} , thus both change attitudes by itself based on voice information attitude change model. If B does not accept the calling, the calling behavior would stop.

Mobile phone short message communication model is described as follows: A receive messages and produces psychological state based on the voice information psychological models, and confirms whether to modify the message content respond with point to point or mass messages or not, thereby the corresponding behavior in generated.

The probabilities of modifying short message is $D_{change}=Get\times[r_1,r_2][i_c,i_m]^T/2\times(1+lgi_3/10)$,

Probability of sending the message is $P_{send}=[x_1,x_2][h_1,h_2]^T/2\times(1+lgi_3/10)$.

Mobile phone micro-blog communication model is described as follows:

A publishes mobile phone micro-blog directly by probability $P_{Wb1}=r_1\times(1+lgi_3/10)$,

or sends other's short messages to micro-blog by probability $P_{Wb2}=i_z\times(1+lgi_3/10)$),

or writes short messages to micro-blog by probability $P_{Wb3}=x_1$;

Then B , the follower of A , reads this micro-blog information by probability $P_{Wb4}=1/S_{ff}\times(1+lgi_3/10)$ (S_{ff} is numbers of B following),

or is commented by all the followers by probability

$$P_{Wb4}=P_{Wb3}\times(\alpha\times\sum S_{ic})/\sum_{t-t_0}S_{ff}\times(1+lgi_3/10)$$

α is random coefficient of preference that mobile phone user comments micro-blog, S_c is the numbers of comments, and S_f is the number of followers of this micro-blog user; or transmits to others by probability $P_{Wb5}=P_{Wb4}\times(\beta\times\sum S_{is})/\sum_{t-t_s}S_{ff}\times(1+lgi_3/10)$

β is random coefficient of preference probability that mobile phone micro-blog users transmit micro-blog, S_s is the number of this micro-blog information, S_f is the number of followers of this micro-blog user.

Propagation Model of Media Agents. Message media Agents have two attributes, one is sending short messages or not, another is rules of transmitting short messages which define the communication behaviors by short message, such as short message nature, sending time, transmitting range and so on.

Due to using anthropomorphic method to model message media Agents, we define their attribute ($Opinion$ and $Uncertainty$) in corresponding to mobile phone users Agents in order to realize the interaction between message media Agents and mobile phone users Agents. In general, message media Agents belong to the mass media, and will be closely to the will of the state with clear attitude and firm position, therefore, $Opinion$ is limited in the interval, such as $[0.9,1]$ 、 $[0,0.1]$ or $[0.45,0.55]$, at the same time, the $Uncertainty$ will generally be very small, we take $Uncertainty < 0.2$ in order to reflect the attitudes of message media Agents which is generally more firm.

As the message media Agents are high-level Agents in mobile phone network, a message media Agent may at the same time impact many mobile phone users Agents.

Propagation Model of Control Agent. The behavior of control Agents may control other Agents and would be defined as a kind of special Agent. In fact, behavior of control Agent is a series decisions and control measures coming from external input.

Like message media Agents, the attribute of control Agent ($Opinion$ and $Uncertainty$) is defined in more extreme intervals, such as $[0.9,1]$ and $[0,0.1]$, at the same time, the $Uncertainty$ will generally be very small, we take $Uncertainty < 0.1$ in order to reflect the attitude of control Agent which is generally more firm than message media Agents and is a kind of more special extreme individual Agent. Other parameters of control Agent, such as credibility $Trust$, range of influence ($Influence$), transmission control strategy ($Tactics$), are selected according to the needs.

Control Agent has two main control strategies: message strategy and micro-blog strategy.

Message strategy: Sending short control messages which would be on behalf of the will of control Agent through controlled message media Agents to mobile phone users; or sending control messages directly to the mobile phone users on behalf of the control mechanism (such as the government); closing mandatorily some base stations in order to make the functions of short message failure; or sending short message to the core of Agents.

Micro-blog strategy: closing mandatorily the mobile phone short message function, or publishing control Agent micro-blog.

4   Experiment and Conclusion

The purpose of our study is to study the actual society by the modeling and simulation, in order to provide some new perspective research tools or the scientific methods to communication and service research and practice of the communication, such as the communication effect evaluation. The focus of the study is on the faith of the public, namely the people's change of attitude.

Considering of the relativity of the effect evaluation, the psychology and the behavior of the Agents are different. So, we use contrast method to compare the effect before communication with effect after communication if the group is same one. At the same time we compare the effects of different methods of transmission. This article takes specific events as the background, the public as the goal, changes of emotion and attitude and changes of behavior as indicators in the same group to research psychological and behavior reaction.

If the sent provocative messages are with uncertainty, important and crisis intensity respectively as 0.8, 0.5, 8, the public's evolution process of attitude and emotion is shown in Fig. 2 and 3. Fig. 2 is the beginning of public's attitude and mood, and Fig. 3 is attitudes and emotional evolution after some time.

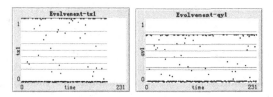

Fig. 2. Initial mood and attitude state distribution

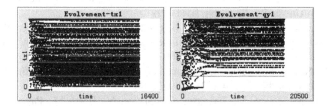

Fig. 3. Mood and attitude state distribution after information

From Fig. 2 and 3, in a crisis situation, the uncertainty of the information is easy to cause impermanence fluctuation of the mood and attitude which would become the trigger of social crisis. Especially after the information spreading with purpose, the number with bad behavior would growth rapidly a accompanied by change of mood and attitude of Agents, which would result further acts outside of information dissemination behavior such as rallies, parades and so on.

5   Summary

Modeling and simulation on information communication is a frontier research topic with important theoretical and practical value, and with great difficulty and challenges. Although the research results are limited and what we have done still needs further improvement, the researches thought and method are original. In the future, we hope that we will carry out more thorough research to provide new thoughts, new methods and practical benefits for modeling and simulation on social research.

Acknowledgments. This research was supported in part by National Natural Science Foundation of China (60874086 and 71073172).

References

1. Zhang, F., Si, G.-Y., Luo, P.: A Survey of rumor Propagation models. Complex Systems and Complexity Science 6(4), 1–11 (2009)
2. Zhang, F., Si, G.-Y., Luo, P.: Research on Rumor Spreading Based on Mobile Phone Short Message in Community structure. In: The 5th Chinese Conference on Complex Networks (CCCN 2009), p. 65 (October 2009)
3. Zhang, F., Si, G.-Y., Luo, P.: Rumor Propagation Model Based on Communication Functions and Finite memory. Journal of System Imulation 23(11), 2482–2486 (2011)
4. Zhang, F., Si, G.-Y., Luo, P.: Study on Rumor Spreading Model Based on Evolution Game. Journal of System Simulation 23(9), 1772–1775 (2011)
5. Barabási, A., Albert, R.: Emergence of scaling in random networks. Science (286) (1999)
6. Mehrabian, A.: Pleasure-arousal-dominance: A general framework for describing and measuring individual differences in temperament. Current Psychology 14, 261–292 (1996)
7. Meng, X., Wang, Z.: Research on Emotion-model Based on Nonlinear State Space Model. Computer Science 135(112), 178–182 (2008)
8. Wilensky, U.: NetLogo. Center for Connected learning and Computer-Based Modeling Northwestern University. Evanston, IL (1999)
9. Onnela, J.P., Saramaki, J., Hyvonen, J., et al.: Structure and tie strengths in mobile communication networks. Proceedings of the National Academy of Sciences of the United States of America 104(18), 7332–7336 (2007)
10. Kumar, R., Novak, J., Raghavan, P., Tomkins, A.: Structure and evolution of blogspace. Communications of the ACM 47(12), S-39 (2004)
11. Leskovec, J., McGlohon, M., Faloutsos, C., Glance, N., Horst, M.: Patterns of cascading behavior in large blog graphs. In: Proc. of the SIAM Int'l Conf. on Data Mining, pp. 551–556. ACM Press, New York (2007)
12. Smith, R.D.: Instant Messaging as a scale-free (EB/OL) (February 27, 2009), http://arxiv.org/abs/condmat/0206378
13. Holme, P., Kmi, B.J.: Growing scale2free networks with tunable clustering. Phys. Rev. E 65(2), 026107 (2002)

An Agent-Based Artificial Transportation System Framework for H1N1 Transmission Simulation

Zilong Cheng, Xiaogang Qiu, Peng Zhang, and Rongqing Meng

School of Mechatronics Engineering and Automation,
National University of Defense Technology, Changsha 410073, China

Abstract. Transportation system has significant impacts on society for its tight connection with travelling behaviors. Constructing an artificial society to study complex social behaviors is a novel approach which has been widely recognised as a key issue in recent years. In this paper we propose an agent-based ATS framework for H1N1 transmission simulation after reviewing the existing approaches. Mathematic models of H1N1 transmission are established to support and simulate individual's micro-decision-making mechanisms. After analyzing the diffusion mechanism of H1N1, an ATS framework which contains four modules is built up based on ACP theory. The four components including the initial agent module, environment agent module, individual agent module and interaction agent module are illustrated in detail. The design schemes of the framework are summed up based on system modeling theory followed by the computation flow based on SIR diffusion model. At last, further research directions of ATS are pointed out.

Keywords: artificial society, infection transmission simulation, H1N1, artificial transportation system modelling.

1 Introduction

With the developing of modern society, it provides us more convenient life as well as more complex social problems. More and more emergency affairs arise which have greatly affected our daily life and the stabilization of society. Transportation simulation research arose since 1960's with macro-model originally. Some pioneers have devoted to explore advanced transportation modeling approaches and plenty of techniques have been applied, including statistics mechanism, differential equation, system dynamic, cellular automata0, robotics-inspired, heuristic and complex networks approach in late 1990's. Many organizations have developed diversiform applications about transportation system research, however, few of them pay attention to the relationship between transportation and infection transmission. What's more, the merely approaches within related literatures only available always concomitancy with strict restricts. Epidemic has attracted great number of attention since the first SIR (Suspected-Infected-Recovered) model proposed in 19270. With the rapid mutation of virus, many new transmission models (SIS, SEIR) have been brought up0. Most of scholars has considered nature environment when design infectious transmission

T. Xiao, L. Zhang, and S. Ma (Eds.): ICSC 2012, Part I, CCIS 326, pp. 313–321, 2012.

model. Actually, transportation system always plays an important role for its enormous impact on human behaviors which has changed traditional ways of infection transmission. Therefore, it is essential to take the traffic system into account when analyzes infection transmission in urban area. Explore advanced methodology to settle infection transmission in transportation system turns into a new challenge to scholars for its complexity, unpredictable and unrepeatable characteristic. Some scientists proposed constructing an artificial society to analysis complex social phenomenon. MAS (Multi-Agent System) is the most promising one among the newly proposed methods which provides us new technology tools to overcome these limitations0. In MAS modeling approach, actors' psychology and demography features are included to depict heterogeneity of individuals. Considering the unrepeatable and unpredictable of transportation system, constructing an ATS (artificial transportation system)0 based on MAS modeling theory is feasible to study capricious transportation phenomenon. We proposed the methodology of using APS (Artificial Population System) to provide individual travel behaviors to ATS. Most of the simulation would be done in ATS layer and high-level decision-making is realized in artificial society layer. Communications between ATS and APS is achieved by interaction agent, and the agent activities in APS would bring on macro-emergence phenomenon in artificial society. Structure of the artificial systems in the artificial society is depicted in the following picture (Figure 1).

This paper deals with complex mutual behaviors between transportation system and H1N1 diffusion in the artificial society by means of proposed an agent-based ATS framework. The rest of the paper is arranged in three main sections. The second section presents the microcosmic interaction model amongst actors. The third section designs the framework of ATS based on ACP (Artificial society, Computational experiments, Parallel execution) theory0. The fourth section summed up the framework designing procedure of ATS followed with a computation example. Conclusions of the paper and its further work are offered at last.

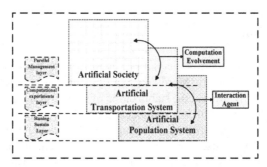

Fig. 1. Layer Structure of Artificial Systems

2   Mathematic Models

In order to reproduce and evolve complex interactions in real traffic system, all kinds of potential activities correspond to a particular probability. Base on the assumption above, we could calculate actors' behavior choice via compartmentalize it into several types. Classical SIR model is introduced to analysis disease transmission which eliminates recovered and dead individuals0. The agent-based mathematical model could execute after obtaining transmission probability of each infection behaviors. The whole model runs on simulate time-step $\triangle t$ which can be altered by simulation requirements. Here, we proposed I_i to denote Individual Infection Index of individual i in the ATS which is made up of three components formally defined as follows.

$$I_i = H \square V \square P_i \tag{1}$$

H indicates leading controlling parameter where variable M indicates human intervention index. Particularly, M=0 when individuals got immunity. E indicates the control parameter introduced by environment condition (such as temperature, humidity, atmosphere pressure) while coefficient λ indicates its impact weightiness, and they together indicate the influencing parameter introduced by nature environment. Its math formula is formally defined as follows.

$$H = \underset{m \in M}{M} \left(\sum_{E_i \in E}^{i} \lambda E_i \right) \tag{2}$$

V indicates traffic transfer index determined by transportation volume while C indicate vehicle correlation index. It is must be emphasized that vehicle correlation index increases as contact network became complexity with the diversity of travel modes. $V_{capacity}$ indicates innate carrying capacity determined by transportation features (including road types, width, length, direction, restriction, number of crossing and depots). φ_0 indicates impact weightiness of vehicles (car, bike, bus) while A_0 the number of corresponding vehicles, $V_{observation}$ the carrying capacity on the road that can obtain by observation. Its mathematic formula is showed in equation (3).

$$V = C \frac{V_{observation}}{V_{capacity}} = C \frac{\sum \varphi_0 A_0}{V_{capacity}} \tag{3}$$

P_i indicates individual infection probability which has close relationship with individual features. The equation below specifies the probability that a particular suspected individual i is infected at a given location, where τ is the duration of exposure, R is the set of infectivity of the infected individuals at the location, N_r is the number of infectious individuals with infectivity r, S_i is the susceptibility of i, ρ is the transmissibility, defined as the probability of a single completely susceptible person being infected by a single completely infections person during one minute exposure. Its mathematic formula is showed in equation (4).

$$P_i = 1 - \exp(\tau \sum_{r \in R} N_r \ln(1 - rs_i \rho)) \tag{4}$$

3   Framework of Artificial Transportation System

The framework of ATS is composed of four primary agent modules: initialization agent module, environment agent module, individual agent module and interaction agent module as showed in the picture (Figure 2). Initial agent module initializing related parameters and default rules as depicted with dotted frames below when the artificial system get started. Environment agent module identifies behaviors and attributes of environment entities. Similarity to other methods, transportation system can be treated as a complex network, links represent roads while nodes represent intersections. Individual agent module describes basic rules, parameters and components of individual agents that are essential to realize desired behaviors and phenomenon. Note that different types of individuals have different infection probability, then ATS presents emergence phenomenon through simple interacting behaviors among agents. For the sake of achieving communication and inter-operation amongst agents, Interaction agent module defines interaction rules and data sharing or exchanging mechanism among all of the agent modules by providing uniform protocols for detection, conversion, transmission and execution.

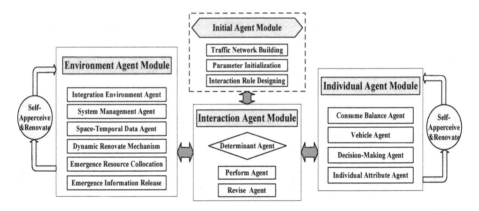

Fig. 2. Framework of ATS towards infection transmission simulation

3.1   Initial Agent Module

Traffic Network Building: According to the demand of experiments, we need build a traffic network topology approximate to the reality based on statistical survey data. Make sure that all of the traffic geography information follows a standard data format which is convenient for subsequent data processing.

Parameter Initialization: This unit chooses proper experiment scale and data type based on pre-specified principle and experiment requirements. Individual agents select initial number of households and vehicles as well as default parameters from database computed ahead.

Interaction Rule Designing: This module establishes communication protocol and function rules based on the state of environment and individual agent. Actors choose routes and vehicles based on the output of consuming balance agent, start infection transmission decision-making mechanism.

3.2   Environment Agent Module

Integration Environment Agent: Traffic entities and nature environment are considered to insure the integrality of environment. The environment agent provides basic environment parameters, such as temperature, humidity, atmosphere pressure, to support computation experiments. When the carrying capacity exceeds the upper limit it is possible to alert to system management agent for further decision.

System Management Agent: This module estimates status of ATS, then generates and issues updating information about traffic and infection transmission in time. In possession of this agent unit, the system model has ability to deal with emergent affairs, when the control index reaches the anticipate value, start-up mode switch mechanism through manual or automatic control. If the unconventional running mode set up, the emergence resource collocation agent would be activated.

Space-Time Data Agent: This module works as a dynamic database to store the space-time information about ATS. Agents can acquire requisite geography and time information as well as upload their newly changes to the database. It is important to note that data accessing format is one of the key point when integration different types of information. Another key point is the efficiency and reliability of data accessing, we propose MYSQL database to provide essential data service.

Dynamic Update Agent: Because ATS works as a DEVS (Discrete Event System) which simulate in certain time-step $\triangle t$, dynamic update mechanism is essential to guarantee the correctness of updating process. After undergoing one behavior mode in a relatively long time, actors are inclined to try another way to accomplish its goal in an alterable statistical possibility. Once it has explored a better one, this agent would store it in the space-time database and take it as default choice in the next time.

Emergence Resource Collocation: In the conventional running mode, this module only shows basic statistical information about the emergence resources. In case of emergence, system management agent triggers the emergence mode. Emergence management system would be touched off and executes scheduled emergence plans, such as optimize and collocate emergence resources.

Emergence Information System: It works as intelligent information system which guides the actors' traveling activities. In the emergence mode, this module puts out new information about transportation system to the actors in corresponding regions. Some useful advices to prevent themselves getting infected are also given.

3.3   Individual Agent Module

Consuming Balance Agent: Actors evaluate comprehensive costs of different travel modes including travel time, cost and feelings before they make a decision. Note that decision-making process obeys the stepwise evaluating strategy on the assumption that only local traffic information is accessible. One likely to choose a lower society cost based on the calculation of related factors.

Vehicle Agent: This module provides feasible travel tools to actors. The basic information (including types, capacity, freedom velocity, departure time) of vehicle deposits in the space-time agent whenever the individual has selected or altered its vehicle. According to the difference of impact weightiness in infection transmission, travel modes are divided into three general types: walking, public traffic and driving. Make sure that individual attributes restrict the travel choice and it transforms in some particular situations.

Decision-Making Agent: This module defines reasoning rules and start-up infection transmission mechanism after actors apperceiving its surroundings. It decides subsequent behaviors based on the judging information obtained from ATS. Normally, it has ability to acquire the state of its neighborhoods, compute the infection probability based on individual attributes, change and refresh its infection state if accumulation infection probability function exceeds infection threshold.

Individual Attribute Agent: All of the major demographic attributes related to the infection transmission are included, such as gender, age, occupation and psychology features. Each kind of traits corresponds to certain impact weightiness and all of them together determine individual infection probability in ATS.

3.4   Interaction Agent Module

Determinant Agent: This module distinguishes credible of the messages before starting the performing function. If the message has passed lifecycle, it drops the invalid message, otherwise, checks its validity and transfer to next agent.

Perform Agent: This module deals with messages from determinant agents. After comprehending and parsing the request, it sends out request information to target agents based on intelligent search methodology.

Revise Agent: Sometimes the experiment intentions or demands altered, the artificial system must be adjusted to accommodate it. Loading data from reality to compare and amend the system parameters to improve its performance.

4   Framework Designing Scheme

In order to produce emergence phenomenon in ATS, all of the models should be established in sequence. The framework designing schemes are as follows:

Table 1. Designing Scheme

1	Traffic System	Traffic Networks Road Mapping Time & Destination Vehicle assignment	3	Agent-based Modeling	Agent Design	Environment agent Individual agent Interaction agent
2	Infection Transmission	Infection Objects Infection Mechanism Describing Method			Theory Support	MAS Approach ACP Theory Sociology Theory
4	Subsystem Integration	Interface to ATS Interface to APS Coordinate System	5	VV&A	Initialization ATS Dynamic Data Loading Computational Experiments	

The designing details are introduced below.

1. The traffic network is constructed from reality which takes GIS as referenced standard. Make sure that it is well mapped with real roads[7]. After defining the demand of transit passengers, such as travel time and destination, actors choose rational travel mode after vehicle assignment.

2. Identifying major objects, attributes and study areas that should be modeled. Classifying and modeling the interacting behaviors for the infection mechanism is determined by the contact network. Similarity to some existing methodologies, agent is atomic units of the model, apperceives surroundings and feedback essential information to support further computation and decision.

3. Analyzing and designing agent models to compute interactions within ATS. Note that all of assignment attributes should obey statistical principle in the aspect of macroscopic. We proposed MAS to construct each kind of agent model together with ACP and sociology theory0.

4. The macroscopic phenomenon is not just a scale-up replication of the simple behavior of individual. After accomplished the designing of components individually, we need integrate ATS and APS by interaction agent module to form an infection transmission simulation framework model. We need designed a coordinator which helps us achieve data exchange and inter-operation during the simulation.

5. It is important to validate the reliability and usability of designed models. To achieve this purpose, we need initialize ATS and let it running with desired computational parameters. At last, we can amend and improve original model to satisfy realistic requirement through multiple times of simulation.

Take H1N1 as an instance, individuals would be infected through close contact within certain time0. The computation flow follows the procedure below.

Table 2. Computation Flow

1 **WHILE**(There are infected and susceptible	10 Compute *infection index* I_i
2 actors who satisfy the infection condition)	11 $I_i = H \square V \square P_i$
3 **FOR** (T ∈ [t,t+Δt])	12 Judge Adapt its state.
4 Compute *traffic transfer index* **V**	13 *Eliminated Recovery and*
5 $V = (\sum \varphi_o A_o / V_{capacity})$	14 *Death individuals.*
6 Compute *dominate control parameter* **H**	15 **End FOR**
7 $H = M (\sum_{m \in M \ E_i \in E}^{i} \lambda E_i)$	16 **End WHILE**
	17 Retain current state.
8 Compute individual infection index P_i	18 **Finally.**
9 $P_i = 1 - \exp(\tau \sum_{r \in R} N_r \ln(1 - rs_i \rho))$	

After executing the procedure above in sequence, the whole system would evolve nonlinear, emergence, self-organization and complexity as it shows below.

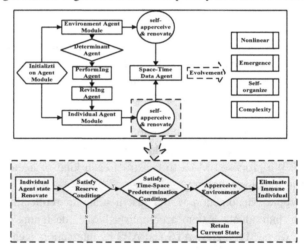

Fig. 3. Evolving Flow Chart

5   Conclusions

In this paper, previously approaches to study transportation and infection transmission were reviewed as well as brought up the novel approach to analysis infection transmission simulation within ATS. The mathematic model is introduced to support individual decision making mechanism. We put forward using individual infection index I_i to quantitative computation and investigation interactions in artificial society. The components of the ATS were described explicitly and the steps to construct ATS for infection transmission were summed up systematic. This framework model will be validated on Repast software toolkit in our future work to make sure the experiments can be replicated by other scholars. There is no doubt that the ATS research will open new avenues to complex system research, it can be used to solve the traffic problems by repeated simulation. More advances from interdisciplinary should be implied to boost the development of ATS.

Acknowledgements. This research is supported by National Nature and Science Foundation of China under Grant Nos. 9102403.

References

1. Maerivoet, S., De Moor, B.: Cellular automata models of road traffic. Physics Reports 41, 91–64 (2005)
2. Epstein, J.M.: Modelling to contain pandemics. Nature 460, 687 (2009)
3. Barthelemy, M., Barrat, A., et al.: Dynamical patterns of epidemic outbreaks in complex heterogeneous networks. Journal of Theoretical Biology 235, 275–288 (2005)
4. Macal, C.M., North, M.J.: Tutorial on agent-based modelling and simulation. Journal of Simulation 4, 151–162 (2010)
5. Wang, F.Y.: Parallel Control and Management for Intelligent Transportation Systems: Concepts, Architectures, and Applications. IEEE Transaction on Intelligent Transportation System 11, 630–638 (2010)
6. Peng, R., Zhao, X.Q.: A reaction-diffusion SIS epidemic model in a time-periodic environment. Nonlinearity 25, 1451–1471 (2012)
7. Lazer, D., Pentland, A., et al.: Computational Social Science. Science 323, 721–723 (2009)
8. Epstein, J.M.: Modelling to contain pandemics. Nature 460, 687 (2009)

Publishing Three-Dimensional City Models on the Web

Kenta Sato[1], Hiroyuki Yamamura[1], Akihiro Tsukamoto[2], Yuzuru Isoda[3],
Susumu Nakata[4], and Satoshi Tanaka[4]

[1] Graduate School of Science and Engineering, Ritsumeikan University,
Nojihigashi 1-1-1, Kusatsu, Shiga, Japan
{is019088,is044082}@cg.is.ritsumei.ac.jp
[2] Kinugasa Research Organization, Ritsumeikan University,
58, Komatusubara Kitamachi, Kita-ku, Kyoto, Japan
atv28073@fc.ritsumei.ac.jp
[3] Graduate School of Science, Tohoku University,
Aoba 6-3, Aramaki, Aoba-ku, Sendai, Miyagi,Japan
isoda@m.tohoku.ac.jp
[4] College of Information Science and Engineering, Ritsumeikan University,
Nojihigashi 1-1-1, Kusatsu, Shiga, Japan
{snakata,stanaka}@media.ritsumei.ac.jp

Abstract. In this paper, we propose a method of Web publishing of three-dimensional city models generated from two-dimensional geographical data. In our approach, the city models are assumed to be historical ones. For an example, rows of houses of Kyoto of the Edo era are generated by determining the areas of the houses based on geographical data and by placing and three-dimensional house models correspondingly. We employed Google Earth as the viewer of the city models. The viewer is embedded into a web page which enables users to access the page to overview the city and look into buildings. Some important documents related to the buildings are also embedded. As an alternative use, we apply the method to generation of city models of tsunami-damaged area in Tohoku district, Japan. The model generation is based on the recovery plan and models are generated by taking changes of terrain in the area into account.

Keywords: GIS, Web publishing, Google Earth, Google Earth API.

1   Introduction

Recently, demands for 3D models are growing in many fields such as research results in the humanities and social sciences, urban environmental planning, and disaster simulation [1]. In our research, we have used GIS data for automatically creating urban 3D models and create a tool for it. To use our tool, we need GIS data on land parcels and their uses and prototype 3D house models [2][3].The housing models are combined with the 3D terrain which is generated from ground elevation points. As an example for our automatic generation, we have done for the *Kyoto* city in *Edo* era, and for the proposed recovery plan proposal of the area which suffered a great deal of damage by tsunami.

T. Xiao, L. Zhang, and S. Ma (Eds.): ICSC 2012, Part I, CCIS 326, pp. 322–330, 2012.
© Springer-Verlag Berlin Heidelberg 2012

Technical innovations associated with the Internet have made it possible for individuals to easily to browse various data. With decent network connection, it is possible to access the large data rapidly via the web browser and thus possible to publish 3D model online. This paper establishes a method to publish 3D models on the web and create a platform for web publishing. Our purpose for, publishing urban 3D city plan using web publishing technology is to, provide system for the general public to share the information.

2   Historical 3D City

A 3D model of the entire Kyoto area is generated using GIS data of Edo era in Kyoto, which is being developed by the "Historical Geographical Information Research" unit of *Ritsumeikan* University's Global COE Program, the Digital Humanities Center for Japanese Arts and Cultures project. This project undertakes to disseminate Kyoto's traditional culture all over the world by distributing the urban 3D model over the Web and placing the tangible and intangible cultural heritage of Kyoto within a 3D model, creating a digital museum using the 3D city as a container.

2.1   Automatic Modeling Tool

A tool to create 3D city models automatically is outlined in the following the example of Kyoto in Edo era.

2.1.1   Input Data

For our tool, we modify and place the prototype model of the house that were created using modeling software based on geometrical and positional information of parcels acquired from the GIS data, which is repeated for all parcels until the entire 3D city model is generated.

1) **GIS data**

As input GIS data of automatic generation, parcel vertices are used in this tool. Parcel vertices are points constituting parcel polygon, having its geographical coordinates and parcel center coordinate as polygon, having its geographical coordinates and parcel center coordinate as attributes (see Fig.1). Since the entire parcel vertices are available, we can fit the prototype exactly on the site, but since the front edge is not given, it is necessary to make appropriate rotation, which is done in relation to the road.

2) **The house prototype models**

The prototype models of the house are created using modeling software. The houses in the Edo era in Kyoto are classified into 9 types.
(*Full Two-Story, Mezzanine, Three-Story, Single-Story, Residential Fenced Residential Fenced Udatu* (see Fig.2).).

2.1.2   Output Data

In our research, we used Google Earth (Google Inc.) for the platform to visualize the 3D city models. The images taken from the satellite are wrapped on surface of the

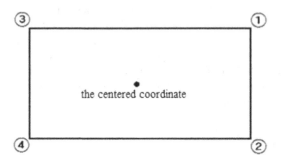

Fig. 1. Parcel vertices

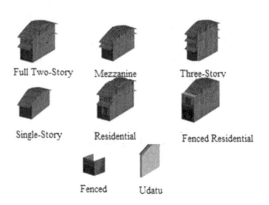

Fig. 2. The prototype models of houses

globe, and entire earth can be examined with the map of high resolution image, and it is well-known for having an easy to use the interface. It allows users to create their own 3D model that can be added on the default Google Earth, or to place 3D model on a server for general public to view the model on Google Earth. For these capabilities, we have chosen to output our 3D models in KML fire format that can be readily used with Google Earth. Figure 3 shows the urban 3D model created by the automatic modeling tool.

2.2   Web Data for Google Earth API

This section explains the method for disseminating the generated 3D model over the Web.

In order to use Google Earth, a user needs to install the software of Google Earth in own PC. But a user can also view Google Earth on a web browser, without downloading software by creating a Web page using Google Earth API. Google Earth API (Application Program Interface) is a library group of a Java Script language offered by the Google Company. If Google Earth plug-in and JavaScript API are used to a web browser, the API is read and Google Earth can be embedded at a web page.

Google Earth API enables to use by web browsers, such as a homepage, displaying the application using Google Earth or its function. It is possible to perform the displaying markers, latitude, and longitude, picture attached to in geographical features, etc. as well as addition of 3D model using this API.

To use this API, an owner of a web page we has to register the Google Maps API key. The API key is sent from Google by registering the homepage embeds Google Earth.

2.3   Results

There are two kinds of models used this time. The urban 3D model created by the automatic modeling tool and the model created with modeling software was used as a landmark. In order to display by Google Earth API, it changed from 3ds form through SketchUp.

A high definition landmark model could not be displayed by Google Earth API. We used the simple model. If a high definition model's is displayed by Google Earth API, it have to read many mark of the peak of a model and it takes too many time or it cannot read. To display 3D city model, we choose the simple model.

When the web page using Google Earth API is accessed, it takes time such as about 10 or 20 seconds to display the 3D city models. The models are arranged on a server, and the models are set as the area near the landmark. There is no influence to display the models via the server. It has not performed yet carrying out of all the town models outputted by an automatic modeling tool. It remains to display the town house of the landmark circumference, and the addition of a town house and the addition of a landmark model are mentioned as a future subject.

The figure.4 which displayed the rows of houses of the Edo period using Google Earth API is shown.

Fig. 3. The model of Kyoto in Edo era viewed in Google Earth

Fig. 4. The model of Kyoto in Edo era viewed in Google Earth

3   Rebuilding Tsunami-Hit Town on the Web

An alternative example using our method aims at supporting the recovery of a tsunami-stricken area by performing automatic generation of the future town based on the proposed recovery plan. The study area is *Onagawa* town, Miyagi Prefecture (Japan) that suffered serious damage from the Tsunami after the 2011 Great East Japan Earthquake. More than 10% of population died and 68% of building totally damaged with the entire town center swept away. Despite its damage, the town drawn up recovery program proposal at comparatively early stage and that is the data source we base on [4].

3.1   Input data

3.1.1   Automatic Modeling Tool
1) **GIS data**

Parcel vertices are used for automatic generation of 3D building models for *Onagawa* town as we did for houses in *Kyoto* of the Edo era. The GIS data before suffering the disaster is obtained from Geographical Survey Institute [5] that has building footprint, and added information required in order to perform automatic generation. The GIS data of the recovery plan were traced from a plan, but the plan did not have land parcels so the parcels were simulated based on average parcel size assumed in the plan but depending on the shape of street block..

2) **The house prototype models**

As a prototype model of Onagawa town, five types of house prototype models of different size and aspect were created by Google SketchUp (see Fig.5). The prototype model used placed on a parcel is selected based on the size of the parcel; if the width or depth are 1.5 times greater than the prototype model, we used one of larger models.

The major difference between Kyoto in the Edo era and *Onagawa* town is that in case of the former, the buildings were mostly on flat land whereas in the latter, much of the buildings are on the slope of the mountain. Automatic generation program does adjust for the elevation of the site but if the slope is steeper, the valley side of the model will lose touch with the ground and the mountain side of the will dig into the ground. Therefore we created a foundation to a building depending on the elevation difference with a parcel, and the building is offset vertically accordingly..

3.1.2   Terrain Model

In automatic generation of *Onagawa* town, our research group also created terrain model since the recovery plan propose to rebuild housing area on artificially modified hills to avoid future tsunami. To do this, digital elevation model from Geographical Survey Institute was used to create TIN model of the terrain and the terrain was modified based on the recovery plan. The points constituting the TIN model were converted to create a 3D model of terrain in COLLADA format which allows texture mapping, and aerial photograph taken on March 19, 2011 by the Geographical Survey Institute is used for the texture of the terrain. By disabling the default Google Earth terrain, this future modified terrain model replaces the current terrain.

The figure 6 will show the foundation model generated by COLLADA.

Fig. 5. The prototype models *Onagawa town.*

Fig. 6. The modified terrain model for *Onagawa town*

3.2   Output Data

The housing model with foundation and the modified terrain model are both output in COLLADA format that are combined and incorporated into KML file that can be viewed on Google Earth (Fig 7).

Fig. 7. Models of the terrain with the future houses in *Onagawa town*

3.3   Web data

We also created Web data of the 3D model of Onagawa town for public viewing using Google Earth API. Apart from generic houses automatically generated by the program, we created landmarks that remained after the tsunami and are expected to continue to be used using Google SketchUp. Ironically, creating landmarks was not a difficult task since only handful of them remained after a tsunami that swept away most of the town center.

Onagawa town and Kyoto of the Edo era has the difference point that the concept of a landmark model is different. The landmark model of Onagawa town used the software for displaying by Google Earth called SketchUp.

Thereby, when performing Web public presentation using API, it was able to display smoothly, without passing other modeling software. And it was able to indicate that the terrain model was outputted in COLLADA format. COLLADA format is able to display into Google Earth, it can soon changing into the format for Google Earth API. The landmark model for 3D city model in Kyoto of the Edo era has to convert into Google Earth. Since the display by Google Earth was a base, Web public presentation was easy in Onagawa town.

Fig. 8. The foundation model with the houses by Google Earth API

4   Conclusions

In this paper, we implemented web publishing of 3D urban models that we created automatically based on GIS data using Google Earth API. Our examples were 3D urban models for past landscape of Kyoto of the Edo era and the future landscape of tsunami-hit town of Onagawa, including automatically generated generic houses, terrain and landmarks.

It has not performed yet carrying out Web public presentation of all the town models outputted by an automatic modeling tool. In others, in Onagawa town , the model before suffering a calamity and the display of the model based on the recovery plan after suffering a calamity are also raised as a future subject, and are due to be mounted using the function of Google Earth.

Although there are various techniques in Web publishing 3D models, Google Earth API was used this time. Many techniques to carry out Web public presentation of the 3D model are being developed, and recently, WebGL has attracted much attention. The experience from our project suggest that the popularity of Web publishing platform also depends on the way 3D models are created as each platform has different specification and 3D models must be optimized accordingly. At the moment, we believe that Google Earth API is the best option to publish geographically large models, and further research is needed to decide which approach is the best for different purposes

References

1. Shibazaki, M., Isoda, Y., Tsukamoto, A., Kosaka, Y., Hasegawa, K., Nakata, S., Tanaka, S.: Modeling, Viewing and Simulating Kyoto Street Models Created from GIS Data. In: 22nd CIPA Symposium, Kyoto, Japan (2009)
2. Isoda, Y., Tsukamoto, A., Kosaka, Y., Okumura, T., Sawai, M., Yano, K., Nakata, S., Tanaka, S.: Reconstruction of Kyoto of the Edo Era Based on Arts and Historical Documents: 3D Urban Model Based on Historical GIS Data. International Journal for Humanities and Arts Computing 3, 21–38 (2009)
3. Kosaka, Y., Isoda, Y., Tsukamoto, A., Okumura, T., Nakata, S., Tanaka, S.: Transaction of the Automatic generation of Urban 3D Model Based on GIS Data- Application in Generation of Kyoto in the Edo era. The Virtual Reality Society of Japan 13, 315–324 (2008)
4. Onagawa-cho Recovery Program,
   http://www.town.onagawa.miyagi.jp/hukkou
5. Geographical Survey Institute, http://www.gsi.go.jp/index.html

Modeling Social Opinion in Online Society*

Mingzhi Zhang and Xiaofeng Hu

National Defense University of China, Beijing 100091, PRC

Abstract. social networks Online provide a globally available, large-scale infrastructure for people to exchange information and ideas. A topic of great interest in internet research is how to model this information exchange and, in particular, how to model and analyze the effects of interpersonal influence on processes such as information diffusion, influence propagation, and opinion formation. Recent empirical studies indicate that, in order to accurately model communication in online social networks, it is important to consider not just relationships between individuals, but also the frequency with which these individuals interact. We study a model of opinion formation in social networks proposed by De Groot and Lehrer and show how this model can be extended to include interaction frequency. We prove that, for the purposes of analysis and design, the opinion formation process with probabilistic interactions can be accurately approximated by a deterministic system where edge weights are adjusted for the probability of interaction. We also present simulations that illustrate the effects of different interaction frequencies on the opinion dynamics using real-world social network graphs.

Keywords: Opinion Dynamics, Social Influence, Complex Network, Agent-based Modeling.

1 Introduction

Online social networks provide information system for people to exchange information, opinion, and ideas, which has created a strongly coupled and strongly interdependent world. An interesting topic in social networks research is how to model these exchanges and, in particular, how to model and analyze the effects of interpersonal influence on processes such as information diffusion, influence propagation, and opinion formation. If one can identify the properties of the network of Internet that shape these process, then it may be possible to alter these properties to achieve a desired outcome, for example to encourage purchase of a product or support of a cause. Early work to characterize interpersonal influence in social networks focused on static, structural properties of the network graph such as vertex degree, distance centrality, and betweenness centrality [1].

However, recent researches indicate that the dynamics of common people interactions may be equal, if not more important than these static properties in

---

* Funded partly by Natural Science Foundation of China under No.71073172, No.61174156, No.61174035.

T. Xiao, L. Zhang, and S. Ma (Eds.): ICSC 2012, Part I, CCIS 326, pp. 331–337, 2012.

determining how information flows [2–4]. It is not sufficient to only consider the network graph derived from relationships such as friendships in Facebook Or Twitter. One must also consider the frequency and timing of interactions between individuals. In fact, the structure of the interaction graph may differ dramatically from that of the relationship graph.

In this paper, we study the process of opinion formation in online social networks and the effects of interaction dynamics on this process. Research on opinion formation in social groups predates the advent of online social networks by decades, and several formal mathematical models of the opinion formation process have been proposed [5–9]. These models all share the assumption that individuals communicate with each other in a synchronized fashion, and the models do not allow for any variation in the frequency of interaction. We consider one such model which was proposed by De Groot [6] and Lehrer [7], and we show how this model can be extended to include interaction frequency. We then prove that, for the purposes of analysis and design, the opinion formation process with probabilistic interactions can be accurately approximated by a deterministic system with no interaction dynamics, but where edge weights are adjusted for the probability of interaction. The benefit of this result is that any analysis or design that has been done for the model with no interaction dynamics can automatically be extended to a network with probabilistic interactions. We highlight several of these design and analysis results in Section 2. We also present evaluations of the effects of different interaction frequencies on the opinion dynamics using real-world social network graphs. These evaluations also illustrate the accuracy of the proposed deterministic model in approximating opinion dynamics with probabilistic interactions.

2   Model Definition

Consider n agents online and an issue about which agents have different opinions. Consider the opinion to be continuous, such that compromising in the middle is possible. Consider further on that all agents have bounded confidence, in the way that they only take into account the opinions of agents which are not to far away from their own opinion. Agent-based models (ABM) of opinion dynamics under this assumptions have been formulated by Hegselmann and Krause [9] and Weisbuch et al[10]. Both models differ in their proposed communication structure but both lead to clustering of opinions in a similar way. The basic models have been extended in several ways [11–16]. But some questions for the basic models remain open: How does the dynamic depends on the number of agents (especially large numbers)? How can we describe the dependence on the initial opinions? [11] conjectured e.g. that a very huge number of agents may force consensus under certain conditions.

2.1   The Agent-Based HK Model with Bounded Confidence

Consider n interacting agents and assume that each agent's opinion is expressed by a real number, say y_i for $i \in \{1, \ldots, n\}$. In bounded confidence interaction, the opinion y_i is affected by the opinion y_j if $|y_i - y_j| \leq r_j$, where the positive number r_i is the confidence bound of agents i. In bounded influence interaction, the opinion y_i is affected by the opinion y_j if $|y_i - y_j| \leq r_i$, where the positive number r_j is the influence bound of agent j. The opinion vector $y \in \mathbb{R}^n_{>0}$ are obtained by stacking all y_i's and r_i's , respectively.

We associate to each opinion vector y two digraphs, both with nodes $\{1, \ldots, n\}$ and edge set defined as follows: denoting the set of out-neighbors of node i by $\mathcal{N}_i(y)$.

- in a synchronized bounded confidence (SBC) digraph, $\mathcal{N}_i(y) = \{j \in \{1, \ldots, n\}$: $|y_i - y_j| \leq r_i\}$; and
- in a synchronized bounded influence (SBI) digraph, $\mathcal{N}_i(y) = \{j \in \{1, \ldots, n\}$: $|y_i - y_j| \leq r_j\}$.

We let $G_r(y)$ denote one of the two proximity digraphs, its precise meaning being clear form the context.

We associate to the SBC and SBI digraphs two dynamical systems, called the SBC and SBI systems respectively. Both dynamical systems update a trajectory $x : \mathbb{N} \rightarrow \mathbb{R}^n$ according to the discrete-time rule for simplicity of numerical simulation

$$x(t+1) = A(x(t))x(t), \tag{1}$$

where the i, j entry of the adjacency matrix $A(y) \in \mathbb{R}^{n \times n}$ for any $y \in \mathbb{R}^n$ is defined by

$$a_{ij}(y) = \begin{cases} \frac{1}{\mathcal{N}_i(y)}, & \text{if } j \in \mathcal{N}_i(y), \\ 0, & \text{if } j \notin \mathcal{N}_i(y), \end{cases} \tag{2}$$

and $|\mathcal{N}_i(y)|$ is the cardinality of $\mathcal{N}_i(y)$. Note that $i \in \mathcal{N}_i(y)$, in other words, every agent has some self-confidence or self-influence. This assumption is a key factor in the convergence of infinite products of adjacency matrices.

2.2   Graph Representation of Networks

In the most common sense of the term, a graph is an ordered pair $G := (V, E)$ comprising a set V of vertices or nodes together with a set E of edges or lines which are 2-element subsets of V.

In modeling opinion dynamics with agents and graphs, agents will be represented by vertices and communications between agents by links between vertices. For we suppose that the interaction between agents be mutual, undirected graphs are used in our model.

Grid Graph. Grid or lattice graph refer to a number of categories of graphs whose drawing corresponds to some grid/mesh/lattice, i.e., its vertices correspond to the nodes of the mesh and its edges correspond to the ties between the vertices. So, a grid graph is a unit distance graph corresponding to the square lattice, so that it is isomorphic to the graph having a vertex corresponding to every pair of integers (a, b), and an edge connecting (a, b) to $(a+1, b)$ and $(a, b+1)$.

The finite grid graph $G_{m,n}$ is an $m \times n$ rectangular graph isomorphic to the one obtained by restricting the ordered pairs to the range $0 \leq a < m, 0 \leq b < n$. Grid graphs can be obtained as the Cartesian product of two paths: $G_{m,n} = P_m \times P_n$. Grid is very important in agent based models, notably in cellular automata, to model local relationship between agents. Normally grid is used with a periodic boundary condition to simulate large systems by modeling a small part, which is the case in our simulation, too.

Random Graphs. At the opposite end of the spectrum from a completely grid graph is a network with a completely random graph, which was studied by Erdös and Rényi (ER) [17]. A large-scale random network does not show highly clustering in general. In fact, the ER algorithm generates a homogeneous network, where the connectivity approximately follows a Poisson distribution.

Small-World Networks. These representative properties of small-world graph [18] are (i) the small average distance between two randomly chosen sites, and (ii) the high clustering coefficient, i.e., the high density of connections within the neighborhood of a node. The small-world model can also be viewed as a homogeneous network, in which all nodes have approximately the same number of edges.

Scale-Free Networks. A scale-free graph is a graph whose degree distribution follows a power law. A key ingredient in scale free network is preferential attachment, i.e., the assumption that the likelihood of receiving new edges increases with the node's degree. The Barabási-Albert model [19] assumes that the probability $P(k)$ that a node attaches to node i is proportional to the degree k of node i, that is $P(k) \propto k^{-\gamma}$ where γ is a constant whose value is typically in the range $2 < \gamma < 3$, although occasionally it may lie outside these bounds. Scale-free networks are noteworthy because many empirically observed networks appear to be scale-free, including protein networks, citation networks, some social networks and the world wide web as well. For those reasons scale free network is chosen in our model to represent agents's communication by means of social networks, mail or other internet tools.

3   The Model and Simulation Results

As we have seen in the previous section, in modeling, grid networks emphasize local neighborhood interactions, while random networks, small-world, and scale-free networks highlight those not geographically restricted, say internet or social networks. To imitate as close as possible real life interactions, we propose to integrate those four networks at the same time in BC model. We also study their impact on the behavior of the consensus threshold through simulation.

3.1   The Coupled Network Model

As said previously, our model is based on mixing four BC opinion dynamics models as following:

- Number of agents: $N = \{0, 1, 2, \ldots, n\}$
- Discrete time: $T = \{0, 1, 2, \ldots\}$
- Opinion formation: $x_i(t+1) = |I(i, x(t))|^{-1} \sum x_j(t) + |J(i, x(t))|^{-1} \sum x_j(t) + |K(i, x(t))|^{-1} \sum x_j(t) + |L(i, x(t))|^{-1} \sum x_j(t)$

with

- For the grid graphs $I(i, x) = \{1 \leq j \leq n \, with |x_i - x_j| \leq \epsilon_{1,i}\}$
- For the random graphs $J(i, x) = \{1 \leq j \leq n \, with |x_i - x_j| \leq \epsilon_{2,i}\}$
- For the small-world networks $K(i, x) = \{1 \leq j \leq n \, with |x_i - x_j| \leq \epsilon_{3,i}\}$
- For the scale-free networks $L(i, x) = \{1 \leq j \leq n \, with |x_i - x_j| \leq \epsilon_{4,i}\}$

3.2   Simulation Results

The simulation is realized with Multi-Agent simulation platform using Matlab. We give the Results for grid network, random network, small world and Scale-Free network as following. In Figure 1, we can see a screen-shot from simulation. The different opinions are colored differently. In judging the consensus we use the notion of consensus probability, which is calculated by dividing the number of agents in the largest cluster by the total number of agents in the system. Of course, this is calculated when the simulation is stabilized, which means there will occur no more opinion changes in the simulation.

The dynamics in an HK process of opinion dynamics starts at both extremes, while in the center nothing happens due to the uniform distribution of opinions. To get clear about the basic dynamics it is useful to study the dynamics onesided (Figure 1). Thus, we regard an infinitely number of agents with equidistant opinions: the natural numbers including zero. If Hegselmann's conjecture is right there must be an for which we observe no emergence of a cluster.

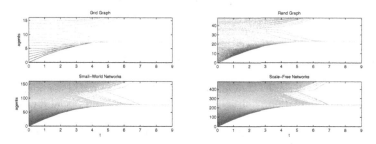

Fig. 1. Dynamics in a HK process of opinion dynamics with the natural numbers including zero as initial profile with four different network topologies

4   Conclusions

Although BC model has been studied heavily among researchers and some of those works have studied the relationship between underlying network structure and consensus threshold, little work has been done on integrating several network structures into a single model. The important part of our model is that we introduced multi-relationship in the opinion dynamics. Despite the fact that only four networks are considered at the first step, this work has shown the possibilities of achieving more complex and realistic network structures by integrating multiple networks. Furthermore the preliminary simulations have shown us that consensus threshold for BC model changes according to the multi-network structures.

Possible future works that we are considering will continue in this direction. These results encourage us to further explore the multi-network structures as a underlying structure of the opinion dynamics models. Besides, we would also like to study the dynamic networks as the result of opinion dynamics.

References

1. Wasserman, S., Faust, K.: Social Network Analysis. Cambridge University Press (1994)
2. Kossinets, G., Kleinberg, J., Watts, D.: The structure of information pathways in a social communication network. In: Proc. 14th ACM International Conference on Knowledge Discovery and Data Mining, pp. 435–443 (2008)
3. Wilson, C., Boe, B., Sala, A., Puttaswamy, K.P., Zhao, B.Y.: User interactions in social networks and their implications. In: Proc. 4th ACM European Conference on Computer Systems, pp. 205–218 (2009)
4. Viswanath, B., Mislove, A., Cha, M., Gummadi, K.P.: On the evolution of user interaction in Facebook. In: Proceedings of the 2nd ACM Workshop on Online Social Networks, pp. 37–42 (2009)
5. French, J.R.P.: A formal theory of social power. Psychological Review 63, 181–194 (1956)
6. DeGroot, M.H.: Reaching a consensus. Journal of the American Statistical Association 69, 118–121 (1974)
7. Lehrer, K.: Social consensus and rational agnoiology. Synthese 31(1), 141–160 (1975)
8. Friedkin, N.E., Johnsen, E.C.: Social in uence networks and opinion change. Advances in Group Processes 16, 1–29 (1999)
9. Hegselmann, R., Krause, U.: Opinion dynamics and bounded confidence models, analysis, and simulation. Journal of Artificial Societies and Social Simulation 5(3) (2002)
10. Weisbuch, G., Deffuant, G., Amblard, F., Nadal, J.: Meet, Discuss and Segregate! Complexity 7(3), 55–63 (2002)
11. Hegselmann, R.: Opinion Dynamics: Insights by Radically Simplifying Models. In: Gillies, D. (ed.) Laws and Models in Science, London, pp. 1–29 (2005)
12. Dittmer, J.C.: Consensus Formation under bounded Confidence. Nonlinear Analysis 47, 4615–4621 (2001)
13. DeffuantG., N.D., Amblard, F., Weisbuch, G.: How can extremism prevail? A study based on the relative agreement interaction model. Journal of Artificial Societies and Social Simulation 5(4) (2002), http://jasss.soc.surrey.ac.uk/5/4/1.html
14. Amblard, F., Deffuant, G.: The role of network topology on extremism propagation with the relative agreement opinion dynamics. Physica A 343, 725–738 (2004)

15. Urbig, D.: Attitude Dynamics with Limited Verbalisation Capabilities. Journal of Artificial Societies and Social Simulation 6(1) (2003), http://jasss.soc.surrey.ac.uk/6/1/2.html
16. Jager, W., Amblard, F.: Uniformity, bipolarisation and pluriformity captured as generic stylized behaviour with an agent-based simulation model of attitude change. Computational and Mathematical Organization Theory 10, 295–303 (2005)
17. Erdös, P., Rényi, A.: On the evolution of random graphs. Publ. Math. Inst. Hung. Acad. Sci. 5, 17–60 (1959)
18. Watts, D.J., Strogatz, S.H.: Collective dynamics of smallworld networks. Nature 393, 440–442 (1998)
19. Barabási, A.L., Albert, R.: Emergence of scaling in random networks. Science 286, 509–512 (1999)

Research on Risk Management Technology of Complex Products SBA Life-Cycle

Aiwen Wang[1,2], Xu-dong Chai[3], Hao Li[1], and Huiyang Qu[3]

[1] Beijing University of Aeronautics and Astronautics, Beijing 100191, China
[2] China Aerospace Science & Industry Corporation, Beijing 100048, China
[3] Beijing Simulation Center, Beijing 100854, China

Abstract. SBA of complex products is a system engineering, which includes collaboration of personnel/organization, management and technology. All the activities involved in equipment system and the life-cycle require the support of comprehensive management. Research on management of SBA life-cycle is introduced in this paper. An evaluation indicator system is given with the analysis of SBA risk. Based on cost breakdown structure (CBS), a method of cost estimation is proposed. Moreover, a schedule prediction method using arrow diagramming method (ADM) and Monte-Carlo simulation is provided. Finally, with the application on SBA of one aircraft, the methods proposed in this paper are demonstrated.

Keywords: simulation-based acquisition, life-cycle, risk, cost, schedule management.

1   Introduction

As the new technology widely applied in spacecraft design and research, the structure of equipment is more complex. The research is more difficult. The cycle of project's acquisition is longer. And the cost of research and acquisition is more expensive. So this change needs us adopt advanced technology and management to improve the competence of acquisition of complex equipment. In 1998, American DoD has come up with the Simulation-Based Acquisition called SBA new mode. Its core is the collaborative work of people, management and technology in life-cycle of product. It's an revolution and innovation based on the traditional culture, process and support environment of acquisition. SBA applies modeling and simulation technology firmly, collaboratively and highly integrated in each department, project and process of equipment's acquisition. It is a new mode of acquisition which includes analysis and definition of need, concept design, detailed design, producing, test and evaluation, utilization, and maintenance until worthless. It represents the developmental direction of complex production in 21th century.

The acquisition of complex equipment is the system engineering which contains several stages: demonstration, research, producing, maintenance, and safe guard. Its life-cycle management technology contains risk management, process management

T. Xiao, L. Zhang, and S. Ma (Eds.): ICSC 2012, Part I, CCIS 326, pp. 338–348, 2012.

and cost management. The risk management is an activity of risk control which includes risk identification, risk evaluation, risk factors and event facing to the whole process of acquisition. The schedule management realize the reasonable management of each activity in life-cycle, and complete the project in time or in advance with limited resource and cost conditions. The cost of life-cycle is the sum of all the direct, indirect, repeated and disposable costs from demonstration stage to discard stage. In general, the cost and schedule of acquisition have the mutual effect. For example, the adoption of new technology increases the cost. The cost risk and schedule risk are the important factors which affect the success of project acquisition. The reasonable control of life-cycle cost and the realization of best performance with the lowest risk, minimum cost and least time are the research goals of life-cycle management technology of acquisition.

This article mainly introduces the research achievements of SBA life-cycle management, which include risk, process and cost management technology of SBA cycle-life. Then the article briefly introduce the initial result of application in spacecraft and gives the conclusion.

2   Current Situation

Along with the coming out of SBA, all countries over the world discuss about the new theory and method to develop the efficiency and decrease the acquisition cost and risk. American researchers has come up with the "spiral development" and "progressive development" tactics, which has been already used in the equipment acquisition process. DoD has also published DoD5000 series files, which define the policy and process must executed and insist on cost as an independent variable called CAIV. The US Army's equipment development, including policy of acquisition, research, produce, test, application, safeguard, adjusting of defense industry, influenced directly or indirectly by these measures.

During the equipment acquisition process, there exist lots of risks. In the 90s last century, by using scientific method and systematical analysis, the US Army has summarized the efficient method to control and manage the risk and also decrease the effect of risk in the acquisition process. Through the active behavior of identifying the factors of risk during the acquisition process, modeling of the key factors of risk such as cost and process, collaborative evaluation method combining quantitative analysis and qualitative analysis, great importance has been made into the following aspects: preventing and releasing and eliminating the negative effect of risk, developing the resistance of acquisition process to the risk.

As the fast development of equipment industry, the cycle-life cost, which leads to the success of complex system's design, must be taken into the key consideration factor. Developed countries such as America has come up with the concept, method and technology of cycle life cost management from 60s last century. Given the same importance as quality and research schedule, cost was followed and controlled during the whole life-cycle of equipment system, and was evaluated and was given corresponding tactics by stages. This method has made a significant profit. Life-cycle cost management has been the important method of American complex system acquisition process.

Schedule management is the core and basic element of project management. The traditional methods such as CPM and PERT were not applicable because the following aspects of SBA: the huge amount, complex constraint, frequency of conflicts of resource, frequent irritation and management. These defaults make the management of schedule of project very difficult.

As an important method to research the complex system, simulation can provide the solution for this kind of problem.

3   Technological Research of SBA Life-Cycle Risk Management

3.1   Technology of SBA Life-Cycle Risk Management

SBA has the following characteristics: wide area, many sessions, huge cost, long period of research, complex system, enormous fee for maintenance. These characteristics result in the high risk of SBA project, which exist inherently in the different stages of cycle-life in SBA.

Risk identification is the most basic and essential part of job in risk management. The risk factors of SBA, including technology risk, cost and schedule risk, supplier risk, external risk exist in all stages of life-cycle. Technology risk exists through the whole process of life-cycle of SBA, including such as the change of design in later stage caused by the immature new technology, and reduction of performance indicator. Cost and technology risk has a strength link. The change of design or performance will increase the cost or delay the schedule. In order to make sure the quality and safety of the equipment production, the equipment research and develop company will choose the corresponding superior supplier and keep the long-term cooperation. So the suppliers' capacity of supply of material and quality of product are the main risk factors in consideration. The large amount of sessions in SBA, the level of technological staff, the normalization of manipulation and the conscience of quality control are the important reasons of the appearance of management risk. External risks are the risk factors which have important effect on SBA but seldom direct connection with SBA such as the change of market and the change of acquisition scheme etc.

This article takes the complex equipment of spacecraft as an example to identify and judge the type of risk, the origin of risk and the scope of risk influence, depending on all the possible risk factors in different stages. Then we form the risk factors system of SBA life-cycle and establish the indicator system of risk evaluation.

Table 1. Indicator System of Risk Evaluation

Type of risk	Content
Technology risk, cost and schedule risk, supplier risk, external risk	1. System indicator amelioration design technology 2. Subsystem accuracy allocation technology 3. test design technology 4. evaluation technology 5. processing design technology 6. produce and assemble technology
Cost risk	1. Repeats of research process leads to the excess of budget 2. The origin of capital of research and development company 3. Inflation leads to increase of cost
Quality risk	1. input of design standardization and design principle 2. control of the research process 3. standardization requirement of product of different stage 4. test evaluation, control of key projects and sessions 5. inspect and analysis of test sufficiency and test of spreadability
Human resource risk	1. Young designers lack of engineering research experience 2. Parallel research of multi equipment lead to human resource in short supply
Endurance risk	1. Guarantee condition of research meet the designer's need or not 2. The safeguard condition of test area meet the requirement of test or not
Supplier risk	1. The degree of dependence to supplier's material or service during the acquisition process 2. Key material sufficient or not
Market risk	1. Change of market's need 2. Change of market competition

3.2   Technology of Cost Estimation in SBA

In order to estimate and analyze the life-cycle cost, it needs to establish Cost Breakdown Structure called CBS depend the whole life-cycle cost. The decomposition structure of life-cycle cost is established by the specially ranked basic unit elements of cost depending on the hardware, software or other project of complex product in a life-cycle. Unit element of cost is the cost term of life-cycle cost. An unit element of cost is the cost element which we can calculate individually.

After the establishment of CBS, corresponding cost model should be used to estimate the cost. The nature of cost model is the mathematical model established by computer. Cost model represents the function between cost and the factors influencing the cost. Generally, the establishment of cost model is the result of integration of Parameter estimation, Engineering estimation, Analogous estimation, Extrapolation estimation, Expert evaluation estimation. Expert evaluation estimation is the top priority choice in earlier stage of SBA and engineering estimation is the top priority choice in later stage of SBA.

Engineering estimation decomposes the system into cost unit elements and estimates the cost of each cost unit element. And then we sum up the cost unit elements to get the total cost. Parameter estimation uses the historical data of similar type product and then establishes the correlate equation between cost and important parameters which represent the characteristics of system. Cost can be estimated by the correlate equation which is called CER (Cost Estimate Relation). CER is the mature method which applied in research of equipment estimation and research cost. In order to establish the links between cost and factors of system, the first step is to make sure the parameters which affect on cost by qualitative analysis. The second step is to find out the priority of each parameter and keep the main parameter and neglect the less important parameter. Then the cost model used in early period can be obtained. The method of parameter estimation can be presented by following formula.

$$LCC = \sum_{i=1}^{n} f_i(p_1, p_2, ..., p_j) \tag{1}$$

LCC represents the cost of life-cycle. f_i represents the estimation formula of cost term i. p_j represents the factor of cost term. For the estimation of cost term f_i we use multiple linear regression:

$$f = \alpha_0 + \alpha_1 p_1 + \alpha_2 p_2 + \cdots \alpha_j p_j \tag{2}$$

α_0 is called regression constant. $\alpha_1, \alpha_2, \cdots \alpha_j$ are called regression coefficient. $p_1, p_2, \cdots p_j$ are the factor of cost term used to estimate the cost term f. When there are n group of historical data, the multiple linear regression model can be represented by:

$$f = \alpha p + \alpha_0 \tag{3}$$

$$f = \begin{bmatrix} f_1 \\ f_2 \\ \vdots \\ f_n \end{bmatrix}, \quad \alpha = \begin{bmatrix} \alpha_1 \\ \alpha_2 \\ \vdots \\ \alpha_j \end{bmatrix}, \quad P = \begin{bmatrix} p_{11} & p_{12} & \cdots & p_{1j} \\ p_{21} & p_{22} & \cdots & p_{2j} \\ \cdots & \cdots & \cdots & \cdots \\ p_{n1} & p_{n2} & \cdots & p_{nj} \end{bmatrix}$$

The cost efficient α adopt method of least squares, which can be represented by:

$$\hat{\alpha} = (P'P)^{-1}P'f \tag{4}$$

So, the formula to estimate the cost is:

$$\hat{f}_i = \hat{\alpha}_0 + \hat{\alpha}_1 \, p_{i1} + \hat{\alpha}_2 \, p_{i2} + \cdots + \hat{\alpha}_j \, p_{ij} \tag{5}$$

3.3   Technology of Schedule Prediction in SBA

In order to represent the order of all the activities during the acquisition process, Arrow Diagramming Method called ADM is adopted.

ADM is a net diagramming method which uses arrow line to represent activities and use node to represent an event. In arrow diagramming, each event is referred to an unique code number. The beginning of the activity which is the tail of arrow is called precede event of this activity. The end of the activity which is the head of arrow is called successor event of this activity. The arrow diagramming is presented by figure 1.

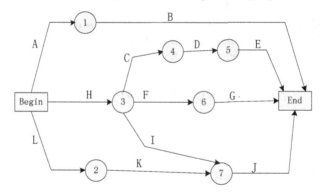

Fig. 1. Arrow Diagramming

During the process of SBA, all the acquisition activities show the uncertainty. The schedule prediction in SBA is to describe the probability by research the effect of the change of uncertain factor to the acquisition of equipment. So the random numbers should be used to describe the uncertainty of each activity. Considerable distribution of random variables should be taken into consideration in order to get the one which is most coherent with the reel situation. In the general situation, there are two characteristics of probability density in SBA's time lasting activities. First, it exists un distribution interval (a, b). The probability density in this interval is always positive. Second, in the interval (a, b), the curve of probability density form unimodal distribution. Gaussian distribution and triangle distribution are the two normal distributions which correspond with these two characteristics. Its sampling formula is as follow:

(1) Gaussian distribution

Sampling formula :

$$x_i = \sigma \cdot \sqrt{-2\ln r_1} \cdot \cos(2\pi r_2^{\,2}) + \mu \tag{6}$$

x_i is the random sample of Gaussian distribution. μ is the expectation value. σ is the mean square deviation. r_1, r_2 are a couple of pseudo random numbers uniformly distributed in the interval [0, 1].

(2)Triangle distribution

Sampling formula :

$$x_i = \begin{cases} a + \sqrt{r_i(m-a)(b-a)}, r_i \le (m-a)/(b-a) \\ b - \sqrt{(1-r_i)(b-m)(b-a)}, r_i > (m-a)/(b-a) \end{cases} \tag{7}$$

x_i is the random sample of Gaussian distribution; a, b, m are the three estimation values ; r_i is the pseudo random number in the interval [0, 1].

After making sure of all the distribution probabilities of every activity, it needs to use Monte Carlo simulation method to do the simulation analysis of schedule in SBA. The calculation of Monte Carlo is as follow:

$$p(\prod_{i=1}^{n} A_i) = \prod_{i=1}^{n} p(A_i) \tag{8}$$

A_i is the random sample of activity in SBA.

4   Example of Application

This article bases on the SBA of complex equipment of spacecraft and will introduce an example of application which use the management technology to scheme demonstration stage of SBA. In this stage, on the base of performance indicator analysis, scheming period, scheming cost and risk evaluation are used as the basic indication of the analysis and decision of scheme. The demonstration process is as figure 2. The full lines represent the management activities. The dotted lines the analysis and demonstration and design of simulation, which are related to technology.

The demonstration of the scheme adopts the combined decision-making method of qualitative analysis and quantitative analysis. It needs to choose a practical scheme from variable schemes. In the first round research of scheme, the performance indicator of spacecraft should be the evaluation basis. The chosen scheme will be applied into project schedule evaluation, cost analysis and risk analysis. Then the period of scheming, the scheme of cost and the risk evaluation will be obtained and be used in the second round of demonstration as the basic indicator.

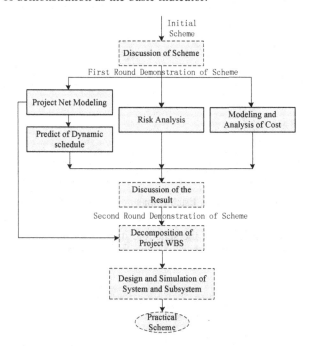

Fig. 2. The Demonstration Process of Spacecraft

The life-cycle cost of spacecraft can be divided into cost of research and development (CDR), cost of production (CP), cost of operating and safeguard (COS) and cost of dispose and recycle (CDR). The life-cycle cost can be presented as:

$$LCC = CRD + CP + COS + CDR$$

CRD is composed by demonstration cost, pre-study cost, design cost, trial-produce cost and test cost. CP is composed by element and material acquisition cost, equipment and facilities acquisition cost, outsourcing cost, produce cost, driving power fuel cost, quality-related costs, cost of depreciation of fixed assets, transportation and packing cost. COS is composed by operation cost and recycle cost. For the design cost, by applying regression method on historical data, the cost regression model can be obtained:

$$Cost = A_0 + A_1 C_{REACH} + A_2 C_{ADVANCE} + A_3 C_{REDESIGN}$$

C_{REACH}, $C_{ADVANCE}$, $C_{REDESIGN}$ represent the cost to reach actual level of technology, actual innovation of technology and the use of different schemes; A_0, A_1, A_2 and A_3 are the cost parameters obtained by historical data.

For the cost not related to design, engineering estimation and Expert evaluation estimation are applied to get the life-cycle cost of spacecraft. The decomposition of establishment of life-cycle cost of spacecraft is as figure 3. The total scheme cost in SBA can be deduced by the cost of each stage.

Fig. 3. The Decomposition of Establishment of Life-cycle Cost of Spacecraft

In order to do the prediction of the schedule in SBA of this spacecraft, we use un example in design stage. The first step is to design the net of stage task diagram as the figure 4.

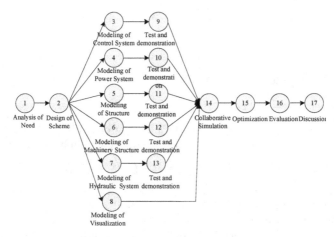

Fig. 4. The net of stage task diagram

Based on the step above, the next step should be obtaining the analysis diagram of the schedule distribution density for each activity by Mont Carol simulation method as the figure 5. Then the same method should be applied to research stage and other stages to get the schedule of complex spacecraft's SBA.

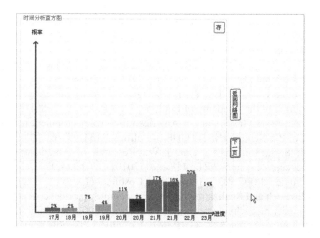

Fig. 5. The schedule distribution density for each activity

The risk analysis in scheme demonstration stage is mainly focusing on technological risk. The experts depend take the risk evaluation indicator system of the figure 1 into consideration and compare the influence level. Then they use layer analysis to get the weight of each indicator and give each risk influence in technology a grade. Then Fuzzy comprehensive evaluation method、 Grey relational analysis method should be applied to get the evaluation value of each scheme.

In the second round of scheme demonstration, experts choose the practical scheme depend on the cost of scheme, the schedule of scheme and the value of risk evaluation. And the simulation result of the project net diagram forms the basis of decomposition of WBS in SBA, which can be used to pilot the multidisciplinary simulation of the system and the subsystems to get the final practical scheme.

5   Conclusions

Through the applying of SBA on complex spacecraft equipment, the demonstration shows that the combination of parameter and other method can efficiently estimate the life-cycle cost; The schedule prediction method based on Mont Carlo simulation method can increase the accuracy of prediction; Identification of risk factor in SBA and establishment efficient risk evaluation system are the bases in risk evaluation. The applying of SBA management technology in demonstration stage can help to analyze and evaluate the different beginning tasks and finally find out the practical scheme.

References

1. Frost, R.: Simulation Based Acquisition, The Road Map. 99S-SIW-147.doc
2. Di, Y.-Q., Li, B.-H., Chai, X.-D., Wang, P.: Research of multi-disciplines virtual prototype collaborative modeling and simulation platform and key technology. Computer Integrated Manufacturing System 11(7), 901–908 (2005)

3. Li, B.-H., Chai, X.-D., Zhu, H.-W., Sun, J.-G., Liang, B.-C., Wu, H.-Z., Peng, X.-Y.: The research of environment supporting technology if SBA. Journal of System Simulation 16(2), 181–185 (2004) (in Chinese)

4. Ren, Z.-Y., Ni, H.-Y.: Inspiration of American acquisition reform to our army. Technology Foundation of National Defense (2), 55–57 (2010) (in Chinese)

5. Zhou, Y.-D., Zhang, D.-P., Li, Y.-H.: Analysis of American progressive acquisition experience. Journal of the Academy of Equipment 19(4), 25–29 (2008) (in Chinese)

6. Dong, H.-L., Zhang, H.: Inspiration of American life-cycle equipment management to our army. Journal of Pla Nanjing INSTITUTE of Politics 3(134), 58–61 (2007) (in Chinese)

7. Hu, J.-X., Li, S.-S., Liu, Z.-T., Yan, J.-W.: Research of American space equipment acquisition risk control system 27(1), 118–120 (2010) (in Chinese)

8. International Standard IEC 300-3-3 Life Cycle Costing 9 (1996)

9. Sun, H.-B.: Research and Realization of Artillery complex product cost estimation method. National University of Technology Graduate Academy (2002) (in Chinese)

10. Zhong, D.-H., Liu, K.-J., Yang, X.-G.: Research of process flexible network's Uncertainty. System Engineering (2), 107–112 (2005) (in Chinese)

Development of System of Knowledge Base for Spherical Plain Bearing

Xuejin Shen, Deguo Li , Shuai Lv, and Yunfei Liu

Department of Mechanical Automation Engineering,
Shanghai University, Shanghai 200072, China
shenxj@shu.edu.cn

Abstract. Presently, applying the Knowledge Base System in manufacturing industry bcomes a tendency. The paper brings the concepts of Knowledge Base System to the industry of spherical plain bearing, and establishes the Knowledge Base System of Spherical Plain Bearing. This system contains four parts of knowledge, i.e., data knowledge, literature knowledge, check knowledge and simulation knowledge. There are four main modules, including the module of data search, module of search and read of literature, module of check calculation and module of finite element analysis. The composition of system structure and flow of system design process are also introduced in this paper. This system is developed on Browser/Server structure. The Knowledge Base System of Spherical Plain Bearing takes the Visual Studio for the man-machine interface, selects the SQL Server 2008 for the storage of knowledge data, and realizes the integration with finite element software of Abaqus to make the analysis of mechanical properties for spherical plain bearing which could provide the basis for its further optimization design. This system is valuable and significant, and will play an important role in the informational construction of spherical plain bearing.

Keywords: Spherical plain bearing, Knowledge base, Database, System.

1   Introduction

1.1   Research Background

Chinese industry of bearing should increase innovational efforts to technology of bearing, apply actively the latest electronic information technology, and accelerate the speed of study and design of new product. It has become the consensus of bearing enterprise that applying software engineering technology to develop a system of bearing for search, calculation, design and analysis, which can easily and intelligently help bearing design engineer to search data and analyze the properties of bearing.

Spherical plain bearing is a standard component and a kind of important industrial base components, which has been widely used in aerospace , transportation, biological and medical treatment and mechanical engineering[1]. Spherical plain bearing is mainly used for supporting parts of low concentricity, large work surface

T. Xiao, L. Zhang, and S. Ma (Eds.): ICSC 2012, Part I, CCIS 326, pp. 349–357, 2012.

pressure and slow swaying and rotary motion. It's generally composed by an inner circle with the outer sphere and an outer circle with the inner sphere, which can bear comparatively large load. The typical spherical plain bearing is shown as figure 1[2]. According to Chinese national standard for spherical plain bearing's classification[3], spherical plain bearing is generally divided into four types : radial spherical plain bearing, angular contact spherical plain bearing, thrust spherical plain bearing and rod end spherical plain bearing.

The related systems of bearing for study and design are mostly about rolling bearing now. With respect to spherical plain bearing, there is no researcher to develop a special software or system for data query, aided design or finite element analysis at present.

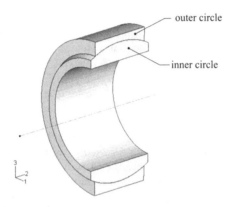

Fig. 1. Structural representation of spherical plain bearing

1.2   Overview of Knowledge Base System

Knowledge Base is called Intelligent Database or Artificial Intelligent Database. KBS (Knowledge Base System), based on the development of related technologies on the two areas of Knowledge Engineering and traditional Database System, is to meet the urgent needs of the knowledge data storage, management and control. So Knowledge Base is the effective combination of Artificial Intelligence and Database.

KBS and MIS (Management Information System) are both developed from Information System. They are both based on the Database System, need data processing, and provide decision-aid information to users from different extent. The main function object of MIS is information, especially the flowing information data. It is not so professional and has no strong need for the stability of information data. It focuses on the range and timeliness of information data. However, the main function objects of KBS are information data of maturity and stability, such as professional data, professional knowledge, predecessors' experience and research results.

KBS, which is a kind of resources integration, includes knowledge information, software, hardware and knowledge engineers. It is a general development tools based on logic. It is especially suited for knowledge system included the large amount of facts and is suitable for the application fields of graphics or CAD. Therefore, it's very suitable for application of mechanical field[4].

1.3   Proposition of Knowledge Base System of Spherical Plain Bearing

The range of mechanical industry is quite wide, and many of the scientific research achievements of mechanical engineering are difficult to reach the sharing of resources. So as to learn these scientific research achievements, people can only take approaches such as attending academic conferences, buying academic periodicals, searching and reading professional academic theses through web site. However, it's still difficult things to further study and use the research process and scientific research results described in paper.

If we put the results of a field of scientific research into one KBS, realize the system integration with the software tools applied, design an interface for KBS which is easily operated, then the problem above could be solved reasonably.

Knowledge Base is not only for the storage of industry knowledge, but also for the organization, optimization and automation of related scientific research achievements. As for machinery industry, there is so much convenience to build a knowledge base system based on computer for each field. It can not only make researchers search the data, information and literature easily and conveniently, but also obtain and apply the real-time research method which is public.

From the above, it's so necessary to bring the concepts of KBS to the industry of spherical plain bearing, and establish a KBSSPB (Knowledge Base System of Spherical Plain Bearing) which can quickly realize the functions such as data search of spherical plain bearing, search and read of literature, check calculation and analysis of performance. And this system should meet the need of quick design and intelligent analysis for spherical plain bearing in bearing industry of China.

2   Analysis of System

2.1   Combination of Knowledge Content

The knowledge of KBSSPB could be divided into four parts: data knowledge, literature knowledge, check knowledge, and simulation knowledge.

Data is the main storage form of knowledge in computer and is the most intuitive knowledge. And spherical plain bearing is standard component. So data knowledge in this system is the most important one. The basic data of the spherical plain bearing include code of spherical plain bearing, overall size parameters, weight, direction and degree of loads, lubricating or not, reference price, information related to manufacturers.

The content of the literature knowledge is from public publications and undocumented publications, generally including journal papers related spherical plain bearing, degree theses, conference papers, bearing manuals, national standards and trade standards, undocumented scientific research achievements, internal production material, design example, research experience, etc. The literature knowledge will be stored in the system's database with the file form.

Before the selection of spherical plain bearing, check calculation is generally required. Check calculation includes load calculation and lifetime calculation. So, check knowledge includes calculating formulas of load and lifetime and the related factor values of calculation formulas.

Simulation knowledge of the Spherical Plain Bearing Knowledge Base System is not simply as to inform the simulation content by the form of text, or provide the operation method or skill information of simulating for spherical plain bearing based on large simulation software. Because the words of simulation knowledge is meaningless and it just gives users how to analyze the force or deformation of spherical plain bearing, in fact customers can't get knowledge really wanted from the text of simulation knowledge itself. It means that the simulation knowledge itself is not the thing which customers expect and the customers' real purpose is to obtain the simulation results. Consider the problems above, the authors made full use of computer technology, realized the integration of knowledge base system and simulation software, and made the encapsulation for simulation knowledge of spherical plain bearing and the operation of simulation software in knowledge base system, finally let the simulation process be automatic in the system, and directly outputted figures of simulation results.

2.2   Analysis of Function Characteristics

The consumers of knowledge base system of spherical plain bearing are not single, and the system function for different consumers are also diversified.

Totally, the function characteristics of this system are as follows:

(1) Can store knowledge data;
(2) Has the interactive function;
(3) Has the type selection function according to the standard of classification;
(4) Can realize the search from selective parameters input;
(5) Can realize the precise search and fuzzy search;
(6) Can search the data of spherical plain bearing through a variety of means;
(7) Can update data;
(8) Can provide the shape of the spherical plain bearing's sample figure;
(9) Can inquiry and read the literature knowledge;
(10) Can directly deal checking calculation;
(11) Can make non-professional users of finite element software easily complete the job of finite element analysis;
(12) Can easily realize maintenance and management of knowledge base.

3   Choice of Development Platform

This system is developed on B/S (Browser/Server) structure. Spherical Plain Bearing Knowledge Base System is a platform to share and apply the knowledge of spherical plain bearing for all kinds of personnel. The users of this system are widespread and discrete, and function of finite element analysis of the system requires background support of large simulation software. So the traditional C/S (Client/Server) structure is obvious limited. The function module of the system would be expanded and updated with the deepening of the research of science and technology of spherical plain bearing. So for a continually updated system, the choice of development based on B/S structure, is not only beneficial to the data update of a knowledge base system, but also beneficial to the update, expansion and perfection of the follow-up function modules of system[5].

This system is based on Windows 7 to complete the development process of entire system, considering compatibility and ease-of-use of the system. The development of this system needs database software to store knowledge data, and needs to realize the links between interface and database through integrated environment and the integration with finite element software.

The establishment of the database platform chooses Microsoft SQL Server 2008 which is the mainstream relational database software in the market. SQL Server is mainly through data table to realize the storage of system data and users' data. "Form" is the core database object of SQL Server, and is the foundation of almost all other database objects.

Visual Studio is an integrated development environment launched by Microsoft. It can be used to create Windows applications and web applications. ASP.NET framework of Visual Studio is a procedure technology based on the compilation by the common language C#. ASP.NET has great function of interface design, and can easily link and visit SQL Server database through simple code backstage. Visual Studio is also presently the most popular Windows platform application development environment. Because of the reasons above, the integrated development environment will choose ASP.NET of Visual Studio.

Abaqus, launched by Dassault Inc., is the good choice of the finite element software. Software of Abaqus can solve problems which are from relatively simple linear analysis to many complicated nonlinear ones. It contains a graphical user interface (Abaqus/CAE) which supports solver comprehensively, and provides four ways of secondary development. One of the four secondary development ways is the script interface of Abaqus based on the language of Python, which can realize almost all function of Abaqus/CAE and directly communicate with the core of Abaqus without graphical user interface of Abaqus/CAE[6].

4   Design of System

4.1   Function Module of System

Through the analysis of system, the main functions of KBSSPB can be summarized as function of data search, function of search and read of literature, function of check calculation, and function of finite element analysis. According to the principle of system function module partition, module of KBSSPB should be divided into: module of data search, module of search and read of literature, module of check calculation and module of finite element analysis. The chart of function module of this system is shown in figure 2.

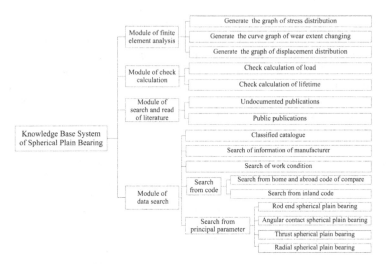

Fig. 2. Chart of function module of KBSSPB

The functions of the main modules shown as above are as follows:

(1) Module of data search. This module can realize the multifarious ways of data search for spherical plain bearing, so that different kinds of consumers could easily apply the function of data search. According to standard classification and data characteristics of spherical plain bearing, nine submodules of data search are designed.

(2) Module of search and read of literature. The coverage of the literature knowledge is very broad, which is the largest source of KBSSPB. This module is often ignored by the design staffs of the knowledge base system, who considers reading of literature is too primitive. In fact, an integrated system should inevitably respect the consumers' habits. With this module, the consumers can obtain almost most of the content they expect. Module of search and read of literature is the great supplement of other modules of KBSSPB, so the relative integrity of knowledge base system is also embodied by this module.

(3) Module of check calculation. Before the selection and use of spherical plain bearing, it is generally required for checking of load and lifetime. It can directly calculate the result of check after the required factors and parameters are input on the interface of this module. This module can spare the trivial jobs of inquiry of computing formula and correlation coefficient for users of spherical plain bearing.

(4) Module of finite element analysis. This module is the greatest merit and innovation of KBSSPB. As to those users, who is in urgent need of the result of finite element analysis through simulation software, but is not good at applying the finite element software, this module seems so valuable. After the required parameters are input on the interface of this module, the system will automatically run the simulation software of finite element analysis in background according to the input parameters, and then the module interface can display or export the graph of stress distribution, graph of displacement distribution or curve graph of wear extent changing.

4.2 Composition of System Structure

Based on the constitution theory of KBS, KBS, which is a kind of resources integration, includes knowledge information, software, hardware and related personnel[7,8]. So the system structure figure of KBSSPB is as shown in figure 3 below.

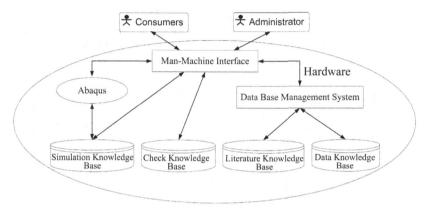

Fig. 3. Chart of structure of KBSSPB

4.3 Technical Route of System Design

The flow chart of system design is mainly as shown in figure 4.

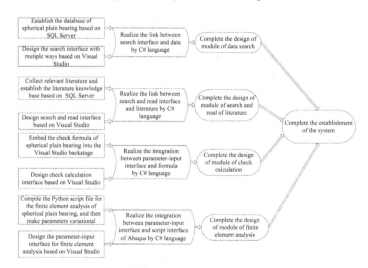

Fig. 4. Flow chart of system design

5   Text Example of System

Take the module of check calculation of KBSSPB for example. Login this system, and then click the "Load Calculation" of "Check Calculation" on the left tree. In this module, firstly choose the drop down list of "Radial Spherical Plain Bearing" for the choice of type of spherical plain bearing; secondly choose the drop down list of "Dynamic Load Rating" for the choice of load type. Then input "87" as the factor of dynamic load rating, "55" as the nominal width of outer ring, "120" as the nominal diameter of sliding spherical. At last, click the button of "Start Computing". So you will see the computed result of dynamic load rating is 574200N, which is shown as figure 5.

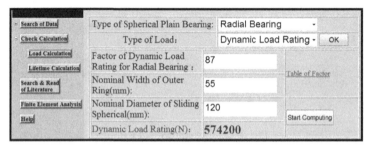

Fig. 5. Interface of load calculation

6   Conclusions

It's quite meaningful to establish a KBS for the spherical plain bearings which are a kind of important industrial base components. KBSSPB is established on the base of the environment integrating Visual Studio, SQL Server and Abaqus. It is divided into four main modules: module of data search, module of search and read of literature, module of check calculation and module of finite element analysis. It can realize multiple ways of data search of spherical plain bearing, quick search and read of kinds of literature, calculation of load and lifetime, and acquirement of the graph of stress distribution, graph of displacement distribution or curve graph of wear extent changing, which are based on the finite element simulation analysis of Abaqus according to the parameters being input. The establishment of the KBSSPB will provide a good comprehensive information platform for the design and application for spherical plain bearing.

Acknowledgements. This work was financially supported by the COSTIND of China (JPPT-115-3-1338), Innovative Team Program of Universities in Shanghai (B.48-0109-09-002) and High and New Engineering Program of Shanghai (D.51-0109-09-001).

References

1. Singh, D.S., Majumdar, B.C.: Computer-aided Design of Hydrodynamic Journal Bearings Considering Thermal Effects. Journal of Engineering Tribology 219(2), 133–143 (2005)
2. Cao, L.: Thermal Analysis and Wear Simulation of Spherical Plain Bearings with Self-lubricating Fabric Liner. Shanghai University, Shanghai (2010) (in Chinese)
3. GB/T304.2-2002: Classification Standards of Spherical Plain Bearing, http://www.kv99.com
4. Xu, J.P., Ma, Y.S., Fan, M.: Introductory Theory of KBS. Science Press, Beijing (2000) (in Chinese)
5. Zhou, Y.W., Qian, M.: Bearing Production Checkout Management System Based on Computer Network. In: 2006 IEEE International Conference on Industrial Informatics, pp. 1149–1152. IEEE Press, Singapore (2006)
6. Cheng, L., Li, H.B.: Second Development of Abaqus Based on the Scripting Interface. Modern Machinery (2), 58–65 (2009) (in Chinese)
7. Jia, X.Z., Luo, T.Y., Lv, F., Liu, H.B.: Research on the Knowledge Base System of Rolling Bearings. Advanced Materials Research 211-212, 87–92 (2011)
8. He, Q., Li, X.Q.: Management of Knowledge Base of Expert System for Fault Diagnosis of Rotating Machinery. Applied Mechanics and Materials 44-47, 2935–2939 (2011)

Using Software Product Line Engineering for Magnitude Modeling and Simulation

Bin Tan, Jun Zhao, Jian-guo Wang, and Litie Tang

Northwest Institute of Nuclear Technology, Xi'an 710024, China
{Tan bin,Zhao Jun,Wang jianguo,Tang litie,tbonln}@hotmail.com

Abstract. Magnitude of space object is an important parameter to the analysis of photoelectricity detection. Multiple, similar software products instead of just a single individual product are needed to be developed in the exploration of such problem. The magnitude modeling problem is given and the Software Product Line Engineering (SPLE) method is introduced to solve the problem. A feature model for magnitude modeling is given, and a variable architecture based on Satellite Tool Kit (STK) is designed. With this approach, exploration analysis of magnitude to photoelectricity detection could be set out.

Keywords: Software Product Line Engineering(SPLE), Magnitude Modelling and Simulation, Satellite Tool Kit.

1 Introduction

Magnitude of space object is an important parameter to photoelectricity detecting. Predicting magnitude by modeling and simulation is often used in the design of spece object. Usually the space objcet is considered as the combination shape of plane, prism and column, and the photoelectricity reflection area could be calculated by integrating reflection facets. Here it is needed to develop multiple,similar software products instead of just a single individual product.There are several reasons of this.Products that are being developed must be adapted for different users, such as designer, detecter, and especially for different shape of space object, and so must provide adapted user interfaes and models. Because of cost and time constraints is not possible for software developers to develop a new product form scratch for each new customer, and so software reuse must be increased. Software reuse is one of the main goals software engineers treat to achieve. Many approaches have been proposed during last decades following this purpose: libraries, objects and classes, components and nowadays Software Product Line Engineering(SPLE).

The basis of SPLE is the explicit modelling of what is common and what differs between product variants[1]. A software product-line is a set of systems that share a common architecture and a set of reusable components. Jointly, they constitute a software platform supporting application development for a particular domain[2,3].

T. Xiao, L. Zhang, and S. Ma (Eds.): ICSC 2012, Part I, CCIS 326, pp. 358–364, 2012.

2   Background

2.1   Magnitude Modeling Problem

The magnitude of stars is measured on a scale where a brightness difference of 100 is represented by a change in the Magnitude of 5. This system was developed in 1856 by N. R. Pogson and is called the Pogson Magnitude Scale. The Sun has a brightness of -26.74, The above results in the formula:

$$M_v = -26.74 - 2.5\log_{10}(E_m / E_0) \tag{1}$$

Where M_v is the magnitude of space object, E_0 is the luminous energy of sun ,and E_m is luminous energy the space object, and E_m can be gained as follow:

$$E_m = \frac{\sigma E_0}{\pi u^2} S_0 \tag{2}$$

Where σ is the diffuse reflection coefficient of space object surface, u is the range form space object to observer, and S_0 is the area efficiently reflecting sunlight. M_v can be expected:

$$M_v = -26.74 - 2.5\log_{10}(\frac{\sigma S_0}{\pi u}) \tag{3}$$

By the formula (3), the M_v is determined by σ, S_0 and u. The magnitude modeling problem is how to calculate S_0, and different requirements for different users. A lot of papers introduced how to compute the value of S_0[4,5,6], the space objects is thinking of ideal geometry shapes, such as plane, column, prism and so on.

2.2   Satellite Tool Kit(STK) for Magnitude Simulation

Magnitude modelling problem involves complex relationship between ground station and space object, and Satellite Tool Kit, often referred to by its initials STK, as a commercial off the shelf software tool, is prefered to solve the problem. STK allows engineers and scientists to perform complex analysis of land, sea, air, and space assets, and share results in one integrated solution. At the core of STK is a geometry engine that is designed to determine the time-dynamic position and attitude of assets, determining dynamic spatial relationships among all of the objects under consideration including the quality of those relationships or accesses given a number of complex, simultaneous constraining conditions. it is now used in both the aerospace and defense communities.

2.3   Two Processes of SPLE

The software product line engineering paradigm separates two processes(Fig.1 shows the two processes): Domain Engineering and Application Engineering. Domain Engineering focuses on a family of systems, Application Engineering focuses on a single system[7].

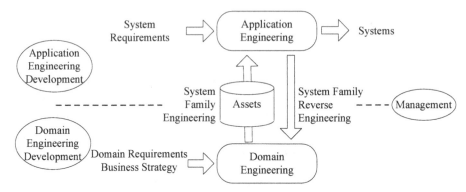

Fig. 1. Reference Framework of SPLE

In SPL development, three main activities are distinguished[8]: core-asset development or domain engineering, product development or application engineering and management. The products are built from core-assets, but also core-assets may be built from existing products. The synchronization between these two activities is arranged by management.

Capturing the variations characterizing the set of products belonging to a product line is a key issue for the requirements engineering of this development philosophy.

The production process is therefore organized in product lines with the aim of maximizing the commonalities of the product family and minimizing the cost of variations.

2.4   Feature Models for SPLE

Definition 1[9]: Features

Features are an abstract concept for describing commonalities and variabilities. What this means precisely needs to be decided for each product line. A feature in this sense is a characteristic of a systme relevant for some Stakeholder. Depending on the interest of the Stakeholders a feature can be for the example a requirement, a technical function or function group or a nonfunctional(quality) characteristic.

Feature models have a tree structure, with features forming nodes of the tree. Feature variability is represented by the arcs and groupings of features. There are four different types of feature groups: "mandatory", "optional", "alternative" and "or".

When specifying which features are to be included in a variant the following rules apply: If a parent feature is contained in a variant,

- all its mandatory child features must be also contained ("n from n"),
- any number of optional features can be included ("m from n, $0 <= m <= n$"),
- exactly one feature must be selected from a group of alternative features ("1 from n"),
- at least one feature must be selected from a group of or features ("m from n, $m>1$").

the graphical notation of feature models can be shown as follows in Fig.2.

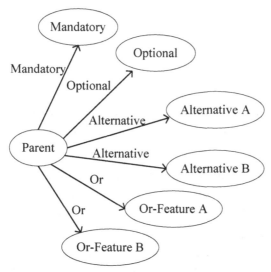

Fig. 2. Structure and natation of feature models

3 SPLE for Magnitude Modelling and Simulation

Feature model for magnitude modelling is shown in Fig.3:

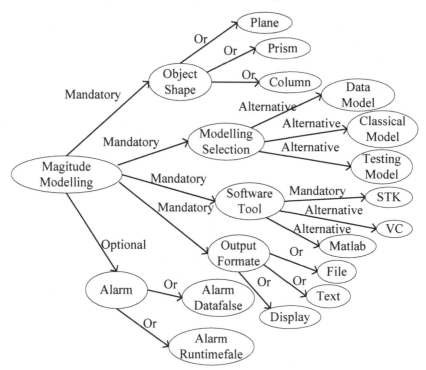

Fig. 3. Feature model for our magnitude modellling SPLE

Each Feature Model has a root feature. Beneath this are four mandatory features-Object Shape, Modelling Selection, Software Tool, Output Formate. When modelling magnitude, it is necessary for setting object shape by any combination of shapes and at least one shape style source is necessary.

Here simple optional features are used, such as the example of the data false alarm. the strict choice among Data model, Classical model and Testing model. STK is needed for all software product, and only one is needed between VC tool or Matlab tool. Output formate coule be combination of file, text,and display.

4   Design a Varible Architecture Based STK

The basic process for STK to magnitude is as follows:

- Set motion parameter of space object,
- Set logitude, latitude and access time of ground station,
- Define geometry parameter, such as vectors and angles between ground station and space object,
- Define reports from STK, which including angles, distance, access time,
- Simulate the magnitude model with Matlab or VC++.

With SPLE method, we design a variable architecture based STK:

- Basic ground station. Creating a new station named StationModel,   as all stations template, and the station attributes such as longitude and latitude are variable quantity.
- Basic space object. Creating a new space object named ObjectModel. And the space object attributes such as shape style and access time are variable quantity.
- Basic scene. Creating a new scene named template, including StationModel and ObjectModel. Define vectors ,angle and reporters between StationModel and ObjectModel. The vectors, angles, and reports could be named as shown in table1,2,3.

Table 1. Vector table

Four prism	six prism	column
ObjBodyX	ObjBodyX	ObjBodyX
ObjBodyY	ObjBodyXOY60	ObjtoStation
ObjBodyZ	ObjBodyXOY180	ObjtoSun
ObjBody-X	ObjBodyXOY120	StationtoSun
ObjBody-Y	ObjBodyXOY240	StationtoObj
ObjBody-Z	ObjBodyXOY300	
	ObjBodyZ	
	ObjBody-Z	

Table 2. Angle table

Four prism	six prism	column
SunObjBodyX	SunObjBodyX	ObjBodyXSun
SunObjBody-X	SunObjBodyXOY60	ObjBodyXStation
SunObjBodyY	SunObjBodyXOY120	SunObjStation
SunObjBody-Y	SunObjBodyXOY180	SunStationObj
SunObjBodyZ	SunObjBodyXOY240	
SunObjBody-Z	SunObjBodyXOY300	
StationObjBodyX	SunObjBodyZ	
StationObjBody-X	SunObjBody-Z	
StationObjBodyY	StationObjBodyX	
StationObjBody-Y	StationObjBodyXOY60	
StationObjBodyZ	StationObjBodyXOY120	
StationObjBody-Z	StationObjBodyXOY180	
	StationObjBodyXOY240	
	StationObjBodyXOY300	
	StationObjBodyZ	
	StationObjBody-Z	

Table 3. Report table

name	FourPrism	SixPrism	Column
Content	Including angle valute of four prism	Including angle valute of six prism	Including angle valute of column

5   Conclusion

Although SPLE is becoming more widely known, there is still uncertainty among developers about how it would apply in their own development contex. In this paper, we proposed our attempt on magnitude modelling in SPLE, where the feature models for magnitude modelling was given, and a varible architecture based STK was designed. With this approach, lots of magnitude modeling researches could be derived, which are useful to exploration analysis on the domain of space object detecting.

References

1. Cza 90, Kang, K., et al.: Feature Oriented Domain Analysis (FODA) Feasibility Study. Technical report CMU/SEI-90-TR-021, Software Engineering Institute, Carnegie Mellon University (1990)
2. Bosch, J.: Design & Use of Software Architectures: Adopting and evolving a product-line approach. Addison Wesley (2000)
3. Buschmann, F., Meunier, R., Rohnert, H., Sommerlad, P., Stal, M.: Pattern-Oriented Software Architecture, vol. 1: A System of Patterns. John Wiley & Son Ltd. (1996)

4. Li, B.-C.: Optical characteristic analysis of space Target. Optical Engineering 80(2), 21–26 (1989)
5. Li, X.-Y., Gao, X.-D., Zhu, Q.-X.: Application of vector method to the calculation of space target ground irradiance. Opto-Electronic Engineering 30(4), 28–30 (2003)
6. Yu, H.-Z., Cheng, Q.-Q.: Research on computing Model of Target Optical Effective Reflective Area. Journal of Spacecraft TT&C Technology 24(3), 15–20 (2005)
7. Czarnecki, K., Eisenecker, U.W.: Generative Programming: Methods, Tools, and Applications. Addison-Wesley, Boston (2000) ISBN 0-201-30977-7
8. Clements, P.C., Northrop, L.: Software Product Lines: Practices and Patterns. SEI Series in Software Engineering. Addison-Wesley (August 2001)
9. Beuche, D., Dalgarno, M.: Software Product Line Engineering with Feature Models, http://www.pure-systems.com

Architecture of Hybrid Cloud for Manufacturing Enterprise

Jingeng Mai[1,2], Lin Zhang[1,2], Fei Tao[1,2], and Lei Ren[1,2]

[1] School of Automation Science and Electrical Engineering,
Beihang University, Beijing, 100191, P.R. China
[2] Engineering Research Center of Complex Product AdvancedManufacturing Systems,
Ministry of Education, Beihang University, Beijing, 100191, P.R. China

Abstract. Cloud manufacturing (CMfg) provides a high-efficiency model to realize manufacturing resources sharing and on-demand using. Though private cloud service platform which has advantages of safety and efficiency is applicable for group enterprise, there is limit of network isolated. In order to increase profits and reduce costs simultaneously, some manufacturing enterprises will combine their private cloud service platforms with public cloud platform to release excess manufacturing resources and abilitiesand obtain more services. After analyzing the architecture of cloud manufacturing service platform, a hybrid cloud infrastructure applied for manufacturing enterprises is proposed, and some functional features of the hybrid cloud platform are described. Furthermore, a mechanism for private cloud combining with public cloud is presented. Finally, some challenges that enterprise might face while operating in hybrid cloud environment are discussed.

Keywords: Cloud manufacturing(CMfg), hybrid cloud, service platform, combination mechanism, linking platform, service confusion.

1   Introduction

With the development of digitization and informatizationtechnologies in the whole lifecycle manufacturing activities, application integration systems[1] with main lines of supply chain management and product management are applied for manufacturing enterprises. Recently, a service-oriented and knowledge based new manufacturing paradigm called Cloud Manufacturing (CMfg)[2-9]is put forward, and promote integration of various information, resource and abilities into a high-efficiency, low consumption and cross-time-space pattern. Using CMfg service platform[3,12,21], manufacturing enterprises can make data, process, equipments and other resources existing in heterogeneous system or platform shared and reusable for all users. And with in-depth research in some key technologies, such as physical resource intelligent perception[5], virtualization[6] and cloud service[7,8],CMfg service platform is applied gradually both in group enterprises and small and medium-sized enterprises (SME) [9].

T. Xiao, L. Zhang, and S. Ma (Eds.): ICSC 2012, Part I, CCIS 326, pp. 365–372, 2012.

SME which is numerous and widely distributed generally connects to public cloud in which distributed manufacturing resources can be virtually described, encapsulated, deployed and centrally stored[10]. Public cloud focuses on integrating resources and capabilities among different enterprises. It has benefits of easy and inexpensive set-up, because services can be obtained on a pay-per-usage model. But it still has risk of privacy leakiness.

Group enterprise which owning comprehensive physical resources and adequate processing capacities and relying more on internal service collaboration, generally builds private cloud for efficient and safe inter-sharing [11]. However, it is a closed system for resources and capabilities sharing, and enterprise can't obtain some low-cost services outside. Meanwhile, some excess resources in private cloud will be idle and waste, because they can't be available for external users.

According smiling curve theory [14], they are the high points in R&D (research and development) and marketing for manufacturing enterprise's value-adding. Though group enterprise owns many departments and subordinate enterprises, it's not enough by sharing resources internal to realize sustainable growth. It's essential to obtain external advantaged resources to promote R&D abilities and reduce costs, and expand market space sustainable. So it's necessary to make enterprise's private cloud combine with other clouds, and that's the mode of hybrid cloud [15-19] in which resources can be shared crossing different clouds.

After analyzing the architecture and functional features of cloud manufacturing service platform, a hybrid cloud infrastructure applied in manufacturing enterprise is proposed, and a mechanism for private cloud combining with public cloud is presented. Finally, some challenges that enterprise might face while operating in hybrid cloud environment are discussed.

2   Review of Private CMfg Service Platform

Li and Zhang et al.[2,11] studied deeply in the architecture of CMfg, and pointed out that the CMfg service platform primarily consists of five layers, including resource

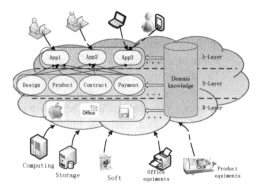

Fig. 1. Structure diagram of private CMfg service platform for manufacturing enterprise

layer, perception layer, service layer, middleware layer and application layer[3,12].The core components are resource, service, knowledge and application, as shown in Fig.1.

- Resource as the foundation

Varies manufacturing resources such as computer and software, are transformed tovirtual resources, such as virtual machine, soft component, model, data, and document.Physicalmanufacturing resources such as drilling machine and milling machine are enabledto be connected intothe networkby using thetechnologies such as RFID andInternet of Things (IoTs), and described as virtual resource calendar[6]. Material, logistics and human resources also can be mappedinto data.

- Service as the interface

Resources and capabilities are encapsulated as services and deployed in CMfg service platform in which services can be discovered and searched using service management tools. Theinterface of services is standardized, so that users can easily invoke services. Meanwhileprocessing equipmentscan be the monitored and operated through these services interface.

- Application as the terminal

In CMfg service platform, there are various applications, such as design, simulation, processing, logistics, business and etc., whose can meet the diverse needs of users.Applications are integrated from varieties of services,and usuallycan be operated through webportaland ubiquitous interaction technologies[13], so that they can be easilyaccessed by using mobile terminals.

- Knowledge as the core

Knowledgebase inmanufacturing domainis constituted of manufacturing knowledge ontology and its formal description [7]. It provides core intelligentsupport for resource virtualization, service management and application integration with the form of data fusion algorithm, fault diagnosis method, and intelligent expert system.

3   Hybrid Cloud Architectures for Manufacturing Enterprise

3.1   Functional Structure

After group enterprises setting up private cloud platforms in their own cloud infrastructures, it is hard to combine their private cloud platforms together because of the respective differences in norms and standards and different privacy requirements. It is a convenient choice to combine private cloud with public cloud which is relatively open.

Private cloud connects physically to external public cloud through high-speed networks and efficient firewall infrastructure (as shown in Fig.2), and joints functionally through a linking platform (as shown in Fig.3) so as to achieve interoperability management of resources, services, applications and knowledge. The functional features of the hybrid cloud for manufacturing enterprise are summarized as follows:

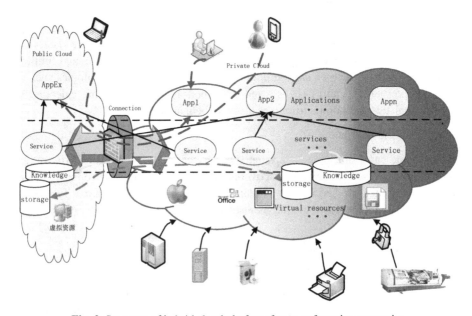

Fig. 2. Structure of hybrid cloud platform for manufacturing enterprise

1. When internal (private) users access to the private CMfg service platform, the function and usage of application and interface of service should be unchanged. It's still handled in private cloud for resource access and perception, real-time data processing and virtualization. In a word,the private cloud platform should maintain its original structure.
2. Internalusers can access tothe public cloud platform, and call for public cloud services as thesame as private cloud services.
3. When external(public) usersaccess to private cloud platform, they can obtain resources, services and applications by permission.

3.2   Combination Mechanism

In order to achieve interoperability in hybrid cloud, acombine mechanism called linking platformis proposed. The linking platform consists of four parts, including resourcesharing management, serviceconfusion management, applicationintegration management and knowledgegathering management. It is a management component for private cloud searching, analyzing and integrating publicservices, deploying its own services, and also searching and extracting multi-domain knowledge existing in public clouds.

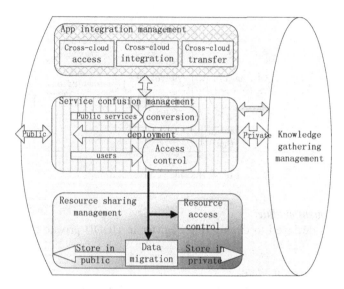

Fig. 3. Structure of linking platform

3.2.1   Resource-Sharing Management

Resource access control module
It is a management mechanism for external user to access internal resource and realizing resources optimal allocation [20], including authentication, resource monitoring, sharing-level evaluation. Sharing-level evaluation refers to assign different levels to resources according classification of internal resources and safety consideration. The levels can be dynamically adjusted based on resource usage and other monitoring information, so as to achieve resource allocationoptimization.

Data migration module
Supported by transmission service interface, structured data (database, etc.) and unstructured data (files, images, etc.) can transmit between differentdata centers.

3.2.2   Service-Confusion Management

Interface conversion module
The essential aim of private cloud linking to public cloud is to call more public services. Firstly, cloud services which have been registered in some public UDDIs (Universal Description, Discovery and Integrations) are found through service search engine in this module. After analyzing services descriptionwith semantic method, it classifies them and extracts some useful information, e.g. basic information,interface information and others. Then, in order to be integrated in private applications, public services are converted referencing to private services interfaces.

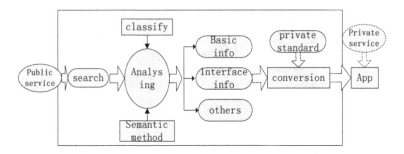

Fig. 4. Interface conversion

Service deployment module
This module is designed to deploy (e.g. register in UDDI) private cloud services in public cloud.

Service access control module
If users request for accessing services, they will be authorized with certain license mechanism. In order to avoid network congestion and services confliction, service monitoring is needed for service flow adjustment, and service scheduling is the key to realize intelligent QoS (quantity of service) management by using intelligent algorithms.

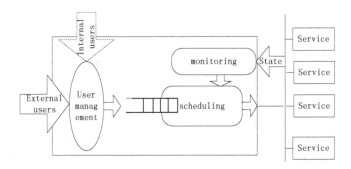

Fig. 5. Service access control

3.2.3   Application-Integration Management

Cross-cloud integration
Services provided by public cloud can be integrated into the private cloud applications.

Cross-cloud access
Users in one cloud can access applications running in other cloud platforms, and be enabled to use any Internet terminal to access application services no whether where.

Cross-cloud transfer
Using transmission and storage services interface and supported by certain license mechanism, applications can transfercross-cloud for deployment and running. And some applications can transferfrom cloud to cloud terminal.

3.2.4   Knowledge-Gathering Management

In hybrid cloud environment, there isvast amountsknowledge in the form of data, algorithms, models, ontology, semantic description and domain knowledgebase. It is essential to search and extract the knowledge distributedin public cloud, becauseit's usual heterogeneous, complex,interdisciplinary and multi-domain. And then, available knowledge should be classified and clustered, and stored in the local knowledgebase.

4   Challenges in Hybrid Cloud

First,it is the challenge oftechnology support, e.g. safety and security. Though, the sharing and reusing of resources are improved, it brings a number of security challengescaused by the structure of enterprise's network changed from closed to semi-open, such as the security of infrastructure (e.g. network, data center), thesecurity of cloud service platform and theaccess security of virtual resources, services and applications.

Furthermore,it is the challenge of business operation model change. In a hybrid cloud, in order to reduce operating costs, manufacturing enterprises will have to adjusttheir organizationstructure and business processes.For example, some departments may be reduced, andsome businessesmay be replaced byrenting services in public cloud. At the same time, business risk will increase, because it's lacking of guaranteeinstability and availabilityby renting public cloud services. So, it is a high-demand for service collaboration management in manufacturingprocess.

5   Conclusions

Though, it's convenient formanufacturing enterprise to buildprivate cloud service platforms for safe and efficientsharingof internal resources, it's essential to combine private cloud with public cloud for the purpose ofR&D abilities improvement, costsreduction and market space expansion.In this paper,a hybrid cloud infrastructure applied in manufacturing enterprise is proposed, and some functional features of the hybrid cloud platform are described. Furthermore, a mechanism for private cloud linking to public cloud is presented.

Acknowledgements. This work was financially supported by the 863 Program project in China (No.2011AA040501), the National Science Foundation of China(No. 61103096), and the Fundamental Research Funds for the Central Universities in China.

References

1. Li, B., Wu, C., et al.: Thedevelopmentof contemporary integrated manufacturing & the implementation strategy of 863/CIMS subject. Computer Integrated Manufacturing Systems (5), 1–7 (1998)

2. Li, B., Zhang, L., Chai, X.: Introduction to Cloud Manufacturing. ZTE Communications (4) (December 2010)
3. Li, B., Zhang, L., Wang, S., Tao, F., et al.: Cloud manufacturing: a new service-oriented manufacturing model. Computer Integrated Manufacturing Systems 16(1), 1–7 (2010)
4. Zhang, L., Luo, Y., Fan, W., et al.: Analyses of cloud manufacturing and related advanced manufacturing models. Computer Integrated Manufacturing Systems 17(3), 458–468 (2011)
5. Li, R.-F., Liu, Q., Xu, W.-J.: Perception and access adaptation of equipment resources in cloud manufacturing. Computer Integrated Manufacturing Systems 4 (2012)
6. Ren, L., Zhang, L., Zhang, Y., et al.: Resource virtualization in cloud manufacturing. Computer Integrated Manufacturing Systems 17(3), 511–518 (2011)
7. Zhang, L., Luo, Y., Tao, F., et al.: Study on thekey technologies f or the construction of manufacturing cloud. Computer Integrated Manufacturing Systems 16(11), 2510–2520 (2010)
8. Tao, F., Zhang, L., Guo, H., et al.: Typical characteristics of cloud manufacturing and several key issues of cloud service composition. Computer Integrated Manufacturing Systems 17(3), 477–486 (2011)
9. Li, B., Zhang, L., Ren, L., Chai, X., et al.: Further discussion on cloud manufacturing. Computer Integrated Manufacturing Systems 17(3), 449–457 (2011)
10. Yin, C., Huang, B., Liu, F., et al.: Common key technology system of cloud manufacturing service platform for small and medium enterprises. Computer Integrated Manufacturing Systems 17(3), 495–503 (2011)
11. Zhan, D., Zhao, X., Wang, S., et al.: Cloud manufacturing service platform for group enterprises oriented to manufacturing and management. Computer Integrated Manufacturing Systems 17(3), 487–494 (2011)
12. Zhang, L., Luo, Y., Tao, F., Li, B.H., Ren, L., et al.: Cloud manufacturing: a new manufacturing paradigm. Enterprise Information Systems (2012)
13. Ma, C., Ren, L., Teng, D., et al.: Ubiquitous human-computer interaction in cloud manufacturing. Computer Integrated Manufacturing Systems 17(3), 544–510 (2011)
14. Shih, S.: Reengineering acer. The World Culture Press, Taipei (1996)
15. Peng, J., Zhang, X., Lei, Z., Zhang, B., Zhang, W., Li, Q.: Comparison of Several Cloud Computing Platforms. In: 2009 Second International Symposium on Information Science and Engineering, pp. 23–27 (2009)
16. Hybrid cloud, http://en.wikipedia.org/wiki/Cloud_computing
17. Sotomayor, B., Montero, R.S., Llorente, I.M., Foster, I.: Virtual Infrastructure Management in Private and Hybrid Clouds. IEEE Internet Computing 13(5), 14–22 (2009)
18. Georg, L.: Hybrid cloud architectures for the online commerce. Procedia. Computer Science (3), 500–550 (2010)
19. Li, Q., Wang, Z.-Y., et al.: Applications integration in a hybrid cloud computing environment modelling and platform. Enterprise Information Systems (2012)
20. Laili, Y., Tao, F., Zhang, L., Sarker, B.R.: A study of optimal allocation of computing resources in cloud manufacturing systems. The International Journal of Advanced Manufacturing Technology (2012)
21. Xu, X.: From cloud computing to cloud manufacturing. Robotics and Computer-Integrated Manufacturing 28(1), 75–86 (2012)

A Study of Fault Detection and Diagnosis for PLC Controlled Manufacturing System

Shiming Qin and Ginam Wang

Ajou University, San 5, Woncheon Dong, Yeongtong Gu, Suwon, 443-749, Korea
taihejiang@hotmail.com, gnwang@ajou.ac.kr

Abstract. Operational faults detect and diagnose to maintenance personals is a difficult thing. In PLC controlled flexible manufacturing systems, there is no inherent automatic fault finding module in controller itself, so additional diagnostic module needs to be develop. Developed fault finding and diagnostic modules depending on measured data from the inspection machines and sensor data. In this work, a fault detection and diagnostic module is described based on internal PLC program signal data which is acquired through OPC Server. The observed or real-time PLC signal data is compared with normal PLC signal data to find out possible faults or deviations. The data acquisition procedure and the techniques used have been explained in this paper.

Keywords: PLC, OPC Server, Fault diagnosis, Hamming Distance, Sequence Checking.

1 Introduction

Flexible Manufacturing Systems (FMS) is generally controlled by logical and sequential functions under the supervision of Programmable Logical Controllers (PLC). The operational faults associated with control processes are often confusing to detect faults and carry out diagnosis tasks. A lot of damage and loss can result before a fault present in the system is detected, hence early detection and diagnosis of faults is important in processing industry. Moreover, it becomes harder to distinguish the root cause of the fault once the fault propagates through the plant. It is the presence of faults in the system, which disrupts the structure of the functional level making it unsuitable for the integration of tasks in the automated manufacturing system.

Hence, this results in the development of automatic diagnosis techniques. In this paper, we present fault detection and diagnosis tool for the PLC controlled FMS. The term *fault* in fault detection refers to the departure from an acceptable range of an observed variable or deviation level of plant operation from normal condition. On the other hand, *fault diagnosis* is a process of identifying and recognizing faults in the system. In addition, it also involves the localization of the fault sources. Faults in manufacturing systems can be divided into general two categories: controller faults and process faults. Controller faults include software bugs and controller hardware faults; in this paper, PLC and PLC program faults. Importantly, basic controller

T. Xiao, L. Zhang, and S. Ma (Eds.): ICSC 2012, Part I, CCIS 326, pp. 373–382, 2012.

hardware faults are common hence; programmable controller and computer manufacturers provide possible diagnostics. In other hand, faults which are external to the controllers are known as process faults. Process faults are broadly defined as the inability of the process to perform in its expected manner. In this work, faults related to process are discussed and diagnostic work performed based on discrete data from process controller. The sensor data in PLC device is acquired through OPC server systematically to perform diagnosis work.

2   Background

In the modern manufacturing, PLC (Programmable Logic Controller) device is well-adopted to a range of automation tasks. These are typically industrial processes where changes to the system would be expected during its operational life and the production systems that feature cost of maintaining is relatively higher than cost of automation [1]. PLC is special-purpose computer, which is designed for multiple input and output arrangements, extended temperature ranges, immunity to electrical noises, and resistance to vibration and impacts. The reason behind increasing popularity of PLC is robustness & flexibility in control. The PLC-program determines automation level of a manufacturing industry. However, because of PLC's inflexible programming system relative to high level languages, its ability in fault detection and diagnosis is limited. The PLC device and control system itself consist no inherent module for fault finding and diagnosis, therefore, additional automated model have to be developed. In this work, the fault finding and diagnosis work in PLC controlled manufacturing system is based on internal data in PLC controller. In the manufacturing systems, PLC is used to control the behaviors of the system. The operating actions of the system and the sequence of these actions are edited beforehand into the PLC control program. As device is set, control program establishes a series of operations of the manufacturing system, which tells the PLC how to control a system.

The control loop of a PLC and the overall model of a PLC controlled manufacturing system can be described as in Figure 1 and Figure 2 respectively [2].

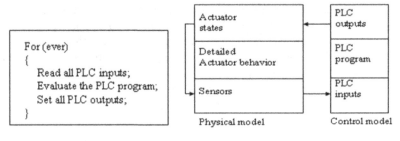

Fig. 1.   Fig. 2.

Fig. 1,2. The overall model for a PLC controlled manufacturing system

In the Figure 2, the PLC controls the manufacturing system according to its control program, which is embedded in the controller, PLC program such as LD (Ladder Diagram) one of widely used programming language in PLC. Here, when a fault occurs, the current states of all sensors or actuators are saved as an array of input, output or flag signals in the PLC memory. In the PLC memory, discrete state signals indicate the operating states of manufacturing system, by which further diagnosis can be carried out. Therefore, the PLC program is the basis of diagnosis in a PLC controlled flexible manufacturing systems.

3   Previous Works

The importance of fault detection and diagnosis has prompted a wide variety of research works and approaches. An overview of different techniques can be found in [3]. In [4], the authors propose a mathematical framework to deal with error monitoring and error recovery in manufacturing systems. Similarly, in [5], a method for detection and prediction of errors is presented. A different approach to diagnostics is used in [6] by H.M. and Y.K., where fuzzy reasoning and X control charts are used. Cause-symptom relations are represented in a fuzzy relation matrix, which is constructed from expert's knowledge or a historical data set. In [7], two methods are developed and combined to implement the whole fault reaction loop from detection to the proposal of a new organization of the manufacturing system.

Hu, Starr and Leung in [8] presents two diagnosis models for control systems for manufacturing systems, one model for combinatorial logic and one for sequential logic. In their paper, they have presented an example of a diagnosis method from the fault-tree analysis field is presented. In [9], Mathias have discussed a method to model event based systems and have described how post-mortem diagnosis based on the use of such models can be performed for PLC controlled equipment. Again, some knowledge based real time diagnostic system for PLC controlled manufacturing systems in reference [10] by Hu, Schroeder, and Starr. In some other works [11], process modeling approach is used to lessen possible manufacturing faults. Tord, Markus, and et have presented discrete modeling approach, for that they have used FSA (finite state automata) in their paper.

From the literature review, most of works can be seen focused on fault detection and diagnosis using different approaches. Although, main objective of fault detection and diagnosis, that is locating possible errors in manufacturing and identifying error nature, less works can be seen focused on their work based on discrete state variables. The internal discrete data, can be used acquired from controller includes operational faults and process faults. The diagnosis of these process faults or conditional abnormalities can only be carried out by measuring state variables. In fact, these variables can not only used to find faults but also to form the basis for more accurate operation fault diagnoses. Therefore, in this paper, we present a complete approach to find faults and diagnosis in manufacturing systems which is based on internal state variables. The process of internal data acquisition is also described in the following sections.

4   Framework

In the framework, in a given manufacturing system PLC is used to control the behaviors of the system. As stated above, when a fault occurs, the current states of all sensors or actuators are saved as an array of input, output or flag signals in the PLC memory. The PLC program is the basis of diagnosis in a PLC controlled flexible manufacturing systems. The set of discrete data recorded in the memory PLC device is considered main source of information for the further analysis. Hence, in the fault detection and diagnosis framework, OPC Server [12] and PLC Guard two sub systems can be seen to acquire data from heterogeneous devices and to work analysis tasks respectively. In the OPC Server, data from different hardware devices can be acquired such as data from the PLC memory in this case seamlessly. For the further processing purpose, acquired data from PLC device is stored into structured format; further detail can be seen in later part of data processing. Developed PLC Guard application involves analysis of acquired data through OPC Server to find out faults and make diagnosis. In this part different techniques are examined and analyzed to achieve objective of this paper. Further detail on the analysis of data can be seen section 5.

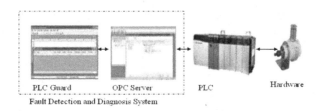

PLC Guard   OPC Server   PLC   Hardware

Fault Detection and Diagnosis System

Fig. 3. Fault Detection and Diagnosis System Framework

OPC is developed by automation software and hardware vendor consortium, OPC is the first automation domain specific component standard (OPC Foundation). OPC standardizes the mechanism for communicating to numerous data sources, whether they are devices on the factory floor or databases in a control room. Vendors can therefore develop a reusable, highly optimized server to communicate to the data source. It can efficiently maintain the data access mechanism. OPC interfaces provide by the server let any client access the server devices. The OPC specification defines a set of standard COM objects, methods, and properties that specifically address requirements for real-time factory automation and process control applications. In OPC's client server model, server applications acquire, contain, and serve data to client applications. OPC servers provide a standard interface to the OPC COM objects, letting OPC client applications exchange data and control commands in a generic way. OPC client applications can communicate with one or more OPC servers from different suppliers. OPC client applications access data the same way, whether the data is coming from an OPC server connected to a PLC (Programmable logic controller system); industrial networks like foundation fieldbus, profibus or devicenet; a supervisory control and data acquisition system; or a production management system.

Every server item on an OPC server has four properties that describe the status of the device or memory location associated with that server item:

Value — The Value of the server item is the last value that the OPC server stored for that particular item.

Quality — The Quality of the server item is a string that represents information about how well the cache value matches the device value.

Time Stamp — The Time Stamp of a server item represents the most recent time that the server assessed that the device set the Value and Quality properties of that server item.

Symbol Name — It is the symbol name of PLC signals. It is the unique identifying attribute that denotes the involved all symbols.

5   Fault Detection and Diagnosis

In the fault detection and diagnosis, the operation and states of the sensor or actuators are monitored continuously. Hence, the methods involved to find possible errors are based on signal values from real operation of manufacturing system. In the Table 1, the normal values for the sensor signal are defined in second row and the observed values are listed in the third row, whereas, first row of the given table describes the signal names. As depicted in Table 1, the variance in the values of signal $S3$ that is 0 in normal conditions, whereas, it changed to 1 in the real-time observation. In this situation, we can indicate an alert to alarm against a faulty sensor or actuator.

Table 1. Sequence checking

Signals	s1	s2	s3	s4	s5
Normal Values	0	1	0	1	1
Observed Values	0	1	(1)	1	1

The working of fault detection and diagnosis techniques applied is based on the internal data in acquired from PLC memory. Furthermore, experimented methods are involved in analysis of data to detect faults and their source identification, for that data value from manufacturing system during its normal operational time is essential.

5.1   Data Acquisition and Pre-processing

Most faults diagnosis applications in the past have focused on fault detection based on steady state data where fault might have existed for a long time in the system and fault might have occurred long before. Therefore, dynamic fault data is used to collect and capture fault data as it occurred. The dynamic fault data is collected including the transition from normal operation to faulty operation. Collection of data using dynamic fault data has been also used in [13]. The main objective in data acquisition is to continuously collect the PLC signal data from OPC server, accessed from PLC device memory and store that information in a data structure.

5.2   Error Detection and Fault Finding

From the section 5, we acquire real operational data values from internal PLC memory through OPC server, and we have complete set of real normal operational, error bug free set of data. In this way, the data value which is acquired continuously from PLC has to be error free, to check that normal operational data value is used. The error in the current operation can be said to be errorless if only it gives data value as recorded in the normal operating time of manufacturing system. Therefore, a methodology to do work needs to be suitable to find differences between two long strings of data set. In this work, hamming distance method is used to solve this problem properly. Hamming distance between two strings of equal length is the number of positions for which the corresponding symbols are different [13]. In other way, it measures the minimum number of substitutions required to change one into the other, or the number of *errors* that transformed one string into the other, it can be given as below.

```
unsigned hamdist(unsigned x, unsigned y)
{
unsigned dist = 0, val = x ^ y; while(val)
{
            ++dist; val &= val - 1;
}
return dist;
}
```

In the hamming distance, the length is considered to be number of differences between two or more strings, it is counted as number of error signals in this work. The hamming distance applied in PLC data applied can be shown pictorially as below.

Table 2. Error detection using hamming distance

Signal	obj1	obj2	obj3	obj4
Normal value	11101	0011	1100	1001
Observed value	11101	0111	1100	1101

Ham_dist=2

In the table 2, normal operating values of PLC signals and observed value in the real manufacturing system can be seen in the table. The signal includes all set of signals recorded during the selected time frame by observer. In the table, the differences between normal value and observed real values from PLC differ in two objects or signals, hence hamming distance value can be seen as 2. Therefore, from this technique, the errors in the observed value can be found in particular object and in a different attributes of that object such as signal value, time value. In the mean time, the sequence of faulty signals can be located and retrieved using time parameters, shown below time chart of signals.

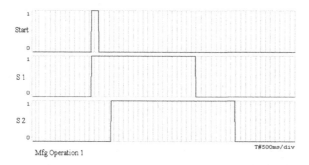

Fig. 4. Time chart of observed signal values

In the figure 4, the time chart of observed signal is depicted can be seen. Since we can traverse the time stamp in our stored database, we can query the time of faulty sequence and retrieve the set of PLC signal values using time parameters. The sequence checking method reduces the time of locating error and debugging it. In the meantime, we can use time chart based on real–time signal values to keep track of accurate sequencing.

5.3   Diagnosis and Debugging

The general goal of fault diagnosis is to localize the source of a fault. Thus, from the fault detection method in previous section, we can find deviation in observed value, now we want to identify the cause of the deviation in this section. In the context of our framework, our specific diagnosis goal is to determine the set of operational assumptions which, normal operation of manufacturing process, if violated, would cause the observed behavior. Since all possible failure modes of the system are numerous and can depend on the material physics of a particular device in a particular piece of equipment, representing all type of errors. The techniques that are described below focuses on the type of errors which can be detected in section 5.2.

5.3.1   Interlock Checking

The operations of work cell in the manufacturing systems are controlled and maintained by switches, *on* and *off* the sensors and actuators. An irregular switching of sensors and actuators can leads to operation shut down. These operations are based on pre-defined interlocking of switches. In this paper, we create a knowledge-base using pre-defined guidelines and interlock information. This knowledge-base information can be compared to the observed set of data. Consequently, any violations of interlock rule can be traced for debugging the PLC based controller system. For instance, the X is a set of states (Symbol Name) and E is a set of events

(Symbol Values), different interlock constraints can be generated in our knowledge-base which are based on the set smooth operational rule of manufacturing systems, can be presented as follows.

$$X = \{s_1, s_2, ..., s_n\}$$
$$E = \{e_1, e_2, ..., e_n\}$$

Interlock Conditions:
$$(s_1 \in X, e_1 \in E) \cap (s_2 \in X, e_2 \in E) = \varnothing$$
$$((s_1 \in X, e_1 \in E) \cup (s_2 \in X, e_2 \in E)) \cap (s_n \in X, e_n \in E) \neq \varnothing$$
$$\neg (s_1 \in X, e_1 \in E) \cap (s_n \in X, e_n \in E) = \varnothing$$

Let the first condition denotes the mutually exclusive State and Events. Similarly, the second expression denotes the combination of OR and AND conditions. The third expression is a combination of NOT and AND constraints. If the observed values of X and E violates any interlock constraint defined in the knowledge-base, it will generate an error message that displays *the symbol name, value* and the *time* of occurrence of the interlock fault.

5.3.1   Pattern Checking

In this process, we mapped the PLC symbol objects collected in the section 5.1. into some specific numerical values. For instance, if M is a set of symbol names and N denotes a set of integer numbers than $M \rightarrow N$, where $N \in \mathbb{N}$. Similarly, a set of binary signal values B= {0, 1} can be mapped to a set of sign values S= {-/+} e.g. $B \rightarrow S$. Converting symbol names, signal value, and signal time i.e. a signal object into some numeric values to ease the task of finding statistical values. In the mean time, we can compute autocorrelation of PLC signal data, depicted in Figure 5. Since autocorrelation is a mathematical tool used frequently in signal processing for analyzing functions or series of values, such as time domain signals. It is useful for finding repeating patterns in PLC signals, such as determining the presence of a periodic signal which has been buried under noise. In this paper, autocorrelation is used to generate a pattern graph, which can be compared with the reference pattern of a normal PLC signal data. As a result, any inconsistency can be traced through the pattern matching techniques.

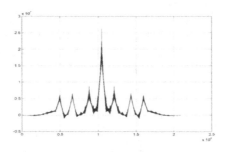

Fig. 5. Generated signal pattern from observed data

As in the Figure 5, in the proposed method, the object signal mapped into numerical values carrying [+/-]. Any faulty PLC signal changes the corresponding sign values, and consequently, the statistical values of a corresponding PLC signal values also changes. As a result, discrepancies between the statistical values of normal and observed PLC signals can be main methods to identify the locations of fault exactly. And which can alarm the user against possible occurrence of operational faults in the system as well.

6   Conclusion

In this paper, we proposed fault detection and diagnosis system for a PLC controlled manufacturing system. Applying the proposed method, we can continuously acquire the stream of PLC signal data from the OPC server, and make a comparison between normal PLC signal data and real-time observed PLC signal data to identify possible cause of operational fault. We described fault detection techniques and diagnosis and debugging techniques with proper examples, hamming distance, sequence checking for fault detection and for diagnosis and debugging we explained interlock checking and pattern checking techniques in this paper. Though, fault detection and diagnosis in this work can meet all requirements for smooth monitoring of PLC based manufacturing systems, however, limitations felt while experimenting can be outlined as collecting optimized sampling data. Optimized sampling in this paper means the sample data which accurately represent the normal data. Since lag of the response time between PLC hardware and PLC Guard program, it was difficult to take optimized sample set; as a result, we have to depend on feasible sample set. Feasible sample set may contain some variance with the normal real-time values. Future work can be resolve the optimized sample set problem and make it more intelligent by designing expert knowledgebase. Meanwhile, we will extend intelligent monitoring and debugging tool by adding more predictive and preventive fault finding features.

References

1. Music, G., Gradisar, D., Matko, D.: IEC 61131-3 Compliant Control Code Generation from Discrete Event Models. In: Proceedings of the 13th Mediterranean Conference on Control and Automation Limassol, Cyprus, June 27-29 (2005)
2. Jarvis, J., Jarvis, D.: Simulation of a PLC-controlled Assembly Line. In: Proc. of 9th European Simulation Symposium, pp. 342–346 (1997)
3. Loborg, P.: Error Recovery in Automation – An Overview. Presented at AAAI 1994 Spring Symposium on Detecting and Resolving Errors in Manufacturing Systems, Stanford, Ca, USA (1994)
4. Kokkinaki, A.I., Valavanis, K.P.: Error Specification, Monitoring and Recovery in Computer Integrated Manufacturing:An Analytic Approach. IEE Proceedings – Control Theory Applications 143(6), 499–508 (1996)
5. Fadel, H.K., Holloway, L.E.: Using SPC and Template Monitoring Method for Fault Detection and Prediction in Discrete Event Manufacturing Systems. In: Proceedings of the 1999 IEEE International Symposium on Intelligent Control/Intelligent Systems and Semiotics (1999)

6. Hsu, H.-M., Chen, Y.-K.: A Fuzzy Reasoning Based Diagnosis System for Control Charts. Journal of Intelligent Manufacturing 12(1), 57–64 (2001)
7. Toguyéni, A.K.A., Berruet, P., Craye, E.: Models and Algorithms for Failure Diagnosis and Recovery in FMSs. International Journal of Flexible Manufacturing Systems 15(1), 57–85 (2003)
8. Hu, W., Starr, A.G., Leung, A.Y.T.: Operational Fault Diagnosis of Manufacturing Systems. Journal of Materials Processing Technology 133, 108–117 (2003)
9. Abdelhameed, M.M., Tolbah, F.A.: Design and implementation of a flexible manufacturing control system using neural network. The International Journal of Flexible Manufacturing Systems 14, 243–279 (2002)
10. Hu, W., Schroeder, M., Starr, A.G.: A Knowledge Based Real time Diagnosis System for PLC controlled manufacturing Systems, City University London, EC1V 0HB, UK. Department of Computing. School of Engineering, University of Manchester, Manchester, UK
11. Alenjung, T., Skoldstam, M., Lennartson, B., Akesson, K.: PLC-based Implementation of Process Observation and Fault Detection for DES. In: Proc. of 3rd Annual IEEE Conference on Automation Science and Engineering, Scottsdate, AZ, USA, September 22-25 (2007)
12. OPC Foundation. OPC Data Access Custom Interface Standard Version 2.05 (EB/OL) (2001-2012), http://www.opcfoundation.org
13. Hamming, R.W.: Digital Filters, Book, 3rd edn.

Walking Speed Recognition System for Transfemoral Amputee Based on Accelerometer and Gyroscopes[*]

Yanli Geng[1], Yang Peng[1], Zuojun Liu[1], and Xinran Wang[2]

[1] Control Science and Engineering College, Hebei University of Technology,
Tianjin 300130, China
[2] Control Science and Engineering College, Shandong University, Shandong, China
gengyanli318813@163.com

Abstract. A sensor system for walking speed recognition is designed. The sensor system is composed of accelerometer MMA7361L and gyroscopes ENC-03, which used to obtain walking information of transfemoral amputee. The sensor system is installed in prosthetic socket. The input signal of intelligence lower limb prosthesis is provided by this system. The signal of sensor system is collected by Quanser semi-physical simulation platform. The signal is decomposed by wavelet transformation and the useful signal is reconstructed. Feature value of that signal is extracted. K-Nearest Neighbor (kNN) algorithm is used in pattern recognition. The results of experiment indicate that the sensor system has advantages of small size, sensitive response, quickly and effectively identify amputees walking speed and so on.

Keywords: Wavelet Packet Transform, K-Nearest Neighbor Algorithm, Walking Speed Recognition.

1 Introduction

With the development of the living standard, transfemoral amputees want high quality prosthesis. Sensors system of intelligent prosthesis can get healthy side and diseased side information. It like sense organ of human and its performance will directly influence safety and comfort of intelligent prosthesis. The previous sensor is used to obtain healthy side or prosthesis information. The sensor which put on the healthy side not only put extra pressure on healthy side, but also causes serious consequences for abnormal gait. The sensor put on prosthesis which used to obtain the motion of prosthesis. The control signal is produced after the movement of prosthesis, so it is only used in passive prosthesis. In this paper A sensor system for walking speed recognition is designed. This system is placed in the prosthetic socket, which could quickly and efficiently collect motion information and identify walking pace. The input signal of intelligence lower limb prosthesis is provided by this system.

[*] This work is supported by Natural Science Foundation of China (61174009) and National Science and Technology Support Program of China (2009BAI71B04).

T. Xiao, L. Zhang, and S. Ma (Eds.): ICSC 2012, Part I, CCIS 326, pp. 383–389, 2012.

2   Design of Walking Speed Recognition System

The composed of two parts data collection and processing, which is presented in Figure 1. Data collection is composed of accelerometer, gyroscopes and data acquisition card. Accelerometer type is MMA7361L and gyroscopes type is ENC-03. Acceleration and velocity signal can get from the sensor. Q-PID card's information collection module is used to collect amputee's hip acceleration and velocity information. Based on SIMULINK which is a simulation tool of MATLAB, this paper presents a simulation model of hip motion measurement system, and the signal is stored in .mat file. Processing unit: The wavelet transformation method is adopted to withdraw signal features, and then used KNN to assort speed.

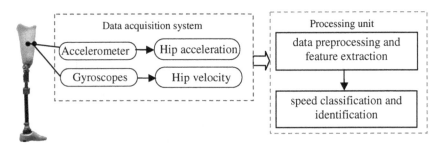

Fig. 1. Walking speed recognition system

Though transfemoral amputee lost their knee and ankle joint, the nerve centers of our brain send motion information to affect side. The motion of hip, knee, ankle is cooperated and coordinated. When we get one joint motion, the lower limb speed is got. Transfemoral amputee wear prosthesis must use prosthetic socket. The prosthetic socket like human's thigh. So the motion of prosthetic socket is the hip motion and motion intention of amputee is detected.

2.1   Hardware Design

The gyroscopes type is ENC-03. This product is an angular velocity sensor that uses the phenomenon of Coriolis force, which is generated when a rotational angular velocity is applied to the vibrator. the maximum angular velocity is +/-300deg/sec., which can fulfill all the speed. The accelerometer type is three Axis Low-g micromachined accelerometer. The MMA7361L is a low power, low profile capacitive micromachined accelerometer. The scale factor is 800mV/ g@ 1.5g. Gyroscopes put on yz plane, which used to obtain the signal of prosthetic socket in sagittal plane. Accelerometer put on xy plant, which used to obtain the signal of prosthetic socket in coronal plane.

Quanser's QPID Hardware-in-the-Loop (HIL) control board is used to collect information. QPID is based on the PCI Express technology for data acquisition applications that require bandwidth to ensure data can be transferred to memory fast enough. With the QPID wide range of inputs and outputs, we can easily connect and control a variety of devices instrumented with analog and digital sensors. Analog input port is used to collect acceleration and velocity.

3 Data Analysis

3.1 Information Acquisition

The QPID are supported by a QUARC Simulink Blockset along with MATLAB. The acceleration and velocity signals are available in versions for us of The MathWorks MATLAB/Simulink software in conjunction with Quanser's QUARC real-time control software. Data acquisition module built in Smiulink shown in figure 2. Firstly QuaRC real-time control software is initialized, and analog signal port is chosen. Secondly HIL Read Analog block is loaded. Finally slope and To File block is added in the module to show the signal and save the data.

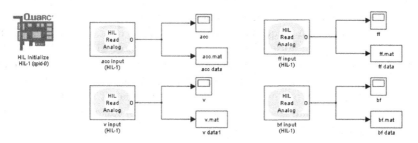

Fig. 2. Data acquisition module

3.2 Data Preprocessing and Feature Parameters Extraction

Mma7361L is used to get acceleration and angle of hip joint. The signal is voltage. There is function mapping relationship between voltage and angle. In this paper x axis is chosen to detected hip movement. zero angle of inclination is vertical of x axis and acceleration of gravity. Incidence angle of x is θ. Component of gravity in sensing direction of x axis is g1(θ).

$$g1(\theta)=g \sin \theta \tag{1}$$

The component of acceleration is proportional to voltage. The scale factor is 800mV/ g@ 1.5g. The angle of inclination is calculated as follow:

$$\theta=(\arcsin(v-1.65)/0.8)*180/3.14 \tag{2}$$

During the walking, the angle of hip change from 40 degree to -10 degree. Using angle measurement device test mma7361. The angle change from 0 degree to 60 degree and the step is 10 degree or 20 degree. The angle is changed from voltage is shown in figure 3. As can be seen from the diagram, mma7361 can measure angle accurately. The movement of hip is detected by mma7361.

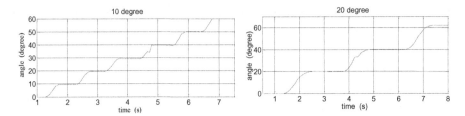

Fig. 3. Standard angle test of mma7361

The sensor system used to recognized walking speed. Subjects walking on treadmill in three velocity(1km/h,2.5km/h,3.5km/h). When subjects walking comfortable collect signal.

Wavelet transform is used to decompose initialize signal. 5-layer wavelet decomposition The function is reconstructed using low frequency coefficient and high frequency coefficient. The method of wavelet analysis is applied to noise signal analysis. Multi level wavelet decomposition of real signals is performed by sym6 wavelet transform. High frequency coefficient of first floor is used for estimate standard deviation of the noise. Tuning the parameters chose global threshold values. De-noise the signal using soft threshold, which provides a theoretical basis for the analysis of noise signals and the measures of noise reduction. Figure 4 shows raw signal , power spectrum of raw signal and de-noised signal of velocity and acc. The de-noised signal can retain characteristics of signal, which can eliminate the dithering and disturbing effectively.

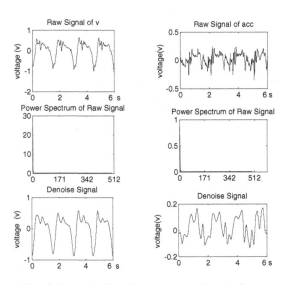

Fig. 4. De-noise signal based on wavelet transform

Wavelet packet is used for data analysis. Characteristic value is extracted from de-noised signal. DB wavelet is used to decompose acceleration and velocity signal and extracted power of raw data. Figure 4 shown that the major power of raw data is focus on 1-10Hz. De-noised signal in figure 4 is reconstructed low frequency signal. This signal contain main characteristic of raw signal. Characteristic value of each speed is extracted. The Feature Vectors are calculated by using standard deviation of the wavelet coefficient. Table 1 shows the characteristic value of accelerometer and gyroscope in different speed.

Table 1. Characteristic value of accelerometer and gyroscope in different speed

Speed		1	2	3	4	5	6	7	8	9
1km/h	acc	0.103	0.102	0.118	0.095	0.1	0.102	0.110	0.101	0.103
	v	0.343	0.351	0.380	0.317	0.296	0.341	0.368	0.336	0.341
2.5 km/h	acc	0.169	0.158	0.166	0.155	0.161	0.158	0.155	0.160	0.153
	v	0.486	0.458	0.463	0.446	0.465	0.451	0.454	0.452	0.439
3.5 km/h	acc	0.276	0.244	0.268	0.282	0.266	0.259	0.268	0.26	0.266
	v	0.606	0.632	0.641	0.633	0.616	0.606	0.641	0.612	0.621

3.3   Speed Classification Based on KNN

The intuition underlying Nearest Neighbour Classification is quite straightforward, examples are classified based on the class of their nearest neighbours. It is often useful to take more than one neighbour into account so the technique is more commonly referred to as k-Nearest Neighbour (k-NN) Classification where k nearest neighbours are used in determining the class. Since the training examples are needed at run-time, i.e. they need to be in In this paper K- Nearest Neighbour is used to classified three speed(slow, normal, fast). Firstly, the subjects walking on treadmill in standard speed. Characteristic value of acceleration and velocity is extracted. This value is the training data. Secondly, the subjects walk in any speed. Characteristic value is extracted using the same method. This value is the sample data. Finally, based on KNN the distance between sample data and training data is calculate. The distance is used to classify walking speed.

k–NN classification has two stages: the first is the determination of the nearest neighbours and the second is the determination of the class using those neighbours. Unmarked vector contain sensor signal characteristic value in each gait algorithm. x_u=[acc, v], acc is characteristic value of acceleration. v is characteristic value of velocity. x_u vector is training data which contain standard speed of acc and v. K- Nearest Neighbour have Training, group and sample vector. Group vector contains three standard speed. Training vector collections of x_u. The characteristic value is divided into three class. y_u=[acc, v], which is sample data which contain characteristic value of whatever speed of acc and v. Subjects walk in any speed and signal is collected. Characteristic value is extracted and classified by trained KNN. Figure 5 shows speed classification.

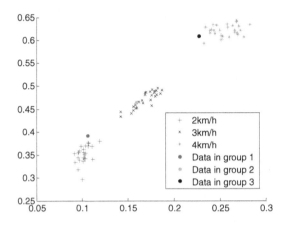

Fig. 5. Speed classification based on KNN

4   Conclusion

Walking Speed Recognition System for Transfemoral Amputee Based on Accelerometer and Gyroscopes sensor is designed. Information acquisition platform is built by Quanser system. The walking data in three speed(fast, normal, slow) is collected. Wave packet is used to de-noised acceleration and velocity and extract the characteristics value. Walking speed is classified by KNN. In this paper using three speed improve KNN, which has good ability of classification in walking speed. In the next research build control platform of intelligent prosthesis. The signal of KNN recognition as input signal to control the pace of intelligent prosthesis. Using sensor system in real-time control.

References

1. Jasiewicz, J.M., Allum, J.H., et al.: Gait event detection using linear accelerometers or angular velocity transducers in able-bodied and spinal-cord injured individuals. Gait Posture 24(4), 502–509 (2006)
2. Godfrey, A., Conway, R., Meagher, D., ÓLaighin, G.: Direct measurement of human movement by accelerometer. Medical Engineering and Physics 30(10), 1364–1386 (2008)
3. Masahiro, Chou, Li-Shan: Dynamic balance control during sit-to-stand movement: An examination with the center of mass acceleration Fujimoto. Journal of Biomechanics 45(3), 543–548 (2012)

4. Huang, H., Kuiken, T.A., Lipschutz, R.D.: A strategy for identifying locomotion modes using surface electromyography. IEEE Transactions on Biomedical Engineering 56(1), 65–73 (2009)
5. Traballesi, M., Porcacchia, P., Averna, T., Brunelli, S.: Energy cost of walking measurements in 96 subjects with lower limb amputations: A comparison study between floor and treadmill test. Gait & Posture 27(1), 70–75 (2008)
6. Martinez-Villalpando, E.C., Herr, H.: Agonist-antagonist active knee prosthesis: A preliminary study in level-ground walking. Journal of Rehabilitation Research and Development 46(3), 361–373 (2009)
7. Yamasaki, H.R., Kambara, H., Koike, Y.: Dynamic optimization of the sit-to-stand movement. Journal of Applied Biomechanics 27(4), 306–313 (2011)
8. Lawson, B.E., Varol, H.A., Goldfarb, M.: Ground adaptive standing controller for a powered transfemoral prosthesis. IEEE International Conference on Rehabilitation Robotics, 123–129 (2011)
9. Sup, F., Bohara, A., Goldfarb, M.: Design and control of a powered transfemoral prosthesis. International Journal of Robotics Research 27(2), 263–273 (2008)

Lumbar Finite Element Analysis and Experimental Study Based on the Biomechanical Properties

Jianping Wang[1], Juping Gu[1,*], and Jian Zhao[2]

[1] Department of Electrical Engineering, Nantong University, Nantong 226019, China
gujup@163.com
[2] Department of Orthopaedics, Affiliated Hospital of Nantong University,
Nantong 226019, China

Abstract. The objectives of this study were to investigate the stress distribution in the lumbar spine before and after the removal of nucleus pulposus, explore the effects of discectomy on the stress distribution and compare biomechanical experiments results with computer simulation results. Three-dimensional finite element model of lumbar L4-L5 was established, the normal and discectomy disc was simulated, the finite element analysis software Abaqus6.9 was used to study von mises stress on the vertebrae and intervertebral disc. Doing biomechanics experiments with sheep lumbar spine whose anatomy and morphology was similar with people, comparing the stress values of the measurement points with simulation results. After discectomy, the human lumbar annulus stress under flexion had an increase of 13.8%, and the sheep lumbar biomechanical experimental results were consistant with simulation results.

Keywords: lumbar spine, finite element, biomechanics, nucleus discectomy.

1 Introduction

Lumbar disc herniation is a common disease of the waist, with a high incidence, low back pain symptoms, which causes a serious impact on the patient's work and learning. For patients with lumbar disc herniation, the doctors often take discectomy to reduce intradiscal pressure, so as to relieve the impact of pain. Short-term effect of discectomy is better, which can ease the pain, but the medium and long-term results are poor. Many patients relapse after a few years, the disc slips again. The study shows that [1], the effective rate of the traditional lumbar disc resection is only 64%, many patients leave with severe low back pain. Discectomy breaks the structure of the disc, which will easily lead to a series of biomechanical changes in the nature, such as height decrease of the disc, stress distribution changes of vertebral, which affect the long-term effects of the surgery.

The lumbar spine has 5 segments, the incidence of lesion is high in lumbar 4 and lumbar 5, in the meantime, the stress of the disc under flexion is 2-3 times that of

---

* Corresponding author.

T. Xiao, L. Zhang, and S. Ma (Eds.): ICSC 2012, Part I, CCIS 326, pp. 390–398, 2012.

upright position[2]. This study will combine the finite element stress analysis and biomechanical experiments to analyze the stress distribution of lumbar L4-L5 before and after discectomy to explore the mechanism of lumbar disc herniation recurrence after surgery, which is benefit for treatment selection, postoperative rehabilitation therapy and maintenance guidance. The biomechanics of the lumbar spine was often studied by computer simulation, we compared the results of finite element analysis with biomechanical experimental results in this paper, indicating that the modeling method was effective and the research approach was feasible.

2   Lumbar Finite Element Modeling and Stress Analysis

2.1   Finite Element Model of Lumbar Spine L4-L5

The DICOM format CT data of the female healthy volunteer was obtained by Siemens 64-slice spiral CT scanning with the thickness of 0.65mm. The data of CT images was got from Mimics software, the lumbar tissue was extracted by threshold and the range of the gray value was 226-1572. Each original image was edge partitioned, selective edited, holes filled and redundant data removed by the modules of Region Growing and Edit Masks of Mimics. The three-dimensional solid model of lumbar spine was smoothed by using Magics9.9 meshing tools. The models of lumbar spine L4-L5 and the disc were shown in Fig. 1 and Fig. 2.

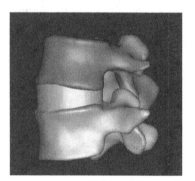 

Fig. 1. The model of L4-5 in Mimics   **Fig. 2.** The model of intervertebral disc

2.2   Materials and Validation

The lumbar surface mesh model was input into ABAQUS before the assignment of the model. After volume mesh processing, the volumetric mesh L4-L5 segments were introduced into the material module of Mimics, the non-uniform, anisotropic nonlinear lumbar model was assigned by using of Mimics assignment function. The relationship between the gray value and density, the modulus of elasticity and density referred to the literature [3], the Poisson ratio was 0.3, the number of materials was 150.

The verification of the finite element model is a very important aspect of the modeling process, the average stiffness is chosen to verify the validity of the model in this study. The average stiffness is the ratio of torque to angular displacement under the load direction, the unit was Nm / °, which makes the research objects comparable even if the loads are different. The average stiffness of this study under states such as vertical compression, flexion, side bending and torsion was between the results of previous studies [4-6], the model was valid.

2.3   Stress Analysis

2.3.1   Loading and Boundary Conditions
There was no relative sliding of the location between the lumbar L4, L5 and the intervertebral disc, the contact type between the disc surface and vertebral body was set to binding contact in the Interaction module of ABAQUS. The lower surface of lumbar 5 was set constraints, displacement and rotation was zero, that was, {U1 = U2 = U3 = 0}, {UR1 = UR2 =UR3 = 0}. The vertical downward load of 500N was applied to the upper surface of L4 uniformly to simulate the upright position force of the person and the torque of 5 Nm was added to simulate the flexion state of human body.

2.3.2   Stress Distribution of Normal Lumbar in Flexion State
Vertebral stress concentrated in the front of the vertebral body in flexion state which was shown in Fig. 3 while the disc stress mainly concentrated at the former lateral which was shown in Fig. 4. The stress cloud in red (the bright parts) corresponds to the greatest force, and the blue (the dark parts) corresponds to the minimum.

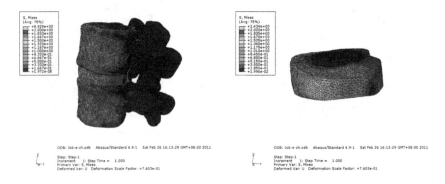

Fig. 3. The stress diagram of L4-5 in anteflexion   **Fig. 4.** The stress diagram of disc

By the graph above, the stress of the disc mainly concentrated in the former part of the lumbar spine in flexion state, the maximum stress of the vertebral body was 8.929MPa, and the maximum stress in the annulus fibrosus was 2.434MPa. The stress mainly concentrated in the front of the vertebra and in the former lateral of the vertebra disc under flexion state while the stress was relatively small in rear parts, uneven distribution of stress would lead to disc herniation.

2.3.3   Lumbar Stress Distribution in Flexion State after Discectomy

The nucleus pulposus was removed to imitate the model of the lumbar spine after discectomy, the same load was imposed to the research object as the normal lumbar spine. The stress distribution graph was got after the finite element analysis of the new model and which was shown in Fig. 5 and Fig. 6.

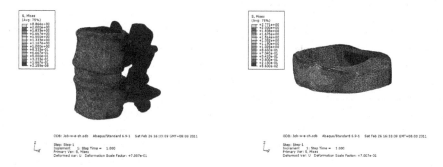

Fig. 5. The stress diagram of L4-5 after discectomy   **Fig. 6.** The stress diagram of disc

By the graph above, the maximum stress of the fibrous ring in flexion improved to 2.771MPa after the removal of nucleus pulposus with the increment of 13.8%. The figure showed the lateral stress was larger than rear stress in the intervertebral disc in flexion state, the movement along with stress difference aroused by residual disc tissue was more likely happen after discectomy which would result in protrusion of residual disc tissue, recurrence of low back pain.

Therefore, patients should pay more attention to the improvement of work habits in daily life after spinal surgery as the stability of lumbar spine was destructed. They should strengthen the protection of the lumbar spine, minimize the frequency of flexion movement, reduce the lumbar injury from uneven excessive stress.

3   Sheep Biomechanical Experiment

It was more intuitive to study the stress distribution in the lumbar spine by biomechanical experiments. Because the anatomy and morphology similarity of the spine between four-legged animals and human beings[7], this paper made a comparison of the sheep lumbar spine biomechanics experimental results with finite element stress analysis results. We illustrated the correctness of the modeling and effective of finite element stress analysis basing on the research.

3.1   Finite Element Analysis of the Sheep

The lumbar spine of the sheep consists of eight segments. This study used the same method to model the 6th to 7th section of sheep lumbar which were similar to L4-L5 of human body. Only single torgue could be imposed to the experimental device, in order to compare with the experimental data of sheep, 5Nm pure bending moment of anteflexion was imposed, and the stress diagram of the sheep lumbar 6-7 before and after discectomy was got after the simulation.

3.2   Sheep Biomechanical Experiment

The L5-8 segments of fresh sheep specimen were intercepted, and the specimens of bone tissue, intervertebral discs and ligaments were retained. The L6-7 sections were used as the research objects. The reason for the interception of the L5 and L8 was the fixation of upper and lower fixed ends of the lumbar spine during the experiment. It would inevitably damage the objects of study during the process of fixing lumbar spine if only L6-7 sections were taken, and which influenced the results of the experiment. Two bases were made by denture acrylic and self-solidifying liquid for denture acrylic, and the 5th and 8th vertebrae of the sheep were embedded in the two bases. Ten strain gauges were pasted on the surface of sheep vertebrae. The specific location was shown in Fig. 7, the left of the diagram represented the front of the sheep lumbar while the right part represented the back of the sheep lumbar.

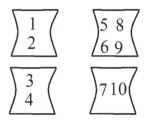

Fig. 7. The location of strain gauges

Two factors were considered in the choice of measurement points. On one hand, in order to improve the accuracy and objectivity of the measurement results, we should choose as many measurement points as possible, on the other hand, the sheep spine was relatively small while the resistance strain gauges and the bases took up some space. Considering the two aspects above, 10 measurement points were chosen in the experiment. The selection of measurement location was based on the results of the finite element analysis as well as practical experience, and positions with large stress were chosen as the measurement points.

Put the model into the corresponding position and the load of the model was achieved by the mechanical testing machine. The testing machine can not impose combined load, so this experiment can only measure the stress of the lumbar spine under pure bending moments. The leads of resistance strain gauges were connected to the strain gauge on the vertebral body to measure the response of each point, which was shown in Fig. 8. The sensitive grid deformed when the vertebral body deformation happened under the applied load, resistance changed accordingly, which lead to the variation of the current, and the strain value was got through the resistance strain instrument. The type of the strain gauge for this experiment was BHF120-1AA and YJ-26 for static resistance strain gauges.

Fig. 8. Experimental operation

3.3   Experimental Results and Data Processing

Each measurement point produced deformation under the applied load, we measured stress-strain value of the points before and after the loading strain. The difference between the value of strain before and after the load was caused by the load. The stress value of each measurement point is the product of the strain value and the modulus of elasticity. Modulus of elasticity of the sheep vertebrae was taken 4.7GPa and we got the stress values from the experiment. The data of the experiment was shown in Table 1 and Table 2. The positive stress value represented that the point bore stretched force and the negative represented the compressive force.

Table 1. Stress under forward bending moment before surgery

	Strain value without loading	Strain value after loading	Difference	Stress value (MPa)
Point 1	-197	-436	-239	-1.1233
Point 2	1904	1400	-504	-2.3688
Point 3	-757	-1103	-346	-1.6262
Point 4	2802	2468	-334	-1.5698
Point 5	-828	-825	3	0.0141
Point 6	3910	3400	-510	-2.397
Point 7	7149	6744	-405	-1.9035
Point 8	-1293	-1286	7	0.0329
Point 9	1949	1976	27	0.1269
Point 10	1475	1427	-48	-0.2256

Table 2. Stress under forward bending moment after surgery

	Strain value without loading	Strain value after loading	Difference	Stress value (MPa)
Point 1	-1658	-1912	-254	-1.1938
Point 2	2112	1762	-350	-1.645
Point 3	-510	-932	-422	-1.9834
Point 4	2878	2759	-119	-0.5593
Point 5	-1302	-1275	27	0.1269
Point 6	2462	2559	97	0.4559
Point 7	5456	5357	-99	-0.4653
Point 8	-1953	-1955	-2	-0.0094
Point 9	2195	2315	120	0.564
Point 10	691	580	-111	-0.5217

3.4   Comparation between Finite Element Analysis and Experimental Results

Comparing the experimental data of each measurement point with the simulation data and results were shown in a form of curve. The dashed line represented the stress values measured, and the solid line represented the finite element analysis results of corresponding points, as shown in Fig.9 and Fig. 10.

It can be seen through the figures that the results of finite element analysis were corresponded to the experimental results. So the sheep lumbar spine model was valid, and methods and results of the finite element analysis were credible.

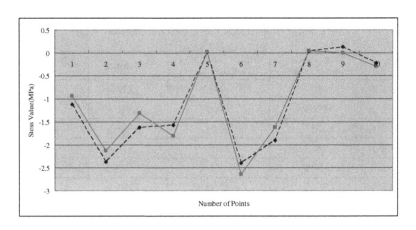

Fig. 9. Stess comparison before surgery

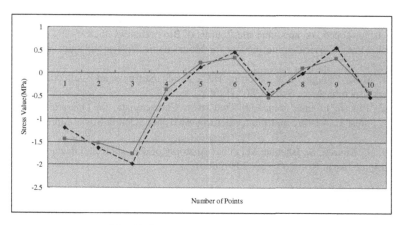

Fig. 10. Stess comparison after surgery

4   Discussion

The clinical treatment of lumbar intervertebral disc is mainly discectomy technique at present, which inevitably leads to the iatrogenic destruction of spinal stability during surgery. The finite element stress analysis of lumbar discectomy help compare lumbar spine biomechanics before and after surgery, assess the stress distribution in flexion state, we can infer the related factors which result in postoperative recurrence of lumbar discectomy.

The data of biomechanics experiment was more objective but also had some contingencies. Through the comparison above, it can be seen that the results of simulation and the experiment were basically the consistent, and the methods and results of simulation were feasible even if there were some errors. There were two sources that lead to the errors: on one hand, the model of lumbar L4-L5 was simplified, the resistance strain gauges used in the experiment occupied a certain area, there would be some errors in finding the corresponding simulation points; on the other hand, the impact of human factors and precision of instruments in the experiment also lead to a corresponding error to the measurement results.

The consistency between experimental results and finite element analysis of the sheep, not only showed the effective of modeling method of the sheep, but also proved the feasibility of building human lumbar model and stress analysis.

Ackowledgements. This study was supported by National natural fund (60975064), Jiangsu 333 (BM2011089) and natural fund of Nantong University (10Z030).

References

1. Korres, D.S., Loupassis, G., Stamos, K.: Results of lumbar discectomy: a study using 15 different evaluation methods. European Spine Journal 1, 20–24 (1992)
2. Wu, J., Qiu, F.: HuangGuSi surgery. People's Medical Publishing House, Beijing (2005) (in Chinese)

3. Morgan, E.F., Bayraktar, H.H., Keaveny, T.M.: Trabecular bone modulus-density relationships depend on anatomic site. Journal of Biomechanics 36, 897–904 (2003)
4. Panjabi, M.M.: Cervical spine models for biomechanical research. Spine. 23, 2684–2700 (1998)
5. Turner, M.S., Clough, R.W., Martin, H.C., et al.: Stiffness and deflection analysis of complex structure. Aero. Sci. 23, 805 (1956)
6. Bao, C., Liu, J.: Lumbar spine subjected stress Characteristic for Operators Using Chain Saw in Forest Harvesting and Finite Element Analysis. Scientia Silvae Sinicae 45, 96–100 (2009)
7. Kumar, N., Kukreti, S., Ishaque, M., et al.: Anatomy of deer spine and its comparison to the human spine. Anat. Rec. 260, 189–203 (2000)

Multi-class Feature Extraction Based on Common Spatial Patterns of Multi-band Cross Filter in BCIs

Banghua Yang, Meiyan He, Yanyan Liu, and Zhijun Han

Department of Automation, School of Mechatronics Engineering and Automation,
Shanghai Key Laboratory of Power Station Automation Technology,
Shanghai University, Shanghai 200072
yangbanghua@shu.edu.cn, {hemeiyan511,lyy8611}@163.com,
295048425@qq.com

Abstract. The CSP (Common Spatial Patterns) has been proved to be an effective feature extraction method in Brain Computer Interfaces. It is widely used for two-class problem. In this paper, the CSP algorithm is expanded to realize the EEG feature extraction for three-class problem. Firstly, the 8 ~ 30 Hz frequency band is divided into eight cross frequency bands and original EEG signals are filtered according to the eight bands. Each filtered signal can be regarded as a new channel. Then the "one to one" strategy is applied to the CSP for three-class problem. Finally, the proposed method is used to analyze the data from BCI Competition IV and the experimental data from our laboratory. The obtained features are input to SVM (Support Vector Machine) for classification. Comparing the proposed method with simple CSP, the accuracy of the former is higher than the latter by 10%.

Keywords: Brain Computer Interface (BCI), Multi-band Processing, Common Spatial Patterns.

1 Introduction

A Brain Computer Interface (BCI) is an interface based on electroencephalography (EEG) which realizes the communication and control between human brain and computers or other devices. In recent years, owing to the developments of brain science, cognitive science, electronic measuring technology and computer information technology, the research of BCIs has developed rapidly and it has attracted more and more attention [1].

The technology of BCIs based on movement imagination is one of research hotspots at present. Some researches show that the mu rhythms and beta rhythms of EEG signals occur the phenomenon of energy reduced or enhanced when people perform different movement or movement imagination. This phenomenon is called event-related desynchronization (ERD) and even-related synchronization (ERS)[2]. The principle of BCIs based on movement imagination takes advantage of ERD / ERS characteristics.

T. Xiao, L. Zhang, and S. Ma (Eds.): ICSC 2012, Part I, CCIS 326, pp. 399–408, 2012.

The CSP (Common Spatial Patterns) has been proven to be an effective feature extraction method in BCIs. However, it can only be used for two-class problem in the pattern recognition. A multi-class EEG pattern recognition is necessary in BCIs. The paper discusses an expanded CSP that can be used in multi-class EEG identification, which takes full advantage of the ERD/ERS characteristics in movement imagination. At present, many researchers use "one-to-else" strategy in CSP to expand it for multi-class identification[3].The principle of "one-to-else" is that one of all classes is regarded as one class, the remaining m-1 (m is the total number of class) classes are regarded as the other class. Then the multi-class problem becomes a two-class problem. The disadvantage of "one-to-else" is that the remaining m-1 is not a single category, which greatly reduces the performance of the two-class CSP. So the "one-to-else" can not get the best classification accuracy. The paper extends the CSP algorithm using the "one-to-one" strategy which avoids the above defect. Then the extended algorithm is applied to the EEG classification for three-class problem. The core of "one-to-one" is to use the CSP to deal with any two classes among m-classes EEG signals. In addition, the necessary precondition for the implementation of the CSP is that we should have enough space domain information, which means that the CSP depends on a sufficient number of channels. Therefore, under the condition of less number of channels (such as the number of channel is 15), the CSP is not very effective if it is used directly. The original EEG signal is filtered using multi-band cross filters in this paper. Each filtered signals is regarded as different channel. Thus the number of input channels for the CSP feature extraction is increased, which meets the requirements that the CSP can obtain obvious features when the number of channels is sufficient. The Support Vector Machine (SVM) is to classify extracted features to test the effectiveness of the proposed method.

2   Introduction of CSP

The CSP was first applied to BCIs by Ramoser etc [4]. The CSP is a spatial filtering method for distinguishing two classes. The algorithm uses the theory of diagonalization of covariance matrix in two-class signal [5]. The main idea of the CSP is to find the optimal projection matrix, which maximizes variance for one class while minimizes variance for the other class. Consequently, the algorithm makes the difference of the two-class reach a maximum.

The original EEG signals of each trial is defined as E_{N*T} , N is the number of the channels and T is the number of samples. The computing process of the CSP is as follows.

Step 1: Calculate the spatial covariance of each trial according to Equation (1)

$$C = \frac{EE^T}{trace(EE^T)} \tag{1}$$

The trace (X) is the trace of the matrix X, which means the sum of the diagonal elements from matrix X.

Then calculate the averages of covariance matrices of all trials within one class (C_l is the movement imagination task of the left hand, C_r is the movement imagination task of the right) according to Equation (2), (3)

$$C_l = \sum_{i=1}^{n} C_{l,i} \tag{2}$$

$$C_r = \sum_{i=1}^{n} C_{r,i} \tag{3}$$

Obtain the covariance of the mixed space C_c

$$C_c = C_l + C_r \tag{4}$$

Step 2: Decompose the covariance matrix C_c

$$C_c = U_c \Lambda_c U_C^T \tag{5}$$

Where Λ_c is a diagonal matrix of generalized eigenvalues, and U_c is a matrix whose columns are the corresponding eigenvectors.

Step 3: Construct whiten transformation matrix and transform the covariance matrix. Firstly construct the whiten transformation matrix P and the spatial coefficient matrix S .

$$P = \Lambda_c^{-\frac{1}{2}} U_C^T \tag{6}$$

Then transform C_l and C_r as follows

$$S_l = PC_l P^T \tag{7}$$

$$S_r = PC_r P^T \tag{8}$$

Finally decompose eigenvalue with S_l and S_r

$$S_l = B\Lambda_l B^T \tag{9}$$

$$S_r = B\Lambda_r B^T \tag{10}$$

Where B is the matrix whose columns are the corresponding eigenvectors.

Then obtain the $N*N$ CSP projection matrix W as $W = (B^T P)^T$. We call each row of W a spatial filter, and each column of W^{-1} a spatial pattern.

Typically, only some spatial filters are selected. For a certain value m, reserved the first m and last m rows of W ($2m$ rows altogether) and removed the remaining middle $N-2m$ rows. The value of m can be changed according to the quality of the EEG signal and the demand of the classifier. However, it can not exceed the number N ($2m<N$) of channels.

The remaining rows form W_{2m*N} matrix with dimension $2m*N$. We can apply this matrix to the original EEG signals E_{N*T}. Finally, obtain $Z_{2m*T} = W_{2m*N}E_{N*T}$ when the original EEG signals E_{N*T} are filtered by W_{2m*N}.

Step 4: Find the feature vector f. The feature vector f can be defined based on log of variance ratio

$$f_p = \log(\frac{\text{var}(Z_p)}{\sum_{i=1}^{2m}\text{var}(Z_i)}) \quad p=1:2m \tag{11}$$

Where $\text{var}(Z_i)$ is the variance of samples in row i. This feature vector is ready to serve as an input for classifier. The CSP can provide a good discrimination between two-class movement imagination tasks. However, the CSP has many advantages only when the number of the channels is sufficient.

3   Data Description

3.1   2008 International BCI Competition Data

The paper uses the Data Sets 2A provided by 2008 BCI Competition IV [6, 7]. This data set consists of EEG data from 9 subjects. The cue-based BCI paradigm consisted of four different types of movement imagination tasks, namely the left hand (class 1), right hand (class 2), both feet (class 3), and tongue (class 4). And each type contains 72 trials, namely the data sets include 288 trials of the training set and 288 trials of test set. The number of channels is 22, the signals were sampled with 250Hz. At the beginning of a trial (t=0s), a fixation cross appeared on the black screen. In addition, a short acoustic warning tone was presented. After two seconds(t=2s), a cue in the form of an arrow pointing either to the left, right, down or up(corresponding to one of the four classes left hands, right hand, foot or tongue) appeared and stayed on the screen for 1.25s. This prompted the subjects to perform the desired movement imagination task. No feedback was provided. The subjects were ask to carry out the movement imagination task until the fixation cross disappeared from the screen at t=6s. A short break followed where the screen was black again. The detailed is elaborated in literature [6, 7]. The paradigm is illustrated in Fig. 1.

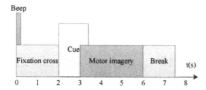

Fig. 1. The paradigm of the experiment

3.2   The Laboratory Experiment Data

The laboratory records the EEG signals using 16-channel electrode cap. The EEG amplifier is a high-precision biological amplifier that is developed in Tsinghua University. The EEG signals are transformed by a 24-bit A/D converter and then are collected through EEG signal acquisition software. The sampling frequency is 1 kHz.

The experiment was conducted by three subjects. The BCI paradigm also consisted of four different types of movement imagination tasks, namely the left hand, right hand, one foot or both feet. The BCI paradigm is similar to the paradigm of the experiment from 2008 BCI Competition IV. And each type contains 75 trials, namely the data sets include 300 trials of the training set and 300 trials of test set.

4   Processing Method

Firstly, the frequency range of 8-30Hz is divided into multiple narrow bands. The original EEG signals are filtered respectively by the multiple narrow bands. The filtered signal in each band is regarded as a new channel, which is equivalent to increase the number of input channels for the CSP. Then the features are extracted using the "one to one" strategy in CSP to the filtered EEG. At last, the features are normalized and output to the classifier. The procedure is as follows.

4.1   Multi-band Cross Filter

The original EEG signals from each channel are filtered by the Butterworth filter through 8 cross bands including 8~12 Hz, 13 ~ 30 Hz, 8 ~ 16Hz, 17 ~ 30 Hz, 8 ~ 20 Hz, 21 ~ 30 Hz, 8 ~ 24 Hz, 25 ~ 30 Hz, which are shown in Fig. 2. We can also select the first six bands. The number of selected bands depends on experience or the classification results. If 8 bands are adopted and there are 15 channels, which forms a 120-channel EEG (15*8). In addition, the bands are overlapped to fully keep the frequency information of EEG signals. The reason why the frequency range of 8-30Hz is chosen is that it contains the mu (8~12Hz) rhythms and beta (8~25Hz) rhythms related to movement imagination.

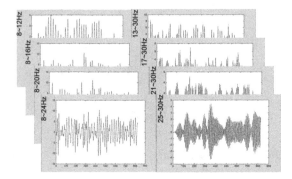

Fig. 2. Eight-band cross filter. The Fig. 2. shows the signals from one of the channels which are filtered respectively by the bands of 8~12Hz, 13~30Hz, 8~16Hz, 17~30Hz, 8~20Hz, 21~30Hz, 8~24Hz, 25~30Hz.

4.2   Training of CSP Filter

The paper adopts the "one-on-one" strategy in CSP, which is similar the CSP method used in two-class. We assume that the labels of the three-class are 1, 2, 3. Any two-class among three classes are calculated using the "one-on-one" strategy in the CSP. Then three combinations can be obtained, they are class 1- class2, class 1- class 3 and class 2- class 3. Three projection matrixes W1, W2, W3 are obtained to the above three combinations, six directions of each projection matrix (the first three directions and the last three directions) are taken. At last, the 18-dimension (3*6) feature vector is obtained according to the three projection matrixes. The time period 2.5s~6s of data for each trial is taken to obtain better performance. The flow chart of the feature extraction is shown in Fig. 3:

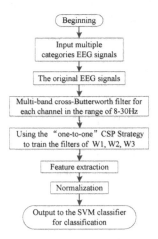

Fig. 3. The flow chart of the feature extraction

4.3   CSP Feature Extraction

The Data sets 2A of 2008 BCI Competition IV is chosen to test the performance of the proposed method. Here the time period of 2.5s ~ 6s is selected for each trial. A matrix of [22 * 875 * 66] is formed owing to that the number of channels is 22, sampling frequency is 250Hz (875= (6-2.5)*250)), and the number of trials is 66. Fig. 4 and Fig. 5 show different results using different methods (method A and method B). The method A (we also call it simple method) includes two steps: (1) Adopt the simple 8-30Hz filter. (2) Use the "one-to-one" strategy in CSP mentioned in 4.2. The method B (the proposed method in this paper) also includes two steps: (1) Adopt the eight-band cross filter mentioned in 4.1. (2) Use the "one-to-one" strategy in CSP mentioned in 4.2. The detailed process can be seen in the Fig.3. As an example, Fig. 4 and Fig. 5 both shows the six-dimensional CSP feature vectors of the left and right hands using the method A and B respectively. The combination of the left and right hand is one of the two classes among the four categories.

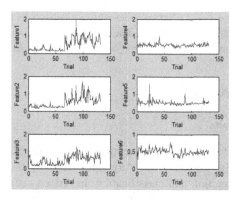

Fig. 4. The six-dimensional feature vector using method A

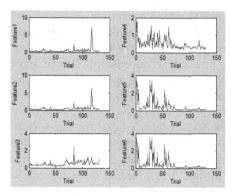

Fig. 5. The six-dimensional feature vector using method B

In Fig. 4, the features of 1, 2, 3, 4, 5, 6 show some difference between the two classes (trials from 1~66 are class 1, trials from 67~132 are class 2), but the difference of these feature is not so distinct. In Fig. 5, the number of channels is regarded as a total of 176(22*8) when the original number of channels is 22. The features of 1, 2, 3 are closed to zero when the subject implements the movement imagination of left hand (trials from 1~66, class 1), and the features of 4, 5, 6 are closed to zero when the subject implements the movement imagination of right hand (trials from 67~132, class 2).

It can be seen from Fig. 4 that the CSP has certain limitation when the number of channels does not reach a certain amount. The step (1) of method B exactly supplements the deficiency of the CSP in frequency domain.

And so, the performance of the feature vector shown in Fig. 5 is significantly improved. Comparing with Fig. 4, the feature vectors shown in Fig. 5 can distinguish the two classes better. In other words, the method B is easier to obtain a good classification effect.

Similarly, in addition, the only first six bands of the eight bands in method B can also be selected for cross-band filters. CSP features resulted from the first six-band is compared with one from the eight-band. The latter can get a better accuracy. And the features from the six-band is superior to the one from method A.

5   Results and Analysis

5.1   Processing Results

In order to prove the effectiveness of the method B, the data of 2008 BCI competition and the laboratory data are analyzed. Any three-class of the four categories are selected for feature extraction and classification. In order to compare the recognition performance, the 18-dimensional feature vector from method A and the 18-dimensional CSP feature vector from method B are both normalized and output to the classifier. The SVM is used for classification, the SVM is a new learning method based on statistical learning theory. It has a rigorous theoretical foundation, can solve the practical problems of the small sample, nonlinear, high dimension and local minima points. For non-linear EEG, the SVM uses the method which is transforming the sample input space into a high dimensional feature space through a nonlinear transformation. Then SVM constructs the optimal linear hyperplane in this new space, so as to realize the linear classification in the feature space [8, 9]. It is an ideal means and tools for classification.

An average accuracy 93% which adopts the method B is obtained through analyzing the data of 2008 BCI competition from three subjects. Fig. 6 shows the result through analyzing data from the three subjects in our laboratory which respectively adopts the method A and method B. In addition, we adopt the six cross-band and eight cross-band filter respectively in the method B, named the method B_1, the method B_2 here.

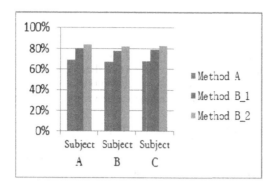

Fig. 6. Recognition accuracy of the data from our laboratory

5.2   Analysis of Results

Fig. 6 shows that the average recognition accuracy using the method B is higher than the method A by about 10%. In addition, when we compare the average recognition accuracy using the method B_1 and B_2, which shows that the result from the eight cross-band (B_1) is better than the six cross-band (B_2). It also shows that the number of channels has a direct impact on the effect of the CSP.

In summary, the method A can't extract the effective feature vectors under the condition of the number of channels is not enough and so the recognition accuracy is low. The method B meets the condition that CSP require more channels. And it makes full use of the time domain and space information of EEG signals. The recognition accuracy of BCI system is greatly improved.

6   Conclusion

This paper researches the algorithm of "one to one" strategy in multi-class CSP based on multi-band cross filter. We deal with data using the method of multi-band cross filter to increase the number of channels for CSP. It preferably meets the condition that CSP requires more channels. And we also extend the using range of the classical two-class CSP to the distinction of multi-class patterns. The classification results of SVM further illustrate that the proposed method is an effective feature extraction method for multi-class patterns. The multi-class pattern can increase the information transfer rate of the BCI system. At the same time, the proposed method improves the classification accuracy of the system.

Acknowledgments. This project is supported by National Natural Science Foundation of China (60975079, 31100709), Innovation project of Shanghai Education Commission(11YZ19), Shanghai University, "11th Five-Year Plan" 211 Construction Project.

References

1. Wolpaw, J.R., Birbaumer, N., Heetderks, W.J.: Brain-computer interface technology: A review of the first international meeting. IEEE Trans. Rehab. Eng. 8(2), 164–173 (2000)
2. Pfurtscheller, G., Brunner, C., Schlogl, A., et al.: Mu rhythm (de) synchronization and EEG single-trial classification of different motor imagery tasks. Neuroimage 31(1), 153–159 (2006)
3. Blankertz, B., Tomioka, R., Lemm, S., et al.: Optimizing spatial filters for robust EEG ringle-trial analysis. IEEE Signal Processing Magazine 25(1), 41–56 (2008)
4. Ramoser, H., Muller-Gerking, J., Pfurtscheller, G.J.: Optimal spatial filtering of signal trial EEG during imagined hand movement. IEEE Transactions on Rehabilitation Engineering 8(4), 441–446 (2000)
5. Fukunaga, K.: Introduction to Statistical Pattern Recognition (1990)
6. Naeem, M., Brunner, C., Leeb, R., et al.: Separability of four-class motor imagery data using independent component analysis. Journal of Neural Engineering 3, 208–216 (2006)
7. Brunner, C., Naeem, M., Leeb, R., et al.: Spatial filtering and selection of optimized components analysis. Pattern Recognition Letters 28(8), 957–964 (2007)
8. Vapnik, V.: Statistical Learning Theory. Wiley, New York (1998)
9. Cover, T.M.: Geometrical and statistical properties of systems of linear inequalities with applications in pattern recognition. IEEE Trans. Electronic Computers 14(3), 326–334 (1965)

Study on the Reproduction of Vocal Fluctuations Using Box-Muller Method for Artificial Synthesis

Tomohisa Okawa[1], Takaaki Kondo[1], Shun Kadoi[1], Kyouhei Kamiyama[1], and Hiroyuki Kamata[2]

[1] Graduates School of Science and Technology, Meiji University, Japan
{ce21104,ce11053,ce21018,kamiyama}@meiji.ac.jp
[2] School of Science and Technology, Meiji University, Japan
kamata@isc.meiji.ac.jp

Abstract. Human speech waveform has been synthesized in many ways. Today, text-to-speech synthesis has become the mainstreams in speech synthesis. However, this technology requires a large amount of data to make high-quality speech synthesis. For this reason, it is impossible to create a synthesized voice of many people. In this study, we aim to create a synthesized speech by focusing on the fluctuations of the vocal cords. By using Box-Muller method, we try to reproduce the fluctuations of the vocal cords. In the Box-Muller method, the average and variance values of the Gaussian function is used. In this paper, we extract the fundamental frequency and frequency variance value from the human voice. We expect that this result can help to reproduce the naturalness of the human voice.

Keywords: Box-Muller method, Fluctuations of vocal cord, Speech synthesis.

1 Introduction

The human voice contains the fluctuations of fundamental frequency, amplitude and human speech waveform. According to a study, these fluctuations are producing the naturalness of human voice[1]. Today, text-to-speech synthesis has become mainstreams in speech synthesis. This technology makes speech synthesis by finding the most suitable combination of sound from database according to the algorithm. It is possible to synthesize the human voice very close to the natural voice. However, in order to synthesize speech sounds more natural, amount of information in the database needs to be increased. So, there arises a problem that the data size becomes huge. For this reason, it is impossible to create a synthesized voice of many people.

In this study, we aim to create a synthesized speech by focusing on fluctuation of the vocal cords. So, when we synthesize the voice, in order to clarify the output of the vocal fluctuations, all other fluctuation was not. By using Box-Muller method, we try to reproduce the fluctuations of the vocal cords. In the Box-Muller method, the average and variance values of the Gaussian function is used. In this paper,

T. Xiao, L. Zhang, and S. Ma (Eds.): ICSC 2012, Part I, CCIS 326, pp. 409–414, 2012.

we extract the fundamental frequency and frequency variance value from the human voice for using Box-Muller method. We expect that this result will be an indicator of reproduction of vocal fluctuations. Using this result, we try to reproduce the voice.

2   Fluctuation of Vocal Cords

At first sight, the human speech waveform seems to be a series of similar shape. However, this form is changing slightly for each shape. Cycle width is also changing as well. The difference in width of the period is called fluctuations of the vocal cords[2]. Method to derive the fluctuation of the vocal cords is shown in the next chapter.

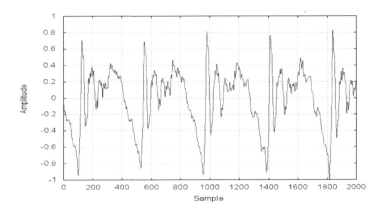

Fig. 1. Human speech waveform of /a/

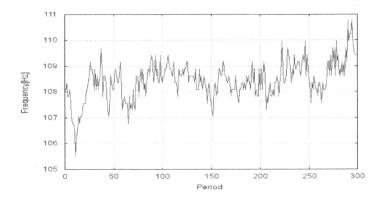

Fig. 2. The vocal fluctuations

3   Reproduction of Vocal Fluctuations

3.1   Extraction of Vocal Fluctuations from Real Speech

In order to detect fluctuations of vocal cords, we find t(0) that the first peak valueis determined. Starting from there, the time until the next peak is 1 component of vocal fluctuation. The cycle fluctuation T(n) is determined from the following equation.

$$T(n) = t(n-1) - t(n) \tag{1}$$

We repeat this procedure and collect the components of vocal fluctuations for simulation.

3.2   Box-Muller Method

We describe the method of reproducing the fluctuation of vocal cords. In this study, we try to reproduce the fluctuation of vocal cords by using Box-Muller method[3]. This method uses the statistical distribution of the fluctuation of vocal cords of human voice.

Therefore, we calculate the fundamental frequency f and variance value σ^2 in order to the statistical distribution. Fundamental frequency f is calculated from the average frequency of the waveform of period 300, the variance value σ^2 is calculated by the following equation.

$$\sigma^2 = \frac{1}{n} \sum_{i=1}^{n} (f_i - f)^2 \tag{2}$$

Here, f_i is the frequency of each cycle. Using this result, we generate a random number according to the normal distribution created by Box-Muller method. How to generate random numbers Z_1, Z_2 by Box-Mueller method is shown below.

$$Z_1 = \sigma\sqrt{-2*\ln x} \cos(2\pi y) + f \tag{3}$$

$$Z_2 = \sigma\sqrt{-2*\ln x} \sin(2\pi y) + f \tag{4}$$

Here, x and y are mutually independent random variables, which are subject to the uniform distribution on (0,1).

4   Result

In this study, we used the voice of the same male voice. We show the result of relationship between the fundamental frequency and variance value from a human voice. This relationship is using the voice data of 300 cycles.

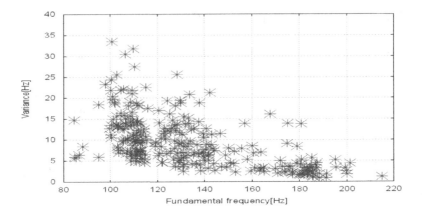

Fig. 3. Relationship between the fundamental frequency and variance value

According to Fig. 3, the variance value is somewhat high when the fundamental frequency is low, and then, the variance value become lower with increasing fundamental frequency. Considering the relationship between fundamental frequency and variance value, we made a synthesis of fluctuations of vocal cords by using Box-Muller method. We show the result of the synthesis of the fluctuation of vocal cords by using Box-Muller method.

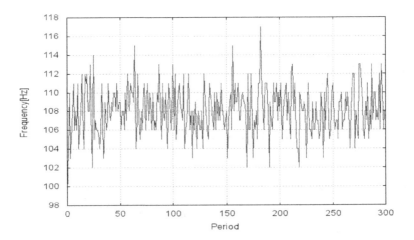

Fig. 4. The synthesized fluctuations(fundamental frequency=108.5[Hz], variance value= 7.35[Hz])

Here, a histogram of the frequency of the vocal cords extracted from real speech and synthesized frequency created by Box-Muller method is shown below.

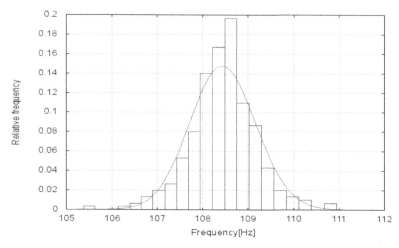

Fig. 5. A histogram of the frequency of the vocal cords extracted from real speech of /a/(Fundamental frequency=108.5[Hz], variance value=7.35[Hz])

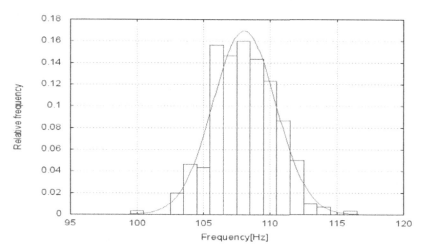

Fig. 6. A histogram of the synthesized fluctuations(fundamental frequency=108.5[Hz], variance value=7.35[Hz])

5   Conclusions

In this study, in order to reconstruct the speech synthesis with highly naturalness, we focused on the fluctuations of vocal cords in a real voice signal /a/. In this result using Box-Muller method, some differences were observed between the reproduced frequency and the frequency of the real voice. Major difference is that real voice has small fluctuations in adjacent frequency, however the fluctuations of the reproduced frequency sometimes becomes large. Also, comparing the histogram, the distribution of synthesized frequency was much the same as frequency of vocal cords.However, there are differences compared with listening to synthetic speech and real speech. By this result, in order to reproduce the frequency of the fluctuations of vocal cords, it is necessary to consider the frequency of the previous cycle, not only to generate a normal random. To reproduce the frequency of vocal cords, distribution of synthesized frequency must be considered something of a time-varying.

References

1. Aoki, N., Ifukube, T.: Frequency Characteristics of Amplitude and Period Fluctuations in Sustained Vowels and Their Psychoacoustic Effects. IEICE A 82, 649–657 (1999) (in Japan)
2. Naniwa, Y., Kondo, T., Kamiyama, K., Kamata, H.: Study on the Artificial Synthesis of Human Voice using Radial Basis Function Networks. IEICE Technical Report NC 110, 199–204 (2011)
3. Box, G., Muller, M.: A Note on the Generation of Random Normal Deviates. Annals Math. Statistics 29, 610–611 (1958)

Shepherding Behaviors with Single Shepherd in Crowd Management

Meng Li[1], Zhiwei Hu[1], Jiahong Liang[1], and Shilei Li[2]

[1] College of Mechanical Engineering and Automation,
National University of Defence technology, 410073 Changsha, P.R. China
[2] Department of Information Security, College of Electronic Engineering,
Naval University of Engineering, 430000, Wuhan, P.R. China
{mengshuqin1984,huzhiwei_nudt,lingjiahong_nudt,stoneli}@163.com

Abstract. Crowd management is to systematically plan and supervise the orderly movement and assembly of a crowd. Shepherding behaviors are a class of flocking behaviors in which one or more external agents (called shepherds) try to control the motion of another group of agents (called a flock), it has a leading application in influencing the behavior and activities of a potentially hostile crowd and bringing a mob engaged in a riot under control. In this paper, we focus on investigating shepherding behaviors with single shepherd in normal situation. In our approach, we use a global dynamic planning algorithm which is the multi-agent planning algorithm in dynamic environment to update the next region occasionally where the flock will be steered to. Also, in order to cope with unexpected events in emergency situation, we combine shepherding behaviors with behavior selection mechanisms which are implemented in rules. The simulation results show that our approach which is validated in an urban circumstance is effective and feasible.

Keywords: Crowd simulation, crowd management, shepherding behaviors, flocking, behavior selection.

1 Introduction

Crowds, ubiquitous in the real world from groups of humans to flocks of insects, are vital features to model in a virtual environment. Various simulation models and architectures have been developed. Whether the behaviors of the crowd are natural and intelligent or not have many relations with the propriety of the crowd models. There are many applications of computer animation and simulation where it is necessary to model virtual crowds of autonomous agents. Some of these applications include site planning, education, entertainment, training, and human factors analysis for building evacuation. Other applications include simulations of scenarios where masses of people gather, flow, and disperse, such as transportation centers, sporting events, and concerts [1].One of the largest areas where crowd behaviors have been modeled is the domain of safety science and architecture with the dominant

T. Xiao, L. Zhang, and S. Ma (Eds.): ICSC 2012, Part I, CCIS 326, pp. 415–423, 2012.

application of crowd evacuation simulators. Such systems model movements of a large number of people in usually closed and well-defined spaces like inner areas of buildings, subways, ships, or airplanes. Their goal is to help designers to understand the relation between the organization of space and human behavior [2].

Crowd management means all measures taken in the normal process of facilitating the movement and enjoyment of people, as well as all measures prepared to be taken in the emergent process of people evacuations. Crowd management can be successful only when viewed as a combination of management of all the crowds, environment and their relationships [3]. This is especially necessary for the crowd incidents in urban circumstances.

Shepherding behaviors are indispensable measures to crowd management. One instance is that army soldiers had to drive a flock of hostile crowd to the place where the mob can do less destruction to the society. Simulating the coordinated behavior of a flock has attracted the attention of researchers in fields such as robotics, games and computer animation. Shepherding behaviors can be found in various forms in nature. An example found in agriculture is a sheep dog guiding a flock of sheep [4, 5, 6]. On all accounts, shepherding behaviors have many important applications in security (e.g., simulation of disaster scenarios and responses); in civil crowd control (e.g., planning evacuation routes for sporting or spectator events); in pollution control (e.g., collecting oil spills); in agriculture (e.g., sheep herding); in transportation safety (e.g., preventing bird strikes); in education and training (e.g., providing immersive museum exhibits and training systems); and entertainment(e.g., interactive games, virtual crowds in cinema) [4, 5, 6].

Our approach is inspired most heavily by Jyh-Ming Lien's innovational research in the domain of shepherding behavior and Bayazit's momentous work on group behaviors in complex environments using global roadmaps, also Avneesh Sud's work is helpful to fulfill this paper. But Jyh-Ming Lien only concerned the local environment information to apply shepherd's steering behavior. And in Jyh-Ming Lien's researches, the shepherd moves like a ghost, i.e., its velocity's magnitude has no restriction which is not the truth to virtual human. Although Bayazit improved the simplistic navigation and planning capabilities in Jyh-Ming Lien's proposed shepherding behaviors with global information, still the agents (shepherd and flock) in Bayazit's work lack the behavior selection abilities when facing unexpected events. Avneesh Sud's research which was mainly concerned about multiple independent agents with distinct goals must be modified to adapt to our approach in which the flock is a collection of intimates.

In our work, we investigate how the global navigation and planning in the form of a multi-agent navigation graph of the dynamic environment combined with finer roadmap-based path planning algorithm enables more sophisticated shepherding behaviors and how behavior selection mechanisms are used to cope with unexpected emergent events.

2 Preliminaries and Shepherding Behaviors with Single Shepherd

A flock is a collection of agents who has its own movement rules while simultaneously reacting to external stimulus such as the shepherd or unexpected events and other obstacles. A *shepherd* is an external agent that controls the movement of the flock, its task is to steer the flock to desired locations. *Shepherding behaviors with single shepherd* are the behaviors in which a single shepherd controls the motion of the flock. It can be illustrated in Fig. 1.

Fig. 1. An example of shepherding behavior with single shepherd: a shepherd control a flock of crowd from initial region (blue contour) to the goal region (white contour)

A *milestone* is any position where the flock will be steered by the shepherd. A *steering point* is any position where the shepherd wants to move himself in order to influence the movement of the flock. As in our paper, the milestones are the output of navigation and planning algorithm in the form of a multi-agent navigation graph. The steering points are computed by finer dynamic roadmap-based path planning. A dynamic roadmap is an abstract representation of the feasible space in a given environment which stores information changing dynamically during simulation.

The *shepherd's locomotion* is the manner in which the shepherd will steer the flock from one region to another region and the flock reacts to the shepherd and external stimulus, while simultaneously guided by its own flocking rules. The shepherd's locomotion is implemented by the *approaching behaviors* and the *steering behaviors*. The approaching behaviors are the manners in which the shepherd will get to the next steering point from its current position in order to influence the movement of the flock. The steering behaviors are the way in which the shepherd will steer the flock from one region to another region.

The flow of shepherding behaviors with single shepherd that can cope with emergent events is as Fig. 2.

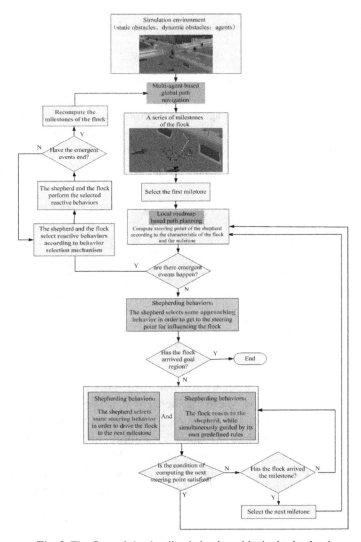

Fig. 2. The flow of shepherding behavior with single shepherd

3   Shepherd's Locomotion and Behavior Selection Mechanism

Shepherd's locomotion is the manner in which the shepherd will move in order to control the movement of the flock. It can be divided into two sub-problems: *approaching behaviors* and *steering behaviors*. In the *approaching* problem, we study how the shepherd goes to the steering point near the flock from its current position. In the steering problem, we study how the shepherd steers the flock toward the milestone [4, 5, 6]. Jyh-Ming Lien proposed three approaching behaviors: *using a straight line, using a safe zone, using a dynamic roadmap* and three steering behaviors: *straight behind the flock, side-to-side behind the flock, turning the flock.* Turning the flock can be divided into *stop-turn steering* and *pre-turn steering*.

3.1   Approaching Behaviors

Using a Straight Line is the way having the shepherd move in a straight line from its current position to the steering point [4]. *Using a Safe Zone* is the way the shepherd using the safe zone to get from its current position to the steering point. A safe zone is the region surrounding the flock outside of which the shepherd will not cause the flock to separate into several flocks. *Using a Dynamic Roadmap* is the way to use micromesh roadmap-based path planning algorithm to compute movement path from its current position to the steering point. These three approaching behaviors are illustrated in Fig. 3.

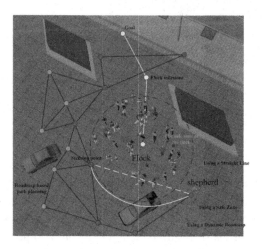

Fig. 3. Three approaching behaviors of the shepherd

3.2   Steering Behaviors

Straight Behind the Flock is the way in which the shepherd moves straight behind the flock. *Side-to-Side Behind the Flock* is the way in which the shepherd moves repeatedly from one side of the flock to the other as it advances behind the flock [4]. *Turning the Flock* the way in which the shepherd try to change the moving direction of the flock. Specifically, let $\vec{v}_f$ be the average moving direction of the flock and let be the desired moving direction of the flock, i.e., the direction from the center of the flock to the next milestone. The angle between $\vec{v}_f$ and $\vec{v}_m$ is represented as . Intuitionisticly, *stop-turn steering* is the manner in which the shepherd places the next steering point ahead of the flock. In *stop-turn steering*, the velocity's magnitude of the flock reduces to zero at first, then the shepherd forces the flock changing its direction to $\vec{v}_m$ in normal velocity's magnitude. In *pre-turn steering*, the shepherd forces the flock changing its direction to $\vec{v}_m$, while the velocity's magnitude isn't changed. The steering point of the shepherd is placed as Fig. 4 when $\vec{v}_m < \vec{v}_f$.

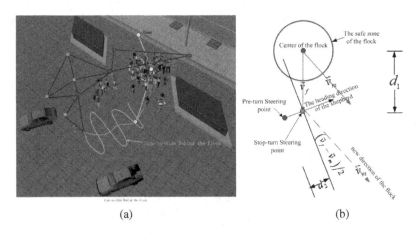

(a)   (b)

Fig. 4. The steering behaviors of the shepherd. *(a) Straight Behind the Flock and Side-to-Side Behind the Flock. (b) Turning the Flock.*

From Fig. 4(a), we can see that *Straight Behind the Flock* method has the problem of causing the flock to become separated, while *Side-to-Side Behind the Flock* can avoid this problem. In Fig. 4(b), how the steering points related with *Turning the Flock* are placed is illustrated, in which d_1 and d_2 are predefined parameters related with influence degree of the shepherd to the flock. It can be cope with in like manner when $\vec{v}_m > \vec{v}_f$. The rules that *Turning the Flock* will be used are as follows:

If $\angle_{fm}$ is smaller than $\angle_{\mu 1}$, **Then** the shepherd selects *Straight Behind the Flock* steering behavior.

If $\angle_{fm}$ is smaller than $\angle_{\mu 2}$, **Then** the shepherd selects *Side-to-Side Behind the Flock* steering behavior.

If $\angle_{fm}$ is bigger than $\angle_{\mu 2}$ and $\angle_{fm}$ is smaller than 90°, **Then** the shepherd selects *pre-turn steering* behavior.

If $\angle_{fm}$ is bigger than 90°, **Then** the shepherd selects *stop-turn steering* behavior.

$\angle_{\mu 1}$ and $\angle_{\mu 2}$ ($\angle_{\mu 2} > \angle_{\mu 1}$) are predefined parameters.

3.3   Behavior Selection Mechanism when Emergent Events Happen

In this paper, priority-based behavior selection mechanism is applied. According to priority order from high to low, we define the following basis behaviors which are implemented in rules to cope with emergent events. When emergent events happen, the shepherd and the members of the flock will select the basis behaviors according to the precondition and priority in Table 1.

Table 1. The basis behaviors used when emergent events happen

Behaviour Type	Rules	Applied agents	Description
succoring	**If** the shepherd finds any agent which can not find its way when fleeing the dangerous area **Then** the shepherd changes its direction to the agent	Shepherd	Helping some members of the flock to find its way
Conceallin g and Cowering	**If** the agent find any large building which can protect it, **Then** the agent stays in the building	Flock	Stay at the place far from the event and physically submissive, quiet.
Watching with Curiosity	**If** the agent's distance from the event is bigger than c_2 and the number of the agents in the dagerous area is bigger than N_1, **Then** the agent changes its direction to the event and its velocity is set to zero	Flock	Watching some target with some attention curiously
congestion behavior	**If** the lateral dispersion is bigger than the clearance of passing through **Then** the agents form a formation (e.g. a column formation) to pass	Flock	The agents form a formation to pass through a narrow space.
Flocking behavior	**If** true **Then** the agent's movement is guided by flocking rules (separation, alignment, cohesion)	Flock	The most initial behaviors that can be found in flocks of birds our fishes.

4   Multi-agent Based Global Path Planning

The *Multi-agent Navigation Graph (MaNG)* is used to provide a novel approach for efficient path planning and navigation of multiple agents in complex dynamic environment depending on the global information. The MaNG computes paths of maximal clearance for a group of moving agents with different goals simultaneously and does not require a separate path planning data structure for each virtual agent [11]. However, Avneesh Sud's concerned only the multi-agent navigation when multiple virtual agents move independently. In our approach, the members of the flock have close relations that guided by flocking rules, i.e., separation, alignment and cohesion rules. In our approach, the flock's underlying congestion is taken into consideration. And we use congestion behaviors of the flock to get the flock through the place where the congestion happens. Our global path planning algorithm is as follows:

Multi-agent based global path planning for flocks

Require: flock P is a set of agents $\{p_i\}$ $i=1,...,N_a$, first-order and second-order Voronoi diagrams, goal region of the flock: g_{flock}, current simulation time T.

1:    for i=1... N_a

2:                compute the current underlying congestion parameters: Lateral dispersion $Lat(T)$ of the

       flock

3:    end for

4:    compute the current center of the flock $center_p(T)$

5:    compute the multi-agent Navigation Graph: MaNG($center_p(T)$) of the flock according to the first-order and second-order Voronoi diagrams and $center_p(T)$

6:    compute a series of Milestones $\{M_i\}$ $i=1,...,N_m$ of maximal clearance for the flock from other obstacles based on the MaNG($center_p(T)$)

7:    compute the clearance of the flock from other obstacles $clear(T)$

8:    if $Lat(T)$ is bigger than $clear(T)$ then

9:                the flock takes congestion behaviors which are implemented in rules:
                If $Lat(T)$ is bigger than $clear(T)$, then the flock form a formation that can
                pass through

10:               end If

11:   end if

12:   return Milestones $\{M_i\}$ $i=1,...,N_m$ and the formation of the flock

---

5   Experimental Results

In our simulation, we employ a human animation software package called DI-Guy. We suppose two cases of scenarios to prove our model: a normal situation and

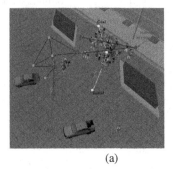   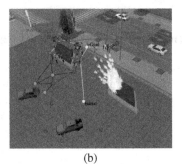

(a)   (b)

Fig. 5. Simulation results in normal situation (a) and emergent situation (b) $\angle_{\mu 1}=10^o$, $\angle_{\mu 2}=20^o$, d_1 is double of the perception distance of the agent $d_2=\frac{1}{4}d_1$, $c_1=\frac{1}{8}d_1$, $c_2=\frac{1}{4}d_1$, $c_3=\frac{1}{2}d_1$

an emergent situation in which a fire near the flock happens when the simulation time is at 60s. Fig. 5(a) gives the superposed snapshots of behavior of the flock and the key steering points (the positions at which the soldier is) of the single shepherd. Fig. 5(b) shows that the single shepherd's moving trajectories (red lines). Simultaneously the flock is separated into four sub-flocks with each one's milestones (the pink dot) are recomputed by global path planning.

6   Summary

In this paper we have presented the shepherding behaviors with single shepherd to crowd management application. In our approach, we incorporated shepherding behaviors with emergent events coping method using several basis behaviors. But, the global and the local roadmap based path planning algorithms still need further researches.

Acknowledgments. This paper was supported by national natural science foundation (61170160).

References

1. Thalmann, D., Raupp Musse, S.: Crowd Simulation. Springer, London (2007)
2. Pelechano, N., Allbeck, J., Badler, N.I.: Virtual Crowds: Methods, Simulation, and Control. Morgan&Claypool Publishers (2008)
3. Shi, J.: Crowd Management for Large-scale Outdoor Events—Multi-agent Based Modeling and Simulation of Crowd behaviors. Ph.D thesis. The Chinese University of Hong Kong, Hong Kong, China (2006)
4. Lien, J.-M., Bayazit, O.B., Sowell, R.-T., Rodriguez, S., Amato, N.M.: Shepherding behaviors. In: Proc. IEEE Int. Conf. Robot. Autom (ICRA), pp. 4159–4164 (2004)
5. Lien, J.-M., Rodriguez, S., Malric, J.-P., Amato, N.M.: Shepherding Behaviors with Multiple Shepherds. In: Proc. IEEE Int. Conf. Robot. Autom (ICRA), pp. 3413–3418 (2005)
6. Vo, C., Harrison, J.F., Lien, J.-M.: Behavior-Based Motion Planning for Group Control. In: IEEE/RSJ, International Conference on Intelligent Robots and Systems, pp. 3768–3773 (2009)
7. Shao, W., Terzopoulis, D.: Autonomous pedestrians. Graphical Models, 246–274 (2007)
8. Vaughan, R.T., Sumpter, N., Henderson, J., Frost, A., Cameron, S.: Experiments in automatic flock control. J. Robot. and Autonom. Sys. 31, 109–117 (2000)
9. Bayazit, O.B., Lien, J.-M., Amato, N.M.: Better Group Behaviors in Complex Environments with Global Roadmaps. In: Proc. Int. Conf. on the Sim. and Syn. of Living Sys (Alife), Sydney, Australia, pp. 362–370 (2002)
10. Bayazit, O.B., Lien, J.-M., Amato, N.M.: Better Group Behaviors using Rule-Based Roadmaps. In: Proc. Int. Wkshp. on Alg. Found. of Rob. (WAFR), Nice, France, pp. 95–111 (2002)
11. Sub, A., Andersen, E., Curtis, S., Lin, M., Manocha, D.: Real-time Path Planning in Dynamic Virtual Environments Using Multi-agent Navigation Graphs. Transaction on Visualization and Computer Graphics, 526–538 (2008)

Finite Element Analysis of Asymptomatic TMJ Disc during Mouth Opening

Shuang Ren[1], Qihong Li[2], and Qiguo Rong[1,*]

[1] College of Engineering, Peking University
Beijing 100871, P.R. China
[2] School of Stomatology, Fourth Military Medical University
Xi'an 710032, China
xixishuang123@126.com, qrong@pku.edu.cn

Abstract. In the temporomandibular joint (TMJ), overloading induced by big mouth opening appears to be important in the casade of events leading to temporomandibular disorders (TMD). In this study, the stress distribution of the disc was explored during big mouth opening. For this purpose, finiteelement models of the disc of different mouth opening degree were used. The disc was loaded with its real displacement for 18 different states of mouth opening. In the model, the posterior zone suffered higher tensile stress, and the stress level increased with the progress of the opening movement. The compressive stress level in the intermediate zone is much smaller, and kept unchanged through mouth opening. Lower tangential stresses were found in the healthy articular disc during mouth opening. This indicates that stress distribution in the articular disc changed with the progress of the opening movement. Excessive mouth opening can induce tissue damage.

Keywords: TMD, articular disc, stress distribution, FEM.

1   Introduction

Functional overloading of the TMJ plays a major role in the etiology of TMD. Condylar resorption and disc perforation are most caused by excessive compressive and shear stresses. and the processof disc displacement may result inbreak of biomechanical equilibrium in the TMJ. Therefore, stress distribution in the TMJ could greatly help us understand the initiation and progression of TMD.

Analysis of joint load distribution cannot be performed experimentally in human. The finite-element (FE) method has been proven to be a suitable tool for approximating the distribution of loads in the structures of the TMJ. It can be used to analyze the stress distribution patterns in the TMJ tissues after application of force or deformation. Most of finite element (FE) analyses were focused on the clenching movement, because the maximum of TMJ loading arises at maximum clenchingbehavior. However, TMJ experiences various loading modes not only

---

* Corresponding author.

T. Xiao, L. Zhang, and S. Ma (Eds.): ICSC 2012, Part I, CCIS 326, pp. 424–431, 2012.
© Springer-Verlag Berlin Heidelberg 2012

during clenching but also during mouth opening. Furthermore, the condylar movement during mouth opening produces remarkable disc motion and deformation. Up to now, few studies have been reported to dynamically simulate the disc behaviors, considering disc displacement and deformation during mouth opening. The aim of this study is therefore to compare the stresses in the disc with different degrees of mouth opening by FE models based on MR images from an asymptomatic TMJ disc.

2   Material and Methods

The right TMJ of a 14-year-old female volunteer was scanned by a MR scanner with no history of TMJ disorders. From the contiguous sagittal slices (3mm) of MR images, the contours of the glenoid fossa, condyle and the articular disc were manually traced for the 19 different positions of mouth opening degrees(6-25mm). And spline fitting points of the glenoid fossa, condyle and the articular disc were traced from every MR images by AutoCAD. Two-dimensional FE models(states NO A1-19) of articular disc for every degree of mouth opening were developed with the ANSYS program, and meshed with quadrilateral element Plane 183. Therefore there were 273 nodes in each contour for one state, and there was a one-to-one correspondence between nodes in every two states. There were totally 5952 nodes and 584 elements for one asymptomatic model.

The material properties of the articular disc were modeled using a linear elastic model reported in the literature [1]. And the Young's modulus of the disc was 44.1MPa, while the Poisson's ratio was 0.4.

To analyze the variation of stress distribution in the articular disc during its movement, the model was not restrained.

Disc loading was simulated by the displacement loading during its movement (Fig.1). Every node on the contour of A1 was constrained by a displacement, which was the difference with the corresponding nodes on the contour of other status.

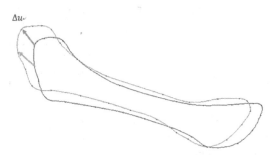

Fig. 1. Disc loading was simulated by displacement. Every node on the contour of A1 was constrained by a displacement, which was the difference with the corresponding nodes on the contour of other status.

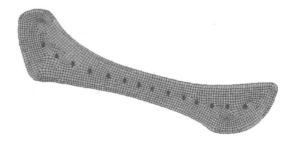

Fig. 2. Path from the anterior band to the posterior band in the disc

Stress analysis was performed by the FE analysis program, ANSYS. The von Mises stress, the first principle stress, the shear stress and the third principle stress distribution in the TMJ disc were evaluated during the movement of the TMJ disc. The stress along the disc were evaluated by establishing a path form the anterior band to the posterior band in the disc(Fig. 2). Stress variation between different status were evaluated by a selecting set of one hundred centralized elements in the anterior, medial, and the posterior zone of the disc, respectively.

3   Results

The maximum principle stress, the minimum principle stress, the von Mises stress, and the shear stress distributions in the disc at states (A02-A19) were displayed in Fig.3. For different degree of mouth opening, the pattern of stress distribution in the disc does not change markedly. The maximum principle stress and the von Mises stress of the anterior band and the posterior band were higher than the medial band. The minimum principle stress of the medial band was a negative value. And the absolute value was lower than that of the anterior band and the posterior band. The stress in the disc was generally well-distributed, and a stress concentration area was located in the lateral part of the disc because of the displacement loading. In the process of the opening movement, the maximum and minimum principle stress of the anterior band and the posterior band were positive and large, which demonstrated that the anterior and posterior band of the disc experienced greater tensile stresses. With different degree of mouth opening, the medial band of the disc experienced compressive stresses, because the maximum and the minimum principle stresses were both negative.

For the different states of mouth opening, the maximum principle stress, the minimum principle stress, von Mises stress and the shear stress of the fourteen marked nodes of the disc were shown in Fig. 4. It can be seen from the figures, that the maximum and the minimum principle stress of the disc along the path of the marked nodes were varied like a parabola, which meant the anterior and the posterior band of the disc experienced larger stress than the medial band. In the process of mouth opening, the disc experienced shear stresses. And the stresses in the anterior band were larger than those in posterior band.

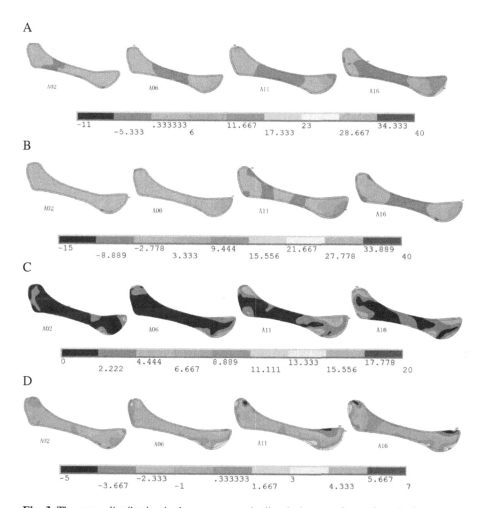

Fig. 3. The stress distribution in the asymptomatic disc during mouth opening. A: the maximum principle stress, B: the minimum principle stress, C: the von Mises stress, D: the shear stress.

Average stress curves of the anterior band, the medial band, and the posterior band of the disc were show in Fig 5.For the anterior band of the disc, as the degree of mouth opening increased, average of the maximum principle stress increased, while the minimum principle stress was positive, which showed that the anterior band mainly experienced tensile stress, and it increased as the degree of mouth opening increased. During the opening process, the anterior band hadexperienced shear stress, which was a small value and not obviously changed with the initial stage. The shear stress of the anterior band increased obviously after state A06, and reached its maximum value in state A15. Von Mises stress of the anterior band had an increasing tendency during the opening process.

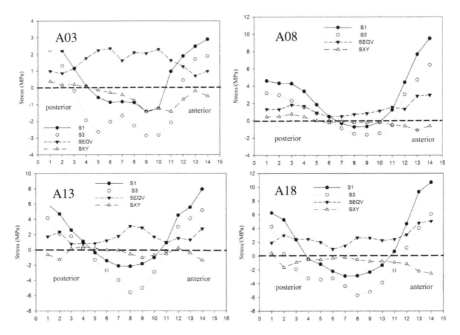

Fig. 4. Stress distribution along the defined path of the disc for different statesof mouth opening

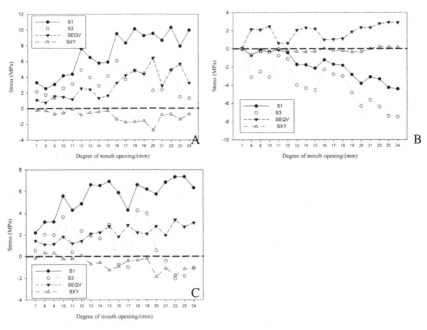

Fig. 5. Average stress of the disc for different states of mouth opening. A:in the anterior band, B:in the medial band, C:in the posterior band.

For the medial band of the disc, the maximum principle stress and the von Mises stress were markedly smaller than those in the anterior and the posterior band during the mouth opening process. The maximum principle stress of the medial band was negative, and decreased gradually as degree of mouth opening increased, which showed the medial band of the disc experienced increasing compressive stress during mouth opening. During the opening process, the medial band experienced a small shear stress, which was not changed markedly.

For the posterior band of the disc, during the mouth opening process, the maximum principle stress was slightly smaller than the anterior band, and it increased gradually during the process, while the minimum principle stress of the posterior band was negative in some opening states. What from the above showed the posterior band of the disc experienced increasing tensile stress, and may experience compressive stress in some states at the same time. The posterior band of the disc experienced an increasing shear stress during the opening process.

4   Discussion

Study of the stress distribution in the TMJ during the functional movement of the TMJ is very important in theory study and clinical treatment. There are wide ranges of study at the present [2], however, most researchers traced the TMJ moving trajectory using mandibular movement kinesiograph(MKG), on the basis of which finite element model was established, and mandible displacement was then loaded in the model to analyze the stress distribution of TMJ. Some researchers applied a rigid motion model, and a simulated force of masticatory muscles was imposed to realize functional movement of the mandible, and then to analyze the stress distribution of TMJ. But these two methods both ignore deformation and displacement of the disc during movement of the TMJ. Because of the structural and functional characteristics of the disc, deformation and displacement of the disc could markedly influence stress distribution of the TMJ. Thus, biomechanical study on the TMJ should fully consider deformation and displacement of the disc [3].

MR images could reflect the shape of the disc, as well as displacement and deformation in different mouth opening states. Finite element model based on MR images is closer to its true shape. This study analyzed the strain of the disc based on its morphological changes. Furthermore, stress distribution was calculated by the constitutive equation, so the results obtained could really reflect actual stress distribution of the disc.

In this study, displacement loading was calculated by coordinate difference of corresponding nodes. However, in practice, a certain node may not move properly to the corresponding node. Therefore, there is a certain error in the accuracy of the model. To seek out the accurate corresponding node is what to be improved in the future.

In this study, stress concentration appeared on the lateral part near the edge of the disc. This may be caused by the boundary effect, and these values were ignored.

These values won't make a difference of the results as there was no boundary node or element selected to analyze.

Mouth opening, which related to mastication, talking and many other functional movements, is the main functional movement of temporomandibular joint. Study on mouth opening has important implications. Opening movement has three stages, small mouth opening, big mouth opening and maximum mouth opening. In the process of small mouth opening, the condylar only rotates; the disc is almost fixed. In the process of big mouth opening, the condylar not only rotates but also glides; the disc along with the condylar moves to antero-inferior direction. In the process of the maximum mouth opening, the condylar stops at the joint turbercle and only rotates.

In this study, the minimum degree of mouth opening is 11mm, while the maximum degree is 29mm. Big mouth opening is simulated in this study, thus the disc and the condylar both have large displacement and deformation. In this study, the first state A01 was chosen as a foundation, and other states were compared with it to analyze stress distribution.

Tanaka's [1]research shows that stress distribution in the asymptomatic joint increases with the increase of opening degree during the opening process. In this study, von Mises stress of the disc increases with increase of opening degree. Thus over-opening of mouth should be avoided to protect the disc from injury.

Disc is made of collagen fibers and elastic fibers, and has good mechanical property to bear large tensile and compressive stress. The bilaminar zone, mainly made of elastic fibers, could afford large deformation. Yet, its tensile strength is low, therefore, abnormal tensile force may lead to injury of the bilaminar zone and then caused TMD [4]. In this study, the maximum tensile stress of the posterior band was located in juncture with the bilaminar zone. It is concluded that temporal posterior attachment of the bilaminar zone is the chief unit to prevent the disc from anterior displacement. Tensile stress in the juncture of posterior band of the disc and temporal posterior attachment mostly loaded in the temporal posterior attachment. This shows the temporal posterior attachment bears increase tensile stress. Currently, we consider that over mouth opening could lead to injury of the bilaminar zone and is one of the induced factor of TMD, which are consistent with the results in our experiment.

Biomechanical properties of the disc ensure that it can bear large compressive stress and tensile stress, but low shear stress. A smaller abnormal stress could lead to injury and deformation of the disc. In this study, posterior and anterior band of the disc bore an increasing shear stress. The shear stress may due to discrepant directions between displacement and traction force. Over mouth opening may caused a shear stress exceeding the tolerance of the disc, and then bring about injury of the disc and TMD.

In conclusion, the model used in this study is appropriate for the finite element analysis of stress distribution of the disc during mouth opening, and the results are reliable. In the mouth opening process, anterior and posterior band of the disc bear an increasing tensile stress and shear stress; medial band bears a low stress. In summary, over mouth opening may cause TMD.

Acknowledgments. This work was supported by Beijing Natural Science Foundation (No.3122020).

References

1. Tanaka, E., Pozo, R., Tanaka, M.: Three-dimensional finite element analysis of human emporomandibular joint with and without disc displacement uring jaw opening. Medical Engineering & Physics 26, 503–511 (2004)
2. Palla, S., Gallo, L.M., Gossi, D.: Dynamic stereometry of the temporomandibular joint. Orthod Craniofacial Res. 6 (suppl. 1), 37–47 (2003)
3. Peter, S.D., Luigi, M.G., Robert, L.S., et al.: Biphasic finite element simulation of the TMJ disc from in vivo kinematic and geometric measurements. Journal of Biomechanics 37, 1787–1791 (2004)
4. Wang, M.Q., Yan, C.Y., Yuan, Y.P.: Is the superior belly of the lateral pterygoid primarily a stabilizer? An EMG study. J. Oral Rehabil. 28, 507–510 (2001)

Simulation of Constant Resistance Knee Flexion Movement

Chengzhu Zhu, Jian Jin*, Yunhao Sun, and Anbing Zheng

School of Mechatronic Engineering and Automation, Shanghai University,
Shanghai 200072
jinjian@staff.shu.edu.cn

Abstract. In the lower limb training process, incorrect training methods can't improve the diathesis of lower limb, moreover, it may make injury to the body of athletes. With the development of sports biomechanics knowledge and computer modeling simulation technology, in the sports training practice coaches make use of human motion simulation methods to carry kinematics and dynamics simulation of athletes lower limb training so that the quantitative training indicators can be got to specific athlete. In this paper a novel human-computer modeling and simulating software—The Anybody Modeling System is adopted. Coupling modeling of human lower limb and training instrument is built, and simulation of training is made. The force status of lower limb muscles are analyzed in the process of constant resistance knee flexion movement, and the results provide a basis to develop quantitative training.

Keywords: biomechanics, computer modeling and simulation, man-machine coupling system, constant resistance training mode.

1   Introduction

In a number of competitive sports, the lower limb quality of athletes play a key role to the pros and cons of competition results. For example ,in hurdle competition, speed endurance, flexibility, muscle strength and coordination of athletes can affect the results[1][2]. A lot training methods of lower limb muscles have been developed, but little quantitative methods are for specific athletes.

So, more and more coaches simulate the exercise process by the sports biomechanics knowledge and computer modeling simulation technology,and make scientific and quantitative training methods for specific athletes. The method have begun to attract attention[3][4].

This article makes the anybody modeling system[5]for modeling and simulating platform, and simulates constant resistance knee flexion movement. The results provide basis for developing extremity quality, fast quality and endurance quality of lower limb muscles.2   Man-machine coupling modeling.

To build muscle training machine-human lower limb coupling model, the establishment of the two, and then couple them through rigid node is needed. Because body movement relates to bones, muscles,ligaments, nerves and other factors, so human body modeling must be simplified to simulate body motion[6]. Lower limb

---

* Corresponding author.

T. Xiao, L. Zhang, and S. Ma (Eds.): ICSC 2012, Part I, CCIS 326, pp. 432–439, 2012.

model including bones, joints and muscles on the research requirements is established. The object have 65 kilogram weight and 170 centimeter stature. Bone quality and size values of the studied object can be found in the Chinese adult body size standards[7]. Mass center and moment[8] inertia of bones can be calculated using duality regression equation. Form of equation such as 1.

$$Y = B_0 + B_1 X_1 + B_2 X_2 \tag{1}$$

e, x_1 is the body weight of object, unit is kilogram; x_2 is the body height of object, unit is centimeter; B_0、 B_1、 B_2 is the coefficient of regression equation(access to the standards of Chinese adults'mass center and inertial parameters[9][10]). Y is the unknown parameter(mass center or inertial of bones).

Human skeleton is connect by joints, so joint modeling is essential to complete human body modeling[11]. In the modeling process joint is simplified as a hinge[12]. In this research, freedom of hip ,knee and ankle joints respectively is three, one and two.

In order to imitate the real human muscles, hill muscle model is introduced and anatomical characteristics of research object is combined. Some parameters (such as muscle strength, beginning and ending points, fiber length, tendon length, pennation angle, etc) of muscles are amended. The model of lower limb is shown in figure 1.

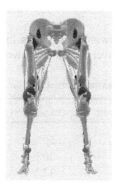

Fig. 1. Human lower limb musculoskeletal mode

Training machine–lower limb coupling model is shown in the figure 2.

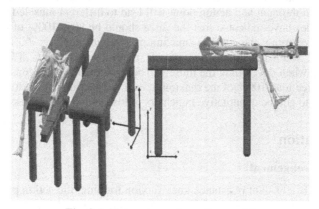

Fig. 2. Initial posture of coupling model

2   Knee Joint Maximum Load

During the constant resistance exercise process, in order to join lower limb and machine arm, some point of lower limb must be selected. When the point and size of load is changed, the training effect will be different. In the trial, three different points are selected as the junction to study the muscle force in different situations. Corresponding position of three point is shown in table 1.

Table 1. The location of three point in leg

Action point	% of lower leg length	Distance to knee joint (Unit: cm)	Distance to centroid (Unit: cm)
1	20%	7.7010	9.0570
2	50%	19.2530	−2.4945
3	80%	0.8040	−14.0460

(The origin of local coordinate system is located in the centroid of leg, positive direction of x axis point to the knee)

The speed of knee flexion movement is 30°/s in the simulation experiment, the maximum value of resistance on every point is shown in table 2.

Table 2. Maximum resistance on three point

Action point	Resistance/Weight
1	50%
2	20%
3	12.5%

Unlike the rigid body system,human body is a complex organism, muscle is the power source to the body movement. When the movement result is the same, the change of action moment and action point will lead to different muscle force status.

Related studies have indicated that the force should be 80%-100% of the maximum load when developing the muscle maximum strength quality; 60%-70% of the maximum load when developing the muscle rapid force quality; 40%-50% of the maximum load when developing the muscle endurance quality. The constant resistance training uses three load:100% of the maximum load, 70% of maximum load, 50% of the maximum load to get the quantitative indicators of lower limb every muscle.

3   Simulation

3.1   Test Arrangement

In the progress of constant resistance knee flexion training, the action point and value of load will all influence the training status of the lower limb muscles. So, after determine the action point and value of load, 9 times simulation tests are arranged. In order to determine the better action point and load value of lower limb muscle quality. Test arrangements are shown in table 3.

Table 3. Simulation test arrangement

Action point load	Load/Maximum load	Action point	Load/Maximum
1	100%	2	50%
1	70%	3	100%
1	50%	3	70%
2	100%	3	50%
2	70%		

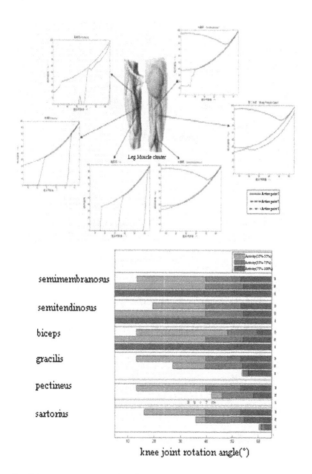

Fig. 3. The trend of lower muscle activation when the load of action point 1、2、3 equals maximum load of 100%

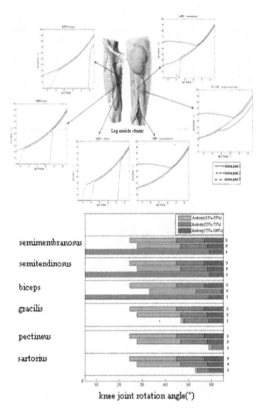

Fig. 4. The trend of lower muscle activation when the load of action point 1、2、3 equals maximum load of 70%

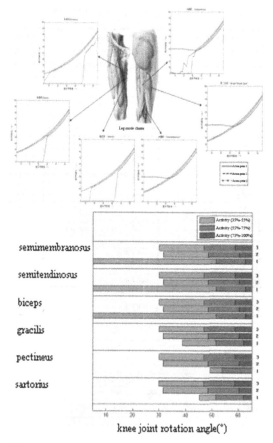

Fig. 5. The trend of lower muscle activation when the load of action point 1、2、3 equals maximum load of 50%

3.2   Simulation Test

According to the different divisions of the load range of the different quality of the development of muscle,muscle activation can be divided into three intervals, for (35%-55%)、(55%-75%)、(75%-100%). Figure 3-5 shows when the action point and value of load changes, the trend of activity of thigh muscles.

3.3   Simulation Results

By comparing with 9 cases, the ideal action point and load to develop muscles of lower limb thigh muscle extremity quality, fast quality,endurance quality are found out, results are shown in figure 4.

In the situation of ideal action point and load the muscle activity distribution as shown in figure 6.

Table 4. Ideal action point and load

Muscle	Extremity quality Action point Load/maximum load	Fast quality Action point Load/Maximum load	Endurance quality Action point Load/Maximum load
Semimenmbr anosus	1 100%	1 70%	1 50%
Semitendinos us	1 100%	1 70%	1 50%
Biceps	1 100%	1 70%	1 50%
Gracilis	3 100%	3 100%	3 100%
Pectineus	3 100%	3 100%	3 100%
Sartorius	3 100%	3 100%	3 100%

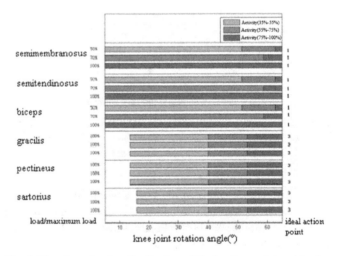

Fig. 6. Muscle activation distribution of ideal action point and load

4   Conclusion

When coaches train lower limb muscle strength for specific athletes, constant training is a commonly used method. Because our human body is a complex organism, it not only includes the rigid bone, but also the flexible muscles, then, human body system is different from common rigid system. Tough the resistance moment loading on body is different, and realize the same action results, but resistance moment acts on different positions, force on human body muscles is completely different. This research is based on lower limb model builded up by human body modeling and simulation platform. The progress of constant resistance knee flexion training is simulated. The ideal action point and load to develop thigh muscles muscle strength, rapid strength, strength endurance quality are found out, which provides theoretical basis for athletes lower limb muscle training .

References

1. Hu, J.P.: Specific strength training of hurdler. Track and Filed (9), 16–17 (2007)
2. Gu, Q.: Some problems in physical strength training for hurdle step. Journal of Wuxi Vocational Institute of Commercial Technology 3(1), 54–55 (2004)
3. Textbook committee of the national sports institute, Sports biomechanics. People's sports press, Beijing (2005)
4. Liu, X.: A review on biomechanics in sports in china. Mechanics and Practice 30(3), 10–15 (2008)
5. Zhou, L., Bai, S., Hansen, M.R., Rasmussen, J.: Modeling of Human Arm Energy Expenditure for Predicting Energy Optimal Trajectories. Modeling Identification and Control 31(3), 91–101 (2011)
6. Luo, X.: The research of human body dynamics modeling and simulation based on ADAMS. Guangzhou industry university, Guangzhou (2006)
7. The standardization and information classification and encoding institute of china, GB10000-88, The people's republic of china national standard China adults body size
8. Lei, J.: Research on human body motion and modeling based on multi-information fusion. China science and technology university, Hefei (2006)
9. The standardization and information classification and encoding institute of china, GB17245-1998, The people's republic of china national standard Mass center of chinese adults
10. The standardization and information classification and encoding institute of china, GB17245-2004, The people's republic of china national standard Inertial parameters of chinese adults
11. LS-DYNA3D User's Manual, Nonlinear dynamic analysis of structures in three dimensions, Livermore Software Technology Corporation (1995)
12. Zhou, X., Drahanich, L.F., Amirouche, F.: A dynamic model for simulating a trip and fall during gait. Medical Engineering & Physics (24), 121–127 (2002)

A Stochastic Lotka-Volterra System and Its Asymptotic Behavior

Liangjian Hu and Juanjuan Zhao

Department of Applied Mathematics, Donghua University,
Shanghai 201620, P.R. China
ljhu@dhu.edu.cn, heiheiiamjj@tom.com

Abstract. In this paper, we investigate a new Lotka-Volterra system

$$dx(t) = \text{diag}(x_1(t), ..., x_n(t))[(b + Ax(t))dt + \sigma x(t)^p dw(t))],$$

where $w(t)$ is a standard Brownian motion, and x^p is defined as
$(x_1^p, ..., x_n^p)^T$. Population systems perturbed by the white noise have recently been studied by many authors in case of $p = 0$ and $p = 1$. The aim here is to find out what happens when $p \geq \frac{1}{2}$. This paper shows environmental Brownian noise suppresses explosions in this system. In addition, we examine the asymptotic behavior of the system.

Keywords: Lotka-Volterra, Brownian motion, stochastic differential equation, asymptotic behavior, Itô formula.

1   Introduction

Population systems are often subject to environmental noise. It is therefore useful to reveal how the noise affects the population system. Consider a population system

$$dx(t) = \text{diag}(x_1(t), ..., x_n(t))[(b + Ax(t))dt + \sigma x(t)dw(t))] \tag{1.1}$$

satisfing

(H1) $\sigma_{ii} > 0$ if $1 \leq i \leq n$ whilst $\sigma_{ij} \geq 0$ if $i \neq j$.

where $w(t)$ is a standard Brownian motion with $w(0) = 0$. As a matter of fact, population system perturbed by the white noise has recently been studied by many authors. Mao, Marion and Renshaw [1] revealed that the environmental noise can suppress a potential explosion. Mao, Sabanis, and Renshaw [2] study the asymptotic behavior of the stochastic Lotka-Volterra model (1.1). On the other hand, Ji and Jiang [5] study the system

$$dx(t) = \text{diag}(x_1(t), ..., x_n(t))[(b + Ax(t))dt + \sigma dw(t))].$$

where $w(t)$ is a standard Brownian motion, and x^p is defined as $(x_1^p, ..., x_n^p)^T$.

Let us now take a further step by considering general type of Lotka-Volterra system

$$dx(t) = \text{diag}(x_1(t), ..., x_n(t))[(b + Ax(t))dt + \sigma x(t)^p dw(t))]. \tag{1.2}$$

T. Xiao, L. Zhang, and S. Ma (Eds.): ICSC 2012, Part I, CCIS 326, pp. 440–450, 2012.

To understand the meaning of the parameter p, we set: $n = 2$, $\sigma = \begin{pmatrix} \sigma_{11} & \sigma_{12} \\ \sigma_{21} & \sigma_{22} \end{pmatrix}$,

$A = \begin{pmatrix} a_{11} & a_{12} \\ a_{21} & a_{22} \end{pmatrix}$. Hence, (1.2) becomes:

$$\begin{cases} \frac{dx_1(t)}{x_1(t)} = (b_1 + a_{11}x_1(t) + a_{12}x_2(t))dt + [\sigma_{11}x_1^p(t) + \sigma_{12}x_2^p(t)]dw(t), \\ \\ \frac{dx_2(t)}{x_2(t)} = (b_2 + a_{21}x_1(t) + a_{22}x_2(t))dt + [\sigma_{21}x_1^p(t) + \sigma_{22}x_2^p(t)]dw(t), \end{cases}$$

where $\sigma_{11}x_1^p(t) + \sigma_{12}x_2^p(t)$ and $\sigma_{21}x_1^p(t) + \sigma_{22}x_2^p(t)$ represent the volatility of growth rate of the two species .

2 Positive and Global Solution

Theorem 1. *Under hypothesis (H1), for any system parameters $b \in R^n$, $A \in R^{n \times n}$, $p > 1/2$, and any given initial value $x_0 \in R_+^n$, there is a unique solution $x(t)$ to equation (1.2) on $t \geq 0$ and the solution will remain in R_+^n with probability 1, namely $x(t) \in R_+^n$ for all $t \geq 0$ almost surely.*

Proof. Since the coefficients of the equation are locally Lipschitz continuous, for any given initial value $x_0 \in R_+^n$ there is a unique local solution $x(t)$ on $t \in [0, \tau_e)$, where τ_e is the explosion time (cf. Arnold [3] or Friedman[4]).To show this solution is global, we need to show that $\tau_e = \infty$ a.s. Let $k_0 > 0$ be sufficiently large for every component of x_0 lying within the interval $[1/k_0, k_0]$. For each integer $k \geq k_0$, define the stopping time

$$\tau_k = \inf\{t \in [0, \tau_e) : x_i(t) \notin (1/k, k) \text{ for some } i = 1, ..., n\},$$

where throughout this paper we set $\inf \emptyset = \infty$ (as usual $\emptyset$ denotes the empty set). Clearly, τ_k is increasing as $k \to \infty$. Set $\tau_\infty = \lim_{k \to \infty} \tau_k$, whence $\tau_\infty \leq \tau_e$ a.s. If we can show that $\tau_\infty = \infty$ a.s. Then $\tau_e = \infty$ a.s.,and $x(t) \in R_+^n$ a.s. for all $t \geq 0$. In other words, to complete the proof all we need to show is that $\tau_\infty = \infty$ a.s. For if this statement is false, then there is a pair of constants $T > 0$ and $\epsilon \in (0, 1)$ such that

$$P\{\tau_\infty \leq T\} \leq \epsilon.$$

Hence there is an integer $k_1 > k_0$ such that

$$P\{\tau_k \leq T\} \geq \epsilon \qquad \text{for all } k \geq k_1 \tag{2.3}$$

Define a C^2-function $V \colon R_+^n \to R_+$ by

$$V(x) = \sum_{i=1}^n (x_i^{0.5} - 1 - 0.5 \log x_i) .$$

The nonnegativty of this function can be seen from

$$u^{0.5} - 1 - 0.5 \log u \geq 0 \qquad \text{on } u > 0.$$

If $x(t) \in R_+^n$, the Itô formula shows that

$$dV(x(t)) = \sum_{i=1}^{n} \{0.5(x_i^{-0.5} - x_i^{-1})x_i[(b_i + \sum_{j=1}^{n} a_{ij}x_j)dt] + \sum_{j=1}^{n} \sigma_{ij}x_j^p dw(t)]$$

$$+ 0.5[(-0.25x_i^{-1.5} + 0.5x_i^{-2}]x_i^2[\sum_{j=1}^{n} \sigma_{ij}x_j^p]^2 dt\}$$

$$= \sum_{i=1}^{n} \{0.5(x_i^{0.5} - 1)[(b_i + \sum_{j=1}^{n} a_{ij}x_j) + (0.25 - 0.125x_i^{0.5})[\sum_{j=1}^{n} \sigma_{ij}x_j^p]^2\}dt$$

$$+ \sum_{i=1}^{n}\sum_{j=1}^{n} 0.5(x_i^{0.5} - 1)\sigma_{ij}x_j^p dw(t)$$

where we write $x(t) = x$. Compute

$$\sum_{i=1}^{n}(x_i^{0.5} - 1)(b_i + \sum_{j=1}^{n} a_{ij}x_j)$$

$$\leq \sum_{i=1}^{n}|b_i|(x_i^{0.5} + 1) + \sum_{i=1}^{n}\sum_{j=1}^{n}|a_{ij}|x_j + \sum_{i=1}^{n}\sum_{j=1}^{n}|a_{ij}|x_i^{0.5}x_j$$

$$\leq \sum_{i=1}^{n}|b_i|(x_i^{0.5} + 1) + \sum_{i=1}^{n}\sum_{j=1}^{n}|a_{ij}|x_j + \sum_{i=1}^{n}\sum_{j=1}^{n}\frac{2}{3}|a_{ij}|(x_i^{1.5} + x_j^{1.5})$$

$$= \sum_{i=1}^{n}(|b_i|(x_i^{0.5} + 1) + \sum_{j=1}^{n}|a_{ji}|x_i + \frac{2}{3}\sum_{j=1}^{n}(|a_{ij}| + |a_{ji}|)x_i^{1.5})$$

and

$$\sum_{i=1}^{n}[\sum_{j=1}^{n} \sigma_{ij}x_j^p]^2 \leq \sum_{i=1}^{n}[\sum_{j=1}^{n} \sigma_{ij}^2 \sum_{j=1}^{n}x_j^p] = |\sigma|^2 \sum_{i=1}^{n} x_i^{2p}$$

moreover, by hypothesis(H1),

$$\sum_{i=1}^{n}x_i^{0.5}[\sum_{j=1}^{n} \sigma_{ij}x_j^p]^2 \geq \sum_{i=1}^{n}\sum_{i=1}^{n} \sigma_{ii}^2 x_i^{2p+0.5}$$

so

$$\sum_{i=1}^{n}\{0.5(x_i^{0.5} - 1)[(b_i + \sum_{j=1}^{n} a_{ij}x_j) + (0.25 - 0.125x_i^{0.5})[\sum_{j=1}^{n} \sigma_{ij}x_j^p]^2\}$$

$$\leq \sum_{i=1}^{n}\{0.5|b_i|(x_i^{0.5} + 1) + \sum_{j=1}^{n}0.5|a_{ji}|x_i + \frac{1}{3}\sum_{j=1}^{n}(|a_{ij}| + a_{ji}|)x_i^{1.5}$$

$$+ 0.25|\sigma|^2 x_i^{2p} - 0.125\sigma_{ii}^2 x_i^{2p+0.5}\}$$

which is bounded when $p > 1/2$, say by K, in R_+^n. We therefore obtain

$$\int_0^{\tau_k \wedge T} dV(x(t)) \leq \int_0^{\tau_k \wedge T} K dt + \int_0^{\tau_k \wedge T} \sum_{i=1}^n \sum_{j=1}^n 0.5(x_i^{0.5} - 1)\sigma_{ij}x_j^p dw(t)$$

since $x(\tau_k \wedge T) \in R_+^n$. Whence taking expectations, yields

$$EV(x(\tau_k \wedge T)) \leq V(x_0) + KE(\tau_k \wedge T) \leq V(x_0) + KT \qquad (2.4)$$

Set $\Omega_k = \tau_k \leq T$ for $k \geq k_1$ and by (2.3), $P(\Omega_k) \geq \epsilon$. Note that for every $\omega \in \Omega_k$, there is some i such that $x_i(\tau_k, \omega)$ equals either k or $1/k$, and hence $V(x(\tau_k, \omega))$ is no less than either

$$\sqrt{k} - 1 - 0.5 \log k$$

or

$$\sqrt{1/k} - 1 - 0.5 \log(1/k) = \sqrt{1/k} - 1 + 0.5 \log k$$

Consequently,

$$V(x(\tau_k, \omega)) \geq [\sqrt{k} - 1 - 0.5 \log k] \wedge [0.5 \log k - 1].$$

It then follows from (2.3) that

$$V(x_0) + KT \geq E[1_{\Omega_k}(\omega)V(x(\tau_k, \omega))] \geq \epsilon([\sqrt{k} - 1 - 0.5 \log(k)] \wedge [0.5 \log(k) - 1]),$$

where 1_{Ω_k} is the indicator function of Ω_k. Letting $k \to \infty$ leads to the contradiction $\infty > V(x_0) + KT = \infty$, so we must therefore have $\tau_\infty = \infty$ a.s. $\square$

Remark 1. When $p = 1$, Theorem 1 turns to be Theorem 2.1 in [1].

3   Boundedness

Theorem 2. *Let hypothesis (H1) hold, $p > 1/2$, and $\theta_1, ..., \theta_n$ be positive numbers such that*

$$\theta_1 + ... + \theta_n < 1/2. \qquad (3.5)$$

Then, for any initial value $x_0 = (x_{01}, ..., x_{0n})^T \in R_+^n$, the solution $x(t; x_0) = x(t)$ of equation (1.2) has the property that

$$\log(E[\prod_{i=1}^n x_i^{\theta_i}(t)]) \leq e^{-c_1 t} \sum_{i=1}^n \theta_i \log x_{0i} + \frac{c_2}{c_1}(1 - e^{-c_1 t}) \qquad \text{for all } t \geq 0, \quad (3.6)$$

where

$$c_1 = \frac{1}{4}(1 - \sum_{i=1}^n \theta_i) \min_{1 \leq i \leq n} \theta_i \sigma_{ii}^2 \text{ and } c_2 = |\theta||b| + \frac{(2p-1)|\theta|^{\frac{2p}{2p-1}} \| A \|^{\frac{2p}{2p-1}}}{2p(2pc_1)^{2p-1}}$$

In particular, letting $t \to \infty$ in (3.6) yields the asymptotic estimate

$$\limsup_{t \to \infty} E(\prod_{i=1}^{n} x_i^{\theta_i}(t)) \le e^{c_2/c_1}. \tag{3.7}$$

To prove this theorem we consider the following lemma.

Lemma 1. *Let hypothesis (H1) hold, $p > 1/2$, and $\theta_1, ..., \theta_n$ be positive numbers such that*

$$\theta_1 + ... + \theta_n < 1. \tag{3.8}$$

Then, for any initial value $x_0 = (x_{01}, ..., x_{0n})^T \in R_+^n$, the solution $x(t; x_0) = x(t)$ of equation (1.2) has the property that

$$E(\prod_{i=1}^{n} x_i^{\theta_i}(t)) < \infty \qquad \text{for all } t \ge 0. \tag{3.9}$$

Proof. Define a C^2-function V $:R_+^n \to R_+$ by

$$V(x) = \prod_{i=1}^{n} x_i^{\theta_i}.$$

It is not difficult to show that

$$LV(x) = V(x)\theta^T(b + Ax) - \frac{1}{2}V(x)(x^p)^T\sigma^T[\text{diag}(\theta_1, ..., \theta_n) - \theta\theta^T]\sigma x^p \tag{3.10}$$

Note that for any $y = (y_1, ..., y_n)^T \in R^n$,

$$y^T[\text{diag}(\theta_1, ..., \theta_n) - \theta\theta^T]y = \sum_{i=1}^{n}\theta_i y_i^2 - (\sum_{i=1}^{n}\theta_i y_i)^2$$

$$\ge \sum_{i=1}^{n}\theta_i y_i^2 - \sum_{i=1}^{n}\theta_i \sum_{i=1}^{n}\theta_i y_i^2 = (1 - \sum_{i=1}^{n}\theta_i)\sum_{i=1}^{n}\theta_i y_i^2.$$

Thus, for $x \in R_+^n$,

$$(x^p)^T\sigma^T[\text{diag}(\theta_1, ..., \theta_n) - \theta\theta^T]\sigma x^p \ge (1 - \sum_{i=1}^{n}\theta_i)\sum_{i=1}^{n}\theta_i(\sum_{j=1}^{n}\sigma_{ij}x_j^p)^2$$

$$\ge (1 - \sum_{i=1}^{n}\theta_i)\sum_{i=1}^{n}\theta_i\sigma_{ii}^2 x_i^{2p} \ge (1 - \sum_{i=1}^{n}\theta_i)(\min_{1 \le i \le n}\theta_i\sigma_{ii}^2)|x|^{2p} = 4c_1|x|^{2p},$$

where c_1 is defined in the statement of Theorem 3.1. It then follows from (3.10) that

$$LV(x) \le V(x)[|\theta|(|b| + \| A \| |x|) - 2c_1|x|^{2p}].$$

Since

$$|\theta| \, \| A \| \, |x| \leq \frac{(2p-1)|\theta|^{\frac{2p}{2p-1}} \, \| A \|^{\frac{2p}{2p-1}}}{2p(2pc_1)^{2p-1}} + c_1|x|^{2p}$$

We therefore obtain

$$LV(x) \leq V(x)[c_2 - c_1|x|^{2p}], \tag{3.11}$$

where c_2 is defined in the statement of Theorem 3.1. For every integer $k \geq 1$, define the stopping time

$$\tau_k = \inf\{t \geq 0 : |x(t)| \geq k\},$$

which by Theorem 2.1 has the properties that, $\tau_k < \infty$ and $\tau_k \to \infty$ almost surely as $k \to \infty$. Now for any $t \geq 0$, the Itô formula shows that

$$V(x(t \wedge \tau_k)) = V(x_0) + \int_0^{t \wedge \tau_k} LV(x(s))ds + \int_0^{t \wedge \tau_k} V(x(s))\theta^T \sigma x^p(s)dw(s).$$

Taking expectations of both sides and making use of (3.11) yields

$$EV(x(t \wedge \tau_k)) \leq V(x_0) + c_2 E \int_0^{t \wedge \tau_k} V(x(s))ds \leq V(x_0) + c_2 \int_0^t EV(x(s \wedge \tau_k))ds,$$

Whence applying the well-known Gronwall inequality gives

$$EV(x(t \wedge \tau_k)) \leq V(x_0)e^{c_2 t}.$$

letting $k \to \infty$ shows that

$$EV(x(t \wedge \tau_k)) \leq V(x_0)e^{c_2 t} \qquad t \geq 0,$$

and the required assertion follows. □

Proof of Theorem 2. we use the same notation as in the proof of Lemma 1, which shows that $EV(x(t))$ is finite for all $t \geq 0$. Moreover, by Theorem 1, $V(x(t)) > 0$ with probability 1, so we must have $EV(x(t)) > 0$ for all $t \geq 0$. In addition, the continuity of $EV(x(t))$ in t can be seen by the continuity of the solution $x(t)$ and the dominated convergence theorem. For convenience, let us set

$$v(t) = EV(x(t)) \qquad \text{for}(t \geq 0)$$

Then $v(t)$ is a continuous positive function of $t \geq 0$. Define the right upper derivative of $v(t)$ by

$$D_+v(t) = \limsup_{\delta \downarrow 0} \frac{v(t+\delta) - v(t)}{\delta} \qquad (t \geq 0)$$

We claim that

$$D_+v(t) \leq v(t)(c_1 + c_2 - c_1 v(t)) \qquad (t \geq 0) \qquad (3.12)$$

To show this, note that

$$V(x) \leq \prod_{i=1}^n |x|^{\theta_i} \leq |x|^{\theta_1 + \cdots + \theta_n} \leq 1 + |x|^{2p}.$$

Then it follows from (3.11) that

$$LV(x) \leq V(x)[c_1 + c_2 - c_1(1 + |x|^{2p})] \leq V(x)[c_1 + c_2 - c_1 V(x)]. \qquad (3.13)$$

On recalling condition (3.5), namely that $\theta_1 + \theta_2 + \cdots + \theta_n < 1$, we observe from Lemma 1 that

$$EV^2(x(t)) \leq \infty \quad for \ all \ t \geq 0$$

Whence it follows from the Itôformula and (3.13) that for any $t \geq 0$ and $\delta > 0$,

$$EV(x(t+\delta)) - EV(x(t)) \leq \int_t^{t+\delta} [(c_1 + c_2)EV(x(s)) - c_1 EV^2(x(s))]ds.$$

Using the Hölder inequality which implies that $EV(x(s)) \leq [EV^2(x(s))]^{\frac{1}{2}}$, we then have

$$EV(x(t+\delta)) - EV(x(t)) \leq \int_t^{t+\delta} [(c_1 + c_2)EV(x(s)) - c_1[EV(x(s))]^2]ds,$$

that is

$$v(t+\delta) - v(t) \leq \int_t^{t+\delta} [(c_1 + c_2)v(s) - c_1[v(s)]^2]ds.$$

Dividing both sides by δ and letting $\delta \downarrow 0$ yields the claimed inequality (3.12). We now compute the derivative

$$D_+[e^{c_1 t} \log v(t)] = c_1 e^{c_1 t} \log v(t) + e^{c_1 t} \frac{D_+ v(t)}{v(t)}$$

$$\leq c_1 e^{c_1 t} \log v(t) + e^{c_1 t}[c_1 + c_2 - c_1 v(t)].$$

Noting that $\log v(t) \leq v(t) - 1$ we obtain

$$D_+[e^{c_1 t} \log v(t)] \leq c_2 e^{c_1 t}, \qquad (3.14)$$

Whence integration yields

$$e^{c_1 t} \log v(t) \leq \log v(0) + \frac{c_2}{c_1}[e^{c_1 t} - 1].$$

Consequently,

$$\log v(t) \le e^{-c_1 t} \log v(0) + \frac{c_2}{c_1}[1 - e^{-c_1 t}],$$

which is the required assertion (3.6), while the other assertion (3.7) follows by letting $t \to \infty$. □

Remark 2. When $p = 1$, $c_2 = |\theta||b| + \frac{|\theta|^2 \|A\|^2}{4c_1}$, Theorem 2 turns to be Theorem 3.1 in [1].

4 Asymptotic Moment Estimation and Pathwise Estimation

Similarly to reference [2], we have the following theorems, which extend Theorem 2-4 in [2] .

Theorem 3. *Let the system parameters $b \in R^n$ and $A \in R^{n \times n}$ be given, and assume that hypothesis (H1) holds, $p > \frac{1}{2}$. Then, for any $\theta \in (0, 1)$, $\theta > 2 - 2p$ there exists a positive constant K_θ such that, for any initial value $x_0 \in R_+^n$, the solution of (1.2) has the property*

$$\limsup_{t \to \infty} \frac{1}{t} E[\int_0^t \sum_{i=1}^n x_i^{2p+\theta}(s)ds] \le K_\theta. \qquad (4.15)$$

Theorem 4. *Let us assume that hypothesis (H1) holds, $p > \frac{1}{2}$. Moreover, let the system parameters $b \in R^n$, $A \in R^{n \times n}$ and the initial value $x_0 \in R_+^n$ be given. Then, there exists a $K > 0$, which is independent of x_0 but not necessarily of the system parameter, such that*

$$\limsup_{t \to \infty} \frac{1}{t}[\log(\prod_{i=1}^n x_i(t)) + \frac{1}{4}\lambda_{\min}(\sigma^T \sigma) \int_0^t |x(s)|^{2p}ds] \le K \qquad a.s. \quad (4.16)$$

where $\lambda_{\min}(\sigma^T \sigma)$ is the smallest eigenvalue of the matrix $\sigma^T \sigma$.

Theorem 5. *Let us assume that hypothesis (H1) holds. Then, for any system parameters $b \in R^n$, $A \in R^{n \times n}$ and any initial value $x_0 \in R_+^n$,*

$$\limsup_{t \to \infty} \frac{\log(\prod_{i=1}^n x_i(t))}{\log(t)} \le n \quad a.s. \qquad (4.17)$$

5 Case $p = \frac{1}{2}$

By observing the proof of the theorems in Section 2-4, we can prove the following properties of (1.2) in case of $p = \frac{1}{2}$.

Theorem 6. *Under hypothesis (H1),let $p = 1/2$ and $\sum_{i=1}^{n} \sum_{j=1}^{n} (a_{ij} + a_{ji}) < 0.375 \sum_{i=1}^{n} \sigma_{ii}^2$. For any system parameters $b \in R^n$, $A \in R^{n \times n}$, and any given initial value $x_0 \in R_{+}^n$, there is a unique solution $x(t)$ to equation (1.2) on $t \geq 0$ and the solution will remain in R_{+}^n for all $t \geq 0$.*

Theorem 7. *Let hypothesis (H1) hold, $p = 1/2$. Let $\theta_1, ..., \theta_n$ be positive numbers such that*

$$\theta_1 + ... + \theta_n < 1$$

Then, when $\sum_{i=1}^{n} \sum_{j=1}^{n} (a_{ij} + a_{ji}) < 0.375 \sum_{i=1}^{n} \sigma_{ii}^2$, $|\theta| \|A\| \leq 2c_1$ for any initial value $x_0 = (x_{01}, ..., x_{0n})^T \in R_{+}^n$, the solution $x(t; x_0) = x(t)$ of equation (1.2) has the property that

$$\log(E[\prod_{i=1}^{n} x_i^{\theta_i}(t)]) \leq e^{-c_1 t} \sum_{i=1}^{n} \theta_i \log x_{0i} + \frac{c_2}{c_1}(1 - e^{-c_1 t}) \qquad \text{for all } t \geq 0, \quad (5.18)$$

where

$$c_1 = \frac{1}{4}(1 - \sum_{i=1}^{n} \theta_i) \min_{1 \leq i \leq n} \theta_i \sigma_{ii}^2 \text{ and } c_2 = |\theta| \|b\|$$

In particular, letting $t \to \infty$ in (6.22) yields the asymptotic estimate

$$\limsup_{t \to \infty} E(\prod_{i=1}^{n} x_i^{\theta_i}(t)) \leq e^{c_2/c_1}.$$

Theorem 8. *Let us assume that hypothesis(H1)holds, $p = \frac{1}{2}$, $\sum_{i=1}^{n} \sum_{j=1}^{n} (a_{ij} + a_{ji}) < 0.375 \sum_{i=1}^{n} \sigma_{ii}^2$. Moreover, let the system parameters $b \in R^n, A \in R^{n \times n}$ and the initial value $x_0 \in R_{+}^n$ be given. Then, there exists a $K > 0$, which is independent of x_0 but not necessarily of the system parameter, such that (1.2):*

$$\limsup_{t \to \infty} \frac{1}{t}[\log(\prod_{i=1}^{n} x_i(t)) + \frac{1}{4}\lambda_{min}(\sigma^T \sigma) \int_0^t |x(s)|ds] \leq K \text{ a.s.,} \quad (5.19)$$

where $\lambda_{min}(\sigma^T \sigma)$ is the smallest eigenvalue of the matric $\sigma^T \sigma$.

It also have

$$\limsup_{t \to \infty} \frac{\log(\prod_{i=1}^{n} x_i(t))}{\log(t)} \leq n \text{ a.s.} \quad (5.20)$$

6   Examples and Computer Simulations

In this section we explore system behaviour using numerical solutions of the stochastic differential function (1.2). In particular, for $t = \triangle t, 2\triangle t, ...$, we employ the Euler scheme

$$x_{\triangle t}(t + \triangle t) = x_{\triangle t}(t) + \text{diag}((x_{\triangle t})_1(t), ..., (x_{\triangle t})_n(t))[(b + Ax_{\triangle t}(t)) \triangle t + \sigma x_{\triangle t}^p(t) \triangle w(t)], (6.21)$$

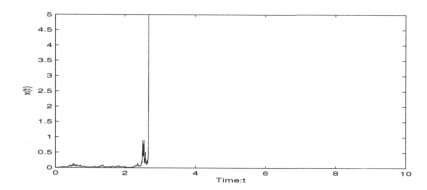

Fig. 1. $p = 0.5,\ \sigma = 1$

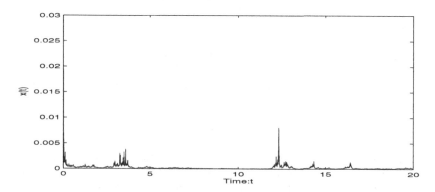

Fig. 2. $p = 0.5,\ \sigma = 10$

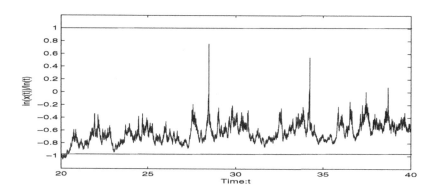

Fig. 3. $p = 0.5,\ \sigma = 10$

with initial condition $x(0) \in R_+^n$ and time increment $\triangle t$. For each time step the vector $\triangle w(t) = (\triangle w(t)_1, ..., \triangle w(t)_m)^T$ represents m independent draws from a Normal distribution with zero mean and variance $\triangle t$. Recent results by Marion *et al* [10].show that, for any finite time and a sufficiently small time step, this numerical scheme will converge to the true solution of (1.2).

Figure 1 and Figure 2 show the results from runs based on the Euler scheme for a one-dimensional example of system (1.2) with $A = b = 1, p = 0.5$ with the initial condition $x_0 = 1$ and step $\triangle t = 10^{-3}$. They show that noise suppresses the explosion. Figure 3 is a sample path of $\log(x(t))/\log(t)$ and illustrates the theoretical results of Theorem 8.

References

1. Mao, X., Marion, G., Renshaw, E.: Environmental Brownian noise suppresses explosions in populations dynamics. Stochastic Process. Appl. 97, 95–110 (2002)
2. Mao, X., Sabanis, S., Renshaw, E.: Asymptotic behaviour of the stochastic Lotka-Volterra Model. Appl. 287, 141–156 (2002)
3. Arnold, L.: Stochastic Differential Equations: Theory and Application. Wiley (1972)
4. Friedman, A.: Stochastic Differential Equations and Their Application. Academic Press (1976)
5. Ji, C.Y., Jiang, D.Q., Hong, L., Yang, Q.S.: Existence, uniqueness and ergodicity of positive solution of mutualism system with stochastic perturbation. Math. Probl. Eng., Art. ID 684926, 18 p (2010)
6. Mao, X.: Exponential Stability of Stochastic Differential Equations. Marcel Dekker (1994)
7. Mao, X.: Stochastic Differential Equations and Applications. Horwood (1997)
8. Mao, X., Marion, G., Renshaw, E.: Convergence of the Euler scheme for a class of atochastic differential equation. Internat. J. Math. 1, 95–110 (2002)
9. Wolin, C.L., Lawlor, L.R.: Models of facultative mutualism: density effects. Amer. Natural 124, 843–862 (1984)
10. Ladde, G.S., Lakshmikantham, V.: Random Differential Inequalities. Academic Press (1990)

Mechanical Model of a Novel Executive Mechanism for Artificial Anal Sphincter System

Enyu Jiang[1], Peng Zan[1,*], Suqin Zhang[2], Jinding Liu[1],
Xiaojin Zhu[1], and Xiaohua Wang[1]

[1] Department of Automation, College of Mechatronics Engineering and Automation,
Shanghai University; Shanghai Key Laboratory of Power Station Automation Technology,
Shanghai, China
[2] Naval Aeronautical Engineering Institute Qingdao Campus, Qingdao, China
{zanpeng,ljd123,enyujiang,x.wang}@shu.edu.cn,
susanzsq@163.com

Abstract. The artificial anal sphincter is used to simulate the normal operation of the anal. It can solve the anal incontinence and relieve patients' life and psychological pressure. The artificial anal sphincter system proposed in the paper is based on a novel executive mechanism. The novel executive mechanism uses a hinge structure to clamp the rectum. To ensure the mechanism's reliability, a mechanical model between the novel executive mechanism and rectum is established to predict the deformation of the rectum when compressed in the radical direction. The results show that the deformation can be controlled by adjusting the spring force.

Keywords: artificial anal sphincter, executive mechanism, mechanical model.

1 Introduction

Anal incontinence (AI) refers to unwanted loss of feces and gases in clinic. The disease has a 3 percent occurrence rate after the surgical incision of rectum or parturition. The rate can reach 90 percent when the surgical incision is operated on elderly [1, 2]. There are about 7.1 percent of general people in America reported suffer from AI. The rate is higher in women and it tends to increase with age [3].

Many methods have been put forward to track with AI, such as medication, anal control valve plug, biological feedback training and colostomy [4]. However, none of the methods yields good enough effect. Since the artificial anal sphincter is put forward, AI has been cracked.

In 1972, Scott developed artificial urinary sphincter to cure urinary incontinence [5]. In 1989, Christiansen found that implanting 800AMS artificial urinary sphincter close to the anus is available to control solid state or semi-solid state faeces [6]. In 1992, Christiansen and Sparso adapted artificial urinary sphincter to artificial anal sphincter [7]. The German artificial sphincter system is a novel hydraulic muscle

---

* Corresponding author.

T. Xiao, L. Zhang, and S. Ma (Eds.): ICSC 2012, Part I, CCIS 326, pp. 451–458, 2012.
© Springer-Verlag Berlin Heidelberg 2012

based on microelectronic and mechanical system [8, 9]. Its novelty lied in that it applied a micro-silicon piezoelectric pump. In the literature [10], an artificial anal sphincter system that utilizes shape memory alloy was discussed. An innovative sandwich structure which is made of SMA is used to clamp anal canal.

In this paper, we present an artificial anal sphincter system based on a novel executive mechanism. First, we will introduce the systematic structure. Secondly, we will discuss the novel executive mechanism. Thirdly, a mechanical model between the executive mechanism and rectum will be established.

2   System Overview

2.1   Key Module Introduction

The artificial anal sphincter system consists of two components. The one which is implanted into the body is called implanted component, the other component is called outside components. The outline of the system is shown in Fig.1.

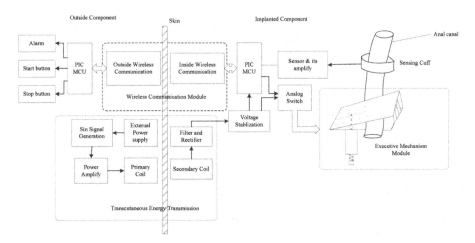

Fig. 1. Outline of artificial anal sphincter system

As we can see, the system is divided into three key modules. The first module is transcutaneous energy transmission module. It is designed to provide driving energy for the implanted component. The second module is wireless communication module. It provides a reliable communication between the two components. The third module is executive mechanism module. It is used to clamp the anal canal.

2.2   The Mechanics of Defection Control

The mechanics of defecation control is shown in Fig. 2. It can be described as follows: The micro-sensor has been always monitoring the pressure of the anal canal. It simulates the function of rectum's nerve and converts pressure signal into electronic signal. The inside MCU simulates the function of human brain. It receives the electronic signal and sends the signal that exceeds threshold to the outside MCU. The outside MCU wars the patient to press "start" button to realize the defection control.

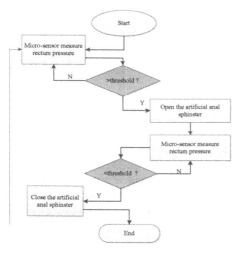

Fig. 2. Mechanics of defecation control

Micro-sensor still monitors the pressure change during the process of defection. When finding the electronic signal is lower than the threshold, the inside MCU will send the electronic signal to the outside MCU again to warn the patient to press the "stop" button to finish the defection process.

3   The Novel Executive Mechanism

Executive mechanism is an important part to simulate the basic functions of nature anal sphincter and realize patients' defecation autonomously. It is also one of the most essential devices in the implanted component. Considering the mechanics of human anal sphincter, the novel executive mechanism must have the following functions.

(1) The novel executive mechanics can hold the anal canal preventing feces and gases leakage reliably in case of occlusion.
(2) The novel executive mechanism can open the anal canal wide enough for passing feces and gases in case of defecating.
(3) The volume of the novel executive mechanism is small enough to be implanted into the patient's body. Certainly, the smaller is the volume the better.
(4) Because the novel executive mechanism is always stuck to the anal sphincter at the most time, it must be compatible with tissues of the patient's body.

Inspired by the sandwich hinge structure in literature [10], we designed a novel executive mechanism which a hinge structure which is formed by two aluminous boards to clamp rectum. The structure of the novel executive mechanism is shown in Fig.3.

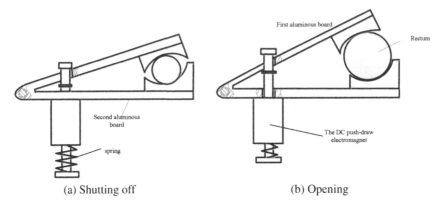

(a) Shutting off   (b) Opening

Fig. 3. Structure of the novel executive mechanism

As is shown in Fig.3, the novel executive mechanism consists of two components: the DC push-draw electromagnet and the hinge structure. The hinge structure is formed by two aluminous boards. The DC push-draw electromagnet is fixed to the second aluminous board. The iron core inside the electromagnet passes through the hole of the second aluminous board and its upper end is embedded into the slotting of the first aluminous board. An arc structure made of silicone rubber is fixed at the end of the two aluminous boards to ensure the stability when clamping the rectum.

When the electromagnet is not electrified, the hinge structure will be put together by the spring force to clamp the rectum. This situation is shown in Fig.3 (a). If the patient needs a defection, patients can electrify the electromagnet to open the mechanism for passing feces and gases. This situation is shown in Fig. 3 (b).

As the executive mechanism will get in touch with the patient's tissue directly, silicone rubber diaphragm is used as the sealing material of the entire mechanism. It also can prevent the mechanism from corroding by complicated environment inside the body.

4   Mechanical Model

For most implanted medical mechanism, motion control is one of the most important problems. As the force is always controllable and active, we need to obtain the mathematical relationship between the force imposed on the rectum and the corresponding deformation.

4.1   Force Analysis of the Mechanism

As we can see from Fig. 3, when clamping the rectum, the novel executive mechanism is actuated by the spring force which is located at about the middle of the aluminous boards. However, the part to clamp the rectum is the terminal of the aluminous boards. We need to establish the quantitative relationship between the spring force and the rectum's internal pressure.

We assume that the rectum is still a cylinder when compressed. The rectum's initial radius is R. When compressed in the radical direction, the rectum will become a cylinder whose radius is $R - \Delta R$. The situation is shown in Fig. 4 (a) (b).

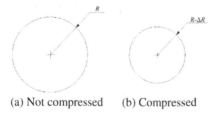

(a) Not compressed   (b) Compressed

Fig. 4. Deformation of intestinal canal at radius

We ignore the weight of the aluminous board, so the force analysis about the first aluminous board is shown in Fig. 5. Two kinds of force are imposed on the board. The force imposed by the spring is F_N, whose direction is vertical to the second aluminous board. The force imposed by the rectum is F, whose direction is vertical to the upper aluminous board. The value of F is given in the following equation:

$$F = pD(R - \Delta R) \tag{1}$$

In equation (1), p is the internal pressure of the rectum and D is the width of the aluminous board.

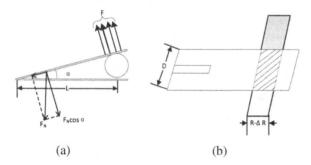

(a)   (b)

Fig. 5. Force analysis of the upper aluminous board

Considering the balance in the vertical direction of the aluminous board, we can easily obtain the following equation:

$$F_N \cos \alpha = F \tag{2}$$

In equation (2), α is the angel of the two aluminous boards.

As the two aluminous boards are very thin, we ignore the thickness. We can obtain the equation of the angle α:

$$\tan \alpha = \frac{2(R - \Delta R)}{l} \tag{3}$$

In equation (3), l is the distance between the hinge and the center of the rectum.

Using equations (1) ~ (3), we can easily get the relationship between F_N and p :

$$F_N \cos\left[\arctan\left(\frac{2R - 2\Delta R}{l}\right)\right] = (R - \Delta R)\,pD \tag{4}$$

Equation (4) explains the relationship of F_N, ΔR and p.

4.2   Radial Compression Model of the Rectum

Human rectum can be idealized as nonlinear, axisymmetric, homogenous, viscoelastic pressure vessels when generating deformations due to external axisymmetric loading distribution. We assume that the pressure imposed on the rectum is through axle center, uniform size and the wall of the rectum is thin enough. The process to clamp the rectum is slow, so the pressure imposed on the rectum is equal to the internal pressure, as is shown in Fig. 6 (a) (b).

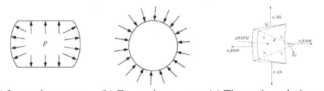

(a) Internal pressure   (b) External pressure   (c) Tiny unit analytic model

Fig. 6. Force Analysis of radical force

As is shown in Fig. 6 (c), we take out a tiny unit of the thin cylinder, where R is the radius of the rectum [11]. The radian is $\Delta\theta$ and the length along the axis is Δl. R_1 is the curvature radius along the axial direction. R_2 is the curvature radius along the direction of circumferential tangent line. p is the equivalent pressure inside the vessel. k is the thickness of the vessel.

In literature [12], the relationship between p and intestinal radical deformation ΔR has been described as:

$$p = \frac{k}{R} \cdot H^{-1}\left(\frac{\Delta R}{R}\right) \tag{5}$$

In equation (5), $H(\cdot)$ is the biomechanical mechanical constitutive relationship between intestinal stress and strain in the radial direction. It shows that the relationship between the stress and corresponding strain is certain.

Equation (5) explains the quantitative relationship between p and ΔR when the rectum is compress in the radical direction.

4.3   Results

Using equation (4) and (5), the quantitative relationship between F_N and ΔR can be derived as follows:

$$F_N \cos\left[\arctan\left(\frac{2R - 2\Delta R}{l}\right)\right] = D(R - \Delta R)\frac{k}{R} \cdot H^{-1}\left(\frac{\Delta R}{R}\right) \tag{6}$$

Arrange the equation (6) to a normal formation:

$$F_N = \frac{D(R - \Delta R)\dfrac{k}{R}}{\cos\left[\arctan\left(\dfrac{2R - 2\Delta R}{l}\right)\right]} \cdot H^{-1}\left(\frac{\Delta R}{R}\right) \tag{7}$$

Equation (7) explains the quantitative relationship between the spring force F_N and the rectum's radical deformation ΔR. We can easily obtain the desired radical deformation ΔR by adjusting the magnitude of the spring force F_N.

5   Conclusions

An artificial anal sphincter system based on a novel executive mechanism is developed. The novel executive mechanism uses a hinge structure to clamp the rectum. A mechanical model between the novel executive mechanism and rectum is established to predict the radical deformation of the rectum when compressed in the radical direction. It must be considered to design a reliable executive mechanism. According to the result, we can control the rectum's radical deformation by adjusting the magnitude of the spring force.

As the equation (7) is not intuitive enough to explain the relationship between the rectum's radical deformation and the spring force, a corresponding curve will be presented in the future work. Furthermore, an axial extension model will also be made and the material properties of human rectum will be considered to get a more convinced result. Future efforts will also be made to take animal experiments and research the rebuilding of the rectum sensation function.

Acknowledgments. This work was supported by National Natural Science Foundation of China (No. 31100708 and 61104006).

References

1. Hofmann, S., Kap Herr, V.: A new method of treatment of anorectal incontinence. J. Pediatr. Surg., 20–134 (1985)
2. Scharli, A.F.: Anorectal incontinence Diagnosis and treatment. J. Pediatr Surg., 22–693 (1987)

3. Nelson, R., Norton, N., Cautley, E., Furner, S.: Community-based prevalence of anal incontinence. JAMA 274, 559–561 (1995)
4. Khaikin, M., Wexner, S.D.: Treatment strategies in obstructed defecation and fecal incontinence. J. World J. Gastroenterol. 12(20), 3168–3173 (2006)
5. Scott, F.B., Bradley, W.E., Tim, G.W.: Treatment of urinary incontinence by implantable prosthetic sphincter. Urology 1(3), 252–259 (1973)
6. Christiansen, J., Lorentzen, M.: Implantation of artificial sphincter for anal incontinence: report of five case. Dis. Colon Rectum. 32(5), 43–436 (1989)
7. Christiansen, J., Sparso, B.: Treatment of anal incontinence by an implantable prosthetic anal sphincter. Ann. Surg. 215(4), 383–386 (1992)
8. Schrag, H., Padilla, F., Goldschmidtb, F.: German Artificial Sphincter System: first report of a novel and highly integrated sphincter prosthesis for therapy of major fecal incontinence. Diseases of the Colon & Rectum 47(12), 2215–2217 (2004)
9. Doll, A., Reimers, S., Heinrichs, M., Goldschmidtboeing, F., et al.: A high performance bidirectional micropump for a novel artificial sphincter system. Sensors & Actuators: A. Physical 130, 445–453 (2006)
10. Amae, S., Wada, M., Luo, Y., et al.: Development of an implantable artificial anal sphincter by the use of the shape memory alloy (SMA). Journal of the American Society for Artificial Internal Organs 47, 346–350 (2001)
11. Jorgensen, C.S., Dall, F.H., Jensen, S.L., et al.: A new combined high-frequency ultrasoundimpedance planimetry measuring system for the quantification of organ wall biomechanics in vivo. Journal of Biomechanics 28(7), 863–867 (1995)
12. Zan, P., Zhang, J., Shao, Y., Yang, B.: Research on the Biocompatibility of the Human Rectum and a Novel Artificial Anal Sphincter. In: Li, K., Jia, L., Sun, X., Fei, M., Irwin, G.W. (eds.) LSMS 2010 and ICSEE 2010. LNCS, vol. 6330, pp. 517–524. Springer, Heidelberg (2010)

Author Index